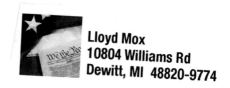

MERCURY
radio arts

Also by Glenn Beck

The Overton Window

Idiots Unplugged: Truth for Those Who Care to Listen (audiobook)

The Christmas Sweater: A Picture Book

Arguing with Idiots: How to Stop Small Minds and Big Government

Glenn Beck's Common Sense: The Case Against an Out-of-Control Government, Inspired by Thomas Paine

America's March to Socialism: Why We're One Step Closer to Giant Missile Parades (audiobook)

The Christmas Sweater

An Inconvenient Book: Real Solutions to the World's Biggest Problems

The Real America: Early Writings from the Heart and Heartland

The Plan to Restore Our Trust, Truth and Treasure

Written & Edited by GLENN BECK and KEVIN BALFE

Illustrations by PAUL E. NUNN

Contributors: PETER SCHWEIZER, TYLER GRIMM, COLIN BALFE, and GARY BROZEK

THRESHOLD EDITIONS - MERCURY RADIO ARTS

LONDON NEW YORK TORONTO SYDNEY

THE DEDICATION

To all the historians who refuse to compromise the truth to be popular, rich, or tenured.

History is rife with those who were called crazy by the establishment. They are almost always the ones who change the world while the establishment is forgotten.

THRESHOLD EDITIONS - MERCURY RADIO ARTS

A Division of Simon & Schuster, Inc.
1230 Avenue of the Americas
New York, NY 10020

First Threshold Editions/Mercury Radio Arts hardcover edition October 2010

Designed by Timothy Shaner, NightandDayDesign.biz

Manufactured in the United States of America

10 9 8 7 6 5 4 3

ISBN 978-1-4391-8719-7
ISBN 978-1-4391-9012-8 (ebook)

THE ACKNOWLEDGMENTS

Special thanks to . . .

Everyone who make the long hours at work worth it: The **VIEWERS, LISTENERS, READERS,** and **INSIDERS.**

Everyone who makes the short hours at home worth it: All of my **PARENTS**, my wife, **TANIA**, and my amazing **CHILDREN**. And to my stepparents, **VINCENT** and **MARY ANN COLONNA**, thank you for being such good role models for your daughter, my wife.

Everyone at **MERCURY RADIO ARTS** *who has helped to turn a sketch on a whiteboard into a world-class company, including:* **CHRIS BALFE, KEVIN BALFE, STU BURGUIERE, DAN ANDROS, LIZ JULIS, RICH BONN, CAROLYN POLKE, PAT GRAY, JOE KERRY, SARAH SULLIVAN, CHRIS BRADY, KELLY THOMPSON, PATRICIA BALFE, JOHN CARNEY, JEREMY PRICE, and CHRISTINA GUASTELLA.**

Everyone whose advice, support, and research made this book possible. I couldn't have put this together without you—and any mistakes are, of course, all your fault: **Brian Riedl, Yaron Brook, Larry Schweikart, David Dougherty, Stephen Moore, Chris Edwards, Dan Mitchell, Erik Prince, Stephen K. Bannon, Steve Kraemer, Fraser Seitel, David Buckner, Andrew Biggs, Professor Owen Smith, Wilson Garrett, Emily Rittenberg, Dan Andros, Pat Gray, Stu Burguiere, Rhonda Adair, Abby Argersinger, Wynton Hall, David Healy, Jr., Grace Hemphill, Jonathan Nicholson, Tim Ward, Casey Wood, Ivan Santana,** and **Tad DeHaven.**

Everyone at Simon & Schuster who makes these books possible (literally), including: **CAROLYN REIDY, LOUISE BURKE, MITCHELL IVERS, ANTHONY ZICCARDI, LIZ PERL,** and **EMILY BESTLER.**

Everyone at Premiere Radio Networks and Clear Channel who allows my voice to be heard by millions every day, including: **MARK MAYS, JOHN HOGAN, CHARLIE RAHILLY, JULIE TALBOTT, DAN YUKELSON,** and **DAN METTER.**

Everyone at Fox News who lets me be myself on television, warts and all, including: **ROGER AILES, BILL SHINE, SUZANNE SCOTT, BILL O'REILLY, JOEL CHEATWOOD, TIFFANY SIEGEL,** and **everyone else on my extraordinary STAFF.**

Everyone else who has helped me over the years in both big and small ways, including: **GEORGE HILTZIK, KRAIG KITCHIN, BRIAN GLICKLICH, MATTHEW HILTZIK, JOSH RAFFEL, JON HUNTSMAN, DUANE WARD, STEVE SCHEFFER, DOM THEODORE, SCOTT BAKER, RICHARD PAUL EVANS, GEORGE LANGE, TIMOTHY SHANER, RUSSELL M. BALLARD, KEN SWEZEY,** along with **ALLEN, CAM, AMY, MARY,** and the whole team at **ISDANER.**

BROKE

THE CONTENTS

Author's Note

"But what do we mean by the American Revolution? Do we mean the American War? The Revolution was effected before the War commenced. The Revolution was in the minds and hearts of the people."

—JOHN ADAMS, 1818

In the history of the world, America's great experiment with freedom has been nothing more than a blink of the eye. Our way of life—unalienable rights, unquestionable freedoms, unimaginable wealth—may seem natural and permanent to us, but, among the billions who have lived, we are the only ones to have ever experienced it.

And now, I fear, we've never been so close to losing it.

I didn't choose to write about this subject because my passion in life is to reform Medicare or cut defense spending. I chose it because it's taken us more than a hundred years to destroy the great American Experiment, and I believe we have only a fraction of that time left to save it.

I'm not an expert in this subject, and my detractors will say that I'm only an entertainer, or I do this just for the money. They couldn't be more wrong. I do shows on Wilson and Coolidge, I talk about Jesus far too much for most people, and I cry on national television. Am I really a ratings genius, or is it more likely that I am just a dad, a husband, a recovering slug, and a concerned American who wants his children to be able to experience what he did?

I guess you will have to decide.

As John Adams once said, revolutions take place in the hearts and minds of the people. To win that battle, we have to usher in a revolution of thought by shifting the debate in America from one about retirement ages and tax hikes to one about individual rights, equality of opportunity, and God's role in our success.

They say that the truth will set you free, but I've found that it will first make you miserable. I say: *Bring it on*. There is much work to be done and many tough choices lie ahead: difficult sacrifices, financial pain, maybe some dark days. It won't be easy, but nothing worth doing ever is.

This book is about understanding that our system of government is broken because we ourselves are broken in spirit, broken in trust, and broken in our faith. It's about understanding that debts and deficits aren't the disease; no, they're just symptoms of the disease. This book is about learning from the past and seeing that "minimum government, maximum freedom" isn't just a catchy slogan. It was once a way of life in America, and it's a way of life that we can have back. My hope is that it will help you to think out of the box politically and motivate you to challenge those who are blocking the doorway to restoration.

The time for trusting others in government based on a "D" or an "R" has long since passed. Trust yourself. Trust your neighbors. Live your life the right way and prepare to witness miracles. God is not done with freedom, and neither am I.

But it all starts with you. You have to find your role, your place in this fight.

Remember, the heroes we read about in history books—Paul Revere, George Washington, Benjamin Franklin—were usually only a very small part of the story. You don't have to ride the horse at midnight yourself to make a real difference. You just have to help make sure that someone else can.

New York City, 2010

PART ONE

THE PAST IS PROLOGUE

"We are perhaps too much inclined to think that [external invasion] is the only way a civilization can die. If the lights that guide us ever go out, they will fade little by little, as if of their own accord . . . We therefore should not console ourselves by thinking that the barbarians are still a long way off. Some peoples may let the torch be snatched from their hands, but others stamp it out themselves."
—Alexis de Tocqueville,
Democracy in America

CHAPTER 1.

Ancient History, Modern Lessons

If history teaches us one thing, it is this: Empires tend to crumble from the inside. If history teaches us two things, it is that very few people ever see it coming.

Perhaps it is because of those two lessons that George Santayana's famous line continually rings true, across civilizations and across the ages: "Those who cannot remember the past are condemned to repeat it."

Time and again, once-great countries have failed because their citizens thought it never could happen to them. They thought they were immune. They thought they were different. They thought they were better.

They were wrong.

That is the danger facing America today. The 2.4 million men and women in our armed forces can and will defeat any foreign enemy we face—but it's no longer *foreign* threats that pose the greatest danger to our future. Indeed, as Tocqueville presciently warned, we are our *own* greatest danger. We are on the verge of "stamping out" ourselves.

In other words: *We have met the enemy . . . and he is us.*

The real battle we are fighting right now is with the laws of economics—and it's a war that can't be won. It's like attempting to fight gravity by constantly jumping: There are slivers in time when it might feel like you're winning, that you've actually changed the laws of nature. Then you crash back to earth and, eventually, get too tired to jump anymore.

Gravity wins. It always does.

Likewise, the laws of economics say that when expenses are higher than revenues for a prolonged

THE AMERICAN EMPIRE:
BY THE NUMBERS
America's share of world GDP peaked at almost **28 percent** in 1951. Today it's roughly **24 percent**.

period of time, there will be repercussions. Sure, there may be fleeting moments when it looks good, when interest rates stay low and credit ratings stay high. Then one day people realize that their money isn't as secure as they thought. Interest rates jump, credit ratings collapse, panic ensues.

> HATE SPEECH?
>
> "If you really want to see when an empire is getting vulnerable, the big giveaway is when the costs of serving the debt exceed the cost of the defense budget."
>
> —Financial historian and Harvard professor Niall Ferguson, who went on to say that he believes this tipping point will happen in the United States within the next six years

The laws of economics win. They always do.

Debt, deficits, unemployment rates, inflation rates, interest rates, and money supply—these are all important indicators because they measure our progress in the battle, but they're not the disease. They're only *side effects* of it. The disease itself, the reason why we're in this economic situation in the first place, is progressivism and all of the free-spending, worry-about-debt-later, utopia-is-within-reach policies that come along with it.

Now we've reached a tipping point. For decades we've been told by leaders and "experts" that debt should be dealt with in the long term, that deficits don't really matter, that jobs will be plentiful, and that America will always be the world's greatest financial superpower. Look where that's gotten us: massive, unfathomable debts; trillion-dollar deficits; a budget less balanced than MSNBC; a job market in which millions can't find work; and a financial system that, by all accounts, was just hours away from the abyss.

Maybe it's time to stop listening to the politicians, professors, and prognosticators and instead pay attention to the only true predictor of the future: the past.

PICTURING THE PRICE

We talk a lot about debt in this book, but part of the problem with this topic is that it's become unrelatable to most Americans. Human minds can scarcely begin to comprehend the scope of the problem we're talking about; but let me try one illustration.

If you were to take $100 bills—not $1 bills or $20 bills, but $100 bills—and stack them seven feet tall and fill in every single inch of an NFL football field from end zone to end zone, that would represent one trillion dollars. Now put thirteen of those fields side by side and you start to picture the size of the debt we've incurred.

That is the price of progressive policies. That is the consequence of our nation's "live large and put it on charge" mentality. That is the result of corruption, lies, and deceit from our self-serving leaders.

British scholar C. E. M. Joad, who studied the collapses of the world's great empires, said that the declines all had several things in common: decadence, weariness, and irresponsibility. To that, British historian C. Northcote Parkinson added that collapses are usually marked by an overcentralized government, heavy taxes, and bureaucracy.

If any of that sounds familiar, then it's time to stop taking for granted that America is infallible and enduring and start acting to make it that way.

When in Rome

During a 2005 appearance at the National Press Club, David Walker, former comptroller general of the United States, explained that "the United States can be likened to Rome before the fall of the empire. Its financial condition is 'worse than advertised.' It has a 'broke business model.' It faces deficits in its budgets, its balance of payments, its savings—and its leadership."

Despite the eye-rolling that normally ensues when anyone tries to mention the fall of the Roman Empire, Walker's warning was not hyperbole; he was dead on. In fact, the parallels between America and the latter stages of the Roman Empire unfortunately go much, much further than most people are comfortable admitting.

THE AMERICAN EMPIRE: BY THE NUMBERS

In 1960, the United States exported **$3.5 billion** more than we imported. In 2009 we imported **$374 billion** more than we exported.

English politician and historian Edward Gibbon wrote one of the most comprehensive accounts of Rome's collapse ever published. *The History of the Decline and Fall of the Roman Empire*, released in six volumes between 1776 and 1788, explained that "human freedom is the first wish of our heart; freedom is the first blessing of our nature." Yet when people shirk individual responsibility and expect more from government, explained Gibbon, they fall prey to tyranny.

And so it was with Rome. "They no longer possessed that public courage which is nourished by the love of independence, the sense of national honor, the presence of danger, and the habit of command," Gibbon explained. "They received laws and governors from the will of their sovereign, and trusted for their defense to a mercenary army."

Gibbon went on to say that the push for intellectual mediocrity further hastened Rome's collapse. "The minds of men were gradually reduced to the same level, the fire of genius was extinguished." Tocqueville had the same observation: "When all fortunes are middling," he wrote, "passions are naturally restrained, imagination limited and pleasures simple. Such universal moderation tempers the sovereign's own spirit and keeps within certain limits the disorderly urges of desire."

It's interesting to note that our Founders were familiar with Gibbon's 1776 work. Thomas Jefferson owned a copy of *Decline and Fall* and kept it in his library in Monticello. He clearly read it, likely several times, since notes from Jefferson have been found in the margins.

TEACHABLE MOMENT

In terms of Rome, Tocqueville was only partially correct. While the state itself was as ruthless and bloodthirsty as ever, it was the *people* who'd become apathetic. They no longer cared enough about their way of life to defend it—and that's an unsustainable foundation for any society.

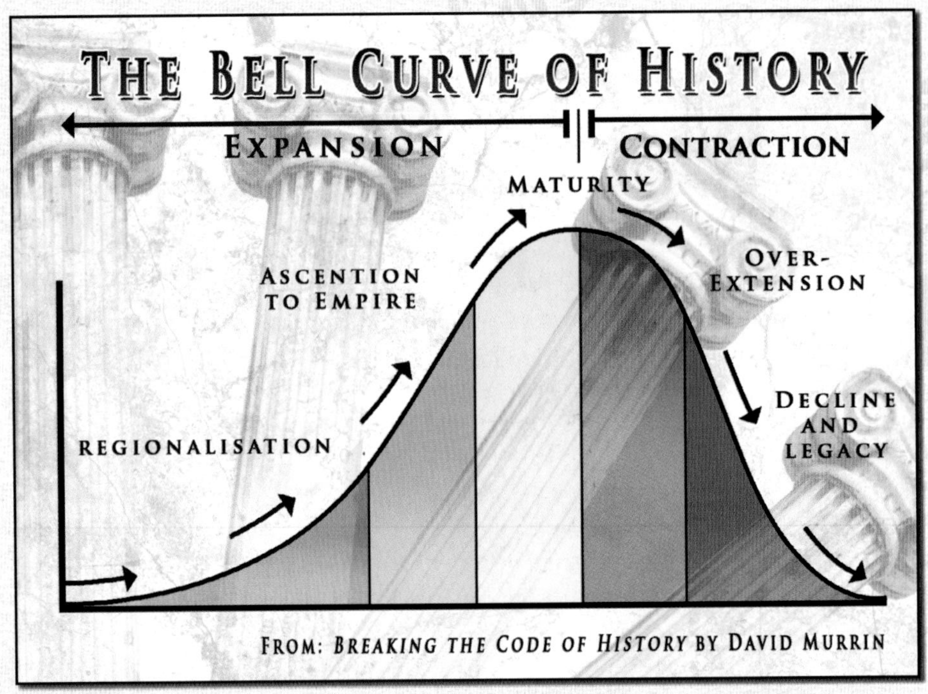

These are important observations, and while they might seem to have nothing to do with economics, they actually strike right at the heart of the problem. A society that seeks to equalize the minds of men doesn't cherish real learning. Education becomes the right of the few, the elite (in Rome's case, the priests; in our case, the Ivy League), and the masses must accept their interpretation.

Likewise, a society that seeks to equalize incentives for work doesn't cherish individualism. In Rome, heavy taxes (some of which were paid not just in money, but in food, goods, or livestock) ate away at the incentive to work hard. By the time Emperor Diocletian forced male children to adopt the profession of their father, all motivation, drive, and individual initiative had vanished.

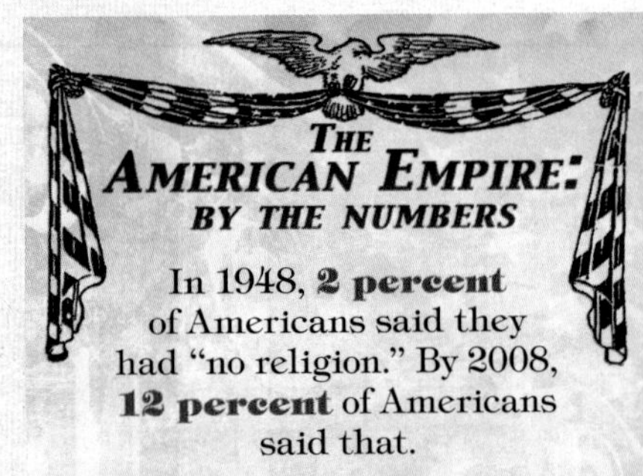

THE AMERICAN EMPIRE: BY THE NUMBERS
In 1948, 2 percent of Americans said they had "no religion." By 2008, 12 percent of Americans said that.

Over time, that inevitably results in the tempered spirit that Tocqueville wrote about, which leads to fewer risk-taking entrepreneurs, lower economic growth, fewer jobs, and, generally speaking, a society that is forced to fund itself via debt rather than productivity.

As Lactantius wrote in the fourth century, "the number of [Romans] receiving pay was so much larger than the number of those paying taxes and that because of the enormous size of the assessments." The result? As one historian put it, "the multiplication of unproductive services such as the administrative bureaucracy [and heavy military spending] combined to place an intolerable strain on the producers of primary commodities."

The explosion of the Roman bureaucracy was fueled by Rome's centralization of power. As the size and strength of government grew, personal ambition withered and a "decline of civic vitality" quickly ensued. People were accustomed to sending huge chunks of their pay to the government and seeing nothing in return.

Those in the cities got an increasing amount of government handouts for their money, a practice that was part of a long-term plan to make people forget about their history. According to Gibbon, "it was artfully contrived by Augustus that, in the enjoyment of plenty, the Romans should lose the memory of freedom."

With individual liberty squelched and businesses increasingly under government control, the Roman economy could no longer achieve the growth necessary to pay its bills. That left their government with one final, desperate move: taxes. Massive, bone-crushing taxes. In fact, Roman taxes became so bad in the later years of the empire that landowners actually fled to barbarian territories, an offense punishable by death, just to avoid paying them.

> **TEACHABLE MOMENT**
>
> This is an interesting parallel to modern-day America. Not only is our bureaucracy growing but our leaders also seem to be solely interested in the rate of employment instead of the return on employment. In other words, putting people to work in unproductive government jobs may be good for headlines, but it leads to a major strain on private business, since those jobs must eventually be paid for via taxes. It's subsidized employment, and it's a lot different than the true entrepreneurial employment that drives real growth.

Taxes and regulations grew so unwieldy that they ended up covering virtually every major area of Roman life, from trade, to farming, to manufacturing, to simple labor. Not surprisingly, the taxes largely became unprofitable for the government, because merchants spent much of their life trying to avoid paying them. As one Roman writer put it at the time, "The whole world groans under the Publicani [tax collectors]."

To placate the Roman people's growing discontent, Emperor Diocletian started offering entertainment and freebies to keep the people calm and docile. They called the ploy "bread and circuses." Feed them, distract them, and maybe they won't realize what you've done to them.

With eyes averted and personal self-initiative suffocated, the Roman government took on public works projects that encroached into every nook and cranny of private life, regardless of whether it was desired or successful. For example, "the frequent and regular distributions of wine and oil, of corn and bread, of money or provisions,

IF IT LOOKS LIKE A REPUBLIC . . .

In 31 B.C., Octavian understood that the institutions of the Roman Republic could no longer hold the empire together. The citizens of Rome were ready for domestic peace, but not for another dictatorship. They still embraced the values of freedom and independence, even though they were no longer living them.

Octavian's solution was to give the people both what they wanted and what he thought they *needed*. Instead of abolishing cherished institutions, he continued them. Representatives were still elected by the people, the assemblies still gathered, the Senate still oversaw some provinces and advised Octavian. As one textbook puts it, "With some truth, Octavian could claim that he ruled in partnership with the Senate. By maintaining the façade of the Republic, Octavian camouflaged his absolute power . . . Moreover, Octavian's control over the armed forces made resistance futile . . .

"In keeping with his policy of maintaining the appearance of traditional republican government, Octavian refused to be called king or even, like Caesar, dictator; instead, he cleverly disguised his autocratic rule by taking the inoffensive title *princeps* (first citizen)."

The people of Rome had gone from being citizens of a Republic to subjects of an Emperor—and it happened without violence, votes. or fanfare.

As the Romans found out the hard way, just because it looks like freedom, doesn't mean it is.

had almost exempted the poorer citizens of Rome from the necessity of labor." Bribery and corruption soon ran rampant. Class warfare and resentment between citizens quickly followed. As historian Michael Rostovtzeff put it, "the peasants hated the landowners and the officials, the city proletariat hated the city bourgeoisie, the army was hated by everybody, even by the peasants."

Much has been written about how complicated the downfall of Rome was, but the recipe was actually pretty simple, and has since been replicated countless times: A great civilization arises. The state encroaches on freedom and demands more power. People take less responsibility for themselves and want more handouts from the government. Taxes go up to pay for the handouts. The size of government explodes and economic growth slows. The government seeks to divert the public's attention from what is really going on to "bread and circuses." Collapse, economic or otherwise, ensues.

Greece Lightning!

The fall of Greece followed a pattern similar to the demise of Rome. Both civilizations displayed a pioneering spirit in their earliest stage of life, both had thriving arts and architecture, and both served as the cradle for many of the concepts we now associate with Western civilization.

THE
AMERICAN EMPIRE:
BY THE NUMBERS
American adults educated in the 1950s ranked **second** compared to other countries. That ranking dropped to **fourteenth** in the 1990s.

It was the Greeks, for example, who developed the ideas of reason and inquiry, which created the groundwork for philosophy and science. They established the foundations of mathematics, including geometry and the rules of numbering. The Greeks were some of the first to establish theaters and develop sculpture as an art form.

The citizen class of Greek societies was relatively free, although it still made extensive use of slaves, and the Greeks gave the world its first democracy. But, as so often happens, freedom could not last in the face of crisis. Once economic troubles came, people turned away from individualism and toward dictators. As one historian recounted, "An economic depression may easily have a dictator in its pocket. Hence, in most of the maritime states of the Greek world the economic crisis led to a tyrant. A Greek tyrant was, almost always, a noble who, to quote Herodotus, 'took the people into partnership.' He pretended to champion the cause of the poor, got himself assigned a bodyguard, drove out or killed the other nobles, and seized the power."

The Greeks suffered from foreign wars, but they also suffered from internal decline. Citizens found it convenient to pick a fight with a neighbor in order to gain slaves, wealth, or property. The Greek historian Thucydides explained that "there were the wicked resolutions taken by those who, particularly under the pressure of misfortune, wished to escape from their usual poverty and . . . coveted the property of their neighbors."

The Greek historian Polybius noted the same thing. "The people have become accustomed to feed at the expense of others," he wrote, "and their prospects of winning a livelihood depend upon the property of their neighbors."

In the end, the virtues of Greek art, law, philosophy, and democracy could not save them from succumbing to that most primitive of the deadly sins: greed. They became their own worst enemy. As we have seen with Arlen Specter and the Republicans, freedom didn't leave the Greeks; the Greeks left freedom.

The Spanish Imposition

During the sixteenth century, Spain was actually the greatest power in Europe. In fact, for more than a century, Spain was more powerful than any other European power since the Romans. Yet, like Rome and Greece, it eventually fell prey to the seduction of the three-headed monster: bloated bureaucracy, centralized power,

The Black Swan

One of the reasons why our Founders set up America the way they did was to protect it from "Black Swans"—the extraordinary, unforeseen events that can only be rationalized in hindsight. By putting power in the hands of the people and limiting the size of government, they were attempting to create a system of safety nets that would hold the country together when faced with the kinds of events that have taken down other great nations.

The problem is that as we've gotten further and further away from that vision, our safety nets have eroded. How do we get them back? Nassim Nicholas Taleb, a professor at NYU's Polytechnic Institute, explained ten ways to insulate yourself from these kinds of events in a book called *The Black Swan: The Impact of the Highly Improbable.*

- *What is fragile should break early while it is still small.*
- *No socialization of losses and privatization of gains.*
- *People who were driving a school bus blindfolded (and crashed it) should never be given a new bus.*
- *Do not let someone making an "incentive" bonus manage a nuclear plant—or your financial risks.*
- *Counter-balance complexity with simplicity.*
- *Do not give children sticks of dynamite, even if they come with a warning.*
- *Only Ponzi schemes should depend on confidence. Governments should never need to "restore confidence."*
- *Do not give an addict more drugs if he has withdrawal pains.*
- *Citizens should not depend on financial assets or fallible "expert" advice for their retirement.*
- *Make an omelet with the broken eggs.*

By my count, America is zero for ten, meaning that we are extraordinarily vulnerable to a cataclysmic event no one sees coming. Afterwards, our leaders will use the Black Swan to blame our system for failing to protect us, but the truth is that it is our leaders who are failing to protect our system.

and skyrocketing taxes. The consequence was massive debt and, by the close of the eighteenth century, Spain was a shell of its former self.

The Spanish empire's decline began when it began to consume more than it produced. By the time that Philip II became king, he found "an empty treasury, stifling taxation, and loans from German and Italian bankers which had mortgaged Spanish income for years ahead . . . the loans absorbed the royal share of the bullion pouring in from the Indies, and, as soon as past debts might be cleared, there were the obligations Philip had contracted to raise money for his wide operations in behalf of the faith."

Before the Spaniards knew it, they were awash in too many state employees,

medical practitioners and priests, and not enough businessmen and entrepreneurs. But the most egregious part of all this government largesse, at least to the citizens of Spain, was the so-called alcabala, which was a 10 percent excise tax on the transfer of all property, including food. Naturally, to avoid the crushing tax, the Spanish soon became professional smugglers. By one estimate, 90 percent of Spanish commerce was evading the tax through clever business measures. Tax avoidance became so bad that the Spanish crown sent soldiers to Catalonia to enforce the new taxation, sparking what became a ten-year civil war.

To get out of their self-created mess, Spain did what any good tax-and-spend, centralized government would: It debased its own currency. Right on cue, the cost of Spanish goods and services ballooned. Spain became a great place to sell stuff to, but a terrible place to buy things from.

> HATE SPEECH?
>
> "Everything you learned, everything you believe and everything driving our political leaders is based on a misleading, outdated theory of history. The American Empire is at the edge of a dangerous precipice, at risk of a sudden, rapid collapse."
>
> *—Paul B. Farrell, columnist on behavioral economics and author,* The Millionaire Code

In discussing Spain's fatal moves toward eventual downfall, one historian summed it up nicely: "The most obvious of the causes of the economic decline of a state is usually the extravagance of the Government."

In other words: frugal government, frugal people; extravagant government, enslaved people.

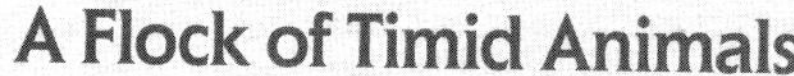

A Flock of Timid Animals

Harvard professor Niall Ferguson recently described the United States as an "empire on the edge of chaos." Could he be right, or is that just more fearmongering coming out of Harvard?

Of course he could be right. Those thirteen football fields filled with endless rows of seven-foot-tall stacks of hundred-dollar bills are essentially monetary soldiers, capable of attacking us from the inside at a moment's notice. Anyone who says otherwise is practicing something far more dangerous than fearmongering: denial.

In many ways, we've already made the same fatal mistakes that past empires have. The centralization of power has already begun to dampen entrepreneurialism, foster entitlement, and incentivize the lack of pride in individual accomplishments

that tends to precede the downfall of most great empires. (Trophies for all participants, anyone?)

The Romans enjoyed growth through conquest. But once the wars ended, so did the spoils, leaving taxation to make up the difference. Americans enjoy growth through business. But between the vilification of profits and the arduous regulations now being imposed, that too is slowing. Taxation will again be forced to make up the difference.

Perhaps the most eye-opening warning about America's precarious position is from Tocqueville himself in 1840:

> *Having thus taken each citizen in turn in its powerful grasp and shaped him to its will, government then extends its embrace to include the whole of society. It covers the whole of social life with a network of petty, complicated rules that are both minute and uniform, through which even men of the greatest originality and the most vigorous temperament cannot force their heads above the crowd. It does not break men's will, but softens, bends, and guides it; it seldom enjoins, but often inhibits, action; it does not destroy anything, but prevents much from being born; it is not at all tyrannical, but it hinders, restrains, enervates, stifles, and stultifies so much that in the end each nation is no more than a flock of timid and hardworking animals with the government as its shepherd.*

Arnold Toynbee, a British historian who wrote the twelve-volume classic *Study of History*, says that societies face a pattern of "challenge and response." A challenge, whether from natural disaster, foreign invasion, or internal erosion, is inevitable and natural, he says. The question is how a nation responds. It is now our chance to provide an answer. We must not be a flock of timid animals—we must be our own shepherd.

Studying the suicidal moves of three once-epic empires—ancient Rome, ancient Greece, and sixteenth-century Spain—reveals that our nation is responding in an all-too-familiar way that will have an all-too-familiar ending. (Present-day Greece can teach us a lot, too.)

The only way out is if, citizen by citizen, the public learns the lessons of history and convinces others that *we are not immune to the laws of economics.* We can still choose individual achievement, limited government, and low taxes—but we have to turn the corner now.

God's hand has been evident throughout America's history, and now there is one more gift to add to the list: Unlike past empires, we've been given the ability to see into the past. Through technology, education, and history books we've been handed a road map that can fend off human nature and lead us toward enduring freedom.

Now we just have to follow it.

"Rather go to bed supperless than rise in debt."

—Benjamin Franklin, *Poor Richard's Almanack*

CHAPTER 2.

Frugal: A Four-Letter Word

One of my all-time favorite Christmas stories is Charles Dickens's classic *A Christmas Carol*. The story's memorable mean-spirited miser, Ebenezer Scrooge, has become synonymous with *tightwad*. But the truth is that Scrooge was not thrifty; he was *greedy*. There is a huge difference between those terms, and it's one that, over time, many people have been conditioned to forget.

Today, those who prize frugality are considered old-fashioned, crusty enemies of progress. Saving, the story goes, is hoarding, and hoarders prevent the economy from growing. If you save money, not only are you boring, you're also contributing to the downfall of America.

But if you're one of those evil savers, cheer up. Frugality may go in and out of style, but it's always been a virtue. While America may currently be experiencing a shift toward the spending side, the pendulum always swings back in the other direction.

Consider a few examples of how frugality has been viewed over time:

> *"I have three precious things which I hold fast and prize. The first is gentleness; the second is frugality; the third is humility, which keeps me from putting myself before others. Be gentle and you can be bold; be frugal and you can be liberal; avoid putting yourself before others and you can become a leader among men."* —Lao Tzu, 600–531 B.C.

> *"Thrift comes too late when you find it at the bottom of your purse."*
> —Seneca

> *"Make all you can; save all you can; give all you can."*
> –John Wesley, founder of Methodism

"He who does not economize will have to agonize." —CONFUCIUS

"If you would be wealthy, think of saving as well as getting."
—BENJAMIN FRANKLIN

"A wise and frugal government, which shall leave men free to regulate their own pursuits of industry and improvement, and shall not take from the mouth of labor the bread it has earned—this is the sum of good government." —THOMAS JEFFERSON

"Economical in the use or appropriation of money, goods or provisions of any kind; saving unnecessary expense, either of money or anything else which is to be used or consumed; sparing; not profuse, prodigal, or lavish."
—*WEBSTER'S* DEFINITION OF *THRIFT*, 1828

Flash forward to today: When most people hear "thrift," they think about thrift stores or thrift clothes, terms that are associated with concepts like "cheap" and "low quality."

America's Founders saw it differently. They *prized* thrift—not just because they saw firsthand what extravagance can lead to, but because they understood that frugality wasn't just about saving money; it was also about saving freedom. If you think of debt as a tie that binds you to others, then it's not a stretch to believe that personal savings yields personal liberty.

"Thrift as a moral virtue and as a utilitarian practice," wrote Professor William Nunn, "was a cornerstone in the development of capitalism as an economic system and individualism as its philosophy."

The father of capitalism, Adam Smith, certainly believed this. In his book *The Wealth of Nations*, Smith argued that robust saving is a basic tenet of economic progress. And it makes sense; you can't have capitalism without, well, capital!

Swapping Government for God

The recent denigration of profits and wealth is right out of the progressive playbook. They make wealth synonymous with greed and profits synonymous with corruption. After a while, people start to think to themselves: *Maybe I don't want to be rich after all.* Wealth isn't something to be admired; it's something to be avoided. So people borrow, they spend, they live the high life, and, sure enough, they are never wealthy. It becomes a self-fulfilling prophecy.

The reason this is so important is that fewer wealthy citizens means fewer jobs.

Fewer jobs means fewer people to take care of others, which in turn allows the government to make a case that it has to step in to fill the void. After all, if individuals were still willing and able to engage in private, willful charity and philanthropy (as used to be the tradition), we wouldn't need government to do it.

Ben Franklin, a frugal yet strong advocate for charity, once wrote, "do not depend too much upon your own industry, and frugality, and prudence, though excellent things; for they may all be blasted, without the blessing of Heaven; and, therefore, ask that blessing humbly, and be not uncharitable to those that at present seem to want it, but comfort and help them. Remember, Job suffered, and was afterwards prosperous."

It seems that many people have forgotten one of the basic principles of a republic: virtue. A large percentage of the population must be virtuous in order for society to properly function. But virtue requires morality, and morality requires adherence to a religion that embraces charity as a pillar of its theology and recognizes a higher power than the government.

The United States was founded on Judeo-Christian principles, which embraced personal giving and charity as fundamental. And that was the way most Americans lived: charity through voluntary giving, in service of God. Then FDR and progressives came along and changed all of that. Charity still meant fulfilling your financial obligation to a higher power, but that higher power went from being God to being the United States government.

Life Mimics Art

Maybe it's time that Aesop's fable about the ant and grasshopper is updated for modern times:

The ant works hard every day during the summer, building his house and storing food for the winter. The grasshopper, on the other hand, watches the ant with amusement and prefers to sing and dance, putting nothing away for the winter ahead.

When the winter comes, the grasshopper has nothing to eat and becomes desperate. He elects a president who promises that spreading the food around is good for everyone. The president demonizes the ant for being greedy and asks how he can live with himself when so many others have so little. An executive order is signed demanding that the ant turn over 50 percent of his food supply to the government. The grasshopper laughs and plays the rest of the winter, getting fat on the ant's assets. The ant is depressed and resentful.

The next summer the ant stops preparing his home and storing his food and instead joins the grasshopper, singing and dancing all day. Unfortunately, all of the other ants make the same decision. The next winter, with no one left to exploit, the grasshoppers and ants all die of cold and hunger.

My apologies to Aesop, but is this really still just a fable?

The government's incessant march toward removing all traces of religion and faith, along with its reluctance to help faith-based charity groups is no accident. It's because that leaves the government itself as the "charity" of last resort. Strip out religion and strip away morality, virtue, and, eventually, personal charity. All that you have left is Washington, D.C.

When Was the Last Time a Poor Person Created Jobs?

Noted titans of American industry like Andrew Carnegie advocated wealth creation as a key driver of private charity. Carnegie amassed his fortune with a simple principle: "Watch the costs and the profits will take care of themselves."

Carnegie valued living below one's means. However, that was not because he wanted to be the richest man on earth—it was because he wanted to help others. "The man who dies thus rich dies disgraced," he once said.

Andrew Carnegie put his money where his mouth was.

Before his death in 1919, Carnegie gave away $350 million—90 percent of his fortune, more than any American before him had ever even possessed. Obama would have loved him, because he really spread it around. He gave millions to Christian groups feeding the poor, millions more to libraries (his donations funded an astonishing 1,700 libraries across the country), and millions to schools like the University of Chicago. Black and Christian schools also received large donations.

> In 1872, when Carnegie entered steel production, the price of steel was $56 per ton. He invented a new production technique that brought costs down and quality up. By 1900, Carnegie Steel was producing steel for $11.50 per ton and had become the world's largest industrial corporation.
>
> TEACHABLE MOMENT

My good friend and mentor Jon Huntsman, Sr., is living his life the same way. He's a multibillionaire who intends to give away the vast majority of his wealth before he dies. The impact he is already having (through his Huntsman Cancer Foundation, among other things) is astounding and, in my estimation, is far greater than any government entity could ever hope for. He is really the perfect example of why we should be encouraging private wealth instead of demonizing it.

Contrary to what progressives would have you believe, the American tradition of thrift was never synonymous with hoarding or being cheap or greedy. It wasn't accumulation for accumulation's sake. On the contrary; thriftiness frees the individual to be generous in giving to God. It is the secret ingredient to charity.

Richard Baxter, a Puritan thinker, put it this way: "Frugality or sparing is an act of fidelity, obedience, and gratitude, by which we use all our estates so faithfully for the chief Owner, so obediently to our chief ruler, and so gratefully to our chief Benefactor, as that we waste it not in any other way."

Doing "well" and doing "good" are not, as Carnegie, Franklin, Huntsman, and so many other wealthy Americans understood, mutually exclusive. Whether or not one subscribes to "trickle-down economics," there's absolutely no doubt that "trickle-down charity" is the most effective kind.

But that reality didn't fit into the progressive agenda. If wealth and private charity worked, then government would remain limited. So the spin and propaganda began. Government programs turned *frugality* into a synonym for *greed.* Those who build wealth, the story went, should feel guilty because there are so many with so little. The results were predictable: More power for the government, more money flowing through their coffers, and plenty of people still struggling.

TEACHABLE MOMENT

The disease of secularism, along with Woodrow Wilson and FDR's embrace of the so-called Social Gospel, as a justification for massive federal spending sprees has fundamentally altered American attitudes toward thrift and savings. As William L. Nunn wrote in 1938:

> *The concept of thrift as originally grounded in Puritan doctrines and in a simple agrarian economy is undergoing a drastic change in the United States today. Long-time or secular economic and social trends accentuated by the recent activities of the governmental agencies and by widespread consumer purchasing on a pay-as-you-use basis are responsible.*

Nunn went on to argue that with the government offering a form of "social insurance," the "practice of individual thrift" was no longer a necessity.

Frugality Fosters Freedom

The Founders understood and embraced the freedom that comes with self-restraint in spending. As historian David Steigerwald notes, Ben Franklin didn't seek wealth because he wanted the trappings of money; his primary objective was to achieve freedom to do as he wished.

Seeing money as a means to achieve freedom radically alters one's beliefs about appropriate levels of government spending. Over time, progressives have successfully persuaded many Americans that government spending is an indicator of our national compassion. But when considered from the classical view of American thrift, the opposite is true: Government spending is really a measure of erosion and encroachment on personal freedom. The more you send to Washington, the less you have available to do with what you want—which ostensibly would include helping others in a real, tangible way.

In his book *Thrift and Generosity: The Joy of Giving,* Dr. John Templeton, Jr., president of the Templeton foundation, offers a great picture of thrift properly understood: "Thrift is not so much a matter of how much we have, but of how we appreciate, value, and use what we have. Everyone, regardless of income level, has opportunities to exercise the virtue of thrift. We practice thrift by monitoring how we spend our time and money and then by making better decisions."

Templeton's words are timely considering that Americans have managed their personal budgets about as well as our politicians have managed the federal one. Consider this: In the early 1980s, the American savings rate was between 10 and 12 percent. After 2005, the savings rate dropped *below* zero (although, to be fair, the increased purchasing of gold makes these numbers somewhat hard to compare). It has recently rebounded slightly, likely because people have again begun to see the merits of having financial freedom.

One of the main instigators of fiscal propaganda was John Maynard Keynes, whose views we'll look at in later chapters. His influential book, *General Theory of Employment, Interest, and Money*, argued what he called the "Paradox of Thrift." Thrift was not virtue, Keynes said, because it undermined prosperity. (Seriously, this was a real argument.) Popular economic textbooks soon began picking up this story line and turning it into economic gospel. As one subsequently put it, "Thrift, which has always been held in high esteem by our economy, now becomes something of a social vice."

As Columbia history professor Richard Hofstadter wrote, "[This view marked] a shift . . . from a working and saving ethic . . . to an ethic which stresses . . . the value of leisure and the pleasure of consumption."

> HATE SPEECH?
>
> "No free government, or the blessings of liberty, can be preserved to any people but by a firm adherence to justice, moderation, temperance, frugality, and virtue; and by a frequent recurrence to fundamental principles."
>
> —*Patrick Henry*

Similarly, in 1963, Nobel Prize–winning economist Paul Samuelson noted that progressives had successfully turned things upside down without the public even realizing it. "In kindergarten we were all taught that thrift is always a good thing. Benjamin Franklin's 'Poor Richard's Almanack' never tired of preaching the doctrine of saving. And now along comes a new generation of alleged financial experts who seem to be telling us that black is white and white is black, and that the old virtues may be modern sins."

It's a perfect summation of progressivism: 2 + 2 equals 5. Sure, your calculator may say "4" but that's only because it doesn't know that times have changed. It was built on old rules, outmoded technology, antiquated theories. In short, your eyes and brain are no longer trustworthy; only the self-proclaimed experts are.

Not everyone, however, was fooled by Keynes's economic sleight of hand. Senator Everett Dirksen, once the head of a savings and loan in Pekin, Illinois, was upset that Keynes considered thrift "a vice rather than a virtue." Dirksen prayed for help in restoring saving to its proper place in the minds of Americans: "Let God give me strength, that I may help to get America back on the beam and elevate thrift to the pedestal it rightly deserves, because thrift and opportunity have been the great horsemen of progress in America."

Back to the Future

Once this new view on saving and thrift became prevalent, it attached itself like an economic cancer to our way of life. And that's where America is today: with a disease that needs to be eradicated from our system.

In the 1950s, consumer debt rose by nearly 200 percent. By 1960, two-thirds of

American households were in some sort of debt. Why? Because consumption had become king. The result was a growth boom in the 1960s, forever hooking politicians on the idea that spending could actually drive America's economy forward.

We now know how that has turned out. Consumer spending makes up roughly 71 percent of the American economy. If we don't spend, we die. That leaves politicians with only one option: to continue to spin spending as a positive. They have to; there's no other choice. Remember what President Bush said after 9/11: *Go shopping. It's our patriotic duty.*

The way forward couldn't be more clear, yet it also couldn't be more difficult: more savings, less spending; more private charity, fewer public handouts. Those are values this country was built on, and while it may seem counterintuitive, they're values that will bring us back to real, sustainable growth.

Frugality ignites freedom. America *must* rediscover that.

Following this path means rejecting Keynes, rejecting spending as charity, rejecting spending as a means to end recessions, rejecting new credit card deals, teaser interest rates, or easy-payment plans. But most of all, it means rejecting the material things we've been conditioned to believe matter the most: things like new televisions, cars, boats, and homes. That doesn't mean we all have to live like it's 1776, but it does mean that we have to understand how those who founded our country viewed economics. After all, those views took our Tree of Liberty from sapling to superpower in record time—they are worth remembering.

So let's go back to the beginning, to a time when Washington was a man not a city, when John Maynard Keynes was still a hundred years away from sucking his thumb, and when debt was considered as toxic as the drinking water.

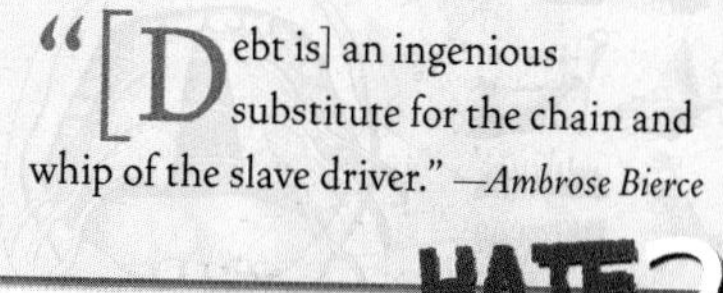

"[Debt is] an ingenious substitute for the chain and whip of the slave driver." —*Ambrose Bierce*
HATE SPEECH?

Welcome to America in the 1700s . . .

"I sincerely believe . . . that the principle of spending money to be paid by posterity under the name of funding is but swindling futurity on a large scale."

—THOMAS JEFFERSON TO JOHN TAYLOR, 1816

CHAPTER 3.

The Founders

A Revolutionary Way to Think about Debt

No one said forming a new country would be easy.

Just ask John Jay.

Jay was the president of the Continental Congress and later went on to become the first chief justice of the U.S. Supreme Court. Back then we were a raucous nation and riots were a regular occurrence. So regular, in fact, that they were often sparked by the strangest of things—for example, as Jay found out, severed cadaver arms.

In 1788, a medical student was sitting in his New York City classroom working on a cadaver arm when another young man peeped into the classroom to see what was going on. Severed arm in hand, the medical student waved the bloody limb at the classroom visitor and jokingly declared that the arm belonged to the Peeping Tom's mother.

The problem?

The Peeping Tom's mother had just died.

The grieving young man dashed home and told his father what he'd just seen. Soon thereafter a mob of angry rioters assembled outside the classroom.

Meanwhile, John Jay was walking around Manhattan, minding his own business and doing typical Founding Father stuff, when he encountered the rioting throng. Rioters' bricks began whizzing through the air, and Jay's head quickly morphed into a bull's-eye. A brick "left two large holes in his forehead," according to accounts at the time, and he "got his scull [*sic*] almost cracked."

Many say that God's hand can be found everywhere in America's founding, and this incident was no exception. Despite his injuries, Jay suffered no brain damage—which is a good thing if you like fiscal responsibility. While Jay may be a lesser-known Founding Father, he was fixated—you might even say *obsessed*—on preventing our fledgling little country from becoming a debt-riddled nation destined for oppression and tyranny.

As Jay saw it, nothing stood to upend the American experiment faster than a nation that bought things it couldn't afford:

> *Let it never be said that America had no sooner become independent than she became insolvent or that her infant glories and growing fame were obscured and tarnished by broken contracts and violated faith, in the very hour when all the nations of the earth were admiring and almost adoring the splendor of her rising.*

Today's big spenders in Washington would have loathed John Jay's fiscal discipline, but they would have really had it out for an even bigger tightwad: Thomas Jefferson.

Like John "Brickhead" Jay, Tom "Tightwad" Jefferson believed that the threat of debt hovered over the nation's neck like a financial guillotine. He felt so strongly about the issue that he dubbed public debt "the greatest of dangers to be feared." He realized that debt is a weapon to be wielded by those to whom it is owed. And this, he understood, is especially dangerous when it is owed to foreign governments or entities. "To preserve our independence," Jefferson said, "we must not let our rulers load us with public debt."

Notice the key phrase he used: "not *let* our rulers." He didn't say "our rulers must not"; he said that it's up to the people to not let them. It's a subtle difference, but an important one, as it underscores the fact that the voting public has stood by while administration after administration has buried us with debt.

> *"I entertain a strong hope that the state of the national finances is now sufficiently matured to enable you to enter upon a systematic and effectual arrangement for the regular redemption and discharge of the public debt, according to the right which has been reserved to the Government. No measure can be more desirable, whether viewed with an eye to its intrinsic importance or to the general sentiment and wish of the nation."*
>
> —George Washington
>
> SORRY STATE OF THE UNION 1792

The Road to Serfdom

There's another consequence of debt that doesn't get talked about much these days, but that Jefferson understood well: Debt forces people to work longer hours to pay it off through taxation. That means less time with one's family, less time to enjoy one's personal freedoms, less time to powder one's wig . . . you know, the fun stuff. Here are Jefferson's own words:

> *We must make our choice between economy and liberty or confusion and servitude . . . If we run into such debts, we must be taxed in our meat and drink, in our necessities and comforts, in our labor and in our amusements . . . if we can prevent the government from wasting the labor of the people, under the pretense of caring for them, they will be happy.*

What's fascinating is that even though Thomas Jefferson himself died cashless under loads of personal debt, he still understood that taking *other* people's money and blowing it on frivolous junk was immoral. It broke the public trust. It poisoned the Tree of Liberty. And he knew from his own personal spending habits that trusting politicians with other people's money (through taxes) was foolish. Jefferson's view was extremely libertarian: "Look, if I want to build a swank mansion with a sweet dome at Monticello with my *own* dough and roll my *own* financial dice, so be it. But I'll be damned if I'm going to swipe *your* wallet to fund *my* pet political projects. That's theft. That's wrong."

Ah . . . financial stewardship. What a novel and bizarre concept.

James Madison, author of the Constitution, also understood the serious long-term problems debt could pose for the new nation. He expressed two major concerns: First, that Americans would not stand for taxes being collected simply to pay for interest on debt (instead of actual government services), and second, that interest payments on debt would show the world we were a creditworthy nation. Why did that worry him? Because Madison worried that once foreign powers knew our payments could be counted on, they'd gobble up our debt and thereby "pretty generally buy out the Americans."

If Madison could only see us now . . .

There's No Such Thing as a Coincidence

One of the common denominators among our Founders was that most of them had been inspired by the genius Scottish moral philosopher and economist Adam Smith. It almost seems providential that Smith wrote *The Wealth of Nations* at the time of America's birth, because our Founding Fathers not only read it, they were deeply influenced by it. Jefferson recommended *The Wealth of Nations* as the "best book on economics." Hamilton paraphrased passages from it in his reports on banking, currency, and manufacturers.

While *The Wealth of Nations* was Smith's best-known book, he'd actually written some prescient passages nearly two decades earlier. "Little else is required," he wrote, "to carry a state to the highest degree of affluence from the lowest barbarism but peace, easy taxes, and a tolerable administration of justice; all the rest being brought about by the natural course of things. All governments which thwart the natural course are unnatural and, to support themselves, are obliged to be oppressive and tyrannical." Put simply, Smith understood the critical ingredient of all economic activity: human nature. He also understood that governments, by their very nature, disrupt free will and free markets because they run on power.

A WEALTH OF KNOWLEDGE

"What is prudence in the conduct of every private family, can scarce be folly in that of the great kingdom."

—ADAM SMITH, *THE WEALTH OF NATIONS*

The Founders, too, had a keen understanding of human nature. They were well steeped in the Judeo-Christian beliefs of human fallibility. As they saw it, Adam and Eve's fall were evidence of human selfishness, and the Pharaoh was evidence of tyranny. They knew that humans are sinful, even depraved creatures who, when armed with the national purse, could do catastrophic economic damage. Starry-eyed, utopian idealists they were not. They understood that there was no guarantee self-government would work. In fact, in some quarters, they were downright daunted and pessimistic. "The weight of self-government," the Federalist declared, "was a burden to which Greek and Roman Shoulders proved unequal." America was still very much an experiment in progress. And debt, the Founders knew, was a surefire way to end it.

A.D.D. Moment

Adam Smith was such a deep thinker that he once fell into a tannery pit while trying to explain division of labor to a friend.

The War on Debt

There's a very good reason why our Founders were so anxious about public debt: America was mired in it at the time of its founding. The cause? The Revolution.

The war for independence wasn't just fought with muskets and cannons; it was a financial fight, too. War is expensive: Soldiers need salaries. Cannons cost cash. But America had almost no money. Things got so bad financially that American commanders often complained that their troops were "almost naked" and had no weapons. To finance the war, we'd taken out loans from both foreign powers and ordinary citizens, who chipped in by buying bonds—a pretty risky endeavor, given that we didn't really even have a government to back them.

These days, it has almost become cliché to say that our fiscal problems could be used against us by our enemies, but back in the revolutionary period, it wasn't a cliché at all; it was an actual strategy. Here's how the *Pennsylvania Packet* described America's financial situation in March 1780:

Britain, foiled in her attempts to conquer America by force, is now carrying on a war of finance. The field of battle is changed for the field of the budget; and the longest purse aided by the best schemes for raising or creating a revenue will in a great measure determine the point . . . The last resource then is finance.

Even back then, our enemy understood that having a strong economy is just as critical to national security as having a strong military. That put our Founders in a really difficult spot: Here were a bunch of ragtag individualists with a blazing dream of self-governance and liberty, and the only chance they had to gain independence was by being completely *dependent* on others for financial support.

Nevertheless, the Founders put their egos aside and hit up investors in both the United States and Europe. Ben Franklin scored a $5.9 million loan from France. Then, with the help of John Adams, he scraped together another $2 million from the Dutch.

Back in the United States, the war had to be financed by individuals, and the wealthy alone wouldn't cut it. As Robert Wright wrote in his book *One Nation Under Debt*, "The number and diversity of holders of U.S. government bonds was impressive in the United States itself and included a variety of professionals, merchants, master artisans, former soldiers, farmers, planters, foreign potentates and investors." The amounts varied. In South Carolina, for example, bonds ranged from $1.04 to $804,000.

These bonds, as you might imagine given the circumstances, had been hastily written. During the war for independence, Robert Morris, the financier of the revolution, and his staff had dashed off handwritten notes to people in exchange for livestock, cloth, and other goods necessary to equip the army.

We're not talking about a well-oiled fund-raising machine here. America was desperate; the nation was *literally* fighting for its existence.

The Brits, of course, realized that they had America by the throat financially, and so they began to apply pressure. They did everything in their power to trash the fund-raising efforts by launching a monetary jihad against American efforts. They counterfeited bonds to make investors nervous, and they blasted the colonist bonds as worthless to sway public perception. The only good use for the bonds, the Brits said, was for wallpaper.

Fortunately, the public realized it was propaganda. People of all kinds turned into investors and snatched up the bonds. In 1795, about 21,500 different entities owned U.S. national bonds. Even Founding Fathers like George Washington, George Clinton of New York, and Caesar Rodney of Delaware owned slices of the revolutionary bond pie. There's nothing like a little personal financial stake to get people motivated.

After the war was won, a debate quickly ensued about how to manage future expenses: Should all expenditures, no matter how pertinent society thought they were, be fully paid for when promised, or was debt okay in certain situations? These were big questions, but a consensus emerged among the Founders over time. The general view was that carefully managed debt could be helpful in two narrow realms: trade or commerce, and in fighting and winning wars. After all, "in war," the Federalists wrote, "the longest purse prevails." Beyond that, debt was to be fiercely avoided.

It was a pretty unambiguous stance, which is why the issue of national debt played only a minor role at the constitutional conventions and no role during the ratification debates. There just wasn't much left to discuss. Except for commerce and wars, debt was off-limits.

One of the main criticisms of the king and the British system among the Founders was extravagance and indulgence among the government. Harvard College president Samuel Langdon preached a sermon to the Massachusetts legislature in May 1775 declaring, "The general prevalence of vice has changed the whole face of things in the British government." He asked, "In what does the British nation now glory?" His answer: "in titles of dignity without virtue, in vast public treasures continually lavished in corruption till every fund is exhausted, notwithstanding the mighty streams perpetually flowing in." He went on to call for eliminating "vast unnecessary expenses continually incurred by its enormous vices." Can you imagine the president of Harvard talking like that today?

Swindling Futurity

Chief among the "Just Say No to National Debt" faction was Thomas Jefferson. For Jefferson, trading future financial prosperity for short-term gain was essentially theft. "The principle of spending money to be paid by posterity under the name of funding is but swindling futurity on a large scale," he said. In fact, Jefferson was such a deficit hawk that he wanted a balanced-budget amendment for the Constitution that would take "from the federal government the power of borrowing."

Some apologists for big federal spending seek historical cover by suggesting that Alexander Hamilton seemed to laud debt. As evidence, they offer up Hamilton's quote that "a national debt, if it is not excessive, will be to us a national blessing." It sounds like damning evidence (other than the "if it is not excessive" qualifier), except for the fact that the quote is now being used completely out of context. Far from praising national spending sprees, Hamilton was actually referring to debt being an opportunity for America to bolster her standing on the international stage by making good on her financial promises.

As Hamilton wrote in his 1790 *Report on Public Credit*, "States, like individuals, who observe their engagements, are respected and trusted, while the reverse is the fate of those, who pursue an opposite conduct."

Hamilton knew that the biggest challenge for early America was liquid capital. The trouble was . . . we didn't have any! It's like the chicken-and-egg quandary that many young people find themselves in today. A good credit score is required to borrow money, but you can't get a good credit score without having money. So, from time to time, Hamilton believed we had to dip into the debt column to build that trust on the international stage.

But there's another Hamilton quote that you won't hear many spending lovers repeat: "The creation of debt should always be accompanied with the means of extinguishment." In other words, when Washington whips out the national credit card in a time of crisis, such as a war, it needs to have a plan for how it's going to pay that money back.

TEACHABLE MOMENT

If Hollywood were around back then, it probably would have had a field day with the relationship between Alexander Hamilton and James Madison. You'd be hard-pressed to find two more different people: Hamilton, in the words of Madison biographer Robert Allen Rutland, "loved the ladies—all the ladies—while Madison was so shy he seemed doomed to bachelorhood." Hamilton was a city guy; Madison liked the country. Hamilton liked being around bankers; Madison liked the company of farmers. Hamilton liked to dress up; Madison was called "the crow" for his incredibly drab dress. And while Hamilton thought some level of debt could be a positive for the country, Madison hated the idea. It's no wonder that these "friends" didn't stay very friendly for long.

Hollywood would also have loved the ending to this story as well, since Hamilton was killed in a duel with Aaron Burr. (Of course, if Oliver Stone were directing, Madison probably would've hired Burr as a hit man.)

A.D.D. Moment

No wonder progressivism got so popular; we could never have survived with such a crazy, antiquated view of debt like that.

It is in that context that Hamilton's frequently misconstrued quotation has to be considered. That is, if we can make good on our financial promises, "a national debt, if it is not excessive, will be to us a national blessing. It will be a powerful cement to our union." If gone unpaid, however, that cement would weigh America down with a reputation as a deadbeat borrower.

Hamilton's view was pretty clear, but in *The Continentalist*, he elaborated further by saying that government funding should be done with a combination of "permanent funds" and grants renewed each year. "Permanent funds are indispensable," he said, "but they ought to be of such a nature and so moderate in their amount as never to be inconvenient."

IS THIS CLEAR ENOUGH?

"Accumulation of debt "is perhaps the NATURAL DISEASE of all Governments. And it is not easy to conceive anything more likely than this to lead to great and convulsive revolutions of Empire." —Alexander Hamilton

Hamilton was, in fact, so worried about a perpetual and growing debt that he came up with an idea to make sure it could never happen: a sinking fund. This fund, which would be separate from the general fund, and would be financed by post-office revenues. These revenues would be completely off-limits to politicians and instead would be used to retire 5 percent of the debt every year until it was paid off.

John "Brickhead" Jay shared the same concerns as Hamilton. Jay had arguably contributed the five most important essays of the Federalist papers and was a diplomat who believed that paying off our debt was important for America's good standing in the world. Fortunately—most of the other Founders agreed. Debt repayment became such a no-brainer that an 1801 Committee on Ways and Means report concluded that "the propriety of pursuing measures for the final extinguishment of the public debt is a position too obviously true to require any illustration." *Too obviously true . . .*

This strategy turned out to be exactly what our fledgling country needed, and foreign countries began taking note of our financial responsibility. In fact, by 1794, Founders' disciplined paying down of the national debt meant America enjoyed the "highest credit rating in Europe." Talleyrand, who would later go on to be the French foreign minister, said that the American bonds "were safe and free from reverses. They have been funded in such a sound manner and the prosperity of this country is growing so rapidly that there can be no doubt of their solvency."

This view would serve America well in the decades to come. Maybe a little *too* well.

Talleyrand Comedy Hour

Mirabeau, a French revolutionary, once said that Talleyrand "would sell his soul for money, and he would be right, for he would be exchanging dung for gold."

Borrowing for Bailouts?

Today, we just assume that debt will be used as a way to "manage" the economy's fluctuations, but the Founders would have laughed in the face of anyone offering that opinion back then. In his farewell address, Washington described public credit as "a very important source of strength and security." He recommended that we "use

TEACHABLE MOMENT

That quote from Talleyrand brings up a really good point that not a lot of people like to talk about: The days of America "growing so rapidly" as to be able to pay off all debts are likely behind us. (That doesn't mean our best days are behind us . . . Gross domestic product and happiness are not mutually exclusive concepts.) Consider the numbers: The average growth rate of our economy from after the Great Depression (1939) through the end of Reagan's Morning in America (1988) was 4.3 percent a year. Looking at it by decade, the United States had similar growth rates in the 1970s (3.3 percent), 1980s (3.1 percent), and 1990s (3.2 percent). The 2000s, however, were not so kind. Growth averaged just 1.9 percent a year. Economists think we'll bounce back with 3.1 percent growth in 2010 and 3 percent growth in 2011, but even if that happens—and it's a very big if—that's still nowhere near the kind of growth we had over most of the twentieth century, let alone during a time like the Industrial Revolution.

The Congressional Budget Office has growth pegged at 2.2 percent a year going forward, a much lower forecast that would pose huge problems for the economy over the long term. Consider the math: If our economy were to grow at 3.5 percent for the next seventy years, GDP would be $162.2 trillion. If we instead grew at 2.2 percent, GDP would be just $66.9 trillion. Small changes, big consequences.

it as sparingly as possible, avoiding occasions of expense by cultivating peace." Furthermore, Washington argued that we avoid "the accumulation of debt . . . by vigorous exertions in time of peace to discharge the debts which unavoidable wars have occasioned, not ungenerously throwing upon posterity the burthen which we ourselves ought to bear."

In 1792, a panic, ignited by land speculators, erupted in the financial markets. "The crash has been tremendous," Jefferson reported. "And bankruptcies continue to increase." In response, Hamilton launched a debt-funded stimulus plan, which included a compassionate bailout for those who bought land next to garbage dumps and the nationalization of a huge chunk of General Buggyworks.

Or, maybe not.

No, instead of using bailouts, Hamilton used a far more powerful policy: *common sense*. He ensured that folks with solid credit got loans, he used government funds to pay off bonds in the open market, and he eased up on the collection of debts owed to the government to keep liquidity in the system.

Wonder of all wonders, it worked.

Our Founders' commitment to cinching America's financial belt and boosting the nation's credit abroad also allowed the United

Founding Wisdom

On the General Welfare clause:

To take from one, because it is thought his own industry and that of his father has acquired too much, in order to spare to others who (or whose fathers) have not exercised equal industry and skill, is to violate arbitrarily the first principle of association, "to guarantee to everyone a free exercise of his industry and the fruits acquired by it."

—THOMAS JEFFERSON

States to grow—literally. By the early 1800s, France was cash-strapped and needed money to fuel its own war with Britain. Having just taken possession of a chunk of land in North America from Spain, France had the perfect bargaining chip to use in funding its war effort. (Napoleon, the first emperor of France, had dreams of colonizing the New World and building an empire, but he knew that, given the war with Britain, the territory would be too hard to defend.)

> "It will afford me a heart-felt satisfaction to concur in such further measures as will ascertain to our country the prospect of a speedy extinguishment of the debt. Posterity may have cause to regret if from any motive intervals of tranquility are left unimproved for accelerating this valuable end."
>
> —GEORGE WASHINGTON
>
> SORRY 1796 STATE OF THE UNION

Having been previously impressed with America's conscientiousness in repaying its debts, Napoleon was ready to make a deal. And what a deal it was. For just four pennies an acre, France sold us 828,800 square miles of land—an area larger than the countries of France, Spain, Portugal, Italy, Holland, Switzerland, and the British Isles combined. It was a little real estate transaction that you probably now know by its more popular name: the Louisiana Purchase.

There was one small catch before the deal of the century could be consummated, however: Napoleon wanted cash up front and America had only about a quarter of the money on hand. To make up the difference, Secretary of the Treasury Albert Gallatin floated bonds, which sold very well, likely due to our stellar credit history. On May 2, 1803, the treaty was signed—adding one more approved use of debt to the Founders' list: expansion.

GOING DUTCH

The National Archives recently found three two-thousand-dollar certificates issued to the Dutch to finance the Louisiana Purchase. The certificates were not stamped or canceled, indicating that we've probably never paid the Dutch back for their investment. Suckers!

Checks and Balances for Our Checking Account Balances

While the Founders obviously got a lot right, they did get one thing wrong: They thought the biggest obstacle to keeping spending under control would come from the president, not the Congress. That fit with their Judeo-Christian beliefs that gave them a crystal-clear understanding of human nature: Politicians, like most individuals, were sinful, self-interested creatures who were not to be trusted spending other people's money.

The Founders had also been shaped by their experience with Great Britain's big-spending king. They did everything in their power to set up the American system in a way that would prevent any American president (our version of a king) from being able to ruin the country with debt. Their solution was to balance the president's power with that of hundreds of representatives from around the country. Hundreds of politicians all to keep one person in check! What they didn't count on, of course, was that the president and the Congress would one day *simultaneously* become reckless with our money.

Overall, of course, the Founders did an amazing job in setting the course for the country. During George Washington's two terms in office, the war debt (including about $25 million in state debts) had reached $75–80 million (about $996 million in 2009 dollars). But, in relatively short order, the Founders got things back under control, while they also built our reputation in the world.

It was a precedent worthy of emulation and preservation, one that could keep strengthening and growing the Tree of Liberty for centuries to come.

There were other people, however, who didn't appreciate those precedents. While they'd not yet been formalized into a group, they would eventually come to be known as progressives, and they had other plans for the Tree of Liberty.

Unfortunately, they involved a saw.

TEACHABLE MOMENT

Back in Washington's days, the federal government owed about $225 per citizen (adjusted to 2009 dollars). Today? Forty-three thousand dollars per person. If this were a game show where I could choose the government showcase or the cash, I'd take the cash.

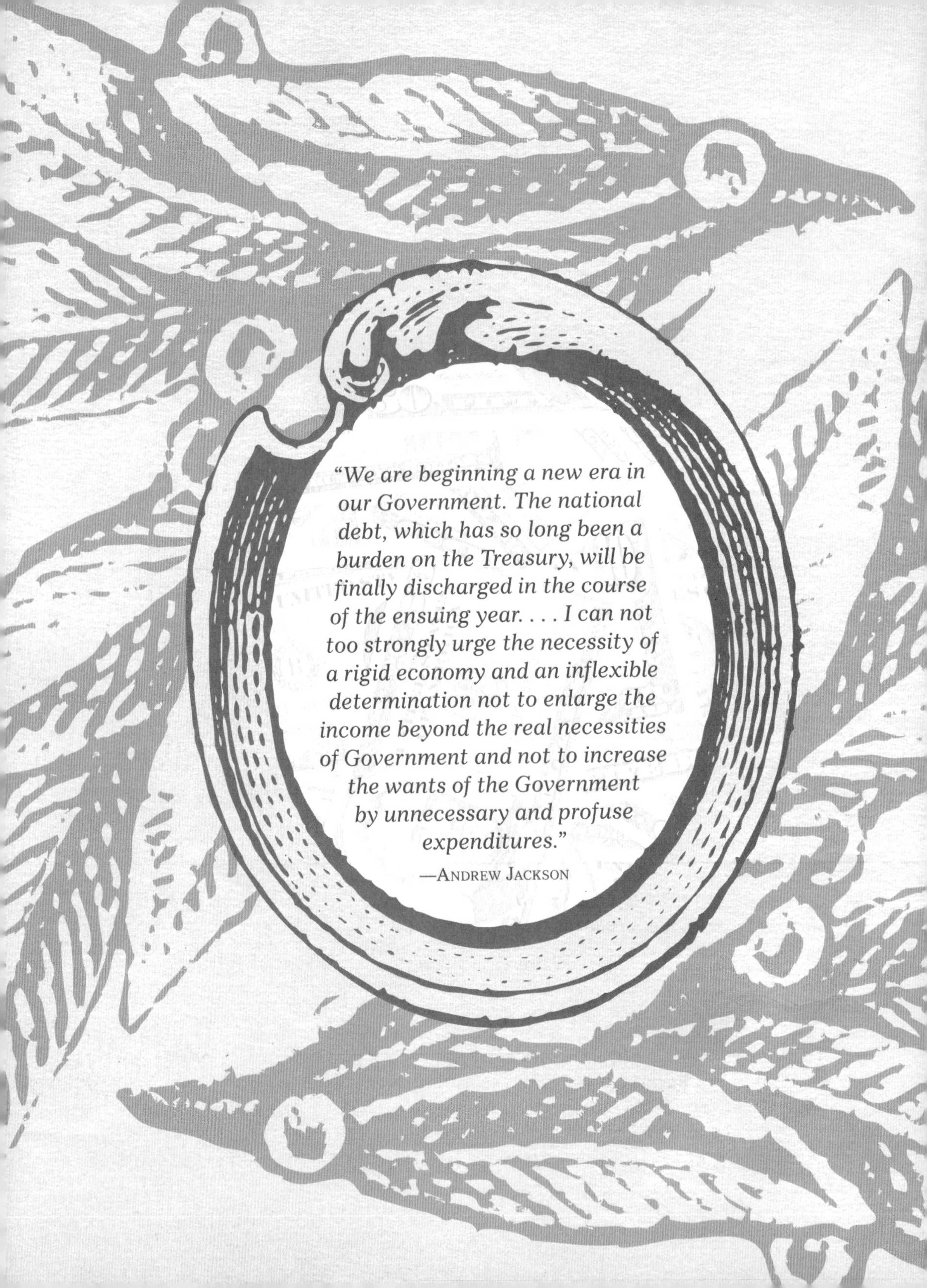

"We are beginning a new era in our Government. The national debt, which has so long been a burden on the Treasury, will be finally discharged in the course of the ensuing year. . . . I can not too strongly urge the necessity of a rigid economy and an inflexible determination not to enlarge the income beyond the real necessities of Government and not to increase the wants of the Government by unnecessary and profuse expenditures."

—Andrew Jackson

CHAPTER 4.

The Nineteenth Century

Old Hickory, Honest Abe, and Harpy Fangs

Don't let that stoic portrait on the face of a twenty-dollar bill fool you; Andrew Jackson knew how to throw a party.

At his inauguration, Old Hickory's raucous band of supporters got so sloshed and wild that they smashed thousands of dollars of fine china and glassware and tracked a trail of muddy footprints all over the White House. The party got so out of control that Jackson had his servants haul the liquor out onto the White House lawn just to get everyone out, so a cleaning crew could get to work.

Starting off an administration with such a costly bash (at least before it was fashionable to do so) might seem to portend bad things for Andrew Jackson's financial stewardship, but nothing could be further from the truth. Jackson despised debt so much that, in 1824, he called it a "national curse" that helped destroy individual liberty in favor of the elites.

Today, that lesson has mostly been lost. Even in the face of increasing joblessness, stagnant incomes, and a deteriorating economy, our leaders view debt as a national blessing that can cure all of society's ills. Unfortunately, forgetting the lessons of the past doesn't invalidate them. History always wins in the end.

"I can not but hope that Congress in reviewing their resources will find means to meet the intermediate interest of this additional debt without recurring to new taxes."
—Thomas Jefferson

SORRY STATE OF THE UNION 1803

Old Hickory's Word: Strong as Oak

Jackson, who was born poor and then orphaned by the American Revolution, staked his political career on a single promise to the nation: "My vow shall be to pay the national debt, to prevent a monied aristocracy from growing up around our administration that must bend to its views, and ultimately destroy the liberty of our country." That promise didn't work out for him during his first run for president in 1824 (he lost), but he continued to live by it after his eventual election.

In many ways, America's seventh president was merely parroting the views of his predecessors. For example, the two presidents before him, John Quincy Adams and James Monroe, had both started a trend toward paying off the debt. Jackson's pledge to do the same, despite how radical it may sound today, was really nothing new. Except for waging wars or buying land, presidents throughout much of the nineteenth century continued the anti-frivolous spending views of our Founders.

We've Been OVERTON WINDOWED

Back in Old Hickory's era, Americans had a much different view on the role of government than they do today. According to noted economic historian Robert Wright in his book *One Nation Under Debt*, "Most Americans believed that government, especially the national government, ought to limit itself to the supply of a few essential public goods, like defense."

There was also a much healthier respect for the Constitution back then, as Progressivism had not yet infected the system. People not only viewed the government's role as limited; they lived it. Instead of a welfare system and an ever-growing list of agencies and programs (HHS, HUD, SSI), people voluntarily helped people: neighbors, charities, churches. Money wasn't raised en masse and put into some general fund; it was raised for specific individuals and families.

Back in the nineteenth century, charity and welfare were viewed as a responsibility of those able to give. In his book *Renewing American Compassion*, Marvin Olasky revealed that nineteenth-century Americans viewed the trip from poverty to prosperity in seven steps: "Affiliation, Bonding, Categorization, Discernment, Employment, Freedom and God." Read the description of these steps, and ask yourself whether these ideals are reflected in the federal government's efforts today.

Affiliation: *Connect people with families and communities that can best relate to them.*

Bonding: *Help people on a one-to-one basis.*

Categorization: *Personalize charity according to individual need.*

Discernment: *Practice responsible giving; know who you are giving to and why.*

Employment: *Demand work. "Labor is the life of society, and the beggar who will not work is a social cannibal feeding on that life."*

Freedom: *This is not the opportunity to do anything with anyone at any time, but is the opportunity to work and worship without governmental interruption.*

God: *God is compassionate, but demands change.*

Even with that extraordinarily restrictive view on using debt, America still managed to expand and grow. Louisiana was purchased. Payments were made for Alaska, the Gadsden Purchase, and the land acquired in the Treaty of Guadalupe-Hidalgo (Arizona, New Mexico, and parts of Utah, California, Nevada, and Colorado). Railroads and canals were starting to rapidly expand—though back then it was private industry that led the way, not the government. Heck, the country even fought a brutal, bloody, and expensive civil war. But again, even with these war expenditures and serious capital investments in land and transportation, the mind-set never shifted: Debt, even when deemed necessary, was the enemy.

TEACHABLE MOMENT

When it came to railroads, the federal government was involved in some of the lines that went to the Pacific coast because they secured the necessary land. But, even then, James J. Hill and his completely private Great Northern Railway was the most profitable. That lesson, of course, has been completely forgotten. These days we just throw billions at Amtrak with no profitability in sight and pretend that it's somehow the way things have to be.

Beyond his own impoverished childhood, Jackson had developed a lifelong hatred of aristocracy that stemmed from an event that occurred during the Revolutionary War. While being held as a prisoner of war, Old Hickory was ordered to shine a British officer's boots. He refused. The officer slashed at him with his sword, and while Jackson was able to ward off the worst of the blow, his left arm was cut to the bone and his head was gashed open. Suffice it to say that that encounter didn't exactly leave him with a warm and fuzzy feeling about English aristocracy.

After he was orphaned, Jackson's views on economics began to take hold. He came to see the accumulation of debt as simply another way to slowly wreak havoc on the rights of man.

A supporter of Jackson once called the idea of mounting public debt "harpy fangs." While he was referring to Greek mythology (Nerd Alert: "Harpies" were winged bird-women with fangs and claws who continually snatched away the food from blind Phineas when he tried to eat), I have a modern-day interpretation: Debt slowly sucks the lifeblood out of a republic, all while beautiful harps play a melody in the background. You are so happy and content with all of the "free stuff" being handed out that you don't realize you will soon be dead.

As 1834 drew to a close, Jackson had accomplished a feat few thought possible: He had paid off the national debt. "Free from public debt," the president wrote, "at peace with all the world . . . the present may be hailed as the epoch in our history the most favorable for the settlement of those principles in our domestic policy which shall be best calculated to give stability to our Republic and secure the blessings of freedom to our citizens."

How did he do it? Surely it must've been through major tax increases, likely on the wealthiest one percent. That, as we all now know, is really the only way to turn things around, right? Strangely, no. Jackson found another way. Instead of new taxes, tariffs, and regulations, he did the opposite: He let entrepreneurs innovate and free markets work. As a result, the American economy grew, virtually free from government interference. The lesson from history is clear: The best way out of debt isn't to grow taxes—it's to grow the tax *base*.

Brother Bankrupting Brother

Unfortunately, the "stability to our Republic" that Jackson gloated about soon came face-to-face with the Civil War. Economically, fighting wars is like gaining weight: Once you start, it's hard to stop. Dieting might help temporarily, but you hardly ever get back down to the weight you were before. Once you start packing on the pounds again, you are starting from a higher weight than last time, thereby creating a vicious cycle that's impossible to get out of without a radical change in lifestyle.

How did Jackson's supporters celebrate the repayment of the debt? With a lavish party in D.C., of course! While that's the way our politicians still celebrate their supposed achievements, there is one big difference between Jackson's parties and the modern-day ones: Every important Democrat attended the debt party in 1835, but Jackson himself stayed home.

War spending is the same way. Each time we fight, we rack up a massive amount of new debt. Even when we subsequently cut spending, it's rare that we ever do enough to pay off the cost of the war. Therefore, the *next* major spending item or war simply adds to the previously bloated total, and so on. The only way to stop the cycle is to take a completely radical approach to our finances—and *radical* isn't a word that is in the vocabulary of most politicians (except those working at 1600 Pennsylvania Avenue . . . though they have a much different vision for *radical* than most of us do).

Before the Civil War, the United States government had never spent more in a single year than $74.2 million (in 1858 dollars). Since the Civil War, however, America has never spent *less* than $236.9 million, which occurred in 1878. In 1865 alone, with the war ending and the occupation of the South beginning, we spent $1.297 billion, the first time in history that any nation ever had a billion-dollar budget.

At the start of the Civil War on April 15, 1861, the federal government was pumping about $172,000 a day into the war effort ($4 million a day in 2009 dollars). By year's end, that number had climbed to $1.5 million a day.

The federal government was hemorrhaging cash at historic levels, yet the war was still being funded "largely (through) domestic financing." Abraham Lincoln's Treasury secretary, Salmon P. Chase, who would later go on to serve as chief justice of the Supreme Court, felt strongly that the Union had benefited from the fact that the debt had previously been paid off, which gave the country a strong credit history. He pledged that, over time, the new mountains of debt would, likewise, be whittled away.

To accomplish that goal, Chase brought back a financing concept pioneered during the Revolution: Instead of simply selling bonds to bankers, he offered them to ordinary citizens as well. Chase did that by breaking the bonds up into denominations as small as fifty dollars, to be paid in monthly installments. The move laid the foundation for the future sales of war bonds during the First and Second World Wars—a source of financing that was critical to our success. But, perhaps more important, Chase's public financing tactic successfully raised two-thirds of the Union's revenues—thereby ensuring that citizens who supported the war effort would pay for it themselves instead of passing the buck to future generations.

RIPPED FROM THE HEADLINES

A NEW WAY TO PAY THE NATIONAL DEBT

—*Chicago Tribune*, July 21, 1865

That fit squarely into Lincoln's view that debt held by American citizens was *far* preferred to debt held by foreign powers. "The great advantage of citizens being creditors as well as debtors, with relation to the public debt, is obvious," Lincoln said in his 1864 address to Congress. "Men can readily perceive that they cannot be much oppressed by a debt which they owe to themselves." That concept may have been obvious back then, but it's pretty obscure now. We no longer seem to care *who* buys our debt, so long as the rates stay low and the money keeps flowing.

TEACHABLE MOMENT

Instead of ensuring that Americans own the debt (90 percent of our War of 1812 debt was held by citizens), we've invited foreign investors in with open arms. As a result, only an estimated 60 percent of our current national debt is held by U.S. entities, thereby leaving the country wide open to the very oppression that Lincoln was concerned about. (I say "estimated" because, as the Congressional Budget Office points out, we really don't know. The numbers are "imperfect"—a fact that should concern all of us.)

Still, the military money machine whirred on. By May 1864, the Navy and War departments were shelling out about $2 million a day, which matched the entire amount the government was raising. But Lincoln, like Thomas Jefferson before him, knew firsthand the perils of personal debt. His failed business ventures had left him to conclude that "debt was the greatest obstacle I have ever met in my life" and he didn't want that same impediment to be put in the way of his country.

Republicans pledged fiscal responsibility, but someone always has to pay. In this case, it was decided that the debts were too large for spending cuts alone (sound familiar?), so, in August 1861, America passed its first income tax. Salmon Chase pushed it through Congress, saying that "a tax of ten or even twenty percent on all incomes [is better than] the rapid accumulation of National Debt . . . and the rapid deterioration of the National credit." But there was some good news—at least for a little while: Chase's proposed tax rates were much higher than what actually passed. Middle-class earners had to pay a whopping 3 percent on income of about $800. Those who made more than $10,000 got creamed with a gigantic 5 percent. And any greedy capitalist who dared to create jobs for others and earned above $10,000 was taxed at the criminally astronomical rate of—ready for this?—10 percent!

"I can not but hope that Congress in reviewing their resources will find means to meet the intermediate interest of this additional debt without recurring to new taxes."
—Thomas Jefferson

SORRY 1831 STATE OF THE UNION

TEACHABLE MOMENT

Abe Lincoln tried several businesses as a young man, among them a partnership to run a grocery store. Lincoln went into debt to buy the business and it never really made money. He walked away from the business after a year, but didn't walk away from his obligations. He not only paid his debt off, but also the debt of his deceased partner, a debt that he was not legally required to repay.

We could joke about how this was quite the Obama-style redistributionist policy, but, as we've now discovered, the joke was really on us. Like almost all progressive policies, this was nothing but a starter home—a bare-bones structure that could be expanded and developed over the years until the end result (a progressive income tax with rates that once went as high as 91 percent) looked nothing like the original. A lot more on that later.

The lesson to take from this is that the national income tax began as an extreme measure authorized to pay for an extreme (and thankfully rare) occurrence: a civil war. And yet, even then, given the dire and essential nature of the cause before them, America's leaders did not use the crisis to saddle future generations with debt. Instead they "soaked the rich" by taking a dime for every buck a wealthy person earned.

HISTORY REPEATING

As Treasury secretary, Salmon Chase frequently got frustrated at the destruction he saw coming. He felt that the government was not prepared nor organized enough and that "neither the President, his counselors nor his commanding general seem to care." Instead, he complained, "they rush on from expense to expense and from defeat to defeat, heedless of the abyss of bankruptcy and ruin which yawns before us." Sound familiar?

The Printing Press and Politicians: A Match Made in Hell

Given the size of the debt that had been incurred, it soon became obvious that even a new income tax wouldn't be enough. So, to fund the war, the North passed the "Legal Tender Act of 1862" and started printing $450 million worth of "greenbacks," so named because of the color of the ink that was used. These notes were not backed by gold but were instead "legal tender notes" backed by the full faith and credit of the federal government.

It was a novel concept, but Treasury secretary Chase hated the idea. He knew that printing money not backed by a hard asset would eventually trigger inflation. "Inflated paper currency," he said, was a "great evil, and should be reformed as soon as possible." But, as before, the war effort took priority. Concerns over inflating took a backseat to concerns over existing, and Chase reluctantly agreed to the act. Like any good politician, Chase, of course, tried to make lemonade out of lemons by putting a picture of himself on the new bill—sort of a miniature political ad in your wallet—in the hope of boosting his name recognition enough to become president one day. (Spoiler Alert: It didn't work.)

While it's often forgotten in history, before this period of government money, "state banks" were the norm. These were actually private banks chartered by individual states. As part of their charters, banks were permitted to print their own money ("notes"), with the value being guaranteed by a gold/silver ("specie") reserve. Because no bank can survive if it keeps a 100 percent reserve, each bank would try to judge how many notes would be redeemed for specie on a given day, and would keep that amount on hand. Typically, that was between 6 and 10 percent of all the outstanding notes.

As is the case today, a bank's reserves are really only part of the reason it is successful—trust is the other. It wasn't the gold that backed the notes, but faith. The "reserve ratio" was more of a test of that faith than any real economic measure that people cared about.

During times of panic, people would run to banks

Here's a story that will sound pretty familiar. After the Civil War, the people like Salmon Chase who agreed to the idea of printing money only as a temporary solution pushed for the government to return to hard currency. The result was the "Contraction Act of 1866" (by the way, how come the names of acts back then were so straightforward? These days we'd call it something dumb like the "Reduction of Paper Money in Circulation and Increase of Specie Instead Because It Will Help Sick Kids Act of 2010") and it allowed for the repossession of greenbacks.

So, why aren't we all paying with notes backed by gold today?

Well, because the economy worsened in 1867 and everyone needed something to blame. The easy target: the Contraction Act. This is going to come as a shock, but politicians collapsed under the pressure and stripped the removal-of-greenback provision from the act.

It just goes to show you that when we do something "temporary" because of an "emergency" we'd better be prepared for it to be permanent.

to exchange their notes for specie. The problem, of course, is that banks didn't have enough to fulfill everyone's orders, so they would occasionally stop converting notes. This was called "suspending," and while it was prohibited by the banks' charters, there wasn't much that anyone could do if all banks did it at once. (Remember, most of the banks during this time were not actually insolvent; they were simply unable to handle a run on their reserves—much like the banks of today.)

THE PUBLIC DEBT AND WHO CREATED IT

—*Chicago Tribune*, August 15, 1868

The key difference between these charter banks and today's banks is that the notes they issued would compete openly in the marketplace against other notes. If a particular bank had a poor reputation, their notes might be worth less, or not accepted by the public at all.

How did you know if a note was worth the $5 printed on it? For that, people turned to something called "Dillistin's Bank Note Reporter," which reported the prices of all known money and was used extensively. Any money trading at more than one percent below par value was considered to not be trustworthy and people would avoid it. Naturally, if you were a businessman and someone wanted to pay you in money you didn't trust, you would "discount" it and demand a higher price for the risk.

These days, there is no competition in money: A dollar is a dollar, regardless of the fact that very little in the way of gold, silver, or other hard assets actually backs up that value.

Competitive money was a very effective and stable system for many years. What ended it? The government's involvement, of course. After printing the $450 million in greenbacks and chartering a slew of new national banks (each with authority to print money), the state banks had to go. The federal government passed a new 10 percent tax on all non-national currency (i.e., notes issued by state chartered banks), effectively giving an unfair advantage to the national banks and driving the private ones out of business.

It's not hard to find that same kind of mentality today. Large, international banks are bailed out because they are "too big to fail" while small, local banks (you know, the ones that don't have big lobbying budgets) are left to fend for themselves. Go government!

The War's Toll: Physically, Mentally, and Financially

Numerous historians have recounted the emotional and psychological toll that the four-year-long whirlwind of human carnage took on Lincoln personally. By the war's end, hundreds of thousands of citizens had been slaughtered and countless more injured or widowed. The cost in blood and treasure is hard for modern Americans to comprehend—and Lincoln knew it was all on him. The death, the debt, the devastation to the nation's land and infrastructure—all of it bore his fingerprints.

"War, at the best, is terrible," Lincoln said in a June 1864 speech in Philadelphia. "And this war of ours, in its magnitude and in its duration, is one of the most terrible. It has deranged business, totally in many localities, and partially in all localities. It has destroyed property and ruined homes; it has produced a national debt and taxation unprecedented . . ."

Tough Love

If you want to really understand how Lincoln viewed our country's obligation to get out of debt, take a look at how he responded to his own stepbrother, who'd hit him up for eighty dollars. After you read Lincoln's letter, think to yourself how someone like George W. Bush or Barack Obama would've responded to the same request.

FROM THE DESK OF
ABE LINCOLN

Dear Johnston:
Your request for eighty dollars I do not think it best to comply with now . . . You are not lazy, and still you are an idler. I doubt whether, since I saw you, you have done a good whole day's work in any one day.

You are now in need of some money; and what I propose is, that you shall go to work, "tooth and nail," for somebody who will give you money for it . . . I now promise you, that for every dollar you will, between this and the first of May, get for your own labor, either in money or as your own indebtedness, I will then give you one other dollar . . .

Now, if you will do this, you will be soon out of debt, and, what is better, you will have a habit that will keep you from getting in debt again. But, if I should now clear you out of debt, next year you would be just as deep in as ever . . .

You have always been kind to me, and I do not mean to be unkind to you. On the contrary, if you will but follow my advice, you will find it worth more than eighty times eighty dollars to you.

—Abraham Lincoln, January 2, 1851

What made Lincoln the iconic leader he was, however, was his ability to recognize that these painful—indeed, excruciating—human and financial costs were still worth it. The Union hung in the balance. Slavery's fate, too. Only stakes of that moral magnitude, Lincoln believed, could justify the kind of debt that, at the time, seemed unthinkable.

Of course, Lincoln, for all his wonderful characteristics, was still a politician. He knew the debt was large, but necessary, and so he did what all good politicians do: He started up the spin machine. "A debt of $600 million now," he explained, "is a less sum per head than was the debt of our Revolution when we came out of that struggle. And the money value in the country now bears even a greater proportion to what it was then, than does the population. Surely each man has strong motive now to preserve our liberties, as each had then to establish them."

Lincoln's comments, while likely intended to alleviate concern among citizens, also reveal that he, like Jackson, understood the power and importance of economic growth as a method of paying down debt. As he explained, a rapidly growing population meant more cash for the Treasury to collect, and therefore each person's share of the overall debt came down. But, even with that understanding, Lincoln knew that future growth couldn't be used as a crutch. It's "no excuse," he said, "for delaying payment [on the nation's bills]."

But Abe's admirable attitude aside, the national debt he had amassed was a *colossus*. In October 1865, Secretary of Treasury Hugh McCullough announced that the national debt stood at $2.8 *billion*, dwarfing anything America had ever seen before. As historian Jay Sexton noted, "The debt's previous high had been in 1815, when it stood at $127 million, thanks to the War of 1812."

These were jaw-dropping and daunting debts and the American people were not accustomed to them. The nation was now spending 42 times more than it had spent just six years earlier, an amount equal to about half of the country's entire gross national product!

In 1865, the Republicans passed a resolution in honor of Lincoln: "Resolved, That the national faith, pledged for the redemption of the public debt, must be kept inviolate, and that for this purpose we recommend economy and rigid responsibility in the public expenditures."

(I'll pause here for a second so you can stop laughing.)

A.D.D. Moment

The logic that population growth decreases the amount of debt "per head" (as Lincoln put it) is something that we're probably going to hear a lot about in the years ahead. With demographics working against them, politicians won't be focused on organic population growth; they'll be focused on growth via immigration. In other words, you are very likely to hear the argument that some kind of amnesty program for illegal aliens is the magic bullet to getting our national debt under control. Two progressive birds, one stone.

Some Things Never Change: *This ad was created from an actual speech given by vocal Lincoln critic Clement Vallandigham.*

Clement Vallandigham

Address to the Peace Democrats, 1864

If you want more taxation, a larger public debt, vote for **LINCOLN.**

If you want renewed drafts of men to carry on the war, vote for **LINCOLN.**

If you want him to take your first, second and third born sons to carry on the war, vote for **LINCOLN.**

If you want to find your currency in a ruined condition, your greenbacks worth thirty cents on the dollar; if you want the price of everything you buy to go up, and everything you sell to go down... vote for the Republican party.

Even in the absence of Treasury secretary Chase, the Democratic and Republican presidents who were elected after the Civil War remained committed to championing his method of getting citizens to pony up small amounts of cash for bonds. And lots of Americans did. By 1880, 71,587 individuals directly owned registered government bonds—a fairly significant number given that the population back then was only about 50 million, but still not rising to the heights of patriotic debt ownership seen during the Revolution.

"The income of the Government, by its increased volume and through economies in its collection, is now more than ever in excess of public necessities."
—Grover Cleveland

Savor those words from Cleveland, a man who was one of the last great fiscally conservative, small-government Democrats. (By the way, back then it was mainly the Democrats who were in favor of a return to hard money, not Republicans. Yep, times have certainly changed.) Cleveland, you might recall, is also the president famous for telling Texas farmers suffering from a drought that they should seek help from citizens, not the government. "Though the people support the government," he said, "the government should not support the people."

SORRY STATE OF THE UNION 1886

A Team Effort

Fortunately for America, which was still finding its sea legs, the nineteenth-century presidents who followed Lincoln were largely committed to chipping away at the nation's massive debt. Their political affiliations didn't matter. Andrew Johnson, who was part of the National Union party, though routinely considered to be a Democrat, cut the debt by $100 million, even though he spent $7.2 million buying Alaska in 1867. Ulysses S. Grant, a Republican, came next. Aided by his fiscally conservative Treasury secretary, who was "fanatically devoted to reducing the national debt and establishing a hard currency," Grant managed to reduce the debt further, down to $2.2 billion—a cut of $500 million.

The next four presidents (Hayes, Garfield, and Arthur—all Republicans—and Cleveland, a Democrat) all pitched in to work the debt down to $1.6 billion by 1892—a full 43 percent below the level it was at in 1865. (During his inaugural address, Garfield said, "By the experience of commercial nations in all ages it has been found that gold and silver afford the only safe foundation for a monetary system." Odds we ever hear that in another inaugural address? Ten million to one.)

Rutherford B. Hayes was called "Rutherfraud" by his sore-loser detractors after a disputed presidential election.

All told, America ran surpluses for twenty-eight straight years following the Civil War. By 1900 the war debt had almost been paid off entirely, and by 1916 the total national debt stood at $1.2 billion, a full 56 percent below its high. While the debt hadn't been completely eliminated, this was still a true bipartisan victory, a powerful testament to the fact that Democrats and Republicans, while having different priorities, all agreed that debt was kryptonite to the America of their dreams.

But as our nation entered the twentieth century, that bipartisan agreement was about to come to a screeching halt.

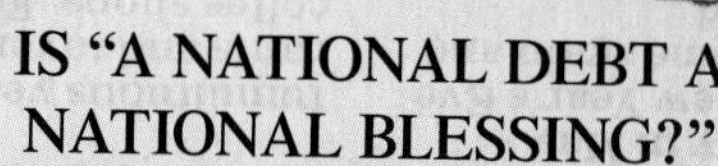
RIPPED FROM THE HEADLINES

IS "A NATIONAL DEBT A NATIONAL BLESSING?"

—*Chicago Tribune*, December 7, 1898

"Remember that God ordained that I should be the next president of the United States. Neither you nor any other mortal or mortals could have prevented this."

—Woodrow Wilson

CHAPTER 5.

America's Debt Progresses the Wrong Way

Woodrow Wilson represents many things to many people.

To leftists, he is a patron saint, one of the holy fathers of progressivism.

To liberal academics, he is a hero, the first and only U.S. president to hold a Ph.D. and to serve as president of a major university (Princeton).

And to me, he is a man who did more damage to the fabric of America than anyone who's come before or after.

To understand how America changed from a country devoted to faith, family, and frugality into a country devoted to freebies, you first have to understand the progressive movement and how it has been working to destroy the bedrock that America was built on.

Progressives Against Progress

On March 21, 1915, President Woodrow Wilson held a White House screening of the infamous KKK movie, *The Birth of a Nation*, which was based on the bestselling book *The Clansman.* After watching the racist flick, Woodrow Wilson, son of a Confederate chaplain, allegedly offered a sterling endorsement. "It is like writing history with lightning," Wilson has been quoted as saying, "and my only regret is that it is all so terribly true."

The film became one of the Ku Klux Klan's greatest pieces of membership propaganda ever. Millions signed up to wear pointy white hoods and hate black people. And, at least according to Civil War historian James McPherson, an emeritus professor at Princeton, Woodrow Wilson, one of progressivism's greatest heroes, deserves much of the credit.

"[Wilson] did see that film," McPherson said. "It was screened in the White House for him and he did endorse it . . . I think his impact on the revival of the Klan and

Did Wilson really give that sterling endorsement of a clearly racist movie? I wasn't there, so I can't say for sure, but there is a pretty lively debate about it online. Many cite evidence of quotes that appeared in papers attributing those words to Wilson, while others say that the endorsement was made up by the filmmakers, who were looking to get publicity. To be safe, let's just assume he never said it. After all, why hate Woodrow Wilson for his racism when there are so many other good reasons to hate him?

TEACHABLE MOMENT

on the popularity of that movement, no matter what he later said, was important."

Such a stinging indictment from one of America's greatest historians—and one who taught at Wilson's own Princeton University, no less—should come as little surprise. For those who care to notice, Wilson's bigotry is well documented: He fired fifteen of seventeen black supervisors who had been appointed to federal jobs and replaced them with whites. He slashed ambassadorships to Haiti and Santo Domingo that had traditionally gone to blacks and gave them to whites. He even issued executive orders to the Treasury Department and postmaster general to segregate the departments. Yes, the left's holy father was, indeed, a bigot—albeit a very *educated* bigot.

Of course, Wilson was hardly the first progressive to not hold African-Americans in high regard. Teddy Roosevelt, for example, showed his true colors during the 1906 "Brownsville Incident."

The 25th Infantry Regiment, which was made up entirely of black troops who'd served America honorably in prior conflicts, was relocated to Brownsville, Texas. The townspeople there didn't appreciate the move, thinking it would upset the racial harmony. One night, a small riot broke out, resulting in the murder of a bartender and injuries to a police officer. The soldiers became immediate suspects.

After questioning and a long investigation, no charges were brought, but all 167 troops (six of whom were Medal of Honor recipients) were recommended to be "discharged without honor." Blacks across America were understandably outraged—but Roosevelt did nothing. In fact, it was worse than that. Roosevelt did nothing until *after* the congressional election was over, hoping to secure as much of the black vote as possible. Only then did he sign an order discharging all 167 troops from service, denying them back pay, and canceling their pensions. When Senator Joseph Foraker of Ohio proposed a bill to allow them to reenlist, Roosevelt denied the effort and turned Foraker into an enemy.

In later years, it became obvious that the soldiers had been framed and that Roosevelt helped ruin the reputations of innocent, honorable men. Sixty-six years after the incident, Richard Nixon signed a bill to correct the historical record and give the 167 men honorable discharges—but Teddy Roosevelt's record will stand forever.

Manifest Destiny?

In H.W. Brands's biography of Wilson, cleverly titled *Woodrow Wilson*, he describes how Wilson thought he was different: "Because he typically believed that he acted according to God's plan, he could evince a certitude his rivals found infuriating . . . Mere mortals wrestled with doubt and confusion, but the self-assured Wilson possessed, to judge by his manor, a direct line to heaven."

I guess that during those phone calls God must have been plying Wilson with great ideas on how to destroy America.

I'm Better Than You

Wilson's bigotry was merely one dimension of his cancerous progressive policies and his elitist persona. In the great tradition of academic leftists, Woodrow Wilson was a supreme narcissist, a man convinced that he was of a superior stock and breed than others. A man with a severe God-complex. "Remember," he told William McCombs, head of the Democratic National Committee, "that God ordained that I should be the next president of the United States. Neither you nor any other mortal or mortals could have prevented this."

What made Woodrow Wilson especially dangerous was that he had taken the faith of his Presbyterian minister father and his mother, the daughter of a Presbyterian minister, and mixed it with a lust for power leavened with a heaping dollop of socialism. In fact, in his own writings, Wilson made no secret about his fixation with power. In his book *Congressional Power*, Wilson wrote, "I cannot imagine power as a thing negative and not positive." Apparently, atrocities at the hands of dictatorial governments and regimes never crossed his mind, even as the country suffered through a world war.

Wilson saw government as a new god, a vehicle through which power could and should be delivered. Writing in his book ominously titled *The State*, Wilson declared "Government does now whatever experience permits or the times demand."

He also mocked what he called the "fourth of July sentiments" of those patriotic dolts who actually believed in the governing philosophy of our Founders. "No doubt a lot of nonsense has been talked about the inalienable rights of the individual," Wilson sneered, "and a great deal that was mere vague sentiment and pleasing speculation has been put forward as fundamental principle."

"In order to avoid a deficit for the ensuing fiscal year, I directed the heads of Departments in the preparation of their estimates to make them as low as possible consistent with imperative governmental necessity."

—William Howard Taft

SORRY 1909 STATE OF THE UNION

All these progressive impulses spoke to a view of government radically different than what any of his predecessors in the White House had held. Progressives believed that government was a means by which they could implement the social engineering that Wilson found preferable by enacting policies designed to "redeem" the masses. "Government is not a machine, but a living thing," Wilson wrote in *Congressional Government*. "It falls not under the [Newtonian] theory of the universe, but under the [Darwinian] theory of organic life."

Expanding the size and scope of the state was, therefore, a natural process, a reflection of the evolving times and the enactment of the Social Gospel, which was the use of religion as rationale for solving many social problems. In this way, taxes were not about simply raising revenue; rather, they were a means of punishing the wealthy for the "sin" of greed and accumulation, thereby creating equality in income.

Wilson didn't usher in progressivism alone: He had lots of help. His secretary of state William Jennings Bryan took the attitude that the wealthy must be punished for their affluence: "If New York and Massachusetts pay more tax under this law than other states, it will be because they have more taxable incomes within their borders. And why should not those sections pay most which enjoy most?"

Education was another conduit for spreading the Social Gospel and progressivism. Amassing children together was a great way to not simply educate, but also to transform a new generation of Americans, prompting liberals like John Dewey to call for a new public education system. "Our problem is not merely to help the students to adjust themselves to world life," said Wilson, "but to make them as unlike their fathers as we can."

This sort of "moral emancipation" should have come as little surprise. In the 1912 election, Wilson ran on the theme of a "second struggle for emancipation" and the need for a "New Freedom." One of the main obstacles in his path, of course, was that rigid, narrow, cumbersome document: the United States Constitution. Fortunately for Wilson, he had that direct line to God.

"Living political constitutions must be Darwinian in structure and in practice," he explained. "Society is a living organism and must obey the laws of Life . . . it must develop. All that progressives ask or desire is permission—in an era when 'development,' 'evolution,' is the scientific word—to interpret the Constitution according to the Darwinian principle."

RIPPED FROM THE HEADLINES

EMPIRE STATE DEBT SHOWS RAPID RISE

—*New York Times*, April, 1914

Put simply, Wilson believed that all that was needed to usher in the radical social engineering he envisioned to create his utopia was for Americans to abandon their "blind devotion to the Constitution." If he could convince the public to do that, all manners of hell could be unleashed. But first, he had to champion the idea that the people behind the Constitution, our Founders, were short-sighted. Sure, they may have been brilliant for their time, but things were different now:

> *While we are followers of Jefferson, there is one principle of Jefferson's which no longer can obtain in the practical politics of America. You know that it was Jefferson who said that the best government is that which does as little governing as possible . . . but that time is passed. America is not now and cannot in the future be a place for unrestricted individual enterprise.*

> *"The people of the United States do not wish to curtail the activities of this Government; they wish, rather, to enlarge them; and with every enlargement, with the mere growth, indeed, of the country itself, there must come, of course, the inevitable increase of expense . . . It is not expenditure but extravagance that we should fear being criticized for."*
>
> —Woodrow Wilson
>
> 1914 SORRY STATE OF THE UNION

That passage is worth reading again because you can almost hear the hinge of history swinging backward, away from everything that our forefathers stood for, fought for, and died for in that one quote. It was a pivot of epic proportions and it paved the way for unprecedented sums of money to be spent on a buffet of social engineering projects designed to control, elevate, and alter the human condition.

A Hostile Takeover of Religion

The kind of perfected condition that progressive thinkers envisioned can be clearly seen in the works of Herbert Croly, founder of the liberal magazine *The New Republic*. Croly said that progressives believed "a better future would derive from the beneficent activities of expert social engineers who would bring to the service of social ideals all the technical resources which research could discover and ingenuity could devise." He wanted to join forces with the ideologists of Christ so they could "plan and effect a redeeming transformation" of society.

Yes, it sounds creepy, because it is. By piggybacking on the language of religion, the progressives gave themselves moral superiority over anyone who disagreed. Taxes became a metaphorical form of "tithing" to the government, which would then launch missions to evangelize and spread the Social Gospel.

It also gave progressives convenient cover for inflicting massive confiscatory taxes on those who had prospered, which they spun as a clear sign of sinful gain.

As William Jennings Bryan put it, "Would it not be fairer for the gentleman to fling his burnished lance full in the face of the toiler, and not plead for the great fortunes of this country under the cover of a poor man's name?"

Wilson even had it in for those who owned automobiles, which he called the "new symbol of wealth's arrogance."

TEACHABLE MOMENT

Another component of the progressives' Social Gospel involved contorting Jesus's biblical commands to *individuals* by turning them into edicts and responsibilities for *governments* to carry out. Ironically, even though many progressives who advocated the Social Gospel did not actually believe scripture was literal, they nonetheless supported what they saw as a Christian society based on the Social Gospel. In other words, they supported the scriptures when it supported them.

One important early proponent of the Social Gospel was Washington Gladden, a progressive Congregational minister from Ohio. As he explained to his followers, socialism was little more than what he called "applied Christianity." And it was applied by using the coercive power of the state, not by individuals and congregations choosing to live out and act on their beliefs.

Others, such as Henry Vedder, author of the book *Socialism and the Ethics of Jesus*, held that Christ was the "Great Leveler," not just spiritually, but in material terms. And Walter Rauschenbusch, a leading proponent of the Social Gospel and the author of *A Theology of the Social Gospel*, explained that the Social Gospel "constitutes the moral power in the propaganda of Socialism."

With the new Social Gospel framework and lingo in place, the social engineers went right to work. Every inch of human life and activity was on the table and up for governmental "improvement." Even seemingly trivial policies, such as dictating to farmers how best to water their crops, became a component of their social engineering mission.

RIPPED FROM THE HEADLINES

WILSON SEES NO DEFICIT

President Wilson sees no prospect of a deficit in the United States Treasury.

—*Wall Street Journal*, February 1915

Wilson's desire to control got so creepy that at one point he decided to create a "new standard of manhood" for American soldiers. The result was a "Commission on Training Camp Activities" that regulated everything from approved soldier recreation to sexual practices, promising "protection and stimulation of its mental, moral and physical manhood."

Wilson didn't want to leave any stone of human responsibility unturned. The government, he said, needed to regulate business and trade, care for the poor and incapable, invoke sumptuary laws, educate the masses, enforce prohibition . . . on and on it went. What America really needed was a "middle ground" between individualism and socialism, because "modern individualism has much about it that is hateful, too hateful to last."

Of course, like any good salesman, it's what Wilson didn't say that was most important: If individualism lasted, then his agenda could not.

But Progressivism Worked . . . Didn't It?

Now that you have a background on how Wilson and other progressives saw the world, it's easier to understand how they used this view to set the country on a course toward economic ruin. When Wilson entered office in 1913, America was in strong fiscal shape. Balanced budgets were the norm. In 1916, U.S. debt amounted to just 2.54 percent of GNP.

Then Wilson got his agenda cranked up. The role and size of government exploded. And so did our budget.

From 1916 to 1919 total federal expenditures rose 2,494 percent and the national debt went from $3.6 billion to a whopping $27.4 billion. World War I, of course, played a role in this expansion, but, like any good progressive, Wilson did not let a serious crisis go to waste. Instead of temporary spending or taxes, as had been the norm (remember, Salmon Chase had pushed through an income tax to fund the troops during the Civil War), Wilson pushed through legislation that would continually expand government without an expiration date.

"We have our enormous debt to pay . . . but while remarkable progress has been made in this direction, the work is yet far from accomplished . . . Perhaps the most important work that this session of the Congress can do is to continue a policy of economy and further reduce the cost of government, in order that we may have a reduction of taxes for the next fiscal year."

—Calvin Coolidge

SORRY STATE OF THE UNION 1924

On October 3, 1913, Woodrow Wilson signed the personal income tax law. At its inception, 98 percent of American families were exempt. A "normal rate" of one percent was charged on incomes above $3,000 ($4,000 for married couples). Above $20,000 in taxable income, however, rates began to rise until they reached 7 percent on incomes over $500,000. Relatively few American families were affected, as only 350,000 1040 forms were filed in 1914.

DEFICIT OF TRU$T

The Federal Reserve System was created in 1913 in response to the panic of 1907. Prior to the vote, Oklahoma's Senator Robert Latham Owen, one of the Fed's organizers, sent out a letter to bankers describing the benefits of the new system. "The first advantage," he wrote, "is protection from panic, because panic will be impossible under this system." It's too bad Senator Owen wasn't alive to see how that worked out in 2008.

By April 1917, with the war as an excuse, new changes were made to the income tax exemptions. The lowest tax threshold went from $3,000 down to $1,000 ($2,000 for married cou-

A GREEK TRAGEDY

While Greece has shown people what eventually happens to a country that can't control its finances, many people don't understand one of the key reasons why Greece was in such bad shape to begin with: taxes. Like many countries, Greeks wanted to have more and more social benefits (like government-run health care) but they didn't want to pay for them. That, along with a culture of corruption among the politicians (sound familiar?), led many Greek citizens to embrace cheating on their tax returns.

In one wealthy suburb of Athens, 324 people checked a box on their return indicating that they owned a pool. But when tax investigators looked at satellite photos, they found a few more pools than that: 16,650 more, to be exact.

Studies have shown that the so-called "shadow economy" in Greece (the transactions that occur under the government's radar) makes up 20 to 30 percent of the total GDP. In the United States that number is estimated at around 8 percent, but, if history is any guide, it will rise right along with tax rates. All of which begs the question: Can ever-expanding entitlements really be paid for with tax hikes, if the proven consequence of tax hikes is tax cheating?

ples), the normal tax rate was bumped up to 2 percent, and the top rate jumped to 67 percent (and then to 77 percent the following year).

From 1917 to 1918, federal revenues went from $1.1 billion to $3.6 billion, an increase of 227 percent. And following the historical precedent of Americans paying for their wars, little public objection arose over the sharply raised taxes.

But all that changed in 1920, when America's new progressive government lowered the financial hammer. The goal wasn't to collect more money (after all, as many progressives will even admit, the higher rates—then at 73 percent for the top bracket—didn't actually produce more revenue); the goal was a new concept in America: redistribution of the wealth.

An analysis of the data reveals exactly what you'd expect in the face of insane tax rates: the wealthy simply shifted their income and sheltered their money. In 1916, when the tax rate for top earners was at 15 percent, the U.S. Treasury reported that there were 206 people in the United States who had million-dollar incomes. But by 1921, when the top tax rate was at a stratospheric 73 percent, only 21 people filed tax returns as millionaires. Hmmm. This proves one of two things: Either 90 percent of the country's millionaires went bankrupt (or died), or millionaires are really, really good at dodging tax rates they consider to be too onerous.

TEACHABLE MOMENT

As David Houston, Wilson's last secretary of the Treasury, put it, "It seems idle to speculate in the abstract as to whether or not a progressive income tax schedule rising to rates in excess of seventy percent is justifiable. We are confronted with a condition, not a theory. The fact is that such rates cannot be successfully collected."

The same trend occurred with those earning between $300,000 and $1 million. In 1916, 1,090 re-

State of the Union Match Game!

Just match the political rhetoric and empty promises to the right president!

1. The whole of the public debt may be extinguished, either by redemption or purchase, within the four years of my Administration.

2. Only by avoidance of spending money on what is needless or unjustifiable can we legitimately keep our income to the point required to meet our needs that are genuine.

3. In my opinion the Government can do more to remedy the economic ills of the people by a system of rigid economy in public expenditure than can be accomplished through any other action.

4. We must have insistent and determined reduction in Government expenses. The first requirement of confidence and of economic recovery is financial stability of the United States Government.

5. Our immediate task is to chart a fiscal and economic policy that can reduce the planned deficits and then balance the budget, which means, among other things, reducing Federal expenditures to the safe minimum.

6. Persistently large deficits would endanger our economic growth and our military and defense commitments abroad. Our goal must be a reasonable equilibrium in our balance of payments.

7. A major reduction in the growth of Federal spending can help dispel the uncertainty that so many feel about our economy and put us on the way to curing our economic ills.

8. The last decade saw domestic spending surge literally out of control. But the basis for such spending had been laid in previous years. A pattern of overspending has been in place for half a century.

9. Last year, government spending shot up 8 percent. That's far more than our economy grew, far more than personal income grew, and far more than the rate of inflation. Unrestrained government spending is a dangerous road to deficits, so we must take a different path.

10. This can't be one of those Washington gimmicks that lets us pretend we solved a problem... If we don't take meaningful steps to rein in our debt, it could damage our markets, increase the cost of borrowing, and jeopardize our recovery.

Answers: 1=C, 2=G, 3=H, 4=I, 5=D, 6=B, 7=J, 8=A, 9=E, 10=F

turns were filed in that range, but by 1921, the number had plunged to 225. As Will Rogers once famously said, "The income tax has made more liars out of the American people than golf has."

Progressive tax rates bucked the ideas of Adam Smith, who understood that such tax schemes were little more than a federal shakedown. As he put it in *The Wealth of Nations*, "When the rule of arithmetical proportion is broken, the door is open to extortion."

A.D.D. Moment

Rogers knew the truth of that statement firsthand. In 1924, he claimed a phony $26,000 deduction for payments to his wife as his secretary. I'm surprised he never ran for office; he would have fit right in.

The Backlash

As often happens when people see the effects of really bad policies, there was a modest return to America's traditional views about debt and the limited roles of government in Wilson's disastrous wake. The debt, which was over $27 billion in 1919, was reduced to $16 billion by 1930 largely due to the work of the presidents who followed Wilson, especially the notoriously frugal Calvin Coolidge. It's also worth noting that this reduction came at a time when it wasn't exactly fashionable to pay off debt. Many European nations defaulted on their war debt, leading Herbert Hoover in 1931 to declare a one-year moratorium on repayments. The United Kingdom, in fact, *still* owes America for World War I, and it's not a trivial amount: $74 billion in today's dollars.

BOND ISSUE FAVORED BY PRESIDENT WILSON

To Meet Part of the Deficit Faced by United States Treasury.

—*Atlanta Constitution*, December 1916

The Mellon Plan

Andrew Mellon served as Treasury secretary under three different presidents: Harding, Coolidge, and Hoover, from 1921 to 1932, the longest run in history.

Prior to taking this role, Mellon had already established himself as one of the most successful businessmen in American history. As secretary, Mellon brought those same skills to bear by championing lower taxes while simultaneously reducing the hefty national debt incurred during World War I.

For Mellon, the country's debt was "a sign of debility and denoted an absence of the essential vigor and foresight which insure future success." He declared it "the policy of the thriftless, the ne'er do-well."

Under his plan (conveniently titled "The Mellon Plan"), he calculated that the entire national debt could be extinguished by 1943. While a little event called World War II got in the way of that dream, Mellon proved that the Founders' views on debt were not quite as antiquated as the progressives wanted people to believe.

Andrew Mellon wrote in his book, *Taxation: The People's Business*, "Since the war, two guiding principles have dominated the financial policy of the government. One is balancing the budget, and the other is the payment of the public debt. Both are in line with the fundamental policy of the government since its beginning." You may want to add Mellon's book to your reading list, and send a copy to your representatives while you're at it.

Unfortunately, progressive policies don't last for four or eight years—they last forever. The income tax and new federal programs were stitched into our fabric, and they couldn't be removed easily. As Harvard professor Gardiner Means put it, "Gradually but steadily, great segments of economic activity have been shifted from the market place to [government] administration." After eight years of Woodrow Wilson's hyper-elitist, progressive social engineering, the Social Gospel's seductions had done what they were designed to do: take power from individuals and hand it over to the planners who were supposedly smarter, more enlightened, and more compassionate organizers of life for the masses. Worse, the idea that the Constitution was outdated and needed constant reinterpretation had produced a new intellectual spawn, the idea of a "Living Constitution," with tenets that are malleable and subjective.

In the June 1887 edition of the *Political Science Quarterly*, Woodrow Wilson foreshadowed his constitutional intentions: "It is getting harder to run a constitution," he wrote, "than to frame one."

What's now known as the Progressive Era came to an end shortly after Wilson left office. In retrospect, we now understand what the progressives of that time didn't: It wasn't really an "era" at all, but a down payment on a much larger payoff still to come. Their movement didn't end, it just took a temporary hiatus so that Americans could forget how poorly those progressive ideas translated from theory to reality.

What progressives needed to become relevant again was something that would shock the conscience of the public, something that would prove the evils of big business, the naïveté of the Founders, and the fallacy of capitalism, all in one fell swoop. What they needed was a major crisis.

And they were about to get one.

"We seldom know, six weeks in advance, what we are going to do."

—President Franklin Delano Roosevelt, explaining his administration's deft economic planning

CHAPTER 6.

Hoover, Keynes, and FDR

The Three Horsemen of the Progressive Apocalypse

Sometimes a nation's mood can be heard in its popular music. In October 1929 the stock market crashed, but that soon seemed to be nothing more than a minor hiccup. Unemployment rose and peaked at 9 percent, but then waned. By June 1930, it had settled back to a very reasonable 6.3 percent. "Happy Days Are Here Again" was a smash hit of 1930—and for good reason: The Roaring Twenties seemed to have carried right into the next decade.

But then something changed. The big-government "solutions" of President Herbert Hoover and, later, Franklin Delano Roosevelt, began to work their black magic. The mood of the economy darkened, and so did the nation's music. In 1931, one of the songs on America's lips was "I've Got Five Dollars." By the next year it was "Brother, Can You Spare a Dime?"

The answer to that musical question, unfortunately, was "No." Most Americans could *not* spare a dime. Federal revenues had dropped from $4 billion in 1927 to $1.9 billion in 1932, a decrease of 53 percent in a matter of just a few years. The economy was in a free fall, and unemployment was once again skyrocketing.

> *"The finances of the Government are in sound condition. . . ."*
> —Herbert Hoover
>
> SORRY 1929 STATE OF THE UNION

A crisis of historic proportions had set in. It would take a passionate leader with economic brilliance, a clear vision, and a strict adherence to our Founders' values if America was to recover quickly.

Unfortunately, we got Herbert Hoover instead.

Engineering a Depression

Herbert Hoover was an engineer-turned-president who believed in the power of planning. He was a tinkerer. Just poke at a problem long enough and you can solve it. Like Woodrow Wilson, Hoover also believed in the power of the "cognitive elite" to solve society's ills. (Before he was elected president, Hoover had helped to feed the people of Belgium in the buildup to World War I.)

When economic catastrophe came to America, he followed his engineer's impulse and tried to "fix" the economy through monetary meddling. He hiked tariffs on imported goods, unleashed government spending, spearheaded new social programs, and championed massive tax increases: The top rate went from 24 to 63 percent during his administration. He did all this with the best of intentions . . . and the worst of results.

"We must have insistent and determined reduction in Government expenses. We must face a temporary increase in taxes. Such increase should not cover the whole of these deficits or it will retard recovery. We must partially finance the deficit by borrowing. It is my view that the . . . additiona[l] taxation should be imposed solely as an emergen[cy] measure terminating definitely two years from Jul[y] 1 next. Such a basis will give confidence in the determination of the Government to stabilize its finance and will assure taxpayers of its temporary character."

—Herbert Hoover

SORRY 1931 STATE OF THE UNION

In addition to the 1932 tax hike, Hoover also put in place new taxes that reeked of desperation, like, for example, an excise tax on *writing* checks! Not surprisingly, the uneducated masses found a way around this brilliant tax by racing to their banks and grabbing their cash. The consequence of this run was that many banks had to be closed down to keep depositors from draining all their reserves. America paid heavily for this and Hoover's other equally disastrous policies. Our deficit, which was $462 million in 1931, jumped to $2.7 billion just a year later.

In a way, Hoover was the grandfather of the New Deal. As the famous progressive newspaperman Walter Lippmann wrote in a 1935 column, "The policy initiated by President Hoover in the autumn of 1929 was utterly unprecedented in American history. The national government undertook to make the whole economic order operate prosperously . . . the Roosevelt measures are a continuous evolution of the Hoover measures." In 1932 the deficit remained over $2.5 billion, and Americans were getting desperate. The only light at the end of the tunnel seemed to be the upcoming presidential election in the fall. It would pit politics-as-usual Hoover against the "reform" candidate, New York governor Franklin Delano Roosevelt, who promised to give American families a "new deal" with the government.

FDR won in a landslide (472 electoral votes to 59) and Americans celebrated what they thought would be a quick end to their economic misery.

Little did they know that it was only just beginning.

Change We Can Believe In

With Hoover's failures so obvious, the backlash that America is so famous for should have been in full effect: lower taxes, less spending, freer markets, more

HISTORY REPEATING

"What's the greatest threat to our still-fragile economic recovery? Dangers abound, of course. But what I currently find most ominous is the spread of a destructive idea: the view that now, less than a year into a weak recovery from the worst slump since World War II, is the time for policy makers to stop helping the jobless and start inflicting pain."

—Nobel Prize–winning economist Paul Krugman, May 2010

individual liberty. But instead of breaking from Hoover's disastrous schemes, FDR expanded them.

While Roosevelt wasn't an engineer like Hoover, he had the same mind-set, believing that central planning and massive government spending could solve virtually any problem. It was a view that both political parties had fallen prey to, and one that, incredibly, still persists today among many progressive economists, despite the overwhelming evidence that it doesn't work.

A.D.D. Moment

Isn't it kind of ironic that "progressive economists" still embrace 1930s thinking?

That FDR would "double down" on Hoover's policies was somewhat surprising, considering the way he'd presented himself to the public. Throughout the 1932 campaign, Roosevelt had hammered Hoover for his economic errors. "Too often," said candidate Roosevelt, "liberal governments have been wrecked on the rocks of loose fiscal policy."

Everywhere he went, Roosevelt billed himself as the commonsense, fiscally prudent choice. In a July 1932 radio address to the nation (still as a candidate), he said, "Let us have the courage to stop borrowing to meet continuing deficits. Revenues must cover expenditures by one means or another. Any government, like any family, can, for a year, spend a little more than it earns. But you know and I know that a continuation of that habit means the poor house."

ACCOUNTABILITY ALERT: FDR took office in 1933. So if we say that his first real budget was 1934, he can claim responsibility for only spending $3.6 billion more than he took in. It's also interesting to note that over FRD's twelve years in office he never ran a surplus. Never.

Stop borrowing? Cover our expenditures? The poorhouse? These kinds of warnings were nowhere to be found once FDR took office. In fact, if he'd followed his own advice, this might be a completely different kind of chapter.

The 1934 election swept 322 Democrats into the House compared with just 103 Republicans. With huge Democrat majorities in both chambers, Roosevelt's big-government wishes became Congress's commands, and his spending spree went forward virtually unchecked. Anything he asked for, he got. The result was predictable and catastrophic: FDR inherited a debt of $22.5 billion in 1933 ($374 billion in today's dollars) and nearly doubled it in just seven years.

TEACHABLE MOMENT

The only real congressional resistance FDR ever encountered was when he tried to ram through his court-packing scheme. Even his supporters in Congress found that one constitutionally offensive.

DEFICIT OF TRU$T

The lack of trust we have in our leaders to follow through on their promises is not exactly a new phenomenon. FDR was Obamaesque in the number of campaign assurances he gave, while also being very careful to never say how he planned to pull them off.

While there are hundreds of examples that can be cited, a speech that FDR gave to farmers during the 1932 campaign sticks out for its sheer audacity. Speaking in front of twenty-five thousand people in Sioux City, Iowa, Roosevelt said:

> ***I shall use this position of high responsibility to discuss up and down the country, in all seasons, at all times, the duty of reducing taxes, of increasing the efficiency of government . . . and getting the most public service for every dollar paid by taxation. This I pledge you, and nothing I have said in the campaign transcends in importance this covenant with the taxpayers of this country.***

By 1936, Roosevelt had jacked up the top income tax rate from 25 to 79 percent—but he'd also increased the threshold for the top bracket from $100,000 to $5 million. Well, that sounds fair, you might think, but, if so, then you're forgetting how progressives work. The initial move was the one that everyone was watching, so FDR compromised. But by 1942 he had a crisis on his hands, and a built-in excuse to do what he really wanted. So not only did the top rate go up again, this time to 88 percent, but the threshold plummeted from $5 million to $200,000.

Those at the bottom were not immune, either—their rate went from 1.125 percent to 4 percent and then eventually to 19 percent, even as the lowest-tax-bracket threshold was cut in half. In other words, everyone got a massive tax hike from this reformer. But it was FDR who got the last laugh: Despite his flat-out lying to the American people, they still kept reelecting him.

Throughout his four-term presidency (America liked FDR so much that the term-limit amendment to the Constitution was ratified upon his departure), Roosevelt operated under the assumption that there was a direct correlation between government spending and the amount of good the government could do. The more government spent and intervened, the more positive benefits it could spread among society. "The New Dealers shared John Dewey's conviction that organized social intelligence could shape society," wrote one noted historian. It was all an effort to reflect "the hope of the Social Gospel of creating a Kingdom of God on earth."

Needless to say, unless God was hoping to create a nearly bankrupt kingdom full of unemployed, hungry, desperate people, their efforts failed miserably.

Smithboating Adam Smith

As a young man educated at Groton, Roosevelt had been indoctrinated with the seductions of the Social Gospel. He'd been taught that poverty was unfair and that it was the government's job to redeem individuals by standing with the poor over the rich, the laborer over the capitalist. In fact, as FDR saw it, the true culprit of the Great Depression had been the "lure of profit" caused by "unscrupulous money changers."

DEFICIT OF TRU$T

"I accuse the present [Hoover] administration of being the greatest spending administration in peace times in all our history—one which has piled bureau on bureau, commission on commission, and has failed to anticipate the dire needs of reduced earning power of the people. Bureaus and bureaucrats have been retained at the expense of the taxpayers."

—FDR, speaking as a candidate for president, September 1932

Roosevelt's administration not only became the "greatest spending administration in peace times in all our history," it also piled on an unprecedented number of new bureaus and agencies. It was almost as though FDR took everything he allegedly hated about Hoover, and then doubled it.

The problem for FDR was that the "lure of profit" was still a beloved concept to most Americans. Free-market capitalism had been the rule since the days when our Founders were inspired by Adam Smith—changing public perception about it would not be easy.

But FDR was up to the challenge.

What he needed, he soon realized, was a respected person who could be the face of a new way to think about government and money. He found his man in the form of a British economic philosopher named John Maynard Keynes.

TEACHABLE MOMENT

We still hear this vilification of capitalism today. In his memoirs, President Barack Obama, looking back on his brief stint at a financial consultancy, wrote that he felt "[l]ike a spy behind enemy lines." Perhaps that explains his apparent "war" on free-market capitalism, but President Obama's decision to appoint people without much private-sector experience is very much in keeping with a Roosevelt-esque view of who is best equipped to run the country.

A.D.D. Moment

It's probably not a coincidence that FDR used the word *hoarding* three times in his executive order requiring the surrender of gold.

Put simply, Keynes believed that savings was akin to hoarding and greed.

He believed that balancing budgets by paying down debts quickly was both unnecessary and counterproductive, and he mocked what he saw as the cult of savings. "The morals, the politics, the literature and the religion of the . . . [nineteenth century] joined in a grand conspiracy for the promotion of saving," said Keynes. "God and Mammon were reconciled. Peace on earth to men of good means. A rich man could, after all, enter into the Kingdom of Heaven—if only he saved."

Keynes flatly rejected America's long-standing tradition of savings and frugality. Instead, he argued that "the sole . . . objective of all economic activity" was consumption. The solution to digging out of economic holes, Keynes believed, was simple: spending. Lots and lots of spending.

The sheer illogic of Keynes's economic "philosophy" is hard to capture in words. Journalist and economist Henry Hazlitt came close, however: "How marvelous is the Keynesian world! The more you spend the more you [have]. The more you eat your cake, the more cake [to eat]."

Most people scratch their heads when trying to understand how Keynes justified the idea that a nation could spend itself into prosperity, but he actually addressed that very question himself in a 1934 *Redbook* article conveniently titled, "Can America spend its way into recovery?" His response:

DO AS I SAY, NOT AS I DO

Of course, like any good progressive, Keynes himself never actually practiced what he preached. As his investment portfolio and sizable savings later revealed, Keynes was a pretty lousy Keynesian! He had no children but he accumulated great wealth that he lived off of and used for further investments.

"Why, obviously! . . . No one of common sense could doubt it unless his mind had first been muddled by a 'sound' financier or an 'orthodox' economist."

By "sound" and "orthodox" he was really referring to people who believed in the Founders' principles on money management: Live frugally, spend rationally, save fervently. It was all part of the plan to tarnish those ideas as "antiquated" or out-of-touch with the new reality. After all, the Founders had never lived through a depression!

Keynes explained that the most important thing was to "get the money spent." What, specifically, it was spent on mattered little. It's a view that has persisted in almost every economic downturn America has been through, including the most recent one. Keynes's pseudo-intellectual drivel went on to say that the behavior that would make "a man poor" (spending more than he earns) could make "a nation wealthy." Solid logic, if you ask me.

Guilt by Association?

"The decadent international but individualistic capitalism in the hands of which we found ourselves after the War, is not a success. It is not intelligent, it is not beautiful, it is not just, it is not virtuous—and it doesn't deliver the goods. In short, we dislike it, and we are beginning to despise it. . . ."

—John Maynard Keynes

Is it possible that people like FDR, Barack Obama, and Paul Krugman could endorse the views and economic theories of a man who believed that capitalism was a failure without themselves believing that? Wouldn't that be akin to someone who endorses the views of a Ku Klux Klan member saying that it doesn't mean they dislike African-Americans?

Keynes argued that individuals and nations are economically very different. An individual has to borrow from someone else, but a nation, on the other hand, can borrow from itself. Like a child borrowing from his parents, the overall debits and credits cancel each other out. Put simply, Keynes believed that national debt—which had long been seen by those old-school "orthodox" economists as sometimes necessary but almost always undesired—doesn't really matter.

Stuart Chase, a Keynesian economist, captured this view well: "If the national debt is all internal, as ours is, the nation can hardly go bankrupt. The American people are on both sides of the balance sheet." It's magic!

If it's true that we simply owe all of this money to ourselves, then we should be able to pay ourselves back. Of course, that part of the equation is never brought up because it would essentially require every debt holder to agree to a one-time final payment of pennies on the dollar in exchange for canceling their bonds. That's probably not going to happen anytime soon.

A.D.D. Momen

Keynes's theory was seductive because it allowed politicians to link their personal ambitions to the idea that spending money was *good* for the economy. As former Treasury official Bruce Bartlett put it: "Thanks to the economics of Lord Keynes, the Democrats could buy their votes with an absolutely clear conscience, in the genuine belief that deficits were good for the economy. This allowed them to, in effect, promise the people something-for-nothing. They could have all the new government programs they wanted and it would not cost a dime, because they were paid for with deficits rather than taxes."

RIPPED FROM THE HEADLINES

GOV. ROOSEVELT MAKES PLEDGE TO SLASH TAXES

—*Chicago Daily Tribune*, September 1932

A New Deal for Socialism

As their embracing of Keynes shows, FDR's wise men believed capitalism was discredited and at fault for the nation's economic woes. Political theorist James Pontuso, who has studied FDR and the New Deal extensively, found that FDR eventually believed that economic collapse was a by-product of capitalism. "Roosevelt," Pontuso explained, "came to doubt the efficacy of an economy made up of small entrepreneurs and businesses."

Part of FDR's solution was to link economic security for all Americans to the Constitution—an idea that our Founders never contemplated. To accomplish that, the free-market system itself would need to be modified. Capitalism, with its focus on individual wealth, could not secure a bright future for all—but the government could. It was a classic "rights of man" versus "rights of men" battle, and FDR chose to fight for the so-called greater good.

As Rexford Tugwell, a member of Roosevelt's Brain Trust and assistant secretary of agriculture, declared, "The Jig is up. The cat is out of the bag. There is no invisible hand. There never was. . . . We must now supply a real and visible guiding hand to do the task which that mythical, nonexistent, invisible agency was supposed to perform, but never did."

Despite how it might look in retrospect, there was far from universal agreement that Keynesianism would actually work. Many saw the illogical nature of it and spoke out. For example, George Humphrey, who became Eisenhower's secretary of the Treasury, saw how silly and dangerous it all was. "I do not think that you can spend yourself rich," he said. Likewise, eminent economists such as Ludwig von Mises saw Keynes as "the Santa Claus fable raised . . . to the dignity of an economic doctrine."

The problem was that economists who wanted to talk sense into people were fighting an uphill battle. The perception at the time, even among reasonable people, was that fascism had "worked" in Italy and was beginning to work in Germany as well. Hitler seemed to have the economy on the road to recovery. It was only in retrospect that people realized that their economic statistics were being enhanced by a rapid military buildup along with the "acquisition" of wealth from the countries they were invading.

As so often happens in politics, the allure of a policy can trump the reality of it. Even though Americans inherently believe that "if something sounds too good to be true, it probably is," that rule is tough to remember when (supposedly) free money is staring you in the face.

CAPITALISM: A HATE STORY

Economic elites don't trust the free market or individuals to make wise decisions, so they say we should toss it aside and trust, well . . . them. Nobel Prize–winning economist Paul Krugman declared in his book *The Return of Depression Economics and the Crisis of 2008* that traditional free-market economics are "obsolete doctrines that clutter the minds of men." Another Nobel laureate, Paul Samuelson, explained that "deregulated capitalism is a fragile flower bound to commit suicide" and went on to claim that free-market supporters were "emotional cripples." Larry Summers, director of the White House's National Economic Council, explained that we needed to the government to save "the market system from its excesses and inadequacies."

Yep, these are definitely the people we should be listening to.

Precious Metals, Worthless Paper

With Keynes providing the cover, there was only one obstacle standing in the way of Roosevelt's unleashing an avalanche of spending: America was the only country left on the gold standard. This meant, for example, that a Frenchman could convert dollars into gold, but an American living in France could not convert francs into gold. The result was that foreign currency flowed into the United States, while gold flowed out, thereby draining our banks' reserves and creating anxiety among investors.

So, just weeks into his first term, FDR ended the requirement that U.S. dollars be converted into gold upon request. That move took America off the gold standard, likely saved our banking system, and forever changed our economic course.

If he had stopped there, we might look back and applaud FDR for making a (rare) sensible decision. But he didn't. Instead, FDR issued an executive order forcing Americans to surrender their physical gold to the U.S. government in exchange for dollars. Why did he do it? It's possible that his rationale was to ensure that private gold (which would've increased in price with U.S. gold out of circulation) wouldn't become an alternative currency. But it's just as possible that he had a dream about confiscating gold and thought it sounded like a pretty good idea.

"Many people have the idea that as a nation we are overburdened with debt and are spending more than we can afford. That is not so. Despite our Federal Government expenditures the entire debt of our national economic system, public and private together, is no larger today than it was in 1929, and the interest thereon is far less than it was in 1929." —FDR

Roosevelt used some nifty word games ("private" debt) to make those numbers work. The truth is much simpler: After adjusting for inflation, the national debt was $16.9 billion in 1929. In 1939, when he made this speech, it was $40.4 billion.

SORRY STATE OF THE UNION 1939

You Never Want a Serious Crisis to Go to Waste

Under the guise of a "national emergency," FDR issued an executive order requiring all Americans to turn in their gold. The order read, in part:

All persons are hereby required to deliver on or before May 1, 1933, to a Federal Reserve Bank or a branch or agency thereof or to any member bank of the Federal Reserve System all gold coin, gold bullion and gold certificates now owned by them or coming into their ownership on or before April 28, 1933 . . .

Whoever willfully violates any provision of this Executive Order or of these regulations or of any rule, regulation or license issued thereunder may be fined not more than $10,000, or, if a natural person, may be imprisoned for not more than ten years, or both.

—Executive Order 6102, April 5, 1933

Throwing Darts

Ditching Adam Smith's tenet of allowing the marketplace to set prices, FDR and his team pursued a reckless course of price setting. Worse, the price setting seemed to be arbitrary, as though throwing a dart at a dartboard were an adequate substitute for sound economics. Henry Morgenthau, Roosevelt's Treasury secretary, recalled that on November 3, 1933, he suggested that the price of gold should rise by 19 to 22 cents. FDR wanted the price rise to be 21 cents. The reason? "It is a lucky number," he said, "because it's three times seven."

Even Morgenthau seemed shaken about the way decisions were being made. As he later wrote in his diary, "If anybody ever knew how we really set the gold price through a combination of lucky numbers, etc. I think they would be frightened." If the public would be frightened over the use of lucky numbers, imagine how they would've felt knowing how little faith FDR had in his own policies. Much of it was little more than guesswork and stabs in the dark. As he later admitted, "It is common sense, to take a method and try it: If it fails, admit it frankly and try another. But above all, try something."

Despite his campaign promises, Roosevelt saw the nation's economic instability as an opportunity to permanently expand the size and power of government and his "trial-and-error" method of governing always pushed in that direction. As Morgenthau put it, a number of high-ranking officials in the Roosevelt administration wanted to transform spending "from a temporary expedient to a permanent instrument of government."

RIPPED FROM THE HEADLINES

LOWER U.S. DEBT OR LOWER TAXES UP TO CONGRESS

Debt retirement versus tax reduction is developing as an issue

—*Chicago Daily Tribune*, September 1924

Economist Thomas Sowell has pointed out that while Hoover was content to just throw money at problems and tinker, FDR's actions created lasting structures laced with inevitable consequences. "The New Deal administration not only set up *policies* to deal with existing economic problems of the 1930s," writes Sowell, "it set up enduring *institutions* to change the way the American economy operated." For example, as historian Arthur Schlesinger, Jr., has noted, "One objective [of New Deal power policy] was to enlarge the publicly owned sector of the power industry . . . as a means of diminishing private control over the necessities of life."

TEACHABLE MOMENT

The most transformative progressives are able to use legitimate emergencies to further both their short- and long-term agendas. With FDR, the Great Depression provided a great excuse to push forward many of the things that would've otherwise only been pipe dreams. But FDR knew that temporary wins wouldn't be enough—his real goal was to pass legislation that would continually and automatically bestow gifts to the public; gifts that people would associate with Democrats, thereby keeping them in power.

We see the same kind of progressive thinking again today as the Obama administration uses legislation like TARP, financial regulation, and health-care reform (all passed under the guise of various "emergencies") to set up new agencies and departments that will again change the way America operates (and, in their minds, *vote*) for decades to come. The difference this time around is that many of us are onto their game.

The Final Reveal

The economic struggles most individuals encountered throughout the Great Depression and its aftermath provided Roosevelt with a golden window of opportunity to leverage economic fears and redefine governmental powers in ways the Founders never envisioned. Remember, the "invisible hand" was a fraud—what people needed was the strong arm of government to make economic security a reality.

It was during this window that FDR finally revealed what his ultimate goal really was: a "second Bill of Rights." The proposed provisions included:

- The right to a useful and remunerative job in the industries or shops or farms or mines of the nation;
- The right to earn enough to provide adequate food and clothing and recreation;
- The right of every farmer to raise and sell his products at a return that will give him and his family a decent living;
- The right of every businessman, large and small, to trade in an atmosphere of freedom from unfair competition and domination by monopolies at home or abroad;
- The right of every family to a decent home;

- The right of adequate medical care and the opportunity to achieve and enjoy good health;
- The right to a good education.

While a "decent home" is still a privilege and not a right, many people have not let go of FDR's utopian vision. Obama advisor and regulatory czar Cass Sunstein has even written a book titled *The Second Bill of Rights: FDR's Unfinished Revolution and Why We Need It More Than Ever.*

In many respects, the second Bill of Rights, proposed in 1944, was not so much an addition to the original, but a replacement of it. Remember the themes that FDR was promoting: capitalism is evil, the Founders hadn't adequately prepared us for a depression, and the Constitution led the American people to the condition they now found themselves in.

RIPPED FROM THE HEADLINES

PRESIDENT PROMISES TO CUT SPENDING

—*Los Angeles Times,* November 1939

Change was necessary. The government would drive it.

In retrospect, this wasn't reform at all, it was a federal takeover of the responsibilities of everyday life that sought to redefine the public's relationship with government. Here's how *New York Times* bestselling financial journalist Bill Bonner, founder of the financial firm Agora, Inc., described it:

> *[The New Bill of Rights] bound ordinary citizens to the federal government in a way that had not been imagined by the Founding Fathers. People came to rely on the state for their daily bread, and to take a much keener interest in the state itself. Traditional virtues—thrift, independence, self-reliance—were replaced with new virtues: political activism and gaming the system. In the second Roosevelt era, people came to expect the state to take care of things at home.*

With American incomes depleted and jobs scarce, many individuals unwittingly embraced the "government-as-nanny-state" model—and who could blame them? Economic pressures were squeezing families from all sides. This was about putting bread on your children's plate, not some ideological debate.

The public believed that these were temporary measures meant to stop the bleeding, not a permanent takeover of the American economy. What Americans were not told, of course, was that the goal for some New Dealers was not economic recovery at all, but economic *transformation.* Walter Lippmann said the New Dealers would "rather not have recovery if the revival of private initiative means a resumption of private control in the management of corporate business . . . The essence of the New Deal," he continued, "is the reduction of private corporate control by collective bargaining and labor legislation, on the one side, and by restrictive, competitive and deterrent government action on the other side." In fact, many of the New Dealers had been advocates of massive government intervention in the economy even *before* the stock market crash of 1929.

RIPPED FROM THE HEADLINES

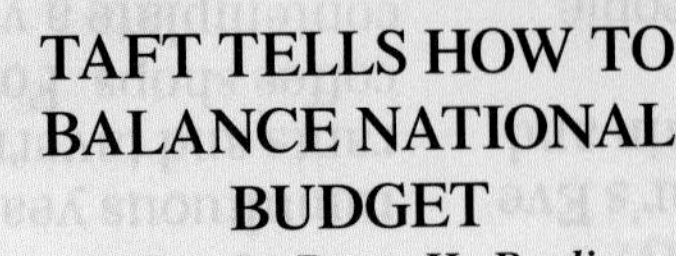

TAFT TELLS HOW TO BALANCE NATIONAL BUDGET

It Can Be Done, He Replies to Roosevelt Dare

—*Chicago Daily Tribune*, January 1940

To achieve these ends, FDR and Secretary of the Treasury Henry Morgenthau turned on the federal spending spigot to full blast. Between 1933 and 1940, Roosevelt more than *doubled* federal spending, from $4.6 billion to $9.5 billion. Federal outlays amounted to 3.7 percent of GNP in 1930; by 1940 they were 9.1 percent.

Many apologists like to argue that FDR's spending spree was the result of World War II, but that is simply not true. Until the actual outbreak of the war, there was little increase in military spending to speak of. Virtually all of the increased federal spending was for domestic programs, along with helping to elect political allies who would further his agenda.

In Pennsylvania, for example, the *New York Herald Tribune* reported, "The Democrats are moving heaven and earth to elect [Joseph] Guffey [to the U.S. Senate] and the whole Democratic ticket." The paper noted that Guffey "does not hesitate to use the enormous sums already poured into the state of Pennsylvania by the Federal government as a reason for voting for Democrats." Guffey even noted on his campaign literature that, under Roosevelt, Pennsylvania had received $678 million in federal money, even though they had paid only $298 million into the U.S. Treasury. This same practice was going on all around the country. The man who oversaw both the Works Progress Administration (WPA) and the Federal Emergency Relief Act (FERA) funds was Harry Hopkins. He admitted that the relief dollars could be used for partisan purposes. "I thought at first I could be completely non-political," Hopkins is quoted as saying by Robert E. Sherwood, a former FDR speechwriter. "Then they told me I had to be part non-political and part political. I found out that was impossible, at least for me. I finally realized that there was nothing for it but to be all-political."

Predictably, spending exploded. In just four years, Roosevelt borrowed almost as much money as all of the dead presidents who came before him combined.

The result of all this spending was a much larger debt, but not much else. In 1939, an exasperated Treasury secretary Morgenthau admitted that the policies were not working:

We have tried spending money. We are spending more than we have ever spent before and it does not work. And I have just one interest, and if I am wrong . . . somebody else can have my job. I want to see this country prosperous. I want to see people get a job. I want to see people get enough to eat. We have never made good on our promises . . . I say after eight years of this Administration we have just as much unemployment as when we started . . . And an enormous debt to boot!

"But you know, you can't eat your cake and have it too. Therefore, in the hope that we can continue in these days of increasing economic prosperity to reduce the Federal deficit, I am asking the Congress to levy sufficient additional taxes to meet the emergency spending for national defense."

—FDR

1940

SORRY STATE OF THE UNION

The Ultimate Stimulus Plan

So if Franklin Delano Roosevelt's massive explosion of spending only made the depression worse, what ended it? The easy answer is World War II, but the real answer is actually more complicated than that.

The war effort required immediate revenue, so Congress passed, and FDR signed, the Current Tax Payment Act of 1943, which created the tax-withholding system that still exists today. The effect was dramatic: While the top tax *rate* increased six percentage points from 1943 to 1944, the amount of tax *revenues* collected soared 82 percent.

Unfortunately, there was still the little issue of an exploding national debt. Putting it in terms of 2009 dollars, the debt went from $659 billion in 1940 to a jaw-dropping $3 trillion in 1946. The debt would not reach those heights again for another thirty-eight years.

TEACHABLE MOMENT

By the end of 2010, America's debt will represent 62 percent of the nation's economy, finally eclipsing the previous all-time high that was reached by FDR during World War II. Congratulations, America.

Roosevelt died during his fourth term in office. He had spent much of his time in charge throwing darts, grasping at straws, and hopping from one failed policy to the next. But, despite his cluelessness, FDR understood one enduring truth about government welfare: Government dependency, he said, could be "a narcotic, a subtle destroyer of the human spirit."

In the decades to follow, progressives (like Lyndon Johnson) who idolized FDR would rise to power. Unfortunately, many of them came to take Roosevelt's view on government dependency as a narcotic very seriously. After all, once you are in the business of dealing drugs, your number-one priority becomes getting as many people hooked on them as possible.

*"I'll have them n**gers voting Democratic for two hundred years."*
—President Lyndon Baines Johnson, discussing the Civil Rights Act of 1964 with two governors

CHAPTER 7.

The 1960s and '70s

A Summer of Love, Two Decades of Spending

Being a progressive really demands a heightened level of self-assurance. Confiscating people's hard-earned money to build a series of government bureaucracies that then redistribute that money as you deem equitable isn't for everyone. It helps to have an ego, to be a little cocky, maybe even a little arrogant.

Fortunately for those in the 1960s who wanted more of everything for everybody, Lyndon Baines Johnson fit the progressive mold perfectly. The evidence? As president, he once relieved himself on the leg of a Secret Service agent. When the agent jumped back in horror, Johnson told him, "That's all right, son. It's my prerogative."

Now *that's* ego.

The Real LBJ

In order to understand why LBJ made his policy decisions, it's important first to understand the way he carried himself and treated others. This story, included in one of the many biographies of LBJ, tells you all you really need to know:

> *[LBJ] felt the need to humiliate others. For Johnson, love too often meant submission; and once a man submitted, Johnson despised him. Crudity was a favorite weapon. With great glee, LBJ described a "delicate Kennedyite" whom he dragged into the bathroom to continue a conversation. He "found it utterly impossible to look at me while I sat on the toilet." LBJ badgered him to come closer so that they could talk. "Then began the most ludicrous scene I had ever witnessed. Instead of simply turning around and walking over to me, he kept his face away from me and walked backward, one rickety step at a time. It certainly made me wonder how that man had made it so far in the world."*

Given that story, I think the same thing can be wondered about LBJ himself.

Lyndon Johnson's soaring sense of personal entitlement also helps to explain his serial philandering and cheating on his wife, Lady Bird Johnson. She once explained to a friend that the trouble was that her husband "loved people" and "half the people in the world are women."

Johnson's extreme elitism also explained why, despite his manufactured civil rights persona, he was really a seething bigot who felt racially superior to the minorities he used for political leverage. Indeed, it's hard to find a modern U.S. president with a worse civil rights record than LBJ prior to becoming a hero of the movement.

Award-winning LBJ biographer Robert Caro recounts that, prior to 1957, Johnson "had never supported civil rights legislation—any civil rights legislation. In the Senate and House alike, his record was an unbroken one of votes against every civil rights bill that had ever come to a vote: against voting rights bills; against bills that would have struck at job discrimination and at segregation in other areas of American life; even against bills that would have protected blacks from lynching."

LBJ: The Benevolent Dictator

[I]f only I could take the next step and become dictator of the whole world, then I could really make things happen. Every hungry person would be fed, every ignorant child educated, every jobless man employed.

—LBJ, SPEAKING TO DORIS KEARNS

But there was more: Johnson considered himself to be so superior to the rest of humanity that he hurled a constant barrage of racist attacks at blacks who served him daily. Johnson's longtime limousine chauffeur and black employee, Robert Parker, wrote in an autobiography that covers the years he spent working for LBJ that Johnson "called me 'boy,' 'n**ger,' or 'chief,' never by my name . . . Whenever I was late, no matter what the reason, Johnson called me a lazy, good-for-nothing n**ger . . . I was afraid of him because of the pain and humiliation he could inflict at a moment's notice."

I relay this story not to smear a former president, but because understanding the role that elitism and narcissism play in progressivism is extraordinarily important. Those who believe that the Founders erred, that the Constitution is imperfect, and the country unexceptional, developed those opinions because of the way they view humanity. They are the enlightened, educated leaders and know what's best for the masses in virtually every facet of life, from relationships to diet to money.

"The American economy is in trouble. The most resourceful industrialized country on earth ranks among the last in the rate of economic growth . . . The current Federal budget for fiscal 1961 is almost certain to show a net deficit."

—JOHN F. KENNEDY

SORRY 1961 STATE OF THE UNION

Minority Vote = Majority of the Vote

Despite his Texas cowboy shtick, Lyndon Baines Johnson was a true progressive at heart. In fact, he wasn't just any progressive, he was a New Deal progressive who wanted to build on what FDR had already started: the transformation of America toward a cradle-to-grave European style of government.

Following FDR, Presidents Truman and Eisenhower attempted to return America to its tradition of fiscal responsibility. In 1946, the national debt had been nearly 122 percent of GNP. But by 1960 it had declined to less than 56 percent. Over the fourteen-year period from 1947 to 1960, America's total deficit was just $740 million (compared to FDR's deficit of $15.9 billion in 1946 alone).

But to progressives, that wasn't an achievement. That was an invitation. By the time LBJ got into office, the crisis in America wasn't economic, but racial. Either way, to progressives, a crisis is always an opportunity, and LBJ was up to the challenge. "This is the next and the more profound stage of the battle for civil rights," he said in a speech at Howard University. "We seek not just freedom but opportunity. We seek not just legal equity but human ability, not just equality as a right and a theory but equality as a fact and equality as a result." What was unsaid, of course, was that LBJ was also seeking a nearly utopian society that he could take credit for—and civil rights were the perfect excuse to push it through.

Johnson was uniquely suited for such progressive undertakings, since he'd grown up learning how to milk the government system. Before successfully running for Congress, LBJ had run a Texas youth program, but, like many progressives, he was missing one important thing from his résumé: He'd never spent any time in his adult life working in the private sector.

> RIPPED FROM THE HEADLINES
>
> **ALARMING RISE IN DEBT STRESSED BY SEN. BYRD**
>
> —*Los Angeles Times*, February 1964

Johnson did have experience, however, in using the welfare state's seductive propaganda to attract key voting blocs. He understood how to appeal to powerful constituencies and special interests that would stand to profit from new social and antipoverty programs. For example, the affordable-housing programs he proposed helped him gain the support of builders, bankers, and real estate agents, who all had strong lobbies in Washington and saw it as a moneymaking opportunity.

Johnson also had experience in targeting large voting blocs for political expediency. He reached out to low-income households and disenfranchised African-Americans and offered them a classic deal with the devil: *Vote Democratic and get free government goodies in return. Help me and you'll be helping yourself.*

The truth was that LBJ couldn't have cared less about the plight of blacks. What he did care about was his image, and he knew that being perceived as a civil rights crusader would help strengthen it. As the *New York Times* recounted, Johnson once explained to an aide the importance of squeezing every last drop of public relations benefit out of his appointment of Thurgood Marshall to the Supreme Court. He knew that stealing black votes away from the Republicans, the antislavery party that Abraham Lincoln once led, was critical to the Democrats' future. "Son," Johnson told the young staffer, "when I appoint a n**ger to the court, I want everyone to know he's a n**ger."

THE UNWASHED, UNGRATEFUL MASSES

"How is it possible that all these people could be so ungrateful to me after I have given them so much?"

—LBJ

LBJ Targets the History Books

Targeting voting blocs with promises is a good start, but to really gain long-term traction, you've also got to reward them for their vote. That, LBJ knew, could be done through federal appropriations, a tactic right out of the drug dealer's handbook: *Give them their first "hit" for free, and thereafter they'll do anything to get more.*

In Johnson's case, the political payback happened to fit right into his agenda. The only problem was that he needed a catchy name for his plan. His idol FDR had "the New Deal," so it would need to be something equally impressive sounding, something that history books could devote entire chapters to, something that would engrave his name next to Teddy's and Franklin's as one of America's favorite presidents, something like *the Great Society.*

Here's how he described it:

> *The Great Society rests on abundance and liberty for all. It demands an end to poverty and racial injustice, to which we are totally committed in our time. But that is just the beginning . . . The Great Society is a place where every child can find knowledge to enrich his mind and to enlarge his talents. It is a place where leisure is a welcome chance to build and reflect, not a feared cause of boredom and restlessness. It is a place where the city of man serves not only the needs of the body and the demands of commerce but the desire for beauty and the hunger for community.*

Another name for that society would be "utopia," but little stumbling blocks (such as the fact that men are inherently sinners) wouldn't stand in LBJ's way. So, to help achieve his vision, Johnson put together more than a dozen different committees that would attempt to answer the question, "What is a Great Society?" As he explained, "We are going to assemble the best thought and the broadest knowledge from all over the world to find those answers for America."

Newsflash: We don't need to *find* the answers, our Founders already gave them to us.

RIPPED FROM THE HEADLINES

'GREAT SOCIETY' NOT A SOLVENT ONE

—*Evening Independent*, January 1965

The Cult of Affluence

It's easy to sit back and wonder why the public was so willing to go along with Johnson's agenda, but the truth is that the pumps had been primed decades earlier. LBJ was simply taking the next logical step. To understand the Great Society, you first have to understand the mind-set shift that occurred in the twenty years leading up to it.

Before the New Deal, most Americans were strongly suspicious of federal power. The grand tradition of self-reliance, free enterprise, local control, and a strong civil society voluntarily helping neighbors in need had persisted throughout American history. While the New Deal presented a more activist government, it was World War II that fundamentally altered the relationship between the American people and their government.

In order to defeat Germany and Japan, federal power expanded like never before. Washington decided exactly what goods industry would produce, and when it would produce it. The federal government even provided Americans with ration books specifying how much meat, gasoline, sugar, and other items they could purchase. It was a scary combination, but big business and government collaborated to run the economy for the sake of winning the war.

After the war, some feared another depression. Instead, the American economy continued to prosper. Luxuries that were rare or nonexistent before the Depression—televisions, long-distance phone service, jet travel, air-conditioning, automatic washers and dryers, interstate highways—became commonplace. Americans moved out of crowded cities and secluded farms into suburban "Levittowns" that had sprung up practically overnight. The GI Bill opened the college doors for millions of war veterans. Polio was cured, and antibiotics made people healthier. Poverty rates plummeted, and incomes rose.

"But by closing down obsolete installations, by curtailing less urgent programs, by cutting back where cutting back seems to be wise, by insisting on a dollar's worth for a dollar spent, I am able to recommend in this reduced budget the most Federal support in history for education, for health, for training the unemployed, and for helping the economically and the physically handicapped."

—Lyndon B. Johnson

SORRY STATE OF THE UNION 1964

As a result, we got spoiled. In what journalist Robert Samuelson calls the "Cult of Affluence," the American people came to take economic prosperity for granted. It began to be seen as their birthright instead of a dream. But there's a major problem with that viewpoint (aside from the fact that it's completely wrong):

FRIEDMAN

CUT SPENDING!

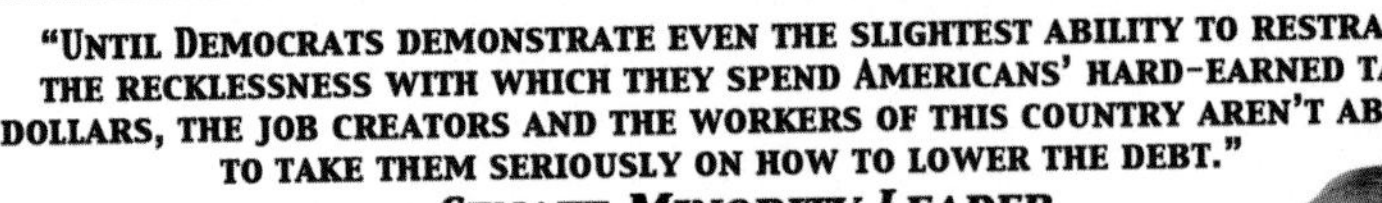

"Until Democrats demonstrate even the slightest ability to restrain the recklessness with which they spend Americans' hard-earned tax dollars, the job creators and the workers of this country aren't about to take them seriously on how to lower the debt."
—*Senate Minority Leader Mitch McConnell, (R-KY)*

"I want the government to stop spending! Stop spending. Stop spending. Stop spending. Stop spending! That's what we want!"
—*Rick Santelli*

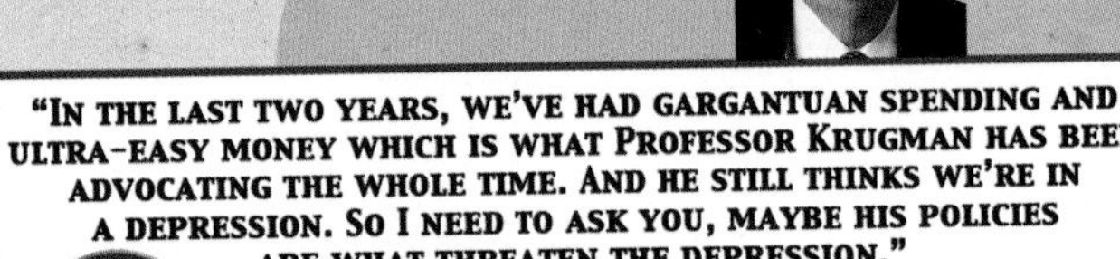

"In the last two years, we've had gargantuan spending and ultra-easy money which is what Professor Krugman has been advocating the whole time. And he still thinks we're in a depression. So I need to ask you, maybe his policies are what threaten the depression."
—*Larry Kudlow (CNBC)*

"Well, it's like the old physicians who continue to bleed the patient and wonder why the patient isn't getting better and then bleeds the patient even more. What we should be doing, yes, we should be cutting back spending because it takes money from productive citizens."
—*Steve Forbes*

"We need to convince markets in the medium and longer term that we have a sustainable fiscal path for balancing our budget or at least bringing our deficits down."
—*Ben Bernanke*

"I was shown the figures the other day by the comptroller of the Pentagon that said that the interest on our debt is $571 billion in 2012, that is, noticeably, about the size of the defense budget. It is not sustainable."
—*ADM. Mike Mullen*

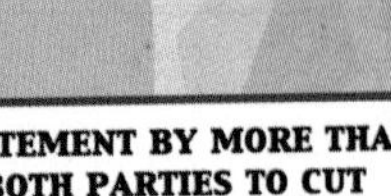

"I gave the President a statement by more than 100 economists urging both parties to cut spending now to boost private sector job creation, the need is clear."
—*House Minority Leader John Boehner, (R-OH)*

"Deficits mean future tax increases, pure and simple. Deficit spending should be viewed as a tax on future generations, and politicians who create deficits should be exposed as tax hikers."
—*Ron Paul, (R-TX)*

"It turns out the rest of the world is straightening out, while the U.S. continues to spend."
—*Raghuram G. Rajan, IMF Economist*

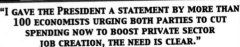

VS. KEYNES

MORE SPENDING!

"SPEND NOW, WHILE THE ECONOMY REMAINS DEPRESSED; SAVE LATER, ONCE IT HAS RECOVERED. HOW HARD IS THAT TO UNDERSTAND?"
—*PAUL KRUGMAN*

"THE ARITHMETIC OF BUDGET CUTS NOW IS JUST TERRIBLE... WE'RE LOOKING AT A U.S. GOVERNMENT THAT, 10 YEARS FROM NOW, WILL PROBABLY OWE SOMETHING LIKE $20 TRILLION. WHETHER WE BORROW $500 BILLION NOW IS NOT GOING TO MAKE A HUGE DIFFERENCE IN THAT POSITION."
—*KRUGMAN ON* THIS WEEK

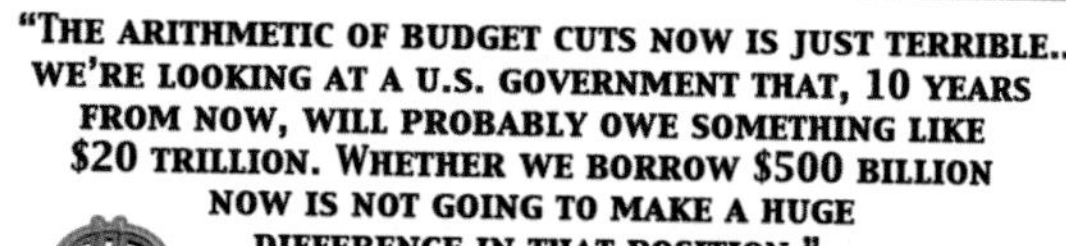

"SO THEN YOU GET THE ARGUMENT, WELL, THIS IS NOT A STIMULUS BILL, THIS IS A SPENDING BILL. WHAT DO YOU THINK A STIMULUS IS? THAT'S THE WHOLE POINT. NO, SERIOUSLY. THAT'S THE POINT."
—*PRESIDENT OBAMA*

"BUT WE'VE GOT EVERYBODY IN THE WORLD CUTTING BACK AND WHAT'S THAT DO WITH THE PROSPECT OF ECONOMIC EXPANSION HERE AT HOME? WELL, IT KILLS IT. IF YOU ARE LOOKING FOR GOOD NEWS, I HAVE ONE SUGGESTION. STOP LISTENING TO EUROPE, STOP LISTENING TO THE CONSERVATIVES. DO WHAT HAS WORKED IN THE PAST."
—*CHRIS MATTHEWS*

"WE MUST DEMONSTRATE A COMMITMENT TO REDUCING LONG-TERM DEFICITS, BUT NOT AT THE PRICE OF SHORT-TERM GROWTH. WITHOUT GROWTH NOW, DEFICITS WILL RISE FURTHER AND UNDERMINE FUTURE GROWTH."
—*TIMOTHY GEITHNER*

"IF THERE IS A WAY OUT OF THIS, I WOULD SAY IT IS THIS: I DON'T THINK WE SHOULD MOVE TO AUSTERITY TOO QUICKLY BECAUSE IT COULD TRIGGER A SECOND RECESSION."
—*PRESIDENT CLINTON*

"IN THIS PERIOD OF TRANSITION FROM THE RECESSION TO RECOVERY, WE CAN'T PULL UP SHORT AND MAKE THE MISTAKE THAT OTHER COUNTRIES AND OUR OWN COUNTRY HAS MADE IN THE PAST BY PULLING OUT OF RECOVERY EFFORTS TOO SOON."
—*DAVID AXELROD*

"I THINK THE TERRIBLE ECONOMIC SITUATION OBAMA HAS INHERITED WAS SO BAD THAT IT [THE ECONOMIC STIMULUS PACKAGE] COULD HAVE BEEN 20 PERCENT BIGGER."
—*BARNEY FRANK, (D-MA)*

"WE OUGHTA BE DEALING WITH LONG TERM DEFICITS IN THE LONG-TERM . . . REPUBLICANS, CONSERVATIVE DEMOCRATS, THE SIDE THAT TALKS ABOUT THE NEED TO REIN IN THE FEDERAL GOVERNMENT, THIS IS NOT VERY RATIONAL."
—*AL HUNT (BLOOMBERG) ON* THIS WEEK

Bloomberg

"IF 'OUT-OF-CONTROL SPENDING' REFERS TO THE RECOVERY ACT AND OTHER JOBS PROGRAMS THAT ARE RESPONSIBLE FOR MORE THAN 2 MILLION JOBS AND ONLY A SMALL FRACTION OF OUR DEFICIT, I'D ASK WHAT THE ALTERNATIVES WERE. WHETHER WE ARE SPENDING OR CUTTING TAXES, CREATING JOBS IN A RECESSION MEANS ADDING TO THE DEFICIT IN THE SHORT TERM."
—*HOUSE MAJORITY LEADER STENY HOYER, (D-MC)*

If prosperity will continue forever, then why not use wealth to end the last vestiges of poverty, to expand health insurance, and to provide more for retirees?

Prosperity was no longer good enough: We demanded utopia.

President John F. Kennedy reflected this hubris in his inaugural address by asserting that "man holds in his mortal hands the power to abolish all forms of human poverty." The paradox was that poverty was already falling and prosperity was already spreading. But once government got involved to push things further, politicians reversed the very factors—like free enterprise, low taxes, and incentives—that had spearheaded the progress in the first place.

In fairness, President Kennedy's vision was more conservative than many have come to believe. He often stated that his goal was to reduce government dependency, not just provide handouts—and he predicted that such new programs would reduce dependency enough to save tax dollars in the long run. It was an economic philosophy that should now sound pretty familiar.

Utopia Through Guilt

The false premise of eternal prosperity allows progressives to use our never-ending wealth as a tool to guilt Americans into spending more and more on the needy. This was not something that was just confined to the 1960s; here's Obama using the same premise during the 2008 campaign:

> ***I think it should be a right for every American. In a country as wealthy as ours, for us to have people who are going bankrupt because they can't pay their medical bills . . . there's something fundamentally wrong about that.***

In his 1964 State of the Union address, delivered only two months after the Kennedy assassination, Johnson proclaimed, "this Administration today . . . declares unconditional war on poverty." "Total victory," he said, was the only option.

This "war" rhetoric perfectly matched the mood of the era. America had won World War II by unifying an all-powerful federal government with a tightly regulated business sector in order to achieve a large national goal, so why not bring back the same model to fight poverty? Once again Washington would establish a national goal, set the course, and the people would fall right into line. It was an extreme version of central planning, and one that citizens of America's rival at the time, the Soviet Union, were already quite familiar with.

Great Society . . . but for Whom?

Johnson's promise to abolish poverty and lead America "upward to a Great Society" had all the markings of a religious pilgrimage. He believed that equality of outcomes could only be achieved by forcing those who worked hard and saved their money (those "dead heads" that Keynesians hate) to redistribute their wealth to others.

The problem with that kind of thinking is that no honest economist would ever support it. Smoothing wealth out among the population might be good for growing voter bases, but it's terrible for economic growth. That left LBJ in a bind: How could he convince the public to support something that the data wouldn't? The answer was simple: *Just change the data.*

Johnson and his team based their views on *The Other America*, a book written by Michael Harrington, a self-professed socialist. In his book, Harrington claimed that millions of Americans were mired in poverty. There was just one problem: His claims lacked serious statistical evidence.

Harrington wrote, "I work on an assumption that cannot be proved by Government figures or even documented by impressions . . . A fact can be rationalized and explained away; an indignity cannot." Right, because who needs data when bleeding hearts are all that's required?

> **High Praise**
>
> ***The War on Poverty arose as much as anything from the socialist tradition of men like Michael Harrington.***
>
> —Daniel Patrick Moynihan, August 1968

As the Great Society sales pitch was being made to the nation, Johnson's progressive allies rallied to his cause to offer spin and false hope. In 1961, Keynesian economist Robert Heilbroner declared, "We are closer than any community in history to attaining that bright goal seen by Keynes—an economy without poverty. Indeed, we are almost there!"

It's no mistake that Johnson chose poverty and civil rights as his two main issues—after all, they were completely intertwined. In 1965, 43 percent of all black families fell under the $3,000 poverty line. Targeting poverty meant focusing on civil rights and equality, and you couldn't have equality without targeting poverty. Politically, it was a match made in heaven.

That fall LBJ won the election over Barry Goldwater in a landslide, resulting in that rarest of all political gifts: the perceived "mandate" from the public to push your policies through quickly. "Look," he said, "I've just been reelected by an overwhelming majority . . . We've got to get this legislation fast. We've got to get it during my honeymoon period."

> *"We must restore equilibrium to our balance of payments."*
>
> —Lyndon B. Johnson
>
> 1968 SORRY STATE OF THE UNION

That's exactly what he did. The next year, with the help of a liberal majority in Congress, Johnson rammed through a host of programs including Medicare, environmental safety regulations, and Operation Head Start, a long-stalled federal-aid-to-education bill. No less a liberal than Ted Kennedy called 1965 a "breakout year" for the progressive agenda.

The following year, LBJ got the Child Nutrition Act passed and, taking a page right out of the progressive playbook, continued expanding the Aid to Families with

Dependent Children program (AFDC). Under Franklin Roosevelt, AFDC had been limited to widows, those who had lost their husbands and now lacked a breadwinner at home to help support the children. That left LBJ and congressional Democrats with an opportunity: Why hook only widows on government support when there are so many other voting blocs that could use a little extra cash?

They began to loosen and expand the rules of AFDC eligibility, eventually getting to the point where any woman living alone with children could take advantage of the program. In so doing, they not only bought a large swath of new votes, they also incentivized out-of-wedlock births and single motherhood.

As Charles Murray described in his classic book, *Losing Ground*, the Great Society incentivized the same negative behaviors that cause poverty in the first place. It's not simply that people engaged in risky behaviors because they dreamed of a lifetime on welfare. Rather, they became less vigilant about preventing harmful behaviors, in the same way that air bags have been shown to make drivers less vigilant about wearing seat belts. No longer would the horrifying possibility of a lifetime of poverty be enough to discourage premarital sex or dissuade someone from dropping out of school. People felt liberated to do whatever felt good and not worry about the consequences. They'd be taken care of either way.

As a result, millions of women suddenly discovered that they could be better off financially by *not* marrying. Even low-income parents who wanted to stay together could maximize family welfare benefits by living together but not walking down the aisle. The results have been predictably devastating: In 1960, only 5.3 percent of all children in America were born out of wedlock. Today that figure is around 40 percent. Read that again—nearly *40 percent* of all babies born in America do not grow up in a household with married parents.

> This kind of entitlement expansion is one of the key tactics that progressives continually use to nudge America in the direction they want. The idea is to get a simple, sometimes even reasonable, program passed. Then, once the structure is in place, the program can be modified and expanded over time until it eventually bears very little resemblance to the original.
>
> **TEACHABLE MOMENT**
>
> The State Children's Health Insurance Plan (S-CHIP) is a great example of this. Originally passed in the 1990s, S-CHIP was initially supposed to be for poor children who had no access to health care. Sounds like a worthy idea, right? It is—and it has tons of support. But, over time, the program was expanded to include middle-class children. States can set income eligibility requirements, and many of them are now at more than 200 percent of the federal poverty rate. In New Jersey it was 350 percent of the poverty level, meaning that a family of four making $77,175 per year was eligible for S-CHIP. Some poverty program.

Think about how little sense this policy makes. Marriage is the greatest "anti-poverty program" ever conceived—families rely on two incomes instead of one—yet LBJ incentivized women to give that up and rely on government support instead. The logic is awful and the results were even worse.

Yet these numbers hide an even greater tragedy. For black Americans—the constituency that LBJ's big-government dependency programs were targeting like a heat-seeking missile—the numbers are even more staggering: In the 1960s, 25 percent of African-American babies grew up without a father in the home. Today, 72 percent of black mothers are unwed.

If you think that happened by accident, think again—LBJ knew precisely what he was doing. All along, Johnson's voting record proved that he had little interest in racial "equality." Instead, he knew that shifting black voters into the Democrat column would be a key component for Democratic victories moving forward. The sad truth is that his strategy actually worked. In 1964, LBJ got 94 percent of the black vote, a record for presidential elections that stood until 2008, when Obama got 96 percent.

In 1965, LBJ signed the Voting Rights Act, and since then no Republican presidential candidate has ever gotten more than 15 percent of the black popular vote.

Throughout his five years in office, Johnson kept whipping out the national credit card and sticking future generations (that's us) with the massive bill.

The five-year price for his Great Society programs, many of which were designed to ensnare and trap the minorities he loved to hate, rang up to an estimated $305.7 billion (in 2005 inflation-adjusted dollars).

Yet the long-term cost to our way of life is far worse than that. The failure of the Great Society and other federal endeavors to "end poverty" and create utopia resulted in widespread irresponsibility. Many now expect business and government to ensure that everyone has a job, health insurance, education, food, housing, continually rising incomes, and a comfortable retirement. The responsibility society has become the entitlement society.

Most reasonable people understand that there is no escaping the trade-off between economic growth and a large welfare state, yet many still react to every recession, every bout of unemployment, and every possibility of government cuts with righteous indignation. People expect government to do everything for them, and then they feel cheated when it fails to do the impossible.

LBJ WAS NO MLK

LBJ served in the U.S. Senate from 1948 to 1961 and hardly had what you could call a good record on civil rights. His voting record against laws that would ban lynching or eliminate the discriminatory poll tax was so poor that the NAACP once sent him a cable: THE NEGROES WHO SENT YOU TO CONGRESS ARE ASHAMED TO KNOW YOU HAVE STOOD ON THE FLOOR AGAINST THEM TODAY.

Johnson also stopped legislation that would have denied federal funds to segregated schools. He opposed President Harry Truman's civil rights agenda and when President Eisenhower pushed through the 1957 Civil Rights Act, Johnson watered it down in the Senate so it became largely unenforceable.

For example, despite the billions spent, LBJ's so-called War on Poverty did nothing to lower the poverty rate. Poor families had more money due to government benefits, but dependency on government for help—which the War on Poverty was supposed to solve—had worsened into a multigenerational *cycle* of poverty.

Ronald Reagan may have summed it up best: "We declared war on poverty and poverty won."

Great Society, Great Cost

By one White House advisor's measure, more than 390 new domestic social programs were added during JFK's and LBJ's administrations, taking the total from 45 to 435 in just eight years.

Two Wars, No Winners

Tragically, LBJ's War on Poverty was not the worst war he ran while in office. In many ways he fought Vietnam as if it were a social problem to be managed, not a war to be won. Eisenhower had committed advisors to Vietnam to fight off the communist insurgency, but it was LBJ who eventually expanded that to half a million.

With the Great Society and the war happening simultaneously, America was committed to guns *and* butter.

Johnson's hubris once again held disastrous consequences. Ho Chi Minh might have been an America-hating communist revolutionary, trained and funded by Moscow, but, to Lyndon Johnson, Ho was a reasonable man; a man he could deal with. "If only I could get Ho in a room with me," he explained, "I'm sure we could work things out."

Johnson's self-deluded confidence in his own persuasive powers and his fundamental misreading of the enemy's intentions cost the nation oceans of blood and treasure. Given his assumption that Ho would be "reasonable," Johnson had designed his policy around that faulty premise.

To have any chance of succeeding in the conflict, the military advised him to massively expand the bombing campaign in the North. Instead, Johnson's God complex led him to choose the bombing targets *himself* during weekly luncheons—Tuesdays worked best for his schedule—with no military representatives present. Johnson and two civilian aides literally sat and handpicked the targets—a process that sounds remarkably similar to FDR's haphazard selection of the cost increase of gold.

The reason for this was simple: Johnson, in his infinite progressive wisdom, wanted "controlled" use of force so as to elicit a "cooperative" response from the enemy. "We should strive to hurt but not destroy [the enemy]," said former LBJ national security advisor McGeorge Bundy, "for the purpose of changing the North Vietnamese decision on intervention in the South."

LBJ saw the bombing not as a military effort but as an act of persuasion, explaining to one aide that his strategy was to view the bombing as "seduction, not rape." Ho was apparently the damsel, LBJ the dashing seeker of his affections. This, of course, assumed that Ho was interested in being seduced and could be persuaded—and you know what happens when you assume.

The idea that Ho was actually a revolutionary bent on victory, hostile to everything that the United States represented, never seemed to cross Johnson's mind. Accounts of LBJ's time in the White House are full of scenes in which the puzzled Johnson asks his aides, "What does he [Ho] want?" as if the communist leader were a county commissioner from Texas who could be bought off.

LBJ proposed a massive development program in the Mekong Delta region of Vietnam, convinced that it would do the trick. "Old Ho can't turn me down," he said to one aide. He told another: "Ho will never be able to say 'no' to a multi-billion dollar development project." But Ho Chi Minh, of course, did just that. Another tragic misstep caused by Johnson's massive ego and arrogance.

By April 1969, American troops in Vietnam numbered 543,000 with a price tag of $61 billion per year—a figure far eclipsing the administration's estimates of a $5 billion maximum per year.

Of course, far costlier than the dollars spent were the lives lost due to a military and public relations strategy designed to persuade the enemy instead of pulverize them. LBJ didn't galvanize Americans by demonizing the enemy, as other war presidents have. He never presented a compelling case as to why it was in America's best interest to wipe out the regime in North Vietnam. Colonel Bui Tin, who served in the North Vietnamese Army, was asked in 1995 what the United States might have done to win. "Cut the Ho Chi Minh Trail," he responded. "If Johnson had granted General [William] Westmoreland's request to enter Laos and block the Ho Chi Minh Trail, Hanoi could not have won the war." Those are painful words of common sense for all American families who lost loved ones in Vietnam.

"Millions of Americans are forced to go into debt today because the Federal Government decided to go into debt yesterday. We must balance our Federal budget so that American families will have a better chance to balance their family budgets."

—Richard Nixon

SORRY 1970 STATE OF THE UNION

Finally, a Real Conservative?

When the reins of executive power were turned over to Richard Nixon, sadly, not much changed. Although he was a Republican who championed a "New Federalism," Nixon was no Andrew Jackson when it came to spending and debt.

Nixon might have been a law-and-order, fight-the-hippies kind of guy, but he also embraced the central tenets of the New Deal. In fact, there is a strong case to be made

The Great Regulator

Columnist Jonathan Rauch has aptly called Nixon "the Great Regulator." In addition to the wage and price controls that prevailed from 1971 through 1974—the largest government intervention ever in peacetime—Nixon also enacted:

> *[In 1969,] the National Environmental Policy Act; in 1970, the Poison Prevention Packaging Act, the Clean Air Amendments, the Occupational Safety and Health Act; in 1972, the Consumer Product Safety Act, the Federal Water Pollution Control Act, the Noise Pollution and Control Act, the Equal Employment Opportunity Act; in 1973, the Vocational Rehabilitation Act and the Safe Drinking Water Act; in 1974, the Hazardous Materials Transportation Act. Nixon opened the Environmental Protection Agency, the Consumer Product Safety Commission and the Occupational Safety and Health Administration.*

that Nixon's economic policies were even more liberal than LBJ's. Building on the Great Society, he nearly *tripled* antipoverty spending, taking it from $37 billion to $100 billion (in 2009 dollars). His "New Federalism," which became a slush fund for state and local governments, pushed community development spending by 206 percent.

Worse, it was Nixon who steered Social Security and Medicare onto their inevitable path toward bankruptcy. A month before the 1972 election, he signed into law a permanent 20 percent increase in Social Security benefits—and then sent all recipients a pre-election reminder of their growing government checks. Medicare spending also rose 246 percent and Medicaid spending climbed 120 percent.

And that wasn't the end of his vote buying. Nixon demanded that his cabinet officials spend tax dollars as fast as possible and he coaxed the Federal Reserve into rapidly expanding the money supply to create an artificial economic boom, a move that contributed to the inflationary chaos of the next decade.

Nixon also made things worse by meddling in the marketplace and forever ruining the monetary system. Specifically, he tried to use wage and price controls to manage inflation, which was a predictable and natural consequence of Lyndon Johnson's guns-and-butter policies.

And then there was the final blow to American financial responsibility: the permanent abandonment of the gold standard.

> Nixon also bloated the White House sta Before Kennedy, it numbered 23. By 1971, under Nixon, it was a ridiculous 5,395, due, in no small part, to keeping up with the demands of the Great Society bureaucrac
>
> TEACHABL MOMENT

By 1944, the major Western powers had signed the Bretton Woods Agreement, whereby a global financial system was created and Allied countries agreed to fix their currencies to the U.S. dollar. Everything was fine until 1970, when confidence in the dollar began to slide. President Charles de Gaulle of France started trading dollars for gold and others soon followed.

The following year, in 1971, Nixon responded to De Gaulle by announcing that the government would no longer convert dollars to gold, thereby taking America off the gold standard for good and freeing up the government to print as much money as it wanted. The result, predictably, was massive inflation, especially from 1979 through 1981, when prices rose at a double-digit rate each year.

But at least Nixon had one better trait than LBJ: He wasn't a racist. Or, at least not an overt one. According to his biography, "Nixon the Quaker detested racism, though he was unconvinced that all races were in fact of equal intelligence. He thought the East Asians might be the most intelligent, followed by the Caucasians, the Indo-Asians, and the Africans; but they all had equal rights." Oh, I see now: It's considered racism only if you don't think someone should have the same rights as you, even if you think there's no genetic way they can be as smart as you are.

If you want to give Nixon a pass on racism, it's much harder to give him one on anti-Semitism. "The Jews are all over the government," Nixon complained to his chief of staff Bob Haldeman in 1971 as his problems were mounting. Washington "is full of Jews," he continued, "[and] most Jews are disloyal." Then, after carving out exceptions for some of his top aides, such as Henry Kissinger, Nixon added, "But, Bob, generally speaking, you can't trust the bastards. They turn on you. Am I wrong or right?"

It doesn't really matter if you're a progressive Republican or a progressive Democrat—the common denominator is disdain for some class of people. And it makes perfect sense: It's virtually impossible to govern from a philosophy of Manifest Destiny without having some serious disdain for intellect, loyalty, and ability of those same masses.

TRIFFIN'S DILEMMA

There are plenty of great books out there to read if you want to know all of the gory, boring details about the 1944 Bretton Woods Conference, which forever changed international monetary policy, but there's one part in particular that's pretty interesting: The conference established the U.S. dollar as the international reserve currency, meaning that all currencies would be valued against the dollar. The dollar, in turn, was tied to the price of gold ($35/ounce)—meaning that the dollar itself had to hold its value over time for the whole system to function.

So far, so good, except that the other outcome of the conference was the establishment of the International Monetary Fund and the World Bank, two entities that were to lend money at cheap rates to developing countries. Where would that money come from? The United States, of course.

In order to lend all that money, we first had to print it. That led to Triffin's Dilemma, which is basically the idea that the United States can't maintain a strong dollar if it also has to print mass amounts of currency. One side had to win out and—drum roll, please—it was the printing/lending/inflation side that was named the victor.

Oh, and one other side note from Bretton Woods: The leader of the British delegation? John Maynard Keynes. We never had a chance.

M.A.E.D.

Aside from the growing nanny state, there was another, less obvious, but equally as dangerous trend emerging. The new buzzword in international economics was *interdependence*. When it came to nuclear weapons and military strategy, we operated under a theory called Mutual Assured Destruction (MAD): You destroy us, we'll destroy you. In theory, it created a standoff that would make a nuclear missile launch less likely.

Elites had been pushing for quite some time to apply the same theory to economics. In other words, if we make countries economically dependent on each other, they will be much less likely to blow each other up.

Professor Carroll Quigley, a legendary teacher at Georgetown whose students included Bill Clinton, wrote about this pattern of interactions in his book *Tragedy and Hope: A History of the World in Our Time*. First published in 1966, Quigley predicted a world in which we would see the "converging of interests" between countries, including the two superpowers, which would begin to move on "parallel paths." Moreover, Quigley declared that this was all part of a coherent master plan. "The powers of financial capitalism," he wrote, "had another far-reaching aim, nothing less than to create a world system of financial control in private hands able to dominate the political system of each country and the economy of the world as a whole."

RIPPED FROM THE HEADLINES

REPORT SUGGESTS U.S. 'GO OFF GOLD' TO FIGHT DEFICITS

—*Los Angeles Times*, August 1971

GOLD LOSES GLITTER AS NEW MONETARY STANDARD IS SOUGHT

The "gold-is-dead" movement is gaining widespread acceptance

—*Sarasota Journal*, September 1971

To save ourselves from nuclear peril, the theory went, we needed to make bank loans to our enemies, create overarching international institutions, and ensure that consumers, governments, and economies would all have a stake in the prosperity of other countries.

President Nixon did just that, signing lucrative trade deals with Moscow in the name of securing peace. (He actually sold them grain at far below world prices in a move that was later called "the Great Grain Robbery.") Nixon also publicly stated his support for the idea that peace could be achieved through a more balanced world:

> *We must remember the only time in the history of the world that we have had any extended periods of peace is when there has been balance of power. It is when one nation becomes infinitely more powerful in relation to its potential competitor that the danger of war arises. So I believe in a world*

in which the United States is powerful. I think it will be a safer world and a better world if we have a strong, healthy United States, Europe, Soviet Union, China, Japan, each balancing the other, not playing one against the other, an even balance.

International loans, interlocking financial systems, and global trade were the paths to peace in Nixon's mind. (Never mind that during World War I and World War II, leading trading partners such as Germany and Great Britain were blowing each other up.) But what no one realized, or at least no one grasped the consequences of, was that a single, giant global economy meant that the fire lines that separate and protect us had to be removed. That left the world vulnerable to a level of financial catastrophe (natural or man-made) that had never before been possible.

A few decades later, that global crisis would begin to play itself out.

Surveying the Damage

Decades after the backlash against New Deal policies and spending had died off, progressives preyed on America's amnesia by pitching a false utopian society where jobs would be plentiful, poverty would be scarce, and the streets would be paved with chocolate (gold was too taboo). Americans, forgetting what really fueled the postwar boom, pretty much bought it.

From 1961 through 1980, annual nondefense spending rose from 9.1 percent of GDP to 16.8 percent of GDP—the equivalent today of a $1.1 trillion budget increase. Not surprisingly, the national debt also rose, from $293 billion to $909 billion—an increase of 210 percent (though, to be fair, the raging inflation of the late 1970s didn't help). Debt was back—and while economic growth, especially in the 1960s, was substantial, it came at a great long-term cost.

By 1981, after enduring decades of JFK, LBJ, Tricky Dick, Ford, and Carter, the great American backlash against liberal policies funded by the future again took hold. The result was an outsider who promised real change: a man who promised to remind Americans that the conventional view on the role of government was wrong, that the Founders were not irrelevant and that their vision was still worth fighting for.

A man who told the country that it was morning in America again.

And while progressives were once again neutralized by the threat of a fierce enemy abroad, economic growth at home, and a reminder that maximum freedom requires minimum government—they had a plan.

This time, they wouldn't wait long to unleash it.

"We don't have a trillion-dollar debt
because we haven't taxed enough;
we have a trillion-dollar debt
because we spend too much."
—Ronald Reagan, 1982[1]

CHAPTER 8.

Reagan, Bush, and Clinton

Read My Lips: Massive Increases in Debt

RONALD REAGAN: A SHINING CITY ON A HILL OF DEBT

The 1960s and '70s were pretty tumultuous: A missile crisis; a hostage crisis, assassinations, a resignation, civil rights, women's rights, a cold war, a hot war, a poverty war, a space race, oil shocks, price controls, inflation, stagflation, and a severe recession.

And that was just for starters.

By the time 1980 rolled around, the American people seemed to be lost. The consumers' confidence index registered 58.7 (a low that wasn't eclipsed for another twenty-eight years), while ABC News/Harris polls revealed both widespread pessimism and widespread agreement on the need for dramatic change.

- 83 percent of Americans said it was likely they'd postpone a major purchase.
- 77 percent thought it was likely that factories would be shutting down within months.
- 93 percent thought it was likely that the average family would have a harder time making ends meet over the next six months.
- 84 percent favored overall cuts to federal spending.
- 69 percent favored cutting federal welfare spending.

In short, times were tough, and most people thought they'd get even tougher. People wanted accountability and responsibility, both from their neighbors and from their government.

Acting on those beliefs, voters threw out Jimmy Carter after one term and elected the original "hope and change" president, Ronald Reagan. The election wasn't even close.

A few months later, President Reagan walked out to the terrace of the West Front of the U.S. Capitol and delivered a bold new message to Americans: "Government," he said, "is not the solution to our problem. Government *is* the problem."

Reagan continued by taking direct aim at the progressives who had governed the country for so long. "From time to time we have been tempted to believe that society has become too complex to be managed by self-rule, that government by an elite group is superior to government for, by, and of the people. But if no one among us is capable of governing himself, then who among us has the capacity to govern someone else?"

"Failure to cope with this problem now could mean as much as a trillion dollars more in national debt in the next four years alone. . . .The deficit problem is a clear and present danger to the basic health of our Republic. We need a plan to overcome this danger."

—Ronald Reagan

1983

SORRY STATE OF THE UNION

It was a message that people were finally ready and willing to hear. For all of its allure, progressivism had failed to deliver on its promise of an ever-expanding suite of services with no costs attached. Keynes had convinced people that more government spending would result in more prosperity, that a "Great Society" could be bought. It didn't happen. He said that inflation and unemployment could not rise simultaneously. But they did. After years of progressive rule, economic growth was slow, debt was high, and both inflation and unemployment were rampant. People were hurting.

Up until Reagan came along, Americans had mostly been willing to allow the government to take more and more of their power. In 1965, when the deficit was just 0.2 percent of our annual GDP, and the Federal Register (which publishes government rules, regulations, meetings, and the like) was just 13,266 pages, most people were satisfied. Polls at the time showed that only 30 percent of the public believed that the government had grown too powerful.

Barry Goldwater, who'd campaigned for president the year before on an "out-of-control-government" theme, paid a heavy political price for sounding the alarm before people even knew they were under attack—losing in an electoral landslide to LBJ. With Democrats now in control of the Oval Office, the House, and the Senate, all barriers to expansion were gone.

Four years later, with the Great Society in full swing, our economy began to suffer under the weight of a bloated government. Deficits, now totaling 2.0 percent of GDP, became the norm and the Register had jumped to 16,850 pages. Within a few short years, LBJ and Congress had enacted literally hundreds of new subsidies—welfare programs, housing programs, urban programs, and education programs, among others. Americans took notice: The percentage of people who agreed that the government was too powerful jumped from 30 percent to 40 percent.

By the election of 1980, Americans had endured eleven consecutive years of deficits and the government's expansion was undeniable. Federal spending, which totaled 19.3 percent of GDP in 1970, had jumped to 21.7 percent in 1980. To keep up with the torrent of new programs and regulations, the Federal Register exploded to over 87,000 pages. Polls that year showed that a majority of the public was now ready to acknowledge what Goldwater had campaigned on sixteen years earlier: The government had simply grown too powerful.

Ronald Reagan, a man who had spent most of his life to that point as a Democrat, was there to tell them they were right.

By the end of his first term in office, Reagan had successfully changed the American mind-set and spirit. Confidence in the White House rose from 15 percent in 1979 to 42 percent in 1984. By the time his reelection campaign came around, many people had taken Reagan's message to heart: He carried forty-nine states and beat Walter Mondale by the largest electoral margin in history.

> *"The federal deficit is outrageous . . . I think the American people are tired of hearing the same old excuses. Together, we made a commitment to balance the budget: now, let's keep it."*
>
> —Ronald Reagan
>
> 1987
>
> SORRY STATE OF THE UNION

Americans were ready to believe that it really was morning again in America.

Reaganomics Report Card

It's impossible to talk about Reagan's years in office without talking about "Reaganomics," a plan designed to combat the slow growth and high inflation that had taken over the economy. It had four key elements:

1. A restrictive monetary policy to stabilize the dollar's value and end inflation
2. A 25 percent tax cut at all income levels
3. A promise to balance the budget through domestic spending cuts and controls
4. An agenda to ease government regulation

By nearly any measure, numbers 1 and 2 were successful. The Fed, led by Paul Volcker, restricted the money supply by jacking up the federal funds rate (the rate at which institutions lend to each other overnight). Over the course of just one year, the rate was doubled, reaching a high of 20 percent in 1981. (For some perspective, the federal funds target range in mid-2010 was 0.00 to 0.25 percent.)

The tax cuts, which were passed as part of the Economic Recovery Tax Act of 1981, did exactly what they were intended to: they brought back economic growth. GDP grew strongly for the rest of the decade. Despite the top income tax rate falling from 70 percent to 28 percent, federal revenues rose 19 percent faster than inflation during the Reagan presidency, from $1.40 trillion to $1.68 trillion (in 2009 dollars). More to the point, inflation-adjusted individual income tax revenues expanded 13 percent—despite the Federal Reserve's contractionary monetary policies.

Some critics have argued that, as a percentage of GDP, federal revenue actually fell, meaning that the cuts failed. Think about how ridiculous that argument is: They are basically claiming that tax cuts didn't work because the economy grew *too fast*. Isn't that the whole point? Lower tax rates encourage working, saving, investing, and productivity—the perfect ingredients for economic growth.

TEACHABLE MOMENT

While comparing revenues, expenses, deficits, and debt to GDP is common because it allows you to make fair comparisons over time, it may not be the best way to measure the power and influence of government. You could easily envision a country with, say, a flat tax rate of 10 percent that essentially operates as a dictatorship. Just because revenue is a small percentage of the economy doesn't necessarily mean that people are any more free.

Under Reaganomics:

- The United States economy grew at an average rate of 3.4 percent a year, beating both the 2.9 percent average rate during the previous eight years and the 2.7 percent over the next eight years;
- The inflation rate plummeted from 12.5 percent to 4.4 percent;
- The unemployment rate fell from 7.1 percent to 5.5 percent as 15 million new jobs were created;
- The prime interest rate fell by one-third;
- Productivity jumped 15 percent;
- The S&P 500 leaped 124 percent; and
- Charitable contributions expanded 57 percent faster than inflation.

In short, tax cuts and a restrictive money policy worked. But Reagan's success with the last two points of his plan was far less impressive.

In Defense of Defense

Classic economic ideological battle lines have been drawn over the years: Adam Smith versus John Maynard Keynes, Milton Friedman versus Paul Krugman (although putting Friedman and Krugman in the same sentence is like putting Edward R. Murrow and Keith Olbermann in the same sentence). But things really start to fall apart when it comes to putting these theories into practice.

Keynesianism has been implemented in various forms throughout the world and over the decades. Likewise, Krugman's theory (basically a supersized version of Keynesianism in which massive government spending is the best stimulus) was essentially our government's response to the 2008 recession.

But when's the last time anyone really tried to run the economy as Adam Smith or Milton Friedman would?

The answer is most likely *never.*

Here's the problem: Presidents can occasionally convince the public and the Congress that tax cuts will inspire growth. Coolidge did it. Kennedy did it. Reagan did it. Bush 43 did it. But only Coolidge followed through on the second half of the equation: *spending cuts*. The rest of them apparently forgot that part.

Point 3 on Reagan's list was to balance the budget. He never even came close.

When the Gipper took office in 1981, the national debt stood at $2.3 trillion (using 2009 dollars). By the time he left office eight years later, it had increased to $4.7 trillion. The reason behind that rise is simple: Reagan ran deficits in every single one of his eight years in office.

So that brings up the all-important question: *Why?* Why would Reagan include tax and spending cuts as 50 percent of his plan and then completely ignore half of that equation? The easy answer is that it was out of his hands. Reagan's budget proposals were one thing, but the bills that actually passed through Congress were something else entirely. The Democrats controlled the House (and, starting in 1987, the Senate as well) and went with him on the politically palatable tax cut side, but not on the politically toxic spending cut side.

But the real story is a lot more complicated than that.

President Reagan once wrote in his diary that "the press is trying to paint me as now trying to undo the New Deal. I reminded them that I voted for FDR four times. I'm trying to undo the 'Great Society.'"

RIPPED FROM THE HEADLINES

REAGAN INSISTS HE'LL WORK TO CUT DEFICIT

President Reagan denied Friday that he is playing politics with soaring federal red ink and declared he is "serious about negotiating a down payment on the deficit."

—Chicago Tribune, January 1984

Protecting the New Deal meant protecting Social Security (the most expensive entitlement), farm subsidies (farmers vote Republican), and veterans' spending (with growing costs from the World War II and Vietnam veterans).

Even among the Great Society programs that Reagan seemed to despise, he ultimately decided that fundamentally reforming Medicare—the most expensive LBJ program—was too politically risky. As a result, a lot of government spending was basically immune from cuts or reform.

Still, Reagan entered the White House seeking modest spending cuts alongside his tax cut proposals. In 1981 he secured $35 billion in domestic spending cuts, even eliminating the failed Comprehensive Employment and Training Act (CETA). The following year, as the deficit rose, Reagan sought deeper cuts. The Democratic Congress offered the president one of their famous deals: For every dollar you raise taxes, we'll cut three dollars in spending.

Reagan reluctantly agreed to the tax increase and signed the Tax Equity and Fiscal Responsibility Act of 1982 . . . but he'd been tricked. A decade later, the president penned a *Wall Street Journal* op-ed and explained what happened.

"Despite the 'assurances,' 'promises,' 'pledges' and 'commitments' you are given, the spending cuts have a way of being forgotten or quietly lobbied out of future budgets. But the tax increases are as certain to come as, well, death and taxes.

"In 1982, Congress wanted to raise taxes. It promised it would cut federal spending by $3 for every $1 in new taxes. Being a new kid in town, I agreed to this. Unfortunately, although the new taxes went into effect, Congress never cut spending by even a penny."

NOT IN MY BACKYARD

The *New York Times* did a great job explaining how Reagan's mandate to cut spending ran into the realities of politics:

The very same people who wanted [spending cuts] also wanted their own goodies preserved. On any particular issue it is the pro-goody faction that is motivated and organized. No one in America wants a subsidy program for peanut farmers, for example, except for a few peanut farmers. But non-peanut farmers don't care that much about this one little program. By skillfully trading their votes for things non-peanut farmers do care about, the congressmen for the peanut farmers were able to save their program. There are dozens of stories like this one. The result is that [budget director David] Stockman was unable to cut the goodies of anyone except those least able to organize and protect themselves: the very poor.

President Reagan's calls for spending restraint were continually undermined by basic special interest politics; undermined by a media that portrayed any minor spending cut as a savage assault on the safety net; and even undermined by his own cabinet members who fought to protect "their turf" against budget cuts.

But the biggest roadblock of all was the Democratic Congress, which used Reagan's number-one priority, national defense, against him.

Reagan firmly believed that the Cold War was bigger than just the U.S.A. vs. the U.S.S.R.—it was a battle of ideologies. It was communism vs. freedom, Marxism vs. capitalism. The winner would determine what kind of world we lived in for decades to come. As Reagan said years before he took office, "If we lose freedom here, there is no place to escape to. This is the last stand on earth."

He reasoned that the national debt wouldn't matter much if we lost the Cold War, and while you can certainly argue about whether he was right, it was what he believed, and he developed his budget to match his principles.

In his book *Reagan's War,* Peter Schweizer recounted Reagan's rationale through interviews with Reagan advisor Ed Meese and his good friend, National Security Advisor William P. Clark:

> *[Disagreements about spending] finally came to a head at a cabinet meeting in the White House. "Mr. President, you have double-digit inflation and double-digit unemployment," warned one cabinet member. "You can't spend all of this money on the military. We have to spend it on social programs."*
>
> *Another cabinet member explained that it would create bad publicity to boost spending on guns while cutting the butter. Congress would probably object; it might bust the budget. The debate raged on until Reagan leaned forward and raised his hand to halt the discussion.*
>
> *"Look, I am the President of the United States, the commander in chief; my primary responsibility is the security of the United States . . . If we don't have our security, we'll have no need for social programs. We're going to go ahead with these [defense] programs."*

Reagan was clear about his priorities from the very beginning. In 1981, he said, "I did not come here to balance the budget—not at the expense of my tax cutting program and my defense program."

This view essentially removed the veto pen from Reagan's hand. If he wouldn't sign the Democrats' domestic spending bills, they wouldn't send him defense spending bills that met his standards. It was, in essence, a domestic version of mutually assured destruction.

Reagan does deserve *some* credit since he did try to rein in spending over the long run, most notably with the Balanced Budget and Emergency Deficit Control Act of 1985. This law, commonly referred to as Gramm-Rudman-Hollings, set specific deficit reduction targets with the goal of running surpluses by 1991. The act was good in theory: It required automatic across-the-board spending cuts ("sequestrations") if the yearly deficit targets weren't met, regardless of what Congress did.

By 1990, the act would have required slashing in excess of 40 percent from spending on defense and domestic programs in order to meet the target levels. That was more than politicians could swallow, so they did what they always do when they don't like the outcome of the game: They changed the rules and weaseled out of their commitment.

Coining a New Economic Theory

Conservatives hate "Keynesianism," because it's become synonymous with huge deficits and a complete disregard for national debt. Liberals hate "supply-side economics," because it's become synonymous with tax cuts for the wealthy. So, allow me to bring America together with a new theory: *Common Sense Economics.*

It's actually pretty simple: You start by cutting taxes, for *everyone*, and, simultaneously, you also make deep cuts in spending. As the tax cuts take hold, the economy grows, because people start hiring, spending, and investing—but you're also spending less so you end up with something that economists believe to be extinct: a surplus.

You're welcome, America.

Actions Speak Louder than Words

The actual numbers over Reagan's terms tell a conflicted story. According to Veronique de Rugy, a senior research fellow at George Mason University's Mercatus Center, "Ronald Reagan sought—and won—more spending cuts than any other modern president. He is the only president in the last [forty-five] years to cut inflation-adjusted nondefense outlays, which fell by 9.7 percent during his first term."

But comparing presidents to each other is a false premise. It's like someone who weighs 400 pounds comparing themselves to someone who weighs 450 and saying that it makes them thin. No, sorry, you're both still fat. "Less bad" is not the same as "good." For fiscal conservatives, presidents should be judged on how they reduced the size, scope, and cost of government over the long term. And by that measure, Reagan didn't do so well.

Over his two terms, total federal spending increased 22 percent faster than inflation. If you look at it as a percentage of GDP (which is only fair because it takes into account how much, or little, the economy is growing), spending actually decreased from 22.2 percent to 21.2 percent.

There is also a point to be made that, while actions speak louder than words, both sides of the equation matter. Plenty of so-called Republican presidents have vowed to restore limited government and reduce spending and have then completely ignored those promises once they realized the political sacrifice they'd have to make to follow through. (Newsflash: You can't significantly cut spending without making a lot of powerful people very, very angry.)

But at least Reagan tried. During his first inaugural address, he told Americans:

> *You and I, as individuals, can, by borrowing, live beyond our means, but for only a limited period of time. Why, then, should we think that collectively, as a nation, we are not bound by that same limitation? We must act today in order to preserve tomorrow. And let there be no misunderstanding—we are going to begin to act, beginning today.*

After four years of seeing his proposed budgets changed and his vetoes overridden, Reagan again stood before America and sounded no less optimistic.

> *A dynamic economy, with more citizens working and paying taxes, will be our strongest tool to bring down budget deficits. But an almost unbroken 50 years of deficit spending has finally brought us to a time of reckoning. We have come to a turning point, a moment for hard decisions. I have asked the Cabinet and my staff a question, and now I put the same question to all of you: If not us, who? And if not now, when? It must be done by all of us going forward with a program aimed at reaching a balanced budget. We can then begin reducing the national debt.*
>
> *I will shortly submit a budget to the Congress aimed at freezing government program spending for the next year. Beyond that, we must take further steps to permanently control Government's power to tax and spend. We must act now to protect future generations from Government's desire*

Having It Both Ways

Watching Republicans and Democrats argue about something like Reagan's economic record is pretty amusing, because it shows you how people automatically fight for their "side" without regard to logic. Republicans want to pretend that virtually everything good that happened from 1981 to 1988 (the surge in employment, the taming of inflation, the economic growth) was a direct result of Reagan and his policies, while all of the bad stuff (the overspending, deficits, S&L crisis) is the fault of Democrats in Congress. Democrats, of course, see it the opposite way. Everything bad was a direct result of Reaganomics, while the positive things had nothing to do with Reagan whatsoever.

to spend its citizens' money and tax them into servitude when the bills come due. Let us make it unconstitutional for the Federal Government to spend more than the Federal Government takes in.

> *"You know, a few of us can remember when, not too many years ago, those who created the deficits said they would make us prosperous and not to worry about the debt because 'we owe it to ourselves.' Well, at last there is agreement that we can't spend ourselves rich."*
>
> —Ronald Reagan
>
> 1988 SORRY STATE OF THE UNION

On March 25, 1986, the U.S. Senate got within one vote of the two-thirds majority needed for a balanced-budget constitutional amendment. But the House never got close, and Reagan certainly never fought for it as much as he implied he would.

One vocal critic of Reagan's handling of fiscal matters was his budget director, David Stockman. After leaving the administration in 1985, Stockman wrote a tell-all book about the Reagan administration's economic policy titled *The Triumph of Politics*. In it, Stockman laments that the administration failed to follow through on the "revolution" in small government that it had promised. "Evidence that the federal government has gone off the deep end in the conduct of its fiscal affairs continues to mount," Stockman wrote. "[I]n eight years direction by the most conservative administration in modern times, the federal government's spending will have exceeded its income by a staggering sum of $1.5 *trillion*." He goes on to say (and try not to laugh), "Historians will undoubtedly find these elephantine figures baffling."

In His Own Words

"Government's view of the economy could be summed up in a few short phrases: If it moves, tax it. If it keeps moving, regulate it. And if it stops moving, subsidize it."

—Ronald Reagan, August 1986

Little did he know, those would actually become the good old days.

Overall, the Reagan experience should prove to those of us who honestly want to solve this problem that no one person can do it alone. It truly has to be a national effort. Thomas Jefferson himself could take the Oval Office in 2012 and, without the firm backing of the people and the unequivocal support of both parties in Congress, our debt would still go up.

THE ETERNAL EXPANSION

Milton Friedman once said, "History shows that over a long period of time government will spend whatever the tax system raises plus as much more as it can get away with."

To combat that, Republicans have at times tried to "starve the beast" by arguing that tax cuts will force the government to spend less. It doesn't work. Common sense dictates that the best way to shrink the size of government is to shrink the size of government. That means tax and spending cuts. There's no other way.

GEORGE H. W. BUSH: A THOUSAND POINTS OF DEBT

My opponent won't rule out raising taxes. But I will. And the Congress will push me to raise taxes and I'll say no. And they'll push, and I'll say no, and they'll push again, and I'll say, to them, "Read my lips: no new taxes."

—Presidential candidate Vice President George H. W. Bush, August 1988, at the Republican National Convention

When George Bush ran for the Republican nomination in 1980 he declared Reagan's economic policies of tax cuts designed to spur growth as "voodoo economics." But when he joined Reagan's ticket as vice president, Bush was loyal and supported his president's policies (which included raising taxes a total of thirteen times in addition to a number of tax cuts).

By 1986, the race to select Reagan's successor had begun and taxation loomed as one of the major issues. Grover Norquist, head of Americans for Tax Reform, had created a no-new-taxes pledge and was asking Republican candidates to sign it. A large number of congressional candidates did just that, including Bush's primary rivals Jack Kemp and Pierre "Pete" du Pont—so Bush, having absolutely no intention to embrace new taxes if elected, signed it as well.

Bush, of course, eventually broke his promise, widening the deficit of trust between the public and our leaders and resulting in many people remembering only this one event of his presidency. Like Reagan, Bush had struck a deal with Congress, promising to support raising tax rates in exchange for spending cuts. Also like Reagan, the spending cuts never materialized. But forgotten in the sound bites and political wrangling are the reasons *why* Bush broke his promise in the first place.

BUSH VOWS TALKS ON HIS FIRST DAY TO CUT THE DEFICIT

President-elect Bush said today that he would open negotiations with Congress on his first day in office in an effort to reduce the Federal budget deficit.

—*New York Times*, November 1988

Unlike Reagan, Bush was temperamentally and politically cautious. He did not consider himself to be a "movement conservative"; he saw his job as president to be the cautious steward of the nation. He was humble and didn't take himself too seriously.

At the White House, he would sometimes carry around a voice-activated stuffed monkey that would sock itself in the head whenever he, the president, began to speak. To friends, he liked to quote the advice he had been given by a former Republican National Committee chairman named Ray Bliss: Always

> “We must make a very substantial cut in the Federal budget deficit. Some people find that agenda impossible, but I'm presenting to you tonight a realistic plan for tackling it.”
> —George H.W. Bush
>
> 1989
>
> SORRY STATE OF THE UNION

wait at least a few days before making a difficult decision because, by then, “you might not have to decide at all.”

That might be a good philosophy for staying out of political trouble, but it's not so good for tackling really tough problems—like the national debt. But for Bush, there was no other way. His often repeated phrase, “it wouldn't be prudent,” wasn't just a throwaway line; it was the way he viewed his job.

These personality traits explain a lot, but the more tangible reason Bush broke his promise is that the high rate of economic growth that Reagan enjoyed over his eight years wouldn't be sustained. Annual GDP growth, which was a healthy 4.1 percent in 1988, plummeted over the next three years to 3.6 percent, 1.9 percent, and then a 0.2 percent contraction in 1991. With growth slowing and spending still increasing, government had to borrow more money to meet its existing obligations.

In 2009 dollars, the national debt rose from roughly $4.7 trillion in 1988 to $6.2 trillion in 1992—a 32 percent increase in just four years. No matter how you slice it, that's not exactly a fiscal record to be proud of. As a percentage of GDP, things look even worse (if that's even possible): The debt grew from 51.1 percent of GDP to 64.1 percent. Like Reagan, Bush was never able to churn out a surplus.

President Bush did not enter the White House with a reputation as a spending hawk. The moderate Bush had a more expansive view of government than Reagan and campaigned on creating “a kindler and gentler” nation (as if President Reagan's America was mean and harsh) and being an “environmental” president. To many, that was code language for expanding government.

At the same time, Bush was also a victim of bad luck. The 1990 recession lowered tax revenues and pushed up the deficit. He inherited a $150 billion tab for the savings and loan crisis and, even worse, he inherited the budgetary time bombs planted by progressives years earlier. Between 1989 and 1993, nominal Social Security costs increased $72 billion (31 percent), Medicare outlays soared $46 billion (50 percent), and interest payments on our debt, a reflection of all the spending we'd done in previous years, jumped up $30 billion (18 percent).

> “We must get the Federal deficit under control . . . This government is too big and spends too much.”
> —George H. W. Bush
>
> 1992
>
> SORRY STATE OF THE UNION

To put all of this another way, of the $163 billion in revenue increases over Bush's term, the increases in the three items mentioned above (none of which Bush had any direct control over) chewed up $148 billion (91 percent) of it. Almost all other spending increases (you may remember Operation Desert Storm) had to be funded by borrowing.

Of course, just like with Reagan, none of this excuses Bush's results—the reality is that he presided over yet another expansion of government—but it does put into context just how little control presidents have once entitlement spending and interest payments are on autopilot.

It's a lesson that, by the time America put Bush's son into the Oval Office, the country would learn all too well.

BILL CLINTON: IT DEPENDS ON WHAT THE MEANING OF THE WORD "SURPLUS" IS

The road to tyranny, we must never forget, begins with the destruction of the truth.

—President Bill Clinton, 1995

Let's get the part out of the way that everyone already seems to know: The Congressional Budget Office (CBO) reports that Bill Clinton ran surpluses from 1998 through 2001. They were the first surpluses in twenty-eight years.

But there's one teeny-weeny fly in the ointment that you won't hear a lot of Clinton supporters point out: Our national debt rose every single year that Clinton was in office.

It started at $6.2 trillion (in 2009 dollars) when he took office in 1992 and ended at about $7 trillion eight years later. Compared to other administrations, a 13 percent increase in the national debt over two terms is something to be celebrated as nearly historic. But in the real world, $800 billion is still a lot of money.

So, how did it happen? How could Clinton claim to be running surpluses while our national debt was still climbing rapidly? The answer lies in how the government calculates its numbers . . . and how politicians spin them.

But first, a big disclaimer: While I'm about to illustrate how Clinton was able to claim surpluses even though our debt was rising, the truth is that *every single president* starting with Reagan has used the same tactics. The only reason Clinton gets singled out, perhaps unfairly, is that he actually reduced spending more than the others and was therefore into "surplus" territory. That makes him a bigger target, but the truth is that you can't criticize Clinton for this without being equally critical of President Reagan and both of the Bushes.

Follow the Breadcrumbs

The complexity of our budget is overwhelming (which I believe is intentional so that the majority of us won't pay attention to it). But when you cut through all the nonsense, there's an extraordinarily simple way to see whether a president was fiscally responsible in reality, or just in sound bites: Look at the balance of our national debt.

Regardless of what else happens during the year, if there's a true cash surplus, then our national debt would be reduced. If there's a true cash deficit, then our national debt would have to go up because we'd have to borrow the money. There's really no other way; you can't have both a surplus and a higher national debt.

"We have to get back to the deficit. For years there's been a lot of talk about it but very few credible efforts to deal with it. And now I understand why, having dealt with the real numbers for 4 weeks . . . If we don't act now, you and I might not even recognize this government 10 years from now."

—BILL CLINTON

1993

SORRY STATE OF THE UNION

Now, back to Clinton. In the fall of 2000, he told America that the recent surplus represented "the largest one-year debt reduction in the history of the United States." He also explained, according to CNN, that the "$5.7 trillion national debt has been reduced by $360 billion in the last three years—$223 billion this year alone." CNN itself reported that "the federal budget surplus for fiscal year 1999 was $122.7 billion, and $69.2 billion for fiscal year 1998. Those back-to-back surpluses, the first since 1957, allowed the Treasury to pay down $138 billion in national debt."

Taken together, those statements clearly imply that Clinton not only ran surpluses and reduced the national debt, but that he reduced it by a record-setting amount.

All wrong.

Let's start with the actual national debt figures. According to the White House Office of Management and Budget, Clinton inherited a national debt of about $4 trillion. Here is his "progress" on the debt over his two terms (in trillions):

September 30, 1993	$4.351	September 30, 1997	$5.369
September 30, 1994	$4.643	September 30, 1998	$5.478
September 30, 1995	$4.921	September 30, 1999	$5.605
September 30, 1996	$5.181	September 30, 2000	$5.629

You might notice something interesting about that string of numbers: *They constantly go up!*

So how exactly does "the largest one-year debt reduction in the history of the United States" mesh with the government's own data showing debt increases? The answer requires someone akin to a forensic accounting expert, but the simple version is that there are *two* kinds of government debt, and Slick Willie, like a bad magician, was trying to get you to only focus on one of them. (There's a good reason why Slick Willie is a nickname for both Bill Clinton and famous bank robber Willie Sutton.)

We get into the details of these two kinds of debt a lot more later, so, for now, this is just a primer for understanding how presidents use this to their advantage.

CLINTON BACKS OFF VOW TO HALVE DEBT

The deficit is much bigger now than it was when I said this.

—*St. Petersburg Times*, January 1993

Our debt comes in two flavors: public debt, which we owe to bondholders and other investors, and intragovernmental debt, which is debt that the government owes to itself. Adding them together gives you our total national debt, which is the number you often see publicized by the media.

Presidents, like Clinton, often choose to focus only on the *public debt* and conveniently ignore the intragovernmental side when making boisterous statements. Why is that convenient? *Because the amount of intragovernmental debt goes up every single year.*

Here's another look at the numbers over the years of the Clinton surpluses, this time showing both kinds of debt:

A Surplus of Lies

Fiscal Year	Claimed Surplus	Public Debt	Intra-governmental Debt	Total Debt Increase
1998	$69.2	↓ $48.1	↑ $161.2	↑ $113.1
1999	$125.6	↓ $82.6	↑ $212.7	↑ $130.1
2000	$236.2	↓ $216.7	↑ $234.6	↑ $17.9

ALL NUMBERS IN BILLIONS

The total of Clinton's "claimed surpluses" over these three years was $431 billion. Yet the national debt rose by a total of $261.1 billion—leaving a difference of $692.1 billion to account for. Looking at Clinton's entire eight years in office makes the numbers even more eye-opening. The White House OMB reports a total deficit of

"For three decades, six presidents have come before you to warn of the damage deficits pose to our nation. Tonight, I come before you to announce that the federal deficit—once so incomprehensibly large that it had 11 zeroes—will be, simply, zero."

—BILL CLINTON

1998

SORRY STATE OF THE UNION

$320.4 billion over the eight-year period of 1993 to 2000. But they *also* report the national debt increasing by $1.6 trillion over that same period.

Something smells fishy in D.C., and you can trace the odor directly to the Social Security Trust Fund.

Ever since the 1983 Greenspan Commission, yearly Social Security surpluses are required to be added in with other revenues (like income taxes), rather than put into that famous "lock box" and held for future payouts. Since Social Security and Medicare tax rates increased steadily (from 12.1 percent in 1978 to 15.3 percent in 1990), the trust funds experienced a major influx of revenue. The Social Security Trust Fund, for example, had a surplus of $7.5 billion in 1985. A decade later, the surplus was $60.4 billion and, just five years after that, it had more than doubled to $152 billion.

The year of that $152 billion surplus? It was 2000. Conveniently that's the same year as the historic Clinton surplus. Coincidence? Not by a long shot. What was happening was that Clinton was simply borrowing every dollar of trust fund surplus and counting it as new income to spend (as the Greenspan Commission had demanded) instead of debt. This "income" then offset the debt he was running up in all other areas and allowed him to make statements like this one, from December 2000:

> *In 1992, the Federal budget deficit was $290 billion—the largest dollar deficit in American history. In January 1993, the Congressional Budget Office projected that the deficit would grow to $455 billion by 2000. The Office of Management and Budget is now projecting a $211 billion surplus for 2000—the third consecutive surplus and the largest surplus ever, even after adjusting for inflation.*

Hans F. Sennholz, an economist who studied under the legendary free-market libertarian Ludwig von Mises, explained the government's accounting gimmick like this:

> *Imagine a corporation suffering losses and being deep in debt. In order to boost its stock price and the bonuses of its officers, the corporation quietly borrows funds in the bond market and uses them not*

RIPPED FROM THE HEADLINES

CLINTON PREDICTS DEBT PAYOFF BY 2013

—United Press International, January 2000

only to cover its losses but also to retire some corporate stock and thereby bid up its price. And imagine the management boasting of profits and surpluses. But that's what the Clinton Administration has been doing with alacrity and brazenness. It suffers sizeable budget deficits, increasing the national debt by hundreds of billions of dollars, but uses trust funds to meet expenditures and then boasts of surpluses which excites the spending predilection of politicians in both parties.

> HATE SPEECH?
>
> "Over the past 25 years, the government has gotten used to the fact that Social Security is providing free money to make the rest of the deficit look smaller . . . [Soon,] instead of Social Security subsidizing the rest of the budget, the rest of the budget will have to subsidize Social Security."
>
> —*Andrew Biggs, a resident scholar at the American Enterprise Institute*

Here's another way to look at this: Last year you made $30,000 at your job and spent $32,000 on living expenses. Your brother, seeing that you were having a hard time, loaned you $10,000 and you gave him an "I.O.U." in return.

Common sense says that your "deficit" for the year was $2,000 and your "personal debt" increased by $10,000. In short, it wasn't a banner year. But our presidents would claim that you didn't have a deficit at all, you had a *surplus* of $8,000. Congratulations! *But what about the $10,000 you borrowed*, you might be wondering? Don't worry about it, politicians would say; it's not real. He's your brother, after all!

> *"We will pay off our national debt for the first time since 1835 . . . If we stay on this ath, we can pay down the debt entirely 13 just years now and make America ebt-free for the first time since Andrew Jackson was president in 1835."*
>
> —Bill Clinton
>
> 2000
>
> SORRY STATE OF THE UNION

The Dividends

Budget gimmicks aside, the truth is that Clinton deserves at least some credit for making real, tangible progress. Research by Brian Riedl of the Heritage Foundation shows that, between 1990 and 2000, three major sources of savings account for nearly all of Clinton's success:

- Defense spending fell by 2.2 percent of GDP;
- Tax revenues rose by 2.6 percent of GDP; and
- Net interest costs on the national debt dipped by 1.0 percent of GDP.

THE PEACE DIVIDEND

Think of Reagan's 1980s defense buildup as an investment that finally paid off when the Soviet Union collapsed. With the exception of brushfires in Somalia, Haiti, and the Balkans, there were no large wars for Clinton to fight or prepare for. As a result, the United States found itself without a major enemy—a luxury it hadn't enjoyed since the 1930s!

Predictably, defense spending decreased substantially. Between 1990 and 2000, spending fell from $491 billion to $376 billion (adjusted for inflation in 2009 dollars). As a percentage of GDP, it fell from 5.2 percent to 3.0 percent (even the subsequent war on terrorism brought the defense budget back up to only 4.9 percent of GDP).

Take that peace dividend away and the results would've been dramatically different. If America had spent 5.2 percent of GDP on the military in 2000, the "surplus" would have been reduced by over $200 billion and the deficit, accounting gimmicks or not, would have been undeniable.

THE TAX AND TECH DIVIDEND

The tax revenue surge is often attributed to the tax increases signed by President George H. W. Bush in 1990 and President Clinton in 1993. But the proof that that's not the case is in the pudding (or, in this case, the data): Between 1990 and 1995, tax revenues did not grow significantly faster than they did during the Reagan years when rates were lower.

Then, in 1995, the Republican Congress put an end to the Clinton spending spree and, in 1997, capital gains tax rates were cut. The combination of all these factors resulted in a soaring stock market and economy.

New business investment fueled the tech boom, resulting in revolutionary companies like Google, eBay, and Amazon being born. Between 1994 and 2000, speculation over the potential of this new breed of Internet companies drove the NASDAQ index up by more than 450 percent. The booming economy and stock market induced a staggering 37 percent inflation-adjusted tax revenue surge between 1995 and 2000—more revenue growth than had occurred in the previous decade *combined*. By 2000, tax revenues had reached a new peacetime record of 20.6 percent of GDP.

As we now know, the good times didn't last forever. In 2000, the bubble burst, ushering in a serious recession that set back revenue and resulted in a costly government response. This was all just in time for the long-run effects to be declared George W. Bush's fault.

POLITICAL RATIONALE GENERATOR

Are you a politician who wants to pass a major economic reform package but just can't seem to convince a skeptical public that socialism is the way to go? You need a better excuse! Just mix and match one problem, culprit and accomplice from the columns below and your package should be law in no time.

Example: "The reason we need to pass [INSERT CUTE REFORM PACKAGE TITLE] *is because of the* ESCALATING COST OF WARS *caused by* THE PREVIOUS ADMINISTRATION *and exacerbated by* ISRAEL.

The Problem	The Culprit	The Accomplice
Our Budget Deficit	*The Previous Administration*	*ACORN*
The Medicare Shortfall	*Special Interests*	*Goldman Sachs*
Stability of Social Security	*Corruption*	*John Boehner*
Escalating Cost of Wars	*Earmarks*	*The BP Oil Spill*
Availability of College Loans and Grants	*Pork*	*Nicotine Addiction*
Steady Unemployment	*The Recession*	*The Toyota Recall*
Falling Value of Dollar Nomination Process	*Greedy Corporations*	*Supreme Court*
Mortgage Fraud	*Uncooperative Congress*	*Closing Guantanamo Bay*
Lack of Transparency In Wall Street Practices	*Talk Radio*	*"Date Night" With First lady*
Shaky U.S. Credit Rating	*Biden Said Something Stupid*	*Greedy CEO's*
Stock Market Volatility	*Sarah Palin*	*California's Economy*
Failing Small Businesses	*Tea Parties*	*The Cambridge Police*
Collapsing Global Markets	*That Damn Joe Leiberman*	*Training Bo the Portuguese Water Dog*
Surging Consumer Borrowing	*The Party of "No"*	*Watering White House Organic Garden*
Bailouts, Bailouts and More Bailouts	*Illegal Immigration*	*Renewable Energy Spending*
Waning Confidence In The Fed	*Lack of Bipartisanship*	*Infrastructure Projects*
Economic Appointees Who Don't Pay Taxes	*The Oil Companies*	*Iran's Nukes*
Lack of Consumer Confidence	*Predatory Lending Practices*	*Tax Cuts on the Rich*
Decline In U.S. Manufacturing	*America's History of Racial Injustice*	*Talking About College Basketball on ESPN*
Diminished Role of Private Sector Influence	*The Haiti Earthquake*	*Israel*

THE INTEREST DIVIDEND

This one is simple, but important. Rising tax revenues and falling defense spending meant smaller deficits. Combined with lower interest rates, this reduced net interest spending from 3.2 percent of GDP to 2.2 percent—a huge savings that Clinton really had very little control over.

In fact, it could be argued that, prior to his inauguration, Clinton didn't even really understand the importance of interest rates to his agenda. At one meeting in early 1992, Clinton was learning about the economic benefits and risks of focusing on deficit reduction. After hearing that one major risk would be slower economic growth, he received some good news: Slow growth could be offset by lower interest rates. Economist Alan Blinder, who was presenting at the time, informed Clinton that the only issue might be the bond markets. If they didn't believe that Clinton was serious about deficit reduction, they may not react the way the White House would want. Clinton was incredulous. According to Bob Woodward's telling of the story, his "face turned red with anger and disbelief. 'You mean to tell me that the success of the program and my reelection hinges on the Federal Reserve and a bunch of f***ing bond traders?' Nods from the end of the table. Not a dissent."

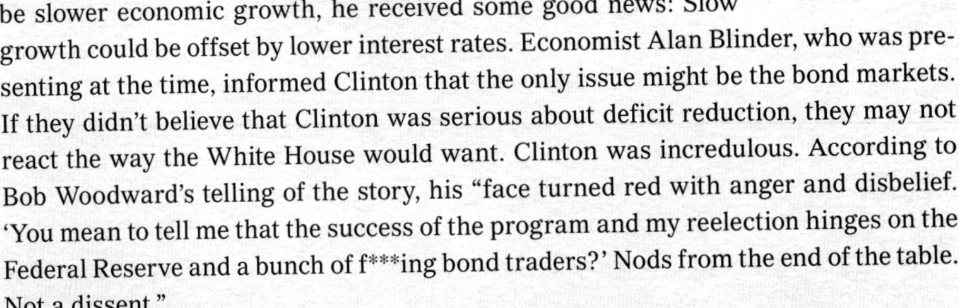

It was an important lesson for Clinton, and one that future presidents would often forget: Ignore investors at your own peril; they are the ones who can ultimately determine your success or failure.

GRIDLOCK IS GOOD?

President Clinton and the Republican Congress's biggest accomplishment may have been that they simply got out of the way. Government gridlock prevented either party from enacting expensive new programs, which, in turn, kept other federal spending relatively constant as a percentage of the GDP. Sometimes a "do-nothing" Congress and White House is the best thing for an economy and a budget.

In fairness, some positive reforms were enacted. In addition to the capital gains tax cuts mentioned above, the president and Congress were able to agree on the 1996 welfare reforms that ended the AFDC entitlement, as well as the 1995 elimination of most farm programs (which President George W. Bush would later reinstate).

A House Divided Cannot Spend

Over the last fifty-seven years, there have really only been two periods of time when any fiscal responsibility was evident in Washington: the Eisenhower and Clinton administrations. Not coincidentally, those were also two periods in which the presidency was often controlled by a different party from the one controlling Congress.

During the worst spending periods, the opposite was true. In 1967 and 1968, for example, LBJ was in the White House and Democrats also enjoyed sizable majorities in the Senate (64–36) and House (248–187). The result? Spending increased an average of 11.6 percent a year over that period.

The largest average decrease, on the other hand, came from the 84th Congress in 1955 and 1956, when spending declined by an average of 4.2 percent a year. Eisenhower was in the White House and Democrats held majorities in both houses of Congress.

Numbers aside, there is commonsense logic to this. If you don't like ever-expanding government, then gridlock is good. I guess maybe our Founders were onto something with this "checks and balances" thing after all . . .

There could have been even more progress: In late 1997, President Clinton and House Speaker Newt Gingrich secretly created a bipartisan plan to permanently rein in Social Security and Medicare. It would provide Social Security personal accounts and convert Medicare into a market-based, premium support program. The idea was for Clinton to offer the plan during his January 1998 State of the Union address, with Gingrich endorsing it immediately after.

So why are Social Security and Medicare both currently still economic disasters? Because six days before Clinton's speech, something happened that would divert America's attention from the budget, and everything else, for a long time to come: The Monica Lewinsky scandal broke.

Republicans and Democrats dismissed talk of any bipartisan compromises and instead armed themselves for political war. As a result, the most promising budget reform in American history died before it could even be unveiled. After that, none of the leaders from that era seriously tackled our budget's underlying structural problems. Like so many before them, they simply kicked the ball down the road.

Unfortunately, America's next two presidents, George W. Bush and Barack Obama, were all too happy to pick that ball up and run with it . . . right off a cliff.

"Congress needs to join with me to bring real spending discipline to the federal budget. Spending discipline requires difficult choices. Every government program was created with good intentions, but not all are matching good intentions with good results."
—George W. Bush, 2005

CHAPTER 9.

W. and O.

The Progressive Era Returns

GEORGE W. BUSH: WARS ON EVERYTHING, EXCEPT DEBT

There are two ironclad rules of government. Rule No. 1: They always try to expand. Rule No. 2: See Rule No. 1.

This eternal truth can manifest itself in a number of different ways. There's the slow and steady, ocean-tide-like expansion that occurs over time. There's also the more aggressive expansion that comes by capturing a mood change among the public, or cashing in "political capital." And then there's the expansion that happens quickly, and sometimes brutally, as the result of an emergency or crisis.

RIPPED FROM THE HEADLINES

IN A SIGN OF CHANGING TIMES, BUSH CALLS FOR MORE SPENDING

The budget . . . strays far from the agenda of small government and fiscal conservatism that the administration advocated on taking office a year ago.

—*New York Times,* January 2002

Most right-leaning administrations generally try to use one of those tactics to their advantage. The most insidious progressive administrations may even try to harness two of them to push their agenda.

The Bush administration exploited all three.

The numbers are not pretty. And, if you consider that they were put up by a man who calls himself a "Republican," they are downright embarrassing. Here's the summary, with everything adjusted for inflation to 2009 dollars:

Total Bush Deficits: $3.3 trillion
Total Increase in National Debt (Bush's *Real* Deficits): $5.0 trillion
Total Bush Spending: $20.5 trillion
Total Inflation-Adjusted Increase of Federal Budget: *Bill Clinton:* 12 percent, *George W. Bush:* 42 percent

Considering that President Bush was the biggest spender since LBJ, no conservative who truly believes in small government can defend Bush's spending record. Sure, you can blame Congress, and it absolutely is a fair target, but remember, from 2001 through 2006 the Republicans controlled the presidency, the Senate (except in 2001 and 2002), and the House. With limited compromise, they could have done as they pleased. Cut waste and bureaucracy? Yep. Force big discretionary spending cuts? Sure. Demand real entitlement reform? Why not? This was the time for a conservative New Deal.

Instead we got a conservative Progressive Era.

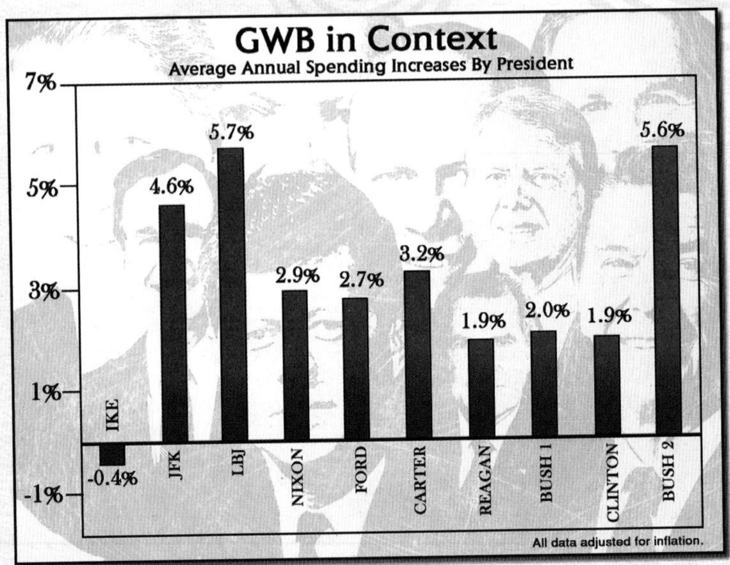

The Autopsy

Bush's economic plan seemed to be pretty simple: tax cuts and then . . . absolutely nothing. It was as though Republicans forgot how to be Republicans once they were in power. Only now, as the political ramifications of their behavior have become obvious, are some finally changing their tune. I hope voters don't let them off that easy.

In fiscal year 2001, the federal government spent an inflation-adjusted $21,500 per household. By the end of Bush's reign eight years later, that number had jumped to nearly $26,000. How did it happen? Four primary factors contributed to the perfect storm:

The Tax Cuts. It's the same old story: Cutting tax rates increases incentives to work, save, and invest; productivity and economic growth increase. Bush's two major tax cuts took place in 2001 and 2003 and were the largest since 1981. In terms of generating economic activity, the evidence of their success (especially the 2003 cuts) is rock solid. In the six quarters prior to the May 2003 tax cuts, nonresidential investment declined every quarter, the S&P 500 fell 18 percent, 1 million net jobs were lost, and the economy grew at an annual rate of just 1.7 percent. In the six quarters following the tax cuts, investment rose every quarter, the S&P 500 leaped 32 percent, 2.3 million net jobs were created, and the economic growth rate doubled to 4.1 percent.

The problem wasn't with the cuts; it was with what happened after. Politicians patted themselves on the back, used their achievement in political campaigns, and then spent *more*, forgetting to follow through on the other half of the small-government equation: *spending cuts*. Ironically, it was that lack of discipline that ensured no further tax cuts could possibly be passed. Thanks, Republicans!

"We owe it to our children and grandchildren to act now, and I hope you will join me to pay down $2 trillion in debt during the next 10 years. At the end of those 10 years, we will have paid down all the debt that is available to retire. That is more debt, repaid more quickly than has ever been repaid by any nation at any time in history."

—George W. Bush

2001

SORRY STATE OF THE UNION

The Tech & Housing Dividends End. Many people forget that Clinton presided over years of a tech boom, and many others don't acknowledge that Bush paid the price for its end. But it was a very real event for the economy. About $5.6 trillion of wealth evaporated as the stock indexes collapsed. The NASDAQ alone fell from more than 5,000 in 1999 to less than 2,000 by 2002, destroying the value of the 401(k)s, pension funds, and mutual funds that people had come to rely on.

The ensuing recession reduced revenue growth from an average of 8.7 percent a year from 1998 through 2000 to an average of -4.1 percent a year from 2000 through 2003. With 1.5 million fewer people working and less tax revenue coming in from individuals and businesses (not to mention a collapsed stock market reducing capital gains and dividend revenues), annual tax revenues fell by $250 billion between 2000 and 2003.

Then, toward the end of Bush's terms, the economy endured the subprime crisis, housing market collapse, and Great Recession, which caused another $10 trillion of wealth to be lost.

In other words, between national security and economic crises, Bush was not exactly able to govern over "eight years of peace and prosperity" as Clinton was.

The War on Terror. The Congressional Research Service has estimated that the total cost of the War on Terror to date (including spending on the wars in Iraq and Afghanistan) is over $1 trillion. That sounds gigantic (and it is), but you have to put it into perspective. While some like to claim that the wars were the reason Bush spent so much, the numbers don't back that up.

If 9/11 and the ensuing wars in Iraq and Afghanistan had never happened, President Bush *still* would have spent $5 trillion *more* (or $2 trillion more in 2009 dollars) than Clinton spent over the course of his presidency. Defense spending only accounted for just over one-third of all *new* spending under President Bush. In other words, the Republicans were going to spend big one way or another. The War on Terror just provided them with good cover.

> **Truth Serum**
>
> **President Bush was the first** president to devote at least 3 percent of GDP to spending on antipoverty programs. President Obama was the second; he pushed it to over 4 percent of GDP.

Spending Like a Drunken FDR. There's one fundamental concept that most politicians have yet to master: *sacrifice*. If you know you're going to a great steak restaurant for dinner, maybe you have a salad for lunch to even things out.

The War on Terror was a national priority; fine, you're not going to hear an argument from me—but then *why not sacrifice in other areas to pay for it*? President

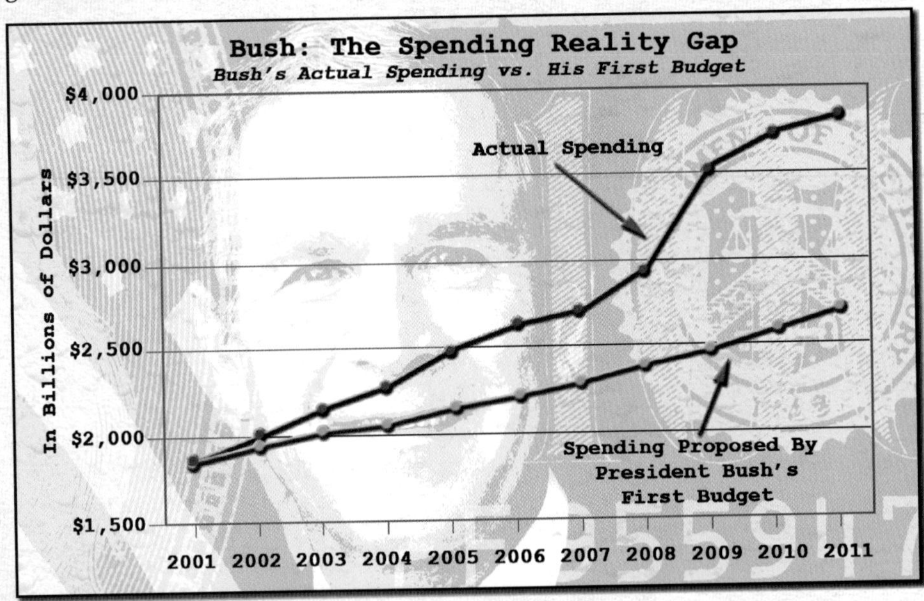

Obama has the same mentality: Extending unemployment benefits was a huge priority for him, fine, but then Obama should have cut spending elsewhere to pay for the extra $34 billion. Instead they just call it an "emergency" and lump it right onto our national debt, all the while talking about how we have to get serious about deficit reduction.

The eight years under Bush illustrate how little willpower politicians have to control their spending. We were fighting *two major wars* and yet we still increased discretionary spending and passed new entitlement programs, even as the existing ones were spiraling out of control.

Bush's first budget (which projected out the next ten years) would have increased federal spending at an average of 3.7 percent a year. That's higher than Clinton's actual average of 3.5 percent a year, but at least it was within a somewhat reasonable range.

Of course, that's not actually what happened.

The Clinton years had left government appropriators feeling richer than they had in years. But with a new sheriff coming into office, and a new crisis to distract the country, the restraints could finally come off. And once they did, all hell broke loose.

Where'd Everybody Go?

When Republicans first took control of Congress in 1995, there were at least five hundred members who supported spending cuts, according to calculations by the National Taxpayers Union. But once Bush took the Oval Office, that number had dropped dramatically—to two. That's right, *two*. Only Ron Paul (R-Tex.) and Jim Sensenbrenner (R-Wis.) voted for less overall spending from 2000 to 2005.

The Decline and Fall of the GOP

In a matter of just over a decade the Republican Party successfully transformed itself into the same corrupt, spineless, big-spending liberals it threw out of Congress in 1994.

The 1995–96 government shutdown was a public relations disaster for a Republican Party that could not match President Clinton's rhetoric. Senator Bob Dole (R-Kans.) finally caved in and agreed to Clinton's spending demands in order to reopen the government, even as President Clinton was himself on the verge of giving in. It was a fiasco for Republicans and resulted in them deciding that even minimal spending restraint constituted political suicide. The "Republican Revolution" died in 1996.

Fast-forward to December 1998. President Clinton had been reelected, the GOP Congress had lost seats in two consecutive elections (despite the Lewinsky scandal), and House Speaker Newt Gingrich (R-Ga.) had just resigned. Most important, the budget deficit that had originally motivated the Republican Revolution was no longer a major national issue.

This was the political environment in which George W. Bush began his 2000 presidential campaign. By calling himself a "compassionate conservative," Bush contrasted himself against the "mean-spirited" Republican Congress still reeling from the government shutdown. The budget surpluses had robbed the GOP of its case for spending restraint (apparently smaller government for its own sake was not on the table), so Bush immediately began promising endless new spending initiatives. The new GOP approach would be to use government spending to buy voter popularity. In other words, they would out-Democrat the Democrats.

Here is how that strategy played out annually:

- 2001: Even after the 9/11 attacks induced a major defense commitment, President Bush sought to buy off "soccer moms" with No Child Left Behind, the largest expansion of federal education spending ever.
- 2002: Farmers were bought off with an 80 percent increase in farm subsidies, reversing the 1996 "freedom to farm" reforms that had phased out subsidies.
- 2003: Seniors were bought off with a Medicare drug entitlement, the most expensive new program since LBJ.
- 2004: State and local government officials were bought off with the most expensive highway bill in American history.
- 2005: No one is quite sure who the target voters were for the president's expensive Mars initiative.
- 2006: Pork project spending—ridiculously considered vital to reelection by lawmakers—reached a record $29 billion, nearly quadruple the 1994 level.[23]

Each large spending bill was intended to buy off another interest group, build Bush's popularity, and expand the Republican majority. How did this strategy work out for them? Well, let's see . . . on election night 2006, voters responded with a historic slaughtering, throwing out the GOP congressional majority due to their reputation as corrupt big spenders. Losses were particularly high among members of the appropriations committees. President Bush's approval rating—nearly 90 percent after 9/11—nearly reached the depths of President Nixon's before the latter's 1974 resignation.

The clear lesson is that you *can't* out-Democrat the Democrats. This should have become glaringly obvious back in 2001, when President Bush signed legislation doubling the K–12 education budget and the Democrats attacked him as cheap for not *tripling* the budget. Whatever reputation for fiscal responsibility the GOP had slowly built up over the past few decades had now been completely destroyed. They sold out their principles for power, and ended up with neither.

It Was More than Just the Spending

Although this book focuses chiefly on economics, no analysis of the Bush administration is complete without a reminder of these gems. Over his two terms, President Bush:

- ***Signed the unconstitutional McCain-Feingold campaign finance bill;***
- ***Signed the highly regulatory Sarbanes-Oxley financial reform bill;***
- ***Essentially nationalized the banking industry in late 2008;***
- ***Imposed steel tariffs;***
- ***Filed a Supreme Court brief supporting affirmative action;***
- ***Tried to nominate moderate Harriet Miers to the Supreme Court;***
- ***Proposed amnesty for illegal immigrants;***
- ***Created a new Department of Homeland Security;***
- ***Added 100,000 federal employees.***

In eight years, President Bush really championed only two significant conservative initiatives: the tax cuts (now threatened by his own runaway spending) and Social Security reform (which never received a vote). Bush's domestic policy record is far more liberal than that of President Clinton and maybe even President Carter. In fact, it is doubtful that an Al Gore presidency could have accomplished as many liberal objectives as President Bush did. Sorry, but sometimes the truth hurts.

Not that the GOP Congress was any better. After completely giving up on the cause of small government, they focused on protecting their power through spending, pork, and perks. For example:

- In 2005, House Majority Leader Tom DeLay (R-Tex.) declared that there was no more wasteful spending left to cut (even though not one program costing more than $1 billion annually had been eliminated since 1996). Later, the GOP Congress refused to create even a nonbinding government waste commission;
- DeLay's "K Street Project" focused the GOP majority on this famous street of lobbyists rather than on Main Street. DeLay demanded that lobbying firms hire more Republicans and donate more to the GOP. In return, Republicans provided these interest groups with tens of thousands of earmarks, and basically outsourced the writing of the bloated highway, energy, and farm bills to them;
- Former GOP representatives Duke Cunningham (R-Calif.) and Bob Ney

(R-Ohio) were sent to prison for accepting bribes and gifts in return for helping friends win government favors;

- Senator Mel Martinez's (R-Fla.) job postings required applicants to write a sample constituent letter defending sugar subsidies;
- The GOP majority refused to even bring President Bush's Social Security reform proposal to a vote;
- Before recess periods, House Republican leadership would distribute talking point packets to their colleagues urging them to take more credit for expanding government;
- In December 2006, Senator Majority Leader Bill Frist (R-Tenn.) sent out a release titled "The Republican Congressional Index: A Dozen Years of Success." This document bragged about the steep education and health budget expansions during the twelve-year Republican congressional majority. Another typical congressional GOP press release: "Largest Federal Funding Increase in History for K–12 Education Takes Effect, Linked to Reform";
- Senator Frist also bragged that GOP reforms had increased government dependency among senior citizens.

During those twelve years of lost opportunities, the few elected Republicans challenging the party's intellectual bankruptcy—such as Tom Coburn (R-Okla.), Jeff Flake (R-Ariz.), Mark Neumann (R-Wis.), and Ron Paul (R-Texas)—were ostracized, threatened, and even kicked off their congressional committees by the party's leadership.

Now that Republicans have seen the consequences of their actions, many are changing their tune, apologizing for their decisions and making all sorts of promises about the future. Only time will tell if this was a Tiger Woods press conference type of staged apology or if it's real, but I do know this: No longer will any politician get the benefit of the doubt simply because he has an *R* after his name.

America Gets Punk'd

A couple of years after Medicare passed in 1965, the calls for expansion started. In June 1967, Secretary of Health, Education, and Welfare John Gardner announced a full-scale study into providing coverage for prescription drugs. Five months later, the Senate Republicans killed the idea, saying that it was far too expensive.

Boy, how times have changed.

It took thirty-six years, but in 2003 the prescription drug expansion of Medicare finally became a reality. And, this time, the charge was led by *Republicans*, a party that no longer seemed to care about price tags.

The following year, *Wall Street Journal* economist Stephen Moore asked the director of the Congressional Budget Office, Douglas Holtz-Eakin, what the total long-term unfunded liability was for the bill. Holtz-Eakin answered with just three words, but they were three words that should instill fear into the hearts of anyone who truly cares about the future of this country: *It is infinite.*

David Walker, who was then the comptroller general of the United States, called the bill "the most fiscally irresponsible piece of legislation since the 1960s." He explained, "We're not being realistic. We can't afford the promises we've already made, much less to be able [to keep] piling on top of 'em. We'd have to have eight trillion dollars today, invested in treasury rates, to deliver on that promise."

Asked by a reporter how much of that eight trillion we actually have, Walker responded, "Zip."

In summary: *an infinite long-term commitment; no money to pay for it.*

"In the coming weeks, I will submit a budget that eliminates the federal deficit within the next five years. I ask you to make the same commitment. Together, we can restrain the spending appetite of the federal government, and balance the federal budget."

—George W. Bush

2007

SORRY STATE OF THE UNION

Massive new entitlement programs that aren't fully funded is nothing new. Both FDR and LBJ had great success in saddling us with trillions they never paid for. But never before have Republicans, a party that supposedly stood for minimum government and maximum freedom, led the way. Why would they be behind such a massive expansion of government? The answer is surprisingly simple: *They wanted to win an election.* Bruce Bartlett, *Forbes* columnist and former Treasury official, explained:

> *The Bush administration was already projecting the largest deficit in American history—$475 billion in fiscal year 2004 . . . But a big election was coming up that Bush and his party were desperately fearful of losing. So they decided to win it by buying the votes of America's seniors by giving them an expensive new program to pay for their prescription drugs.*

"Expensive" is a big understatement. According to the 2009 U.S. financial statements, David Walker was only off by a little bit: Medicare Part D is currently underfunded by $7.2 trillion.

One of the scariest parts of this whole debacle is how the bill was forced through Congress over the objections of conservatives, who actually wanted to be able to continue to look at themselves in the mirror. Bartlett explained:

> *When the legislation came up for [an important vote on a motion to proceed] . . . it was failing by 216 to 218 when the standard 15-minute time allowed for voting came to an end. What followed was one of the most extraordinary events in congressional history. The vote was kept open for almost three hours while the House Republican leadership brought massive pressure to bear on the handful of principled Republicans who had the nerve to put country ahead of party. The leadership even froze the C-SPAN cameras so that no one outside the House chamber could see what was going on.*

Republicans not wanting the public to see what they were doing is pretty funny, since what they were doing was selling out their long-cherished principles and values for short-term political gain. No one should have been surprised—the parties had been melding together for years—but to those who still thought that the words *conservative* and *Republican* were synonymous, it was a huge wake-up call.

The Senate eventually passed the bill with fifty-four votes. Only eight Republicans voted no. Lindsey Graham, one of the Republicans who allowed the bill to move forward by giving a key vote on an earlier motion that would have killed it, was one of them. Why vote yes to move forward and then vote no on the final bill once it already has enough votes to pass? I guess you'll have to ask the senator himself, but I do know this: After all of the debating, arm-twisting, procedural motions and backroom dealing was done and the monstrosity of a bill finally passed both houses of Congress, it went to the desk of a man who claimed to be a fiscally conservative, small-government Republican. He could have vetoed it. Instead he signed it, saying, "Medicare is a great achievement of a compassionate government and it is a basic trust we honor . . . Each generation benefits from Medicare. Each generation has a duty to strengthen Medicare. And this generation is fulfilling our duty."

What he neglected to mention is that *no* generation has ever fulfilled its duty to pay for it.

Republican Regulation of Freedom

Bush apologists will offer plenty of excuses for his spending, but there's another area in which he grew government that no real conservative can ever defend: regulations. If you use the Federal Register as an approximate measure

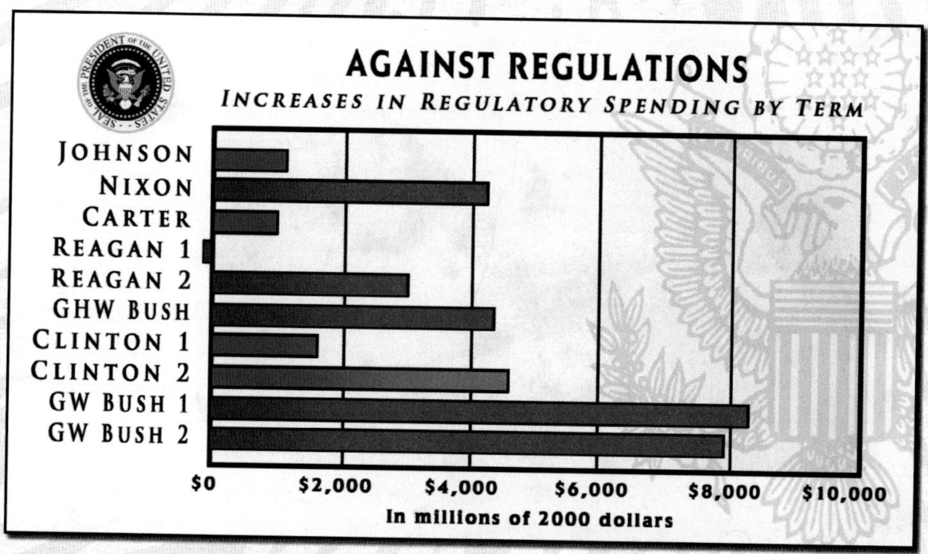

for how intrusive the government is becoming in our everyday lives, then the Bush administration was a disaster. In 2008, the Register reached an all-time high of over 79,400 pages, up from 64,438 pages just seven years earlier when Bush took over.

Why care about regulations? Because they cause red tape, bureaucracy, and, very often, hidden expense. Every time a business has to comply with a new rule, it incurs a cost, one that usually gets passed along to consumers. And those costs are not insignificant. Economist Mark Crain estimates that compliance with regulations cost $1.172 trillion in 2008. To put that into perspective, total corporate tax revenue for that year was $304 billion.

But the costs extend beyond compliance—the rules also have to be enforced. While Clinton had cut the government's regulatory staff by 969 employees, Bush *added* 91,196 people! Every one of those new employees gets a salary and benefits that add to our federal budget deficit. It's no surprise then, that according to Veronique de Rugy of George Mason University's Mercatus Center, "The Bush team has spent more taxpayer money on issuing and enforcing regulations than any previous administration in U.S. history."

BUSH PLEDGES EFFORT TO BALANCE BUDGET BY 2004

—*Washington Post,* April 2002

Give Me Government, or Give Me Death

While plenty of crises are exploited by government, there's no doubt that the financial crisis—or at least the market's reaction to it—was very real. In September 2008, the Dow Jones Industrial Average crashed 1,200 points and big banks like Lehman Brothers, Bear Stearns, and Citibank teetered on the brink of bankruptcy. (Spoiler Alert: Lehman and Bear no longer exist.) Who then swooped in to save the day? The same Bush administration economic dream team that never saw the crisis coming in the first place. It's like the plot of a bad horror movie . . . and the ending is just as predictable.

Guest Check!

Table No.	No. Persons.	Check No. 082774	Server.

Sticker Shock Expenditure	Inflation Adjusted Cost
Marshall Plan	$115 billion
Louisiana Purchase	$217 billion
Moon Race	$237 billion
S&L Crisis	$256 billion
Korean War	$454 billion
The New Deal	$500 billion (est.)
Gulf War II	$597 billion
Vietnam War	$698 billion
Total:	$3.07 trillion
Financial System Rescue:	$3.7 trillion

Taxpayer Copy — Thank You!

Table No.	No. Persons.	Check No. 082774	Server.

We were told that we were facing the mother of all economic crises. We were told that, without action, the entire financial system could collapse. We were told that we'd seen nothing like this since the Great Depression.

Then we were told something else: The government had a plan that could save us. And it was simple: We just had to use taxpayer dollars to bail out everyone who happened to have a lobbyist, a negative balance sheet, and a financial IQ of less than 80.

We were living through the largest experiment in Big Government in fifty years, bigger than the Great Society, bigger than the Apollo moon mission, bigger than the Vietnam War. In the end, our politicians gambled $3.7 trillion (and counting) of our money in an effort to save us from the misery that their own ineptitude had caused.

In the middle of it all, a supposedly conservative president sat down with the media and told the nation that he "abandoned free-market principles to save the free-market system." It was not exactly George W. Bush's finest hour.

The original bailout plan was drafted by Secretary of the Treasury Hank Paulson, the former head of Goldman Sachs. It had come together almost literally overnight and practically on the back of an envelope. The bank presidents were summoned to Washington, gathered into a boardroom, and commanded to sign on to the scheme. "No" was not an option.

DEFICIT OF TRU$T

Peter Orszag, the guy put in charge of balancing the budget in the Obama administration—the same guy who said that the Obama-care bill will "save the government money"—co-authored a 2002 study saying that the chances of taxpayers ever taking a loss on Fannie and Freddie mortgage guarantees was about "one in a million."

But where will you come up with the $700 billion, people wondered. Don't ask, he'd tell them; just trust me. Let us spend the money . . . *or the economy will cease to exist*. It's the only way.

The congressional leadership, the Bush White House, and officials at the Federal Reserve Bank scurried around in those weeks during the fall of 2008 like rats on a sinking ship. Now, many years and many trillions of dollars later, the ship is still taking on water. Some 5 million Americans have lost their jobs since the great bailout began, and another 8 million or so have dropped out of the workforce completely or can't find a full-time job. The real unemployment rate is close to 18 percent. The stock market and housing market are still in chaos. Incomes have continued to fall.

It was, we can now safely say, one of the biggest frauds in American history. A supposedly capitalist country organized as a republic was actively strong-arming private companies into taking money, forcing others into mergers they didn't want, cutting deals with unions, penalizing private bondholders, and hiring a czar to monitor compensation.

And the timing couldn't have been worse. Not only had a Republican president started America on a fast track toward socialism, but he was about to hand power over to a man who was salivating at the chance to use a crisis to fulfill his promise to "transform" America.

For conservatives, a really bad situation was about to get a whole lot worse.

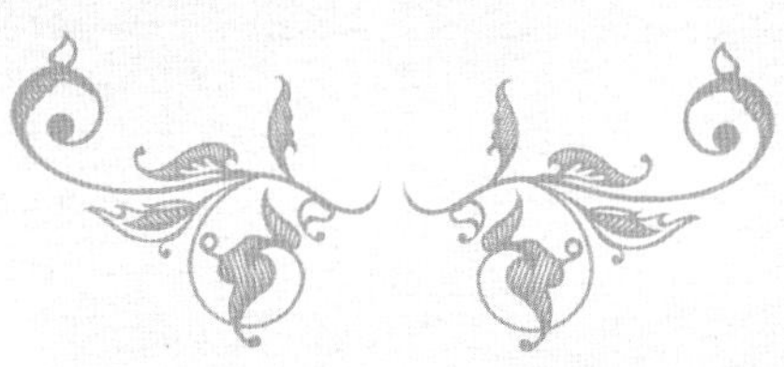

BARACK OBAMA: WE'RE CALLING YOUR BLUFF

Next year, when I start presenting some very difficult choices to the country, I hope some of these folks who are hollering about deficits and debt step up. Because I'm calling their bluff.

—BARACK OBAMA, JUNE 2010

The Bush administration's use of crises to further its agenda did not go unnoticed by Barack Obama. After the election in November 2008, his incoming chief of staff, Rahm Emanuel, told an audience of top CEOs, "You never want a serious crisis to go to waste." He further explained, "Things that we had postponed for too long, that were long-term, are now immediate and must be dealt with. This crisis provides the opportunity for us to do things that you could not do before."

That was the understatement of the century.

In retrospect, it should have been more obvious as to how this would play out. Barack Obama, a man who has made no excuses for the fact that he sees major social and economic injustices in America, was about to take over the country in the middle of a crisis. You don't need a Hollywood writer to guess what would happen next.

Time put Obama on its cover with a cigar and a top hat looking like a dapper Franklin Roosevelt. It was fitting symbolism, because Obama had a New Deal of his own in mind: Right out of the gate his first proposal was audacious and spectacularly irresponsible: a nearly $1 trillion spending plan—disguised as a "stimulus package"—with money going to a virtual all-you-can-eat buffet of liberal causes. It was twenty-five years' worth of stale Democratic spending proposals repackaged and marketed as stimulus.

There would be money for the National Endowment for the Arts, Head Start, unemployment insurance, renewable energy subsidies, turtle crossings, a fund for federal bureaucrats to purchase a new fleet of cars, a bailout of the pork industry (how appropriate), new labor union jobs, and housing aid that would be ciphered through corrupt left-wing "welfare

"If we had taken office in ordinary times, I would have liked nothing more than to start bringing down the deficit. But we took office amid a crisis. And our efforts to prevent a second depression have added another $1 trillion to our national debt . . . I'm absolutely convinced that was the right thing to do. Families across the country are tightening their belts and making tough decisions. The federal government should do the same. So tonight, I'm proposing specific steps to pay for the trillion dollars that it took to rescue the economy last year."

—BARACK OBAMA

SORRY 2010 STATE OF THE UNION

lobby groups" like ACORN. It was eight years of progressive dreams passed in one fell swoop.

The bill was signed into law within forty days of the new presidency (it was an emergency, after all!). Some federal agencies saw their budgets stretched by 80, 90, and 100 percent. It was as if Washington, D.C., had won the lottery—and, in a way, it had. A free-spending, Marxist president with an inherited crisis is just as good as a Powerball ticket . . . if you live inside the Beltway.

Government workers began singing "Happy Days Are Here Again"—just like Americans had in 1930 when they thought the worst was behind them. But all of that singing and optimism must have distracted them from reality: Americans were hurting. Badly. And they were about to let their government to know it.

PLEASE STOP ASKING FAIR QUESTIONS

The *New York Times* interviewed Obama in March 2009, shortly after his first budget was released.

Q. The first six weeks have given people a glimpse of your spending priorities. Are you a socialist as some people have suggested?
A. You know, let's take a look at the budget—the answer would be no.

Q. Is there anything wrong with saying yes?
A. Let's just take a look at what we've done . . .

Q. Is there one-word name for your philosophy? If you're not a socialist, are you a liberal? Are you progressive? One word?
A. No, I'm not going to engage in that.

It was an artful dodge, but I wonder what Obama would've said if they'd instead asked, "Are you trying to become a benevolent dictator by taking over health care and the financial industry, as some people have suggested."

Keying on Keynes

Obama's gluttony of spending was inspired by someone who should be pretty familiar to you by now: John Maynard Keynes. (While we've been pretty hard on Keynes in this book, the truth is that he'd probably be horrified to see how his ideas had been bastardized by the new generation of economists who see no end in sight to the virtues of government spending. In fact, Keynes himself once suggested "25 percent [of GDP] as the maximum tolerable proportion of taxation." That is far lower than where we are now, once state and local taxes are factored in.) Wasting money was virtuous; thrift and efficiency and paying the bills on time was an evil, deadly poison. It was the 1930s and '40s all over again.

Economic sanity was nowhere to be found—especially among the elected elite and the academics they hold up to parrot their beliefs.

President Obama's budget would result in a 100 percent increase in publicly held national debt within a decade.

If we work really, really hard and stick to Obama's 2010 budget, we'll run deficits totaling **$82,219 per American household** through 2020.

In January 2009, Obama, as president-elect, was publicly making the case for a far larger stimulus package than the $130 billion one he'd pitched during the campaign. To bolster his argument, two of his economic and finance advisors threw together a "study" analyzing what would happen to our economy with and without the stimulus.

At the time, total nonfarm payroll employment stood at 134.3 million. Here's what the advisors concluded would happen by the fourth quarter of 2010 under each scenario:

	Without Stimulus	**With Stimulus**
Jobs	133.9 million (down 0.4 million)	137.6 million (up 3.3 million)
Unemployment Rate	8.8 percent	7.0 percent

While we're not yet able to measure the results as of the fourth quarter of 2010, here are the preliminary figures:

Jobs	130.5 million (down 3.8 million)
Unemployment Rate	9.5–10.1 percent

The total Obama jobs deficit—promised jobs minus actual jobs—is 7.1 million. I can hear it now: *But imagine how bad it would've been if we didn't pass the stimulus!*

Four days after the report was issued, Obama himself began using it as the basis of his predictions; telling an audience that his plan would create 3.7 million jobs—almost double his previous estimate.

Nobel-Winning Nonsense

How did everyone's favorite economist, Paul Krugman, react to the report? He wrote in the *New York Times*, "Their report is reasonable and intellectually honest, which is a welcome change from the fuzzy math of the last eight years." He then called the possible 8.8 percent unemployment rate they predicted without the stimulus "disastrous."

The report may or may not have been "intellectually honest," but it was definitely something else: "laughably wrong."

In typical Washington fashion, the prediction originally created by Obama administration economists was turned into fact and then deposited into the echo chamber of liberal politicians and advisors.

- **Peter Orszag, former White House Budget Director:** "I want to again emphasize the reason that we think it's about the right size is it will help create 3 million to 4 million jobs."
- **Jared Bernstein, chief economic advisor to Vice President Joe Biden:** "It's not a promise; it's a pretty standard economic analysis. And actually, this part is not rocket science. I know there's lots of economic forecasting that's awfully tough to understand. This isn't it."
- **Senator Harry Reid:** "This bill creates 3.5 million jobs."
- **Senator Chuck Schumer:** "And it's a very significant stimulus; 3.5 million to 4 million jobs is a lot of jobs."
- **Larry Summers, director of the National Economic Council:** "Yeah, the plan will create 3 million to 4 million jobs more than the economy otherwise would have had, and that's before you get to the financial recovery approach."
- **David Axelrod, senior advisor to the president:** "Well, look, I think, in its broad context, the goal the president set was a plan that would create 3 million to 4 million jobs to help offset those dismal numbers that you just showed everyone. And I think that we're on track to do that."

Not only is there no accountability for all the people who made these ridiculous predictions, but they are still out there making more of them, promoting new stimulus plans and predicting more job gains.

> **In His Own Words**
>
> ***My plan is detailed and specific when it comes to cutting spending. In fact, all my new spending proposals would be more than paid for by spending reductions.***
>
> —BARACK OBAMA, JULY 2008. THE 2010 DEFICIT IS NOW PROJECTED AT A RECORD $1.47 TRILLION.

Politics of the Past

By the summer of 2010 the shine of Obamanomics had really started to fade. Everyone outside Washington felt it. The economy wasn't healing. Jobs were harder to find than ever. Half of the unemployed were out of work for more than six months. There were more than 1 million Americans who weren't even bothering to look for jobs. Incomes fell by 3.4 percent under the first year of the stimulus. Nearly 20 million American workers couldn't find a job, or couldn't get a full-time job, or stopped looking. Employers were virtually on strike.

Yet the delusion rolled on. Vice President Biden, who had said "in my wildest dreams, I never thought [the stimulus package] would work this well," put his dunce cap back on and went on a "Summer of Recovery" tour. Some recovery: The economy lost 221,000 jobs in June and another 131,000 in July. Obama went to Racine, Wisconsin, and told a gathering of underemployed workers that things would have been worse if the spending blitz hadn't happened. He said the stimulus kept the unemployment rate from rising to 15 percent. Pretty convenient, since just a year earlier his own economists said the unemployment rate wouldn't go above 9 percent. It also directly contradicts the more recent studies by the president's own Council of Economic Advisors, which argues that the stimulus had perhaps a 1 percentage point impact on the unemployment rate.

Republicans, starting to realize that the country was sick and tired of the nonstop spending barrage (or at least starting to understand that spending wouldn't help them in the upcoming midterms), finally began to balk. Obama responded as only someone who wants to get beyond the politics of the past could: He labeled Republicans as lovers of the wealthy and haters of the poor.

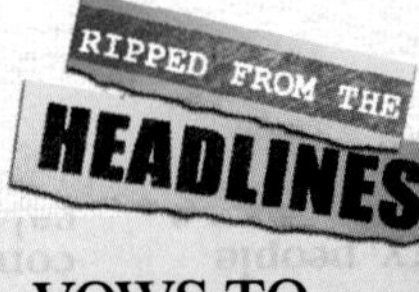

OBAMA VOWS TO SLASH WASTEFUL U.S. SPENDING

—*Forbes*, November 2008

During a weekly radio address Obama said:

> *The Republican leadership in the United States Senate chooses to filibuster our recovery and obstruct our progress. And that has very real consequences.*
>
> *Think about what these stalling tactics mean for the millions of Americans who've lost their jobs since the recession began. Over the past several weeks, more than two million of them have seen their unemployment insurance expire.*
>
> *They say we shouldn't provide unemployment insurance because it costs money. So, after years of championing policies that turned a record surplus into a massive deficit, including a tax cut for the wealthiest Americans, they've finally decided to make their stand on the backs of the unemployed.*
>
> *They've got no problem spending money on tax breaks for folks at the top who don't need them and didn't even ask for them; but they object to helping folks laid off in this recession who really do need help.*

Barack Obama may be a lot of things, but he's not a dummy. He knew that if he could change the argument from one over debts and deficits to one over morality, then he could win. Unfortunately, there is the small matter of those pesky little facts that keep getting in the way.

First, on the idea that leadership chooses to "filibuster our recovery": The president basically said that approving extensions to unemployment insurance is the key to the recovery. If that were true, then why didn't he just have far more money devoted to that in the original stimulus plan, instead of all those "shovel-ready" projects?

Second, he skillfully used the line "they say we shouldn't provide unemployment insurance . . ." That's completely false. In case no one has noticed, we *already* provide unemployment insurance. A lot of it. In California, for example, someone can normally obtain up to twenty-six weeks of help. But now, according to the *Los Angeles Times*, "Congress has approved four extensions for a total of 53 additional weeks. States with very high jobless numbers, such as California, became eligible for 20 weeks on top of that, for a total of 99 weeks." This isn't a debate about *providing* insurance—99 weeks is almost two years. It's about whether we should *indefinitely* provide insurance—especially when it can't be paid for.

And lastly, the president who was supposedly beyond partisanship made the argument that we've all been waiting for: *Republicans want the poor and unemployed to pay for tax cuts on the rich.* Yep, those are definitely the kinds of accusations that are going to bring this country together. Who wouldn't want to make tough sacrifices after a pep talk like that?

Bush Didn't Spend Enough?

Ronald Reagan incurred $2 trillion of debt in the 1980s. But that debt accomplished two missions of great long-term consequence: First, it financed the Cold War military buildup that helped free the world from communism; and second, it financed tax-rate reductions, which helped rebuild the U.S. economy after the dreadful stagflation of the 1970s. Under Reagan, the national wealth increased by at least $9 trillion.

And that's the big economic difference between Reagan and Obama. With Obama, there are no pro-growth or pro-business tax cuts in his agenda. The mentality is to target the wealthiest citizens (because there aren't enough of them to matter at the polls) and redirect the money through welfare and entitlement programs.

The Obama administration and congressional Democrats defend their record deficits and debt by arguing that, during the Bush years, critical government "investments" were neglected. Deficits, we are told, were a result of the Bush tax cuts and the War on Terror, while Republicans devised an ugly plot to "starve the beast" of government.

No Money Down!

It's no accident that the Obama administration uses investment terminology when talking about their spending. An "investment" sounds much better than a "giveaway" or "handout." Here are a few examples:

Obama: "We will create millions of jobs by making the single largest new investment in our national infrastructure since the creation of the federal highway system in the 1950s."

Obama: "[I] will call for major investments to revive our economy, create jobs, and lay a solid foundation for future growth."

Obama: "The way I see it, providing coverage to 11 million children through CHIP is a down payment on my commitment to cover every single American."

Biden: "There's going to be real significant investment, whether it's $600 billion, or more, or $700 billion. The clear notion is, it's a number no one thought about a year ago."

I hate to ask a dumb question, but which programs were starved, exactly? Most budget items grew by 4 or 5 or 6 times the rate of inflation (21 percent).

Bush's So-Called Neglect: Federal Spending Increases from 2001 to 2009

Inflation-adjusted to 2009 dollars

National defense	81 percent
Income security programs	51 percent
Medicaid and SCHIP	63 percent
Veterans' benefits	72 percent
Health research and regulation	68 percent
Highways and mass transit	39 percent
International affairs	69 percent
Community and regional development	90 percent

Creative Solutions: Spend and Tax

So what is the Obama strategy to balance the budget, which is consuming 25 percent of national output, up from 20 percent a decade ago? Answer: *new taxes.* But even liberal think tanks agree that taxing will not be enough to cover the nearly $1.5 trillion budget deficit this year. According to the Tax Policy Center, a left-leaning think tank, "Washington would have to raise taxes by almost 40 percent to reduce—not eliminate, just reduce—the deficit to three percent of our GDP, the 2015 goal the Obama administration set in its 2011 budget."

Okay, fine, but there's one major problem with that: Obama has promised to only raise taxes on couples making more than $250,000 a year and on individuals making more than $200,000. According to the Tax Policy Center, "The top two income tax rates would have to more than double, with the top rate hitting almost 77 percent, to get the deficit down to 3 percent of GDP" if Obama held to that promise.

The numbers just don't add up. The *Wall Street Journal* has determined that taxing the top 2 percent of wealthiest Americans at a rate of 100 percent—that is, taking everything they've got and assuming they still go on working and investing for basically a zero after-tax income—would run the federal government for less than six months.

It doesn't take an economist to realize that if you won't cut spending, and you can't get enough from just taxing the rich, then the only thing left is expanding tax increases to the middle class. How will they do that? Simple. It's already being whispered about in the hallowed halls of Congress: a value-added tax, or "VAT" for short.

The VAT is a version of a national sales tax that gets added at each stage of a product's production and is ultimately paid by the final consumer. The Tax Foundation says that a U.S. VAT to get rid of the deficit would have to reach at least 18 percent. Think that sounds like a crazy rate? Think again—the United Kingdom's VAT will be rising from 17.5 percent to 20 percent next year. In announcing the increase, their finance minister said, "This single tax measure will, by the end of this parliament, generate over 13 billion pounds a year of extra revenues. That is 13 billion pounds we don't have to find from extra spending cuts or income tax rises."

No cuts, no income tax hikes—just pay more money on everything you buy . . . what a deal!

Deal or not, you can't argue with the allure of a VAT for shortsighted, self-serving politicians. They can pass it and seriously argue that they never voted for a tax *increase* and that they fought hard to maintain government services.

What they won't tell you is that, like most new taxes, the VAT won't lower the deficit or help eat away at the national debt. Instead the money will be spent on a host of brand-new services. Randy Holcombe, an economics professor at Florida State University, recently studied the effects of the VAT in other countries. He found that the rates almost always rise after the tax is initially introduced (no surprise), but that government spending also increases and economic growth decreases.

> **Truth Serum**
>
> *Treasury Secretary Timothy Geithner:* **"I don't believe [tax hikes on the wealthy] will have a negative effect on growth."**
>
> After the 2003 Bush tax cuts (from 2003 to 2007), tax revenues grew $500 billion faster than inflation.

Don't fall for the scam. The VAT will be spun as a way to pay for the mistakes of the past, but all it will really do is add another one to the list.

Sound Economics vs. "Fairness"

I understand that taxes are a political issue and that Obama is a politician first—I just wish he would admit that. But think about this tax debate logically. On the one hand, you have Democrats saying that raising taxes during a recession is an awful idea—that was a central talking point during the stimulus debate. On the other hand, you have Democrats saying that it's okay to raise taxes on the wealthiest Americans because, as Secretary of the Treasury Timothy Geithner said, "[those increases won't] have a negative effect on growth."

And on a third hand, you have almost all politicians saying that we need to make sacrifices to get our deficit under control.

Which is it? Either tax increases stimulate growth or they don't. Either they will close the deficit or they won't.

Confusing the issue even further is that Obama's former chief economist, Christina Romer, has shown in her research that raising taxes to grow the economy is a fool's errand. One of her papers concludes that "tax cuts have very large and persistent positive output effects." She also says that it was the Herbert Hoover tax *increases* that helped plunge the economy into the Great Depression. According to Romer: "The revenue act of 1932 increased American tax rates greatly in an attempt to balance the budget, and by doing so dealt another contractionary blow to the economy."

The truth, of course, is that, as we saw with FDR and Social Security, this discussion isn't about economics; it's about politics—and it's a shining example of why we keep losing ground.

Hope

A president's first long-term budget is a blueprint, a reflection of his agenda, his aspirations, and his hope to leave the country in a much better place than he found it. But that's not what Barack Obama's first budget was. To anyone with a fiscally conservative bone in their body, the document read as if it were written by Hugo Chávez or François Mitterrand. It was a socialist fantasy, a literal handbook on how to bankrupt a country in ten easy steps.

This first budget, released in early 2009, called for $42 *trillion* of government spending over the next decade. Even the president's historic tax increases would not keep up with this soaring spending—the national debt would rise by $9 trillion. In Washington, the saying was that a trillion is the new billion. Bumper stickers began to appear that read: PLEASE DON'T TELL OBAMA WHAT COMES AFTER A TRILLION!

A.D.D. Moment

Can you guess what this sea-of-red-ink budget was titled? "A New Era of Responsibility." At least President Obama has a sense of humor.

Obama was proposing that the government borrow more money in the next ten years than it had in the first 225—and he made no apologies for it. Answering questions aboard Air Force One in March 2009, Obama said, "So if you look at our budget, what you have is a *very disciplined, fiscally responsible* budget, along with an effort to deal with some very serious problems that have been put off for a very long time."

I added the emphasis above to highlight just how deceitful it is to call a budget that commits America to ten more years of massive deficits "very disciplined" and "fiscally responsible." I wonder what, exactly, *irresponsible* spending would look like?

Wait, wait, I take that back. No, I don't.

The president's next budget, released in 2010, was even more reckless. Over the following decade, it proposes to:

- Spend $45 trillion;
- Push the debt held by the public to 90 percent of GDP; more than twice its current level;
- Raise taxes by $3 trillion;
- Raises taxes on small-business owners and upper-income taxpayers by an average of $300,000 over the next ten years;
- Borrow 42 cents on every dollar spent;
- Add an additional $74,000 of debt per household.

And these figures were likely optimistic! They assume an economic boom is just around the corner, which would create trillions of dollars more in wealth (and thus, much more tax revenues) than mainstream forecasts predict. His budget endorsed Congress's $800 billion cap-and-trade bill but leaves the cost out of its tables. It claimed $132 billion in vague "program integrity savings." It bragged about $7 billion in program terminations and cuts the previous year, and proposed $23 billion more for the current year—without mentioning that every saved dollar went into new government

Real vs. Claimed Deficits
By Fiscal Year, in Billions

	Budget Year	Real Deficit	Claimed Deficit	Difference
PRESIDENT CARTER	1978	$72.7	$59.19	
	1979	$54.98	$40.73	
	1980	$81.18	$73.83	
	1981	$90.15	$78.97	
		$299.02	$252.71	$46.31
PRESIDENT REAGAN	1982	$144.18	$127.98	
	1983	$235.18	$207.8	
	1984	$195.06	$185.37	
	1985	$250.84	$212.31	
	1986	$302.20	$221.23	
	1987	$224.97	$149.73	
	1988	$252.06	$155.18	
	1989	$255.09	$152.64	
		$1859.58	$1412.23	$447.35
PRESIDENT BUSH SR.	1990	$375.88	$221.04	
	1991	$431.99	$269.24	
	1992	$399.32	$290.32	
	1993	$346.87	$255.05	
		$1554.06	$1035.65	$518.41
PRESIDENT CLINTON	1994	$281.26	$203.19	
	1995	$281.23	$163.95	
	1996	$250.83	$107.43	
	1997	$188.34	$21.88	
	1998	$113.05	- $69.27	
	1999	$130.08	-$125.61	
	2000	$17.91	-$236.24	
	2001	$133.29	-$128.24	
		$1395.97	-$62.90	$1458.88
PRESIDENT BUSH	2002	$420.77	$157.76	
	2003	$555.00	$377.59	
	2004	$595.82	$412.73	
	2005	$553.66	$318.35	
	2006	$574.26	$248.18	
	2007	$500.67	$162.00	
	2008	$1017.07	$458.45	
		$4217.25	$2135.05	$2082.2
PRESIDENT OBAMA	2009	$1885.11	$1844.19	$40.92

Over the last twenty-one years, **budget deficits have averaged $210 billion a year**, after adjusting for inflation. But in 2009, President Bush gave President Obama a $1.2 trillion deficit. Obama then increased that by almost the exact historical average—$210 billion.

spending; not a nickel went toward deficit reduction. Finally, his budget assumed large yet totally unspecified discretionary spending cuts happening at some point in the future, never the present.

President Obama was highly critical of the $3.7 trillion in deficits that President Bush ran up over his eight years in office—and he was right to be. Yet Obama's budget proposal calls for borrowing $7.6 trillion should he remain in office for the same amount of time that Bush did. If that comes to pass, Obama would have added more to the national debt than every president before him . . . *combined*. If this is Obama's blueprint, then we better all start wondering what the building is going to look like once construction is finished.

Americans don't want to be deceived, but we do want hope. We want to know that if we do our part, work hard, play by the rules, live within our means, then things will turn out all right in the end. But Obama's budget shows that that's not the case. If we do everything right and if all of his projections are perfectly accurate (something that we all know is a long shot), then we'll be worse off in ten years than we are today. We'll have continuing deficits, more debt, and a much bigger hole to dig out of.

Is that any way to live? Is that any way to run a country?

Hope can come only from knowing that you are on the right track, knowing that you are fighting valiantly and that, despite long odds, it's a fight that can be won. Hope can come only from knowing that everyone is fighting toward the same end

I'M SERIOUSLY SERIOUS

To show he was getting tough, President Obama also called for a freeze in government spending. Finally, some tough decision making!

Wait, the freeze lasts for only three years? And it exempts *all* entitlement spending, such as Social Security, Medicare, and Medicaid, which are driving long-term spending? And it also exempts discretionary spending on defense, homeland security, and veterans? So it applies only to the 12 percent of the budget spent on things like air traffic control, education, and national parks? And those programs just received $300 billion in stimulus spending, which doesn't count toward the freeze? And the savings over ten years would be just $250 billion? And that represents just 3 percent of the $9 trillion in *additional* deficits projected to be run up over that time?

Oh.

goal, knowing that you've got the best technology, the best experts, and the best team on your side. Hope can come only from knowing what you are really up against so that you can devise a plan to beat it.

In other words, hope can come only from knowing the truth, and that's exactly what I am about to give you.

OBAMA TO SEEK SPENDING FREEZE TO TRIM DEFICITS

—*New York Times,* January 2010

PART TWO

THE CRIME OF THE CENTURY

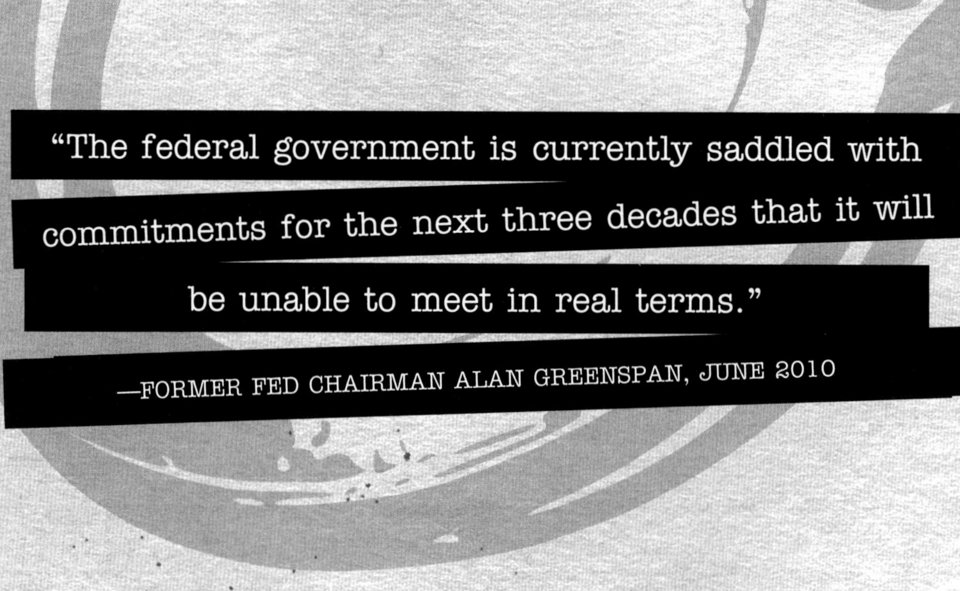

“The federal government is currently saddled with commitments for the next three decades that it will be unable to meet in real terms.”

—FORMER FED CHAIRMAN ALAN GREENSPAN, JUNE 2010

CHAPTER 10.

The Truth

By now you've seen the pattern of lies, broken promises, and outright corruption that has been epidemic in America for decades. It's obvious that the battle over small vs. large government was waged a long time ago—and the small-government side lost. What we're debating now is something far more serious: the survival of the last free country on Earth.

With those kinds of stakes, the last thing we can to do is let our politicians continue to deceive us. America has a life-threatening disease—we don't need to be coddled, we need to be leveled with.

Consider this chapter the first step toward doing just that.

Where We Are Now

There's a lot of talk in the media about the financial legacy we're leaving behind for our children and grandchildren. That's fine, and it's obviously important, but we need to realize that the threat is far more imminent than that. This isn't a battle for the next generation; it's a battle for *this* generation.

> HATE SPEECH?
>
> "The longer we wait, the more severe, the more draconian, the more difficult the adjustment is going to be. I think the right time to start is about 10 years ago."
>
> —*Fed chairman Ben Bernanke, January 2007*

Unfortunately, if history is any guide, it's a battle we're going to lose unless there is a radical, and likely very painful, change in course. The truth is that for seventy-two out of the last hundred years, our government has spent more money than it has taken in. If you shorten the time period, the statistics get even worse: Over the last fifty years, we've run deficits forty-four times (88 percent), and, over the most recent ten years, we've run deficits in nine of them. That's astonishing when you really think about it—financial restraint and accountability has been, by far, the exception instead of the rule for a very long time.

Our $3.8 Trillion Budget

The Relative Size of Major Expenses

Social Security
$738

National Defense
$738

Income Security
$567

Medicare
$498

Trans-
portation
$91.55

Veterans
Benefits
$122

Net Interest
$251

Health
$381

Science
$31.02

Natural
Resources
$39.52

International
Affairs
$67.39

Agriculture
$25.42

General
Govt.
$28.94

Energy
$8.81

Allowances
$60.50

Community
$21.88

Commerce
$-111,796

Administration
Affairs
$53.46

Education
$122

Based on the FY2011 Budget, in Billions.
Includes offsetting receipts where appropriate.

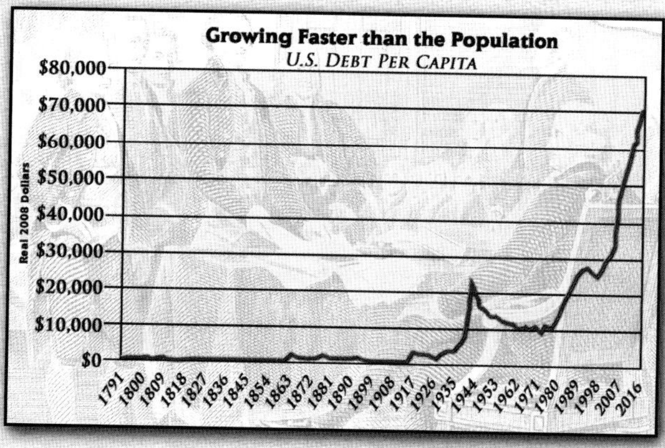

While fingers can be pointed at any number of people or parties, there's really only one group that bears ultimate responsibility: us. The American people have been, for the most part, willing to sit idly by as our leaders spent away our future. Sure, we didn't sign the checks or make the backroom deals, but we didn't hold people accountable, either. Decade after decade we express outrage and shock over our financial condition, yet we continue to elect the same people again and again and expect different results. It truly is, as Einstein once said, the very definition of insanity.

Mandatory Bankruptcy

Bear with me for thirty seconds of boring budget appetizers before we get to the main course. There are two terms that are immensely important to understand: *mandatory spending* (sometimes also called "direct spending") and *discretionary spending*. Despite their names, these terms don't refer to the relative merits of the spending (i.e., there is some discretionary spending that is extremely important, and some mandatory spending that's not). They refer to legislative processes.

When Congress creates a mandatory-spending program (i.e., the Social Security Act of 1935), it determines two things: first, who will be eligible to participate in the program, and second, what the benefit formula (which is used to figure out how much each participant receives) will be. From there, the program runs *permanently* on autopilot. Annual spending is not determined by Congress or the White House, but instead by demographics. Costs are a function of how many people are eligible, how many actually sign up, and where they fall in the benefit formula. So, for example, if the poverty rate increases, more people enroll in food stamps, the cost of the program automatically increases, and the increased funding becomes a mandatory government obligation.

> "Under our Alternative simulation, debt held by the public as a share of GDP could exceed the historical high reached in the aftermath of World War II by 2020—10 years sooner than our simulation showed just 2 years ago."
>
> —*Government Accountability Office*
>
> HATE SPEECH?

In practical terms, mandatory spending is essentially hands-off. It continues to grow according to existing law and can't be touched without a specific act of Con-

> "Roughly 93 cents of every dollar of federal revenue will be spent on the major entitlement programs and net interest costs by 2020. By 2030, net interest payments on the federal government's accumulating federal debt exceed 8 percent of GDP—making it the largest single expenditure in the federal budget."
> —*Government Accountability Office*

HATE SPEECH?

gress to change the eligibility rules or benefit formulas (and good luck with that).

By contrast, discretionary programs are budgeted annually by Congress and the president. If they want to spend $500 billion on defense this year, they must pass an appropriations bill (and get it signed by the president) that provides the Defense Department with that amount. This, of course, ensures that the system of checks and balances envisioned by our Founders is adhered to every year. Congress passes a bill; the president signs or vetoes it. But autopilot spending gets around this essential part of our constitution by forcing future administrations (and generations) to accept decisions made well before their time by politicians who may now be either retired or dead.

It truly is a modern-day version of taxation without representation.

As any budget expert will tell you, no honest discussion about getting the country back on a sustainable track can happen without talking about mandatory spending, of which entitlement programs are the most common form. Why? Because, as you'll see, these types of programs make up a large (and growing) part of our annual spending. Unfortunately, they're also generally considered to be the third rail of politics, because they are so well defended by their supporters. As a result, most politicians (other than second-term presidents with nothing to lose) pretend they don't exist and instead focus on small, symbolic cuts that will have almost zero effect on our long-term problem.

Forty-two cents of every dollar spent by the federal government in 2010 will be borrowed.

In 2010, autopilot programs (including the programs that we'll call the Big Three: Medicare, Medicaid, and Social Security) will eat up 56 percent of our federal budget, and that does not include the interest that we pay on the money we have to borrow to

UNLIKELY ALLIES: GLENN BECK AND THE *NEW YORK TIMES*?

Yes, even the *Times* seems to get it. This is from a recent editorial criticizing the Obama administration for not setting their spending-cut goals higher:

The discretionary spending singled out has actually been trending downward as a share of the economy for several decades . . . If the public is encouraged to believe that discretionary spending is the main problem—and cutting it is the real answer—there will never be adequate political support for the tough decisions ahead. —New York Times, May 2010 meet those commitments. For context, total spending on national defense and education makes up 22 percent of the budget.

> "We can't grow our way out of this. We could have decades of double-digit growth and not grow our way out of this enormous debt problem. We can't tax our way out. . . . The reality is we've got to. . . cut spending or increase revenues or do some combination of that."
>
> —*Erskin Bowles, White House chief of staff under President Clinton; co-chairman of President Obama's debt and deficit commission*

HATE SPEECH?

2010 Selected Entitlement Spending

Program	**Cost**
Social Security	$721.5 billion
Medicare	$457.2 billion
Medicaid/SCHIP	$284.5 billion

Deciding how to spend our money as a country is very much like deciding how to spend our money as a family. Some things are necessities (food, shelter, clothing) and some are extravagances (flat-screen TV, tennis bracelet, smoothie maker), which we could easily cut back on in tough times. But America's priorities seem to have reversed themselves sometime in the late twentieth century. Instead of focusing on necessities, like national defense, we let our extravagances, like entitlement programs, take priority.

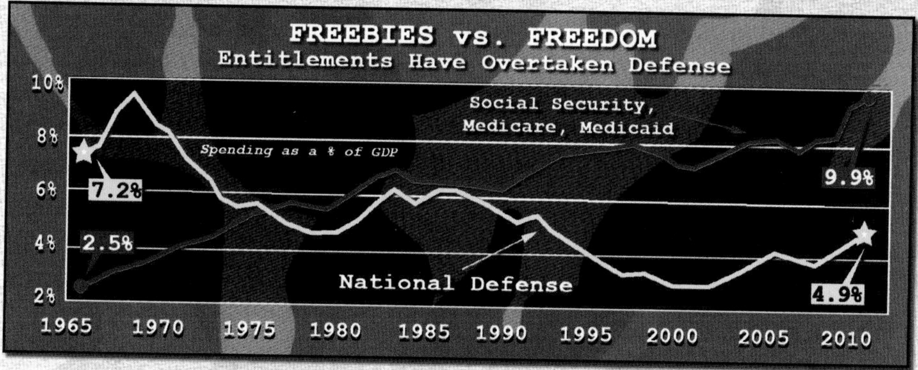

Original chart by Brian Riedl at the Heritage Foundation, data from White House OMB

In the backward way that Washington doles out our money, they first give large agribusinesses their full farm-subsidy entitlements and the wealthiest seniors their full Medicare drug entitlements—and then use whatever scraps are left for discretionary items like body armor for our troops. This isn't just irrational, it's immoral—a sad reflection of how far America's values have come from the days of our founding.

Predictably, the surging cost of these autopilot mandatory programs has been squeezing out the discretionary programs. Since the early 1960s, Washington has consistently spent about 20 percent of GDP a year, yet the composition of this spending

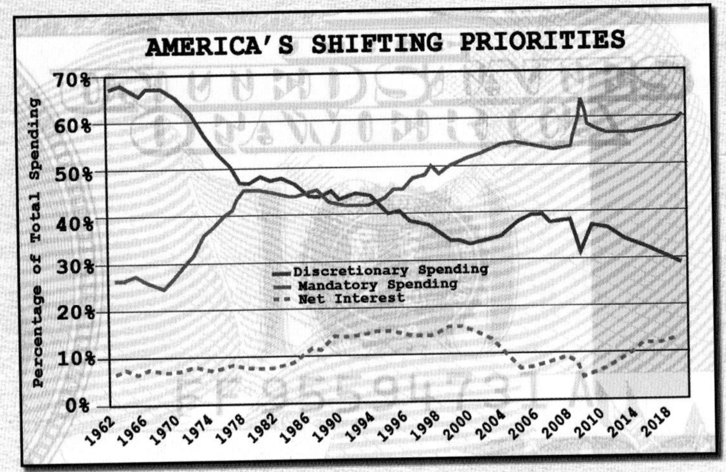

has changed dramatically. In 1962, two-thirds of all federal spending went toward discretionary programs, and only one-third went toward mandatory programs. Back then, the largest discretionary program was national defense, and it accounted for *half* of all federal spending. But, over time, the entitlement seeds we've planted have flourished. Social Security costs grew faster than the economy; Medicare and Medicaid benefits were created and expanded; and President Lyndon Johnson's Great Society further enlarged the welfare state. As a result, the ratios began to change.

Mandatory spending, plus net interest on the debt, now comprises two-thirds of the budget, while discretionary spending has been squeezed into the remaining one-third (with defense comprising just one-fifth of all spending).

The national security state has officially been replaced by the welfare state.

Unfortunately, it's only going to get worse. Over the next few decades, as 77 million baby boomers (10,000 per day) begin retiring into Social Security, Medicare, and (often) Medicaid, these programs' costs are projected to double to 20 percent of GDP. (And that doesn't even take into account the new ObamaCare costs.)

> **TEACHABLE MOMENT**
>
> The other way to look at this is to consider that all of the revenues we expect for 2010 ($2.165 trillion) will only cover three budget categories: defense ($855 billion), Social Security ($715 billior and Medicare ($451 billion). Everything el we spend on, from the education of our kids to the eradicatic of our diseases, will require deficit spending. *Everything.*

By putting two-thirds of all government spending on autopilot, where it can grow with no oversight, no constraints, and no limit, Congress has essentially lost control of its own budget. No other government in the world writes a blank check for its pension and health-care programs, and for good reason: It's an obvious road to ruin.

Pork: Not Just the Other White Meat

Despite all the promises made to the contrary, earmarks continue to add to our debt. According to research conducted by Citizens Against Government Waste and Taxpayers for Common Sense, spending bills included nearly ten thousand pork projects costing taxpayers $16 billion in 2010.

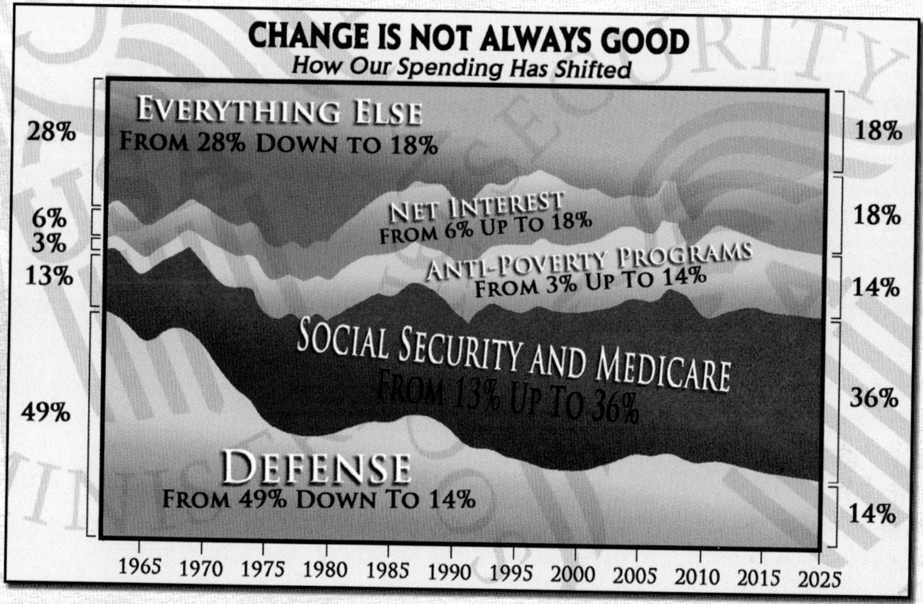

Original chart by Brian Riedl at the Heritage Foundation, data from the White House OMB

That's obviously outrageous and should stop immediately, but here's the problem: Earmarks and pork distract us from the larger financial issues we face because they are perfectly prepackaged for media consumption. The dumb museums and idiotic research projects make perfect sixty-second news segments, but when you compare $16 billion in earmark spending to the projected 2010 deficit of nearly $1.5 trillion, you quickly realize that earmarks are primarily a distraction. It's like being so focused on a scrape on your arm that you don't realize that you've also been shot in the chest.

In 1990, Washington spent $22,027 per American household (adjusted for inflation). In 2010 we'll spend $30,543, an **increase of 39 percent** in just two decades. Are you getting 39 percent more for your money?

None of that is to say that we shouldn't hold our politicians accountable for their waste and, more important, for their corruption and broken promises, but the more we all focus on the left hand building needless bridges, the more we're ignoring the right hand as it does real long-term structural damage.

An Interesting Look at Interest

As Albert Einstein once said, "The most powerful force in the universe is compound interest." When you're saving money, it's a powerful force for good, but

> **Tricks of the Trade**
>
> **Be wary of anyone talking about future interest payments only in terms of a percentage of our spending. Why? Because overall spending is increasing, so that can make the percentage seem artificially low. A better way to look at it is by either comparing our interest payments to revenue or GDP, or by simply looking at the actual number of dollars we're spending on interest year to year (adjusting for inflation).**

when you owe more than you can pay, it's a powerful force for bankruptcy.

In 2009, net interest payments on our national debt comprised about 8.6 percent of our total revenue. The problem, of course, is that there is no end in sight to our deficits, and therefore no way to pay down the balance we owe. So, it compounds. Fast.

According to the Congressional Budget Office (CBO), the interest on our debt will at least double in the next ten years, reaching 20 percent of revenue in 2020. The problem with that analysis is that it assumes interest rates will stay pretty low. What if they don't? A less rosy projection that assumes higher rates puts interest payments at 22.4 percent of revenue *in just three years*! Think about that: 22 cents of every tax dollar you send to Washington would be sent right back out to investors, many of them in other countries. No wonder our Founders were worried that debt could lead to our destruction.

The really scary numbers start to pile up when you consider what happens if interest rates rise even more than the CBO thinks—not a far-fetched scenario if you believe that investors are likely going to demand higher rates to compensate them for their increased risk. In that case, the White House has calculated that every one percent rise in interest rates would add $845 billion in deficits over a ten-year period.

If that were to happen we would start to enter very dangerous territory: The government would be forced to borrow even more money, requiring even higher interest rates to outbid everyone else looking to borrow from the same pool of money. That quickly ushers in a vicious cycle: Interest rates rise, making our deficits worse, making interest rates rise even higher, and a textbook death spiral ensues.

> Think interest rates will always stay low? Think again. After consuming 7 percent of the federal budget in the 1960s and '70s, interest payments doubled to 14 percent of the budget in the 1980s and '90s. (The prime rate was over 21 percent in 1980!) When interest rates eventually came down, the cost of servicing the debt dropped back to 5 percent of the budget . . . but, in this case, what goes down must come up.
>
> TEACHABLE MOMENT

The other problem with rising interest rates is that using more money to pay interest on debt means that less is available to provide tax relief or to fund the programs we actually *care* about. The beauty of this particular consequence is that it's not a partisan issue at all. Republicans may care about completely different budget items than Democrats do (say, the DOD vs. the NEA), but once interest rates hit a certain point, it won't matter. *Every* budget item will have to be cut, if not completely eliminated, in order to not default on our loans.

Assuming that we can maintain a reasonable interest rate on our debt—a very large assumption given that federal debt levels are set to exceed $20 trillion by 2020—the news isn't exactly positive. While the percentage of our spending consumed by interest may triple, the actual amount we pay would more than *quadruple*, rising from $188 billion in 2010 to $768 billion (adjusted for inflation) by 2020.

> **TEACHABLE MOMENT**
>
> There are two ways that politicians and others can quote our interest payments: gross or net. In 2009, for example, we paid $383 billion in interest on our debt. But some of that money was actually paid to other agencies as interest on borrowings from places like the Social Security Trust Fund. And some of that amount was also offset by any Federal Reserve profits (which hit a record $45 billion in 2009). The net result was an actual cash payment to investors of $187 billion.
>
> Why am I boring the snot out of you by telling you this? Because hearing numbers without knowing their context is at best confusing and, at worst, misleading.

If you still aren't convinced that interest payments are a major issue going forward, consider the kinds of investment decisions we are *already* being forced to make. This chart, put together by the Heritage Foundation, compares our average monthly interest payments with the entire *annual* budget for some federal departments.

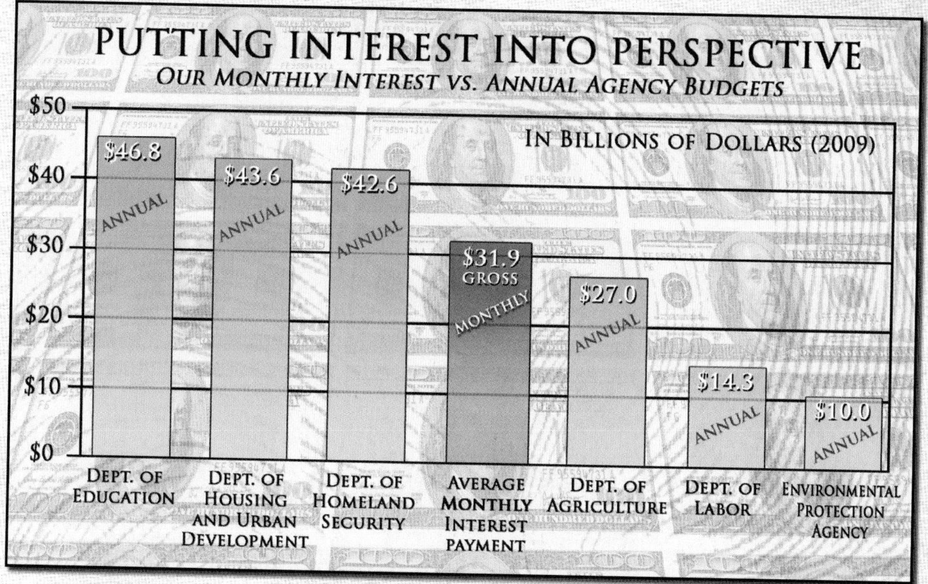

Original chart by Brian Riedl at the Heritage Foundation, data from White House OMB and Treasury Dept.

Decisions over the allocation of dollars isn't just some hypothetical scenario that economists debate for some future year when we'll all be dead, it's a real-life problem with real-life implications . . . and it's happening right now.

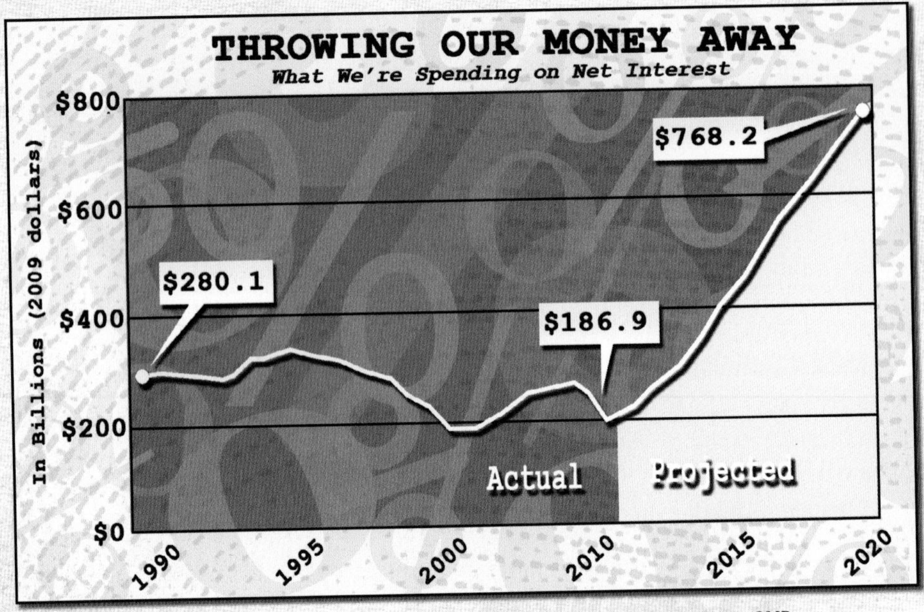

Original chart by Brian Riedl at the Heritage Foundation, data from White House OMB

The Big Unknown

If you've ever applied for a loan, you know that your interest rate is dependent upon your credit score. The same principle applies to our country. We currently enjoy the highest credit score from the major ratings bureaus, but that can no longer be taken for granted.

Standard & Poor's, one of the major credit-monitoring companies, provides ratings for a variety of organizations—from corporations to countries. These ratings help investors determine the riskiness of a potential investment and, consequently, the level of interest they should demand in return. S&P rates borrowers on a scale from AAA to D, with intermediate ratings being offered at each level between AA and CCC (e.g., BBB+, BBB, and BBB-).

Here's the important part: A rating below BBB means that the investment is not considered to be "investment grade" and is instead "speculative grade." CCC is the lowest rating offered by S&P, and it implies that the investment is "extremely speculative."

Investment Grades:
AAA: the best-quality borrowers, reliable and stable
AA: quality borrowers, a bit higher risk than AAA
A: economic situation can affect finance
BBB: medium-class borrowers that are currently in satisfactory condition

In addition to the rating, S&P also offers an outlook for each country they monitor. Changing a rating or an outlook is actually a pretty big deal and doesn't happen very frequently.

As the chart below shows, the United States still has the highest rating and a stable outlook, but many other major economies are experiencing downgrades. Greece, for example, was given a junk rating by S&P, while Spain and Portugal both had their ratings downgraded, all in April 2010. Those moves caused the interest rates on each country's bonds to jump, which, in Greece's case, threw their budget into even more turmoil, thereby forcing the European Union to quickly put together a bailout package to calm nervous investors.

S&P CREDIT RATINGS & OUTLOOKS

One important thing to notice on this chart is how the cost of financing goes up as credit ratings go down. While it's not a perfect formula (Japan is an outlier for many very complex reasons), it's clear that a high credit rating is important if you want to keep your borrowing costs low.

Country	Rating (Foreign Long Term)	Outlook	Public Debt to GDP	Cost of Debt*
United States	AAA	Stable	52.9%	2.2%
Germany	AAA	Stable	77.2%	2.2%
United Kingdom	AAA	Negative	68.5%	2.3%
Spain	AA	Negative	50.0%	2.9%
Japan	AA	Negative	192.1%	0.8%
Republic of Ireland	A+	Negative	63.7%	4.1%
China	A+	Stable	18.2%	n/a
Italy	A+	Stable	115.2%	3.0%
Portugal	A-	Negative	75.2%	3.4%
Russian Federation	BBB	Stable	6.9%	5.0%
Iceland	BBB-	Negative	95.1%	n/a
Greece	BB+	Negative	113.4%	6.7%

*Average rate of two- and ten-year bond yields.

The Tipping Point

While no one knows exactly when the agencies would downgrade the United States' rating, Moody's recently offered a few hints at what they're looking at. The key indicator, they said, is the percentage of our revenue that is consumed by interest payments. The threshold they are looking for is . . . drum roll please . . . between 18 and 20 percent. That range may sound familiar from the last section on interest rates, because it's exactly where the CBO thinks we'll be by 2020, if not a lot sooner. If true, a credit rating downgrade could be a lot closer than many "experts" think.

TEACHABLE MOMENT

Moody's, another of the major credit-rating agencies, recently warned that the United States' rating could be in jeopardy if economic growth were to be slower than the Obama administration projects. While many hope that a potential downgrade is years away, there is a case to be made that an immediate downgrade would actually be the best thing that could happen to us.

Martin Weiss, chairman of the Weiss Group, which, among other things, owns an independent credit-rating agency, recently wrote an open letter to the three major credit agencies advocating for a downgrade of U.S. long-term debt. "By reaffirming the government's triple-A rating," he said, "the three leading rating agencies help entice savers and investors to pour trillions more into a potential debt trap, or, at best, to be severely underpaid for the actual risks they are taking. The rating agencies give policymakers a green light to perpetuate their fiscal follies, further degrading our government's ability to meet future obligations. And, they help create a false sense of security overall. Recognizing and confronting our nation's financial troubles with honesty is the necessary first step toward solving them."

Of all the reasons that a downgrade makes sense—and, make no mistake, a downgrade would cause unbelievable chaos in the markets—the most important one is the idea that it will stop providing cover to our politicians. How can a country, a state, a corporation, or a person with massive deficits budgeted for as far as the eye can see merit the highest possible rating? They can't—an individual in the same financial condition as our country would never be able to borrow another dollar—but as long as our rating continues to be artificially influenced by our reputation, politicians will continue to believe they have an excuse to stick with the status quo.

HATE SPEECH?

"While we see limited risk of a U.S. sovereign debt downgrade in the next 2–3 years, beyond that we cannot be so certain." —*Société Générale*

I.M. Freaking Out

The International Monetary Fund (IMF), a group of 186 member-nations, recently issued a (long and really boring) report called "Fiscal Monitor: Navigating the Fiscal Challenges Ahead." It's too bad that they write at such an academic level that

Reviewing the Reviewers

As Martin Weiss pointed out in his open letter, there are at least four examples of major failures by ratings agencies, proving that they are sometimes not able to see disaster until it's already happened. Let's all hope they are not blinded enough to allow another one to happen without warning.

1. In the early 1990s, major life and health insurance companies were not downgraded in most cases until after they'd already failed.
2. Enron. According to the *New York Times,* "Credit-rating agencies . . . saw signs of Enron's deteriorating finances by last May [of 2001]. But the agencies—Moody's Investors Service, Standard & Poor's, and Fitch Ratings—did little to warn investors until at least five months later, long after more problems had emerged and Enron's slide into bankruptcy had accelerated.

   "Not until mid-October did the three credit-rating agencies begin to warn investors of Enron's deteriorating condition, and not until Nov. 28, just days before Enron filed for Chapter 11 bankruptcy protection, did they lower their debt ratings below 'investment grade.'" By the time the downgrade finally happened, Enron's stock price was already under four dollars.
3. The mortgage crisis. Credit agencies gave mortgage-backed securities their highest ratings, thereby giving a false sense of security to investors. We all know how that worked out.
4. Investment banks. Agencies gave the bonds of failing banks, like Lehman Brothers and Bear Stearns, investment-grade ratings until the day of their demise.

it doesn't get much play in the media, because their data is refreshingly honest, especially because they put each country's economic position into its proper worldwide context.

One of the key indicators that the IMF looks at is something called "Gross Financing Needs." The idea is to figure out how much money each country needs to raise each year based not only on their deficit, but also on the maturity length of their existing bonds. If a country has a large budget deficit (like the United States does) and a short maturity length on their bonds (again, like the United States does), then they'll need to issue more new debt than a country with a small deficit or longer maturities.

Not surprisingly, the United States is in the second worst shape of all advanced economies, needing to raise 32.2 percent of our annual GDP to keep everything up and running. That's worse than Greece (21.5 percent), Portugal (21.8 percent), and Spain (20.7 percent), the three countries that routinely get the most headlines about their economic problems. The only country more dependent on issuing new debt than the United States is Japan, which needs to raise 64 percent of its GDP. Hopefully, for their sake, borrowing costs will stay as low as they are, because if they start to creep up, Japan could be in big, big trouble.

From our perspective, this conclusion is pretty unsettling. Think of it like the difference between having a five-year adjustable-rate mortgage on your house or a thirty-year fixed-rate mortgage. The shorter mortgage opens you up to interest-rate risk, the idea that rates may be much higher when you are forced to refinance. By having a low rate locked in for decades, you can more easily budget your future spending. Similarly, with short maturities on our Treasury bonds, we are much more exposed to interest rates than other countries. A jump in rates would mean much more damage to our budget than it would to others.

Future deficits are related to spending, not revenues. Spending is projected to be 6.2 percent of GDP above the historical average in 2020, while revenues are expected to be 0.2 percent above the average. In other words, we're going to be taking in more money than usual a decade from now, but we'll be spending far more than usual. Why are we still debating how to fix this?

A Lot of Work to Do

There's a table in the IMF report that should be on the front page of every newspaper in the country, yet almost no one besides policy wonks has probably ever seen it. Put simply, the table shows the amount of GDP that each advanced country will need to cut from its deficit in order to be at a sustainable level of debt in 2030.

For the United States, it's not pretty. We would need to make an adjustment equal to 12 percent of our GDP over the next twenty years to maintain the IMF's target level of debt. That's $1.7 trillion—an amount larger than the entire economy of many advanced countries. For comparison, Greece, Spain, and Portugal, all require adjustments of less than 10 percent of their GDP.

I told you this chapter was all about the truth, so here it is: Aside from Japan, the United States has the most work to do of any country in the world to get back onto a sustainable path. $1.7 trillion won't be found by freezing some spending or cutting a little waste, it will only be found through major structural reforms to the programs and agencies that many people currently rely on.

All Debt Is Local

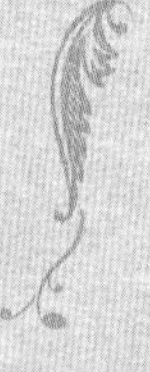

If our national debt were the only major financial problem we were facing, it would be a lot easier to turn things around. In most countries, you pay your taxes to the government and that's that. If there's trouble, the government implements some austerity measures and things can turn around fairly rapidly. But here in America, that's not the way things work. We don't answer to just one government; we answer to several of them.

America's state and local governments are, for the most part, in pretty sad shape. That shouldn't be surprising, since all levels of government have become so interdependent on each other. Instead of being self-sufficient, states have, in many cases, become slaves to Washington, unable to function without D.C.'s never-ending supply of money.

The best evidence of this might be what happened in 2010 when, under pressure over deficit spending, the government was unable to pass an extension of $24 billion in Medicaid assistance to states; assistance that was first granted as part of the stimulus package. Facing this proposition, governors from around the country were alarmed. The budgets they'd created (which were ugly to begin with) took support from Washington for granted. Without it, they claimed, things would be a disaster. Here's how the *New York Times* described it:

According to the Center on Budget and Policy Priorities, total budget shortfalls (unlike the federal government, states can't run deficits) for 2011 and 2012 are **likely to reach $300 billion.** That's about the size of the entire economies of New Zealand, Peru, and Ecuador, *combined*.

> *Gov. Edward G. Rendell of Pennsylvania . . . penciled $850 million in federal Medicaid assistance into the revenue side of his state's ledger, reducing its projected shortfall to $1.2 billion. The only way to compensate for the loss, he said in an interview, would be to lay off at least 20,000 government workers, including teachers and police officers, at a time when the state is starting to add jobs.*
>
> *"It would actually kill everything the stimulus has done," said Mr. Rendell, a Democrat. "It would be enormously destructive."*

California governor Arnold Schwarzenegger was even more optimistic about help from Washington: He penciled $1.5 billion into his budget. When he realized that none of that might be coming, he wrote a letter to Congress calling the move "both cruel and counterproductive." Governor David Paterson of New York was equally aggressive. He projected $1.1 billion in federal funding, an assumption that left him scrambling to figure out how to close a budget gap that will now likely be over $10 billion.

CALIFORNIASTAN?

"The cost to insure California's debt with credit default swaps is now higher than debt of developing countries, such as Kazakhstan, Lebanon and Uruguay. It costs $277,000 per year for five years to insure $10 million in California debt, compared with $172,000 for Kazakh debt."

—Reuters, early 2010

The State of Our States

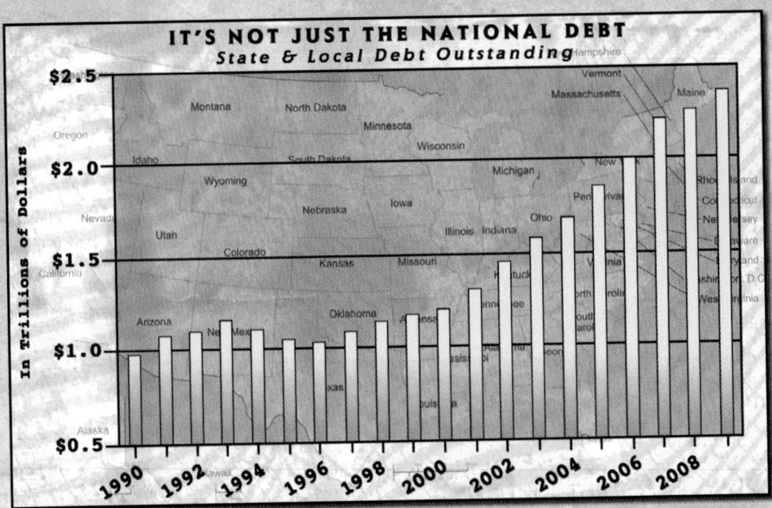

Original chart by Chris Edwards, Cato Institute, based on National Income and Product Accounts

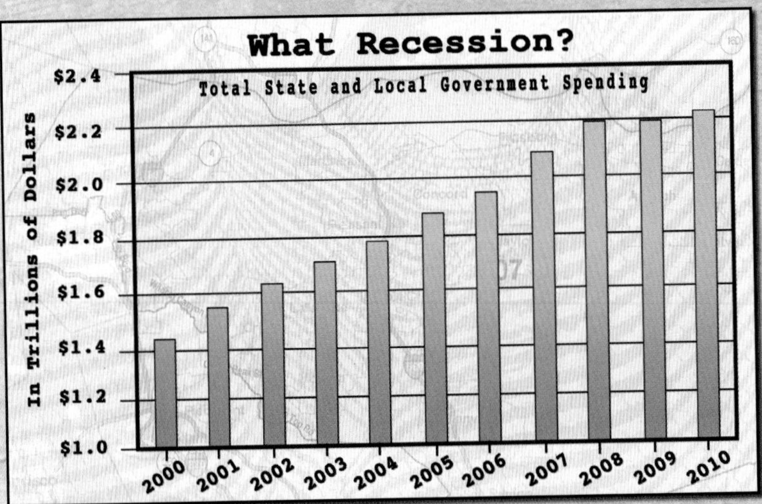

Chart by Chris Edwards, Cato Institute, based on National Income and Product Accounts

Despite the recession and all of the noise about "slashing spending" and laying off public employees in droves, the reality is that state and local spending has been slightly up over the last three years. That, of course, is after a massive run-up (58 percent) over the last decade. As a result, state and local debt is now at an all-time high, up 138 percent since 1990 levels.

In 1916, the entire national debt could've been paid off by the richest man in the country at the time, John D. Rockefeller. Today, the two richest men, Bill Gates and Warren Buffett, could combine every penny they have and not even be able to pay three months of interest on our national debt.

A.D.D. Moment

The point is this: There is simply not enough money to pay the debts that have been incurred. We can shift burdens from unions to states, from states to Washington, and from Washington to wealthy taxpayers, but it won't be nearly enough. Shifting problems doesn't solve them.

There's also a certain irony to a governor complaining that the federal government is not sending enough money to their state. After all, federal money isn't exactly the "free" money that governors seem to think it is—it's *our* money; it's taxpayer money. It doesn't really matter whether Medicaid gets paid for by states via income and sales taxes, or by Washington via income taxes: It still ultimately gets funded by taxpayers. The arguing and name-calling in the media by politicians is only for show. If governors can get the feds to pay, they can claim success in balancing their budget, and if Washington can get states to pay, they can claim large cuts in federal spending. Either way, this is all purely done for election cycle sound bites. Taxpayers lose no matter who "wins."

Huge Returns, No Risk . . . Call Now!

In 2008, states reported that their public-employee pensions were underfunded by a total of $438 billion, a grotesquely high number that, given the shape that most state budgets are in, is huge cause for alarm. But $438 billion is actually the *good* news. Here's the bad: Independent estimates put the real amount that state pensions are unfunded by at over $3 trillion. Why the enormous discrepancy? There are lots of reasons, but the main one is that states assume that their funds will have amazing future returns . . . with no risk.

As anyone who has tried to invest money recently understands, finding a no- or low-risk return is extremely hard. Treasury bonds? You'll get between 0.3 and 3.5 percent a year depending on how long you want to lock your money up for. Municipal and state bonds? Almost as bad. Corporate bonds or the stock market? Maybe, but not without tons of risk. Gold or commodities? The same. Yet, despite

TEACHABLE MOMENT

About 80 percent of state pensions are "defined benefit" plans. These plans basically guarantee workers a certain payout in retirement that is based on a percentage of an employee's final salary, along with the number of years they worked for. That is different from a "defined contribution" plan, in which workers pay in a specific amount, but their payout is determined later based on a multitude of factors. The problem for states is that defined benefits are, well, already defined . . . as in guaranteed.

How did these kinds of plans get so popular? It's actually common sense. Politicians, unable to hand out massive pay increases or other lavish benefits to buy the votes of unions, used pensions instead. Guarantee someone a payment four decades from now and no one cares. You get reelected, the budget stays balanced, and the workers get a guaranteed lottery ticket. Everybody wins! Except the taxpayers . . .

In most states, public-employee pension benefits are guaranteed by law, legal precedent, or the state constitution . . . In short, once earned there is a near zero probability that **benefits will not be paid in full.**
—American Enterprise Institute, 2010

that reality, the median investment return factored in by state pensions is 8 percent a year. Eight percent! With no risk! "Optimistic" doesn't even begin to describe that projection.

That ridiculous rate is one big reason why pensions are in much worse shape than people assume. In New Jersey, for example, the 8.5 percent future return that they are assuming means that their pension is currently in the hole by $32 billion. But if you nudge that return to 10.5 percent, voilà, the pension would be fully funded! Nudge it the other way, down to a more realistic 2 or 3 percent, and you can imagine that the underfunded amount would be a lot more than $32 billion. When you're talking about numbers this large, slight tweaks to the variables can have an enormous effect.

The big problem with all of this, and the reason why it's in this chapter, is that taxpayers are legally obligated to make up any difference between what's been promised and what can actually be paid. When states like Rhode Island, which has total government obligations equal to 63 percent of its GDP, can no longer afford to make pension payments, they'll turn to their general fund for help. But that would be a complete disaster. Unthinkable cuts in services would need to happen almost immediately. (In Illinois, for example, pension payments would eat up *half* of the state's revenue, thereby requiring massive cuts in everything from education to health care.)

Think politicians would ever go for that? Of course not! That leaves one final option: the federal government. Washington will bail these states out. (After all, what politician is going to be the one on local news breaking a promise to seventy-six-year-old Ethel who worked in the public library for forty-one years?) And they'll borrow more money to do it.

There is an exit strategy, however: As state finances continue to get hammered, politicians are finally taking a hard look at their pension obligations. All sorts of reforms have been implemented, but the changes so far only apply to newly hired workers, not those who are already scheduled to collect billions.

The one exception is Colorado, which has made reforms to existing pensions as well as future ones. The retirees, of course, sued the state, and the case, which could set a precedent for the rest of the country, is now pending. If Colorado prevails, other states may realize that these benefits are not

Some have speculated regarding an eventual **federal bailout of state public-sector pension funds.** Such a step is not unimaginable given the scale of funding shortfalls.
—American Enterprise Institute, 2010

Carlsbad Decisions

Ever wonder why so many cities are in so much trouble? Consider the offer that Carlsbad, California, made to their police and firefighters. According to the *North County Times*, those workers have "a '3-percent-at-50' retirement plan, meaning that emergency services workers who retire at age 50 can get 3 percent of their highest salary times the number of years they have worked for the city. City officials have said that in Carlsbad, the average firefighter or police officer typically retires at age 55 and has 28 years of service. Using the 3 percent salary calculation, that person would receive an annual city pension of $76,440."

as sacrosanct as originally thought. If the retirees win, then, well, I hope you like your job, because we'll all be working a lot longer to pay for these benefits.

Of course, there is another solution for cash-strapped states, and leave it to the geniuses in New York to find it. Here's how it works:

Step 1: Make ridiculous promises to state employees.
Step 2: Watch as your pension fund becomes massively unfunded.
Step 3: Find yourself unable to make enormous contributions while still keeping your state up and running.
Step 4: The *New York Times* describes this step pretty well: "In classic budgetary sleight-of-hand, [New York] will borrow the money to make the payments to the pension fund—from the same pension fund."

No, you're not missing anything; it really is that idiotic of an idea. New York wants to borrow $6 billion from the pension fund, and then use that money to make the contributions they owe to the same fund, along with interest that will cost billions more.

But wait, there's still bonus idiocy to come! Remember how I explained that most state pensions assume an 8 percent return on their money every year? Yeah, well New York is one of those states. Unfortunately, when you are supposed to *pay* that ridiculous rate, it's not quite as appetizing. So, instead of paying the money back to the pension fund with 8 percent interest, they plan to pay it back at between 4.5 and 5.5 percent. But don't worry, they say: The stock market will be up huge in the future and that'll make up for the difference.

Sure it will.

HATE SPEECH?

"Half the states' pension funds could run out of money by 2025, and that's assuming decent investment returns. The federal government should be worried about its exposure. Are these states too big to fail? If something isn't done, we're facing another trillion-dollar bailout."

—*Professor Joshua D. Rauh of the Kellogg School of Management at Northwestern University*

A TRUE GLOBAL PANDEMIC
UNITED STATES
PUBLIC DEBT: $7,581,480,000,000
PUBLIC DEBT AS % OF GDP: 53.7%
TOTAL WORLDWID
$039,083,5

HIGHER DEBT

LOWER DEBT

DEBT BALANCE

A Chart Is Worth a Thousand Books

Instead of continuing to blabber on about how dire things are at virtually all levels of government, I instead want to show you a few charts and graphs that should speak for themselves.

DEBT TO GDP

What happens when government debt passes the value of an entire year's worth of economic output? Who knows, but if bond guru Bill Gross is right, it will be the start of something that he calls a "debt super cycle." That doesn't sound good.

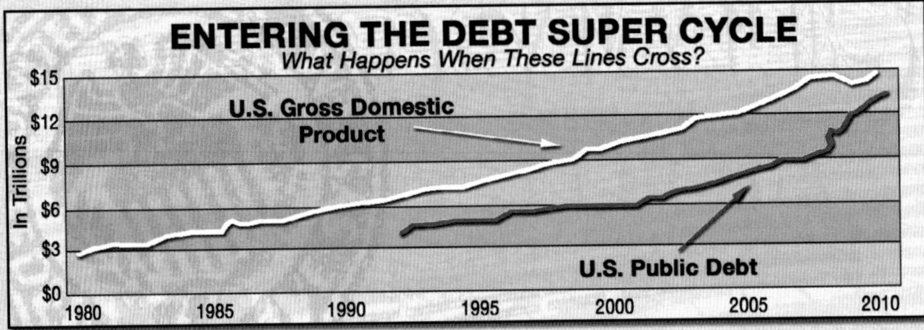

Original chart by Brian Riedl at the Heritage Foundation, data from Census & OMB

FEDERAL SPENDING AND HOUSEHOLD INCOME

This one speaks for itself: While households have enjoyed a modest increase in income, our government has been anything but modest. When people talk about the "unsustainability" of our lifestyle, this is the chart that backs them up.

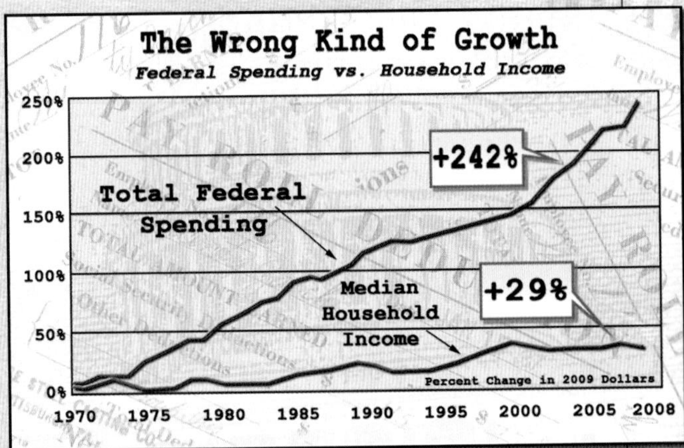

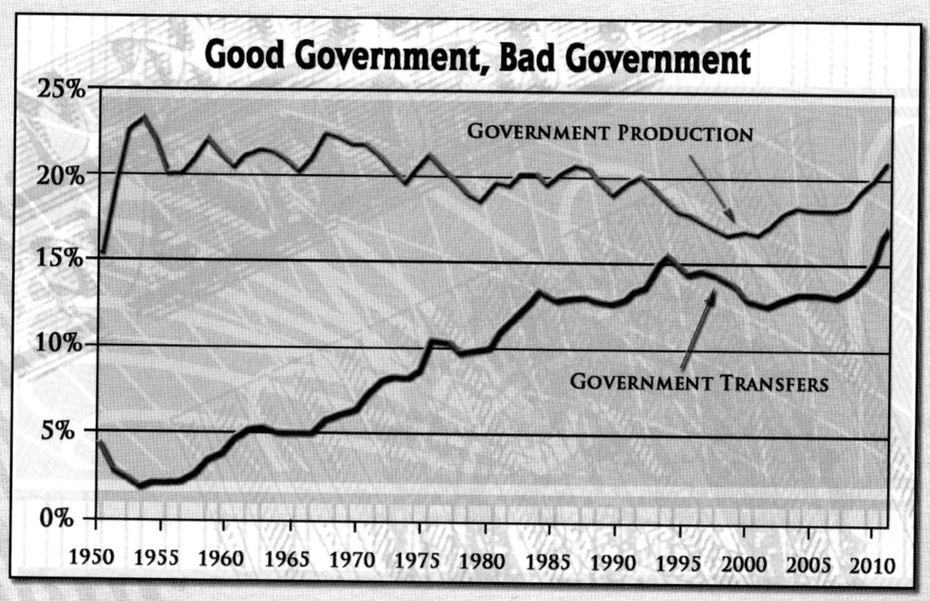

THE TWO FUNCTIONS OF GOVERNMENT

Governments in the United States do two basic things: They produce stuff (like postal services and national defense) and they transfer money between parties (farm subsidies, ethanol subsidies, etc.). The transferring of funds can also be called "democratic theft" since it's a legalized way of taking money from one person or group and giving it to another politically selected person or group. The sum of these two lines is total government spending.

In an ideal world, each of these lines would be constantly at a low level. If one line is growing, it should be the "production" line. In our case, both lines are way too high, and the transfer line has grown much more rapidly over the years than the production line. Not good.

HATE SPEECH?

"Timely attention to [budget deficits] is important, not only for maintaining credibility, but because budgetary changes are less likely to create hardship or dislocations when the individuals affected are given adequate time to plan and adjust. In other words, addressing the country's fiscal problems will require difficult choices, but postponing them will only make them more difficult."

—*Fed chairman Ben Bernanke, April 2010*

GOLD AND DEBT

The point of this one is pretty simple: While the metric tons of gold in our reserve has stayed fairly constant for over thirty years, our national debt has not. Of course, the *value* of our gold reserve is always changing based on the price of gold, but we no longer seem that interested in backing our debts up with anything other than "the full faith and credit of the United States government." I don't know about you, but I'll take the gold.

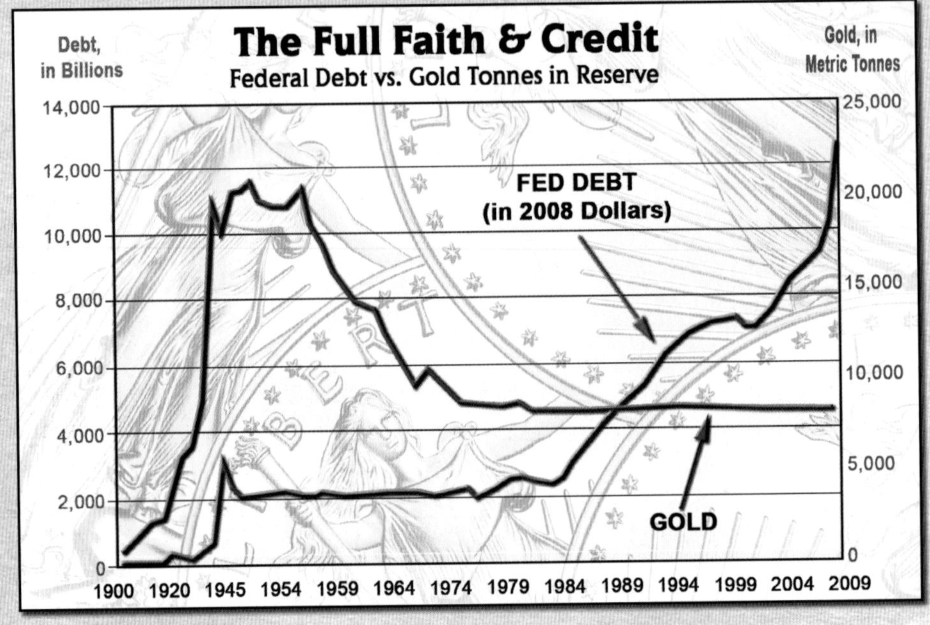

THE COST OF DELAY

Here's a good (and by "good" I mean "terrifying") way at looking at the consequences of continuing to argue over what to do instead of just doing it. If we had started in 2009, we'd need to adjust either our spending or revenue (or a combination of the two) a total of 8.1 percent of GDP to close our budget gap. That'd be really painful for a lot of people. But if we wait, it only gets worse. Starting reductions in 2030, for example, would require 50 percent more pain—equal to 12.1 percent of GDP—than if we started now.

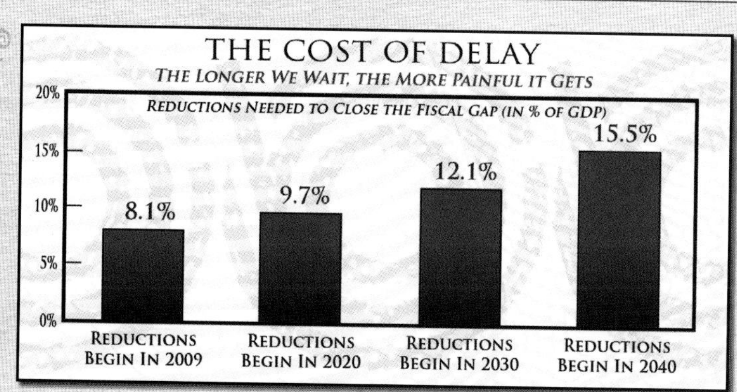

Unfortunately, the numbers are likely even worse than the chart shows. Why? Because the analysis doesn't take into account that our economic growth would likely slow under massive deficits and mounting debt, resulting in less revenue coming in than the government expects.

THE ADJUSTED MONETARY BASE

According to the St. Louis Fed, "The adjusted monetary base is the sum of Federal Reserve deposits and vault cash held by domestic depository institutions, currency held by the public, and an adjustment for the effect of changes in reserve requirement ratios." This is also the data point that the Fed can most directly control.

If it's felt to you like we've printed a few more greenbacks recently, you're right. The good news (if you can call it that) is that most of this new money is being held by banks and not put into circulation. That's *good* news because that hockey stick full of money would likely cause massive inflation if it were all released at once.

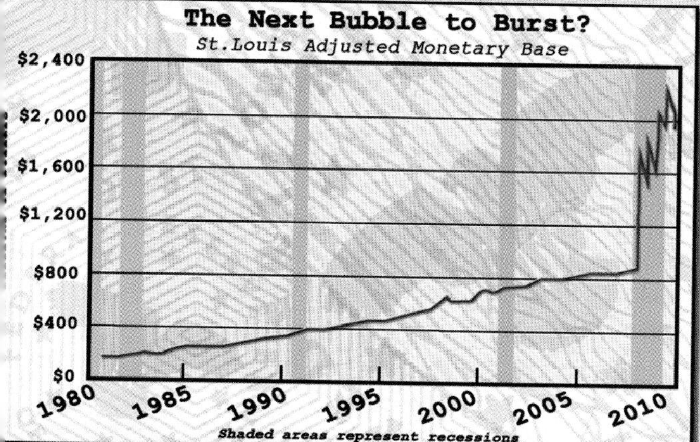

So now we walk a very fine line: We have to somehow bring the money supply back to normal levels without triggering another crisis. That should go well.

THE REAL BOTTOM LINE

When you look at the entire spectrum of debt that we've incurred, it roughly breaks down this like:

National debt	$13 trillion
State and local debt	$2.5 trillion
State and local pensions (unfunded)	$3 trillion
Social Security	$7.7 trillion*
Medicare	$38 trillion*
Total U.S. debt	**$64.2 trillion**
Total GDP of entire world	**$61.0 trillion**

**These amounts are to cover commitments made for the next seventy-five years, not forever.*

The unvarnished truth is that we owe more money than all of the economies in the world produce over an entire year, combined. Given that reality, it's almost comical to hear people debate whether we should spend more or save more; whether a program should expand 5 percent or 10 percent; or whether some variable, like the retirement age, should be tweaked. It's the very epitome of rearranging the deck chairs on the *Titanic*.

Our leaders not only can't see the forest for the trees; they can't see the forest *fire*, either. The few who do understand how dire things are generally believe that it's better for the public to stay in the dark while the elites fix things. So they confuse. They complicate. They belittle and denigrate the messengers instead of debating the message itself.

> HATE SPEECH?
>
> "Unless taxation reaches levels that would be unprecedented for the United States, current spending policies are unlikely to be financially sustainable over the next 50 years."
>
> —*Congressional Budget Office*

But now that you know the truth, you have an obligation to spread it. To educate your family, friends, and neighbors. To make others understand that America is not immune from the laws of economics. That freedom, our gift from God, did not come with a lifetime warranty.

All great struggles are eventually determined by the will of those who know to speak out. This one is no exception. Dietrich Bonhoeffer, a German who was executed by the Nazis for his warnings about Hitler, summed up this obligation better than anyone:

Silence in the face of evil is itself evil.
God will not hold us guiltless.
Not to speak is to speak.
Not to act is to act.

You bought this book because you wanted to know. Now that you do, it's your responsibility to speak. It's time to act. From here on out, silence about this crime means you're no longer just a witness; you're also an accessory.

"The basic premise behind the "game" of Three Card Monte is that you have three cards, for example, two black fours and a red ace. You shuffle the cards around on the table, and the "mark" or "sucker" tries to pick the odd card, in this case, the red ace. The sucker bets money on whatever card they think is the money card, they lose, and you take their money."

—ANDRU LUVISI, PRACTICENOTINCLUDED.COM

CHAPTER 11.

The Cover-Up

If the pillaging of America is a crime, and if the evidence of that crime is insurmountable and undeniable, then why haven't there been any consequences for those responsible?

Because of the cover-up.

Like all good political scandals, the cover-up in this case is as bad as the crime itself. Politicians realized long ago that the public wanted more benefits but didn't want to pay for them, so they have done everything in their power to deliver a Utopia free from financial burden. Whenever their conspiracy is threatened they embark on a mission to hide, manipulate, and obfuscate the truth.

Things have gotten so deceptive in Washington that the best analogy to show the way our budget really works might just be the game three-card monte. In that famous con, the "dealer" (who has all the power and control, just like our leaders) shows you a "money card" (the queen of hearts, for example), along with two other cards. The three cards are then rearranged around the table in front of you and the dealer asks if you know where the money card is.

Of course I do, you think to yourself. *I was following it the whole time!*

You put your twenty dollars up, the dealer flips over the card you chose, and . . .

You lose.

The truth is, no matter how transparent and fair you thought the game was, you never had a chance of winning. It was rigged from the start. If you had somehow picked the right card, the dealer's accomplices at the table would've grabbed your money and run.

ENRON 101

ACTUAL QUOTES FROM GOVERNMENT FINANCIAL STATEMENTS

"Since the actuarial calculations for social insurance costs are not reported as liabilities on the Balance Sheet, the corresponding costs also are excluded from the cost of government operations."

—Understanding the Primary Components of the Annual Financial Report of the United States Government

And that brings us back to the federal budget, which is coincidentally designed very much like a street con.

Card One: The Unified Cash Basis Budget

This method of budgeting is very similar to how you probably keep your personal checkbook. When you write a check, you record it as an expense; when you receive a check, you record it as income. It's actually pretty simple and, with a few exceptions, it's how the government creates its annual budget. When you hear that we had a "$400 billion deficit," they are generally talking about cash, meaning that the government spent $400 billion more than it received over one specific fiscal year.

Unfortunately, like anything that's simple, this method has some very large flaws. For example, let's say that you want to go on vacation in January, so you take out a $2,000 loan in December. Under the cash basis of accounting, the money you received would show up as an asset on your financial statements—you're $2,000 richer! What this method doesn't account for, of course, is that you will very soon be paying that money back out. The $2,000 isn't an asset at all; it's a liability.

When it comes to our government, that's a pretty neat trick to be able to employ. Money they are receiving now (as a result of, say, Social Security taxes) is accounted for as revenue, even though that money is clearly earmarked to pay future benefits. In fact, Social Security, as you saw during the Clinton-era chapter, is one of the prime ways that politicians are able to make things look better than they are. The large surplus that Social Security has been running each year helps to offset the enormous deficit being run up by the rest of the government. If we were being truthful, that Social Security money would be held as a liability, just like that $2,000 you received as a loan for your vacation next year.

The key thing to remember about the cash basis is that it lets income and expenses land in different reporting periods—an accounting quirk that's very convenient if you're in the business of convincing people that things aren't really as bad as they think.

Card Two: The Modified Accrual Basis Budget

This method provides a more accurate picture of finances because, with a few exceptions, it measures income and expenses when they are actually earned or incurred. If you hire a snowplow driver to clear your driveway on December 31, your books will account for the expense in that year, even if you don't pay the driver until January.

The one exception to this is taxes: Instead of accounting for how much the government *thinks* they'll receive in any given year, they don't actually account for tax revenue until it is officially collected (hence the name "*modified* accrual basis"). In a strange departure from the norm, this is actually a smart way to do it, since tax revenue is very hard to estimate in any given year.

For reasons far too complex to get into in a book that is trying not to put you to sleep, the federal government uses *both* cash and modified accrual methods and then creates an awesome report with six ridiculously complicated financial statements that are supposed to bring it all together.

Naturally, neither the cash basis nor the modified accrual basis completely accounts for long-term commitments to programs like Social Security and Medicare. For that, you have to go to yet *another* set of statements.

A.D.D. Moment

Here's a sample quote from the instructions to a federal financial report (and be thankful you don't have to read this stuff for a living): "The primary purpose of the Statement of Changes in Cash Balance from Unified Budget and Other Activities is to report how the annual unified budget surplus or deficit relates to the federal government's borrowing [debt held by the public] and changes in operating cash." Ohhhh, why didn't you just say so?

TEACHABLE MOMENT

Cash vs. Accrual 101

(Please skip this section if you majored in accounting.)

	Cash	Accrual
Reports	Income/expenses when cash is actually received or paid.	Income/expenses when transaction is agreed to.
Provides	A snapshot of finances at a given moment in time. How much you have; how much you need to borrow.	A longer-term view of all obligations made that year. Information on resources used that year.
Fails to Account For . . .	Resources used that year but not yet paid for.	How much has to be borrowed to finance government activities that year.
Accounts for Cost of Retirement Benefits of Current Federal Employees?	No	Yes
Used by . . .	Government officials and the Congressional Budget Office for budgeting.	Private-sector corporations and businesses. Modified version used by federal government when reporting results (not for budgeting).

If you don't think the choice of accounting method matters, think again. ShadowStats.com, a group that attempts to deconstruct official government numbers, calculates that our 2009 deficit would've been $4.1 trillion if the Generally Accepted Accounting Principles that apply to public corporations were used. Compare that to the $1.4 trillion the government actually reported and you start to see how important esoteric accounting concepts really are.

A.D.D. Moment

It's important to ask politicians what accounting method they are using when they quote numbers or projections. (Please note: Neither Glenn Beck nor Mercury Radio Arts, Inc., is responsible for the embarrassment, awkward silence, or police activity that will likely ensue after asking a politician about accounting methods.)

Card Three: On Budget/Off Budget

This is where the dealer's sleight of hand really comes into play. When considering the annual deficit, the government considers three major items to be "off budget": Social Security payroll taxes, Social Security benefit payments, and the net balance of the U.S. Postal Service. To add to the confusion, the costs of running the Social Security Administration (SSA) are classified as "on budget," meaning that it's hard to match up the costs of administering Social Security with the revenues the program actually takes in. (Which, of course, is exactly what those who run entitlement programs want.)

The total federal deficit is the sum of the on-budget deficit (or surplus . . . hahaha) and the off-budget deficit (or surplus).

The surplus of Social Security payroll taxes over benefit payments is known as an "off-budget" surplus and is invested in special Treasury securities held by the Social Security Trust Fund. So far, so good, but here's the rub: The government then lends that surplus to itself and spends it as it would any other revenue.

This is how that might work in a more personal scenario: Imagine if, for forty consecutive years, you invested $5,000 in your 401(k). Each December you then lent yourself that $5,000 to go on a nice vacation. On the day you retire, your 401(k) consists of nothing more than forty sheets of paper that each say "I.O.U.: $5,000." Think you could you retire on that?

ENRON 101

ACTUAL QUOTES FROM GOVERNMENT FINANCIAL STATEMENTS

"*By law, Social Security's and the Postal Service's activities are considered off-budget.*"

—*Understanding the Primary Components of the Annual Financial Report of the United States Government*

That is what the government does with Social Security. They spend the money, stick an I.O.U. in the Trust Fund, and pretend like everything is fine. Worse, they treat the money they borrow each year (the $5,000 you used for your vacation in our example) as true income, while *also* pretending that money will be available for your retirement. There's a very simple term for this: double-counting. (Some might also use words like "fraud," "cover-up" or "cooking the books.")

Here are some real numbers to put it all in perspective: In 2008, the government ran an on-budget $642 billion deficit. But by raiding their off-budget surplus of $183 billion they were able to report—and the media highlighted—a *total* budget deficit of "only" $459 billion. The problem, of course, is that the $183 billion in surplus is not a surplus at all; it's money being withheld from all of our paychecks with the understanding that it will be used to pay benefits to us and others in the future. By borrow-

Do As I Say, Not As I Do

If you're a CEO and you think you can fudge the books in order to make yourself look better, we're going to find you, we're going to arrest you, and we're going to hold you to account.

—PRESIDENT GEORGE W. BUSH, 2002

The fiduciary duty that the government has to taxpayers is the same as a corporation has to its shareholders. After all, the U.S. government is basically the largest publicly owned entity in the history of the world. Shouldn't the same consequences apply to those in government who break the rules or distort the truth as apply to those in private industry?

ing that money and using it to cover other expenses, the government undercounts the true deficit while simultaneously leaving the Trust Fund with a pile of I.O.U.s. In three-card monte street-con parlance, you just got cheated/jacked/scammed/owned/suckered/played/burnt/flimflammed/jackjohnsoned.

This is a pretty important concept, so consider one more example: You owe $1,000 to Peter for something you bought from him a long time ago. Instead of paying him directly, a company (just for the sake of illustration, let's call them "Gederal Fovernment, Inc.") agrees to be the intermediary and garnish $100 out of your paycheck each week. Once they've collected the full $1,000 they intend to transfer the entire amount to Peter.

As Gederal Fovernment, Inc. garnishes each $100 from you, they'd logically put that money into an account and hold it as a liability. But what if instead you found out that this company had spent all of the money they'd garnished from you to pay for their annual company picnic? Think about where that would leave each of the three parties: Peter is still owed $1,000, you've paid a thousand dollars and have nothing to show for it, and the company probably has to declare bankruptcy, thereby wiping out all of the commitments they've made.

It's a pretty ugly scenario, but it's really not far off from what the government does with Social Security year in

ENRON 101

ACTUAL QUOTES FROM GOVERNMENT FINANCIAL STATEMENTS

"Certain material weaknesses in internal control over financial reporting and other limitations on the scope of our work resulted in conditions that prevented us from expressing an opinion on the fiscal year 2009 and 2008 financial statements other than the Statements of Social Insurance."

—GAO audit report of 2009 financial statements

In the world of publicly traded companies that statement is called a "disclaimer of opinion" from an auditor. It's very rare, and very bad. Think: stock-price collapse.

and year out. The only reason there hasn't been a bankruptcy is that the government has a very useful tool that private companies don't: a printing press.

Divide and Conquer

While those are the three major tricks that the government can use to distort and confuse, there are plenty of smaller gimmicks at their disposal as well. For example, when you look at the debt clock in Times Square, or see the national debt reported by the media, you will usually see a figure around $13 trillion (or much higher depending on when you are reading this). That figure represents the sum of two different kinds of debt.

The first, and most important kind, is called "debt held by the public." When the government spends more money that it has, it makes up the difference by borrowing. This borrowing is done by selling debt instruments through the Treasury Department (i.e., 10-, 20-, 30-year Treasury bills). This is genuine debt that *must* be repaid to investors. Debt held by the public currently totals about $8.6 trillion.

The other category of debt is called "intragovernmental." This is simply money that one part of the government borrows from another part. The scenario that we just laid out about Social Security fits into this category. When the government raids the Trust Fund to pay for regular operating expenses, the I.O.U.s it issues would be labeled as "intragovernmental" debt.

The intragovernmental holdings currently total about $4.5 trillion.

The key is to understand that when politicians talk about debt, they may very well only be talking about the "debt held by the public" category. That, of course, is misleading, because all of the I.O.U.s scattered throughout the government will eventually need to either be repaid or shredded. Either way, the only number that really counts is the total.

> **ACTUAL QUOTES FROM GOVERNMENT FINANCIAL STATEMENTS**
>
> ENRON 101
>
> "*The federal government's financial condition and fiscal outlook have deteriorated dramatically since 2000. The federal budget has gone from surplus to deficit and the nation's major reported long-term fiscal exposures—a wide range of programs, responsibilities, and activities that either explicitly or implicitly commit the government to future spending—have more than doubled. Current budget processes and measurements* do not fully recognize these fiscal exposures *until payments are made.*" —GAO report, December 2007

Filling the GAAP

TEACHABLE MOMENT

Let's imagine for a second that the U.S. government was bound by the same accounting rules as publicly traded companies. They would be forced to adhere to something called "GAAP," or, as we called it earlier, "Generally Accepted Accounting Principles." These are a common set of accounting principles, standards, and procedures that public companies must use to compile their financial statements.

The reason these practices were created is so that investors would have consistency when assessing the financial outlook of various companies across various industries. Car Manufacturer A can be compared to Biotech Company B, because both account for their revenue, expenses, assets, and liabilities in exactly the same way.

Call me crazy, but we are all investors in this country—wouldn't it be nice if we could assess its health in the same way we look at Microsoft or General Electric? Of course it would, but the government instead relies on something called FASAB, the "Federal Accounting Standards Advisory Board," for its guidelines. Unfortunately, FASAB is bound to use the accounting rules that the Congress and White House set—no matter how irrational those rules are. The result is a set of financials that can't even be compared to other governments, let alone to public companies.

I Have Some Good News and Some Bad News

The good news first: Many of the most important financial numbers are available to the public each year via something called "The Financial Report of the United States Government," which is audited by the GAO. The bad news can be best summed up by Bruce Bartlett, a Treasury official under the first President Bush. "This report," he complained, "gets almost no media coverage whatsoever, despite the fact that it reveals far more about the sorry state of the federal government's finances than the budget does." In other words, if a truthful report is issued, but no one reads it, does it make a difference?

The GAO also issues its own report, "The Federal Government's Long-Term Fiscal Outlook," which challenges the Congressional Budget Office's assumptions and offers its own scenario based on its estimation of economic factors. Unfortunately, no one seems to care. In fact, the strategy from the government seems to be to issue numbers, statements, and reports in so many formats and from so many different entities that they simply hope to wear people out with confusion and exhaustion. So far, and I don't say this about the government much: Job well done.

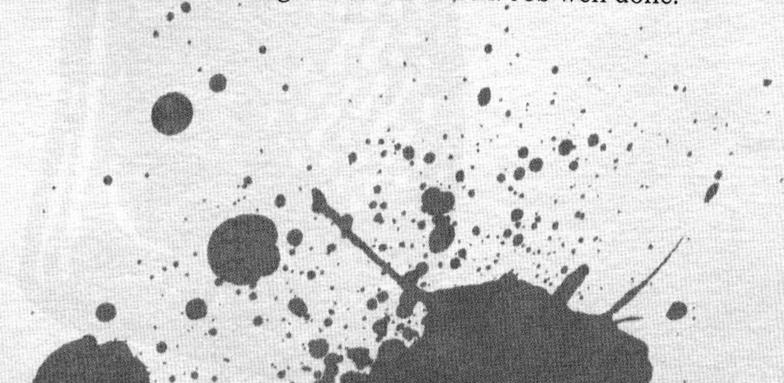

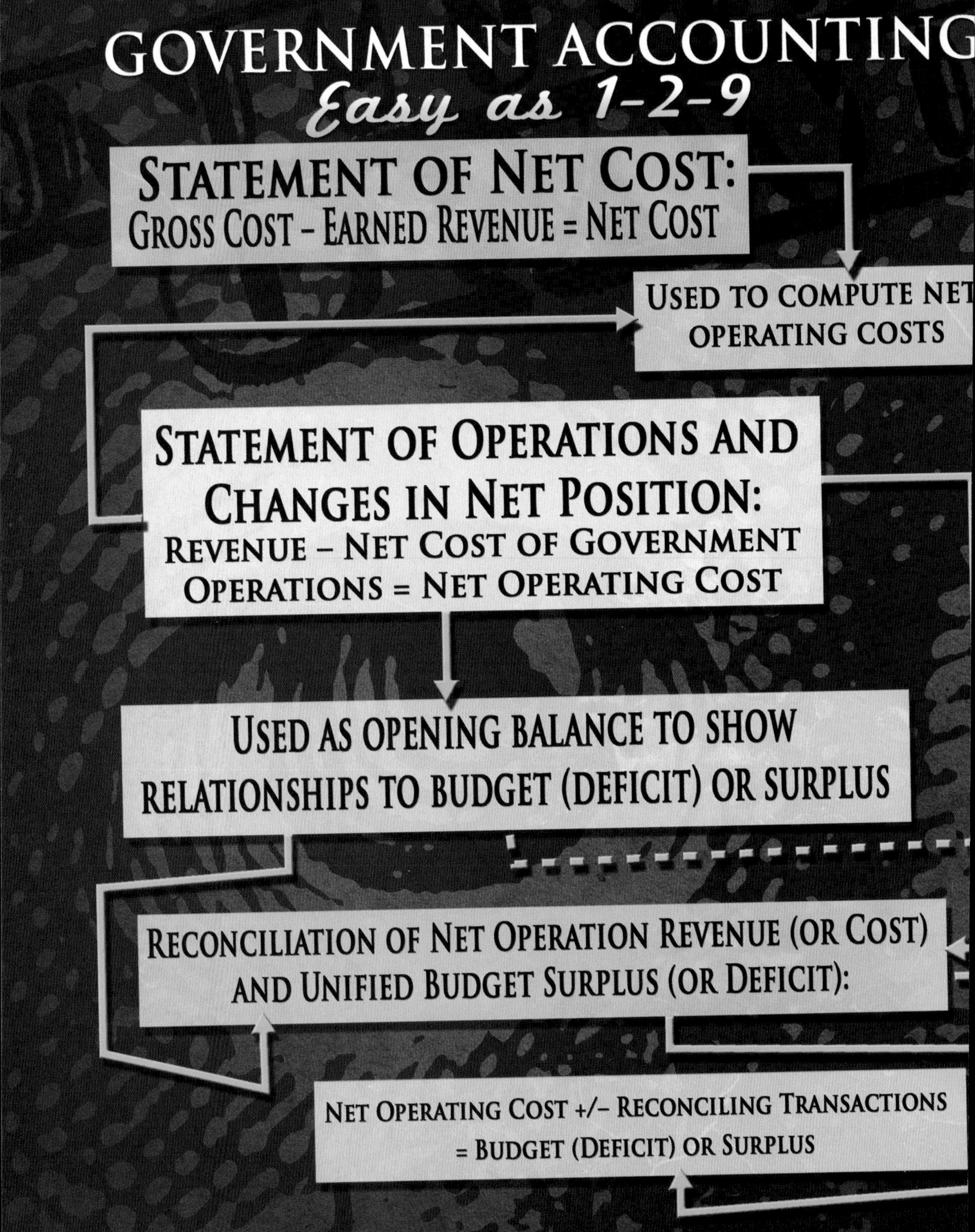

GOVERNMENT ACCOUNTING

Easy as 1-2-9

STATEMENT OF NET COST:
GROSS COST – EARNED REVENUE = NET COST

USED TO COMPUTE NET OPERATING COSTS

STATEMENT OF OPERATIONS AND CHANGES IN NET POSITION:
REVENUE – NET COST OF GOVERNMENT OPERATIONS = NET OPERATING COST

USED AS OPENING BALANCE TO SHOW RELATIONSHIPS TO BUDGET (DEFICIT) OR SURPLUS

RECONCILIATION OF NET OPERATION REVENUE (OR COST) AND UNIFIED BUDGET SURPLUS (OR DEFICIT):

NET OPERATING COST +/– RECONCILING TRANSACTIONS = BUDGET (DEFICIT) OR SURPLUS

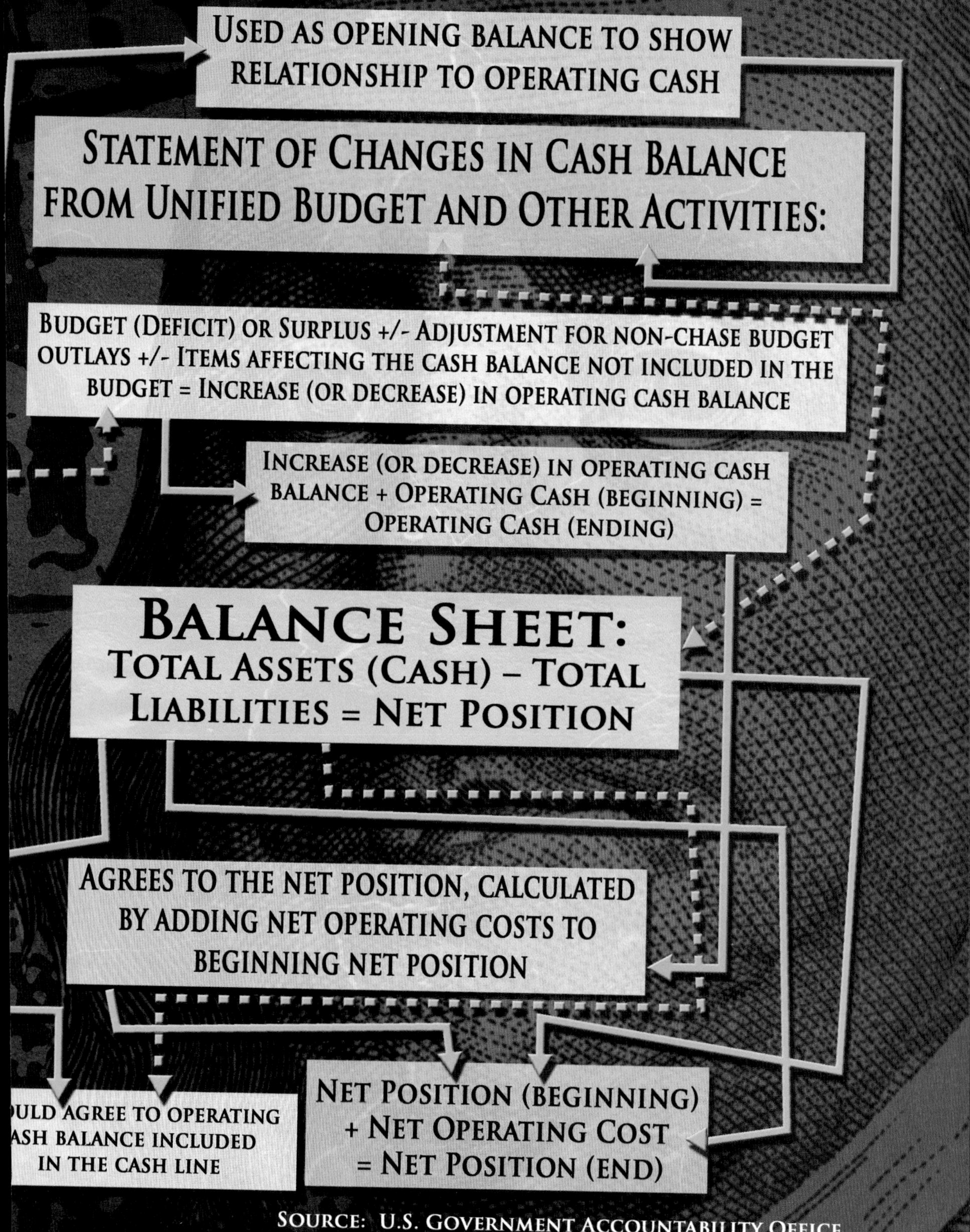

USED AS OPENING BALANCE TO SHOW RELATIONSHIP TO OPERATING CASH

STATEMENT OF CHANGES IN CASH BALANCE FROM UNIFIED BUDGET AND OTHER ACTIVITIES:

BUDGET (DEFICIT) OR SURPLUS +/- ADJUSTMENT FOR NON-CHASE BUDGET OUTLAYS +/- ITEMS AFFECTING THE CASH BALANCE NOT INCLUDED IN THE BUDGET = INCREASE (OR DECREASE) IN OPERATING CASH BALANCE

INCREASE (OR DECREASE) IN OPERATING CASH BALANCE + OPERATING CASH (BEGINNING) = OPERATING CASH (ENDING)

BALANCE SHEET:

TOTAL ASSETS (CASH) – TOTAL LIABILITIES = NET POSITION

AGREES TO THE NET POSITION, CALCULATED BY ADDING NET OPERATING COSTS TO BEGINNING NET POSITION

ULD AGREE TO OPERATING ASH BALANCE INCLUDED IN THE CASH LINE

NET POSITION (BEGINNING) + NET OPERATING COST = NET POSITION (END)

SOURCE: U.S. GOVERNMENT ACCOUNTABILITY OFFICE

FLY-OVER STATE SOLUTIONS

We might hope to see the finances of the Union as clear and intelligible as a merchant's books, so that every member of Congress and every man of any mind in the Union should be able to comprehend them, to investigate abuses, and consequently to control them.

—President Thomas Jefferson to Secretary of the Treasury Albert Gallatin

The comedians at the Treasury Department included that quote at the beginning of a 254-page report on our 2009 finances. In fairness, they included a "Citizen's Guide" at the beginning that tries to relay some numbers in a way that doesn't require a Ph.D., but who would ever log onto an obscure government website to read it?

The truth shall set you free—but what if the truth is nearly impossible to find?

Instead of using complex, archaic accounting rules, the federal government should be forced to print a simple "statement to shareholders" every year and include it with each citizen's annual Social Security statement. This report would detail our country's financial statements using GAAP, and provide year-over-year comparisons.

The current Treasury report includes a letter from Timothy Geithner, the secretary. Unfortunately, as a political appointee, he's not exactly an unbiased, independent observer. In fact, his 2009 letter has parts that sound more like Soviet propaganda than harsh reality. For example:

> *Largely because of the Recovery Act and financial stabilization policies, GDP went from contracting at an annual rate of 6 percent at the beginning of 2009 to growing by nearly 6 percent at the end of the year. Confidence in our financial markets and institutions has been largely restored. Borrowing costs for many . . . have fallen significantly. Job losses are moderating.*

I have a better idea. Along with the financial statement we include a letter to shareholders from both the majority and minority leaders of the Senate so that Americans can see how the numbers are interpreted by both the left and right and then draw their own conclusions.

Pay-Go, a Green Light for Spending

Congratulations! You've made it past the accounting! Your reward is that we get to move onto the really good stuff. Pay-Go (or PAYGO, short for "pay-as-you-go spending") is one of my all-time favorite examples of how politicians try to look fiscally responsible while simultaneously spending us to death.

In June 2009, President Obama implored Congress to be more responsible with its spending. (Seriously!) "Congress can only spend a dollar," he explained, "if it saves a dollar elsewhere . . . Paying for what you spend is basic common sense."

Pay-Go, which existed as a statute from 1991 through 2002, is the idea that Congress can only spend a dollar if it saves or raise a dollar elsewhere. It's supposed

DEFICIT OF TRU$T

"When I became Speaker of the House, the very first day we passed legislation that made PAYGO the rule of the House. Today we will make it the law of the land . . . So the time is long overdue for this to be taken for granted. The federal government will pay as it goes."

—Speaker of the House Nancy Pelosi, February 4, 2010

to ensure that future spending is deficit-neutral—it doesn't have any impact whatsoever on the existing debt—and, if our politicians weren't such spineless weasels, it might actually work.

In its 1990s form, Pay-Go required that the White House track all new entitlement spending and tax legislation. If, at the end of a year, things didn't balance out, a series of automatic spending cuts would be triggered. The concept itself was a good one: Make spending cuts mechanical so that no politician or party has to take all the blame. It's built-in political cover.

Unfortunately, it didn't work out that way.

DEFICIT OF TRU$T

"Statutory PAYGO is the guaranteed mechanism to make Congress balance its checkbook like families all across this great nation have to do."

—Representative Baron Hill (D-IN); February 4, 2010

First, politicians exempted major categories of mandatory spending, including Social Security, from the rule. Cuts in Medicare spending, the other large area where an impact could actually be made, were limited to just 4 percent. Pay-Go had no teeth and was therefore widely ignored. Over the twelve years it was law, Congress spent $700 billion *more* on entitlements than it cut or raised. At the end of each year, when the automatic triggers were set to go off (which would have exposed their two-faced irresponsibility), they would sneak language into a spending bill that would cancel the automatic triggers.

That wasn't the exception—it was the rule. It happened every single time.

Since Pay-Go was so obviously pointless, it went away in 2002, but Democrats, sensing that voters were coming back around to fiscal responsibility, brought Pay-Go back as a rule in 2007. They must've liked the PR value of that so much that, just a couple of years later, they turned Pay-Go back into an actual law.

Call it a rule, regulation, or law, it's all semantics to politicians; they'll find a way around whatever doesn't fit their agenda.

A.D.D. Moment

The truth is that Pay-Go, if actually enforced, would be quite problematic for the career longevity of many politicians. How can you deliver the benefits and entitlements you promised voters if you actually have to fund them? You can't—which is why Pay-Go is used only when it's convenient for everyone. According to the House Budget Committee, since 2007, "Pay-go has been waived or circumvented for $1.3 trillion in deficit increases; and when applied it has been used mainly to justify chasing higher spending with higher taxes."

Waivers and exceptions aside, there are other good reasons why Pay-Go is not only a failure, but also an illustration of everything wrong with Congress. First, de-

DEFICIT OF TRU$T

"I believe in PAYGO. If I start a new program I will pay for it. If I intend to cut taxes for the middle class, then we're going to close some of the tax loopholes for corporations and the wealthy that are not working for shared prosperity. So we're going to have fiscal discipline." —BARACK OBAMA, MARCH 27, 2008

spite its cute little name, the new version of Pay-Go applies only to new entitlement programs, *not* to any of the discretionary funding that pays for the day-to-day operations of our government. So, for example, if the government wants to increase spending on highways or pay for an SEIU museum, Pay-Go has nothing to say about it.

Second, even when Pay-Go applies, it doesn't *really* apply. Entitlement programs like Medicare can continue to grow every year with no corresponding cuts, as long as they don't grow over something the weasels call a "baseline." In this case, the baseline is 6 percent. As long as total entitlement spending doesn't grow by more than 6 percent a year, Pay-Go can't touch it.

Finally, let's say that Congress wants to expand an entitlement, Pay-Go miraculously somehow applies, and they don't issue a waiver or some other pronouncement to get out of it. Think it works then? Of course not! When Congress passed a major expansion of the State Children's Health Insurance Program (S-CHIP) costing $33 billion, they got past Pay-Go rules with a really cool math trick: They counted the next ten years of tax increases as revenue, but they counted only five years of spending.

DEFICIT OF TRU$T

When Speaker of the House Nancy Pelosi said, "The federal government will pay as it goes," she was just kidding! Don't you get it?? It's like saying "Al Gore will live a green lifestyle." Of course he won't! Hahahahaha! It's comedy gold!

Unfortunately, the joke is really on us. When you're done laughing, check out the table below, which lists the instances in which the House of Representatives avoided their own Pay-Go rule during the 110th Congress. In some cases the legislation was just *too important* to worry about the deficit, so they issued a waiver. In other cases, they simply ignored Pay-Go altogether. The total damage was over $400 billion, though, thankfully, not all of these bills were eventually enacted into law.

Legislation	Date Passed	Non-Offset Amount
Auto Bailout (H.R. 7321)	12/10/08	$3.9 billion
Unemployment Insurance Ext. (H.R. 6867)	10/3/08	$5.7 billion
Emergency Econ. Stabilization Act (H.R. 1424)	10/3/08	$110.4 billion
Economic Stimulus II (H.R. 7110)	9/26/08	$23.9 billion
Disaster Tax Relief Act (H.R. 7006)	9/24/08	$8.1 billion
2008 Alt. Minimum Tax Patch (H.R. 7005)	9/24/08	$64.6 billion
Housing and Econ. Recovery Act (H.R. 3221)	7/23/08	$24.9 billion
Senate Restaurant Employees (S. 2967)	7/10/08	$3 million
2008 War Supplemental (H.R. 2642)	6/19/08	$70.9 billion
Unemployment Insurance Ext. (H.R. 5749)	6/12/08	$10.0 billion
Farm Bill (H.R. 2419)	5/14/08	$2.9 billion
Economic Stimulus I (H.R. 5140)	2/7/08	$124.4 billion
2007 Alt. Minimum Tax Patch (H.R. 3996)	12/19/07	$50.6 billion
S-CHIP (H.R. 3963)	10/25/07	$3.1 billion
2007 War Supplemental (H.R. 2206)	5/24/07	$6.0 billion

Source: GOP House Budget Committee

A BUREAUCRACY TO MONITOR OUR BUREAUCRACY

LOTS OF PEOPLE ARE WATCHING OUR BUDGET...
GO UP IN FLAMES

FEDERAL BUDGET

BUDGET REVIEW DIVISION

JOINT COMMITTEE ON TAXATION

COMMITTEE ON APPROPRIATIONS

DEPARTMENT OF THE TREASURY

I.R.S.

GOVERNMENT ACCOUNTABILITY OFFICE

CONGRESSIONAL BUDGET OFFICE

OFFICE OF INFORMATION AND REGULATORY AFFAIRS

OFFICE OF MANAGEMENT AND BUDGET

FEDERAL ACCOUNTING STANDARDS ADVISORY BOARD

OFFICE OF FEDERAL FINANCIAL MANAGEMENT

CONGRESSIONAL RESEARCH SERVICE

SENATE COMMITTEE ON BUDGET FINANCIAL MANAGEMENT SERVICE

JOINT COMMITTEE ON TAXATION

SENATE FINANCE COMMITTEE

Whenever They Get Around to It

In 1974, Congress passed the Congressional Budget and Impoundment Act, which sought to mandate specific rules and a timetable for budgeting. The act requires that Congress formulate a budget by April 15 of each year (coincidentally, the same day Americans' taxes are due) and pass a budget by May 15.

Want to take a guess at how well that's worked out? According to the nonpartisan Committee for a Responsible Budget, "[B]etween Fiscal 1976 and Fiscal 2010, Congress met that deadline only six times. On average, the House and Senate fail to meet the April 15 deadline by more than a month. In Fiscal 1991, they missed the deadline by a whopping 177 days, finally passing a resolution on Oct. 9, 1990."

Because appropriations are based on a budget being passed, this delay has serious consequences for responsible and transparent budgeting. The process is forced to be done hurriedly later in the year, making it easier for waste to slip through the cracks and for politicians to rush through needless spending, knowing that there won't be enough time for a comprehensive review or for public outrage to derail their plans.

As the Committee for a Responsible Budget notes, "The deadline debacle is another indication that the budget process is broken. Congress cannot finish its business on time and ultimately makes spending decisions based on what is expedient and what allows the House and Senate to adjourn at the end of the year. Is it any wonder that the federal deficit and debt are spiraling out of control?"

No, it's not.

Emergency!!!

While there are a ton of gimmicks and techniques that can be used to hide spending, the most revered and pervasive of them all is to declare something an "emergency." This simple designation allows funding to happen without being subject to many of the normal budget rules.

Emergency requests are handled during what's called a "supplemental appropriations process." There is a legitimate purpose for these kinds of requests, namely wars and natural disasters; the kinds of things that simply can't wait until the next

DEFICIT OF TRU$T

"I am committed to restoring a sense of honesty and accountability to our budget. That is why this budget looks ahead 10 years and accounts for spending that was left out under the old rules—and for the first time, that includes the full cost of fighting in Iraq and Afghanistan. For seven years, we have been a nation at war. No longer will we hide its price."

—President Obama, February 2009

"This will be the last supplemental for Iraq and Afghanistan. The process by which this has been funded . . . will change."

—White House spokesman Robert Gibbs, April 2009

Just over a year later, Obama requested a $33 billion supplemental to fund the war in Afghanistan because his new "surge strategy" would be more costly than anticipated.

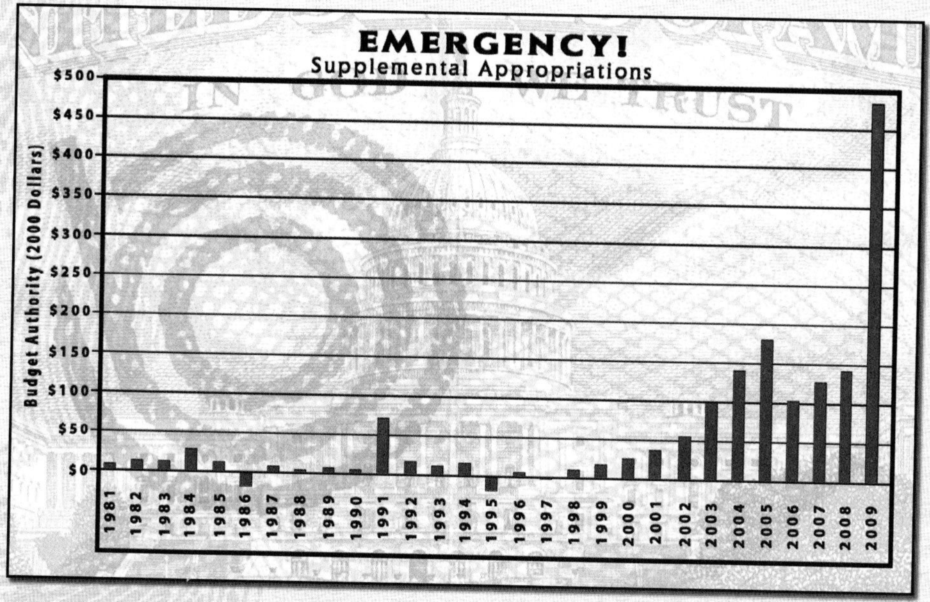

budget cycle to be funded again. But like everything Congress gets their fingers into to, the use has been expanded to the point where the original intent is not even recognizable anymore.

These days, supplementals aren't the exception, they're the rule. Dr. Veronique de Rugy, an economist and budgetary expert, found that "each year over the last two-and-a-half decades, Congress and the president have enacted between one and eight supplemental spending bills, ranging from $1.3 billion in FY 1988 to $120 billion in FY 2007."

More often than not, modern-day supplementals contain spending that probably wouldn't have passed muster under normal budgetary procedures. But with the "emergency" designation attached, there is usually little scrutiny and a far greater sense of urgency to get the bill passed. "For instance," Dr. de Rugy explains, "the War Supplemental Appropriations Act (2003) appropriated $348 million for 29 projects unrelated to the war, such as $110 million for the National Animal Disease Center in Ames, Iowa. The Emergency Supplemental Appropriations Act for Defense, the Global War on Terror, and Tsunami Relief (2005) contained $1.13 billion for projects that had nothing to do with defense or tsunami relief, including $55 million for wastewater treatment in De Soto County, Mississippi and $25 million for the Fort Peck Fish Hatchery in Montana."

The reason this kind of spending can get through with little oversight is that emergency appropriations don't include the kind of detail about how the funds will be used as regular presidential budget requests do. Remember, *this is an emergency*!

The effect of appropriations on the deficit is no small matter. The Congressional Research Service found that "had supplemental appropriations been fully offset since 1981, federal debt held by the public could have been reduced by about 18% or $830 billion. This could have reduced interest payments to the public by $35 billion per year." Thirty-five billion dollars, by the way, is enough to fund NASA and the EPA for an entire year . . . with $6 billion (the entire GDP of Nicaragua) still left over.

Rapid-Fire Fraud!

One reason this cover-up has been so successful for so long is that there is a nearly unending supply of techniques that can be used to keep it going. Budget tricks are limited only by the imagination of those who want to keep the truth hidden. What follows is a description of a few of the more popular gimmicks in rapid-fire fashion:

PLAYING WITH THE CALENDAR

Don't have any budget left for an expense? Just delay it! By waiting until the first day of a new fiscal year to cut a check, programs can be made to look like they cost far less than they actually do. Like all of these gimmicks, this one is eventually exposed, but politicians who use it simply hope they're retired on a golf course by the time that day of reckoning finally comes.

Want an example of this technique in real life? During the last week of FY 2006, $5.2 billion was due to Medicare providers. Instead of cutting those checks as usual, the payments were halted for six days, thereby pushing the expense into FY 2007 and making the '06 numbers look a heck of a lot better than they actually were.

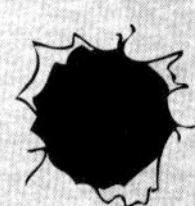

THE MAGIC ASTERISK

In 1981, Ronald Reagan's budget director, David Stockman, couldn't find the savings needed to balance the budget within a couple of years, so he invented "the magic asterisk." In practice, it wasn't really "magic" at all; it was simply an asterisk placed into the budget with the phrase "Future savings to be identified" written next to it.

In his memoir, Stockman recalled, "If we couldn't find the savings in time—and we couldn't—we would issue an IOU. We would call it 'Future savings to be iden-

ENRON 101

Actual Quotes from Government Financial Statements

"The U.S. Government is a party to major treaties and other international agreements. These treaties and other international agreements address various issues including, but not limited to, trade, commerce, security, and arms that may involve financial obligations or give rise to possible exposure to losses. A comprehensive analysis to determine any such financial obligations or possible exposure to loss and their related effect on the consolidated financial statements of the U.S. Government has not yet been performed."

—A Citizen's Guide to the 2009 Financial Report of the U.S. Government, note 22

tified.' It was marvelously creative. A magic asterisk item would cost *negative* $30 billion . . . $40 billion . . . whatever it took to get a balanced budget in 1984 after we toted up all the individual budget cuts we'd actually approved."

This paved the way for increasingly imaginative future budget trickery.

EVEN DAVID COPPERFIELD WOULD BE JEALOUS

This is a really neat trick. When you want to make your program sound less expensive, simply phase it in. For example, when Medicare Part D cost estimates were made in 2003, they were based on a ten-year time frame. The problem was that the program wouldn't even fully phase in until 2006. That made the ten-year cost sound much lower than it really was, since there would be little or no expenses for at least two of those ten years.

But the truth always catches up eventually; the program is estimated to cost $952 billion over the *next* ten years.

A MINUTE TO PASS, A LIFETIME TO PAY FOR

Washington's cash-based accounting results in short-term thinking with long-term consequences. After the 2003 debate over the new Medicare drug entitlement (Part D), lawmakers congratulated themselves on a bill that "only" cost $395 billion over ten years. The problem with that math is that they'd just created a *permanent* new entitlement, not just a ten-year one.

The true cost of the bill was a lot more eye-opening, but you'd be hard-pressed to find anyone gloating about it: $7.2 trillion in unfunded liabilities over seventy-five years or $15.5 trillion if you wanted to be crazy and fund the program's commitments in perpetuity.

FLY-OVER STATE SOLUTIONS

Here's a nutty idea: When Congress and the White House want to debate a new entitlement, with spending that will be on permanent autopilot, they should have to calculate and release the long-term cost of the program, not just the ten-year cost. Tell us what it will cost over 10, 20, 50, 75, and 100 years, along with how much of that cost is currently "unfunded." And, if you want to get really wild, require that all programs are fully funded for their eternity. Don't stick future generations with the bill; make the generation that wants the goodies sacrifice and pay for them.

You know the old saying *garbage in, garbage out*? The same concept applies with accounting. If you play with the variables enough, you will eventually get the headline you are looking for to leak out to the media.

Here's another good example. When President Obama was working with Congress to craft the health-care bill, he knew that it would be scored by the Congressional Budget Office over a ten-year budget window. He also knew that a cost over a trillion dollars would be politically unsellable. But there was one big problem: The cost *was* over a trillion dollars (early drafts of the bill were scored at $1.6 trillion). It was time to get creative.

In order to lower the ten-year cost, the benefits were phased in over time, while the revenue was counted immediately. The result was that the House version counted only seven years of expenses and the Senate bill counted just six, meaning a substantially lower ten-year total cost. Like with Medicare Part D, what was not trumpeted by Obama or the media, of course, is what the program will cost over the following ten years, when *all* revenues and expenses are recognized. Unfortunately, we're all about to find out.

THE WASHINGTON MONUMENT PLOY

When the federal government threatened cuts to the budget of the National Park Service, they responded that they would have to close the Washington Monument, one of the most popular tourist attractions in the nation's capital. This episode gave birth to the "Washington Monument ploy," which refers to the time-honored tradition of politicians responding to threats of spending cuts by declaring that the most popular programs would be the first to go.

Here are some recent examples:

- From the *Lansing State Journal* in Michigan: "DHS Director Marianne Udow said the state must make a difficult decision: cut money for food banks and homeless shelters for the living or cut money for burials for the dead. 'It's a terrible choice to have to make,' Udow said." Just two weeks earlier, Michigan was planning to spend $38 million on iPods for schoolchildren.
- In 2008, California governor Arnold Schwarzenegger said that the state's budget would force the closure of forty-eight of the state's parks, the firing of seven thousand state employees, and the release of thirty-seven thousand prisoners. This is widely believed to have been "a stunt designed to gain public support for raising taxes."
- In 2009, a Taxpayer Bill of Rights was on the ballot in Maine. It would have capped state spending, so Commissioner of Public Safety Anne Jordan falsely claimed that the measure would "eliminate a one-time payment of $50,000 to the families of law enforcement officers, firefighters or EMTs who die in the line of duty."
- The mayor of South Bend, Indiana, in an attempt to increase local income taxes for more funding, declared that, without tax increases, the city would have to close all public pools, all summer playground sites, and lay off police officers and firefighters.
- As New York state attempted to work out a budget, Governor David Paterson took to the radio to warn about what would happen if Republicans didn't get on board and the government was forced to shut down. "Eventually the banks aren't going to pay based on IOUs, and you now have no money to pay your police, you have no money to pay your correction officers, your firefighters, your emergency health care workers . . . You could have anarchy, literally, in the streets when the government shuts down," Paterson said.

As you hear these kinds of threats from politicians—threats that are likely to become more frequent and more draconian as the need for painful budget cuts becomes even more obvious—just keep in mind that responsible spending is not the cause of crisis and chaos, *irresponsible* spending is.

> ENRON 101
>
> **ACTUAL QUOTES FROM GOVERNMENT FINANCIAL STATEMENTS**
>
> *"If the [Securities and Exchange Commission] had jurisdiction over the White House we might have all had time for a course in remedial economics at Allenwood Penitentiary."*
>
> —Reagan budget director David Stockman

THE STATUTORY DEBT LIMIT

In 1940, the debt limit was set at $43 billion. It has since been raised ninety-nine times. Today the debt limit is $14.3 trillion—291 times higher than the original "limit."

The debt limit itself is set by Congress and is supposed to tell the Treasury Department how much debt it is allowed to sell. But, like parents who keep moving a curfew back every time their child is late, the limit no longer has any real teeth since it's basically raised whenever necessary.

There is one very interesting aspect of this limit that everyone should keep in mind, however: What if a majority party in Congress actually grew a spine and decided to stop allowing this limit to go up? What if they put their foot down and said *no more, enough is enough—figure out how to manage the $13 trillion you already owe*?

The short-term answer is pretty easy to figure out. We'd be unable to issue new debt, spending would be necessarily slashed, America would likely lose its AAA credit rating, and markets around the world would panic.

But what about the long-term answer? Would refusing to raise the debt limit finally send the message to all involved that there is no more money? Would it change

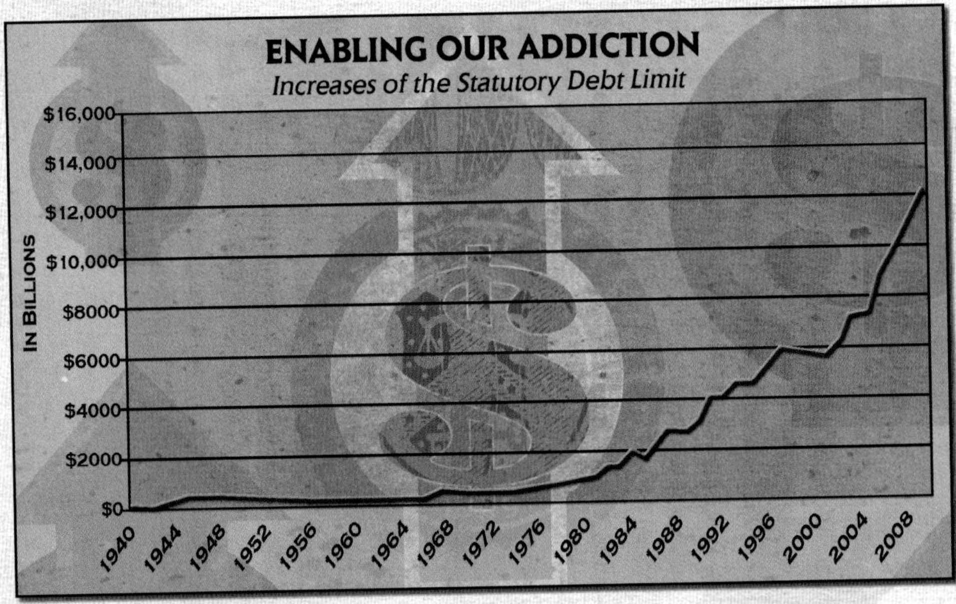

the way everyone involved thinks about the future role of government? Would it force people to look back to the Constitution, to individual charity and free-market innovation? Would it compel politicians and policy makers to think in a completely new and radical way about what is really important, and how it's funded?

If history is any indication, we'll never know.

But it sure is fun to dream about.

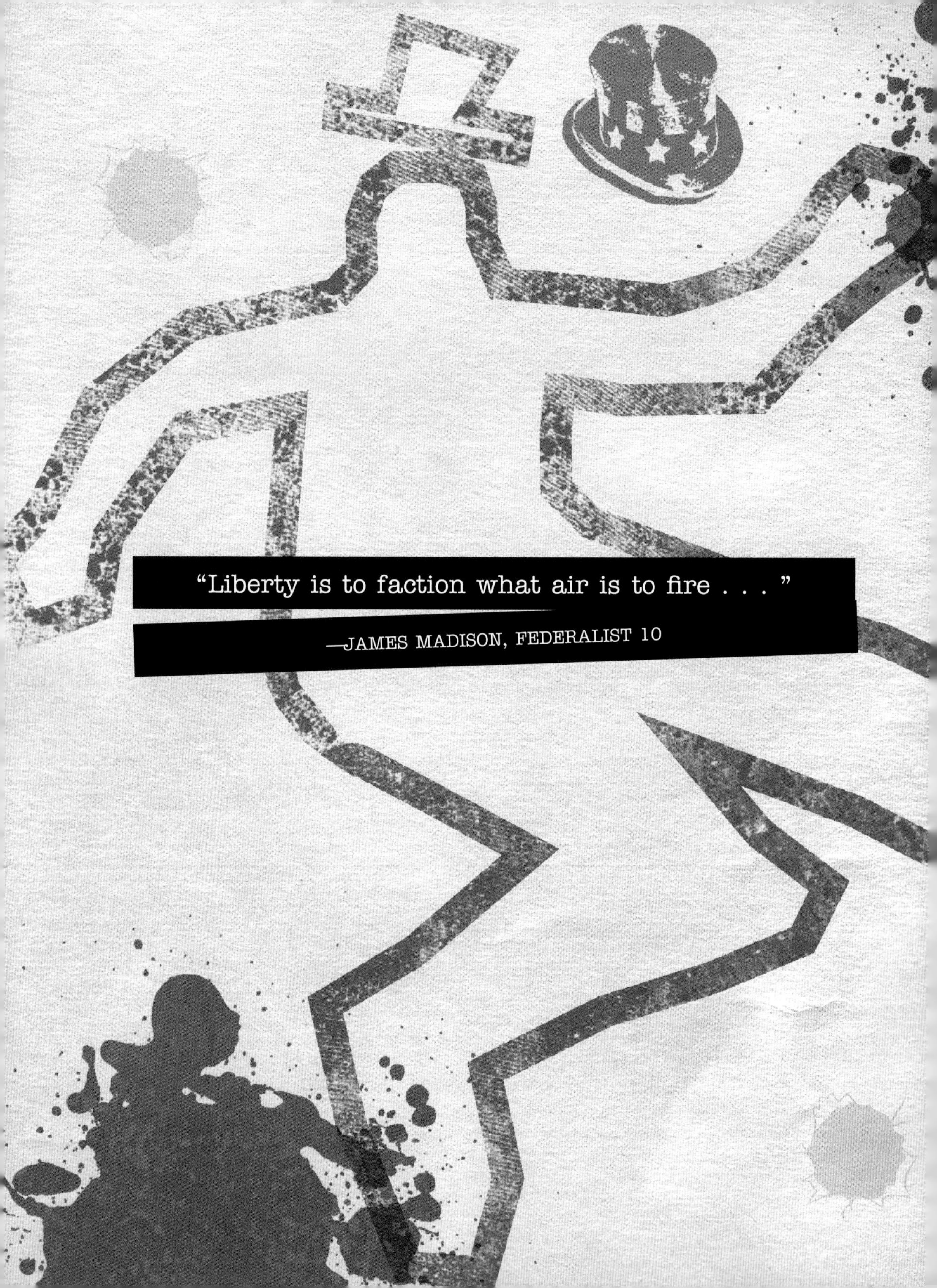
"Liberty is to faction what air is to fire . . . "
—JAMES MADISON, FEDERALIST 10

CHAPTER 12.

The Murder Weapon

Lobbyists. Special interest groups. Activist organizations. Advocacy campaigns. The mere mention of these words outrages many Americans. Blaming them for whatever ails us has almost become a national pastime.

A very quick search of the headlines reveals special interests being blamed for everything from government gridlock, to overspending, to stalled health-care reform, to the demise of an energy tax, to the lack of immigration reform. A more thorough search would likely also find them responsible for the exact *opposite* of all those things.

Our Founders thought long and hard about advocacy groups or what they called "factions," but, as the Madison quote at the start of this chapter shows, they ultimately realized that special interests will always exist wherever there is freedom.

Liberty is to faction what air is to fire.

Fire can be both a blessing and a curse. We can cook with it and warm ourselves, but it can also burn, destroy, and kill, so we have to manage it. We've developed firefighters, fire hydrants, fire extinguishers, fire alarms, fire escapes, and fire drills. Controlling fire isn't easy, but eliminating it would require eliminating the supply of air that feeds it. That's not exactly a good trade-off if you enjoy breathing.

Likewise, special interest groups have positives and negatives, but the only way to eliminate them completely would be to destroy the democracy and freedom that nourish them. Again, that's not exactly a good trade-off. Instead we need to manage and control the effects of these groups and use them to our advantage.

RIPPED FROM THE HEADLINES

"LOBBYIST SWARM" CALLED GREATEST IN YEARS; THEY THRONG THE CORRIDORS OF THE CAPITOL

—*New York Times*, May 1932

The Chicken or the Egg?

It's one of life's eternal questions: Are you fat because you eat a lot, or do you eat a lot because you're fat? The same question can be applied to lobbyists and the government: Does government expand because the number of lobbyists keeps rising, or does the number of lobbyists keep rising because the government keeps expanding?

Unlike the brainteaser about why we're all fat, I actually have an answer on the lobbying question. It's the latter: *Big government causes big lobbying.*

From 1998 through 2009—a period of rapid government growth—annual lobbyist spending more than doubled, to $3.5 billion, and the number of registered lobbyists in Washington peaked at nearly 15,000.

As Washington increasingly intervenes in our lives and our businesses, more lobbying groups organize for the purpose of protecting themselves from the government's increasing power. Whether it's the National Rifle Association protecting our gun rights, the Club for Growth protecting our economic freedom, or Microsoft protecting itself from a government lawsuit, the end goal almost always starts out the same: preservation of some specific freedom or liberty that the government may infringe upon.

Despite the way this chapter is titled, and despite the fact that there are a lot of things that need to be done better, special interest groups are *not* the murder weapon. They may, in some cases, be an accomplice, a co-conspirator, or an enabler, but the actual murder weapon involved in this crime is the progressive idea of the government as a provider.

Investing in Yourself

Because government has become so big and intrusive, groups have found that money spent on lobbyists is generally money well spent. According to one study, $1 spent on lobbying yields on average $220 in return—a 22,000 percent profit. Beats the stock market, don't you think? And it's profitable, too, at least for politicians. By one estimate more than thirty elected members of Congress have *family members* who are lobbyists. As *USA Today* put it, "No rules or laws prevent lawmakers or their staffs from being lobbied by relatives."

Just thinking out loud here, but maybe the reason there's no law against lobbying your relatives is that the people who'd have to pass the law are being lobbied by their relatives not to?

Lobbying for Lobbyists

As we start to transition from seeing the truth about our problems to actually solving them, it's important to first understand the role that special interest groups will play in crafting those solutions. Not only do they have the ears of the people who will need to make the tough decisions that lie ahead, but they also control the purse strings. They are often world-class marketers, masters of public relations and spin, and they will do everything in their power to fight for their cause—or against their opponents'.

I am a strong believer in the marketplace of ideas. If the game is not rigged, all information is widely available, and the brokers are honest, the best ideas should prevail over time. Of course, we all know that that's not the way it always works in the real world. Sometimes the game *is* rigged. Sometimes the players *are* corrupt. Sometimes information is buried or distorted. And yes, sometimes bad ideas become law.

But none of that means that competition among ideas isn't still the best system out there. When important issues come up, special interests form coalitions to argue their side. Depending on the topic, those arguments might happen publicly in television spots and press conferences, or they might happen quietly, behind closed doors. Either way, from a politician's standpoint, these groups serve a useful purpose: They are able to boil often complicated issues down into basics and explain their position succinctly.

Good politicians—I'll give you a second to stop laughing—are not necessarily experts on the intricacies of complicated issues, but they can weigh all the evidence they hear from groups on both sides and then reach their own conclusion. If this were a trial, the lobbyists would be the attorneys and the politicians would be the judge and jury.

Yes, I understand that this is somewhat of a simplistic view. I understand corruption, the influence of campaign donations, and the fact that some groups get access and others don't. But, in most cases, those are problems with our *politicians*, not problems with the groups themselves.

Remember, special interests, for all their faults, simply represent different factions of the public. If you're not an explicit member of one group, then chances are you're represented by another. Want lower taxes, fewer gun regulations, or more nuclear power plants built? You're represented by special interests. Want the opposite of all those things? You're represented by special interests, too. One man's special interest is another man's protector of rights.

Lobbyists are a natural part of democracy, and that's why they've been around for almost as long as Congress itself. And it doesn't take Joy Behar–esque intelligence to figure out why: Profits can be significantly affected by legislation. Nudge laws in the right direction and you could be rich; watch them go the other way and you could be bankrupt.

There seems to be general agreement that among the first lobbyists to petition government officials was William Hull. Hull was a Revolutionary War veteran hired by a group of other Massachusetts veterans to

TEACHABLE MOMENT

The Willard Hotel in Washington, D.C., has claimed that the term *lobbyist* originated there. President Ulysses S. Grant would often drink brandy and smoke cigars in the hotel's lobby and people would frequently mill around for a chance to bend his ear on an issue. It's a good story, but it's not where the term came from. The truth is that it originated in Britain and referred to one of the lobbies of the House of Commons where lawmakers would gather. I still think we made out okay, though, I'll take winning the revolution over winning an argument about word origins any day.

work on their behalf to receive back pay they were owed. Despite the fact that vets from other states were also owed money, Hull seemed to be the only one representing any vets at all. Sensing an opportunity, he wrote to veterans groups around the fledgling country and urged them to send their own representatives. Presto, lobbying had made it to America.

It took some time (and probably quite a few questionable tactics), but in 1876, Congress finally required lobbyists to register with the government. Seventy years after that, the Federal Regulation of Lobbying Act passed, requiring greater disclosures, including a reporting of their expenditures so that people could clearly see the alliances that had been formed. Other reforms followed, and while there is still plenty that needs to happen, lobbying has come a long way since deals were done in the Willard Hotel.

BAD IDEA JEANS

In 1850, Samuel Colt, the firearms maker, gave a pistol to the son of a congressman, hoping it might provide a little incentive to extend his patent. Aside from that kind of gift probably being illegal today, there was one other small problem: The congressman's son was just twelve years old.

Exposing the Wizard

Things have obviously changed quite a bit since the Lobbying Act was passed. While lobbyists are more prevalent and powerful these days, technology has also allowed the public more access than ever to see what's really going on. Websites like OpenSecrets.org (run by the Center for Responsive Politics) make it their mission to bring transparency to the process. Want to know the interest groups lobbying for pro-choice? They'll show you the top contributors, how much they spent, and which politicians and parties were on the receiving end. And you can do the same for pro-life groups.

That brings me to the reason that I care enough about special interest groups to put them in this book: They represent both the key to our future and the roadblock to it. When entitlements eventually weave their way back into the public debate before the 2012 election, it will be these groups that will be fighting either for the status quo or for reform. Knowing who they are, and why they exist, will be a key to nudging the debate in our favor.

Here is a primer on some of the groups that have made an impact in previous entitlement debates. There's a lot more where these came from, but next time you see a TV ad telling you that "Republicans want to deny seniors access to antibiotics," I suggest you stick around until the end and see who paid for it.

DEFICIT OF TRU$T

"The Republicans are here for the special interests, we're here for the people's interests."

—House Speaker Nancy Pelosi

AMERICANS UNITED FOR CHANGE

AMERICANSUNITED FOR CHANGE

www.americansunitedforchange.org

Formed in 2005, Americans United For Change (AUFC) was originally called "Americans United to Protect Social Security." The group was set up by Democratic congressional leaders, unions, and senior groups to blitz President Bush's plan to allow personal accounts for Social Security.

The group engaged in guerrilla-warfare-style politics to target members of Congress who supported reform. It told voters that benefits would be cut through an evil process of privatization. During the height of the debate, it organized 224 events in sixty-five target districts in three weeks.

- AUFC is largely supported by the American Federation of State, County and Municipal Employees, a large and powerful union of government workers.
- Since Barack Obama was elected, AUFC has played an instrumental role in helping to push forward his agenda. It has had major media campaigns dedicated to all the major liberal issues: health-care reform, financial reform, the Employee Free Choice Act (which makes it far easier to unionize workers), and "clean" energy.
- Its mission, in their own words:

> *AUFC has challenged the far-right conservative voices and ideas that for too long have been mistaken for mainstream American values. In the process, we helped create a groundswell for a return to the traditional progressive values that have defined America—economic fairness, opportunity, national and economic security and democratic leadership.*
>
> *Today we are building on that success through national campaigns that utilize grassroots organizing, polling and message development, earned and paid media, online organizing, grass-tops outreach and paid and volunteer phones to pass the transformational legislation coming out of the Obama White House.*

No, Not Really

According to the AUFC website, "We are not a partisan organization nor are we allied with any political party."

Really?

No, not really. Also according to the website, "The chief mission of Americans United For Change for the next two years is to amplify the progressive message—to contribute to a grass roots groundswell for progressive policies."

Okay, see, they're progressives, not Democrats!

Here is what's not on their website, but was reported by the *Washington Post*: "The takeover of the Democratic National Committee by Barack Obama's campaign continues apace with the hiring of communications operative Brad Woodhouse at the national party committee . . . For Woodhouse, who has been running the issue-oriented progressive group Americans United [For Change] for the last several years, his new post is a return home."

I can definitely see how they wouldn't call themselves a partisan organization.

NATIONAL COMMITTEE TO PRESERVE SOCIAL SECURITY AND MEDICARE

www.ncpssm.org

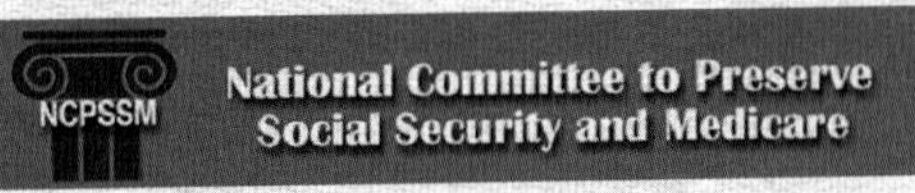

This organization was started by James Roosevelt, the son of Social Security's founder, FDR. Its intent is to "protect, preserve, promote and ensure the financial security, health and the well being of current and future generations of maturing Americans."

- 81 percent of the group's funding since 1990 has gone to Democrats.
- The group asserts that Social Security's finances will be fine and that the situation "in no way constitutes a crisis."
- The group is strongly opposed to privatization of Social Security, asserting this would make the program more expensive for taxpayers and mean a decrease in benefits.
- Committee president Barbara Kennelly said in a July 2010 interview that raising the retirement age would be discriminatory because white males are the ones who have easier jobs and can work longer.
- The group's current top recipient of money is Nancy Pelosi.

GRAY PANTHERS

www.graypanthers.org

The Gray Panthers was launched to oppose the Vietnam War but have expanded to become a powerful force in grassroots advocacy for progressive goals.

- It says its mission is to "work for social and economic justice and peace for all people." Their vision is to "create a humane society that puts the needs of people over profits, responsibility over power and democracy over institutions."
- It explains that their growth came as a result of "publicly challenging the status quo from a progressive, even radical, point of view."
- The group is extremely opposed to cutting Social Security or Medicare benefits. Its members would like to see a drastic increase in government handouts. A resolution posted on its website (yes, seriously) explains:

> *BE IT RESOLVED, that Gray Panthers opposes any and all efforts to reduce the effectiveness and reliability of the Social Security Program.*
>
> *BE IT FURTHER RESOLVED, that Gray Panthers supports exploration of a variety of methods to safeguard against shortfalls in the Social Security system, including lifting of the cap on income subject to social security tax, inclusion of State and Local government employees, and other measures that enhance the program.*

- It also includes this resolution in regard to Medicare:

> *BE IT RESOLVED, that the Gray Panthers advance the position that the entire 2003 Medicare Modernization Act must be repealed, and that this position be emphasized whenever we discuss Medicare in our national or local groupings.*

What? Repeal Medicare Part D? Yes, but don't get too excited—they want it repealed so that it can be replaced with something far larger and more expansive. Part D, which is already breaking the bank, apparently isn't comprehensive enough.

AMERICAN ASSOCIATION OF RETIRED PERSONS (AARP)

www.aarp.org

The AARP's mission is to "enhance the quality of life for all as we age, leading positive social change, and delivering value to members through information, advocacy, and service."

- In 2008 (the latest year for which there is data available), the AARP had over $1 billion in revenue.
- The AARP is arguably the strongest supporter of preserving Social Security's status quo.
- The AARP has become a dominant force in politics and claims over 40 million members, making it one of the largest membership organizations in the United States.
- The AARP lost tens of thousands of members due to its support of ObamaCare.

- Lobbying: 2008—$27,900,000; 2009—$21,010,000;
- AARP will likely become the largest source of health insurance for Medicare recipients.

AMERICAN MEDICAL ASSOCIATION

www.ama-assn.org

The AMA played an extremely important role in lobbying for ObamaCare. On its website, the group says, "Fulfilling a long-time advocacy goal of the AMA, passage of the Patient Protection and Affordable Care Act will expand health insurance coverage to 32 million more Americans by 2019. During 2010 and beyond, the AMA will continue its work to facilitate expanded coverage."

- The AMA had revenues of $228 million in 2008 (the latest year for which IRS data is available). Ironically, the AMA lobbied hard *against* the creation of Medicare. In 1961, it launched "Operation Coffee Shop" using then-actor Ronald Reagan's voice in radio ads explaining how socialized Medicare would lead to totalitarianism. However, since it came to be law, the group has since fought hard against any attempts to cut benefits.
- The AMA runs a spin-off grassroots group called the "Patients Action Network," which has 800,000 members who advocate for protecting Medicare and finding ways to legislate expanding health-care coverage.
- According to the Center for Responsive Politics, the AMA agrees with Republicans on issues such as medical malpractice reform, but has recently "begun to shift support to the Democrats, favoring their attempts to pass patients' rights legislation and expand Medicare payments."
- Since 1990, the AMA has given $26 million in campaign contributions.
- In 2010 (as of July), the AMA spent $15 million lobbying. In 2009, they spent $21 million.

60 PLUS ASSOCIATION

www.60plus.org

60 Plus bills itself as the conservative alternative to AARP. The group is a strong proponent of personal accounts for Social Security and is open to many reforms that do not include raising taxes. AARP has accused it of being a front organization for the pharmaceutical industry.

- Has about 5.5 million "activists."
- When approaching policy in general, 60 Plus favors a "less government, less taxes" approach.
- The group is a very strong supporter of eliminating the death tax.
- As a group, 60 Plus was a strong advocate against ObamaCare, arguing that it would have serious negative implications for senior citizens, estimating a half-trillion-dollar cut in Medicare.

SENIORS COALITION (TSC)

www.senior.org

It says its mission is "to protect the quality of life and economic well-being that older Americans have earned while supporting common sense solutions to the challenges of the future."

- Its focus is on protecting the Social Security Trust Fund and saving Medicare from bankruptcy.
- TTSC claims have to 4 million members and to be the "nation's leading free-market senior education and advocacy organization."
- TSC supports the idea of personal accounts for Social Security and insists on a Social Security "lock box" so that government can no longer raid the trust fund.
- In 1995, the director of government affairs for TCS testified before Congress that "if we want to protect the integrity of Social Security the only way is through a Balanced Budget Amendment."
- TSC has been called a right-wing front group funded by the pharmaceutical industry and developed through the direct mail business of its

founder, Richard Viguerie. (Viguerie, by the way, wrote a book called *Conservatives Betrayed: How George W. Bush and Other Big Government Republicans Hijacked the Conservative Cause.*)

- TSC rallied support among seniors and members of legislation that would prohibit attempts to force the Social Security Administration to pay out benefits to illegal aliens.

TEACHABLE MOMENT

In 1969 lobbyists spent an average of $9,560 per lawmaker. In 2009 they spent $6.4 million per lawmaker.

The Crime-Scene Evidence

Knowing who is going to be fighting for and against you is only half the equation. The other half is having the facts to back up your position. When it comes to entitlement programs, that's even more important than usual because of how powerful and well organized the lobbies are. Whenever their programs come under attack they fight back with everything they've got: TV commercials, newspaper editorials, rallies, public protests, even events targeting specific individuals or politicians.

The only defense against these kinds of tactics is the truth. And while most of us know that entitlements like Social Security and Medicare are murdering our finances, many don't know how to make the right arguments against people who rely on emotion instead of fact. While it's not worth getting into every single doomsday number or detail of these programs—we can leave that to the economists and policy wonks—it is worth understanding where these programs came from and how they ever got so out of control to begin with.

As Martin Luther King, Jr., once said, "No lie can live forever"—well, these programs are based on the biggest lie of all: that money can be shuffled around from

A REMINDER . . .

Keeping all of this straight can get tough at times, so before we get into the specifics, here's a quick reminder on how the entitlement programs work.

Entitlements are "mandatory" spending and have a special autopilot status in the federal budget. They are allowed to grow *automatically* every year, without limit or oversight, and largely outside the federal budget process. Each year, Congress begins by automatically accepting whatever growth may occur in these programs—essentially giving them the first claim over federal revenues. After all yearly entitlement costs have been paid, lawmakers then determine how much money will be left over for discretionary programs (which are currently 40 percent of the budget and declining) in the upcoming year. The rest of the year is devoted to passing the appropriations bills for these "lower-priority" discretionary items—you know, the unimportant things like national defense, homeland security, the courts, and veterans' health care.

person to person, from states to Washington and from trust fund to trust fund without consequence. It's time for that way of thinking (or, in this case, *not* thinking) to finally end. Progressive thought has brought us straight to the brink—only an equal but opposite force can move us away from it.

Prosecution Exhibit A: Social Security Insurance

We can never insure one-hundred percent of the population against one-hundred percent of the hazards and vicissitudes of life. But we have tried to frame a law which will give some measure of protection to the average citizen and to his family against the loss of a job and against poverty-ridden old age. This law, too, represents a cornerstone in a structure which is being built, but is by no means complete.

—Franklin Delano Roosevelt, signing the Social Security Act into law on August 14, 1935

The way we now think about Social Security is not really what FDR intended. These days, Social Security is assumed to be there to help fund your retirement, but back in the days of the New Deal, Social Security was simply a welfare program. Read FDR's quote again, "protection . . . against loss of a job and against poverty-ridden old age." Social Security was nothing more than a poverty entitlement disguised as a retirement program and then given a fluffy-sounding name.

But if that was really the case, then why hide it?

The New Dealers had a lot of reasons, but the most important was that welfare had a stigma to it. If something was looked at as a handout, the theory went, then some people would be too ashamed to take advantage of it. (I know that's hard to believe, but you have to remember that this was happening during a time when people still had shame; a time when relying on the government was still looked at as something you tried to avoid.)

SENATE APPROVES BENEFITS FOR ALL AGED 70 OR MORE

The Senate, in an unexpected move, voted today to pay Social Security benefits to all persons 70 or more years old, whether or not they have ever paid any Social Security taxes.

—*New York Times*, March 1966

Social Security insurance got around that stigma with a simple premise: If *everyone* is covered under the program, then no one individual can be singled out. Georgia senator Walter F. George explained it like this: "Social security is not a handout; it is not charity;

it is not relief . . . As an earned right, the individual is eligible to receive his benefit in dignity and self-respect."

But the word games didn't end there. To further get around the idea that we were simply redistributing wealth or underwriting the poor, the money taken from workers was called a "contribution" instead of a "tax." You were *contributing* to your own future! In fact, most people don't even realize that the "FICA" line they often see on their pay stubs for Social Security actually stands for the "Federal Insurance *Contributions* Act." Remember: *If you change the language, you change the debate. If you change the debate, you change the country.* FDR did exactly that.

It Could be Worse . . .

We could be France. The legal retirement age there is sixty, and only 50 percent of people work past fifty. Their pension system, not surprisingly, is in even worse shape than ours.

The other important thing to understand about the history of Social Security is that it wasn't created to be the best possible program—it was created to ensure that it would endure long enough to be expanded. Other countries had retirement programs that were subsidized by general revenues, but FDR knew that, over time, funding it that way would become so costly that it would always be a target to be cut. "Those taxes were never a problem of economics," Roosevelt said. "They are politics all the way through. We put those payroll contributions there so as to give the contributors a legal, moral, and political right to collect their pensions . . . With those taxes in there, no damn politician can ever scrap my Social Security program. Those taxes aren't a matter of economics, they're straight politics."

Smart. Very, very smart.

If people feel like they've paid into something, they'll be much more reluctant to cut it because they consider it a return on their investment. If, instead, it were a tax that went into a general fund and was redistributed through some random welfare program, people would be much more willing to cut it when times get tough.

The problem is that this is not at all the way Social Security really works. What you pay into the program over time may be taken into account in the benefit formula, but that money isn't held in a fund for you where it gathers interest until your retire. In fact, that most basic of problems was evident from the very beginning.

According to the Social Security Administration website, Ida May Fuller of Vermont was the first person in history to receive regular monthly benefits. "Miss Fuller, a Legal Secretary, retired in November 1939. She started collecting benefits in January 1940 at age 65 and lived to be 100 years old, dying in 1975."

So far, so good. But then the SSA explains the economics of her account. "Ida May Fuller worked for three years under the Social Security program. The accumu-

Mr. Ponzi Would Be So Proud

It's not exactly creative to refer to Social Security as a Ponzi scheme, especially when you consider that it was being called that just three years after it was created. The following excerpt is from an editorial that appeared in the *Reading Eagle* in August 1938:

No one will be told that the government does not take this money and keep it for the old age or for the needy day of the washwoman, but spends it as fast as it comes in for battleships, cooling systems, salaries, mileage of congressmen and all the miscellaneous expense of government.

Those whose money is thus in government custody cannot get excited about it because they know the government's ability to raise money is still better than, say, the Boston wizard of finance, Mr. Ponzi, who once tried a similar idea in a private way, and went to jail for it.

lated taxes on her salary during those three years was a total of $24.75. Her initial monthly check was $22.54. During her lifetime she collected a total of $22,888.92 in Social Security benefits."

Now, I'm not as smart as Paul Krugman, but doesn't this math set off some alarm bells? Weren't people looking around and saying to themselves: *Hey, wait a second, if someone lives past their life expectancy, or if people start to live longer in general, aren't we really going to be screwed?*

Ida May Fuller received over 92,000 percent more than she put in and yet people want you to believe that no one noticed or saw an immediate economic red flag. The truth, of course, is that *everyone* saw the warning signs—they just didn't care. The point wasn't to make Social Security infinitely solvent; the point was, as FDR said, to create "a structure . . . [that] is by no means complete."

It wasn't complete because the math didn't even come close to working. In 1935, less than 6 percent of the population was age sixty-five or older. But by 2008, that percentage had more than doubled to 12.8. And it's not going to get better any time soon. According to the Urban Institute, "The number of Americans ages 65 and older will more than double over the next 40 years, reaching 80 million in 2040. The number of adults ages 85 and older, the group most often needing help with basic personal care, will nearly quadruple between 2000 and 2040."

When Social Security first started paying out benefits, the regular retirement age of sixty-five also happened to be the average life expectancy. That's why it was called *insurance*. If you lived longer than you planned for, this safety-net insurance policy would be there to back you up. Even though the taxes paid were called "contributions," a more accurate term might actually have been "premiums." Americans made up one big insurance risk pool and the government knew that those who died early would end up paying for those who lived longer.

But things have changed. While everyone loves to complain about our health-care system, it's helped move the life expectancy back fifteen years! The problem is that the official retirement age has barely budged (it is scheduled to gradually rise to 67 by 2025). We have reached the point where many Americans now spend one-third of their adult lives in taxpayer-funded retirement. Why? Because FDR and his brain trust didn't index the retirement age for life expectancy, a simple idea that would've made the program far more economically viable. Again, that wasn't an oversight—it was intentional. As with ObamaCare and the "missing" public option, the idea wasn't to make the legislation perfect; it was to get something on the books that could later be tweaked and expanded.

It all adds up to a disastrous financial outlook. According to the Congressional Budget Office, the Social Security Trust Fund will pay out more in benefits than it receives in payroll taxes in 2010. As in *this year.* As in, much earlier than most "experts" had been projecting.

That, of course, doesn't make Social Security insolvent; what makes it insolvent is that the Trust Fund *has no money in it*. Remember, the fund is a joke, a vault filled with $2.5 trillion in worthless I.O.U.'s because Congress already spent the money. Starting this year, when the new funds coming in no longer cover our obligations, cash will have to come out of other areas. The Social Security surpluses that have subsidized the rest of the federal budget since 1983 will be replaced with chronic and expanding deficits that require annual taxpayer bailouts.

Experts say that by 2037, the "fund" will be completely exhausted—though if their track record is any indication, it will likely happen much sooner without major changes. It's going to be a tough problem to solve, and it'll be made a lot harder by the

ADOPT A RETIREE!

Brian Riedl of the Heritage Foundation sums up the demographic challenge facing America like this:

The first of 77 million baby boomers have already begun retiring. Combined with longer life spans, these retirements drive down the ratio of workers supporting each retiree. In 1960, five workers funded the benefits of each retiree. Today that ratio is 3:1, and by 2030 it will be just 2:1. To understand what a 2:1 worker-to-retiree ratio means, imagine a boy and a girl born today, in 2010. In 2030, they marry and start a family. This young couple will have to support themselves, their children—and the Social Security and Medicare benefits of their very own retiree. The costs will be enormous, especially given the steep rise in health care costs that plagues Medicare.

fact that anytime a politician brings up the idea of reform he immediately becomes a target. Even George W. Bush, a second-term president with not much to lose, couldn't make any progress with even a modest reform proposal. It seems those pesky elections that are always looming just around the corner are constantly weighing on politicians' minds.

The good news is that, while reform will require sacrifices all around, Social Security *can* be put onto a sustainable path.

The bad news is that, for all its problems, Social Security is actually the least of our entitlement problems.

Republicans Hate Entitlements!

Are you sure about that? When the Social Security Act was signed in 1935, it was done with the support of 81 Republicans in the House. When Medicare passed in 1965, 70 Republicans voted in favor. More recently, the Republican-controlled Congress passed Medicare Part D by a 54–44 vote. According to the *New York Times*, "Eleven Senate Democrats, most of them moderates, joined 42 Republicans and one independent in voting for the legislation; 9 Republicans and 35 Democrats voted against it."

Prosecution Exhibit B: Medicare and Medicaid

[Medicare] is a feasible and dignified way to free the aged from the fear of financial hardship.

—Lyndon B. Johnson, 1965

It seems as though each time that progressives are allowed to run wild for a few years they leave us with at least one program that's like a ticking time bomb for our budget. The New Deal gave us Social Security, Barack Obama has given us ObamaCare, and the Great Society left us with the biggest budget bomb of them all: Medicare.

Like Social Security three decades earlier, Medicare was originally pitched in 1965 as a way to provide for the elderly poor without calling it welfare. It was also pitched as being economically responsible. Neither claim turned out to be true.

Six months before the Medicare bill was passed, cost estimates were about $1.1 billion for the next two years and "several billion dollars spread over this decade." The day after the Medicare bill was signed into law, newspapers across the country printed a wire story calling it a "$6.5 billion bill." The long-term cost, the House Ways and Means Committee said, would be $12 billion by the year 1990—a figure that even took projected inflation into account.

The reality, as we now know, was far different:

U. S. ESTIMATES MEDICARE COST FAR TOO LOW, INSURERS FIGURE

What will the government's Medicare program cost? Nobody knows for sure, b[ut] a substantial segment of the insurance i[n]dustry believes government estimates m[ay] prove to be quite a bit short of the mar[k]

—*Chicago Tribune*, May 8, 1965

- The actual cost over the two years after it was signed was not $1.1 billion; it was $2.8 billion.
- The actual cost over the rest of the decade wasn't "several billion"; it was $13.2 billion.
- The actual cost in 1990 wasn't $12 billion; it was $98 billion.
- And the total size of the program today isn't the "6.5 billion" that was claimed at the time; it's $457 billion a year—ten times more, even after factoring for inflation.

DEFICIT OF TRU$T

It was obvious that we were in trouble when, just five years after it was signed into law, a story appeared in the *Chicago Tribune* saying, "An estimate that one part of the Medicare program for the next 25 years will cost 131 billion dollars more than originally forecast was reported today."

The trustees of Social Security and Medicare/Medicaid (yes, these programs actually have trustees!) summed up Medicare's overall financial health pretty nicely in their 2009 annual report:

Medicare's financial difficulties come sooner—and are much more severe—than those confronting Social Security. While both programs face demographic challenges, rapidly growing health care costs also affect Medicare . . . As a result, while Medicare's annual costs were 3.2 percent of Gross Domestic Product (GDP) in 2008, or about three quarters of Social Security's, they are projected to surpass Social Security expenditures in 2028 and reach 11.4 percent of GDP in 2083.

Let's do a little back-of-the-envelope math. The trustees say that Medicare will cost 11.4 percent of GDP in 2083, but what does that actually mean? Well, a program that ate up 11.4 percent of the 2009 GDP ($14.3 trillion) would've cost $1.63 trillion. That is quadruple Medicare's current $457 billion budget. In today's dollars, financing that additional $1.2 trillion in Medicare spending would cost every single American household an additional $10,000 a year in additional taxes.

Ouch.

Some people look at this whole debacle differently and make the claim that Medicare recipients are getting back just what they paid into it through their payroll taxes.

Those people are completely wrong.

DOUBLE OUCH

If we assume a growth rate in our economy of 3.5 percent for the next 74 years (yes, that is very optimistic), then in 2083 our GDP would be $186.1 trillion. Thus 11.4 percent of that means a total Medicare cost of $21.2 trillion per year.

Medicare has three main parts: Part A (hospital insurance), Part B (mostly outpatient services), and Part D (prescription drug coverage). (Don't worry, they didn't forget about Part C, which is called "Medicare Advantage," it's just a combination of Parts A and B.) The payroll tax funds *only* Medicare Part A—and even that is in deficit. Medicare Parts B and D are not "social insurance" in any way, shape, or form, and they are certainly not "earned" over time through any kind of payroll contributions. Instead they are funded by seniors, who pay for 25 percent of the program through premiums, and, of course, by all of us taxpayers who finance most of the other 75 percent through general tax revenues. That is virtually no different than any other run-of-the-mill welfare program.

Of the $31,406 that Washington will spend per household in 2010, $9,949 will be spent on Social Security and Medicare alone.

TEACHABLE MOMENT

Part D

Assuming you like the idea of Medicare, there is a good case to be made for it covering prescription drugs. After all, it makes little sense for a health insurance program to cover heart surgery but not the medication that could prevent the heart problem in the first place. On the other hand, the vast majority of seniors already had drug coverage through their Medigap insurance policies, and federalizing those benefits had long been considered unaffordable for taxpayers.

That all changed in 1998, when the Clinton surpluses immediately began burning a hole in Congress's pockets. Near the top of their wish list was, you guessed it, prescription drug entitlements. After Al Gore endorsed this idea during his 2000 presidential run, "compassionate conservative" George W. Bush quickly followed suit.

By 2003, President Bush knew he had to deliver on his promise before the next election. The original budget surpluses that had prompted the proposals in the first place were gone, but that didn't matter much to the senior-pandering president and Republican Congress. After initially insisting on market-based Medicare reforms in return for the new entitlement, President Bush eventually gave up on them and signed into law a new entitlement that was estimated to cost $400 billion over ten years—without the government setting aside a single nickel to pay for it.

States, which already struggle financially almost every year, are not spared the costs of these retiring baby boomers. Because Medicare does not cover long-term care, such as nursing homes, state-run Medicaid programs will end up absorbing these costs. Yet Washington's Medicaid budget covers only 57 percent of the program's actual cost, with states paying the other 43 percent.

RIPPED FROM THE HEADLINES

MEDICARE COSTS OVER ESTIMATES

Social Security officials conceded Tuesday that the cost of Medicare and Medicaid are running way over original estimates.

—*Hartford Courant*, July 2, 1969

Overall, the long-term costs of Social Security, Medicare, and Medicaid are unfathomable. The Congressional Budget Office (CBO) projects that even if the growth of health-care costs eventually slows, the federal cost of these three programs will grow from 9 percent of GDP in 2009 to 19 percent of GDP by 2050 and to 26 percent by 2082. For context, over the past fifty years, total federal spending on *everything* has averaged just 20 percent of GDP.

Half a Conservative?

To be fair, House Democrats wanted an $800 billion entitlement, so you can make the case that by Bush reducing it to $400 billion he fought really hard for fiscal responsibility. Then again, you could also make the case that CNN's Rick Sanchez is a talented broadcaster, proving that just because you can *make* a case doesn't mean it's an accurate one.

To finance this cost increase, the CBO estimates that the income tax brackets would have to rise to 25 percent for low-income families, 63 percent for the middle class, and 88 percent for upper-income individuals, small businesses, and corporations. Plus the 15.3 percent payroll tax, plus state and local taxes. A lot of people facing those kinds of tax rates (me included) may just decide to stay in bed and not bother working. Think that's a veiled threat? Go ahead, call my bluff.

TEACHABLE MOMENT

As federal Medicaid spending doubles to nearly 4 percent of GDP, state Medicaid costs will double as well. Washington will be pressured to bail out these growing state expenses, but that would merely substitute federal tax increases for state tax increases. The taxes will still come out of the same pockets—ours.

The Prosecution Rests

There is no trick. We can't promise to work less, raise pensions and erase deficits.

—French labor minister Eric Woerth, 2010

Back in 1995, a senior fellow with the American Enterprise Institute wrote a syndicated newspaper column titled "The Demographic Deficit." In it he made the case that while Social Security and the like are indeed a Ponzi scheme, there is, he said, "nothing inherently wrong with a Ponzi game." The problem, he explained, is that the game can't continue because the demographics don't work. More workers are retiring than are entering the workforce. But "reforms need not be draconian . . . What is needed is an artificial generation of young adults."

Where would this "artificial generation" come from? Robots, perhaps? Nope—*immigrants*. His proposal was to take in more immigrants over the next twenty-five

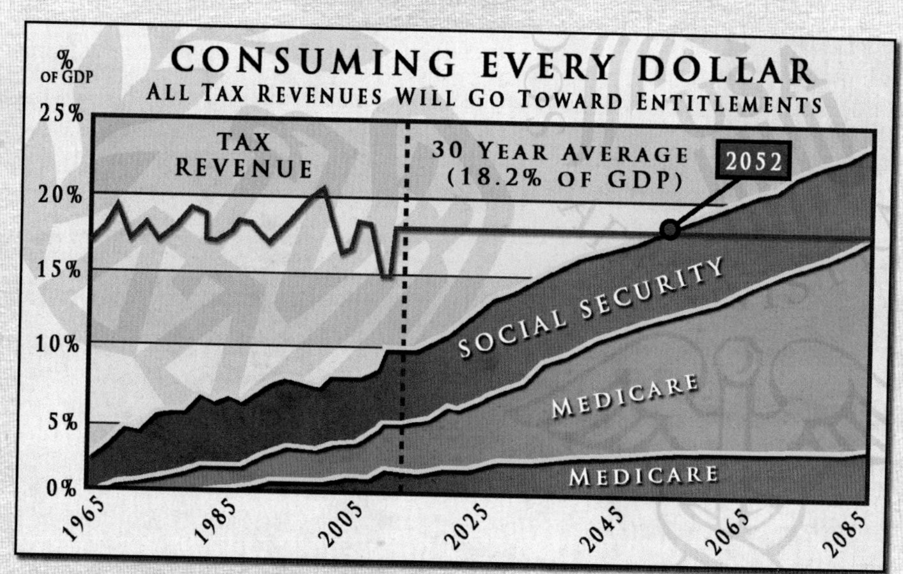

Source: Brian Riedl at the Heritage Foundation, based on projections from the CBO

Above: Without change, by 2052, every single dollar of federal tax revenue will be used to pay for Social Security, Medicare, and Medicaid benefits—we won't even be able to pay the interest on our debt.

years because they "typically arrive in America at about age 25, work hard and pay pension payroll taxes for 40 years before retiring."

Sounds awesome—I can see the proud look on our Founders' faces now: Centuries of sacrifice and bloodshed all so that we can mass-import immigrants to pay for our gluttony.

The only thing worse than being the originator of a Ponzi scheme is being the person who knows the truth about the scam and looks the other way. But solving our problems through immigration or other so-called painless fixes does just that: *It continues the con.* Immigrants can't pay our bills even if we somehow thought that was a good idea; the fiscal hole we've dug is way too large.

The only people who can pay our debts is . . . us.

Entitlement spending is one of those issues for which you'd be hard-pressed to find anyone, regardless of politics, who doesn't consider it a huge problem. Unfortunately, that's where the agreement usually ends. Some on the left think the easy fix is to jack up tax rates on the superrich (which would not provide nearly enough money),

and some on the right think we should slash benefits, jack up the retirement age, or both—policies that, let's be honest, would never get through Congress anytime soon.

If we continue to wait, then, one day soon, Americans will realize that we no longer have ultimate control over reforming our own programs. The investors who hold our debt and decide our future will be able to dictate the changes they want to see in order to keep interest rates at a sustainable level. As in Greece, people will one day wake up and realize that the benefits they thought were secure are now simply gone.

As the enormity of these problems begins to capture the attention of the public (which likely won't happen until people actually begin to personally feel the pain) we are going to hear all kinds of solutions from politicians and experts. Most of them, like the various immigration proposals, will be minor reforms that merely further a particular agenda.

You'll know the real solution when you hear it, because it is going to sound awful. Pain will be inflicted on a tremendous number of people, most of whom did nothing to deserve it. There's no way around that, but you're going to be told that there is, that there's a magic bullet of quick and painless answers out there. In reality, these solutions will do nothing more than push the problems off to future generations. We cannot let that happen. That would be as much a moral catastrophe as it would be a financial one. It's incumbent upon us to solve it.

Remember, during the American Revolution and Civil War, Americans sacrificed their lives, fortunes, and sacred honor for something they desperately wanted.

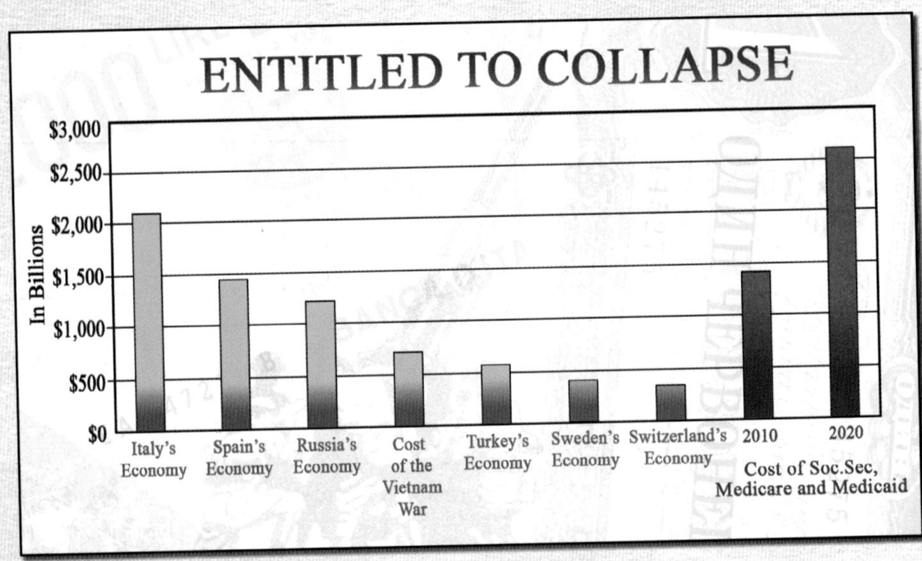

STRAWMAN BECK!

Don't think that anyone is really out there trying to make the case that our entitlements are completely fine and that no hard work is needed? Well, check out this email from liberal activist group MoveOn.org, sent in July 2010:

Dear MoveOn member,

Social Security is under attack and we need to fight back against the lies.

Have you heard that Social Security is going bankrupt? Driving up the deficit? In crisis?

Well none of that is true. These are all myths that opponents of Social Security have been spreading to scare people into accepting benefit cuts this fall. But the myths are taking hold—so we have to fight back with the facts.

Myth #1: Social Security is going broke.

Reality: There is no Social Security crisis. By 2023, Social Security will have a $4.6 trillion surplus (yes, trillion with a 'T'). It can pay out all scheduled benefits for the next quarter-century with no changes whatsoever. After 2037, it'll still be able to pay out 75% of scheduled benefits—and again, that's without any changes. The program started preparing for the Baby Boomers' retirement decades ago. Anyone who insists Social Security is broke probably wants to break it themselves.

This is exactly the kind of thinking that's brought us to this point. *Everything's fine, go back to sleep.* How is a program that, by MoveOn's own set of facts, is sustainable for ony the next twenty-five years (notice they say "quarter-century" to make it sound more impressive) without change not in need of reform?

Another "myth" it cites: "The Social Security Trust Fund has been raided and is full of IOUs." And what is MoveOn's so-called reality? "Not even close to true," it writes, "The Social Security Trust Fund isn't full of IOUs, it's full of U.S. Treasury Bonds."

I think someone needs to explain to MoveOn that a bond *is* an I.O.U.: You give someone cash and they give you a piece of paper called a bond promising to pay you back in the future. MoveOn also fails to mention the key point that makes all of this so much worse than a typical I.O.U. scenario: The government has issued these bonds *to itself*.

They knew that true liberty cannot be handed to you or bought from others; it can only be earned.

But now our politicians seem to believe the opposite. They are unwilling to sacrifice their own lives or fortunes, but they are more than happy to sacrifice the lives and fortunes of their children and grandchildren. It goes without saying, but anyone willing to do that has long since sacrificed their sacred honor.

It's time to say enough is enough. It's time to stop allowing our names to be tarnished for eternity by a group of people who don't even seem to believe in the very principles that so many before them gave everything they had for.

It's time for a plan.

FRIEZES
8'
12 DRUMS
37'

PART THREE

THE PLAN

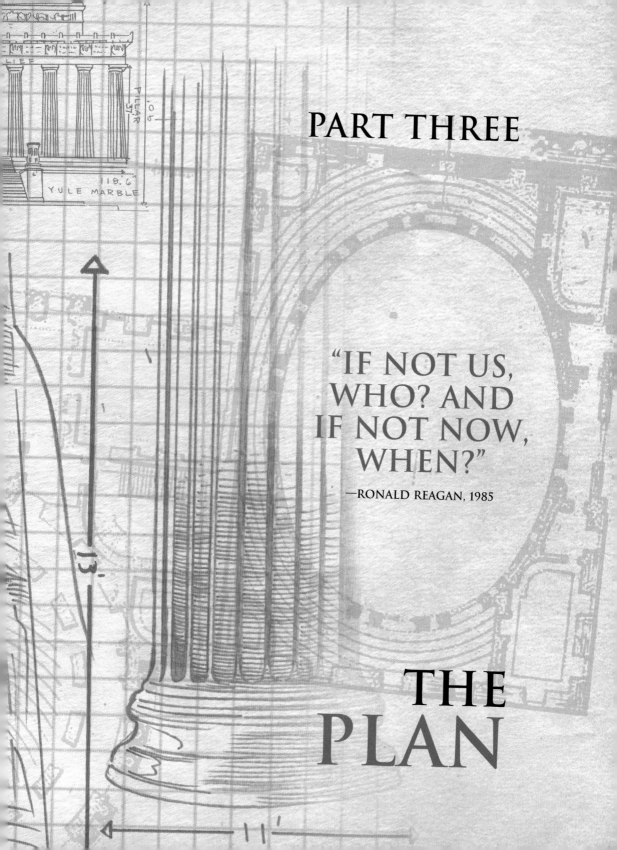

"IF NOT US, WHO? AND IF NOT NOW, WHEN?"

—RONALD REAGAN, 1985

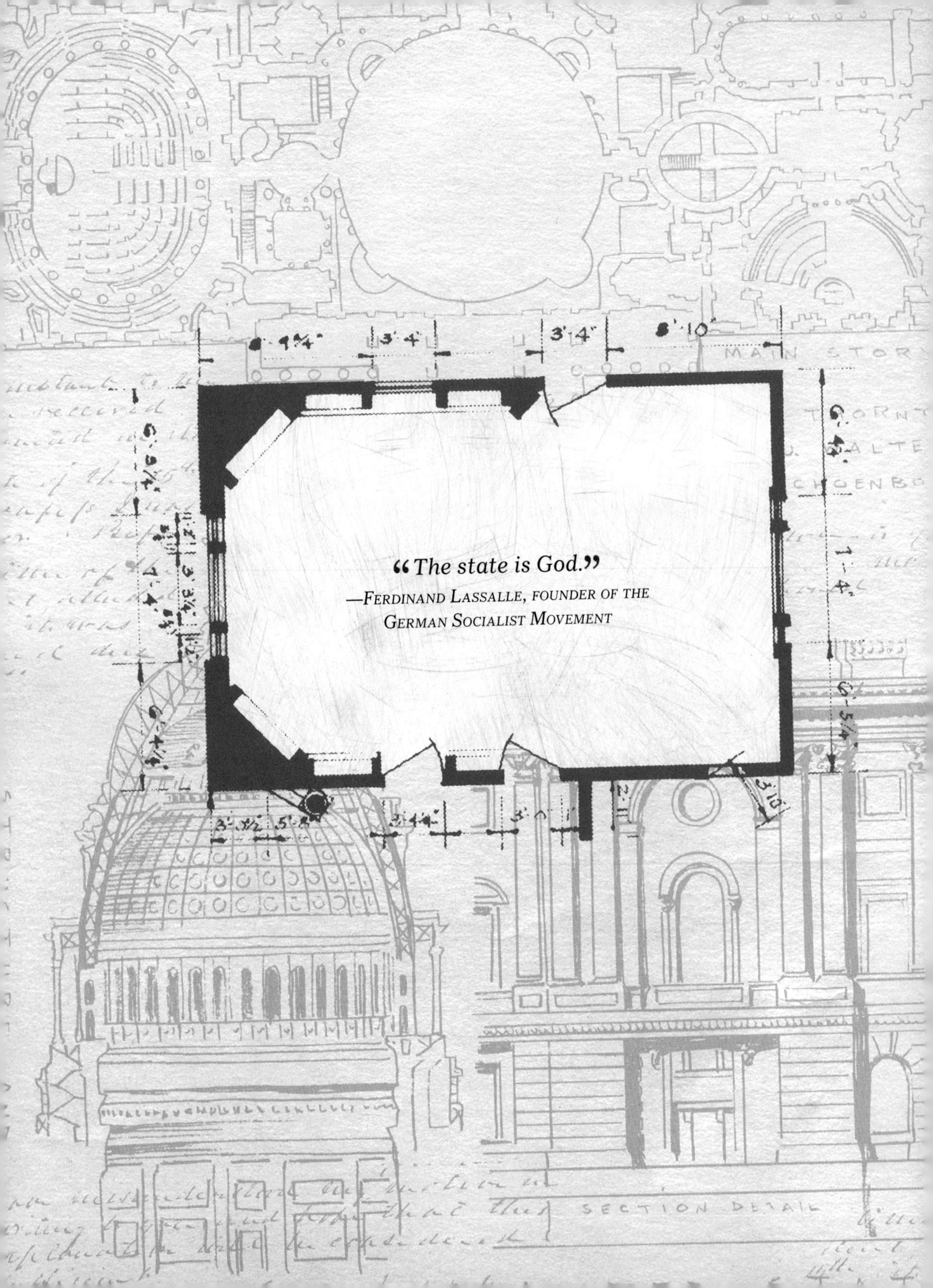

“The state is God.”

—Ferdinand Lassalle, founder of the German Socialist Movement

CHAPTER 13.

Step One: The Rights of Man or Men?

You don't fight fire with fire; you fight it with water. And you don't fight bad math with more math; you fight it with logic.

It might seem odd to start off this plan with a focus on individual rights instead of a recipe for Medicare reform or a list of specific programs that can be cut—but it's time this debate is reframed from one about numbers and esoteric policy decisions to one about individual rights and freedom.

If the ultimate goal of every law that a government creates and every dollar that it spends is to help people pursue happiness, then shouldn't our focus be on that—*what makes us happy*—instead of endlessly tweaking reimbursement levels and retirement ages?

The truth is that there is no way a $13 trillion debt will ever be paid off through budget surpluses. While it would be great to one day throw a party to celebrate the elimination of our national debt like Andrew Jackson did, that's just no longer a reality. We are not going to be running a trillion-dollar surplus anytime soon—and we're certainly not going to run thirteen straight years of them. Our real goal should be to balance the budget permanently and create an environment that will spur another era of economic growth. Over time, the size of our economy will make the size of our debt seem reasonable in comparison.

When all is said and done and all of the numbers have been crunched, the single best

Putting It All into Perspective

"I'm convinced that today the majority of Americans want what those first Americans wanted: a better life for themselves and their children; a minimum of government authority. Very simply, they want to be left alone in peace and safety to take care of the family by earning an honest dollar and putting away some savings. This may not sound too exciting, but there is something magnificent about it. On the farm, on the street corner, in the factory and in the kitchen, millions of us ask nothing more, but certainly nothing less, than to live our own lives according to our values—at peace with ourselves, our neighbors and the world."

—RONALD REAGAN, 1976

thing that could happen to America is for us to stop thinking like a staid, old blue-chip company and instead start thinking like a hungry start-up. The world has changed and we need to adapt by creating a business environment that attracts entrepreneurs and investors to this country in droves. That means competitive tax rates, easier compliance, less red tape, and the elimination of the bureaucracy that makes so many would-be entrepreneurs decide to give up, but it also means a relentless, nearly obsessive pursuit to restore individual rights to their proper place in our society.

That, of course, is easier said than done. Progressives have had a century to tangle us up in regulations, massively complex tax laws, and crushing federal benefits that make any small business owner think twice about their career choice. They've evolved original intent, tarnished the reputations of our Founders, and successfully fooled millions of Americans into making a false choice between "the greater good" and their own good. It won't be easy to unwind ourselves from all of that, but it *can* be done.

That brings me back to why I am starting with a focus on individual rights. The title of this book, *Broke*, is not simply a reference to our financial situation; it's a comment on our entire society. Our budget mess is simply a side effect of the mess we've made out of our political system and our broken set of values and principles. To fix ourselves financially we first have to fix *ourselves*—and that means a return to the only plan that really matters: the one laid out in our Constitution.

Think about it as though you're managing the construction of a building. Architects and engineers have spent a long time crafting the blueprints. Every measurement, angle, and spec is perfect. If you follow their plan, the building will be strong and lasting.

Instead, you deviate from it. You guesstimate some measurements, you use whatever materials are around, and you build according to the advice of whoever decides to stop by that day. Do you think the building will endure?

From the outside, your structure would probably look like a monstrosity. Fixing it would seem impossible—but it's not. You have the original blueprints. Sure, it

POLICIES OF THE PAST

Barack Obama and others can complain all they want about how the "policies of the past" brought us to this point—but that's a pretty shortsighted view. The real policies of the past have all been progressive: bigger government; less individual freedom; more centralized power. If Obama wants to solve our nation's troubles he should focus more on the original "policies of the past"—the ones written into the Constitution.

would take years of hard work—but the building can eventually be restored to its original design.

Likewise, our task for restoring America is daunting, but the architects left us a blueprint in the form of a constitution. We just have to be willing to follow it.

As I met with expert after expert to talk about this section of the book, I was struck by how many of the good ideas that came up can be found right in the Constitution itself. Over time, I came to realize that progressives have so successfully changed and confused the meaning of what our Founders wanted that most people don't even know what the truth is anymore. That is a recipe for disaster for any country, and we are seeing the consequences of it now.

The policy details behind the changes we need can and should be worked out by experts who are guided and informed by only two things: common sense and the Constitution. That's why, while others will come at these problems from the bottom up with detailed policy papers and briefing books, I am coming at them from the top down. We need a long-term plan to get Americans back to thinking about this country in the way our Framers intended it, a plan to restore individual rights, equality of opportunity, and faith to their rightful places.

Only once we successfully change the debate from one about rich vs. poor and Republicans vs. Democrats to one about freedom vs. serfdom and God vs. government will we also have a real chance to change our future.

Defining Rights

". . . that all men are created equal, that they are endowed by their Creator with certain unalienable Rights, that among these are Life, Liberty and the pursuit of Happiness."

We all know that famous phrase from the Declaration of Independence, but it's funny how, over the years, people have lost sight of four important things about it:

1. We are "created" equal. We don't live as equals or die as equals; we are only created that way.
2. We have the right to "pursue" happiness, not a guarantee of it;
3. Our rights are "unalienable," which means they cannot be taken or given away by any man or government.
4. Only five words were capitalized: Creator, Rights, Life, Liberty, and Happiness. I don't believe that was an accident—the Founders were

ensuring that everyone understood that those words deserved a common level of respect. Our rights come from our Creator, and those Rights provide us with access to Life and Liberty and the ability to pursue Happiness.

Some argue that the Declaration itself is not a part of the Constitution. While it may be true that it was not assigned an actual article number, our Framers intended for the words of the Declaration to be incorporated into the law of the land. In 1794, Samuel Adams said, "Before the formation of this Constitution it had been affirmed as a self evident truth, in the declaration of independence, very deliberately made by the Representatives of the United States of America in Congress assembled that 'all men are created equal, and are endowed by their Creator with certain unalienable rights.' This declaration of independence was received and ratified by all the States in the Union and has never been disannulled."

Declaring Our Spirit

"While [the Declaration] may not have the force of organic law, or be made the basis of judicial decision as to the limits of right and duty, and while in all cases reference must be had to the organic law of the nation for such limits, yet the latter is but the body and the letter of which the former is the thought and the spirit, and it is always safe to read the letter of the Constitution in the spirit of the Declaration of Independence."

—U.S. Supreme Court, ruling in Cotting v. Godard (1901)

Our Founders' own experiences with England made them understand an important truth about human nature that formed the basis for the American experiment: The greatest violator of individual rights in the history of the world is the government. The uniqueness of the constitution they developed was in the fact it did everything in its power to help assure that America would not suffer the same fate.

But we have anyway.

Ask the average person on the street: What are your individual rights? You'll get a lot of different answers, but I sincerely doubt you'll get the right one. Your individual right is the right to live your life in whatever way you choose, so long as it does not infringe on the rights of others to do the same. Everything else that the average person will likely mention is only a consequence of the right to live life free from interference.

Once you start to look at rights in this way, your entire perspective changes. You can no longer look at everything that government does and propose tweaks or reforms, because that forces you to concede that those things are within the government's purview to begin with. Instead you have to start with a blank piece of paper and ask yourself, *What are the things that governments should do according to the definition of individual liberty as outlined by our Founders?*

TEACHABLE MOMENT

American notions of rights stand in contrast to those that flowed from the French Revolution, which ignored God and declared that the rights of men were derived from government. When you remove God from the rights equation, tyranny naturally follows. Individual rights turn into collective rights. Instead of the government being subservient to man, man becomes a slave to government. That's one reason why the American Revolution ended with the freest country on earth, while the French Revolution ended in guillotines.

To me, the list is pretty short: military; judiciary; patent and copyright protection and international relations. That's about it.

Admittedly there is no perfect answer; you may disagree with some of the things on my list and you may have others to add. But the point is that the proper role of government encompasses fewer than ten items—not ten thousand.

When you apply that standard to what America has become today, you are left with some pretty troubling questions: What is the proper role of government in providing health care, welfare, affordable housing, or retirement security? What is its role in limiting smoking, posting calorie counts, or demanding seat belts be worn? Should the government be able to deny a prescription drug to sufferers of a disease because it is not "FDA approved"? Should they run public schools and force all people in a geographic area to pay for them via property taxes? Should they even collect property taxes in the first place? After all, who has given the government authority to regulate and tax private land transactions?

The answers, if you didn't guess, are all *no*. And while the questions could go on and on, the sad truth is that none of them is being asked. Instead we debate how entitlements can cover more and more people, how we can find new ways to make sure people are not allowed to harm themselves, and, if we're really lucky, how we can hold property taxes steady for a year.

That must change, and so must our entire notion of what "freedom" and "compassion" really are. In today's society, our Founders would be considered radicals. Their ideas and interpretation of the very Constitution they wrote would now seem, at best, insane and, at worst, borderline seditious. But that is the kind of radical thinking required to spit ourselves out of the perpetual motion machine and throw ourselves off from a course that leads to an inevitable end, one that everyone sees coming yet no one seems willing to do anything about.

Living Constitution, Dead Republic

Our Founders believed that individuals control the government, not the other way around. As French theorist Frédéric Bastiat wrote, "Life, liberty, and property do not exist because men have made laws. On the contrary, it was the fact that life, liberty, and property existed beforehand that caused men to make laws [to protect themselves] in the first place."

But the best evidence of all showing how our Founders viewed individual rights is the Constitution itself. At the time of its drafting, most of the Founders did not want to include a Bill of Rights. Why? Because to them it was obvious that the government should not infringe on individual rights, since the Constitution did not grant that power to them. Including a Bill of Rights, they believed, would actually give more weight to the view that any rights not specifically listed would be fair game for infringement. That was obviously not their intent. As Ayn Rand wrote:

> *The government was set to protect man from criminals—and the Constitution was written to protect man from the government. The Bill of Rights was not directed against private citizens, but against the government—as an explicit declaration that individual rights supersede any public or social power.*

That presents a pretty difficult problem for progressives. If people believe that the individual is supreme and that their rights supersede all others, and, worse of all, that those truths are hardwired into the fabric of the Constitution, then how can you introduce new group rights, such as entitlements?

The answer, it turned out, was to slowly evolve the meaning of the Constitution by arguing that the Founders simply could not have fathomed what this country would eventually grow into. In 1985, Supreme Court justice William Brennan, Jr., expressed this view when he said, "For the genius of the Constitution rests not in any static meaning it might have had in a world that is dead and gone, but in the adaptability of its great principles to cope with current problems and current needs."

Another Supreme Court justice, Oliver Wendell Holmes, went even further by doubting the fundamental belief that man was ever even endowed with unalienable rights. "All my life," he wrote, "I have sneered at the natural rights of man."

This is an extraordinarily dangerous argument because, if successful, it pretty much invalidates the actual words written in the Constitution. Once those words are no longer sacred, then the role of government no longer has to be limited. That leads right into the misguided idea that entitlement programs and a growing welfare state would somehow have been permissible to our Founders,

NEW DEAL FORCING REASSESSMENT OF U.S. CONSTITUTION AS LIVING FORCE

Rooseveltian Program Hinges on Flexibility of This Basic Code in American Social Structure

—*Christian Science Monitor*, September 19

which is completely untrue. As Thomas Jefferson once wrote, "If we can prevent the government from wasting the labors of the people, under the pretense of taking care of them, they must become happy."

In promoting entitlements, progressives have relied on the same two tactics that they always do: word games and emotions. A "living" Constitution implies that the alternative would be a "dead" Constitution, and who wants that?

As with most progressive arguments, it's a false choice. The opposite of a living Constitution isn't a dead one—it's an eternal one. If you want to join in the word games, try this: A "living Constitution" implies that it will someday die; an "eternal Constitution" will be around forever.

Judge, Jury, and Executioner

Preying on emotion is the other tactic that is often used to pull us away from the Constitution. For example, which argument do you think is easier to make to the public: that our courts should step in to protect the weakest and least fortunate among us, or that our courts should turn their heads and ignore poverty and suffering?

It's common for people to petition the courts to help with some societal issue, and judges are often tempted to intervene because it's difficult to watch suffering that could so easily be avoided. But the Founders never intended for problems to be solved by courts—they intended for them to be solved by people themselves, or, in extreme cases, by direct representatives of the people. If enough people believed that, for instance, all children should receive $50,000 from the government on their sixth birthday, then that would be enacted through legislation that's crafted by elected representatives who are accountable to voters for their actions. An appeal directly to the courts to demand that the government take care of these children should fall on deaf ears.

"[Progressives] saw in constitutional interpretation the opportunity to rewrite a Constitution that showed at every turn the influence of John Locke and James Madison into a different Constitution, which reflected the wisdom of the leading intellectual reformers of their own time," writes University of Chicago Law School professor Richard Epstein. "They consciously used their intellectual powers to rewrite, not understand, key provisions of the Constitution."

Think about how that plays out in real life. If one of our foundational documents can be changed according to the "wisdom of the . . . reformers of [our] own time," then we no longer have a foundation. The Constitution is not meant to sway in the wind as new fads come and go; it's meant to be steady as rock. In 1976, Supreme Court justice William Rehnquist gave a speech in which he addressed this head-on:

> *It is always time consuming, frequently difficult, and not infrequently impossible to run successfully the legislative gauntlet and have enacted some facet of one's own deeply felt value judgments. It is even more difficult for either a single individual or indeed for a large group of individuals to succeed in having such a value judgment embodied in the Constitution. All of these burdens and difficulties are entirely consistent with the notion of a democratic society. It should not be easy for any one individual or group of individuals to impose by law their value judgments upon fellow citizens who may disagree with those judgments. Indeed, it should not be easier just because the individual in question is a judge.*

Believe it or not, our Founders anticipated that, from time to time, their document might need modification to keep up with the times. That's exactly why they included this neat thing called the amendment process. They spelled out exactly how the Constitution could be updated, *right in the Constitution itself*. They made the process difficult, but not impossible—an appropriate bar to meet when you're looking to permanently amend the supreme law of the land.

But for progressives, that is a huge problem. They know that the vast majority of Americans would reject their vision if they were actually allowed a vote on it. We are still a center-right country, after all. That's why a living Constitution is so appealing—it allows them to circumvent pesky things like votes and bills and instead appeal right to the judiciary. Finding a single activist judge is a heck of a lot easier than getting three-fourths of the states to approve a constitutional amendment.

Supreme Logic

"[T]he living Constitution is genuinely corrosive of the fundamental values of our democratic society."

—William Rehnquist

The Fifth Freedom: Logic

In the early 1980s, two communists, Alexander Natta, a leader of the Italian Communist Party, and Mikhail Gorbachev, sat down to talk. Gorbachev's staff kept notes of the conversation. Natta told Gorbachev that, in the West, the main result of the growing welfare state was that "a bureaucratic apparatus, which serves itself, has swelled." He went on to note that the welfare state bureaucracy functioned in a way so as to "protect its own interests and to forget about the citizens' interests."

He was right, of course, and we've seen that observation play out in real life over the last three decades. More and more citizens petition for redress and, more and more, the government acts only to accumulate more power and control. Tea parties and town hall meetings are no longer viewed by most politicians as being serious forums for the exchange of ideas. They are nuisances organized by a vocal minority.

Of course, the welfare state didn't come out of the blue; it was born out of progressive efforts to redefine what "rights" individuals really possess. Without an expanding view of rights, from man to *men*, we'd never have a need to expand government to the extent we have. After all, if the only role of government is to protect us from criminals or from a violent infringement of our rights, then why would we need an ever-expanding, centralized bureaucracy?

IS THIS TOO VAGUE?

"The laws of nature are the laws of God, whose authority can be superseded by no power on earth."

—George Mason

For progressives, the welfare state is ultimately not about meeting the immediate needs of the destitute; it's about ensuring that citizens serve the interest of the state instead of the other way around. Their objective is to create mass dependence on the government in exchange for individual liberty—and, don't look now, but they are succeeding! Not only are autopilot entitlements growing out of control, but we also now have more people dependent on the government than people paying taxes to support it.

As with most of the things destroying America, this shift can easily be traced back in history. In 1941, Franklin Roosevelt gave a speech called "The Four Freedoms." In addition to talking about fundamental ideas like freedom of speech and religion, FDR included two new progressive ideas: "freedom from want" and "freedom from fear."

This is a perfect example of the word games that are so crucial to success for progressives. Take "freedom from want"—who doesn't long for that? You picture yourself lying on a lounge chair by the pool, being fanned by fig leaves with your every desire fulfilled by a personal staff. But then you think about it a little longer: If there's universal freedom from want, then what is the staff doing there? Do they really *want* to wait on me? Who cleans the pool, washes the towels, and sweeps the deck? Who built my lounge chair or picked the fig leaves? You see where I'm going—freedom from want, like a "living Constitution," is a false premise, a term perfectly constructed for a public relations campaign.

Ayn Rand once pointed out another great way to distinguish whether a right is in accordance with the Constitution: simply ask the question "at whose expense?" after the right is proposed. For example, try asking that question after someone proposes a universal right to a college education. *At whose expense?* The same thing applies

SUPERSAVER COMBO PACK!

Here's an example that combines everything we've talked about: activist judges, appeals to emotion, promotion of a living Constitution, and freedom from want.

In a case that eventually went to the Supreme Court, Circuit Judge Joseph Hatchett ruled on a lawsuit against a local welfare office that had placed a child in an abusive foster home. In his opinion, Hatchett equated a child placed in a foster home to a prisoner placed in a cell, writing:

> *[The Fourteenth Amendment] must draw its meaning from the evolving standards of decency that mark the progress of a maturing society. With contemporary society's outrage at the exposure of defenseless children to gross mistreatment and abuse, it is time that the law give to these defenseless children at least the same protection afforded adults who are imprisoned as a result of their own misdeeds.*

Aside from this being a tragedy, it's also a perfect example of progressivism at work from the bench. Who here wants a child to be abused in a foster home—raise your hand. No takers? Okay, that means we're all on the same page so far. Now the question becomes, how do you best ensure that doesn't happen, and who gets punished for the fact that it did? On the first question, the best way to stop something from happening is to pass a law with a strict penalty. So far, so good—child abuse is definitely against the law, and the penalties are severe. On the second question, assuming there is no negligence or other laws broken, the punishment should apply to the *actual criminal*. That is where this ruling goes off the rails.

In holding the state responsible, the judge is inferring that the state has a responsibility to protect people from each other. As Chief Justice Rehnquist wrote, that's simply not the case. The Fourteenth Amendment was intended to "to protect the people from the state, not to ensure that the state protected them from each other. [It provided] no affirmative right to governmental aid, even where such aid may be necessary to secure life, liberty, or property interests of which the government itself may not deprive the individual."

In 1968, while testifying about crime, Ronald Reagan captured the essence of this argument. "We must reject the idea that every time a law's broken, society is guilty rather than the lawbreaker. It is time to restore the American precept that each individual is accountable for his actions."

---

to other rights that FDR proposed in his "Second Bill of Rights," such as the right to food, clothing, and recreation. *At whose expense are those things provided?*

Asking that same question about individual rights yields an entirely different answer. Your right to life and liberty does not come at the expense (financial or otherwise) of anyone else.

If you still think you'd like to experience "freedom from want" then consider that, as German economist and university professor Wilhelm Röpke wrote in *A Humane Economy*, there is one group of people who enjoys it every day: prisoners. Think about it. Food? Covered. Shelter? Taken care of. Medical treatment? Totally free. Money? Not necessary.

Prisoners have all of their material needs met, but are they really "free"? Of course not. Are they really happy? Doubtful. Röpke explained:

> *Freedom from want means no more than the absence of something disagreeable, rather like freedom from pain or whatever else may occur to us. How can this be put on par with genuine "freedom" as one of the supreme moral concepts, the opposite of compulsion by others, as it is meant in the phrases freedom of person, freedom of opinion, and other rights of liberty which we cannot conceive of truly ethical behavior and the acceptance of duties?*

"Freedom from want" doesn't mean happiness and contentment, which is what most people think of; it means exactly the opposite. When your wants (which are impossible to eliminate unless you're dead) are provided by others, then you are, by default, reliant on those others. If the government gives you free food every month then you inevitably become dependent upon it for that food. That's not freedom at all: It's serfdom.

Samuel Adams saw this very early on as a potential danger. "The Utopian schemes of leveling [redistribution of wealth] and the community goods [state ownership of property]," he wrote, "are as visionary and impractical as those which vest all property in the Crown. [These ideas] are arbitrary, despotic, and, in our government, unconstitutional. Now, what property can the colonists be conceived to have, if their money may be granted away to others, without their consent?"

It's a great question—if something you own can be taken away without your consent, do you really own anything at all?

In 2005, Adams's fear reached a tipping point as the Supreme Court ruled against the property rights of an individual in favor of the desires of a group. The case was *Kelo v. New London* and it revolved around whether eminent domain could be used to take private land and give it to another private entity, in this case a developer. By a 5–4 margin, the court ruled it could and Susette Kelo involuntarily lost her land and her little pink house.

The ends in this case don't justify the means. If the developer had put up a mall that was now paying millions in taxes, it still would have been

How much of a focus are group rights now as opposed to individual rights? The American Civil Liberties Union's website lists five "Key Issues." Among them are: Racial Justice, Prisoners' Rights, and Immigrant's Rights (the others being National Security and Drug Reform).

wrong to trump Kelo's rights for group gain. But in this case, the ends are at least worth considering. Pfizer, which was to be the anchor of the new development, ended up merging and closing their existing facility adjacent to the new land. As of now, the entire parcel sits vacant and useless, a sorry testament to the danger of putting groups ahead of individuals.

Positive Rights, No Responsibility

Those who push so-called positive rights are really pushing the idea that people have a right to things like health care, welfare, affordable housing, etc. In other words, the things that government attempts to provide through entitlement programs.

The reason they use the term "positive rights" is that it implies the opposite is "negative." What they don't tell you is that negative rights are also commonly known by another name: *natural rights.* Those are the unalienable rights that come directly from the Creator. Positive rights, on the other hand, don't come from your Creator; they come from man and, consequently, can be taken away by man.

Take government-mandated health care, for example. That is clearly a positive right because it immediately fails the "Ayn Rand test" (i.e., *At whose expense?*). If someone receives a medical test or prescription drug for free, or at a significantly discounted rate, then someone else is subsidizing that. And if someone is being provided a service at a regulated rate, then someone else is *providing* that service at a rate they were not able to freely control.

But, there's another big difference between positive and natural rights: responsibilities. Positive rights don't demand any. Natural rights, like the right to life, for example, imply that we all have a duty upon us to not take that right away from someone else. But where is the responsibility with positive rights like universal health care or welfare payments? Your responsibility is simply to ensure that you meet the government's eligibility guidelines.

THE RIGHT TO HEALTH CARE, REVISITED

One way to debate those who argue that we have a duty to provide social programs such as health care for the poor is to turn the entire argument around on them. What is a right to health care? Is it to go to a preselected doctor and pay a prearranged price for the service you need, assuming that the service has been preapproved by some bureaucrat? Or, is a true right to health care that all citizens are free to negotiate their own insurance contracts outside the constraints of their workplace or state; that people can choose their own doctor, their own tests and drugs, and shop around for those services? Is a legitimate, constitutional right to health care a monstrous government agency regulating and monitoring everything people do, or is it the exact opposite of that?

Positive rights, by their very nature, infringe on liberty. To give something of value to someone (e.g., free health care), you must take something (in this case, wealth) from others. Entitlements don't just mandate receiving; they also mandate giving. How is a doctor free to pursue his or her life and career if the government has regulated virtually every aspect of the industry, including the fees they can charge?

From God to Man

"In the supposed state of nature, all men are equally bound by the laws . . . of the Creator: They are imprinted by the finger of God on the heart of man."

—SAMUEL ADAMS, 1794

The Economics of Freedom

Progressives want to divide our world into political rights and economic rights. They say they support freedom of speech, yet they seem to be fine with eliminating our economic freedom. But the two concepts are intertwined. You cannot make people dependent on you financially and still pretend that they are free to do as they choose.

For example, if the U.S. government were a primary investor in my radio program, don't you think there might be a conflict of interest? How could I feel free to criticize the president when he is essentially paying my salary? The same concept applies in everyday life. As more people become reliant on the government for their food, shelter, or income, there are fewer people left who feel they can speak out freely against them. Nobel Prize–winning economist Milton Friedman summed up this whole idea much better than I ever could:

> *Viewed as a means to the end of political freedom, economic arrangements are important because of their effect on the concentration or dispersion of power. The kind of economic organization that provides economic freedom directly, namely, competitive capitalism, also promotes political freedom because it separates economic power from political power and in this way enables the one to offset the other. Historical evidence speaks with a single voice on the relation between political freedom and a free market. I know of no example in time or place of a society that has been marked by a large measure of political freedom, and that has not also used something comparable to a free market to organize the bulk of economic activity.*

In other words, there is no real political freedom without economic freedom. The two go hand in hand. If we are not free to engage in the profession we want, to spend as we want, to invest as we want, then in what sense can we really be considered free?

Put Your Money Where Your Mouth Is

Progressives pushing positive rights usually hide behind a philanthropic smoke screen. They do it "for the children" or to "help the least fortunate" or to "save the poor." But the truth is that their goals have little to do with helping people and everything to do with seizing power.

Sound like a strong condemnation? Consider this: Traditional Americans are *much* more generous with charities than self-described progressives. In his book *Who Really Cares?,* former Syracuse University professor and current president of the American Enterprise Institute Arthur Brooks found that traditional/religious conservatives were by 25 percentage points more likely than progressives to donate money to help the poor and by 23 percentage points more likely to volunteer their time for the same. The annual gap in giving was large: $2,210 for traditionalists, $642 for progressives.

During the height of the Great Depression, FDR spoke frequently of the need for people to be generous to help their fellow man. But a look at his tax returns reveals that he was far more interested in being generous with other people's money. In 1935, for example, he made more than $75,000 (about $1.2 million in today's dollars), and yet he donated just 2.5 percent of his income to charity.

A New Standard

The worth of every expense and budget item, whether I address it in this book head-on or leave to others to debate, has to be measured against the principle of individual rights. Is Social Security really an individual right, or does it, in fact, *infringe* on our rights by involuntarily sequestering a worker's money? Is a federal Department of Education really part of the proper role of government, or is its involvement in education exactly what is causing failing schools and deteriorating local budgets?

There are a lot of questions that need to be addressed—and many people are not going to like the answers. But I am also a realist. I understand that we cannot go from where we are to where we need to be overnight, or maybe even within our lifetimes. The transition to a country of group rights and entitlements took a hundred years; it may take that long to shift back.

In spite of my belief that individual rights have to be the standard we live by, I am not calling for the immediate elimination of welfare, Medicare, Social Security, or a host of other programs. I know that's not realistic and wouldn't positively contribute to the debate we all need to have. But that doesn't mean that I'm going to shred my values. I am convinced that this issue has a right and wrong answer and that choosing incorrectly has eternal consequences. To paraphrase Thomas Jefferson, in matters of style I will swim with the tide and be happy to compromise, but in matters of principle, I will stand like a rock.

Educate Yourself

Throughout this section of the book I am going to provide you with some places you can go to educate yourself further on each topic. Visit *glennbeck.com/broke* for easy access to the links and sources included below.

- Ayn Rand wrote often about individual rights. This page, from the Ayn Rand Center, will link you to several of her articles, the most important of which is titled "Man's Rights":
  http://www.aynrand.org/site/PageServer?pagename=arc_ayn_rand_writings

- David Kelley, *A Life of One's Own: Individual Rights and the Welfare State* (free preview):
  http://books.google.com/books?id=tgReibe9U_kC

- Milton Friedman, *Why Government Is the Problem* (free):
  http://books.google.com/books?id=vIPVuMtTV6cC

- Ludwig von Mises, *Omnipotent Government* (free preview):
  http://books.google.com/books?id=QoOMaqfdpT4C

- William Rehnquist, *The Notion of a Living Constitution*, from a 1976 speech at the University of Texas School of Law (free):
  http://www.law.harvard.edu/students/orgs/jlpp/Vol29_No2_Rehnquist.pdf

- Wilhelm Röpke, *A Humane Economy* (free):
  http://mises.org/books/Humane_Economy_Ropke.pdf

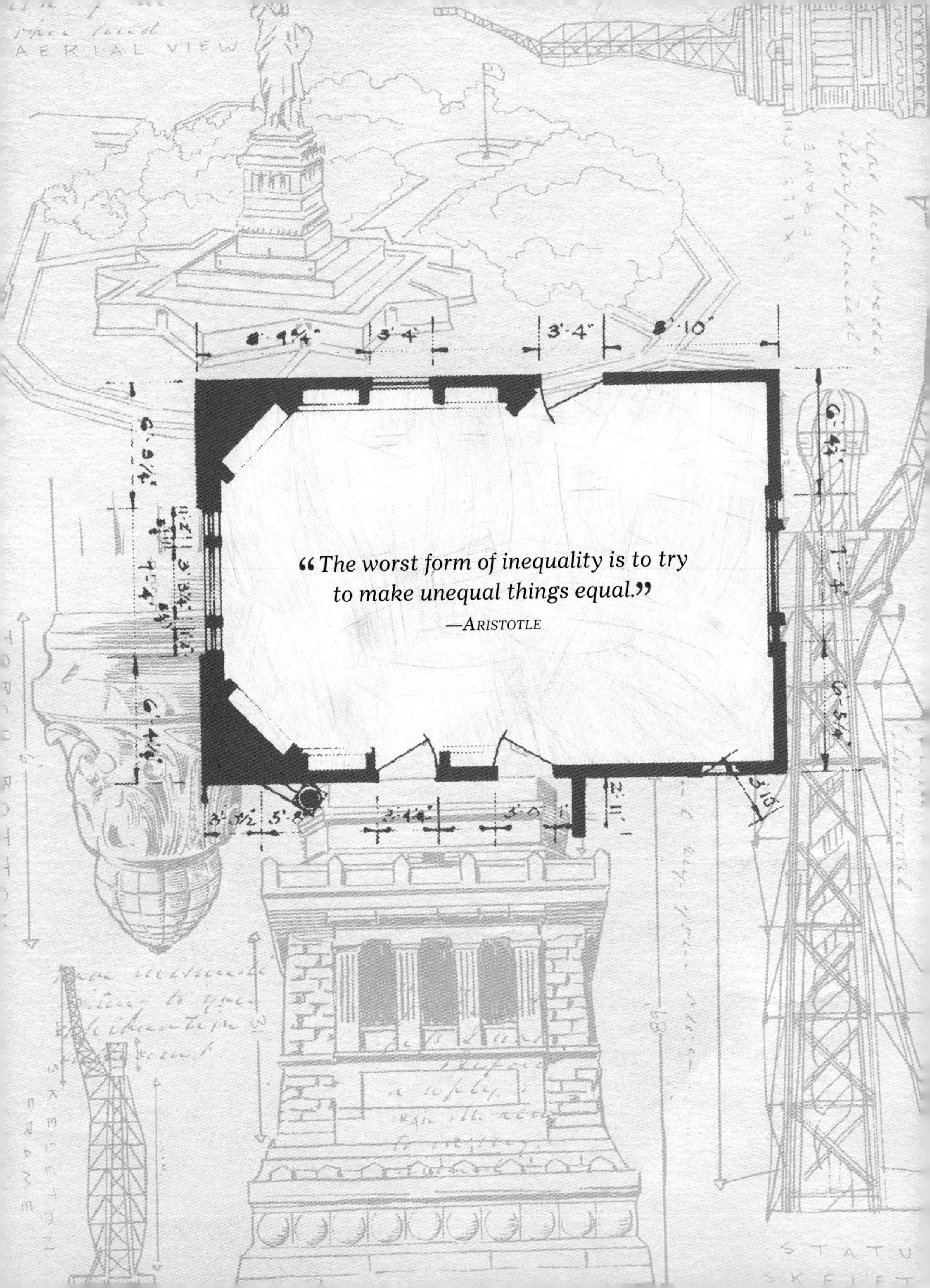

“The worst form of inequality is to try to make unequal things equal.”

—ARISTOTLE

CHAPTER 14.

Step Two: Opportunity vs. Outcome

Step two of the plan starts in the same place that step one did: the Declaration of Independence. *All men are created equal.* How could such a short, seemingly straightforward phrase cause so much debate?

Over the years, progressives have intentionally conditioned Americans to believe that "equality" should be society's ultimate goal, the axis upon which all political agendas should spin. But this is just another example of their word games: Promoting "equality" implies that the opposite choice is "inequality"—thereby invoking images of discrimination, racism, and sexism. I don't know of too many people who support those things—and that is exactly the reason why embracing "equality" is such a smart political tactic.

Of course, by this point in the book you probably realize that this is just another false-choice argument contrived by progressives. We are not being forced to choose between equality and inequality: We're choosing between equality and diversity.

If Only We Had . . .

History has shown that, until recently, equal creation at birth has always been the prevalent view in America. In an 1813 letter to John Adams, Thomas Jefferson wrote, "A constitution has been acquired, which, though neither of us thinks perfect, yet both consider as competent to render our fellow citizens the happiest and the securest on whom the sun has ever shone."

What does that have to do with equality? Simple—our Founders believed that the words of the Constitution guaranteed Americans enough natural rights to be *happy* and *secure*. Jefferson did not write Adams complaining that "Americans won't be happy until the Constitution is amended to provide welfare or health care or a federal department to run education"—he wrote saying that it's *already* competent. And that was just two and a half decades after the Constitution was ratified. Equality to our

Jefferson Owned Slaves!

It's virtually impossible to talk about Jefferson and equality without someone bringing up a question about slavery. After all, how could a person who believed that all men are created equal own up to two hundred slaves?

The long answer would fill an entire book itself, but Professor Douglas Wilson, co-director of the Lincoln Studies Center, took a stab at a simple version. He believes that the question itself needs to rephrased: Instead of asking how Jefferson could own slaves, we should be asking how he could have possibly been as outspoken against them as he was. Wilson wrote:

> *How did a man who was born into a slave holding society, whose family and admired friends owned slaves, who inherited a fortune that was dependent on slaves and slave labor, decide at an early age that slavery was morally wrong and forcefully declare that it ought to be abolished?*
>
> *The rephrased question reveals that what is truly remarkable is that Jefferson went against his society and his own self-interest to denounce slavery and urge its abolition. And, crucially, there is no hidden assumption that he must in some way have believed in or tacitly accepted the morality of slavery.*

Founders had nothing to do with where we all would end up in life; it had to do with crafting a document that gave us all the tools we needed to succeed.

Tocqueville, who visited America in the early nineteenth century, wrote that our balancing act between freedom to flourish or to be a total slacker is uniquely American and in sharp contrast to Europe: "In America it is freedom that is old—equality is of comparatively modern date. The reverse is occurring in Europe, where equality, introduced by absolute power and under the rule of kings, was already infused into the habits of nations long before freedom had entered into their conceptions."

European countries had become used to "equality of outcome"—which might sound okay until you learn that the outcome itself is not very good. Would you prefer to have a society where 25 percent live in wealth, 25 percent in poverty, and 50 percent in the middle, or would you prefer a society where 100 percent of the population lives sparingly? As Tocqueville wrote in apparent amazement, "Americans are so enamored of equality that they would rather be equal in slavery than unequal in freedom."

At Gettysburg, Lincoln continued to solidify America's stance, declaring that the country was "conceived in liberty, and dedicated to the proposition that all men are created equal." He did not, of course, mean that we are all born with equal athletic talents, levels of intellect, or personal drive and ambition; rather, that we must all be equal before the law, that we must all have an equal opportunity to flourish in whatever ways we so choose. John F. Kennedy understood this meaning well, telling college graduates in 1963, "All of us do not have equal talent, but all of us should have an equal opportunity to develop those talents."

And that's really all that people can ask for in life: a level playing field upon which to pursue their dreams. But that seems to be where the problems usually begin for progressives. Promoting a level playing field isn't quite as sexy as promoting "equality" because things like group rights, entitlements, and a living Constitution are simply not possible without championing the idea that the outcome is just as important as the opportunity.

There is, however, a nearly foolproof way to make progressives stumble over their own logic and, no surprise here, economist F. A. Hayek found it.

> *From the fact that people are very different it follows that, if we treat them equally, the result must be inequality in their actual position, and that the only way to place them in an equal position would be to treat them differently. Equality before the law and material equality are therefore not only different but are in conflict with each other; and we can achieve either one or the other, but not both at the same time.*

In other words, if your goal is to move everyone up two spaces, then true equality under the law would say that you have to move the wealthy, middle class, and poor all ahead by the same amount. But that, of course, would still leave you with inequality, just a different degree of it. The only way to truly make people the same is to apply a different standard to each person, depending on their circumstance—a philosophy that's about as far away from true free-market capitalism as you can get.

It's our responsibility to remind Americans that we are great not because we are equals, but because we are different. The melting pot is not just a description of how different nationalities blended together; it's also a metaphor for our whole way of life. America has something that virtually no other country can lay claim to: strength through diversity. So why are we running from it?

America Is Exceptional? Not So Much

There are three types of Americans: those who believe in American exceptionalism (the idea that America is uniquely blessed, which sets us apart and above every other country in opportunity, freedom, and promise); those who believe that America is no better or worse than other nations; and those who simply don't care.

I want to focus on the second group because their view, quite frankly, is dangerous. If you don't believe that America is exceptional then you would have no problem embracing equality of outcome on a global scale. While I don't think anyone actively supports allowing people to starve in Africa, it's worth understanding that a global view of equality means degrading Americans' standard of living. There's really no other way: Third-world countries are not going to become financial superpowers anytime soon, so the only real way to create international equality is to move us in their direction.

FOR JUST THE PRICE OF A CUP OF COFFEE A DAY . . .

One example of international equality of condition is the Global Poverty Act (which, for the time being, has fortunately died in Congress). The act's mission, in part:

To require the President to develop and implement a comprehensive strategy to further the United States foreign policy objective of promoting the reduction of global poverty, the elimination of extreme global poverty, and the achievement of the [U.N.] Millennium Development Goal of reducing by one-half the proportion of people worldwide, between 1990 and 2015, who live on less than $1 per day.

By some estimates, the United States' contribution would have totaled 0.7 percent of our GNP, in addition to our existing foreign-aid budget. And who was the sponsor of the Global Poverty Act in the Senate? You probably already guessed it: Barack Obama.

Progressives have contempt for American exceptionalism because it flies in the face of cultural relativism, the holy grail of everything they believe in. To claim that America is "better" is to commit the worst of progressive sins: making a moral and cultural judgment that holds America in higher regard than other nations. "I believe in American exceptionalism," President Obama once said, "just as I suspect that the Brits believe in British exceptionalism and the Greeks believe in Greek exceptionalism."

Progressives see "equality" as a cultural and moral leveler, as a statement that there can be no "better" or "worse" nations or people—but that is not at all what the Founders intended. John Locke, who perhaps influenced the Founders more than anyone, said that equality simply meant that the government was "respecting people as equals."

Equality vs. *Equality*

The fault line between American and European beliefs about equality is deep and wide. The American Revolution emphasized equality before the law. The French Revolution emphasized egalitarianism, or equality of condition. The American Revolution produced the most powerful nation the world has ever known. The French Revolution ended in disaster.

There's a very good reason for this: Equality of outcome is the enemy of individual rights. How are you free to make decisions if your good decisions are reversed and your bad ones are vetoed? As Lord Acton put it, "The finest opportunity ever given to the world was thrown away because the passion for equality made vain the hope for freedom."

The failure of European notions of equality has not stopped American progressives from trying to bring it here. In September 1932, FDR (it always seems to come back to FDR, doesn't it?) declared that Americans needed to engage in "a reappraisal of values." Among them was this very idea of equality of outcome. He explained:

> *Our task now is not discovery or exploitation of natural resources, or necessarily producing more goods. It is the soberer, less dramatic business of administering resources and plants already in hand . . . of adjusting production to consumption, of distributing wealth and products more equitably . . . The day of enlightened administration has come.*

He went on . . .

> *The Declaration of Independence discusses the problem of government in terms of a contract . . . Under such a contract rulers were accorded power, and the people consented to that power on consideration that they be accorded certain rights. The task of statesmanship has always been the redefinition of these rights in terms of a changing and growing social order.*

Money Doesn't Matter, but I Want More of It

Wilhelm Röpke, author of *A Humane Economy*, summarized what happens when government begins to target anything that surpasses some predetermined standard of success:

> ***The language of the old paternal government is still current and so are its categories, but all this is becoming a screen that hides the new crusade against anything which dares exceed the average, be it in income, wealth, or performance. The aim of this social revolution is not achieved until everything has been reduced to one level, and the remaining small differences give even greater cause for social resentment.***

It is ironic that progressives, who denounce "materialism," are actually hypermaterialists themselves. The only equality yardstick that seems to matter to them is money and other worldly possessions.

I can't even begin to tell you how much I wish I had been on national TV during FDR's administration. I swear, the red phone would be ringing nonstop. Between distributing our wealth more equitably and redefining our rights based on how society changes (as though rights are something malleable that a president has control over), FDR was essentially trying to compress all Americans toward an economic center.

LBJ, as usual, took things even further. In his 1965 commencement address about equality for African-Americans at Howard University, Johnson said, "To fulfill these rights we seek not just freedom but opportunity. We seek not just legal equity but human ability, not just equality as a right and a theory but equality as a fact and *equality as a result*" (emphasis mine).

The reason we could not achieve that goal, LBJ believed, was some external "unseen forces" that help certain people and suppress others. These invisible forces justify using the power of the state to impose an equality of outcome wherever it can. After all, as Johnson said, "For what is justice? It is to fulfill the fair expectations of man."

TEACHABLE MOMENT

Fair expectations? I won't dare ask who gets to decide what the definition of *fair* is.

LBJ, of course, didn't come up with this concept himself; it had been around in various forms for a while. But John Rawls, who was arguably the most influential liberal political philosopher of the twentieth century, furthered the idea in his 1971 book, *A Theory of Justice* (now required reading for any college philosophy student . . . or White House employee).

The book was based around a thought experiment whereby people would determine how government should be set up in order to bring about political and economic justice. The trick, however, is that participants had to reach their conclusions behind a "veil of ignorance," meaning that they did not know how their life would turn out; whether they'd be a bum or a billionaire. Rawls concluded that there are two basic principles necessary needed for a society to function "justly":

1. The Liberty Principle. This is the idea that people should have political freedoms such as free speech, freedom of the press, and be treated equally under the law. Not many people take issue with this.

2. The Difference Principle. Because participants in the thought experiment did not know their outcomes, Rawls claimed that the "just" decision these people came to was that wealth should be distributed so that the worst off benefit the most.

In essence, it's this theory that progressives are trying to implement through all of their social programs and tax systems. The only problem is that we are no longer in a thought experiment.

There's a very good reason why progressive, big-government presidents like FDR and LBJ loved the idea of equality, and it has nothing to do with what good guys they were. Equality means power because equality requires enforcement.

LBJ, who used civil rights issues for his own political advantage, understood this concept very well. What good are equal rights if you don't have all sorts of commissions, agencies, and groups to monitor them? Likewise, creating equal outcomes requires a very strong central authority to implement the laws, ensure that everyone is obeying them, and punish those who aren't. Economist Thomas Sowell once put it like this:

> *The question becomes, are you going to have everyone play by the same rules, or are you going to try to rectify the shortcomings, errors and failures of the entire cosmos? Because those things are wholly incompatible. If you're going to have people play by the same rules, that can be enforced with a minimum amount of interference with people's freedom. But if you're going to try to make the entire cosmos right and just, somebody has got to have an awful lot of power to impose what they think is right on an awful lot of other people. What we've seen, particularly in the 20th century, is that putting that much power in anyone's hands is enormously dangerous.*

Whenever conservatives or libertarians talk about these kinds of ideas, the vitriol from the other side bursts out. They scream about racism and hate and wonder how we will ever protect the mentally handicapped, the diseased, or the people who've been struck by catastrophe without safety nets. But it's a false argument. Equality of opportunity doesn't need to overlook the weakest among us. There is clearly a constitutional (and, certainly, moral) role for government in helping certain groups of people.

Hayek—a staunch libertarian, and one of the most revered free-market economists of all time—actually believed that there should be some kind of social safety net provided by the state. But don't get too excited, liberals: His conception of a social backstop is quite different from Barack Obama's.

In *The Constitution of Liberty,* Hayek asserted that the state should provide assistance, within reason, for the weak, sick, or those who were victims of unforeseeable (that's a key word) disasters. But he strongly argued against the rationale that because some in society are born into poor families, while others are born into rich families, it means that the former have a right to the assets of the latter. In other words, Hayek would probably have agreed that there was a role for the government in Hurricane Katrina's aftermath, but that increasing taxes to pay for public schools to give out iPods is probably unwise.

Here is Hayek, in his own words:

> *There are good reasons why we should endeavor to use whatever political organization we have at our disposal to make provision for the weak or infirm*

or for the victims of unforeseeable disaster. It may well be true that the most effective method of providing against certain risks common to all citizens of a state is to give every citizen protection against those risks. The level on which such provisions against common risks can be made will necessarily depend on the general wealth of the community.

It is an entirely different matter, however, to suggest that those who are poor, merely in the sense that there are those in the same community who are richer, are entitled to a share in the wealth of the latter or that being born into a group that has reached a particular level of civilization and comfort confers a title to a share in all its benefits. The fact that all citizens have an interest in the common provision of some services is no justification for anyone's claiming as a right a share in all the benefits. It may set a standard for what some ought to be willing to give, but not for what anyone can demand.

America: Where the Real "King" Is a Dead Singer

Thomas Jefferson once wrote, "There is a natural aristocracy among men. The grounds of this are virtue and talents." Not that I need to clarify TJ's point, but he meant that, unlike his motherland, nobility in America wasn't based on birthright: It was based on individual success and achievement.

Our Founders believed that individuals all possess different abilities, ambitions, and levels of work ethic. And that was a *good* thing. In fact, their main concern was over what Jefferson called an "artificial aristocracy" made up of people who were born wealthy or into the right family, but lacked virtue or talent. They worried that these people, if put into positions of power in government, would become a danger to the country because they had not *earned* their position.

Jefferson's solution was surprisingly simple:

> *I think the best remedy is exactly that provided by all our constitutions, to leave to the citizens the free election and separation of the [natural aristocracy from the artificial], of the wheat from the chaff. In general they will elect the really good and wise. In some instances, wealth may corrupt, and birth blind them, but not in sufficient degree to endanger the society.*

I guess I first have to point out that Jefferson was wrong about one thing—Americans no longer tend to always elect the "good and wise"—but he was right about everything else. Unlike Europe, our social hierarchy has overwhelmingly been based on merit. That's the very essence of the American Dream: Work hard for your success and you not only earn respect, you also may earn a fortune. But achieve suc-

Do You Still Recognize Your Country?

America has already moved so far from legislating opportunity to legislating outcomes that it's hard to tell which bills were actually proposed (and/or are now law) and which ones we made up. (Answers are at the bottom of the page.)

1 H.R. 4287: Enhancing Livability for All Americans Act of 2009
To establish an Office of Livability in the Office of the Secretary of Transportation, and for other purposes.

❑ *REAL* ❑ *FAKE*

2 H.R. 1321: Healthy Americans Act
To provide affordable, guaranteed private health coverage that will make Americans healthier and can never be taken away.

❑ *REAL* ❑ *FAKE*

3 H.R. 3890: Reorganizing Prosperity Act
To further close the gap between classes and provide low-income families with the appropriate environment to share in economic prosperity, and for other purposes.

❑ *REAL* ❑ *FAKE*

4 H.R. 3681: Maslow Hierarchy Act of 1988
To establish the means for each citizen to achieve the levels noted in Maslow's 1943 Hierarchy of Needs including but not limited to food, family, and health, and for other purposes.

❑ *REAL* ❑ *FAKE*

5 H.R. 2233: Health Empowerment Zone Act of 2009
To authorize the Secretary of Health and Human Services to designate health empowerment zones, and for other purposes.

❑ *REAL* ❑ *FAKE*

6 H.R. 1040: A Living Wage, Jobs for All Act
To establish a living wage, jobs for all policy for all peoples in the United States and its territories, and for other purposes.

❑ *REAL* ❑ *FAKE*

7 H.R. 1500: Helping Families Afford to Work Act
To amend the Internal Revenue Code of 1986 to increase and make refundable the dependent care credit.

❑ *REAL* ❑ *FAKE*

8 H.R. 1362: Nine to Five for 99 Percent Act
To ensure a living wage for each citizen by requiring the option of a forty-hour minimum workweek for all nonfarm employees.

❑ *REAL* ❑ *FAKE*

9 H.R. 4122: Graduation for All Act
To support high-need middle and high schools in order to improve students' academic achievement, graduation rates, postsecondary readiness, and preparation for citizenry.

❑ *REAL* ❑ *FAKE*

10 H.R. 9251: Restoring the American DREAM Act
To provide for Directed Relief from Economic and Market declines to those impacted by the significant financial crisis.

❑ *REAL* ❑ *FAKE*

(Answers: Fake bills: 3, 4, 8, 10)

cess through luck or birthright (e.g., Paris Hilton) and, while you may still earn that fortune, you won't be able to buy any respect with it.

But the welfare state and entitlement culture is changing that entire equation. Individual achievement is no longer celebrated as it once was. Why give the best player on the team a trophy when that might hurt feelings? Instead, give *all* players a trophy and celebrate mediocrity. Unfortunately, when you cherish mediocrity for too long you eventually become mediocre yourself.

Whose Dream Is It?

One thing that has been lost over time is that the American Dream is a dream by *individuals* to be able to accomplish whatever they want. Too often it's our government coming out with legislation to "help people fulfill the American Dream" when, by their actions, they are ensuring that can never happen. A push toward equality is the worst thing that could ever happen to the Dream. How many people do you know who dream of the day that they can finally be mediocre?

We must turn our backs on that way of thinking. Celebrate diversity, not only in appearance, but in aptitude and ability. Celebrate accomplishments, not only when the least talented succeed, but also when the most talented do. And celebrate hard work, certainly when it pays off, but especially when it doesn't. Those three values have been taken from us and twisted. If we can restore them, we can restore America.

A Deadly Sin That's Not So Deadly

Some progressives, like famed professor and liberal theorist Ronald Dworkin, are so serious about equality that they've developed a simple test to determine whether it's being achieved: envy. If envy exists, then so does inequality.

Using "envy" as the benchmark test is yet *another* progressive word game (are you detecting a trend here?). Envy is one of the seven deadly sins, so who could possibly be in favor of it?

But envy is really the wrong standard to apply. Envy is a human condition that can't be eliminated. Unless everyone is *exactly* the same in every possible way, then some form of envy will always exist.

Envy, of course, can lead to anger and bitterness and demands that you get what your neighbor has—which is exactly what lead to the downfall of ancient Greece. But, in the hands of someone who believes in themselves, envy can also be one of life's greatest motivators. Jealous of the guy who's dating the girl you like? You're motivated to lose those last ten pounds. Jealous of your co-worker who makes more money? You're motivated to work harder and longer. Jealous of your teammate who hits more home runs? You're motivated to get stronger and spend more time at practice.

A distinction has to be made, however, between envy and another one of the deadly sins: greed. Envy for the sake of simply accumulating more stuff is not what this country is all about. But envy for the sake of the reward it brings, for the chance to reap the fruits of your own labor and ideas, is *exactly* what this country is about.

The problem with trying to eliminate envy is that, even when we succeed, we fail. If a teacher takes all of the students who got "C's" on a test and marks them up to an "A," are those students really better off? Have they really reaped the rewards of their own talent and hard work? Progressives don't seem to understand that designing identical trophies is not the issue; the issue is whether you were handed it for participating or whether you earned it by being the best.

Most progressives won't actually mention the role that envy plays in their push for classlessness. One who did was James Duesenberry, who sat on LBJ's Council of Economic Advisors and was former chairman of the Harvard economics department. In other words, Duesenberry was no slouch.

He believed that a group's sense of economic well-being was based on how well the group above them was doing. If the group above them was successful, a "sense of deprivation" was created and it became necessary to bring the more prosperous group down. One way to do that was through the progressive income tax.

Economist E. J. Mishan of the London School of Economics furthered Duesenberry's theory. He wrote, "Ideally, of course, the tax should suffice to cover all the initial and subsequent claims necessary to placate everybody in the lower-income groups, and the stronger is this envy of others, the heavier must be the tax."

THE UNITED STATES OF DWORKIN

Here's how Dworkin would design his utopian society if, God help us all, he ever got the chance. It's based on a hypothetical scenario he outlined when describing how you could truly have equality of resources.

The first step would be an auction, in which all participants start with the same amount of currency. At the end, everyone has purchased their share of resources according to their own tastes and desires. Sounds great—except Dworkin says we now have a big problem. See, some participants in the auction simply aren't as smart or talented as others. As a result, they may have bid incorrectly, resulting in an uneven outcome and, of course, envy among the participants. *Hey, how did that guy get all of the cake and I got stuck with broccoli?* We can't have that.

To achieve equality even when talent levels are different, Dworkin introduces an insurance pool. Before the auction starts, participants use some of their assets to purchase a policy that will cover them should they turn out to make unwise decisions. At the end, those who did great keep their stuff, and those who did poorly turn to the insurance policy to make up the gap. And, just like that, everyone is equal.

So, according to Mishan, tax rates wouldn't be based on economic need; they'd be based on the degree of envy of those below you on the income ladder. Sounds like a pretty strong foundation to build an enduring country on.

Two University of Chicago law professors, Walter Blum and Harry Kalven, wanted to research this idea further, so they asked people a simple question: If America suddenly became three times richer overnight, but the change in the relative distribution of money did not change, would redistribution still be pushed?

The clear answer? *Absolutely.* "It initially appears that what is involved is envy, the dissatisfaction produced in men not by what they lack but by what others have." Basically, what Blum and Kalven discovered is that everything is relative. If you think you are well-off but then someone moves next door who seems like they have even more, then you suddenly become envious and in favor of redistribution.

Progressive Brainteaser

Here's a brainteaser: When do progressive think that equality is a bad thing?

Give up? *Taxes.* Whenever a new graduated tax is proposed, progressives take the moral high ground, saying things like *The people who have benefited from America's prosperity the most refuse to help those who are struggling!* But the moral high ground should actually be claimed by the very people who are being targeted. Everyone believes in equal treatment under the law at an abstract individual level—we all think, for example, that a rich person should do the same amount of jail time as a poor person for the same crime—but why doesn't equal treatment apply when it comes to a new social program? Why is it okay to tell a wealthier person that they will pay a 10-percent tax, while others pay nothing?

It may not be advertised this way, but economic equality doesn't really work without the rich funding it through tax rates that are anything but equal. As Hayek said, it's impossible to demand equality without treating people differently.

We know where this false journey toward equality ends because Tocqueville described it long ago:

> *After having thus successively taken each member of the community in its powerful grasp and fashioned him at will, the supreme power then extends its arm over the whole community. It covers the surface of society with a network of small complicated rules, minute and uniform, through which the most original minds and the most energetic characters cannot penetrate, to rise above the crowd. The will of man is not shattered, but softened, bent, and guided; men are seldom forced by it to act, but they are constantly restrained from acting. Such a power does not destroy, but it prevents existence; it does not tyrannize, but it compresses, enervates, extinguishes, and stupefies a people, till each nation is reduced to nothing better than a flock of timid and industrious animals, of which the government is the shepherd.*

Our only defense is to open up enough eyes to what is really going on. We've already seen how the language has been shaped and changed by progressives: positive rights, a living Constitution, freedom from want, equality as a positive, and envy as a negative. Maybe it's time to fight back with some word games of our own—words like *diversity, success, motivation*, and *personal achievement*.

We can talk about "fixing" the budget and reforming social programs all we want, but those programs are simply a manifestation of the progressive push toward equality. Until that is exposed for the false idol that it is, no budget plan will ever go anywhere.

In other words, we cannot reform entitlements without first reforming equality.

If we are unsuccessful, or, worse, if we do nothing, then I guarantee you that envy will be nothing compared to the next deadly sin we will face . . . wrath.

Educate Yourself

- Alexis de Tocqueville, *Democracy in America* (free)
  Vol. 1: *http://books.google.com/books?id=xZfiBEzcPTEC*
  Vol. 2: *http://books.google.com/books?id=KO8tAAAAIAAJ*

- F. A. Hayek, *The Intellectuals and Socialism*
  http://books.google.com/books?id=7AsHAAAACAAJ

- Jeremy Waldron, *God, Locke, and Equality* (free preview)
  http://books.google.com/books?id=ROAfJfNfUq8C

- Helmut Schoeck, *Envy: A Theory of Social Behaviour*
  http://books.google.com/books?id=0pkQAQAAIAAJ

- John Kekes, "Dangerous Egalitarian Dreams," *City Journal*, 2001 (free)
  http://www.city-journal.org/html/11_4_urbanities-dangerous.html

- Robert Nozick, *Anarchy, State, and Utopia* (free preview)
  http://books.google.com/books?id=hAi3CdjXlQsC

- Thomas Jefferson's letter to John Adams, 1813 (free)
  http://press-pubs.uchicago.edu/founders/documents/v1ch15s61.html

- Thomas Sowell, *Economic Facts and Fallacies*
  http://books.google.com/books?id=kNFpQgAACAAJ

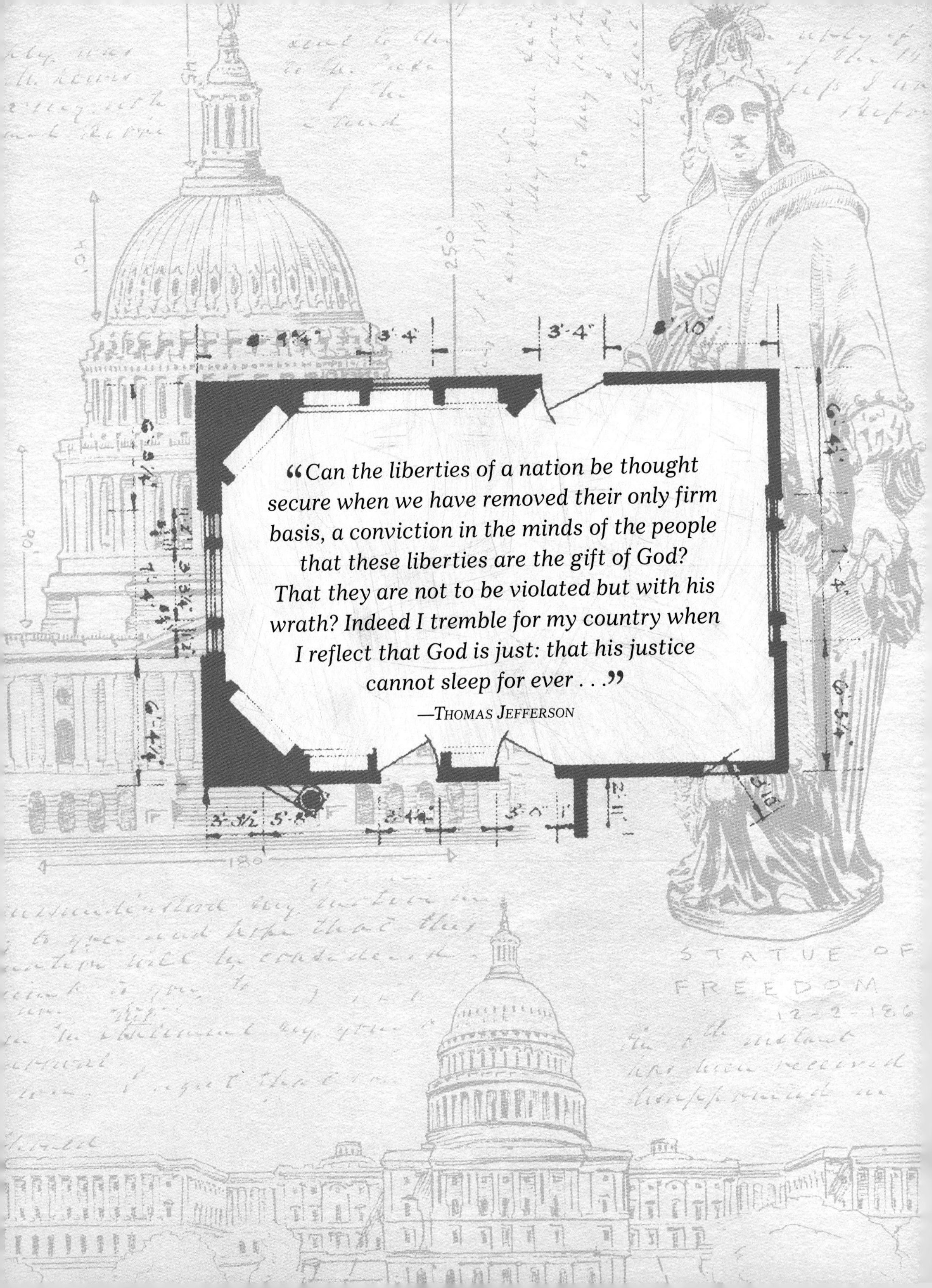

"Can the liberties of a nation be thought secure when we have removed their only firm basis, a conviction in the minds of the people that these liberties are the gift of God? That they are not to be violated but with his wrath? Indeed I tremble for my country when I reflect that God is just: that his justice cannot sleep for ever . . ."

—Thomas Jefferson

CHAPTER 15.

Step Three: Faith in America

When was the last time you trembled while thinking about God?

If it's been a while—*why*? Did God issue some sort of statement that since humans are doing such a great job here on earth, He's decided to no longer judge them? Did He declare that He will cease to admonish or reward leaders and nations for their actions?

The answer is no—He didn't suddenly change His mind. He didn't read liberal blogs and decide that he's no longer important, and He didn't much care for all the court decisions trying to remove Him from society.

He doesn't waver, falter, or flip-flop like John Kerry on a campaign trail because His truths are absolute. It's we who have changed.

It doesn't take a religious scholar to see that America has turned away from God. In fact, it takes only about five minutes of channel surfing, a browse past the magazine rack, or a quick scan of the "spam" folder in your email to figure that out. And, possibly for the first time in this book, the blame does not solely fall on progressives. While they make an easy target because they often openly mock God and religion in general (yes, I do "cling to guns and religion," thanks for asking), each and every one of us has contributed to this neglect. Be honest—if the priorities of your life were graphed on a pie chart, how big of a slice would God get?

My intention is not to lecture you. I'm as guilty of this as anyone. Believe me, there's nothing I would like more than to sleep in on Sunday morning, play with the kids, and then pop in a DVD. We're all at fault for our shifting priorities—it's in our very nature to turn toward false idols like money, possessions, power, or celebrity.

Throughout history, the consistent consequence of disobeying God's law has been clear. Adam and Eve were kicked out of the Garden. When the Israelites didn't fully follow the Lord, God burned with anger and made them wander the desert until the entire generation who had done wickedness in His sight were "consumed."

> **Are We Still on God's Side?**
>
> ***"My concern is not whether God is on our side, my greatest concern is to be on God's side, for God is always right."***
>
> —Abraham Lincoln

Why would we think our spiritual neglect today will get some sort of free pass from God when no other generation throughout history ever has? If you believe, as I do, that the Founders' work in creating this nation was divinely inspired, then you should also believe that God is not going to look kindly at the dismantling of what He created.

If we want a different result than other civilizations, then we need to make different decisions. Virtue must replace vanity; godliness must replace greed and gluttony; fear and trembling must replace power and arrogance.

God set this nation apart and God expects us to take care of the gifts we are given. But don't expect to see punishment through fire or flood if we don't—God allows us to reap the rewards or suffer the consequences of our own decisions. To God, none of us is too big to fail.

The path toward healing does not begin with some unnamed hedonistic progressive activist—it begins with *you*.

Now, at this point you may be saying to yourself: *This is a cool story and all, Glenn, but isn't this a book about fixing our economy*?

Yep, it sure is—but our financial renewal cannot begin without a spiritual renewal. We are broke because we are broken. We are like a ship lost at sea, bobbing in the waves and moving in whatever direction the prevailing wind blows. To reach our destination we need a North Star—a fixed object that can lead us in the right direction.

And that North Star is God.

Founding Faith

Like individual rights and diversity, faith was a bedrock principle at our country's founding. It was the glue that kept our Republic together. The Founders understood that sins could never be eradicated through legislation. As the Bible reminds us, "*All* have sinned, and come short of the glory of God" (emphasis mine). The Founders' Judeo-Christian heritage told them that men are not perfect, so don't waste time trying to make them that way.

Here is how James Madison, the primary author of the Constitution, put it in Federalist 51:

> *But what is government itself but the greatest of all reflections on human nature? If men were angels, no government would be necessary. If angels were to govern men, neither external nor internal controls on government*

would be necessary. In framing a government which is to be administered by men over men, the great difficulty lies in this: You must first enable the government to control the governed; and in the next place, oblige it to control itself.

That really puts into perspective the Founders' mind-set as they drafted our Constitution. The only difference between America and all the other countries that have tried to develop systems to control both the masses and the government itself is religion. A strong belief in something greater than man acts as a natural brake on unconstrained capitalism. You don't rob or scam another person because you fear both the temporary punishment of the state and the eternal punishment of your God.

A common way of looking at the necessity for religion in a republic is what is called the "Moral Calculus." In short, a republic can function only if a sufficient percentage of the population is virtuous. But virtue requires morality and morality requires religion, or at least a belief in a higher power to which we will ultimately be accountable. As Benjamin Franklin, who, by his own admission was a Deist, once said, "Only a virtuous people are capable of freedom. As nations become corrupt and vicious, they have more need of masters."

Guidance from . . . Where?

A 2007 Pew poll asked: "When it comes to questions of right and wrong, which of the following do you look to most for guidance?" Just 29 percent of people said "religion."

Professors Donald S. Lutz and the late Charles S. Hyneman once studied 15,000 political items that were published or written by the American Founders. They also reviewed 2,200 books, pamphlets and newspaper articles on politics from the period surrounding the Revolution. What they found was that the most commonly referenced source in these materials was the Bible, making up 34 percent of all citations. The most cited writers and thinkers were not deists or agnostics, but Christian thinkers like Montesquieu and Blackstone.

Far from shying away from a spiritual influence, our Founders embraced it. They believed that the reason the Constitution would work in America was that our love of religion made us unique from any other country in the history of the world. As John Adams said, "Our constitution was made only for a moral and religious people. It is wholly inadequate for the government of any other."

SORRY, FRANCE

Gouverneur Morris, one of the most important Founding Fathers, believed that the U.S. Constitution would not work in France because the French had (clear your throat) "low moral character."

Speaking of France, Alexis de Tocqueville seemed to marvel at the role religion played in America in the early nineteenth century. I apologize for including so much of his description of that experience, but I think it's critical to understand that religion was not simply represented by a prayer before dinner or an hour on Sundays. It was woven into the very fabric of our society. Tocqueville wrote:

> *Whilst the law permits the Americans to do what they please, religion prevents them from conceiving, and forbids them to commit, what is rash or unjust.*
>
> *Religion in America takes no direct part in the government of society, but it must nevertheless be regarded as the foremost of the political institutions of that country; for it does not impart a taste for freedom, it facilitates the use of free institutions . . . I do not know whether all the Americans have a sincere faith in their religion, for who can search the human heart? but I am certain that they hold it to be indispensable to the maintenance of republican institutions. This opinion is not peculiar to a class of citizens or to a party, but it belongs to the whole nation, and to every rank of society . . .*
>
> *The Americans combine the notions of Christianity and of liberty so intimately in their minds, that it is impossible to make them conceive of one without the other.*

While I believe we can blame only ourselves for the way faith has been tossed aside, there's no doubt that progressives understand the role of religion in American history well and have worked hard to whitewash it. After all, if people can rely on each other for help, moderate their excesses, and govern according to God's rules, then what need do they have for a strong central government?

How Times Have Changed

From a *New York Spectator* account of a court proceeding in 1831:

The Court of Common Pleas of Chester County (New York) a few days since rejected a witness who declared his disbelief in the existence of God. The presiding judge remarked, that he had not before been aware that there was a man living who did not believe in the existence of God; that this belief constituted the sanction of all testimony in a court of justice and that he knew of no cause in a Christian country where a witness had been permitted to testify without such belief.

Separating Church and State or Church *from* the State?

I'm confused. Tocqueville said that religion was regarded as a "foremost political institution" in the early nineteenth century, but how could that be, given that our Founders built an enormous wall between church and state?

The answer lies in the fact that the meaning of "separation of church and state" (a term that does not appear in the Constitution itself, or any other federal document, for that matter) has completely changed over time. It's like a game of telephone tag where someone says "No government religion" at one end and, by the time the message gets to the last person, it's recited as "No religion in government."

The First Amendment was intended to apply solely to the federal government so that it could not overrule state churches and establish a national religion. Why was that deemed necessary? Because, at the time the Constitution was ratified, at least ten of the thirteen states had some provision recognizing Christianity as the official or recommended religion in their state constitutions and would have failed any modern test of separation of church and state.

In fact, reading many of the state constitutions of that time is an eye-opening exercise. The 1780 Massachusetts Constitution, written by John Adams, declared, in part:

> *[the] good order and preservation of civil government essentially depend(s) upon piety, religion, and morality . . . by the institution of public worship of God and of the public instructions in piety, religion, and morality. . .*

North Carolina's 1776 Constitution went even further, leaving no doubt as to their intentions:

> *No person who shall deny the being of God, or the truth of the Protestant religion, or the divine authority of either the Old or New Testaments, or who shall hold religious principles incompatible with the freedom and safety of the State (e.g. Pacifism), shall be capable of holding any office, place of trust or profit, in the civil department, within this State.*

State governments were free to put as much or as little separation between themselves and religion as they desired—it was only the power of the federal government to mandate a *national* religion that concerned the Founders.

So where does the famous "separation of church and state" line come from? It was actually in a letter written by Thomas Jefferson to the Danbury Baptists in 1802. The Baptists, concerned that the government might interfere with their right to worship, had appealed to Jefferson for advice.

In assuring them that their rights were as unalienable as the rights of any religion, he wrote the Baptists and told them that the first amendment ensured their freedom and that there was a *"wall of separation between church and state"* . . . that would prevent the government from ever interfering in their right to worship the way they pleased.

Like many of the words of our Founders, the meaning of Jefferson's letter has been completely changed over the years to suit the agenda of those who would prefer that he was talking about religion infiltrating our government instead of the other way around.

It's also important to note that our Founders backed up their words with actions. One day after passing the First Amendment, which contains the "establishment" clause that has been used to claim they did not want any religion in government, Congress declared a public day of prayer. Don't you think it would be pretty odd to declare a public day of government-sponsored prayer if you'd just created a constitutional amendment banning the government from sponsoring prayer?

Godless Capitalism

"If we ever forget that we are One Nation Under God, then we will be a nation gone under."

—Ronald Reagan

While our Founders embraced Judeo-Christian beliefs, this is not a plea for people to practice or convert to any specific faith. I really couldn't care less if you are a Jew, a Mormon, a Roman Catholic, or a Wiccan—the point is to believe in and honor the God of your choosing, because it is our Creator who gave us our rights. (Okay, maybe I do care a little bit if you're a Wiccan.) As soon as God is taken out of the equation, then nothing is left but man. And if our rights come from man, they can be taken away by man.

That is why anyone who really understands individual liberty, like Penn Jillette, for example, should support America's embrace of faith, even if they don't believe in God themselves. Thomas Paine, who, by all accounts, was not a fan of organized religion, nevertheless understood that faith and liberty go hand in hand. "Spiritual freedom is the root of all political liberty . . . " he said. "As the union between spiritual freedom and political liberty seems nearly inseparable, it is our duty to defend both." Our agendas—ensuring that no man can infringe on another's natural rights—are the same, even if our beliefs aren't.

WITHOUT A COMPASS

A 2009 survey revealed that the only religion that grew in every state since 1990 was "the nones"—which is composed of people who said they have no affiliation to a specific religion. Twenty million more adults identified themselves that way in 2009 than in 2000.

Faith is more than just a belief in a specific religious doctrine; it's something that fills us from the inside. It makes us whole. If you strip that away, something has to fill the void. More than fifty years ago, philosopher José Ortega y Gasset wrote, "Without commandments, obliging us to live after a certain fashion, our existence is that of the 'unemployed' . . . By dint of feeling itself free, exempt from restrictions, it feels itself empty . . . Before long there will be heard throughout the planet a formidable cry, rising like the howling of innumerable dogs to the stars, asking for someone or something to take command, to impose an occupation, a duty."

That's a pretty good description of exactly what progressives are going for. Nature abhors a vacuum, so if spirituality does not fill a person, then things like envy, greed, and a sense of entitlement will.

To move toward that vacuum, progressives push reason instead of religion, government instead of God, and taxes instead of charity. They agree with Freud, who said of religion, "Let us put away childish things," and they work to kick God out of our schools, bar Him from our courtrooms, boot His likeness off our town squares, and lock Him out of government completely.

Progressives have gone to absurd lengths to dim the North Star that has been guiding us as a nation for more than two hundred years. Back in 1981, the president of Yale University told incoming freshmen that the Moral Majority, which was then a politically active group of evangelical Christians, were "peddlers of coercion." The *Los Angeles Times* pulled Johnny Hart's cartoon *B.C.* when, for Easter, he depicted a caveman writing a poem that read: "never to mourn the Prince who was downed, / For He is not lost! / It is you who are found." They didn't run it because, in the words of the newspaper's spokesperson, the cartoon was "insensitive and exclusionary."

And then there are the well-publicized pushes to rip the Ten Commandments from courthouses, remove mangers from public display, and eliminate references to Christmas from our schools and the phrase "under God" from the Pledge of Allegiance.

In Utah, the 10th Circuit Court of Appeals recently ruled that roadside crosses memorializing the deaths of Highway Patrol troopers are unconstitutional. "We hold that these memorials have the impermissible effect of conveying to the reasonable observer the message that the state prefers or otherwise endorses a certain religion," the court wrote.

I've even had my own experience with this supposed "wall of separation." During the organizing of an event at the Kennedy Center in Washington, I was told that no prayers could be recited from the stage. Prayers are not exactly baptism or communion; they're prayers—things that millions of people say every day. Presumably, if you are paying to come to my event (an event that was called "Divine Destiny," by the way) then you'd probably be okay with an appeal toward God at the beginning of the program. The whole idea of watering down religion in the hope of not upsetting people has just gone way too far.

Some of the religious targets of progressives seem pretty silly—I mean, who could *really* be offended by a manger set up on a lawn or crosses memorializing deceased heroes? But that's part of their whole attack: remove all references, from the massive to the mundane, so that, over time, religion is extracted from our lives.

The late Christopher Lasch, who was no conservative, asked, "What accounts for [our society's] wholesale defection from the standards of personal conduct—civility, industry, self-restraint—that were once considered indispensable to democracy?" His answer: "the gradual decay of religion would stand somewhere near the head of the list."

And he pointed to a familiar villain as the culprit: liberal elites. "Among elites," Lasch wrote, "[religion] is held in low esteem—something useful for wedding and funerals but otherwise dispensable . . . The elites' attitude to religion ranges from indifference to active hostility."

The Pelosi Gospel

"They ask me all the time, "What is your favorite this? What is your favorite that? What is your favorite that?" And one time, "What is your favorite word?" And I said, "My favorite word? That is really easy. My favorite word is the Word . . . And that Word is, we have to give voice to what that means in terms of public policy that would be in keeping with the values of the Word. The Word. Isn't it a beautiful word when you think of it? It just covers everything. The Word."

—Nancy Pelosi, May 2010

The Social Gospel

At the heart of this change is the Social Gospel, a theory that the book *American Progressivism* describes like this:

> *Social Gospel embraced evolutionary theory (although not it's "survival of the fittest" determinism) and saw orthodox religion as insufficient for the times. Social Gospel posited evolution as a divine plan for rational social advancement, and suggested that it become possible, through an empowered central state, to realize the Christian hope that "thy will be done on earth as it is in heaven." Social Gospel adherents considered it to be their mission to fulfill in this life the New Testament's call to bring about the perfect kingdom of God.*

Morals Based on Man

"The moral teachings of Christianity have exerted an incalculable influence on Western civilization. As those moral teachings fade into cultural memory, a secularized morality takes their place. Once Christianity is abandoned by a significant portion of the population, the moral landscape necessarily changes."

—R. Albert Mohler, Jr., president, Southern Baptist Theological Seminary

The question now becomes: The moral landscape changes into *what*?

The socialism preached in the Social Gospel is far more dangerous than atheistic socialism because Social Gospel followers believe they are bringing about God's will. The atheist may take away our economic freedom, but the Christian socialist will do that while also taking away our freedom to worship. They must dilute and twist the real Christian message and replace it with this idea that the state can somehow usher in God's will.

The logical conclusion of this process is that when the state ushers in God's will, as determined by the state, politicians become the priests and the state itself becomes God. At that point there is no role for churches, since secular schools and universities will provide all religious instruction. That will lead to full Social Justice where all people other than the ruling elites will live equally as serfs, without individual liberties, private property, or most importantly, freedom of religion.

Restore Faith, Restore America

Real faith renews our spirit of hard work and independence. Faith restores the idea of a society based on merit and reward. The Bible says, "If a man will not work, he shall not eat" (2 Thessalonians 3:10). Jesus dignified work when he said "the worker deserves his wages" (Luke 10:7). In the parable of the talents He actually condemns those who don't do the best with what they have been given. The one who invested and doubled his five talents is praised, and He faults the one who is given five talents but does nothing with them.

With a spiritual reawakening, we can take responsibility for ourselves again, embrace the virtues of hard work, and reignite purpose and direction in our country. With faith there are no bailouts for failure because failure is not negative. With faith, there are no entitlements because neighbors help neighbors.

The Puritans used to sing a hymn that included this verse:

Dare to be a Daniel,
Dare to stand alone;
Dare to have a purpose firm,
Dare to make it known.

Following World War II, George Orwell—who was not exactly a libertarian—commented that the hymn needed to be updated with the word *Don't* added to the beginning of each line. Even he saw that the British people were losing that sense of individual purpose and boldness that had served them so well for so long.

Have we?

Only God knows what he has planned for the future of America, but I know that we can't fix our broken country without His help. It's no coincidence that our economic decline can be charted right alongside our spiritual decline or

Biblical Wisdom

Regardless of anyone's religious affiliations (or lack thereof), the Bible is full of unquestionable truths about life, love, and money:

- ***"The debtor is slave to the lender."* (Proverbs 22:7)**
- ***"The plans of the diligent lead to profit as surely as haste leads to poverty."* (Proverbs 21:5)**
- ***"Like a bad tooth or a lame foot is reliance on the unfaithful in times of trouble.* (Proverbs 25:19)**
- ***"Be sure you know the condition of your flocks, give careful attention to your herds; for riches do not endure forever, and a crown is not secure for all generations."* (Proverbs 27:23)**

that our reliance on big government can be charted side by side with our retreat from God.

As the Founders struggled over the language of the Constitution in 1787, Ben Franklin addressed George Washington with these words:

> *I have lived, Sir, a long time and the longer I live, the more convincing proofs I see of this—that God governs the affairs of men. And if a sparrow cannot fall to the ground without his notice, is it probable that an empire can rise without His aid? We have been assured, Sir, in the Sacred Writings that "except the Lord build the House they labor in vain that build it." I firmly believe this; and I also believe that, without His concurring aid, we shall succeed in this political building no better than the builders of Babel.*

Do we still believe that or do most people now think that an enduring America can be built in the image of man? Do we still respect the need for His approval, or are we trying to build our own tower into the sky without His help?

America's founding was a miracle and her survival through dark days of depression, civil war, and enemy aggression proves that the guiding spirit of God's hand is still with us. But the more we turn from Him, the more likely it is that the next time the sky gets dark, there will be no North Star to guide us toward safety.

Educate Yourself

- David Barton, *The Myth of Separation*
  http://books.google.com/books?id=THGlAAAACAAJ

- John Eidsmoe, *Christianity and the Constitution*
  http://books.google.com/books?id=Vt4KAAAACAAJ

- Michael Novak & Jana Novak, *Washington's God* (free preview)
  http://books.google.com/books?id=b-rW2EWXleIC

- Stephen L. Carter, *The Culture of Disbelief: How American Law and Politics Trivialize Religious Devotion*
  http://books.google.com/books?id=nDz_esG-T2gC

- Steven Waldman, *Founding Faith* (free preview)
  http://books.google.com/books?id=cAjl7EEXzd8C

- Vincent Phillip Munoz, *God and the Founders*
  http://books.google.com/books?id=tq6UOwAACAAJ

- William J. Federer, *Back Fired: A Nation Founded on Religious Tolerance No Longer Tolerates the Religion of Its Founders* (free preview)
  http://books.google.com/books?id=QA1aNWKtfSoC

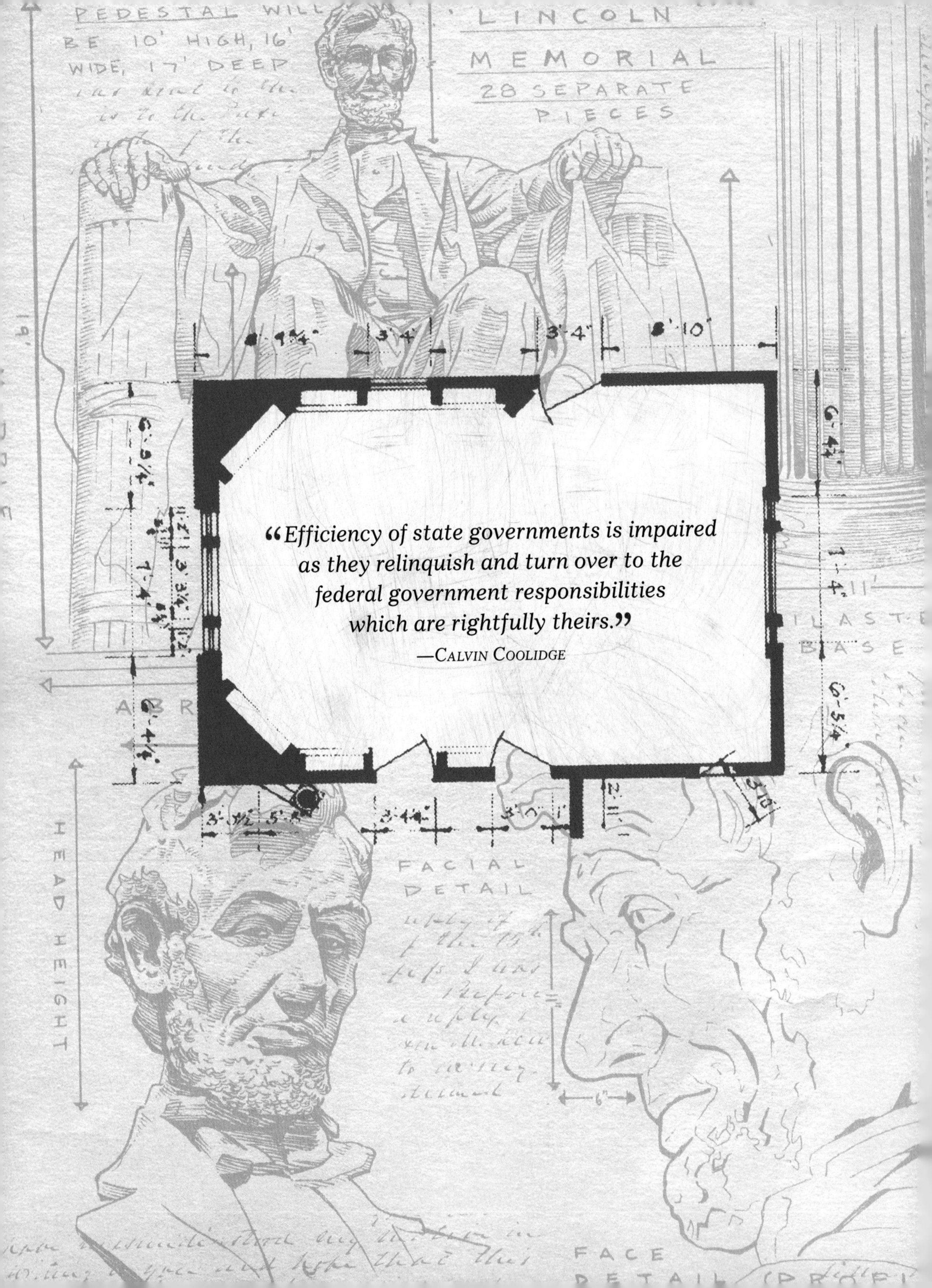

“Efficiency of state governments is impaired as they relinquish and turn over to the federal government responsibilities which are rightfully theirs.”

—Calvin Coolidge

CHAPTER 16.

Step Four: Decentralize and Disconnect

The world of innovation and the world that is our federal government are on two separate bullet trains headed in opposite directions. Technology is getting smaller, faster, and is doing more with less; the federal government is getting bigger, slower, and doing less with more. The new trend in business is decentralization; the trend in government is exactly the opposite.

Over the last century the government has taken control of virtually everything it could get its hands on, from education to energy, from finance to health care. It's hard to understate the enormity of what has happened, but consider this: The number of federal regulators has more than tripled over the last fifty years to keep up with the government's growth.

And yet, for all the talk about innovation and technology, most of government's policy prescriptions remain surprisingly clunky and outmoded. When they want to "fix" the auto industry, they appoint a czar. When they want to tackle environmental issues, they appoint a czar. Health care? Green jobs? Bank bailouts? Czar, czar, czar.

It's ironic, but to cut through the bureaucracy and get things done, politicians like to create another level of bureaucracy.

That, of course, is the opposite of how successful companies operate. The tendency in business is toward shifting away from centralized technology and a top-down management style and replacing it with a looser, flattened, decentralized management. Out with the old mainframe computer, in with the iPad; out with middle managers in corporate headquarters, in with franchise owners or branch managers who have real authority.

The reason this trend is happening is simple: It works. Just look around at the companies that are doing well. I can guarantee you that very few of them have a centralized bureaucracy with workers paid to punch the clock instead of innovate, create, and make informed decisions.

Take Johnson & Johnson, for example. It has 76 years of sales increases, 25 consecutive years of adjusted earnings increases, and 47 years of dividend increases. Not too shabby. And right there on its website, the hypersuccessful company gives away one of the most important reasons for its success: "Johnson & Johnson is organized on the principles of decentralization management."

CEO William Weldon told a conference at the Wharton School of Business that the decentralized approach sparks innovation "in that it allows different people with different skills, different thoughts, to bring together different products and technologies to satisfy the unmet needs of patients or customers."

Lou Gerstner, CEO of IBM in the 1990s, turned that company around by decentralizing it. "Let's decentralize decision making wherever possible," he once told managers. Gerstner's "Total Quality Movement" empowered employees and forced them to take responsibility for their actions—and it worked: IBM's stock price increased by a factor of almost ten under his leadership.

Technology is decentralizing power and giving individuals more choices and freedom at lower costs and higher quality. The Internet itself is about as decentralized a system as could ever be created (although some are even trying to centralize control of that).You can pick the applications you want on your cell phone, do your banking online, buy virtually any product on the planet from anywhere else on the planet, and get news from a whole host of sources, some as small as an individual, some as large as a Fortune 500 corporation. And that's exactly the point: Decentralization helps create more freedom.

We are in the midst of a revolution in decision making and control and the reason is simple: Decentralization improves performance, generates new innovations, and empowers individuals by encouraging them to take on greater responsibility in return for greater potential rewards. Decentralization is taking hold everywhere—except in Washington.

ADAPT OR DIE

It's too bad there aren't more true capitalists in government. If there were, they might understand the term *creative destruction* and be more concerned about whether it applies to countries in addition to companies.

Coined by Austrian economist Joseph Schumpeter, *creative destruction*, according to the *New York Times*, describes "how capitalism destroys companies as more innovative ones succeed." Kodak, for example, used to be a leading camera company, but they failed to adapt to digital. Meanwhile, a startup like Netflix was able to take down a powerhouse like Blockbuster precisely because it was able to see that what Blockbuster was doing would soon no longer work.

It's not hard to see the lesson in this for America.

DE-CENTCOM

The U.S. military is probably one of the most top-down centralized organizations in the world. And for good reason—I don't think any of us wants some go-getter in the field deciding to initiate a nuclear strike. But, even with the obvious constraints, things are changing.

The military is putting a renewed emphasis on empowering junior officers, instead of having them simply wait for orders from on high. In the introduction to the U.S. Army Leadership Manual, then Army Chief of Staff General Eric Shinseki explained that the U.S. military has found that "practicing this kind of decentralized execution based on mission orders in peacetime trains subordinates who will, in battle, exercise disciplined initiative in the absence of orders. They'll continue to fight when the radios are jammed, when the plan falls apart, when the enemy does something unexpected." General Shinseki concluded that officers "should empower your subordinate leaders: give them a task, delegate the necessary autonomy and then let them do the work."

This new effort—empowering noncommissioned officers (NCOs) so they can respond to fast-moving situations on the ground rather than getting on the radio and waiting for instructions from back at headquarters, is working. In Iraq, General David Petraeus guided the surprisingly successful surge by decentralizing operations. He met with junior officers and empowered them to do what they think is best, even if that meant cutting through the military bureaucracy. He delegated decision making down to the proper level by encouraging leaders to innovate and adapt based on the situation.

Don't look now, but it worked—and it can work for government as well.

The Original Management Consultants

Like most of the good ideas that we are now rediscovering, decentralization was first embraced by the ultimate innovators: the Founders. They believed deeply in empowering individuals, not only because it would result in decision making closer to the actual problem, but also because spreading power out ensured that it could never be amassed in one place.

I mentioned earlier that I was struck in researching this book by how many of the best ideas that came up can already be found in the Constitution. This one is no exception. The Tenth Amendment, ratified in 1791, was created to act as a safety net, a second layer of protection just in case people would eventually be dumb enough to not understand that the whole intent of the Constitution was to limit federal power. It reads:

> *The powers not delegated to the United States by the Constitution, nor prohibited by it to the States, are reserved to the States respectively, or to the people.*

It's simple, straightforward, and, just as the Founders feared, almost entirely ignored.

The system by which the states were supposed to be laboratories of democracy, mostly free from federal interference, is called "federalism" and its benefits were defended in the aptly titled *Federalist* Papers. In number 39 ("Conformity of the Plan to Republican Principles"), for example, James Madison wrote:

> *Each State, in ratifying the Constitution, is considered as a sovereign body, independent of all others, and only to be bound by its own voluntary act. In this relation, then, the new Constitution will, if established, be a federal, and not a national constitution.*

If our Founders wanted to create a purely national government (even with states still in existence), then they would have set up a majority-rules system. The president would be elected based on a national popular vote, as would senators and representatives. Instead, presidential elections are handled via electoral votes based on state population. Representatives are assigned the same way. Only the Senate provides a true equal balance of representation among the states at the national level. This was an entirely new concept in government: a system with some national features, and some federal features. It wasn't a democracy, it was a *true* republic—the first ever to be tried on the planet—and it was genius.

HATE SPEECH?

"[The states are] the most competent administrations for our domestic concerns and the surest bulwarks against antirepublican tendencies."

—*Thomas Jefferson*

The Founders had seen the freedom-robbing consequences of what centralization under a powerful king had meant. They understood that liberty expands as centralization contracts. So they went small. They took government local. They wanted the lowest-level decision makers to be the first ones to decide.

But they also recognized that some problems that start in the states are truly of national importance, which is why the federal government was not stripped of all its power. In fact, Article Six of the Constitution declares that the Constitution itself is the supreme law of the land, a clause that gives the government tremendous power to defend the rights that are spelled out in the document. *But only those rights.* Everything else, as the Tenth Amendment made clear, was to be left to the states or to the people.

It's that distinction that seems to have confused people over the years, and Ronald Reagan addressed it head-on in a 1987 executive order on federalism:

It is important to recognize the distinction between problems of national scope (which may justify Federal action) and problems that are merely common to the States (which will not justify Federal action because individual States, acting individually or together, can effectively deal with them).

The trick, of course, is how you define each of those problems. Poverty, a problem common to all states, is to me a local issue. Leaders in West Virginia can understand and react to the plight of coal mine workers better than a bureaucrat in D.C. can. Leaders in Detroit know the intricacies of the auto business and what it's going to take to help laid-off workers. Leaders in New York City have seen firsthand the consequences of market collapses and federal regulation of Wall Street and can help those displaced workers transition their lives. It's a perfect recipe for accountability and for ensuring that decisions are made based on the realities of a specific situation instead of the generalities of an entire country.

But others contend that poverty is a problem of national scope that can best be handled by the federal government through large aid programs. Of course, those people don't want to cut state aid and have the feds take over; they want *all* levels of government involved—something that, as we've seen, not only doesn't work, but is also massively expensive.

The key thing to remember is that neither federal nor local control can ever *eliminate* a problem like poverty. Those who declare that as a goal may have a bleeding heart, but they also likely have a bleeding brain. So the question becomes, which system gives us the best chance at using taxpayer money most efficiently and effectively?

By that standard, I believe it's no contest: Federal aid can never compete with local assistance. For a while, most of our leaders seemed to agree with that. Before the Civil War, petitions to the federal government for aid or for subsidies were rarely approved. In 1817, for example, President James Madison vetoed a road and canal construction bill for being unconstitutional. Even for a time after the war, presidents still took the idea of states' rights pretty seriously. Grover Cleveland famously turned down a request to help Texas farmers trying to recover from a terrible drought and he routinely scolded those looking for federal funds to enhance their local communities.

BLEEDING BRAIN, EXHIBIT A

“*There are 37 million people living in poverty in America. Alleviating poverty is the cause of my life.*”

—Former Senator John Edwards

Edwards also seemed to be pursuing another cause in life, but we'll leave that for another book.

Poverty 1, America 0

"I have called for a national war on poverty. Our objective: total victory."

—President Lyndon Johnson

You would think that people would eventually realize that national wars on things like poverty and drugs only result in more poverty and drugs. If you don't want to simply fight things like homelessness, drug addiction, or crime, but instead actually *beat them* then you have to start from the bottom up. It's about cities and states doing what is best for their communities, not a career politician in Washington deciding how to dole out federal aid money. Wars are not won from central command; they're won by the soldiers on the field.

Why It Works

Professor Lino Graglia of the University of Texas Law School once explained that keeping power decentralized and at a local level "controls the tyranny" and produces greater diversity and respect for individual preferences. "It can be shown arithmetically," Graglia wrote, "that as an issue is decided by larger units, involving more people, the likelihood increases that fewer people will obtain their preference and more will be disappointed."

Let me put that into more relatable terms: You and your spouse are deciding which school to send your child to. You have four choices: public, charter, private, or home school. The two of you agree that, for various reasons, you want to go the home-schooling route—but personal decisions are no longer allowed; your entire extended family must decide for you.

Over a long weekend, the whole family flies into town, gets together in a room, and debates what to do about not only your child, but two others as well: one who's a cousin from California, and another who's a cousin from Detroit. The family hears from all of the different parents who lobby for their choice: The cousins from California prefer a private school, while those from Detroit were recently laid off and can afford only the public option.

At the end of the weekend, the family decides that the best compromise seems to be the charter school. It's cheaper than the private option and of a higher quality than the public option. The decision is announced and is binding on all three sets

We've Been Overton Windowed

"When the Constitution was adopted, the states were very strong, largely independent political entities, and the national government was relatively weak. Because federalism is a technique or attempt to share political power among sovereignties, to argue for federalism in that context was to argue for greater national power. Today the situation is reversed, with the national government having achieved virtually complete sovereignty, and to argue for federalism now is to argue for greater local power."

—Professor Lino Graglia, University of Texas Law School, 1982 of parents, and none of them like the result. Had they each decided according to their own needs and circumstances, things would have turned out much differently.

It's an extreme example, of course, but it's not that far off from the way federal programs really operate. It's one-size-fits-all and it forces the states to accept suboptimal solutions simply because the "group consensus" in Washington has dictated a specific agenda.

Professor Graglia went on to explain that local control also means less overall government spending. Why? Because the costs of local government programs are felt more immediately by taxpayers and therefore result in less waste and fewer spending sprees. You can see proof of this in property taxes. They are always under intense scrutiny because people believe they can actually influence them. Property taxes aren't sent off to some no-name processing center in a faraway state; they're sent right to the town hall. Politicians who spend that money better do it wisely.

TEACHABLE MOMENT

When you make everyone responsible for something, no one is responsible for anything. Every good manager knows that you can't announce to the whole office, "We're all responsible for maintaining the copier," because that ensures that you'll be out of paper and dry on toner in no time. And then the finger-pointing will start. To get something done, someone needs to be personally responsible.

Guess what: Government works the same way. Remember the debacle after Hurricane Katrina? I don't know about you, but dealing with a cataclysmic disaster seems to me like the exact thing we have government around for. Yet, after Katrina, there were plenty of agencies that were on site but powerless. There was more finger-pointing than there was problem solving. The buck didn't stop anywhere so neither did the blame. Meanwhile, people suffered.

The trouble with federal control is that it blurs accountability. Pennsylvanians who receive money from the federal government figure that people in Texas, California, and Florida are paying for it, thereby making it a net gain for Pennsylvania. But, of course, the people in Pennsylvania are paying for programs implemented elsewhere. It's all a big sham, an illusion to make people feel like they are somehow getting free money from Washington, when in reality all we are doing is shuffling money around the country so that politicians can create better campaign commercials.

TEACHABLE MOMENT

When's the last time you heard a Democrat in Congress get excited about tax relief? It almost never happens—but turn the issue to *property* taxes and ask a local politician instead of a national one and you suddenly see a different side of people.

"I will not be satisfied until we find a way to bring property taxes down. You want property tax relief? Come and get it! Come and get it!"
—Massachusetts governor Deval Patrick (D)

Our Money Takes an Expensive Vacation to D.C.

We covered lobbyists earlier, but the largest and most influential lobbying group in the country is made up of state and local governments. Over 88,000 different entities exist in the United States and most of them receive some kind of federal aid.

Unlike the early days of America, states are no longer shy about asking the feds for help. In fact, there is an entire industry called "grantsmanship" built around it. When Washington lets it become known that money is available, the states come begging.

Aside from the larger problem of this making our states more and more dependent on the federal government, there's another issue: taxation with very little representation.

Think about it: Income-tax dollars go from you to Washington, where they are appropriated out to various big-budget items. From there, they're refined into grants and programs, drawing everyone from state and local politicians to trade groups to unions to Washington to lobby for the money. Grant recipients are selected (I'm sure there's definitely no political horse-trading going on) and the money then starts flowing. The problem is that federal tax dollars, instead of benefiting the nation as a whole, could easily go to finance some specific initiative in a state across the country—a state where you have absolutely no representation.

The situation has gotten so bad that states now like to brag about their bounties as though grabbing as much cash as you can is a good thing. In Massachusetts, Governor Deval Patrick listed "$33.6 Million [in federal funds] for Community Development Block Grants" as a headline on his website. In Wisconsin, Governor Jim Doyle announced "$51 Million in Federal Education Funding." And in New York, Governor David Paterson bragged about applying to the federal government for "$540 Million in Public Safety Grant Requests to Improve Broadband Communications."

The special interest groups, of course, love this system. If you're a lobbyist for education or road construction, you no longer have to go on a tour of fifty state capitols to plead for cash; you can just go to Washington and lobby there.

Central Control: A Lobbyist's Dream

"It seems quite clear that special interests can get a stronger hold at the federal level than they can at the state level. All one needs at the federal level is to find a few skillful congressmen and one senator, and one is assured a billion or so annually in the federal budget. This is less likely to be true at the state level because the sums are more palpable and the notion of budgetary restraint, the notion that money spent on this means money taken away from that, is more familiar. And, of course, states cannot print money, as the federal government can."

—Harvard Law School professor Charles Fried

THE STATE AID BOOMERANG

THE JOURNEY OF TAX DOLLARS TO D.C. AND BACK

REGULATIONS AND MANDATES

814 GRANT PROGRAMS
$449 BILLION IN 2007

50 STATE GOVERNMENTS
88,000 LOCAL GOVERNMENTS

GRANTS AND CONTRACTS

WAGES

LOBBYING BY STATE AND LOCAL GOVERNMENTS, UNIONS, AND TRADE ASSOCIATIONS

BUSINESSES, NONPROFITS, AND INDIVIDUALS

16 MILLION EMPLOYEES

TRADE ASSOCIATIONS AND INTEREST GROUPS

EMPLOYEE UNIONS

ORGANIZATIONS OF GOVERNORS AND MAYORS

SPENDING ADVOCACY

VOTERS

ORIGINAL CHART BY CHRIS EDWARDS AT CATO

Bureaucracy as a Business

Progressives want us to believe that while businesspeople and the private sector are self-serving and profit-seeking, bureaucrats are just trying to benevolently fix other people's problems. We all know from experience that that is simply not true.

There is a school of economic thought, called Public Choice Theory, that explains what a sham the idea of bureaucrats working for the greater good is. Many economists who support the theory, including James M. Buchanan, have won the Nobel Prize. So take that, Krugman.

TEACHABLE MOMENT

Bureaucrats and politicians don't immediately profit the way a business does, but they are self-serving in other ways. They look for opportunities to expand their power and institutionalize their ability to continually extract money from others. Professor Fred McChesney of Northwestern University likens bureaucrats and politicians to the scoundrels in William Faulkner's novel *The Reivers*. At night, scoundrels would go out to the country road and water it down. The next day, when a passing car sank into the mud they created the night before, they would show up with a mule and offer to pull it out—for a hefty price, of course. Not wanting to leave their cars behind and walk, the drivers were forced to pay.

A more contemporary name for this kind of thing is "scam."

One way bureaucrats in Washington seek to institutionalize power is by continually promising money to the states—with strings attached. Think about the absurdity of this: Not only is Washington simply returning money to a state that it took from taxpayers in the first place, it often returns that money with additional requirements that, guess what, give the feds even more power and control.

Many of the federal "aid programs" that are so often bragged about by politicians require states to set up new boards and agencies to direct these activities. And this is not exactly a new idea. To get money through the 1916 Highway Act, for example, states were required to create, fund, and run highway departments, and then regularly file reports back to Washington to update them on their progress. We've also seen how the federal government will provide highway funds in exchange for states agreeing to their nanny-state regulations, like a 55-mph speed limit.

More recently, in 2009, Louisiana governor Bobby Jindal announced that he was declining federal stimulus money because Louisiana would have been required to raise taxes. Virtually the same thing happened again in 2010: The federal government passed an "emergency" $26 billion state-aid package that was spun in the media as keeping teachers employed. "We can't stand by and do nothing," President Obama said, "while pink slips are given to the men and women who educate our children or keep our communities safe."

That kind of language is not used by accident. It's intentionally meant to put massive heat on state politicians to accept the money, whatever the cost. The $26 billion, for example, may include requirements that states accepting the money cannot cut their education budgets in the following year. "It would be prudent in not committing entirely to the idea of taking this money unless we know . . . what the impact is and the potential unintended consequences," Michael Drewniak, spokesman for New Jersey governor Chris Christie, said after being asked by the media why the governor wasn't enthusiastically grabbing the money being offered.

TEACHABLE MOMENT

After seeing all the strings attached to the federal stimulus money, states like New Jersey seem to be smartening up. But so are the feds. The $26 billion state-aid package included a provision whereby the state *cannot* turn the money down. If they don't accept it then the money will, according to the bill, "bypass the state government" and flow straight to recipients chosen by the U.S. Department of Education.

A Competitive State

Federalism is a far better system because, as Professor Charles Fried of Harvard Law School explained, it allows people to "vote with their feet." If, for example, the people of Vermont want to outlaw french fries, and the courts say that's okay, then people who want french fries can go to New Hampshire or Massachusetts to get them. If, on the other hand, the federal government outlaws french fries, you need to leave the country.

The free-market system works because businesses compete for customers. The competition, in turn, drives prices down and quality up. The federal government, on the other hand, is a monopoly. Don't like Social Security? Tough. Can't get a straight answer from OSHA? Too bad. Don't ever want to receive Medicare benefits? You're paying anyway. State competition is the only opportunity we have available to provide citizens with a way to get around the monopoly.

There's probably nowhere in the country where the benefits of state competition can be seen as much as here in the Northeast. Between New York City, Connecticut's Fairfield County ("the Gold Coast"), and the greater Boston area, there is a lot of highly concentrated wealth. There are also a ton of taxes. That leaves people like me with a choice: Do I want to live in Manhattan and pay an enormous city income tax (in addition to state and federal taxes), do I want to live in Connecticut and pay only state and federal, or do I want to move my company to New Hampshire and pay only federal income tax? It's nice to have a choice in tax rates; it would be nicer to have a choice in even more areas.

New Jersey, which has always been a high-tax state, is beginning to see the benefits of being competitive. If Governor Christie is successful in lowering the cost of living and doing business in that state, I can guarantee you that people will flock there. New York will lose more of its tax base and New Jersey will gain. It's competition at its finest.

A NICE PLACE TO VISIT

New Yorkers, fed up with high taxes (next year, the combined federal, state, and local tax burden for top-earning New Yorkers will be over 53 percent) and poor services, have been fleeing the Empire State in droves. Between 2000 and 2009, 1 out of every 7 New Yorkers left the state for good. And you know what? I love New York, but this is a good thing. People are voting with their feet. If anything will make politicians understand that people will not put up with "tax and spend" forever, it's the mass exodus of taxpayers.

Obviously, there are certain things that only the federal government can do. We can't have competing armies or competing judicial systems, but that's why the federal government exists in the first place. Remember, the list of things they should do is pretty short: national security, judiciary, international relations, and patents and copyrights. Competition among states in those areas would be a disaster. And that, in fact, is a pretty good litmus test for figuring out whether a program or agency should be at the state or national level: If competition would be a bad thing, then the feds should probably have it.

Aside from continually pushing our leaders to ask that question about each and every thing the federal government does, we must also reshape this entire debate. Never lose sight of the fact that we have the Constitution on our side! Others can complain and harass and name-call, but our Framers agreed with *us*. Progressives have so successfully tarnished the idea of federalism that the default standard now seems to be that power automatically rests with the federal government. If you want local control, you have to fight for it. That's the *opposite* of how this should work. The default standard should be that power rests with the states and people. If the federal government wants a new program, agency, or initiative, then they should be forced to make the case as to why that power must reside in Washington. As in a criminal trial, the onus must be on the federal government to demonstrate, beyond a reasonable doubt, that something must be nationalized in order for it to work properly.

A.D.D. Moment

That litmus test is probably not foolproof, but let's test it out with an example: Would competition among states for fighting poverty be a good thing or a bad thing?

Good, of course! If Ohio comes up with a great program, then other states can adapt it. There's no reason there can't be national organizations to collect and share information and best practices; it's just that the actual funding and execution of ideas must happen locally.

The Politics of Control

The first four topics we've covered in the plan so far all have something important in common: They push America toward control by elites. Think about it: From the degrading of individual rights, to a push toward "equality" for everyone, to the

They've Cracked the Code!

A *Time* article from 2002 explained that Ronald Reagan and lots of other prominent Republicans were actually all racists speaking in a cryptic language that only other racists could understand: "[A campaign speech Reagan gave] was a ringing declaration," they wrote, "of [Reagan's] support for 'states' rights'—a code word for resistance to black advances clearly understood by white Southern voters."

In 2007, Bob Herbert wrote in the *New York Times* about the same incident, "[Reagan] was tapping out the code. It was understood that when politicians started chirping about 'states' rights' to white people in places like Neshoba County they were saying that when it comes down to you and the blacks, we're with you."

Since there seems to be so much confusion, let me try to explain this in a way that even the media can understand: These days, "states' rights" is not code language for anything other than returning rights to the states. In fact, I'm not sure if the media has noticed, but segregation and slavery, which is what I assume they're referring to by playing the race card, are actually *illegal*. You can give states all the rights you want and they're not coming back.

minimizing of the role of God in society, to transferring power from states and cities to a central bureaucracy, it's all laying the groundwork for a new kind of aristocracy.

But to get there, progressives must continue to buy off various voting blocs by redistributing wealth. And that's why federalism is such a big deal. "State aid" is just a really nice, really friendly way of talking about wealth redistribution without really *talking* about it. After all, if you take tax dollars from a wealthy person in Boston and send it to an antipoverty program in Arizona under the guise of "state aid," then what have you really done other than redistribute wealth?

Some people might wonder why progressives would care whether that redistribution happens nationally or locally. If the state of Arizona takes tax dollars from a rich person and funnels it to that same antipoverty program, isn't that just as good?

No—and here's why: State tax rates are, for the most part, not as graduated as the federal system. Remember, in the federal tax system, almost half the population pays nothing and the top 10 percent finances over 70 percent of our country's revenue. That's not the case in all states—and some states don't have income taxes at all and instead rely on property or sales taxes, which, much to the chagrin of progressives, have flat rates.

Howard Chernick, a professor at Hunter College who specializes in studying public aid, explained clearly why progressives fear more state control of tax dollars:

> *In a decentralized federal system such as the United States, the realization of distributional goals requires the joint fiscal effort and cooperation of several layers of government. If fiscal responsibility for redistribution were left*

entirely to subnational levels of government, then states with weak fiscal capacity or limited preferences for redistribution might choose benefits and levels of access that fall below minimum.

The federal government is not going to willingly give up the power it has accumulated. In fact, it's not even going to give it up unwillingly. The only way that we can return to the power-sharing arrangement envisioned by our Founders is if people demand that their states stand up for their constitutionally guaranteed rights. That means taking extraordinarily strong stands on issues that, in the past, would've seemed like no-brainers. It means turning down federal aid, not participating in so-called compulsory national programs, and suing to demand that every federal initiative meets the Tenth Amendment test.

In some cases, this is already happening. Missouri voters, for example, recently passed Proposition C, the Health Care Freedom Act, which allows citizens there to opt out of ObamaCare. The vote, much to the surprise of the national media, wasn't even close: 71 percent supported it. There are similar efforts afoot in other states, such as Oklahoma and Utah. In addition, at least fourteen attorneys general are suing the federal government over the constitutionality of ObamaCare.

There's also a fire growing in states like Montana, South Dakota, and Wyoming where governors (representing both political parties) signed legislation declaring that federal regulations of firearms don't apply if the weapon is made and used in their state. This may not seem like a big deal if you don't forge your own weapons, but it reasserts the sovereignty of the state and seeks to curtail the power of the federal government.

There's an old riddle that you've probably heard before: How do you eat an elephant? *One bite at a time.*

The same logic applies here. Looking at everything that America faces seems overwhelming, to say the least. But the beauty of our system is that the Founders set it up to be self-healing. We don't have to fix every other state—we just have to fix our own. We don't have to fix 300 million other Americans—we just have to fix ourselves.

If we are better people and hold our local politicians to the Constitution, then we've done 99 percent of the work. Remember, even national figures like senators and congressmen are really just local politicians whom we've sent to represent us. Judge them on how they perform for their districts, not on how well they're doing climbing the political ladder in D.C. or how many important committees they've weaseled their way onto.

Hundreds of years ago, our Founders developed a system of power sharing that was unique to the world: a republic—not just in name, like the Romans once had, but also in function. It was a system set up to endure the test of time and of tyrants; a system that would set national goals but rely on local execution; a system that ensured the federal government could never grow too large because it didn't even have the power to give itself more power.

Progressives have destroyed this system over time, but those of us who want to restore it have one big advantage: the system was designed to heal itself. Violence and aggression aren't required because the prescription for fixing the Constitution is the very power of legislation that it grants. Our Framers knew that, despite their best efforts, we would reach a point where power had been amassed in the hands of a few—and they gave us the tools to amend their document and ensure that the people and states could again harness the powers that had been reserved for them.

All it takes are some creative ideas and the strong will of people to implement them. In the next chapter I lay out the ideas . . . I just need you to provide the will.

Educate Yourself

- *The Federalist Papers* (free)
  http://thomas.loc.gov/home/histdox/fedpapers.html

- *The Anti-Federalist Papers* (free)
  http://www.wepin.com/articles/afp/

- Forrest McDonald, *E Pluribus Unum: The Formation of the American Republic, 1776–1790*
  http://books.google.com/books?id=lICaAAAAIAAJ

- Forrest McDonald, *States' Rights and the Union: Imperium in Imperio, 1776–1876*
  http://books.google.com/books?id=yjiGAAAAMAAJ

- George W. Carey, *In Defense of the Constitution*
  http://books.google.com/books?id=hYCEQgAACAAJ

- Thomas E. Woods, Jr., and Kevin R. C. Gutzman, *Who Killed the Constitution? http://books.google.com/books?id=hdJcr-ye0ZYC*

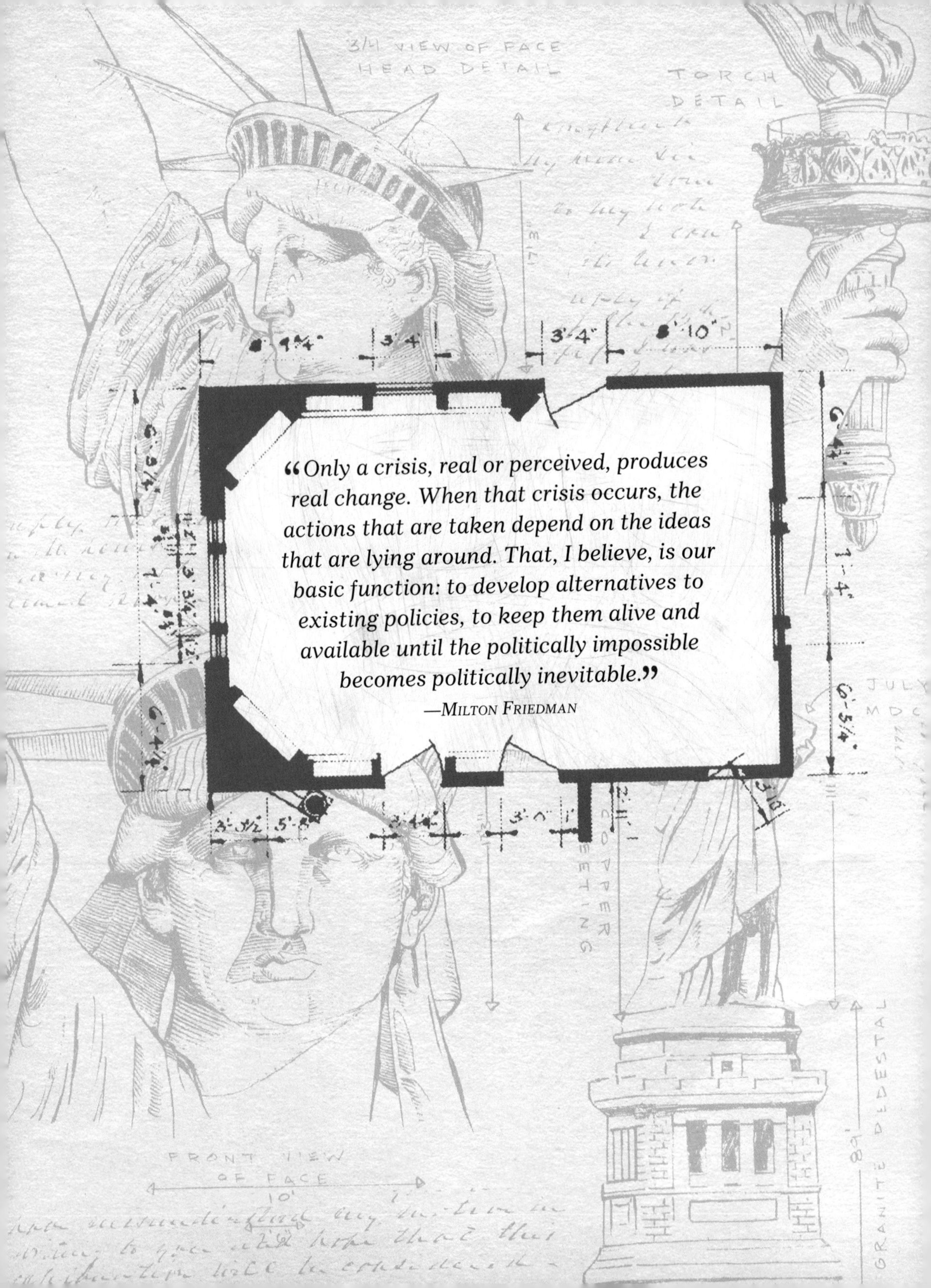

"Only a crisis, real or perceived, produces real change. When that crisis occurs, the actions that are taken depend on the ideas that are lying around. That, I believe, is our basic function: to develop alternatives to existing policies, to keep them alive and available until the politically impossible becomes politically inevitable."

—Milton Friedman

CHAPTER 17.

Step Five: A Taste of Their Own Medicine

Progressives have consistently used claims of a crisis to further their agenda, so maybe it's time to give them a taste of their own medicine. We are in a crisis *right now*, and it doesn't need to be exaggerated or embellished: It's a constitutional crisis.

We are so far removed from the actual language and intent of the Constitution that it's no wonder our system is broken. The emergencies that people want immediate reactions to (the jobs crisis, debt crisis, and corruption crisis) are only consequences of our constitutional crisis.

So, to borrow a phrase from Rahm Emanuel, let's not let this serious crisis go to waste.

A lot of great ideas to strengthen our founding document have been proposed, but there are several that I think have a real chance at being politically possible and, once implemented, actually effective. In other words, these are not ideas that will be easy to pass but then act as nothing but window dressing and, conversely, they're also not ideas that might sound appealing but that are completely unrealistic (i.e., "vote them all out").

Just keep in mind that nothing will happen overnight and, while that can be frustrating, we must all keep pushing in the same direction. If we do our job, make our case, and never give in, then Milton Friedman's observation will eventually be our path to restoration as the politically impossible someday becomes the politically inevitable.

Pass a Balanced-Budget Amendment

"I wish it were possible to obtain a single amendment to our Constitution. I would be willing to depend on that alone for the reduction of the administration of our government to the genuine principles of its constitution; I mean an article taking from the Federal government the power of borrowing."

—Thomas Jefferson

I really don't like the idea of tinkering with our Constitution. I think it says what it needs to say in the simplest form possible. But sometimes there's no other choice. Sometimes, as Jefferson wrote years before he ever thought of a balanced-budget amendment, "when a long train of abuses and usurpations, pursuing invariably the same Object evinces a design to reduce them under absolute Despotism, it is their right, it is their duty, to throw off such Government, and to provide new Guards for their future security."

We don't need to throw off the government, but we do need to provide for our future security by reining in its ability to bankrupt us—and it looks like a balanced-budget amendment is what it's going to take to do that.

Nobel Prize–winning economist James Buchanan says that our nation's chronic deficits are the result of a "structural flaw in our fiscal politics" and that "the structural flaw requires structural correction, that is, constitutional constraint that will, effectively, change the basic rules for the fiscal game."

The problem is that we've gotten to this place not because of any problem with the Constitution, but because of the evolving interpretation of it. A "living" Constitution requires that our government constantly provide services equal to the societal norms of the time. That takes a lot of money to accomplish. In earlier times, the cost would've been a deal breaker, but as Keynesianism took hold, that was no longer an issue. As Buchanan pointed out:

> *Politicians prior to World War II would have considered it to be immoral (to be a sin) to spend more than they were willing to generate in tax revenues, except during periods of extreme and temporary emergency . . . There were basic moral constraints in place; there was no need for an explicit fiscal rule in the written constitution.*

But now, with the moral constraints long gone, there *is* an explicit need for a law. Our leaders have run deficits in 44 of the last 50 years and the Obama budget projects them to continue for another decade straight. It's no longer a question of whether they can balance the budget on their own—every ounce of data proves they cannot—so it's time to balance it for them.

A constitutional amendment, while daunting to actually pass, would be the most effective and enduring way of guaranteeing that our leaders cannot spend us into serfdom. It doesn't have to be complicated, but there are a few things that have to be addressed to prevent the weasels from finding loopholes:

1. Spending cannot be higher than the prior year's amount, plus the rate of inflation and population growth.
2. If, at the end of a given fiscal year, the estimates were wrong and the budget is still not balanced, the difference would automatically be cut from the budget for the next fiscal year according to a very specific, predetermined formula.
2. An exception can be included for a war *declared* by Congress, or a national calamity. The benchmark for meeting the definition of the latter would need to be quite high, think something in the range of 90 percent of members of Congress agreeing. That may seem like an unrealistic bar, but how many politicians would have voted against declaring 9/11 or Hurricane Katrina a national calamity?
4. Federal expenses cannot be pawned off on the states.

What's amazed me most about this particular issue is that it really seems to be something that anyone who honestly cares about our financial health would get behind. I understand there might be some disagreements about the wording, but the premise itself should have bipartisan appeal. In fact, the only way someone could argue against it (besides a strict constitutionalist who doesn't want to ever touch the Constitution), would be to make the case that this amendment would necessitate significant reforms to the entitlement programs. But isn't that exactly the point?

Oh, and there's one other influential group of people who always want to argue against this kind of amendment: Congress.

And that might just be the best reason of all to fight for it.

STOP THE PRESSES!

No, literally, I mean stop the presses. Stop printing money.

But, since we're here, I think I've found something that Senator Lindsey Graham and I actually agree on. Unless he's changed his mind (which does seem to happen quite often, depending on the election calendar), he proposed, along with Senator Jim DeMint, a balanced-budget amendment in 2007.

The bill so far has sixteen co-sponsors, all of them Republicans. Where are the rest of the Republicans? And where are the Democrats, especially the Blue Dogs who know that this kind of spending is unsustainable? If you see any senators, ask them why they are not signed on to this.

Pass a Term Limits Amendment

"As long as members have the chance to spend their lives in Washington, their interests will always skew toward spending taxpayer dollars to buy off special interests, covering over corruption in the bureaucracy, fund-raising, relationship building among lobbyists, and trading favors for pork—in short, amassing their own power."

—SENATOR JIM DEMINT

Since we're already talking about constitutional amendments, let's add another one: term limits.

The Founders believed that public service was just that—a way to *serve* the public, not to be served *by* the public. Today we think of politicians in designer suits, privy to all kinds of access and special treatment, living in beautiful D.C. town houses, but that's not the way it was ever intended to work. After our founding, politics was a part-time endeavor and those who participated were not defined by their role in government, but by their real career. Doctors, farmers, businessmen—these were people from varied backgrounds and experiences who devoted some of their time in service to their country.

When the first Congress was supposed to meet in New York on March 4, 1789, to tally Electoral College votes for the presidential election, only eight of the twenty-two senators and thirteen of the fifty-nine representatives showed up. Where was everyone else? Tending to their daily lives. They had fields to plow, businesses to run, and families to take care of. In fact, during the early part of our history, senators and congressmen were paid by the days they actually worked ($6 a day) as an incentive to get them to come to Washington more often. In 1815, members of Congress began receiving a salary ($1,500 a year, which is about $21,116 in today's money), but that was it. No one was getting rich off their political career because politics wasn't thought of as a profitable endeavor; it was thought of as temporary stewardship of the country. Members served, made the tough choices, and then went back to work and got on with their lives.

Does that in any way resemble the way it now works? When you look at Barney Frank or Charlie Rangel do you immediately think of him as a private citizen, or as a professional politician?

Like it or not, we now have a political class that's drunk on power and all of its trappings. Very few politicians

Reason #5,891 That We Need Term Limits

"Looking back over the past eight years, we've done a lot of legislation here where actually bills have been passed before we knew the numbers."

—SENATOR CHRISTOPHER DODD (D-CONN.)

have the courage to make difficult choices and serve the needs of the people first because they always have their eyes on the next election or the next fund-raising cycle. Members of Congress barely get into office before they have to start campaigning for reelection.

The solution? Term limits. Written into the Constitution. In ink.

I can already hear the strict constitutionalists weeping . . . *He's proposed TWO amendments and we've barely even started!* I get it, I get it, we don't like to touch the sacred document when we don't have to. But, believe me, we have to. What is the good of keeping the Constitution pristine if it eventually becomes irrelevant?

So what would my dream amendment actually say? Simple: Representatives would be limited to three total terms (six total years) and senators would be limited to two total terms (twelve total years).

Senator Jim DeMint proposed that exact language in November 2009. The bill currently has just three co-sponsors (just to give them a little credit, it's Senators Brownback, Coburn, and Hutchinson) and is on a fast track to nowhere. Illinois Democratic senator Dick Durbin was pretty blunt about its chances. "It's a great issue to talk about, but it's not going to happen," he said. Coincidentally, Durbin himself has now served thirteen years in the Senate, just over the maximum allowed by the proposed bill.

Come to think of it, maybe that's not such a coincidence after all.

The first thing that should be obvious is that, like the balanced-budget amendment, the reason this has never gone anywhere is that the people it would hurt the most (members of Congress) are also the ones who have to pass it. That's why, during campaign cycles, we must ask this question to get all candidates on the record: "Yes or no, do you support a term-limits amendment to the Constitution?" And I would expand that to asking current members as well—make them say publicly that they support career politicians and the status quo.

Reason #5,892 Why We Need Term Limits

"I love these members, they get up and say, 'read the bill.' What good is reading the bill if it's a thousand pages and you don't have two days and two lawyers to find out what it means after you read the bill?"

—House Judiciary Committee chairman John Conyers (D-Mich.)

It's pretty ironic that presidents, who have no spending authority, are limited to eight years in office, yet the people with the power to actually spend our money are free to serve for as long as they can keep getting elected.

In the House, Representative John Dingell is the longest-serving member in history, having been on the job more than 19,400 days (and counting) and has outlasted eleven U.S. presidents. "The nice thing about having been around here awhile," says

POWER GOES TO THEIR HEADS

I don't have an official study on this, but it stands to reason that the longer you're around, the more likely you are to eventually find yourself in a scandal. Take, for example, Representatives Charlie Rangel and Maxine Waters, both of whom were charged with ethics violations in 2010. Rangel is a twenty-term lawmaker and Waters has been around for ten terms. That's an awful lot of "experience" in finding ways to bend the rules for your own benefit.

Dingell, "is you learn how the place works. You learn the buttons that you push and the levers you pull." Yeah, that's awesome.

Before his recent passing, former Klansman Robert Byrd spent fifty-one years in the U.S. Senate and cast more than 18,600 votes. During a 2006 interview, Byrd said, "If I could live another 100 years, I'd like to continue in the Senate." Combined, Byrd, whose nickname was the "Prince of Pork," and Representative Dingell have spent more than a century in Washington.

Some critics of term limits like to argue that career politicians can bring a wealth of experience in navigating difficult legislation to successful passage. That, of course, is utter nonsense. For one, it assumes that passing more laws is, by definition, a net positive. And what good is "experience" when all it produces is bigger and more expensive government? With every term on the job, politicians become more beholden to powerful interests and make more promises to win reelection. That's hardly the "experience" we want or need.

There's a dirty little secret about Washington that no one inside the Beltway is going to tell you: Politics isn't rocket science. There's a Senate and House rulebook. You study it, do homework on key issues, vote your values, and get on with it. We don't need people with "experience," we need people with principles—and term limits are the best way to ensure that's exactly what we get.

Pass a Line-Item Veto Amendment

I know, this is getting ridiculous, but this is the last amendment I'm supporting (for now), I swear.

The line-item veto has been talked about for years and the power was even handed to Bill Clinton for a time. But, in 1998, the Supreme Court ruled the practice unconstitutional, which is why the only way to get it back is to actually amend the Constitution.

The reason we need this should be pretty obvious: Congress loves to hide the pig inside the blanket. In other words, they like to take legislation that has wide support (defense bills are a favorite) and then wrap it in all sorts of fat. Since the president needs the underlying legislation to pass, they usually take a lesser-of-two-evils approach and pass the whole thing rather than risk sending it back to Congress, where it might be radically changed, or even killed altogether.

The line-item veto would hand presidents a cost-cutting "scalpel" that would allow them to go into a bill and carve out just the fat. As the only elected official in the entire spending process who has term limits, the president should ideally be in the best position to put the future of the country ahead of his or her career.

There is, no surprise, a lot of debate about the idea. Some people say it would give the president too much power by letting him veto specific items and enact "revenge" against certain lawmakers. Others say that it could actually *increase* overall spending because the president could horse-trade with members by letting them put through their little pet projects in exchange for their vote on a massive presidential initiative (for example, a public option for health care, or Medicare Part E . . . which you know is coming).

While those may all be valid concerns, they're all worries about what *might* happen in the future. Excuse me for being logical, but I'm more concerned about what's *already* happened in the past and is continuing to happen right now. Does the line-item veto have downsides? Possibly—but the downsides of *not* giving presidents this power are far more certain and far more serious.

A More Perfect Union

Since I've now proposed three constitutional amendments, it's worth recapping why this process exists in the first place.

Unlike the idea of a living Constitution, whereby judges impose their own judgments on society, the constitutional-amendment process was specifically designed to keep the country on the right course. In his famous farewell address, George Washington explained the importance of having the means to amend the Constitution:

> *This Government . . . containing within itself a provision for its own amendment, has a just claim to your confidence and your support. Respect for its authority, compliance with its laws, acquiescence in its measures, are duties enjoined by the fundamental maxims of true liberty. The basis of our political systems is the right of the people to make and to alter their constitution of government. But the constitution which at any time exists till changed by an explicit and authentic act of the whole people is sacredly obligatory upon all.*

The brilliance of our amendment process is the unprecedented level of support it requires from the American people. And that's an important point. Progressives, such as Herbert Croly, have actually complained that the amendment process is too difficult (ostensibly because they couldn't get enough support for their radical ideas). Croly at one point supported a plan pushed by Senator La Follette whereby the Constitution could basically be amended by a simple majority of the popular vote. Thankfully Americans saw through that for the sham of an idea it was—but the point is that we make updating the Constitution hard for a reason.

Have a Backup Plan

The three amendments I just outlined are my dream list of reforms, but, let's face it: We haven't ratified a constitutional amendment since 1992; it's not likely we're going to ratify three of them in the next few years. So, while we're doing the hard work to get those amendments into the national debate, there are a few other practical things that we should be pushing for as well.

THE SAFE ACT

Introduced in May 2010 by Representative Lamar Smith (R-Tex.), this bill would attempt to do the same thing that a balanced-budget amendment would, but without going through the formal process. The downside of that is obvious: Without an amendment, politicians can usually find a way around the law (as they did with the Gramm-Rudman-Hollings Act back in the Reagan era; see sidebar). But the upside is that this bill, which already has sixty-five cosponsors (all of them Republicans . . . why?), actually has a real chance of being passed within a relatively short time span.

Like any good piece of legislation, this bill has a cute acronym: "SAFE," which stands for "Save America's Future Economy Act of 2010." (They had to work "Future" in there to make the acronym work, but this is about our *current* economy, not just the future.) Its goal is simple:

> *To amend the Balanced Budget and Emergency Deficit Control Act of 1985 to limit the year-to-year increase in total Federal spending to increases in the Consumer Price Index and population.*

The Cato Institute's Chris Edwards, who has testified before Congress on spending-cap plans like this, explains how the act would work:

> *[Smith's bill] would cap growth in all spending including defense, nondefense, and entitlements. If spending this year was $3.70 trillion, inflation was 2 percent, and population growth was 1 percent, then federal spending next*

REMEMBER, WE'VE FAILED BEFORE

As a reminder why trying to balance budgets through legislation can be a fool's errand, the "Balanced Budget and Emergency Deficit Control Act of 1985" (more commonly known as the Gramm-Rudman-Hollings Act) was a failure. Like the SAFE Act, it looked great on paper, but Congress got their dirty hands into the provisions and opened up all kinds of exceptions and loopholes. The act eventually became unsustainable because it would have forced deep across-the-board cuts to make up for the spending excesses. The lesson is clear: If we try this again without an amendment, the law needs to be crafted in such a way that Congress will be unable to tweak the rules every time they want to make an exception.

> *year would be limited to $3.81 trillion. If Congress failed to get spending under the limit by the end of the year, the president's budget office would be required to apply an across-the-board cut, or sequester. . . . The idea is simply that the government's budget shouldn't grow faster than the average family's budget.*

The other benefit of a bill like this is that a spending limit would put all of us on the exact same page in terms of our budget expectations and would let us hold those accountable who don't play by the rules.

The problem, of course, is that "limits" and Congress and don't play well together. Remember the statutory-debt limit that I wrote about earlier? Sure, Congress has to vote to give themselves the authority to raise it every time they need more money, but they've had absolutely no problem doing that. Who's to say the same thing wouldn't happen here?

Still, even with all the reservations, the SAFE Act would be a great first step on the way to a balanced-budget amendment and I hope that all politicians who aren't yet signed on are asked why they don't support restraining our spending.

THE GWBV

Sure, it's not quite as catchy as the "SAFE" act, but this one didn't have a name, so I gave it one. It's the "George W. Bush Veto" and it comes from an idea that Bush proposed back in March 2006.

The idea is to get around the unconstitutionality of the line-item veto by giving the actual veto power to Congress, but also giving the president "freezing" authority. The *Washington Post*, which actually supported Bush's idea (should that make me nervous?), summarized it like this:

> *Under his proposal, the president could not nix part of a spending bill; he could, however, temporarily freeze a spending item and request that Congress rescind it. Congress would be obliged to act on such requests quickly, without amendment and with no possibility of filibuster. If a majority of both houses of Congress stood by the provision, the president's action would have no consequence. If, on the other hand, the spending were a single member's pet project—a bridge in Alaska, say—Congress as a whole might not stand by it. The bill, in other words, gives the president not a line-item veto but a device for forcing individual votes on line items buried within larger spending packages.*

Forcing individual votes on line items would shine some light in dark areas of the budget that most members want to keep that way. It would also hold *everyone* accountable because the president could no longer sign a fatty bill and claim, "Well, I didn't want all of these frivolous programs, but we have to keep America safe and so I had no choice." Now he would have a choice, and by not freezing items that don't belong or are excessive, the president can be held just as responsible as the members.

RETURN IMPOUNDMENT AUTHORITY

Prior to 1974, presidents could impound funds and refuse to spend money that Congress had authorized if they thought it was frivolous or unnecessary. The first president to use the mechanism was Thomas Jefferson. In 1803 he told Congress that he did not need to spend the $50,000 that they had appropriated for gunboats because there had been a "peaceful turn of events."

All presidents up through Richard Nixon possessed and used this provision. It empowered them to be a responsible spender of the people's money and to trim the fat wherever they saw fit. In 1966, LBJ (yes, *that* LBJ) impounded $5.3 billion out of a $134 billion budget, including $1.1 billion in highway funds and $760 million in funds for things like housing and education. I guess that even a stopped clock is right twice a day.

When Nixon came along and started vetoing spending bills, members of Congress became irritated. After one of Nixon's vetoes was overridden, the Treasury secretary announced publicly that Nixon would instead impound the amount of spending over and above the amount he'd requested. That did not make Congress happy and they began moving to take away the impoundment authority that presidents had been using since the beginning.

Supremely Helpful

In ruling the line-item veto unconstitutional in 1998, three justices (Scalia, O'Connor, and Breyer) wrote a dissenting opinion in which they seemed to be offering a suggestion on how to achieve the same end without provoking a court case:

> ***Had the Line Item Veto Act authorized the president to "decline to spend" any item of spending contained in the Balanced Budget Act of 1997, there is not the slightest doubt that authorization would have been constitutional.***

In other words, if we'd simply rescind the Impoundment Act instead of trying to create new veto authority, there wouldn't be an issue. Maybe it's time we take them up on their advice.

After Watergate, Nixon was no longer in much of a position to fight and the Congressional Budget and Impoundment Control Act of 1974 was passed, putting the final nail in the coffin for a president's ability to trim the fat.

In May 2010, the Obama administration proposed the "Reduce Unnecessary Spending Act of 2010." (The RUSA? What kind of terrible bill-naming is that?) It would basically amend the 1974 Impoundment Act to allow the president to propose a package of rescissions to any spending bills. Congress would then have to vote up or down on each rescission without offering any amendments.

This seems to be an updated version of the GWBV and, unfortunately, it's also meeting the same fate, as Obama's bill hasn't gone very far in either the House or the Senate. I guess that does prove one thing: Congress's defense of its spending has nothing to do with which party is in the White House. After all, without term limits, most members of Congress know they'll be around a lot longer than the president anyway.

PAY-GO: PAY OR PLAY

This one is really simple: Either expand the "pay as you go" spending law to encompass *all* federal spending (not just selective discretionary items) or eliminate it altogether. The way it is now is completely pointless since the only thing it does is allow politicians to claim they support offsetting new spending with cuts elsewhere (or tax hikes) while never having to make any difficult decisions. We have to stop giving them this kind of political cover to hide behind.

Pass a Commonsense Lobbying Bill

When Tom Daschle got booted out of office, he went to work at lobbying firm Alston & Bird. Within two years, Daschle had earned $2.1 million for his services. As majority leader of the United States Senate, he used to make $193,400 a year.

Daschle is not alone. The revolving door between "public servant" and big-money lobbyist whirs with dizzying speed. According to Public Citizen, "between 1998 and 2004, 43% of former lawmakers became lobbyists." Of the 62 members of Congress who left office in 2008, 16 now work as lobbyists. Of those 16, 13 are Republicans. (A large reason for the disparity is that Republicans lost seats 6-to-1 that cycle.)

We need a lobbying bill that has two main objectives:

1. To force any nationally elected politician to be at least four years removed from office before he can work as a lobbyist. This would take most of their appeal to lobbying firms away because their insider

contacts would be much less relevant after four years. It would also prevent people from using political office only as an entryway into a lucrative lobbying career, which happens all too often.

2. Family members of current members of Congress cannot be lobbyists. Period. It's almost embarrassing that this has not already been outlawed. A recent CBS News investigation revealed, "19 federal lobbyists closely related to members of Congress, including dads, wives, brothers, sisters, sons, daughters, in-laws and more."

   Although lobbyists cannot directly lobby their relatives, that rule is really just for show. If your daughter is a lobbyist for a defense contractor and you sit on a committee that can approve a project her company is pitching, isn't that a pretty big conflict of interest?

The only members of Congress who would be against a bill like this are those who believe that it will eventually cost them a lucrative career. Those aren't the kind of people we want representing us anyway.

All in the Family

Here are a few of the family connections between lobbyists and members of Congress that *CBS News* found:

SENATOR BYRON DORGAN (D-N.D.)
Wife: Kimberly, lobbyist as of 1998
Client: American Council of Life Insurers

Senator Dorgan was considered a key vote against so-called cramdown legislation, an issue his wife lobbied on for the ACLI in 2009, according to a Federal Election Commission lobbying report filed by the Council.

REPRESENTATIVE DAVID OBEY (D-WIS.)
Son: Craig, lobbyist

Obey heads up the powerful House Appropriations Committee, which oversees nearly all federal spending.

REPRESENTATIVE STEVEN LATOURETTE (R-OHIO)
Elected in 1994
Wife: Jennifer, lobbyist (former LaTourette chief of staff)
Clients include: Spokane Transit Authority, Airports Council International–North America, Federal Technology Group

LaTourette also serves on the powerful House Appropriations Committee.

Want to Wage War? Declare It

The last time Congress passed a declaration of war was during World War II. That's both fiscally and morally reprehensible. Who are we as a country if we can't even sign a piece of paper before we go kill people?

Wars are not just a commitment of young lives; they're also a massive financial commitment. As we've seen, our deficits usually soar during war times—not just because of the actual defense spending but also because progressives like to use wartime spending as cover for spending on pet projects and entitlements (see: FDR, LBJ, GWB).

Without returning to the constitutional framework for declarations of war (i.e, "Congress shall have the power to . . . declare war), a balanced-budget amendment becomes severely weakened because all the Congress needs to do is deem appropriations as "emergency spending," thereby ballooning deficits.

The concern that divisive partisanship might stop a president from getting a declaration of war for a legitimate cause of national security is highly unlikely. In fact, in the six times since World War I that Congress passed declarations of war (all six declarations happened in 1941 and 1942), every single one passed with virtually unanimous support. (Fun war trivia: the only declaration that was not unanimous was the Declaration of War against Japan one day after they bombed Pearl Harbor. There was one dissenting vote in the House. Funny, I didn't realize that Dennis Kucinich was that old.)

If the cause is just, the Congress will support it. And if it doesn't, because of politics or any other petty reason, then we have even more problems than I thought.

A Binding Commission

> *"For far too long, Washington has avoided the tough choices necessary to solve our fiscal problems—and they won't be solved overnight. But under the leadership of Erksine and Alan, I'm confident that the Commission I'm establishing today will build a bipartisan consensus to put America on the path toward fiscal reform and responsibility."*
>
> —PRESIDENT OBAMA, FEBRUARY 2010

In creating the "National Commission on Fiscal Responsibility and Reform," President Obama is taking a step in the right direction. Unfortunately, it's just a baby step. And it actually may not even be in the right direction.

Here's the problem, of the 18 members of this commission, 12 are current members of the House and Senate. Sure, they're split between the parties, but they're still *politicians*, i.e., the very people who've gotten us here. The other 6 members were appointed by President Obama and include two former politicians as the co-chairs (Erskine Bowles and Alan Simpson), a former union leader (Andy Stern), a (well-respected) democratic economist who worked for LBJ and Bill Clinton (Alice Rivlin) and, finally, two business leaders (Republican Dave Cote from Honeywell and Democrat Ann Fudge, former CEO of Young & Rubicam).

To summarize: All 18 members are politically active and 14 of the 18 are current or former politicians. In addition, their recommendations are nonbinding, meaning the president and Congress can pick and choose what they like and dismiss the rest. This is completely the wrong way to come up with new, creative solutions that can be accepted by the American people and, in fact, may do nothing other than provide cover for Democrats to raise taxes without any equally painful spending cuts.

Obama Has a Commission?

Funny how things change once you're president. Remember this quote from then candidate Barack Obama?

"John McCain's big solution to the crisis we're facing is—get ready for this—a commission," Obama told the crowd. "A commission. That's Washington-speak for we'll get—we'll get back to you later."

—Barack Obama, September, 2008

Obama has now created four different commissions of his own, including one on the Gulf oil spill. I guess that means he'll get back to us later?

We need a real budget commission that is made up of political outsiders (primarily entrepreneurs and executives) and is handed real power to make long-term structural changes (not just recommendations for getting our short-term deficits under control, which is what the Obama commission is tasked to do).

This is not exactly a new concept; private-sector commissions have worked before. In 1981, President Reagan created a special commission called the Private Sector Survey on Cost Control (better known as the Grace Commission). The commission was made up of 161 executives and included thirty-six task forces. The entire cost of this commission ($75 million) was paid by private companies—at no cost to the government.

After three years, the commission produced recommendations with nearly 2,500 cost-cutting and revenue-enhancing recommendations that would save the federal government $424 billion in the first three years and would rise to $1.9 trillion in savings later. Peter Grace, the head of the commission, found that the Office of Management and Budget didn't even know how many social programs were in existence. They'd estimated 120–130 but, as Grace said, "We later found out that there are 963 different social programs, and you can get [enrolled] in 17 of them at the same time if you try hard enough."

The vast majority of the commission's recommendations were completely ignored by Congress.

Redraw the Battle Lines

Members of Congress almost never lose. Their reelection rates run upwards of 90 percent or more even while their approval rates are generally 20 percent or less. The simple fact is that we don't really select them; they select us.

One of the main reasons for the absurd incumbent reelection rates is that the shape of our congressional districts is determined by politicians in state legislatures. To gain an advantage for their party, they twist and shape the lines of these districts according to party affiliation data so that their side can win as many seats as possible. There is even software available to help politicians get the districting lines drawn in a way that will help their party the most.

It started back in 1812 with Elbridge Gerry, the governor of Massachusetts. He supported legislation that redrew the districting map to help his party by creating a shape so contorted that it looked like a salamander. His opponents called the design a "Gerry-mander" and the term has stuck ever since.

Needless to say, this is not exactly what our Founders had in mind when they designed our republic. In fact, in a 1964 Supreme Court ruling, the majority scolded Georgia for the way they'd gerrymandered their districts:

> *While it may not be possible to draw Congressional districts with mathematical precision, that is no excuse for ignoring our Constitution's plain objective of making equal representation for equal numbers of people the fundamental goal for the [national] House of Representatives. That is the high standard of justice and common sense which the founders set for us.*

Thankfully there is some good news brewing in, of all places, California (yes, really, California). In 2008, voters there passed Proposition 11, which upended the practice of gerrymandering for state legislators. The job of shaping districts in California now falls to a fourteen-member commission ("the Citizens Redistricting Commission") that will be chosen like a jury. And guess what? Members of the commission can't come from the "political class." It's a simple, elegant solution to a problem that has become a national epidemic. Now let's expand it to the national level.

JEFFERSON'S VISION

Thomas Jefferson had his own vision for how the country would be divided and governed: wards. Each ward, which would comprise approximately 100 families, would act like its own mini republic. According to Jefferson, each ward would include:

GERRYMANDER-SHAM-MOCKERY!

OF ALL THE GERRYMANDERED DISTRICTS ACROSS THE U.S., THESE ARE OUR TWO FAVORITES. WE'VE RENAMED THEM FOR YOUR CONVENIENCE.

THE OUTER BANKS RORSCHACH TEST

THE CHICAGO JAWS OF LIFE

SOURCE: THE NATIONAL ATLAS

> *A justice, chosen by themselves, in each, a constable, a military company, a patrol, a school, the care of their own poor, their own portion of the public roads, [and] the choice of one or more jurors to serve in some court. . .*

Jefferson believed that the smaller you created the political units, the better off you would be. There would be more connection among individuals to the process, more frugality over the spending of resources, and more concern shown for other members of your unit. Looking back, it's hard to argue that Jefferson was wrong.

Jefferson lobbied for his approach and was partially successful. Next time you fly over the heartland, take a look down at the perfect squares of townships chiseled into the landscape.

Citizen Bonds

Part of the reason our national debt is more of a threat now than it's been in the past is that so much of it is owned by foreign entities, primarily foreign governments. A new government debt product that is made available only to U.S. citizens would go a long way toward putting a dent in that problem.

Having more U.S. holders of our debt would also better align the interests of the citizens and government. If our generation wants to declare a war or institute a new entitlement program then our generation has to pay for it, just as our forefathers sacrificed and paid for the things they wanted. No more passing the debt burden on to our children by using foreigners as the enablers.

Some critics will say that we need foreigners to continue buying our debt because we have so much of it to issue and they'll help keep interest rates low. But those critics are only proving my point. If our debt isn't quite so easy and cheap to issue, then maybe we'll start thinking more about it.

The "Stop Empowering Influential Unions" (SEIU) Act

The biggest challenge posed by unions is not in the private sector, where they have been on the decline for some time; the big action is on the public side.

Unions represent about 37 percent of public-sector workers, and only 7 percent of those in the private sector. Why are unions on the decline in private business but growing in government? Simple: In the private sector the excessive demands of unions are checked by free-market competition. If they become unreasonable and drive up costs at one car company, for example, people will buy cheaper and better-built cars from a competitor.

But in government, there is no competition. If they drive up demands for pensions or benefits, who is going to provide a counterbalance? That's why there is no check on union power.

And here's the problem: When public employee unions come making their demands, they don't negotiate with those who are paying the bills (taxpayers), but with politicians, many of whom are eager to buy their support in the next election by giving them exactly what they want.

But let's step back from the obvious conflicts and instead look at why we have public unions in the first place. After all, does it really make sense that we even allow government employees to unionize? They're *public* employees.

It all happened because of a 1962 executive order signed by President John Kennedy. (That's right, this is not a result of a *law*—but a presidential order.) As Dan Henninger wrote in the *Wall Street Journal*, "This [executive order] changed everything in the American political system. Kennedy's order swung open the door for the inexorable rise of a unionized public work force in many states and cities."

Today, public-employee unions are literally bankrupting us. We cannot have public employees negotiating against taxpayers—it just makes no sense.

Part-Time Politicians

The Constitution simply says that Congress needs to meet one time a year. That's it. And for most of our country's history, because of the travel and logistics, Congress met for a very limited time. But as government started to grow, so did the amount of time that members of Congress spent in Washington. They now meet for an average of 140 days a year—but that includes only the time they are actually in session. It doesn't include fund-raisers, meetings with lobbyists, or "fact-finding" trips overseas. In short, members of Congress are spending a lot of time in Washington listening to each other (and special interests) and not much time back home listening to the people they represent.

So, let's turn that around. We can't force them to stay in their districts (although ankle bracelets are pretty appealing) but we sure can give them some incentives to stay home with their constituents. Here are a few ideas for doing just that.

PROHIBIT FUND-RAISING WHEN CONGRESS IS IN SESSION

Seventeen states have rules that prohibit members of the state legislature from fund-raising when they're in session. This really hits lawmakers where it hurts; politicians see fund-raising as the lifeblood of their reelection chances. So let's apply this idea to the national level. Tell members of Congress that they can't raise money while they're meeting and, guess what, they magically won't want to meet so much!

UTILIZE TECHNOLOGY

There's no reason why much of the nation's business can't be accomplished by leveraging the latest in secure meeting technology. The White House Situation Room uses it; the military uses it; major corporations use it. Why can't Congress?

This would not be a replacement for regular meetings of Congress, of course, but it would allow members to physically spend more time in their districts while still participating in votes, hearings, and debates remotely.

LIMIT THE LENGTH OF CONGRESSIONAL SESSIONS

Large states such as Texas and Florida have part-time legislatures that meet on a fixed schedule. In Florida, for example, the legislative session is ninety days. We need to put Congress on the same kind of strict time limit: 120 days to do their business. Period. Leaving members of Congress in Washington for long periods of time is like locking teenage boys in a room with a bottle of whisky: We're just asking for trouble.

The only reason for *not* flip-flopping the amount of time politicians spend in Washington versus their districts is that politicians would rather be inside the Beltway. But who does that really benefit—them, or the people they are elected to serve?

Maybe you think this idea sounds unworkable. Fine, then let's break up Congress entirely. We allow it to meet in Washington just once per year; the rest of the time members stay in their districts. Think that's unworkable as well? Fine—I can do this all day but, in the end, something drastic must be done or our republic will die. Our Founders may have given us an exceptional country, but part of the deal was that we would be smart enough to learn from our mistakes and course-correct for the future—and we are failing miserably.

Of course, we could avoid all of this by simply passing term limits. If politicians can't stay in office forever then I really couldn't care less how often they're in Washington. With term limits, they'll *want* to spend more time at home because that's where they'll have to be when their political careers are over since we've also stopped them from joining the lobbying circuit.

Everything I've laid out in this chapter would help to rein in the power of Congress and the federal government as a whole. It's the kind of commonsense stuff almost all politicians would claim to support individually, yet, as a group, these things never seem to go anywhere. That's why those of us who know how this story will end have to form our own de facto lobbying group and ensure that politicians understand their two choices: vote to limit their own power, or lose it altogether.

In the meantime, we have a large and growing national debt to worry about. While we work toward long-term structural change, we also have to make the short-term cuts and sacrifices that will give us the runway we need to get them passed. So, with that in mind, it's time to turn from big-picture principles and proposed legislation to the actual budget. Most people say there's just not that much we can cut. We'll see about that.

Educate Yourself

- The California Citizen's Redistricting Commission
  http://www.wedrawthelines.ca.gov

- DeMint/Graham Balanced Budget Amendment (S.J. Res 27)
  http://www.govtrack.us/congress/bill.xpd?bill=sj111-27

- DeMint Term Limits Amendment (S.J. Res 21)
  http://www.govtrack.us/congress/bill.xpd?bill=sj111-21

- Save America's Future Economy Act of 2010 (SAFE)
  http://www.govtrack.us/congress/bill.xpd?bill=h111-5323

- James M. Buchanan, "Clarifying Confusion About the Balanced Budget Amendment," *National Tax Journal*, September 1995
  http://ntj.tax.org/wwtax/ntjrec.nsf/009a9a91c225e83d852567ed006212d8/68f7f882cd48d258852567ef0057a8a5/$FILE/v48n3347.pdf

- James Q. Wilson, *Bureaucracy: What Government Agencies Do and Why They Do It*
  http://books.google.com/books?id=1aR54vBa2E4C

BROKE

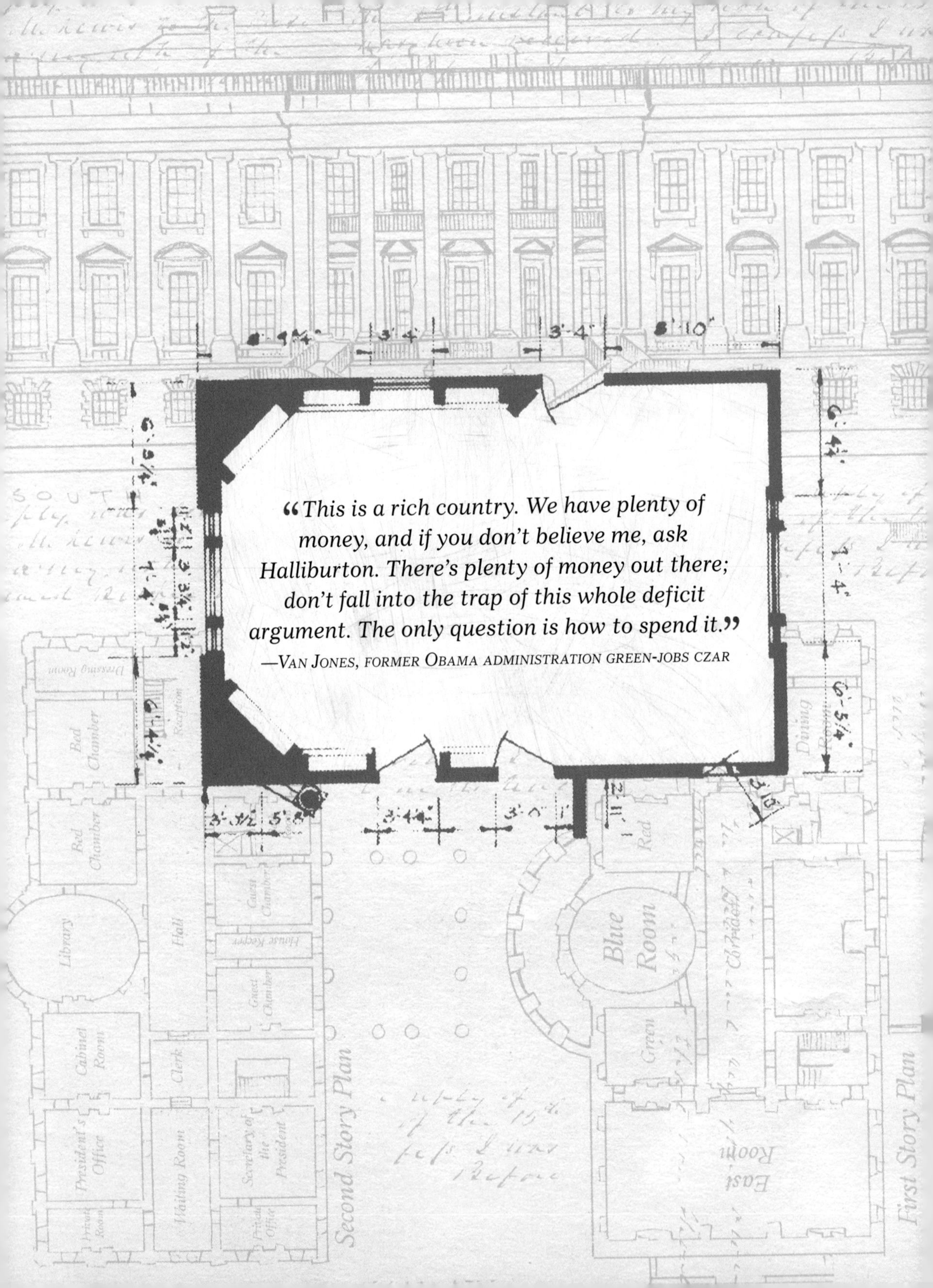
“This is a rich country. We have plenty of money, and if you don’t believe me, ask Halliburton. There’s plenty of money out there; don’t fall into the trap of this whole deficit argument. The only question is how to spend it.”
—Van Jones, former Obama administration green-jobs czar

CHAPTER 18.

Step Six: Scalpels, Hatchets, and Chainsaws

Let's get the bad news out of the way first: There is no small answer to our problems. We've known about our disease for decades now, and yet we've never gone to see a doctor. We knew surgery would be the only answer, so we kept waiting, kept procrastinating, kept hoping for a miracle cure—but it never came.

Now we find ourselves in need of radical, painful reforms that will be so large, and happen so rapidly that to many it may look like a revolution is taking place. Not with blood and violence, but with policies and ideas. That might sound insane, but Barack Obama has said essentially the same thing. He uses words like *change* and *transformation,* and his wife talks about us not being allowed to go back to the lives we had before. Use whatever words you want to make it sound acceptable, but our Founders would have called it *revolution.*

I believe we have three options: We can keep denying our problems (I was very good at this in my own life for a long time and would be happy to lend some advice) by doing the exact things that brought them on. We can give up, which is what many people are hoping and expecting us to do. Or we can take them head-on and realize that whatever pain we endure is just delayed payment for our decades of extravagance.

I choose to take them head-on. I choose to fight and sacrifice for what I believe in. If you agree, then I have a few ideas on how to get started.

Just Stop

Believe it or not, it's a lot harder than you might think to balance our budget. That in itself is concerning, since it shouldn't take this much sacrifice just to get a budget—any budget—balanced. The issue, as we've talked about before, is that so much of the budget (including Social Security, Medicare, and interest payments) can't be touched. That leaves us focusing not only on a small portion of the overall pie, but also on the portion that so many powerful people, from politicians to special interests, guard with their lives.

There is plenty of pain to go around and plenty of ways to divide that pain up, but make no mistake—we're all going to have to share in it. (To update Barack Obama's line, "I think when you spread the pain around, it's good for everybody.") That not only prevents the natural reaction of "Why are you only targeting my favorite program?" but it also makes it a lot easier to make the significant cuts we need, not just the "scalpel" type cuts that our politicians seem to like so much.

It might sound cliché, but before we can cut anything, we have to find a way to close the deficit of trust that so many of us (me included) have with our leaders. Many Americans would be more than willing to sacrifice financially for our future (yes, even with tax hikes), *but only if we had an ironclad guarantee that the extra money would be used to permanently reform our budget and pay down our debt.* That last part is key because, without a formal agreement, no one is willingly going to hand more money over to Washington. We've played that game before and know how it ends.

My favorite idea for how to bridge the gap in the short term is to have whatever money is raised from our sacrifices go directly into a special fund that is administered by an independent board. The board's only mission is to protect the money from Congress and use it in a predetermined way to pay down the debt and get the budget onto a sustainable track.

So, what are those sacrifices, exactly? Well, the first and most important thing we can do right now is: *Just stop spending.* If you have lung cancer, you don't continue to smoke—but that's exactly what we're doing. Every single ounce of available data shows that we are in this position because of the spending we've done over the last few decades, yet we not only continue to do it, we are doing it at a rate never before seen in our history.

No more. Are people going to be angry? Of course they are—every dollar spent by the government is received by someone who is not going to be pleased when it's gone. But it's time to embrace the "greater good" argument that progressives love so much and forget about making individuals mad.

Obama Froze Government Spending!

Sure he did . . . and Ron Paul voted for Medicare expansion. The truth is that the Obama spending freeze is a three-year hold that applies only to 13 percent of the federal budget. Over the first year, it would save $15 billion (out of a $1.5 trillion estimated deficit)—exactly one percent. I'm not complaining, I'll take the $15 billion—but let's not pretend that this is some really difficult sacrifice. A *real* freeze would apply to *all* expenses of the *entire* federal government.

Critics will say that this would be catastrophic, since over 70 percent of our economy is made up of consumer spending. Even though I'm talking about government spending, I won't argue their premise. For a while, jobs will be lost and things will look dire—but that's how you know you are truly setting things right. Cancer patients undergo chemotherapy, a lengthy, barbaric process that makes them feel worse than they did before. But it's for a reason. You take the poison so you can try to eradicate the disease.

What we don't need are more gimmicky spending freezes or warnings about how we'll get serious "next year"—actions speak louder than words . . . so JUST STOP SPENDING. NOW!

Want to Really Get Radical?

How about a *real* system of checks and balances? The House of Representatives gets to vote only on revenue measures and the Senate gets to vote only on spending measures. If one or the other gets out of whack, the whole country would know exactly whom to hold accountable.

A Living Wage?

Progressives love to complain about the gap between the incomes of the rich and poor, but if the press had been doing its job, then Americans would have realized a long time ago that the most outrageous gap in this country is the one between federal workers' wages and everyone else's.

The average federal employee earned $81,258 per year in 2009. The average private-sector worker made $50,462. When you add in the benefits, the gap grows even wider. The average private-industry employee gets about $10,500 per year in benefits but federal employees receive a staggering $42,000 or more. The disparity in total compensation has grown from 66 percent in 2000 to 101 percent in 2009.

When you look at direct job-to-job comparisons (there are so many positions in government that don't even exist in the private sector), total compensation (salaries and benefits) for federal employees is 50 percent higher than for their private-sector counterparts. It's true that some of the difference can be attributed to the skill and education levels of federal employees, but even after taking that into account, there's still a large disparity.

Somehow we've turned the idea of public service into a lucrative career. Even worse, we've made the idea of collecting your salary in taxpayer dollars something that people are *drawn* to.

SCALPEL, PLEASE

The Heritage Foundation has estimated that bringing federal compensation in line with market rates would save almost $47 billion in 2011.

There's also that pesky little economic law of incentives and subsidies. Incentivizing people to work for the government means fewer of them are going to start their own businesses or innovate inside private companies. In other words, we are pulling people away from productive careers (some of whom would then likely hire additional workers themselves) and giving them taxpayer-funded jobs that, let's face it, are often unproductive in terms of actually growing the economy.

How do you close this gap? Well, the unions are a big problem. It makes no sense that we have public employees unionizing to negotiate against . . . the public. It's time we start negotiating with federal employees the way we negotiate in the private sector when the company is facing bankruptcy: Work with us or we all go under. If you consider that taking the printing press away from our federal government would,

The Priority Pyramid

We should start to look at the federal budget as a pyramid. At the top are the very few things that we must spend on to survive. These would pretty much match my list of vital responsibilities of the federal government (national defense, courts, intellectual property, international relations). As we start to move down the pyramid, more budget items get introduced, but they are less of a priority.

Like a family in a crisis that would devote all of its resources to things like food, shelter, and clothing, we need to refocus our attention to the top of the pyramid. After paying for the autopilot entitlement commitments (plus interest), we use whatever is left to budget for those things that are both constitutional and essential to our survival. Then we assess. How much money is left? Any? If so, what's next on the priority list? If there's nothing left, we stop right there.

To use real numbers, here's how this might look for 2011 (all numbers are in billions):

Total Expected Revenue	**$2,567**
Less:	
Mandatory spending	($2,165)
Expected interest payments	($251)
What's Left	**$151**
Constitutional priorities:	
Defense	($750)
Intellectual property	($12)
Courts/justice	($57)
International affairs	($54)
Funds Remaining to Spend	**($722)**

To translate the above from math to English: *There is no money left*. The mandatory spending is so large that it takes away from any ability we have to even choose what things should be priorities for us. That's why the debate on those programs needs to change from "You can't take away my benefits" to "If we pay your benefits, we can't have a court system."

Once entitlements are reformed and we've paid for the things that the federal government is responsible for, we'd have a few options for the remaining money: We could continue down the pyramid and fund additional programs; we could reduce tax rates or eliminate specific taxes; or we could pay down the national debt. But, as of now, none of those options is even available to us.

technically, make it bankrupt, then it's not a stretch to say we need to start taking a much harder line.

President Obama has proposed increasing federal pay 1.4 percent next year, which would be small historically, but would still push pay higher and, given the low inflation, possibly make the public/private gap even wider. Some Republicans want to cancel raises altogether, which would save $2.2 billion.

Truth Serum

After adjusting for inflation, total pay for federal employees **has grown 36.9 percent** since 2000. Private-worker pay? 8.8 percent.

I believe we go even further: Freeze pay for all existing personnel until market wages catch up, then cap future annual increases at the amount that private pay rises. For new employees, sorry, but the pay scales change right now.

Put Away the Scalpel, Get Out the Hatchet

George Washington had four cabinet departments. Since then, we've added fourteen new departments and gotten rid of only two. (The Navy Department became part of the Department of Defense in 1949 and the U.S. Post Office became a federal corporation in 1971.) Yes, we have a few more people living here than we did in Washington's day, but the key question to ask is whether a department's purpose is in line with the principles of our Constitution. In the vast majority of instances, the answer is *no*.

There are several agencies that can have their responsibilities disseminated among either existing departments or brought down to the state level, where they'll be cheaper and have more of an impact. But there are two cabinet-level departments that should be cut altogether: energy and education.

DEPARTMENT OF ENERGY

Jimmy Carter created this mission-creeping monstrosity to rid us of our dependence on foreign energy and to regulate oil prices. How is that working out? Yeah, not so well—which is exactly why it has changed its entire agenda.

Look at the front cover of the department's *FY 2009 Agency Financial Report*. Right there, in plain view, it says: *Working to Save the Planet*.

They're not just out to save America, mind you, but the whole *planet*! That's a pretty ambitious agenda for an agency that can't even seem to get nuclear power plants authorized to be built.

Some of the DOE's functions, like maintaining and producing nuclear weapons, need to be integrated into other areas—like, I don't know, the people at the Pentagon who are in charge of our nuclear weapons. But most of the DOE's tasks can be privatized or eliminated altogether. The Strategic Petroleum Reserve, for example, could easily be managed by an outside entity. In fact, President Clinton pushed that exact idea more than fifteen years ago.

The DOE has also become a major conduit for corporate welfare. As part of President Obama's "stimulus package," the Department of Energy is shoveling billions of dollars in loans and grants into auto industry coffers—including $5.9 billion to Ford so they can reengineer factories in five states, and $1.6 billion to Nissan for a factory in Tennessee. "Transforming the American auto industry will not be easy, but we know it can be done," said Secretary of Energy Steven Chu in making the announcement.

Just one question: *Why in God's green earth is the Department of Energy in the auto subsidy business?* If we want to hand money to private auto companies (and we don't), then shouldn't that run through the Department of, say, *Transportation*?

The DOE also runs a $300 million appliance-rebate program along with a $5 billion "Weatherization Assistance Program" aimed at "weatherizing" homes for "low-income families and creating green jobs." Again, that's not a priority for a bankrupt country, and certainly not a job of the DOE.

In all, the Department of Energy received $37 billion in extra funding as part of the stimulus plan, more than doubling its entire annual budget. The stated mission of the money was to help deal with "economic uncertainty, U.S. dependence on oil, and the threat of a changing climate." Matching each of those goals up to the Constitution yields some pretty interesting results:

- ***Economic uncertainty:*** I don't see any mention of funneling money to a government agency to protect against something that is a normal part of life. If you manage your budget well then you are *always* prepared for uncertainty.
- ***U.S. dependence on oil:*** I suppose you could make a case that this is a national security threat and so the federal government has a role, but it has failed at solving this for decades. Why would we think that throwing more money at it would solve things now?
- ***The threat of a changing climate:*** I've *scoured* the Constitution and can't seem to find a reference from Madison talking about how the government should try to change the weather.

Since its founding, the DOE has spent $750 billion (in 2010 dollars)—a majority of which has gone into the search for alternative energies. And what do we have to show for all that time and money? Almost nothing. Electric cars, which seem to be all the rage these days, are powered by a technology that was around long before the DOE was ever created.

The first step toward eliminating this agency is to privatize or disseminate its key tasks. There aren't that many, so it should be pretty easy. For example, the DOE operates twenty-eight national laboratories that do a lot of important research. During the Clinton administration, a DOE Task Force recommended privatizing those labs since much of their research also has business applications. Great idea—let's do it now and turn an expense item into a new federal revenue stream.

THE DEPARTMENT OF EDUCATION

I know it's shocking that someone wants to shut down the DoEd—but there's a good reason this has been talked about so much over the years: The department is unconstitutional.

The U.S. Constitution is crystal clear: *Any powers not granted to the federal government belong to the states.* So where, exactly, does the document enumerate the power of administrating a national education system to the federal government? For almost two hundred years, education was a state and local matter and the results were pretty encouraging (all that local schooling did was result in America becoming the world's greatest superpower). We developed one of the best education systems in the world.

And then along came Lyndon Johnson and his use of civil rights as a pretext for expanding government powers in all sorts of ways, including into education. LBJ tied education to fighting poverty and civil rights. He proposed (and Congress supported) a federal program to help low-income families with education subsidies. By the time Jimmy Carter took over, the window had shifted so much that he was able to actually promise and deliver on a new federal department to direct education policy. Supporters swore that the department would be small and would merely play an oversight role in coordinating local education. They lied.

The most fascinating part of the DoEd's birth is that even committed liberals saw the department for what it was: a boon to labor unions that in no way served schoolchildren. The late senator Daniel Patrick Moynihan (D-N.Y.) declared, "This is a back-room deal, born out of a squalid politics. Everything we had thought we would not see happening to education is happening here."

Several other notable liberals were concerned as well. Congresswoman Pat Schroeder (D-Colo.) said, "No matter what anyone says, the Department of Education will not just write checks to local school boards. They will meddle in everything. I do not want that." And that was from a liberal Democrat! Congressman Joseph Early (D-Mass.) accurately predicted that a "national Department may actually impede the innovation of local programs as it attempts to establish uniformity throughout the Nation."

Even the *New York Times* wrote an editorial against creating the new department: "The supporters of a separate department [of education] speak vaguely of the need for a federal policy on education. We believe that they misunderstand the nature of American education, which is characterized by diversity."

Given all the criticism, why did it still pass? The late congressman Benjamin Rosenthal (D-N.Y.) said it was for a simple, yet all-too-familiar reason: "not wanting to embarrass the president."

When the DoEd was formed, its initial budget was $13.1 billion (in 2007 dollars) and it employed 450 people. In 2010, the estimated budget is $107 billion and the department has a jaw-dropping 4,800 employees.

How important are these government workers to the day-to-day operation of the country? In November 1995, when the federal government shut down over a budget crisis, 89.4 percent of the department's employees were deemed "nonessential" and were sent home.

Of course, if all this money were producing exceptional results we might be having a different discussion. It would still be unconstitutional (the ends don't justify

A FAMILIAR ACCOMPLICE

Between 1908 and 1975, more than 130 bills were introduced to Congress to create the Department of Education. They all failed. So why did the 1979 bill succeed? Simple: the unions, specifically the National Education Association (NEA). According to D. T. Stallings in *A Brief History of the United States Department of Education:*

> *In 1972, the massive union formed a political action committee, and in 1975 it joined forces with other unions to form the Labor Coalition Clearinghouse (LCC) for election campaigning. Along with other members of the LCC, the NEA released 'Needed: A Cabinet Department of Education' in 1975, but its most significant step was to endorse a presidential candidate—Jimmy Carter—for the first time in the history of the organization.*

The *Wall Street Journal* later reported an admission by one House Democrat that "the idea of an Education Department is really a bad one. But it's NEA's top priority. There are school teachers in every congressional district and most of us simply don't need the aggravation of taking them on."

So let me see if I have this right: Because some lawmakers didn't want to be aggravated thirty years ago, we now have to deal with a massively expensive government agency that is doing nothing to help our kids. Does that pretty much sum it up?

the means as far as that document is concerned) but at least we'd have a reason to figure out how to perform the same tasks in a constitutional way.

But the results are not exceptional; in fact, they're nonexistent. Test scores for reading have remained completely flat and math scores are up just one percent. As Maris Vinovskis, President Bush's and Clinton's senior advisor to the Department of Education, conceded, "if the value added by the federal government . . . doesn't really help the kids, who needs us?"

Great question—the answer is *no one.* Returning educational oversight to the states would not only be great for taxpayers, it would be great for kids.

Who cares more about whether your school is serving the needs of a community than the community itself? Who would ever think that some faceless bureaucrat in Washington could fix a problem with a public school in the north end of Hartford more than the people of Hartford?

Progressives; that's who.

Remember, they believe that Americans are a bunch of uneducated, bitter morons clinging to their guns and religion. If we controlled our own schools locally then our kids would all be learning about creationism and the role of religion in the founding of the country. AGGGGGHHHHHH!

As Richard L. Lyman, president of Stanford University at the time of the DoEd's founding, said, "the two-hundred-year-old absence of a Department of Education is not the result of simple failure during all that time. On the contrary, it derives from the conviction that we do not want the kind of educational system that such arrangements produce."

President Reagan tried to get rid of the Department of Education but he could never get Republican senators to go along with it. "Education is the principal responsibility of local school systems, teachers, parents, citizen boards, and state governments," he said. His goal was to "insure that local needs and preferences, rather than the wishes of Washington, determine the education of our children."

I couldn't agree more. Let's stop having taxpayer money sent to Washington so that it can be siphoned off, diluted, and then funneled right back to us along with specific rules on how we can spend it. I propose a five-year phase-out of the DoEd that will culminate in power and control restored to the states and communities, where it belongs.

Get It Off Our Books

Some of the things we are spending boatloads of money on still need to be done, but not in Washington. That leaves two options: Move the responsibility to the states, or privatize it.

THE STATES

We've already covered some of this, but the states should be handling a lot more than they currently are. In fact, if it were up to me, we'd flip-flop the entire way our taxes are paid. Our federal tax bill should be relatively small, covering only those essential responsibilities of the federal government; but our state tax bill, depending on where we choose to live, would rise. Want to be in a high-tax, high-service state because school test scores are amazingly high and the roads are paved with gold? That's your choice. Want to be in a low-tax state because you're homeschooling and don't own a car? You can choose that, too.

When local users have to consider how to spend their own money, they suddenly become a lot more frugal. Right now, if a politician successfully earmarks some federal bill to build a $40 million otter museum in your state, everyone celebrates. But what if the taxpayers in that state had to decide whether to spend that same $40 million of their own money on the otter museum—would they still do it? Maybe—and if they decide to (as communities often decide to float bonds to pay for new stadiums), then more power to them. But force *them* to make that decision and I guarantee that you'll see a fast change in the attitude toward spending money.

There is no shortage of specific programs that can go back to the states, but here are a few:

- ***Federal housing programs:*** A few years ago I might've had to explain why this is a bad idea. By now it should be pretty obvious. The American dream *is not* homeownership, nor was it a constitutional dream of our Founders, which is why the document is silent about the right to a nice house—so let's stop incentivizing it.
- ***Federal highway/mass transit:*** $41.3 billion proposed for 2011. In 1956, Congress passed and President Eisenhower signed the Federal-Aid Highway Act of 1956 to create a national highway system. The act was supposed to expire in 1972 but—shocker—that never happened. Construction of Ike's dream was formally completed in 1996 with the 160,000-mile "national highway system," but the spending keeps cranking right along.

  Back in 1987, President Reagan vetoed a highway bill because it had 121 earmarks.

  Compare that with the 2005 highway bill that contained 6,376 earmarks that cost $24 billion. Included was a horse-riding facility in Virginia, a snowmobile trail in Vermont, and a day-care center park-

and-ride program in Illinois. Don't shoot the messenger, but Republicans controlled Congress that year.

The CBO estimates that simply shifting 25 percent of the funding responsibility to the states would save $93 billion over the next decade. Great—let's do it, but why stop at 25 percent? After all, who knows best how to get people around their territory faster than the people who own that territory? If a state wants a new bridge, a wider roadway, or a new off-ramp, then the people who will benefit from those things should pay for them. I guarantee you that there won't be any more "bridges to nowhere" if the people who are going nowhere have to foot the bill for them.

Ending federal highway programs also means ending the federal gas tax ($0.18/gallon) and letting the states pick up the slack if they need to.

- ***Federal agriculture subsidies:*** $10–30 billion a year. I love farmers. They built this country and they feed our people. And one of the character traits I love about them most is their independence. But let's be honest: too many of them have become hooked on federal farm subsidies.

Agriculture subsidies were first put in place during the Great Depression, when the situation in rural America was terrible. Farm families had incomes that were half that of the rest of America. But today things are much different. USDA statistics show that the income of farm households is higher than the national average. The largest 10 percent of recipients of agriculture subsidies collect 72 percent of all payments. In other words, a few operators are getting a lot of cash.

Farm subsidies really don't go primarily to small farmers; they go to large operators and landowners. It's an important distinction because it allows wealthy celebrities who own farmland to cash in government checks. Did you know, for example, that David Rockefeller, the billionaire, gets a government check for growing corn? Other billionaires

Cultivating Fraud

The agriculture subsidy program is also riddled with fraud. A report by the Government Accountability Office found that in 40 percent of cases they studied, the USDA was not even reviewing applications to see if they were legitimate. As a result, they were making billions of dollars in payments to people who were either not farming or were dead. Another investigation by the *Washington Post* found more than $15 billion in wasteful spending and payments of $1.3 billion to people who did not even farm.

who have cashed USDA checks include Seagram's patriarch Edgar Bronfman, Sr., and Paul Allen, co-founder of Microsoft. Former NBA star Scottie Pippen and David Letterman have also been on the gravy train, as well as six U.S. senators.

PRIVATIZE

Here's a rule of thumb: If you can Google something and find a private company to do that task, then that's probably where the responsibility for it should be. Profit motive has a funny way of making companies act efficiently. In fact, giving some tasks to companies can often turn an expense item into a revenue item.

There's also the monopoly issue. When the federal government does something, it not only generally has a monopoly, it also has an unfair advantage because it doesn't have to worry about making money. What entrepreneur is going to compete with the government when he knows that he is up against a nearly limitless pile of money?

As with decentralizing tasks to states, there is no shortage of examples for what can be privatized or licensed, but here are a few:

Military Arsenal Production

Army ammunition plants and arsenals can be turned into federal corporations. This will boost innovation and save taxpayers money. The RAND Corporation estimates that this would save us $1 billion right away, and perhaps $3 billion over the long term. Canada has already done this; we should be next.

Ports

In 1983, Great Britain privatized 19 ports and formed the Associated British Ports. These private ports actually pay taxes and earn profits. They are advanced and highly efficient. About two-thirds of the cargo headed into Britain goes through them.

In the United States, nearly all ports are still government owned. One big reason for that has been national-security concerns (you might remember the controversy that ensued over the Dubai Ports World deal from 2006). I'll admit, I was concerned about the United Arab Emirates owning American ports, and I think the concerns are still valid—no one wants to sell out our security for money. But if we take politics out of it and look at it rationally, there's no reason we can't address both issues. First, as in the case of Dubai, we always have the option to say no to any bidder that raises suspicions. Second, any federal asset that poses a security risk can still receive oversight by the government (private airports, for example, still have Transportation Security Administration employees running security).

And finally, deals can be crafted so that the security side of the asset is still handled by the government (i.e., we can still man radiation checkpoints) while the actual operations of the asset are managed by the private corporation.

Transportation

In 1987, Great Britain privatized London's Heathrow Airport as well as several other airports by creating the British Airports Authority. Other countries have followed suit—but the United States is not one of them.

Building airports is an expensive business. Denver's new international airport, for example, cost three times what it was supposed to. Taxpayers coughed up $685 million. Compare that with an entirely private airport opened in Branson, Missouri, in 2009. It cost $155 million to build and includes service from several discount airlines. The CBO estimates that just eliminating grants to medium and larger airports would save us about $10.7 billion over the next decade.

In 1996, Canada privatized its air traffic control system. Nav Canada now does a great job running the Canadian system and it's funded by charging a fee to airlines that use it. They get top marks for efficiency and safety. U.S. air traffic control, on the other hand, needs serious technical upgrades and is marred by bureaucracy.

And then there's Amtrak. I could write an entire book just on Amtrak, but one thing is clear: This whole scam where we set up a corporation and fund it with tax money? It doesn't work.

A POISON PILL

In his book *One Nation Under Debt,* economist Robert E. Wright had what sounds like a great idea for how to make decisions about spending: Let the taxpayers decide. Literally.

If you have a 401(k) plan, you probably know that you can specifically select how your contributions are invested. Wright asks, Why we can't do the same with our tax dollars? Why not include, with each individual return, a form that allows taxpayers to select among national discretionary priorities, ranging from debt reduction to farm subsidies to road building to education? We then consolidate that info and develop budgets based on our priorities. If most people really want to fund corporate welfare programs or pay billionaires to grow food, then that's exactly what we'll do. If people would prefer something else, then those programs get phased out.

This concept, and others like it, are seductive, but they're really just traps. America is a republic, yet this idea treats us as though we're a democracy. It may sound like semantics, but it's not. Our Constitution calls for a careful balance among the people, the states, and the federal government—and ideas like this destroy that balance.

The real issue is not in the way we decide how much to spend, or where to spend it, but in who we've elected to make the decisions for us. We don't like that our voices are not being heard, so we are trying everything we can think of to change that. But the problem is not the system; it's the people. If we put people with values and principles into office and term-limit them so they don't lose those values, then the rest will take care of itself.

The Low-Hanging Fruit

When it comes to waste, one of my favorite sayings applies: *A small hole can sink a big ship.* Cutting waste and pork in and of itself will not balance our budget or pay off China, but it is certainly a start to real financial responsibility and, even better, might help to prove to people that we're finally taking this seriously.

IMPROPER PAYMENTS

According to the Government Accountability Office, the federal government made at least $98 billion in "improper" payments in 2009. The largest program with improper payments was . . . wait for it . . . Medicaid, where $24 billion, or nearly eight cents of every dollar, was "improperly spent" in 2009.

INEFFECTIVE PROGRAMS

In 2008, federal auditors researched and rated every government program, as part of the "Expect More" initiative. They found that 22 percent of them, representing $123 billion in annual spending, did not positively impact the communities they were intended to.

A REAL SCALPEL

Every couple of years the CBO releases a report called "Budget Options," which provides a whole bunch of decisions we could make to save or spend money, along with the pros and cons of each. The savings side of it seems to be pretty much routinely ignored, but I decided to take a quick breeze through it. Here are a few random ideas from the CBO. Try to decide if your life could possibly continue without these programs:

- *Eliminate National Science Foundation Spending on Elementary and Secondary Education*
  Total ten-year savings: $931 million

- *End Department of Energy Research on Fossil Fuels*
  Total ten-year savings: $7.9 billion

- *Prohibit New Enrollees to the Department of Agriculture's Conservation Stewardship Program*
  Total ten-year savings: $10.9 billion

- *Eliminate Subsidized Loans to Graduate Students*
  Total ten-year savings: $18.8 billion

There's plenty more where that came from, but I think you get the idea. There are hundreds of billions in programs out there that can be eliminated without causing hardship to most people. It's the "low-hanging fruit" of our budget, and it's time we went and picked it.

The Third Rail

> *"Government is the great fiction through which everybody endeavors to live at the expense of everybody else."*
>
> —Frédéric Bastiat

We all know that even if we did everything I've suggested in this book, we'd still have a real long-term issue because of Medicare and Medicaid and, to a lesser extent, Social Security. We can't truly fix America without fixing those programs.

But while the solutions will ultimately be painful, the first step isn't: We have to talk about it. The fact that these programs are called the "third rail" of politics because your political career dies if you bring them up is not only unacceptable, it's un-American. We are a country that debates the tough issues and makes the tough choices. We don't shy away from a debate just because it may irritate some powerful interest groups.

To that end, you have to hand it to Congressman Paul Ryan (R-Wis.) for putting out a comprehensive, well-supported plan that not only covers the easy stuff, but also hits on the third rail. It's called the "Roadmap for America's Future" and while it offers a lot of ideas that I support, it's even more important that I support his overall premise as to *why* things have gotten so far from the Constitution: progressives.

Of course, Paul Ryan is still a politician and, while he offers up a lot of great ideas, he can only go so far. He's got bipartisanship, consensus building, and all that other fun stuff to worry about. But I don't, so I can follow Ryan's thesis to its logical end: If progressivism caused this crisis, then rooting it out of the system is the only way to truly end it.

Predictably, progressive economists like the *New York Times's* Paul Krugman don't like Ryan's plan. One of Krugman's complaints is that Ryan is not being honest about the ultimate fate of Medicare:

> *And [Ryan's plan is] evasive: when you propose replacing the whole Medicare system with a set of vouchers, the defensible response to someone who says that you'll end Medicare as we know it is to say "Yes, and we should," not start flailing while denying that you're doing any such thing.*

Okay, how's this: *Yes, and we should.*

I'm sorry that someone has to say it, but if the current Medicare system is a financial disaster of epic proportions, then how is fiddling around the edges going to make it less of a disaster? The obvious problem is rising health-care costs, but the more basic problem is that America was never built to support entitlement programs in the first place. We are trying to retrofit a hulking V-8 engine into a Model-T Ford and it's just not working.

YOUR RIGHTS FROM GOD DO NOT INCLUDE HDTV

"Today there is much focus on our rights. Indeed, I think there is a proliferation of rights. I am often surprised by the virtual nobility that seems to be accorded with those grievances. Shouldn't there at least be equal time for our Bill of Obligations and our Bill of Responsibilities? . . . It seems that many have come to think that each of us is owed prosperity and a certain standard of living. They're owed air-conditioning, cars, telephones, televisions."

—Justice Clarence Thomas, in a speech to students

But I also clearly understand the political realities. The current Medicare system is not going away anytime soon, at least not until the scope of the deception becomes obvious to everyone. And I'm compassionate—we cannot simply strip away benefits that so many people, especially the elderly, are relying on. These people played by the rules—they had no way of knowing that the game itself was a scam.

So, that leaves us in a position of having to make commonsense decisions in the short term, while working toward the ultimate long-term solution, which is to change the way people think about the proper role of government in their lives.

I'm not going to be naïve enough to think that I can solve even the short-term Medicare issue in this book. I'm no expert in medical insurance, health-care costs, or tort reform—but I do have six principles that I think we need to stand by, even when the debate gets ugly:

1. *Affordable health care should still be a priority.* Just because I don't believe that the federal government should be in the health-care business doesn't mean that I don't believe we should work to make high-quality health care available to everyone. The difference is simply in the approach. While progressives think that the best way to cover everyone is through regulations, mandates, and price controls, I think the exact opposite policies will get us much closer to where we all want to be.
2. *Allow informed decisions.* We're caught in an endless loop: Health-care costs are rising quickly, so the government implements more and more regulations that obscure the real price of services and take

power away from consumers, thereby causing health-care prices to rise further. It's insanity. If you want costs to come down then force people to take an interest in what they are paying. It's really not that hard—if everything I need done is covered by insurance, then what do I care what the cost is? Why would I ever call different MRI providers to compare scan prices? Why would I ever ask about whether generic drugs are available or double-check with my doctor to see if I *really* need another blood test or if the one from two months ago will suffice?

It seems like a simple thing, but health-care costs are out of control because no one has the ability to control their own specific costs. Turning the whole system around by empowering consumers to compare costs and benefits will drive down prices while increasing quality.

Twinkies Aren't Covered

If you substitute something we all buy every day, like food, for health care, it becomes a lot easier to understand why costs are rising so rapidly.

Imagine if your employer were to take $12,000 per year out of your paycheck and then sign you up for a "food plan." Your options are limited: a few assorted restaurants and one large grocery store that you are covered at. Any time you go to those places, you pay only a small co-pay, something around $10 or $20, no matter what you actually buy.

A few things would likely happen under a system like this:

- ***You would be robbed of choice. Heard great things about the new Mexican place down the street? Sorry, you're not covered there. Want vegetarian-only options and you're willing to pay more? Sorry, we have only one plan choice.***
- ***You would buy more food than you need, since the vast majority of what you'll pay is set at the beginning of the year and the food co-pays are tiny. Not sure if you really want the apples? Just grab them anyway and throw them out if they go bad. Who cares, they're free.***
- ***Most of the restaurants you eat in and stores you shop at won't even display prices. The cost is irrelevant to you. It's like being on a cruise ship—all the food is included, so eat up.***
- ***Since you don't care about individual prices, stores and restaurants jack them up. A bag of lettuce for $34? Sure, why not! The people who run the food plan might argue, but how can they ever figure out what the "market price" should be if the market itself lacks any competitive pricing?***

In summary, fixed-price, noncompetitive plans result in lack of choice, higher prices, and overconsumption. That's exactly how our health system works with third-party payers, and it's exactly why it's collapsing.

3. *Back to the states.* I know I sound like a broken record, but centralizing power and authority in Washington is perhaps the worst mistake we've made over the last century. Thomas Jefferson once explained the logic behind the way the Founders spread out power like this:

   Let the national government be entrusted with the defence of the nation, and its foreign and federal relations; the State governments with the civil rights, laws, police and administration of what concerns the State generally; the counties with the local concerns of the counties, and each ward direct the interests within itself.

   It is by dividing and subsiding these republics from the great national one down through all its subordinations, until it ends in the administration of every man's farm by himself; by placing under every one what his own eye may superintend, that all will be done for the best.

   You'll notice he never explicitly mentioned any entitlement programs—but if he had, their administration clearly would've fallen to the state or county level.
4. *Turn off cruise control.* How can a budget—*any* budget—ever be balanced if a large chunk of the expenses can't be touched? Instead of being on perpetual "autopilot," Medicare should be budgeted in two- to three-year increments. Not only would that allow us to easily adapt to changing financial conditions, it would also allow us to create budgets that bear some resemblance to reality.
5. *It's not about the poor.* The whole entitlement argument in some ways needs to be reset. The group that we spend the most on for these programs is not the poor—it's the middle class. We can debate what to do about those who are most financially strapped, but let's not sensationalize the issue by making people believe that reform is going to leave the poor without access to antibiotics or food.
6. *Change minds, not numbers.* In 1790, Americans drank only about 2.5 gallons of liquor per person per year. But thirty years later, America had developed a bit of a drinking problem. According to professor James Q. Wilson, "By 1820, Americans were drinking at the prodigious rate of 10 gallons of liquor a year for every man, woman and child in the country. Violence and disorder, not surprisingly, rose alarmingly."

In response, did the government pass a bunch of meaningless and unenforceable laws? Did it impose price controls or a national alcohol agency? No. Instead it pushed to create "internalized inhibitions, reinforced by social sanctions."

Put simply: *They changed the cultural attitude toward alcohol.*

Groups such as the YMCA, churches, and other civic organizations campaigned for change by making the issue a question of personal character. And guess what—it worked. Drinking rates went back down. "Between 1829 and 1850 [alcohol consumption] fell from 10 gallons to 2.1 gallons [per person] a year."

We need to do the same for entitlements. People used to have a sense of pride in *not* accepting handouts from the government. It was a last resort, and bad one at that. It wouldn't be a great first step if that sense of pride returned.

GUESS WHICH PRESIDENT SAID . . .

"The lessons of history, confirmed by the evidence immediately before me show conclusively that continued dependence upon relief induces a spiritual and moral disintegration fundamentally destructive to the national fiber. To dole out relief in this way is to administer a narcotic, a subtle destroyer of the human spirit . . . It is in violation of the traditions of America."

—Franklin Delano Roosevelt (seriously.)

If you listen to the experts, Social Security is a lot easier to fix than Medicare, but how long will those fixes last? If we make changes now to tax rates, retirement ages, or payouts, who's to say that in another few decades our kids won't be asked to sacrifice again? After all, we played this game in 1983, made reforms, and now here we are again.

Beyond that lack of trust in this program, which is set up like an upside-down pyramid since more people will be collecting than working, there is also too much intellectual dishonesty out there right now. I hate to keep going back to Paul Krugman, but he is the apparent economic voice for most progressives right now. In blasting Alan Simpson, co-chair of the Obama Deficit Commission, Krugman wrote:

> *So there are two ways to look at Social Security. You can view it as a standalone program, in which case payroll tax revenues and the trust fund accumulated out of those revenues are at the center of the story; or you can view it as just part of the federal budget, in which case the relative size of retirement benefits and payroll tax receipts has no special significance—benefits are just one federal expenditure, payroll taxes just one source of federal revenue . . .*

But here's what you can't legitimately do: you can't switch views in midstream. You can't say that Social Security is just part of the federal budget, so the trust fund is meaningless—then say that because there's no real trust fund, Social Security is in crisis when payroll receipts fall short of benefits.

This is intentional confusion at its very best. Far be it from me to question a Nobel Prize winner at his own game, but Professor Krugman is dodging the only important part of the whole debate: *There is no money in the trust fund.*

You know the story by now: The Social Security surpluses have been spent by Congress over the years, meaning a trust fund full of government bonds. But in all of the professor's admonitions about how we're *allowed* "to look at Social Security," nowhere does he ever say how we *should* look at it: as a fund that will have more expenses than revenue, with no cash reserves to make up the difference.

My point is simply that it's difficult to solve even so-called easy problems when people refuse to acknowledge the truth. Beyond that, I believe that Congressman Ryan has the right idea: Give choice and power back to workers while still protecting those who need it most. If you want the gory policy details, you can read his entire plan via the link at the end of this chapter.

State's Evidence

Right now there are more than five million state and local workers who are exempt from the Social Security system. (Don't get too excited; Congress closed the opportunity to opt out in 1983.) Galveston County in Texas opted out of Social Security for its public employees in 1981. Workers there have their money put into conservative fixed-rate guaranteed annuities instead and—guess what?—they're doing great. Even after the stock market plunge in 2008, county employees had netted out much better than those in Social Security.

I had Rick Gornto, who designed the Galveston plan, on my television show back in October 2009. He told me that a Galveston worker making $75,000 a year would get monthly checks for about $4,500. Under Social Security, that same worker would get around $1,645 a month. Galveston's program is safe and works great. So why doesn't the government learn more about it? Well, according to Gornto they've already studied it but "this issue of privatization versus public option that you're talking about is really more of a political issue rather than an economic issue."

Exactly right—which is why the fine print is not even worth debating until politicians stop playing the "only government can do it right" game.

$ $ $ $ $

If there's one thing I can leave you with from this chapter it's that the idea that we can cut our budget only by inflicting massive pain on the poor is laughable. There are literally hundreds of billions of dollars of items that can be cut before we ever even have to make an extremely difficult decision.

But make no mistake: We *are* going to have to make extremely difficult decisions. Entitlements can't go on the way they are, but the secret to reform is not in just changing retirement ages or tax rates, it's in changing the minds of Americans; it's in convincing people that they don't need the government; that, in fact, the government will only prevent them from ever achieving their dream. If we can make that case, then the rest will take care of itself.

Educate Yourself

- Chris Edwards, *Downsizing the Federal Government* (free preview)
  http://books.google.com/books?id=aCG7Z5XETewC

- James Sherk, "Inflated Federal Pay: How Americans Are Overtaxed to Overpay the Civil Service"
  http://www.heritage.org/Research/Reports/2010/07/Inflated-Federal-Pay-How-Americans-Are-Overtaxed-to-Overpay-the-Civil-Service

- Paul Ryan's "Roadmap for America's Future"
  http://www.roadmap.republicans.budget.house.gov

- Steve Forbes and Elizabeth Ames, *How Capitalism Will Save Us: Why Free People and Free Markets Are the Best* (free preview)
  http://books.google.com/books?id=KQsLxskq3xsC

- Wayne Allen Root, *The Conscience of a Libertarian* (free preview)
  http://books.google.com/books?id=vmyGTXhzzF8C

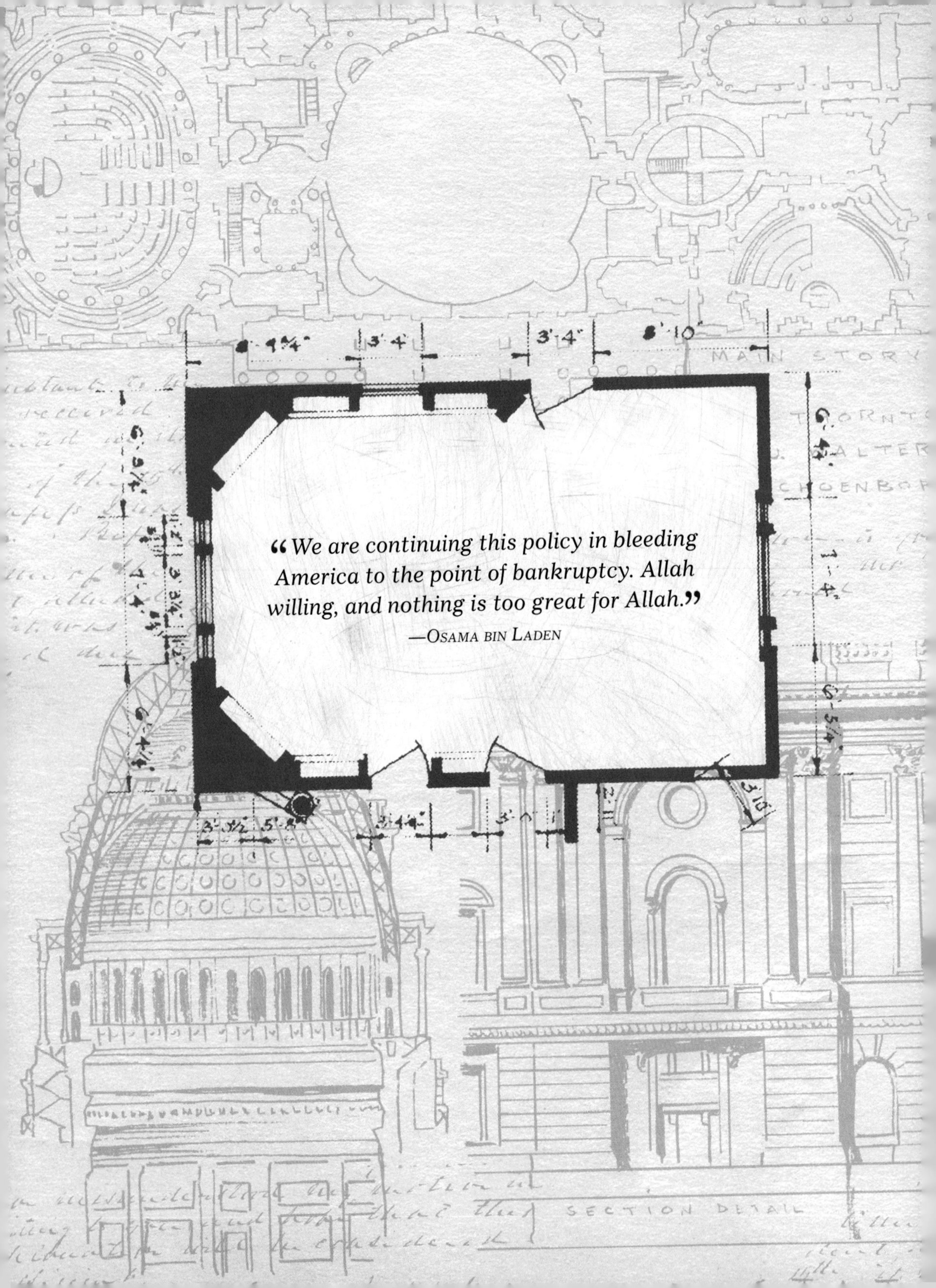

“*We are continuing this policy in bleeding America to the point of bankruptcy. Allah willing, and nothing is too great for Allah.*”

—Osama bin Laden

CHAPTER 19.

Step Seven: Declare War on Defense Dollars

Nothing matters more than national defense.

Nothing.

National defense is the cradle inside which all our freedoms rest. Not to be too dramatic, but you can't freely worship, work, or speak if you're dead.

As Thomas Paine reminded us, "Those who expect to reap the blessings of freedom must, like men, undergo the fatigues of supporting it." That means sacrificing, if necessary, in other areas to ensure that our defense budget is never strained.

But there is a right way and a wrong way to spend money. While the size of our commitment is important, it's how those resources are used that matters most. Ronald Reagan once said, "Government always finds a need for whatever money it gets." Nowhere is that more true than when it comes to defense. Give them $1 billion and they'll spend it all; give them $1 trillion and they'll spend all of that, too. Our job is to ensure that we're providing an amount commensurate with our mission and that it's being spent as effectively and efficiently as possible.

As I promised at the outset of this book, our financial situation demands shared sacrifice: sacrifice that will cross age groups, racial groups, and, especially, political groups. If Democrats are going to be asked to make difficult choices in cutting their favorite programs, then Republicans need to be asked to do the same. Nothing can be off-limits—and that includes national defense, which has historically been something of a sacred cow to most on the right.

The reason for opening up the $750 billion defense budget for a hard look is simple: Our financial condition is itself a national security issue. Admiral Mike Mullen, chairman of the Joint Chiefs of Staff, recently said, "Our national debt is our biggest national security threat." At about the same time, a group of military officers met to lay out a national security strategy. Their top recommendation to protect our nation? "Restore fiscal responsibility."

Even Secretary of Defense Robert Gates, someone you'd think would be pushing for as much military money as possible, has said that "we can't have a strong military if we have a weak economy." Updating Reagan's line for modern times, he went on to say, "it just underscores the message that I've had for the Congress over the last couple of years that a dollar that they make us spend on stuff we don't need is a dollar we can't spend on what we do need."

If you'd prefer to hear that same message from a liberal politician instead of members of the armed forces, then consider the words of House Democratic majority leader Steny Hoyer: "It's time to stop talking about fiscal discipline and national security threats as if they're separate topics: Debt is a national security threat, one of the greatest we know of."

RIPPED FROM THE **HEADLINES**

DEBT IS GREATEST DEFENSE THREAT, AMERICA WARNED

A special Republican report tonight warned that the most serious weakness in the armor of American national defense is the existence of a national debt of 44 billions of dollars.

—*Chicago Tribune*, March 1940

Throughout history, economics has been used in warfare almost as long as bullets have. We've already covered how England tried to win the Revolutionary War by bankrupting the colonies, but this strategy has been used in more modern times as well. In 1939, Joseph Stalin wrote, "We have outstripped the principal capitalist countries as regards technique of production and rate of industrial development. That is very good, but it is not enough. We must outstrip them economically as well. And we must do it in the next ten or fifteen years."

During the Cold War, it was America that used this strategy. We forced the Soviets to try to keep up with us on defense spending, and then we waited as they collapsed under their own weight once global oil prices declined, drying up one of their main sources of income.

These days, the tables have been turned again. Osama bin Laden, who participated in that bankrupting of the Soviets while they occupied Afghanistan, is now using the same strategy on us. In bragging about the financial return of the 9/11 attacks, bin Laden said, "Every dollar of al Qaeda defeated a million dollars, by the permission of Allah, besides the loss of a huge number of jobs. As for the economic deficit, it has reached record astronomical numbers estimated to total more than a trillion dollars."

In addition to our deficits, a good portion of our national debt is owed to China, a communist country that is not exactly an ally. Former Treasury secretary Hank Paulson revealed in his memoir that, after Russia invaded Georgia in 2008, Russian president Vladimir Putin tried to convince the Chinese government to dump Fannie Mae and Freddie Mac securities as a form of economic warfare against us. And when

President Obama met with the Dalai Lama of Tibet, the Chinese government made clear that as a form of retaliation they might stop buying our debt.

I can envision a time a few decades from now when our grandkids will look back at our relationship with China and think, "How could they have let that happen?" I'd much prefer we answer the question now.

Dwight D. Eisenhower once defined something that he called "The Great Equation":

> *Spiritual force, multiplied by economic force, multiplied by military force is roughly equal to security. If one of these factors falls to zero, or near zero, the resulting product does likewise.*

If Eisenhower was right, then we're in trouble. We've already addressed the spiritual and economic sides of the equation, so that leaves only the military. As painful as it might be for those who think this topic should never be addressed, the truth is that money doesn't buy happiness, nor does it win wars. Then again, the amount of money isn't really the issue—if we can't buy good defense for $750 billion a year then something is seriously wrong. The issue is the overall principle of national defense that the money is being spent in support of. Until we refine and agree on that, no amount of money will ever be enough.

SecDef Common Sense

"I may want to change things, but I'm not crazy. I'm not going to cut a carrier, okay? But people ought to start thinking about how they're going to use carriers in a time when you have highly accurate cruise and ballistic missiles that can take out a carrier that costs between $10 and $15 billion and has 6,000 lives on it."

—Secretary of Defense Robert Gates

The Beck Doctrine

Warriors aren't whiners. Our soldiers, sailors, airmen, and marines are the best damn people on the planet. Period. Hell, they've signed up to *die* for us if necessary. "Who else but an idealist," said President Reagan, "would choose to become a member of the Armed Forces and put himself or herself in harm's way for the rest of us?"

We need to look out for their financial interests because they are too selfless to do it for themselves. When President Reagan was facing tough budget decisions back in the early 1980s, he said he got literally hundreds of letters from soldiers telling him, "If giving us a pay cut will help our country, cut our pay." That gives me shivers just to write it. These men and women love America in a way that many of us will never understand.

Try to imagine someone at the Department of Health and Human Services or the Department of Energy making that offer. In fact, forget about government workers; try to imagine a private citizen offering their pay to be cut to help our country's finances.

Reagan's response to our soldiers back then is the same as it should be now: "I wouldn't cut their pay if I bled to death." In other words, we are going to take a hard look at the defense budget, but pay for our rank-and-file troops is off-limits.

TEACHABLE MOMENT

In 2010, pay for a new private or basic airman is $17,366 per year. A corporal with three years of experience in the Army receives $25,128 and a sergeant-level employee with five years of experience receives $37,104. For comparison, the 2008 poverty level for a family of three was $17,163 per year. For further comparison, the Department of Labor was recently looking for a staff assistant. The job pays a minimum of $51,000 for the first year.

The great news is that we can save mountains of money without penalizing the people who are doing the hard work. Like the rest of this plan, the key is starting from the top down. President Obama may claim to want to take a scalpel to the budget, but that's pointless without first putting the budget side by side with the Constitution. If the goals and projects we are funding are not consistent with the overall role of government, then we don't need a scalpel—we need a chainsaw.

The Constitution does not encourage us to save all of mankind or reorganize the world. The Founding Fathers recognized that the world is a dangerous place and that, from time to time, America would need to be prepared to fight to maintain its freedom. But they were also quite clear that they did not regard America as an empire. Nor were they interested in a crusade. On July 4, 1821, John Quincy Adams set out to simply explain America's role in the world:

> *[America] goes not abroad in search of monsters to destroy. She is the well-wisher to the freedom and independence of all. She is the champion and vindicator only of her own . . . She well knows that by once enlisting under other banners than her own, were they even the banners of foreign independence, she would involve herself, beyond the power of extrication, in all the wars of interest and intrigue, of individual avarice, envy, and ambition, which assumes the colors and usurp the standard of freedom.*

The Constitution simply says we are to "provide for the common defense." Obviously, that doesn't mean we can or should simply pull our troops from everywhere we have them stationed. That would not only put allies in harm's way; it would also be a slap in the face to all the troops who've given up so much to serve and protect.

BIPARTISAN DEBT THREATS

"We cannot sustain this level of deficit financing and debt without losing our influence, without being constrained in the tough decisions we have to make, it's time to make the national security case about reducing the deficit and getting the debt under control."

—Hillary Clinton, May 2010

So, before I pull out my scalpel *or* my chainsaw, here are my basic principles for national defense:

- **We mind our own business.** We are not on the hunt for new enemies in the world. America will be your best friend and will treat you fairly if you do the same to us.
- **The enemy of my enemy is *not* my friend.** We are not going to prop up corrupt or dangerous governments simply because they happen to hate countries that hate us.
- **We sacrifice our values at our own peril.** We are going to conduct ourselves consistently with our values. That means not befriending countries that we don't agree with simply because they have something of value. Yes, Saudi Arabia, I'm talking to you.
- **If you mess with us, we will fight to win.** America's military arsenal is unparalleled in human history, but the last time the full might and muscle of our armed forces was released was World War II. Since then wars have been fought "humanely" with an eye toward minimizing damage. The results have not been pretty.

  That ends now. If America is provoked into a war, then we fight with everything we have. War is hell and should never be taken lightly. But when it's declared (and it must be *declared*), America must crush its enemy.
- **We will not rebuild the rubble we reduce you to.** If you provoke America and we unleash our full arsenal, you will be reduced to rubble. We will not waste our time or resources rebuilding your country afterward.

I think these principles all fit pretty well with the vision laid out by John Quincy Adams and any spending we do should be in direct support of them. America's foremost goal should always be peace and prosperity and we must break free of this perpetual cycle of military operations that is helping to bankrupt us. As we've seen, when America has been at war, domestic government spending has surged. Even when we win, we lose.

James Madison understood this well. In 1775 he wrote:

> *Of all the enemies of public liberty, war is perhaps the most to be dreaded, because it comprises and develops the germ of every other. War is the parent of armies. From these proceed debts and taxes. And armies, debts and taxes are the known instruments for bringing the many under the domination of the few . . . No nation could preserve its freedom in the midst of continual warfare.*

RIPPED FROM THE HEADLINES

SOVIET BORROWS HEAVILY AS OIL AND DOLLAR FALL

In effect the Soviet Union finds itself racing in an outer lane of a circular track while its adversary has the advantage of an inner lane.

—*New York Times*, December 1987

Sending the Wrong Message

Our largest overseas expenditures don't come from fighting wars, but from nation-building and occupation. The cost of the Iraq War has been estimated at between $1 trillion and $3 trillion. Nation-building operations account for about 80 percent of those costs. The actual combat represents just 20 percent.

The nation-building role we've assumed is a result of our experiences after World War II, when it was necessary to rebuild Japan and Germany because of the threat posed by the Soviet Union and communism. But the threat of global domination on that magnitude doesn't exist anymore. Sure, terror groups

Offering Guns, Not Butter

In his famous treatise, *The Art of War*, the ancient Chinese general and strategist Sun Tzu wrote, "Winning a hundred victories in a hundred battles is not the acme of skill. To subdue the enemy without fighting is the acme of skill."

We are big on "doctrines" in this country (I've already given you mine), but one of the best was Reagan's. (It was creatively called "the Reagan Doctrine.")

The idea was simple: arm and equip our allies who are already fighting our enemies for their own self-serving reasons. Reagan, for example, supported insurgents in Nicaragua, Afghanistan, and other places around the world, and succeeded in kicking the Soviets out of those countries with very few American soldiers being put at risk.

The principle grew out of the experiences of World War II when Bill Casey, Reagan's CIA director, had been a member of the Office of Strategic Services, a predecessor to the CIA. "I believe that it is important today to understand how clandestine intelligence, covert action, and organized resistance saved blood and treasure in defeating Hitler," he wrote. "These capabilities may be more important than missiles and satellites in meeting crises yet to come . . ."

would love safe harbors in poor, dysfunctional countries, but guess what—there are always going to be terror groups *and* poor, dysfunctional, chaotic countries. If the groups are eradicated from Afghanistan or Somalia they'll move to Niger or Liberia.

That's why nation-building as a result of the War on Terror won't work—it's a never-ending cycle of war and rebuilding. And the precedent it sets for other countries in need is terrible. It's actually reminiscent to the plot of *The Mouse That Roared*, wherein a tiny country declares war on the United States because it wants international aid from America. It's a funny movie, but it's basically the way our policy can be interpreted by the rest of the world: Just make America angry because we'll bomb you (compassionately), and then rebuild you much better than you ever were before.

Has Anyone Seen My $2.3 Trillion?

> "*Given America's difficult economic circumstances and parlous fiscal condition, military spending . . . can and should expect closer, harsher scrutiny.*"
>
> —Secretary of Defense Robert Gates

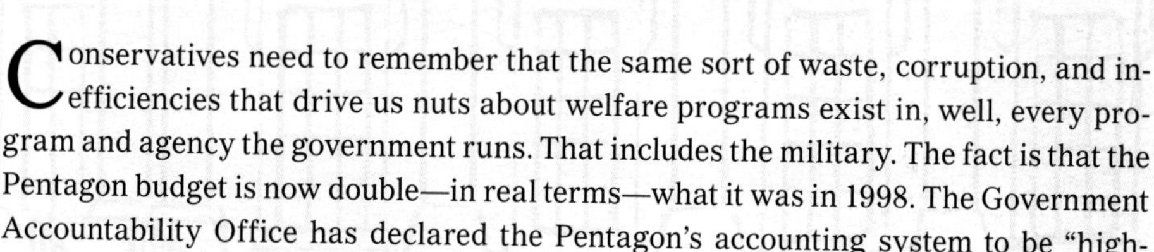

Conservatives need to remember that the same sort of waste, corruption, and inefficiencies that drive us nuts about welfare programs exist in, well, every program and agency the government runs. That includes the military. The fact is that the Pentagon budget is now double—in real terms—what it was in 1998. The Government Accountability Office has declared the Pentagon's accounting system to be "high-risk" for the past fifteen years.

Jim Minnery, an accountant who works for the Defense Finance and Accounting Service, has turned into something of a whistle-blower. Earlier this decade he attempted to track down $300 million that had seemed to vanish. "We know it's gone," he said, but we don't know what they spent it on.

But far from getting support from the top for his mission, Minnery's superiors questioned why he was bothering looking for the money. "The director looked at me and said, 'Why do you care about this stuff?' It took me aback, you know? My supervisor asking me why I care about doing a good job," Minnery told CBS News.

Is Gates the Guy?

You have to give Secretary of Defense Robert Gates credit. He seems to really be trying to reform the Pentagon's budget. The Air Force, Army, and Navy have been told to each identify $28.3 billion in efficiencies over the next five fiscal years. Nonservice defense agencies have to come up with another $17 billion, which means a total of $102 billion that Gates is trying to cut, almost all from overhead.

Minnery was eventually reassigned and, he says, the Pentagon simply wrote off the missing money. But he wasn't done talking. In 2006, he told the *Defense Industry Daily*, "[The Pentagon's] systems can't keep track of who they've sold stuff to, who owes them, who they owe."

The size of the numbers we're talking about is staggering. On September 10, 2001, Secretary of Defense Donald Rumsfeld tried to make people understand the unbelievable scope of the problem by announcing that the Pentagon was unable to track $2.3 trillion worth of transactions. The Defense Department's own auditors have said that they cannot account for a full 25 percent of their annual expenditures.

> **Check Under the Cushions**
>
> *"With good financial oversight we could find $48 billion in loose change in that building [the Pentagon], without having to hit the taxpayers."*
>
> —Retired Vice Admiral Jack Shanahan

And try this one on for size: In July 2010 the Pentagon admitted that it cannot account for $8.7 billion in Iraqi funds.

Senator Tom Coburn, a defense hawk, has called for greater "due diligence on national defense spending" and says we need to "reduce wasteful, unnecessary, and duplicative defense spending that does nothing to make our nation safe." He's right. The Pentagon's books are more of a disaster than Afghanistan—bring in the best accountants and technology teams in the world and clean them up.

The Shock and Awe Commission

I understand that it's not exactly revolutionary to say "clean up Pentagon waste," but for all the talk, it never seems to happen. If we really got in there and started digging, who knows what we'd find. And that's the whole point: We don't even know what we don't know. That is no way to run a three-quarter-trillion-dollar budget.

As a first step, I propose that Congress appoint a fifty-person special commission (I refuse to call it a "blue-ribbon panel") with a very specific recipe:

- 10 appointees are current military personnel, ideally from all different levels of the bureaucracy so that all points of view can be considered. No more than 5 of these appointees can be "flag officers" (officers who've been nominated by the president and confirmed by the Senate) because they are too entrenched in the current way of doing things.
- 10 are retired military personnel. They will lend experience and will likely be more open to speaking out honestly.
- 10 are partners from the world's top accounting firms (KPMG, Ernst & Young, etc.). They understand how to structure processes like pur-

chases and accounts payable and can institute proper controls so that our auditors can issue reports each year.

- 10 are partners from the world's top management-consulting firms (Bain Capital, McKinsey, etc.). These people understand how to incorporate best practices from the corporate environment. They'll make our Pentagon more streamlined, more efficient, and more able to react to the emergencies they are there to address.
- The final 10 are smart, talented people who are selected because they are innovators in their fields, but have absolutely no knowledge of defense systems. They are there to question everything. Why do we need a new "Ford" class of aircraft carriers? What will the F-35 really do? Why does it cost so much? Wouldn't drones be cheaper? These people will be annoying, but invaluable.

Their mission would also be very specific: To take one year and develop a set of recommendations that are binding. The only way to prevent a specific recommendation from taking hold would be a two-thirds majority vote of Congress—thereby forcing politicians to publicly associate their names with the status quo. This group would also pass background checks and have access to classified material since I have a sneaking suspicion that marking something "classified" is really a convenient way to ensure that waste never has to be accounted for.

I'm No SecDef, But . . .

I know that it's easy to sit back and write about these kinds of things from my couch when there are real jobs, real lives, and real careers at stake. Up to this point I've given you the fifty-thousand-foot view—the Founders' take on defense and the principles that I think we should adhere to when deciding how to spend—but now it's time to get specific. It would be ridiculous to claim that I could give you every example of how to cut costs or waste at the Pentagon. I did, after all, just suggest a fifty-person team work on that very issue for a year, but I also don't think it's fair to just say "cut, cut, cut" without at least providing a few real-world examples.

Since I'm not an expert in this area (which is actually a benefit), I turned to Erik Prince, a former Navy SEAL and the founder of the private military company Blackwater (now "Xe"). In an interview, I asked him for some examples of things that the Pentagon could do better. The remainder of this chapter is based on the insights and experiences he offered to me during an interview about how to make the military more efficient without compromising our security.

MATCH DECISION MAKERS TO COSTS

The socialist bad habit of separating costs from users and decision makers has infected the Defense Department, too.

The Navy was performing vertical replenishment services (a fancy way of describing how warships are restocked from helicopters) using two choppers, thirty-five personnel in the field, and another seventy staff members stateside waiting or preparing to deploy. The Navy then outsourced that task to a private contractor, who used the same two choppers but just eight people total in the field and three stateside.

Bipartisan Debt Threats

"This country cannot continue to run trillion-dollar deficits. We're now looking at in excess of one trillion dollars, the likelihood is we'll go to two-trillion-dollar deficits. We cannot do that and expect that we can remain a powerful nation . . . This country will not have the resources to confront the problems that we need to confront for the future."

—Director of Central Intelligence Leon Panetta, 2009

Why the difference? Because the Navy admiral who staffed the original mission didn't have to use his budget to pay for the people. The Navy Bureau of Personnel paid the personnel costs so, at least to the admiral, they were free. Of course, when you're not paying for something, you tend to not only use more of it, but you don't use it as efficiently as you otherwise would. (Think, for instance, about how you use electricity in your home versus when you stay at a hotel.)

The solution here is fairly simple: Like most large businesses, each manager in the field should have a budget that they are accountable for.

AL GORE WOULD NOT BE PLEASED

One of the largest costs for the military is fuel, but the Air Force has taken "burn rate" to a whole other level. The way they conduct support for operations in Iraq or Afghanistan is like mowing your lawn with a Porsche Cayenne. Sure, you can do it, but it costs a whole lot more than necessary and, at the end, your lawn looks exactly the same as it would if you'd used a $200 mower.

That analogy fits pretty well in describing how we treat air support in Afghanistan. The massively expensive fighters we use there require huge airfields, large support and maintenance staffs, and aerial refueling, which requires a whole additional level of support.

Worse, it's all mostly for show. The Defense Department could buy fifty proven, state-of-the-art turboprop attack aircraft equipped with the finest in electronics and equipment for about $500 million. Basing them on unimproved strips around Afghanistan close to where they are needed would alleviate the need for jet engines while simultaneously giving us an advantage in being able to respond faster to a call from the ground.

Because of fuel costs, the payback in switching aircraft types is only about seven months. Once you factor in the reduced manpower for support and maintenance, and the reduced costs of repairing damage to an aircraft that only costs $10 million (instead of a $100 million fighter jet), the real payback period is likely even a lot shorter than that.

As the United States begins to transition out of Afghanistan, its forces would be able to take over an effective, low-cost platform for air support instead of the "air show" capability we currently have.

Again, it's the chasm between the spenders and the users that is primarily driving this kind of insanity. Switching to the right equipment for the mission would save billions a year, reduce collateral damage, and decrease fuel burn by more than 90 percent.

> **Bipartisan Debt Threats**
>
> ***"Unless our rates of expenditure are sharply reduced, we will bring on the type of collapse that will leave us defenseless before our foe. Excessive expenditures thus become the chief menace to our national security."***
>
> —President Dwight Eisenhower

HOW MANY ADMIRALS DOES IT TAKE TO . . .

The Defense Department is typical of all government entities in that it too has become bloated and top-heavy. The department currently consumes about 40 percent of its annual budget in overhead costs. Though the military currently has fewer than 3 million personnel in reserve and active status, the command structure is about the same size as it was during World War II, when the United States had nearly 15 million personnel.

To put things in even simpler terms, the Navy now has more admirals (315 flag officers) than ships (264). That sounds more like a jobs program than a defense agency.

In an era when technology is allowing global private-sector organizations to run multiple billion-dollar enterprises in multiple time zones with very little overhead cost, the military is stuck with a pre-digital-age organizational chart that keeps getting thicker with layers of bureaucracy, all of which are trying to fix the same problem but only making things worse.

General Petraeus may have successfully decentralized bureaucracy in organizing the Iraq surge, but that mentality has not yet spread across the Pentagon. It's still the same old turf battles about the same old issues.

BUYING VOTES WITH LIVES

After reading any of the defense industry publications you can instantly spot the programs that were sold on politics instead of merit. Some defense contractors actually run promotional advertising boasting how many congressional districts their overpriced systems are made in. Not how efficiently lethal they are, or how many lives they could protect, but how much pork they can offer to each member that votes for it.

It's gotten so bad that the "systems integrators" will actually build or arm-twist their vendors into building a facility in the district of a key vote or appropriator to get it approved. Is that really how we want our defense suppliers selected? Is that really how we want our tax dollars spent? No wonder Congress has a 16 percent approval rating.

Is Anyone Counting?

How many defense contractors does the Pentagon actually use? No one seems to know (which is a problem in itself), but by one outside estimate, it's approximately 790,000.

Gates is now beginning to take this issue head-on. In August 2010, he announced that funding for private contractors would be reduced by 10 percent in each of the next three years. That's left lobbyists for those companies, along with politicians themselves, scrambling to protect their turf. "They're going to come full force," said Dave Levinthal of the Center for Responsive Politics about lobbyists.

RUN THE BACK OFFICE LIKE A PRIVATE COMPANY

There are tremendous similarities between government-run health care and the government-run military programs. Health-care costs continue to rise because government regulations and bureaucracy stifle innovation and efficiencies. Just compare Lasik or plastic-surgery procedures (all privately paid) with Medicare- or Medicaid-dominated procedures—it's no contest: The costs of private procedures have come down and quality has dramatically improved.

The same concept applies to the way the military runs their operations. Unlike a private corporation, they can't just acquire goods from the vendor that gives them the best terms, they have to go through an entire procurement process. It's so full of red tape and abuse that some lawmakers believe that reform would not only save the Pentagon $135 billion over five years, but it would also help get equipment to troops in the field far faster.

Debt, Defense, Decline

"This is how empires decline. It begins with a debt explosion. It ends with an inexorable reduction in the resources available for the Army, Navy, and Air Force. Which is why voters are right to worry about America's debt crisis."

—Harvard economist Niall Ferguson

The way to change this is to change the incentive structure. For example, September is a golden month to be a government contractor because September 30 is when the fiscal year ends. Budgets have to be fully spent by then because if they're not, then chances are their budget will be cut the following year.

It's an insane perversion of how a real budgeting process should work. If a department is able to achieve its objectives without spending its fully budgeted amount then it should be congratulated and rewarded, not penalized. It's a basic management technique that every world-class company understands.

The Pentagon is like any other dysfunctional organization—no one is going to step up unless they see things changing. Blowing the whistle gets you nothing but a reassignment to a research center in Antarctica, so good people keep their mouths shut and put in their time. But once people see that a real effort is under way to change the culture (and that it's being managed outside the political process), innovators who have been frustrated and paralyzed by the bureaucracy will rise up and provide real leadership.

The truth is that we can have a far *more* capable military for 30–50 percent less than what we are paying now—without cutting a dime of soldiers' pay. Sound crazy? Consider this: If 40 percent of the Defense Department's budget is spent on overhead, then just reducing the markup on that to the same maximum markup permitted to private contractors (15 percent) could save nearly a quarter of the budget with no real loss of combat power.

There's no doubt that there are a lot of places to cut and many areas to improve. We just need two things to get started: real leadership, especially from outside the Pentagon, and political will, especially from Republicans who all too often want to cut everywhere except defense.

Sometimes, when you're starving, even the sacred cows have to be slaughtered.

Educate Yourself

- A. J. Bacevich, *The new American militarism: how Americans are seduced by war* (free preview): *http://books.google.com/books?id=YYIn7sXgcBMC*

- Dana Hedgpeth, "Defense secretary's planned cuts upset investors and defense contractors," *The Washington Post*, August 11, 2010 *http://www.washingtonpost.com/wp-dyn/content/article/2010/08/10/AR2010081006290.html*

- David M. Walker, *Comeback America: Turning the Country Around and Restoring Fiscal Responsibility* (free preview): *http://books.google.com/books?id=7Ga0TEYaScIC*

- Secretary of Defense Robert Gates, from a speech given May 7, 2010 *http://www.defense.gov/Transcripts/Transcript.aspx?TranscriptID=4621*

“The present tax code[s] . . . artificially distort the use of resources, inhibit the mobility and formation of capital, add complexities and inequities which undermine the morale of the taxpayer, and make tax avoidance rather than market factors a prime consideration in too many economic decisions.”

—*John F. Kennedy, 1963*

CHAPTER 20.

Step Eight: Spit Ourselves Out of the System

Our current tax system is a disaster.

That is not a controversial statement, yet this somehow is: *We need to reform it.*

Why the disparity? Because progressives have been successful at convincing people that "reform" is code language for cutting taxes for the rich. Nothing could be further from the truth.

Tax historian Charles Adams once wrote:

> *Nothing reflects a nation more faithfully than its tax system. A society can best be evaluated by examining who is taxed, what is taxed, and how taxes are assessed, collected, and spent. Those in control of the political process invariably bear lighter tax burdens than those on the outside.*

If that's true, if our tax system really is a reflection of our society, then what does that say about who've we become? Are we really a society that believes in using the tax code as a weapon against political enemies? Are we really a society that is willing to tacitly approve of corruption by looking the other way when the powerful take advantage of us? Are we really a society that takes pride in seeing the most successful people brought back down toward the average?

If the answer to any of those questions is yes, then I don't know who America is anymore. But if the answer is no, then our task is simple: We have to make our weakness our strength. Right now, the tax code is something to be dreaded, if not outright feared. But what if we could turn that around? What if the tax code were to become one of America's greatest assets, a reflection of our core beliefs and values? What if instead of penalizing success, it rewarded it? What if instead of taking weeks to comply with, it took seconds?

That is our mission. Not simply to "reform" the system, but to transform it into something that, by its very nature, will attract the best and brightest back to America. The system as it stands today is unworkable, unproductive, and unsustainable.

That's why we've got to spit ourselves out of it.

Yeah, but the 47th Would Have Matched

A few years ago *Money* magazine went to 46 tax experts to prepare a tax return for a hypothetical family. What they got back were 46 different returns. None of the tax preparers could agree on how much the family owed in taxes.

The System Stinks . . . but We Can't Change It

Government has certain critical costs that must be funded. (Remember: I am for "limited government," not anarchy.) But *how* we collect taxes is almost as important as how *much* we collect. Economist Henry George, writing in the nineteenth century, noted that "the mode of taxation is, in fact, quite as important as the amount. As a small burden badly placed may distress a horse that could carry with ease a much larger one properly adjusted, so a people may be impoverished and their power of producing wealth destroyed by taxation, which, if levied, in any other way, could be borne with ease."

Anytime someone proposes large-scale tax reform, the attacks begin immediately. But, without yet arguing for a specific plan, look at what the status quo has brought us: endless piles of forms, parallel tax systems, credits, deductions, loopholes, and penalties. Critics whine about the gap between the rich and poor, yet they refuse to change the very system that is causing that gap in the first place! They complain about the middle class disappearing, yet they have no problem maintaining the very tax policies that are forcing it to happen. They constantly protest that the wealthy don't pay enough, yet they fight to maintain the ridiculously complex structure that allows the most wealthy to reap the most benefit.

What I am trying to say is that the very people who hate our tax system also seem to be its biggest supporters. Perhaps they're just scared of change, worried that it might upset the delicate applecart that they've balanced welfare programs on. Or perhaps they know that the activist groups that support them rely on the current tax code for their survival. I don't know the reason, but I do know that we are not engaging in a debate with honest brokers.

Outsource the Helpdesk?

The Treasury inspector general for tax administration reported that 43 percent of all tax questions asked of the IRS in a special study received wrong answers or no answer at all.

So, to move forward, we need to move the critics to the side. We need to reframe the debate so that instead of people telling us why our ideas won't work, they should be forced to explain how the status quo does. Believe me, they won't have an answer other than to resort to partisan nonsense.

Closing the Glass Door

Those who fight to maintain the current tax system don't want us to realize that they are trying to close the glass door to their exclusive club. Think about it: Who do you think benefits most from all the deductions, exemptions, preferences, shelters, and other loopholes in the current tax code? Here's a hint, it's not the minimum-wage worker down the street, or the middle-class guy with two kids and a decent house in the suburbs. It's the people who are *already* wealthy. It's the people who can speed-dial lawyers, lobbyists, and accountants anytime they need to.

RIPPED FROM THE HEADLINES

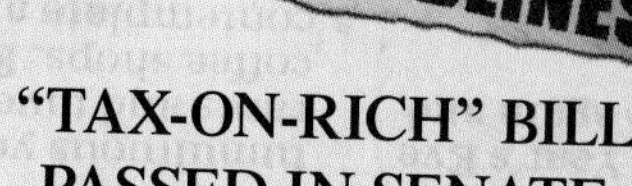
"TAX-ON-RICH" BILL PASSED IN SENATE

—*Los Angeles Times*, August 1935

Wealth is the key to the club, and with our current tax code getting even more progressive, there won't be many more available. As Milton Friedman once pointed out:

> *These [progressive] taxes are much less taxes on being wealthy than on becoming wealthy. While they limit the use of the income from existing wealth, they impede even more strikingly—so far as they are effective—the accumulation of wealth. [High taxes] give an incentive to avoid risk and to embody existing wealth in relatively stable forms.*

A WASTE OF TIME

The federal tax code with all its amendments, rules, and regulations is now nore than *9 million words long*. Complying vith all of those words is time consuming. he IRS estimates that we spend a cumuative 7.6 million hours each year dealing ith the tax system. That's the equivalent of early 4 million full-time workers.

In other words, the more progressive the tax system, the more likely it is that those aspiring to wealth will never get there. Remember, our taxes are especially heavy on wealth that is earned, saved, or invested, but not nearly as punitive on income that is consumed. If you already have a lot of money and want to enjoy a lavish lifestyle, the tax system won't hit you especially hard. But for those still trying to get to the promised land—progressive taxes are your worst enemy.

Here's an extreme example to show you what I mean: Suppose a middle-class woman hits the Powerball jackpot and decides to take the lump-sum payout option of $100 million. She gets her check, pays about $50 million to all the various governments with their hands out, and goes on her way.

From that point on, she is essentially home free. If she spends money she may pay some sales tax, and if she invests it poorly (i.e., doesn't spend a million to hire a great attorney and accountant), then she may pay some capital gains tax, but she's mostly done with the progressive tax code (as well she should be; she just paid $50 million).

Now, contrast her luck with another middle-class woman who never hits Powerball but works hard. Every year she earns a little bit more money, and every year she pays a little more in tax. How can she possibly build wealth? In any year that she does extremely well (say she receives a $100,000 bonus), she'd pay far more in taxes, leaving much less for her to save.

The progressive tax code almost forces you to win the equivalent of a lottery jackpot to really make it big in America. Not only is that unfair; it's also a terrible way to run a country. How much incentive do people have to take risks or to work extra hard when every time they look up they see the glass door to the club slowly shutting?

Efficiently Inefficient

If you are trying to raise, say, $100 billion in taxes, you would want to raise it as efficiently as possible. If it costs you $20 billion to collect it, that's inefficient and wasteful; wouldn't it be far better to raise that $100 billion with only $5 billion in costs? Well, the Office of Management and Budget estimated that the compliance cost for the current tax system is $200 billion. We only collect about $1.2 trillion in personal income taxes. That's inefficient and foolish—but it also may be a vast understatement. According to the Tax Foundation, compliance will cost us $338 billion this year.

The reason for this is simple: Politicians keep making the tax system more complicated. The number of words of tax law and regulation—and this is just for the income tax—jumped from 718,000 in 1955 to more than 7 million in 2005.

Equality Through Taxes

"We think [letting tax cuts on the wealthy expire] is the responsible thing to do because we need to make sure we can show the world that they're willing as a country now to start to make some progress bringing down our long-term deficits."

—Timothy Geithner

After you cut through all the mind-numbing data and statistics, you finally reach the central problem: Our income-tax system is no longer about maximizing revenue for the government; it's about redistributing wealth to create a more just society.

Ever since the Progressive Era our leaders have been fiddling with the tax code to promote "economic equality." By penalizing some groups and rewarding others, they are able to use the tax system as a kind of social-engineering tool. And by encouraging some behaviors and discouraging others, they are able to increase dependence on the government and decrease self-reliance.

This goes to one of the core differences between progressives and those who celebrate capitalism: Many progressives believe that successful people don't deserve their wealth. The odd thing is that this bias only seems to apply when you're talking about investors, entrepreneurs, and business owners. After all, I haven't seen much criticism of Brad Pitt or Julia Roberts for making tens of millions of dollars for a single movie, of Eminem for selling millions of albums, or of Derek Jeter for playing a game. Instead, progressives seem to recognize that these people have unique talents and gifts and that their salaries compensate them for that. In a free market, uniqueness equals value.

Flashback!

After Woodrow Wilson created the income tax he raised rates, and the number of millionaires in the country magically declined overnight. FDR had the same experience. The state of Maryland just learned this lesson the hard way. It increased the tax rate on millionaires, and all of sudden the number of millionaires living in Maryland plunged by a third. The government collected $100 million less from that group than it was expecting.

But highly successful business leaders and entrepreneurs have unique talents as well. How many people have the genius and drive to build a company in their garage and grow it into a Fortune 500 behemoth? Surely that takes at least as much talent as Justin Bieber, and as much hard work as, say, Jerry Seinfeld put into his sitcom.

It's time to stop bashing businesspeople—they are, after all, creating the jobs that everyone else is clamoring for more of. Yet instead of incentivizing them to create more, we punish them when they do.

NOBEL PRIZE–WINNING NONSENSE

"Isn't keeping taxes for the affluent low also a form of stimulus? Not so you'd notice. When we save a schoolteacher's job, that unambiguously aids employment; when we give millionaires more money instead, there's a good chance that most of that money will just sit idle."

—Paul Krugman

I assume by "give millionaires more money" what he *really* meant was "allow millionaires to keep more of the money they've earned."

Austrian economist Ludwig von Mises once said that "the only way [progressives know] to do away with poverty . . . is to take away—by means of progressive taxation—as much as possible from the well-to-do. In their eyes the wealth of the rich is the cause of the poverty of the poor."

That cause-and-effect relationship is, of course, completely untrue. It's like making the claim that skinny people cause the fat of the obese. Even if you eliminated all the skinny people (or forced all of them to become fat themselves), there is no reason to think that the fat people wouldn't just stay that way.

Let's say that our politicians actually understand that concept and realize that, while they can never make the fat people skinny, they can definitely make the skinny people fat. To them, equality is equality; who cares if people are all fat or all skinny, as long as they are all the same.

To meet their goal, politicians implement a series of policies that force the skinny to eat a minimum number of calories per day that's based on their height, weight, body fat percentage, and genetic markers.

Fast-forward ten years later and something strange will have happened: Some of the skinny people will have become fat; none of the fat people will have become skinny; and all of the fat people will have become even more obese. Why? Because the skinny people will find loopholes in the policies, or they'll work harder at burning calories so that the policies have less of an impact on them. It's much harder to be skinny if *you're already* skinny. But the fat people won't have that ability. To become skinny, not only would they have to avoid all of the policies forced to make them gain more weight, they'd also have to figure out a way to actually lose weight. It's just not going to happen.

It was a convoluted example, but the point is that taxes can't force equality because God made people different and no law made by man can ever change that.

The other issue with progressive rates is that the wealthy do all they can to shelter income from their reach. The higher the rates go, the more time and money people spend in trying to find tax shelters (which are perfectly legal if done correctly). A lot of the really wealthy people I know have decided to just load up on tax-free municipal bonds even though the interest rates are very low.

The problem from an economic perspective is that things like municipal bonds

The Lengths Some People Will Go

The behavior of rich people can teach us a lot about what's wrong with our tax system. Even wealthy progressives like George Soros enjoy playing the tax-avoidance game. The hedge fund he founded, the Quantum Fund, is actually incorporated on the tiny island of Curacao in the Dutch Antilles.

The Kennedy family has played this game as well. They built much of their wealth through Merchandise Mart, a commercial real-estate enterprise. But the *Chicago Tribune* reports that back in 1947, Joe Kennedy divided the company up and domiciled it in—get this—not Massachusetts, California, or even Florida, but *Fiji*. Why Fiji? Obviously there were tax benefits to housing it there. When Joe Kennedy died, the family's fortune was said to be between $300 million and $500 million. How much did they pay in inheritance taxes? Just $134,330.90, according to the *New York Times*. Do the math: That's about .0004 percent.

You can simply dismiss these people as hypocrites, but the fact that so many people go to such great lengths to avoid paying taxes here should tell us something about our system, and how much money we're losing as a result of it.

are not optimal investments. Do we really want rich people making it easier for state and local politicians to issue more debt, or would we rather have those rich people creating jobs, building factories, and starting businesses?

Let's say you're wealthy and your accountant gives you two choices: Give me $100,000 and I'll be sure that you don't pay an ounce of tax on it, thereby saving you nearly $40,000; or pay the tax on your $100,000, then take the remaining $60,000 and try to invest it in stocks, bonds, or a new business.

If you choose option two, then you'd need to obtain a return of nearly 70 percent on your money just to get back to even. That makes it a pretty easy decision, doesn't it?

Rewarding Tax Avoidance

"We've got a tax code that is encouraging flight of jobs and outsourcing."

—Barack Obama, 2004

And that, in a nutshell, is the whole problem: Our tax code should be promoting *growth*, not creative means of avoiding taxes. As John F. Kennedy reminded us when he cut taxes back in the early 1960s, "a rising tide lifts all the boats." What JFK left out is that a rising tide also pushes more water onto the shore where it can be collected. More prosperity and growth is good for *everyone*—including the government.

WINNING THE BATTLE, LOSING THE WAR

In 1991, politicians desperate for more revenue had the bright idea to impose a "yacht tax." *Let's hit these rich people where it really hurts*, some progressive genius surmised: *Let's increase the cost of their yachts!*

And then the law of unintended consequences took over. Since yachts cost more, demand for them plunged, sending sales through the floor. Boatbuilders began to struggle. Some shut down, some moved overseas, but either way, American jobs were lost. By 1994 the tax was rescinded, but the damage had already been done.

To recap, class-warfare attacks on the rich only result in the lower and middle classes losing the war. The only people who were hurt by taxing yachts were those entrepreneurs who owned boatyards or made boat parts, along with the middle-class workers who lost their jobs.

The same concept happens with higher income- and corporate-tax rates. When there is less incentive to produce and create jobs, the Donald Trumps of the world are not the ones who wind up hurting the most.

Lifting all ~~Yachts~~ Boats

One of the many fundamental weaknesses of progressives is that they tend to have a static view of human nature. They figure, "Well, if we raise taxes by ten percent, we are going to get 10 percent more revenue." Sounds logical, right? Maybe, but it's completely wrong. Behavior changes because incentives matter. Progressives will admit this when it's convenient (i.e., "cash for clunkers" was essentially a tax incentive program) but they ignore it when it comes to income tax rates.

That's one reason why tax increases hardly ever bring in the amount of revenue that advocates claim they will. When rates rise, people shift their money from productive areas to less productive areas to avoid paying taxes. That means, for example, the rich stop investing in their businesses and instead put an increasing amount of their money into tax-free municipal bonds.

W. Kurt Hauser of the Hoover Institution at Stanford University has demonstrated that there is "a close proportionality between revenue and GDP since World War II, despite big changes in the marginal tax rates in both directions." Federal tax receipts between 1950 and 2009 averaged 17.9 percent of GDP and maxed out at 20.6 percent (in 2000) even though the top marginal tax rate for federal income tax was all over the board—going from a low of 28 percent to a high of 92 percent over that time period.

In other words, despite all the changes to the tax laws, rates, and income brackets over the years, the only thing that *really* matters in terms of how much the government collects is our GDP. That's why it's time to stop playing these games with the minutiae of tax law and instead adopt a system that will help raise the water level of the entire pool.

Unfortunately, that doesn't seem to be what most of our politicians are really interested in doing. That's why, for example, instead of looking at the facts and his-

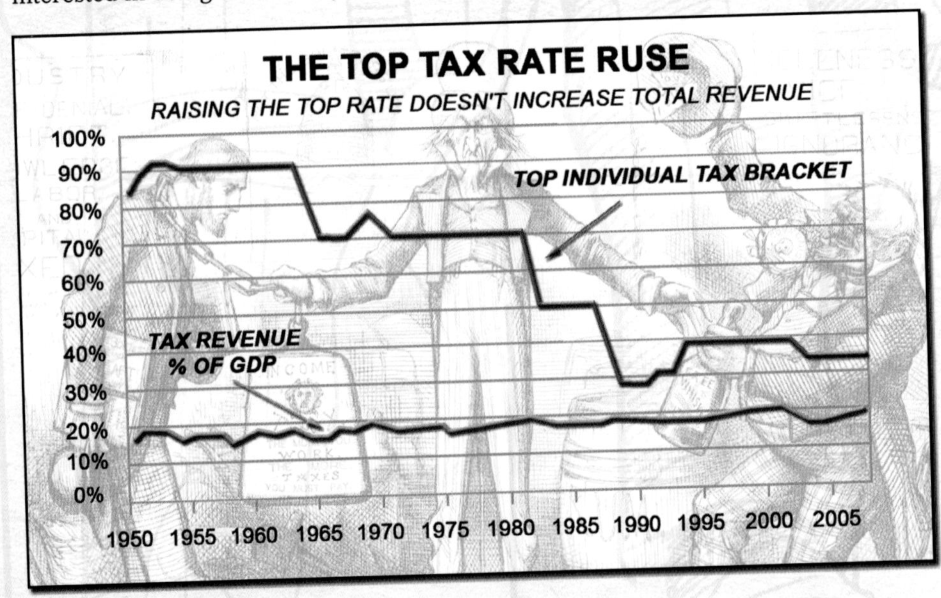

torical data, they fall back to making the same old arguments and reciting the same old talking points.

Every time there's a budget crisis (and even sometimes when there isn't) you hear a similar refrain: *It's time to make the rich pay their fair share!* But there are two problems with that logic. First, the wealthy already are paying more than their "fair share": The top 1 percent pays 35 percent of the taxes and the top 10 percent in income pay a whopping 71 percent of the federal income taxes. And second, putting the whole financial burden on the rich won't solve the problem. Even if the federal government were to take every single penny from the top 1 percent of earners, it would yield only a little less than $2 trillion. The government spends that in eight months.

We're Hiring!

As David Keating of the National Taxpayers Union pointed out, the tax industry has "more workers than are employed at the five biggest employers among Fortune 500 companies—more than all the workers at Wal-Mart Stores, United Parcel Service, McDonald's, International Business Machines, and Citigroup *combined*." Ready for another shocking comparison? The IRS has more employees than the CIA and FBI *combined*. (That says a lot about the priorities of the people in Washington.)

And therein lies the whole problem: There aren't enough rich people to solve our problems. That's why instead of trying to destroy them, we should be figuring out how to make more of them.

There's another issue about the progressive tax code that isn't talked about much because it's not politically correct, but it needs to be said: *Everyone* who earns money needs to pay tax. According to 2009 data from the Congressional Budget Office (which goes through tax year 2006), the bottom 20 percent of earners paid an effective tax rate of *negative* 6.6 percent in federal income tax (i.e., they actually received more money back through credits than they paid in taxes). In terms of the overall revenue collected from individual taxes, the bottom 40 percent of the country contributed *negative* 3.6 percent. In other words, the other 60 percent of the country paid 103.6 percent of the taxes collected.

I am not going to play the "fairness" card because I think that just distracts us from the bigger problem: when you don't pay any tax (or, in this case, when you receive money back) you are not invested in this country's economic growth, nor are you concerned about its spending. But when *everyone* pays, even if it's a very modest amount, then everyone is motivated in the same way. There is also the issue of decision-making. If nearly half the country pays little or no tax and receives entitlements, then how can a leader who is pro-tax cuts and pro entitlement reform ever get elected?

I Was for Job Creation Before I Was Against It

Capitalists believe that competition is healthy. It increases quality and service and reduces prices. But what many people fail to realize is that competition doesn't just happen between companies; it also happens between countries. Businesses and entrepreneurs are no longer constricted to deciding whether to relocate to Maryland or Texas; they can choose from Maryland, Texas, Brazil, or England.

The global economy and new technology have changed all the rules. Broadband technology affords businesses the ability to have teams of people all working together simultaneously in real time from all over the planet. That means companies can up and ditch America faster and easier than ever.

The good news is that America still has more going for it than almost any other country. All else being the same, companies would rather be located here because of our relative security, our educated workforce, our mass population of consumers, and the ability to attract new investors. But those features are being duplicated in other countries. Given the lack of jobs around the world, and the desire for governments everywhere to attract business, we need to be thinking about how to make America the place to be headquartered. But instead we are doing the opposite.

American businesses currently pay some of the highest corporate tax rates in the world. According to the Tax Foundation, once you factor in both federal and state taxes, the rate exceeds 39 percent. In the developing world, only Japan has higher corporate tax rates—and our advantage may not last much longer. Japan's new government announced its intention to lower the corporate tax rate by 10 to 15 percentage points.

The news is the same in Europe. Sweden, often seen as a hopelessly socialist country, even has lower business taxes than us—currently 28 percent. Over the last two decades, many European countries have begun to understand that corporations create jobs and have moved to lower tax rates. The average corporate rate in the European Union is now less than 25 percent.

RIPPED FROM THE **HEADLINES**

SALES TAX BACKED TO BALANCE BUDGET

A temporary sales tax on items other than food, housing and those already subject to Federal excises was urged today by the Committee for Economic Development if the levy was found necessary to achieve a balanced budget in the fiscal year 1953.

—*New York Times*, April 1952

There is one simple truth that many politicians, on both sides of the aisle, do not seem to understand: *You can't be* for *jobs but against those who create them.*

Reread that sentence again and let it sink in. You cannot give speeches about job creation and simultaneously vilify those who actually do the creating.

Taxing companies doesn't simply result in that money magically coming out of profits and going right to Washington. Instead tax increases are passed along to consumers in the form of higher prices, or, worse, they are offset by restructurings or layoffs. What is the point of getting extra tax dollars if the result is that jobs are lost? The lost income tax, Social Security tax, and Medicare tax on those eliminated jobs, combined with the costs of supporting these now jobless workers through unemployment insurance or other welfare programs, means that any extra corporate tax revenue will be partly—or even completely—offset by other factors.

The other problem with sticking it to corporations is that, like individuals, corporations figure that when taxes get too high, they will stash their money somewhere else . . . like a country with lower tax rates. Remember Enron? They got in trouble for creative accounting, largely to show profits that didn't exist, but they also didn't want to pay tax on those inflated profits.

Enron embarked on a "huge tax-avoidance scheme" by creating a jaw-dropping 881 subsidiaries abroad—most of them in obscure little island countries that served as tax havens. By doing this they avoided paying about $2 billion in federal taxes, a gimmick that also allowed them to report higher false profits. But this isn't a slam on tax havens; that's just the free market at work (Enron also had lots of subsidiaries in Delaware). The slam is on the tax law itself for incentivizing companies to go through so much trouble to avoid paying the money they would otherwise send to us.

None of Your Business

The most frustrating part of the whole corporate-tax debate is that, even though we have some of the highest corporate tax rates in the world, we still don't generate nearly as much revenue from the corporate tax as progressives think. The current figure is only about 12 percent of federal revenues—meaning that the entire corporate tax system could be eliminated and we'd still collect at least 88 percent of the income we budgeted for (and likely a lot more, given the new jobs that would be created).

Confiscating Their Weapon

"The United States, and most of the rest of the developed world, is in need of a tectonic shift in fiscal policy. Incremental change will not be adequate."

—Alan Greenspan, 2010

If we were starting a country from scratch and putting "best-practice" policies into place, we'd start by agreeing that the tax code should be about one thing: raising revenue efficiently and fairly. Our current code couldn't be further from that.

What we need, as Greenspan said, is a "tectonic shift"—and I believe that the idea of a flat income tax could be just that.

Before I go any further, let's take a deep breath because I know that the flat tax immediately conjures up different images for different people. Progressives have been so successful in putting propaganda out about this idea that most people don't even know what it really means anymore.

Some critics try to argue that a flat tax is unfair because it would result in the rich and poor paying the same amount. I don't know if they're deliberately lying, or just trying to confuse people, but that's not even close to being accurate. A flat tax means that everyone pays the same tax *rate*. If you make twice as much taxable income as your neighbor, you pay twice as much tax. And if the rich guy in town makes 100 times more than you, he pays 100 times more in tax. It is a policy that mirrors a principle I really like: equal justice under the law.

Steve Forbes has proposed a flat tax in which individuals and companies would pay a flat 17 percent of their income in taxes. Period. No deductions. No loopholes. No credits. No exemptions. Nothing. The only preference in the flat-tax system is a generous allowance based on family size.

At Least He Was Honest

Things have become very complicated with taxes in recent years. But even back in the 1930s it was confusing. At least for FDR. Along with his 1937 tax return, President Roosevelt sent the following note:

I am wholly unable to figure out the amount of tax for the following reasons. The first twenty days of January, 1937 were part of my first term in office and these twenty days the income tax rates as of March 4, 1933 apply. To the other 345 days of the year 1937, the income tax rates as they existed on January 30, 1937. As this is a problem in higher mathematics, may I ask that the Bureau let me know the amount of the balance due?

Try that the next time you file your taxes and let me know how it works out.

Under Forbes's plan, a family of four would pay no federal income tax on their first $46,165 in income. I'm not sure where I would like to see that limit set since I would like to see *everyone* pay at least some tax, but the point is that we can easily alleviate concerns about a flat tax hitting the poor too hard. Adults and children would also get standard exemptions.

Two scholars at Stanford University, economist Robert Hall and political scientist Alvin Rabushka, have pushed for a 19-percent flat rate. Their plan also has an allowance for families, but it's smaller than Forbes's plan, largely because they want to reassure critics that the politicians would still collect as much money as they do from the current system.

The specific rates and allowances can easily be debated later; it's the principle of treating everyone equally that's important to me. The flat tax provides all Americans with equality of opportunity—no longer would there be discrimination based on how someone earns, spends, or invests their wealth. It would also get the government out of the business of using the tax code as a weapon, or to manipulate behavior. And, best of all, a flat tax would eliminate the loopholes that fund the special interests that so many people on both sides of the aisle claim to hate.

The Same Tax Base

The first thing to understand (because this is where the attacks always start) is that this is *not* some kind of plan to save us all boatloads of money. In fact, it would basically raise the same amount of revenue as the current system. But instead of the 1040, the Schedule A, Schedule B, Schedule C, Schedule D, etc., Forbes's plan would replace all that with two postcards: one for households and one for businesses. All the money and energy that goes into finding ways to avoid taxes would be freed up to work on productive things, like expanding businesses or investing.

Better still, tax evasion and tax avoidance will go down. As Hall and Rabushka wrote, "At 40 cents on the dollar, dishonesty is lucrative. At 19 percent, most people would relax. Evasion and avoidance are far less profitable at 19 percent than at 40 percent." Some progressives believe that compliance can be handled through enforcement by the IRS, but every piece of available data shows that's not the case. Evasion is driven by tax rates. Period. When crime doesn't pay, people don't commit as many crimes.

Would the rich pay less under this plan? Maybe some would, but it depends on how they earn their wealth and how much they are spending to hide it. If someone makes $100 million a year right now but pays just $10 million in federal income tax, then the flat tax would actually represent a steep increase to them.

Either way, the point is to stop looking at equality and fairness (which clearly does not work) and start looking at the overall tax base. If we can have a system that benefits everyone, then why does anyone care exactly how much, say, Keith Olbermann pays in taxes? Arbitrary definitions of fairness aren't the issue, economic growth is—and that's the real power of the flat tax.

RIPPED FROM THE HEADLINES

INCREASED INCOME TAX RATE ONLY SOLUTION TO U.S. BUDGET PROBLEM

Neither the administration nor the Congress shows any sign of being willing to vote the taxes which are absolutely essential if the budget is to be balanced.

—*Los Angeles Times*, March 1959

As Hall and Rabushka put it, "With taxes taking no more than nineteen cents from each additional dollar at every income level, most people will pursue those economic activities that bring the highest return and the most satisfaction, rather than the ones that minimize taxable income."

The flat tax has had a broader political appeal than most people think. One of the first flat tax bills introduced in the Senate was by Dennis DeConcini, a Democrat from Arizona. On April 5, 1982, another Democrat, Congressman Leon Panetta from California, introduced a flat tax bill. In 1992, while he was running for president, former California governor Jerry Brown came out with a flat tax. Brown is no supply-sider, but he saw that special interests had created huge loopholes in the tax code and that the tax code was too complex.

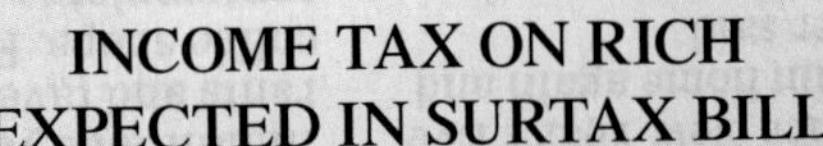

INCOME TAX ON RICH EXPECTED IN SURTAX BILL

Measure Would Prevent Individuals From Escaping All Federal Payments

—*Baltimore Sun*, July 1969

Answering the Critics

Some people believe that a flat tax would hurt charitable contributions because they would no longer be deductible. But Hall and Rabushka found that only about 60 percent of charitable contributions were actually claimed as deductions on tax returns. Besides, only about one-third of Americans even itemize their taxes, so most people give to charity solely for reasons of the heart. That would not change under the flat tax.

Moreover, history shows that lucrative deductions are not the key to charitable giving. Ronald Reagan slashed the top income tax rate from 70 percent to 28 percent, which meant that the after-tax cost of giving a dollar to charity jumped from 30 to 72 cents. But what followed was an increase in charitable contributions. As Hall and Rabushka wrote, "Sustained, strong economic growth, which increased the real income of the average American, was the most important factor in the sharp rise in giving, far more important than any tax break."

The second objection that's been made involves the mortgage-interest deduction. Critics say that eliminating it would wreak havoc on the housing sector. While it's true that some people currently take on a higher mortgage because they know they can count on the interest deduction, let's look at what that's brought us: a huge housing bubble and subsequent collapse. It's precisely because of government interference in interest rates, tax deductions, and mortgages that the housing market is about as far from a truly free market as you can get.

In any event, the home-mortgage-interest issue is a bit overblown. With a flat tax, interest rates would go down because money would be taken out of tax shelters and put into productive investments. So while taking away the mortgage tax deduction may make housing more expensive, lower interest rates would make the next payments less expensive.

There's also the fact that, under a flat tax, interest income would no longer be taxable. As a result, investors wouldn't need to demand a

FALSE FEARMONGERING

Home ownership in the United States stands at about 67 percent of the population. In comparison, the rate of ownership in the United Kingdom and Australia is about 69 percent and 67 percent in Canada. Yet mortgage interest is not deductible in any of those countries.

higher rate of interest to compensate them for taxes. That means going from, for example, 6-percent mortgages that are deductible to 4.5-percent mortgages that are not deductible. Six of one, a half dozen of another. Either way, it's not the big issue that critics try to make it into.

Not Just a Theory

It's also important to look around at the worldwide evidence for the flat tax, since at least thirty jurisdictions have already implemented some form of it. Not all of them are perfect; some still have unwieldy systems, but with just one rate. That's obviously an improvement over what we are dealing with, but a truly effective flat tax means the elimination of double taxation and special interest loopholes.

That's why the flat tax systems in places such as Hong Kong, Estonia, and Slovakia are good models. The leaders of those countries have largely succeeded in putting in place low tax rates and systems that have no special favors *or* penalties. As a result, investors and entrepreneurs can concentrate on building wealth and creating jobs.

Some people argue, by the way, that a national sales tax would be the best tax reform plan. Proposals like the fair tax are very appealing and they share many of the same principles of a flat tax, such as one low rate, no double taxation, and no special loopholes.

Estonian Envy

"They've got a tax system here that is transparent, open and simple. I am amazed to be in a country that has been able to effect a flat tax in such a positive way."

—President George W. Bush during a **2006** visit to Estonia

My hesitation about the sales tax is that I don't trust politicians. We already know that the crowd in Washington would love a value-added tax (VAT) in addition to the income tax. Well, I worry that they would see the national sales tax as an *additional* source of revenue, not a replacement for what we now have. Sure, they might promise to get rid of the income tax, but instead they'll pull a bait and switch.

I'm fine with the national sales tax idea, but the deficit of trust is just too big right now, so I'd support it only if we simultaneously got rid of the Sixteenth Amendment and replaced it with something so ironclad that even justices like Sotomayor and Kagan would have no choice but to say that the income tax is unconstitutional.

While that's a nice idea in theory, seeing that we can't even get a watered-down balanced-budget amendment through Congress, I'm not going to hold my breath waiting for it to happen.

The flat tax would eliminate virtually everything we hate about our current system (aside from actually having to hand your money over in the first place).

It would be simple and fast to comply with.

It would get rid of the special exemptions, loopholes, and kickbacks that benefit primarily lobbyists, special interests, attorneys, major corporations, and America's wealthiest citizens.

It would ensure that Congress writes bills without regard to tax handouts or penalties.

It would prevent the tax code from being used as a weapon against individuals or companies.

It would put a jolt of life into an economy that, by all accounts, has become stagnant.

It would incentivize businesses to expand here, thereby creating jobs and a bigger tax base.

And, most important, it would make it easier for the middle and lower classes to move up and for the wealthy to stay wealthy.

Does all of that sound too good to be true?

It is . . . because the very things that make the flat tax a great deal for taxpayers make it an awful one for the politicians who would have to support it.

Educate Yourself

- Alvin Rabushka's blog on the flat tax
  http://flattaxes.blogspot.com

- Arthur Laffer, Stephen Moore, and Peter Tanous, *The End of Prosperity: How Higher Taxes Will Doom the Economy—If We Let It Happen* (free preview)
  http://books.google.com/books?id=EU5gY-JY-mwC

- Dan Mitchell, Center for Freedom & Prosperity, "The Global Flat Tax Revolution" (free video)
  http://www.youtube.com/watch?v=qBAr0MzRFU0

- Robert Ernest Hall and Alvin Rabushka, *The Flat Tax* (free preview) *http://books.google.com/books?id=4Cr-x6ZlVOEC*

- Steve Forbes, *Flat Tax Revolution: Using a Postcard to Abolish the IRS* (free preview) *http://books.google.com/books?id=jOIq84fao2oC*

CONCLUSION

Our Story Continues

"Four regiments are enough to conquer the whole of America . . ."

Those fateful words were uttered by the British general Thomas Gage prior to the American Revolution. Around the same time, Colonel James Grant rose in the British House of Commons and assured his colleagues that he "he had served in America—knew the Americans very well [and] was certain they would not fight, they would never dare to face an English army and did not possess any of the qualifications necessary to make a good soldier."

Meanwhile, in the House of Lords, the Earl of Sandwich was also busy calming the nerves of his countrymen. "Supposing the Colonies do abound in men," he asked them; "what does that signify? They are raw, undisciplined, cowardly men. I wish instead of forty or fifty thousand of these brave fellows, they would produce in the field at least two hundred thousands, the more the better, the easier would be the conquest . . . Believe me my Lords, the very sound of the cannon would carry them off . . . as fast as their feet could carry them."

They were, of course, all wrong. The Americans may not have had as many men, supplies, munitions, or experience, but they had something that the British didn't: passion for their cause.

The colonists were willing to sacrifice their lives in pursuit of true freedom. The British were happy to be subjects of the king.

The colonists were willing to sacrifice their fortunes for a chance at building the world's greatest economy. The British felt they were already wealthy enough.

The colonists were willing to sacrifice their sacred honor to stand before the world and pronounce that rights to life and liberty could come only from God. The British were happy to take orders from a man.

Today, we find ourselves in nearly the same position, but under completely different circumstances. Depending on where you look around the country, you'll find either passion or apathy. You'll find millions willing to sacrifice their lives and fortunes for true freedom and you'll find millions of others who would trade freedom for security at every chance they get. You'll find Americans who believe that our sacred honor is everything, and you'll find Americans who would sell out their neighbors for an extra dollar from the government.

We are the colonists. And we are the British.

Progressives expect us to do nothing, and they doubt both our cause and our conviction to it. They believe they have created and executed on a plan to take this country from self-sufficiency to serfdom; from pursuit of happiness for all, to guaranteed happiness for none—and that no one can stop it.

But they've miscalculated on one key thing: We have a passion for liberty. We will not be the generation that lets true freedom slip from our grasp. Progressives expect us to do nothing—and that will be their biggest mistake.

There's no doubt that the problems we face are daunting, but our grandfathers faced worse. World wars, communism, a nuclear crisis—this country has seen the worst that man has to offer—and we've overcome it every single time.

Remember, nothing is inevitable. Nowhere is it etched in granite that America will fall. Nowhere has a book been written that contains the last chapter of our story.

History is not static. It is written by God and it is based in virtue. If we can fix ourselves, we can fix our country. If we can restore honor in our own lives, we can restore it across the entire country.

But we have to act. If you are waiting for a hero, then you are waiting for our demise. You *are* the hero. Our story is being written as we speak—find your place in it and remember that you don't have to be the lead character to make a difference.

As Frederick Douglass once said during another period of American struggle, "Find out just what any people will quietly submit to and you have found out the exact measure of injustice and wrong which will be imposed upon them."

Our government has found out how much injustice Americans are willing to quietly accept. But it has yet to see what happens when we've had enough.

THE CITATIONS

Facts Can Be Stubborn Things

Chapter 1: Ancient History, Modern Lessons

PAGE 3: "met the enemy . . . and he is us" I Go Pogo, "We Have Met the Enemy . . . and He Is Us," *igopogo .com*, accessed July 23, 2010, http://www.igopogo.com/we_have_met.html. ŏ **"it's roughly 24 percent"** Angus Maddison, *The World Economy: A Millennial Perspective/Historical Statistics* (Paris: Organization for Economic Co-Operation and Development, 2007).

PAGE 4: "'exceed the cost of the defense budget'" Scott Condon, "Sobering Opening for Aspen Ideas Festival," *Aspen Times*, July 6, 2010, http://www.aspentimes.com/article/20100706/NEWS/100709901/1077&ParentProfile=1058.

PAGE 5: "imported $374 billion more than we exported" U.S. Bureau of the Census, "U.S. Trade in Goods and Services—Balance of Payments (BOP) Basis," *census.gov*, June 10, 2010, http://www.census.gov/foreign-trade/statistics/historical/gands.txt. ŏ **"kept it in his library in Monticello"** Jefferson Encyclopedia, "Near-Perfect Republic (Quotation)," *wiki.monticello.org*, accessed July 23, 2010, http://wiki.monticello.org/mediawiki/index.php/Near-perfect_republic_(Quotation). ŏ **"notes from Jefferson have been found in the margins"** Kevin J. Hayes, "How Thomas Jefferson Read the Qur'an," *Early American Literature* 39, no. 2 (2004), 247–61.

PAGE 6: "The Bell Curve of History" David Murrin, *Breaking the Code of History* (West Sussex, UK: Emergent Asset Management Ltd, 2010), 59. ŏ **"By 2008 12 percent of Americans said that"** Frank Newport, "This Easter, Smaller Percentage of Americans Are Christian," *gallup.com*, April 10, 2009, http://www.gallup.com/poll/117409/easter-smaller-percentage-americans-christian.aspx.

PAGE 7: "'strain on the producers of primary commodities'" Cyril E. Robinson, *A History of Rome From 753 B.C. to 410 A.D.* (London: Methuen, 1935), 410. ŏ **"a 'decline of civic vitality' quickly ensued"** Solomon Katz, *The Decline of Rome and the Rise of Medieval Europe* (Ithaca, N.Y.: Cornell, 1955), 79. ŏ **"'Romans should lose the memory of freedom'"** Edward Gibbon, *The History of the Decline and Fall of the Roman Empire, Volume 2* (London: G. Cowie and Co. et al., 1825), 278. ŏ **"'groans under the Publicani [tax collectors]'"** Jim Nelson Black, *When Nations Die* (Carol Stream, IL: Tyndale House, 1994), 65. *See also* Charles Adams, *For Good and Evil: The Impact of Taxes on the Course of Civilization* (Lanham, MD: Madison, 1999), 81. ŏ **"they called the ploy 'bread and circuses'"** David Stone Potter, "Bread and Circuses," **in** *Life, Death, and Entertainment in the Roman Empire* (Ann Arbor, MI: University of Michigan, 1999). ŏ **"regardless of whether it was desired or successful"** Guglielmo Ferrero, *Ancient Rome and Modern America: A Comparative Study of Morals and Manners* (New York: Putnam, 1914), 89–90.

PAGE 8: "'by taking the inoffensive title princeps (first citizen)'" Marvin Perry, Margaret Jacob, James Jacob, Myrna Chase, and Theodore H. Von Laue, *Western Civilization: Ideas Politics and Society, Volume 1: To 1789* (Boston: Houghton Mifflin, 2009), 142. ŏ **"'citizens of Rome from the necessity of labor'"** Edward Gibbon, *The History of the Decline and Fall of the Roman Empire, Volume 2* (London: G. Cowie and Co. et al., 1825). ŏ **"'hated by everybody, even by the peasants'"** Jim Nelson Black, *When Nations Die* (Carol Stream, IL:Tyndale House, 1994).

PAGE 9: "establish theaters and develop sculpture as an art form" W.G. Hardy, *The Greek and Roman World* (Cambridge, MA: Schenkman, 1962), 4. ŏ **"'and seized the power'"** W.G. Hardy, *The Greek and Roman World* (Cambridge, MA: Schenkman, 1962), 9. ŏ **"'coveted the property of their neighbors'"** Thucydides, *The History of the Peloponnesian War*, ed. M.I. Finley, trans. Rex Warner (New York: Penguin, 1972), 87. ŏ **"'depend upon the property of their neighbors'"** Polybius, *The Rise of the Roman Empire, Introduction by F.W. Walbank, trans. Ian Scott-Kilvert (New York: Penguin, 1980), 309.*

PAGE 10: "ten ways to insulate yourself from these kinds of events" Nassim Nicholas Taleb, "Ten Principles for a Black Swan-Proof World," *Financial Times*, April 7, 2009, http://www.fooledbyrandomness.com/

tenprinciples.pdf. ṍ **"eighteenth century, Spain was a shell of its former self"** John Steele Gordon, *Hamilton's Blessing: The Extraordinary Life and Times of Our National Debt* (New York: Penguin, 1998), 2. ṍ **"'his wide operations in behalf of the faith'"** Edward Dwight Salmon, *Imperial Spain: The Rise of the Empire and the Dawn of Modern Sea-Power* (New York: Henry Holt, 1931), 111–12.

PAGE 11: "level of trust has dropped to 29 percent" Pew Research Center for the People and the Press, "Press Accuracy Rating Hits Two Decade Low: Public Evaluations of the Media: 1985–2009," *people-press.org*, September 13, 2009, http://people-press.org/report/543/. ṍ **"not enough businessmen and entrepreneurs"** Reginald Trevor Davis, *Spain in Decline 1621–1700* (London: MacMillan, 1957), 93–94. ṍ **"sparking what became a ten-year civil war"** Charles Adams, "Beware the Ides of April: High Taxes and the Decline and Fall of Practically Everybody," *Policy Review* 68 (1994). ṍ **"but a terrible place to buy things from"** Reginald Trevor Davis, *Spain in Decline 1621–1700* (London: MacMillan, 1957), 95. ṍ **"'usually the extravagance of the government'"** Reginald Trevor Davis, *Spain in Decline 1621–1700* (London: MacMillan, 1957), 102. ṍ **"'at risk of a sudden, rapid collapse'"** Paul B. Farrell, "Collapse of the American Empire: Swift, Silent, Certain," *MarketWatch*, March 9, 2010, http://www.marketwatch.com/story/the-rise-and-certain-fall-of-the-american-empire-2010-03-09?pagenumber=1. ṍ **"an 'empire on the edge of chaos'"** Scott Condon, "Sobering Opening for Aspen Ideas Festival," *Aspen Times*, July 6, 2010, http://www.aspentimes.com/article/20100706/NEWS/100709901/1077&ParentProfile=1058.

PAGE 12: "'hardworking animals with the government as its shepherd'" Alexis de Tocqueville, *Democracy in America, Volume 2* (New York: Vintage, 1990).

Chapter 2: Frugal: A Four-Letter Word

PAGE 15: "'and you can become a leader among men'" Lao Tzu, *The Sayings of Lao Tzu*, trans. and with an introduction by Lionel Giles (London: Orient Press, 1904), 35. ṍ **"'find it at the bottom of your purse'"** Theodore Roosevelt Malloch, *Thrift: Rebirth of a Forgotten Virtue* (New York: Encounter, 2009), 1. ṍ **"'give all you can'"** John Templeton, Jr., MD, *Thrift and Generosity: The Joy of Giving* (Philadelphia: Templeton Foundation Press, 2004), 6.

PAGE 16: "'will have to agonize'" Theodore Roosevelt Malloch, *Thrift: Rebirth of a Forgotten Virtue* (New York: Encounter, 2009), 61. ṍ **"'not profuse, prodigal, or lavish'"** Theodore Roosevelt Malloch, *Thrift: Rebirth of a Forgotten Virtue* (New York: Encounter, 2009), xix–xx. ṍ **"'and individualism as its philosophy'"** William L. Nunn, "Revolution in the Idea of Thrift," *Annals of the American Academy of Political and Social Science* 196 (March 1938): 52–56.

PAGE 17: "'Job suffered, and was afterwards prosperous'" John Bach McMaster, *Benjamin Franklin* (New York: Chelsea House, 1980), 125.

PAGE 18: "'profits will take care of themselves'" Paul S. Boyer, Clifford Clark, Sandra Hawley, and Joseph F. Kett, *The Enduring Vision: A History of the American People, Volume 2: From 1865*, Concise (Boston: Wadsworth, 2010), 408. ṍ **"'dies thus rich dies disgraced'"** Andrew Carnegie, *The "Gospel of Wealth" Essays and Other Writing*, ed. and with an introduction by David Nasaw (New York: Penguin, 2006). ṍ **"Carnegie gave away $350 million"** National Park Service, "Carnegie Libraries: The Future Made Bright," *nps.gov*, accessed July 21, 2010, http://www.nps.gov/history/nr/twhp/wwwlps/lessons/50carnegie/50carnegie.htm. ṍ **"an astonishing 1,700 libraries across the country"** National Park Service, "Carnegie Libraries: The Future Made Bright," *nps.gov*, accessed July 21, 2010, http://www.nps.gov/history/nr/twhp/wwwlps/lessons/50carnegie/50carnegie.htm. ṍ **"brought costs down and quality up"** Paul S. Boyer, Clifford Clark, Sandra Hawley, and Joseph F. Kett, *The Enduring Vision: A History of the American People, Volume 2: From 1865*, Concise (Boston: Wadsworth, 2010), 408.

PAGE 19: "'purchasing on a pay-as-you-use basis are responsible'" William L. Nunn, "Revolution in the Idea of Thrift," *Annals of the American Academy of Political and Social Science* 196 (March 1938): 52–56. ṍ **"achieve freedom to do as he wished"** David Steigerwald, "Did the Protestant Ethic Disappear?: The Virtue of Thrift on the Cusp of Postwar Affluence," *Enterprise and Society* 9, no.4 (December 2008): 788–815. ṍ **"savings rate dropped below zero"** Charles Steindel, "How Worrisome Is a Negative Savings Rate?" *Current Issues in Economics and Finance* 13, no. 4 (May 2007), http://www.newyorkfed.org/research/current_issues/ci13-4/ci13-4.html.

PAGE 20: "'now becomes something of a social vice'" Campbell R. McConnell, *Economics* (New York: McGraw-Hill, 1960), 261–62. ỗ **"'frequent recurrence to fundamental principles'"** Moses Coit Tyler, *Patrick Henry* (Boston: Houghton Mifflin, 1898), 208. ỗ **"'old virtues may be modern sins'"** Paul Anthony Samuelson, *Economics: An Introductory Analysis* (New York: McGraw Hill, 1958), 237. ỗ **"'the great horsemen of progress in America'"** David Steigerwald, "Did the Protestant Ethic Disappear?: The Virtue of Thrift on the Cusp of Postwar Affluence," *Enterprise and Society* 9, no.4 (December 2008): 788–815.

PAGE 21: "households were in some sort of debt" David Steigerwald, "Did the Protestant Ethic Disappear?: The Virtue of Thrift on the Cusp of Postwar Affluence," *Enterprise and Society* 9, no.4 (December 2008): 788–815. ỗ **"roughly 71 percent of the American economy"** David J. Lynch, "Consumer Spending at 71% of GDP As Other Sectors Sink," *USA Today*, October 10, 2009, http://www.usatoday.com/money/economy/2009-10-11-consumer-spending_N.htm. ỗ **"'the chain and whip of the slave driver'"** Ambrose Bierce, *The Devil's Dictionary* (New York: Oxford, 1999).

Chapter 3: The Founders

PAGE 22: "'but swindling futurity on a large scale'" Thomas Jefferson, "To John Taylor," in *The Works of Thomas Jefferson*, Federal Edition, vol. 11 (New York and London, G.P. Putnam's Sons, 1904–1905), http://oll.libertyfund.org/title/807/88161/2005262 on 2010-07-15.

PAGE 23: "declared that the arm belonged to the Peeping Tom's mother" "Medicine: Doctors' Riot," *Time*, May 11, 1942, http://www.time.com/time/magazine/article/0,9171,790468,00.html. *See also:* "The Doctor's Riot 1788," *The Riots of New York City*, http://thehistorybox.com/ny_city/riots/riots_article7a.htm; James Rupp, "Grave Robbers, Alexander Hamilton, John Jay and the Doctor's Riot," July 15, 2010, http://americanhistory.suite101.com/article.cfm/grave-robbers-alexander-hamilton-john-jay-and-the-doctors-riot; and Whitfield J. Bell, "Doctors Riot, New York, 1788," *Bulletin of the New York Academy of Medicine*, vol. 47, no. 12 (December 1971), http://www.ncbi.nlm.nih.gov/pmc/articles/PMC1749932/pdf/bullnyacadmed00213-0055.pdf. ỗ **"'left two large holes in his forehead'"** Dan T. Coenen, "Fifteen Curious Facts about *The Federalist Papers*," *Advocate* (University of Georgia School of Law, 2007), 3, http://digitalcommons.law.uga.edu/cgi/viewcontent.cgi?article=1001&context=fac_pm. ỗ **"'got his scull [*sic*] almost cracked'"** Whitfield J. Bell, "Doctors Riot, New York, 1788," *Bulletin of the New York Academy of Medicine* 47:12 (December 1971), 1571, http://www.ncbi.nlm.nih.gov/pmc/articles/PMC1749932/pdf/bullnyacadmed00213-0055.pdf. ỗ **"Despite his injuries, Jay suffered no brain damage"** Robert E. Wright, Ph.D., *One Nation Under Debt: Hamilton, Jefferson, and the History of What We Owe* (New York: McGraw-Hill, 2008), 112.

PAGE 24: "'almost adoring the splendor of her rising'" Robert E. Wright, Ph.D., *One Nation Under Debt: Hamilton, Jefferson, and the History of What We Owe* (New York: McGraw-Hill, 2008), 118. ỗ **"'the greatest of dangers to be feared'"** Thomas Jefferson, "Letter to William Plumer, July 21, 1816," *The Writings of Thomas Jefferson*, ed. Andrew A. Lipscomb, vol. 15, (1903), 47, http://www.bartleby.com/73/383.html (accessed July 15, 2010). ỗ **"'we must not let our rulers load us with public debt'"** Thomas Jefferson, "Letter to Samuel Kercheval," in *The Writings of Thomas Jefferson*, ed. Lipscomb and Bergh, vol. 15 (Washington, D.C., 1903–1904), 39, http://etext.virginia.edu/jefferson/quotations/jeff1340.htm. ỗ **"the general sentiment and wish of the nation"** George Washington, "Annual Message, November 6, 1792" http://www.thisnation.com/library/sotu/1792gw.html.

PAGE 25: "'under the pretense of caring for them, they will be happy'" Milton and Rose Friedman, *Tyranny of the Status Quo* (New York: Avon, 1985), 35. ỗ **"Thomas Jefferson himself died cashless under loads of personal debt"** Robert E. Wright, Ph.D., *One Nation Under Debt: Hamilton, Jefferson, and the History of What We Owe* (New York: McGraw-Hill, 2008), 14. ỗ **"trusting politicians with other people's money (through taxes) was foolish"** Robert E. Wright, Ph.D., *One Nation Under Debt: Hamilton, Jefferson, and the History of What We Owe* (New York: McGraw-Hill, 2008), 14. ỗ **"Americans would not stand for taxes being collected simply to pay for interest on debt"** Robert Allen Rutland, *James Madison: The Founding Father* (Columbia, MS: University of Missouri, 1997), 75. ỗ **"thereby 'pretty generally buy out the Americans'"** Ron Chernow, *Alexander Hamilton* (New York: Penguin Press, 2004), 296–297. *See also:* Robert Allen Rutland, *James Madison: The Founding Father* (Columbia, MS: University of Missouri, 1997), 75. ỗ **"Jefferson recommended *The Wealth of Nations* as the 'best book on economics'"** John Chamberlain,

The Roots of Capitalism (Indianapolis, IN: Liberty Fund, 1976), 85. ȍ **"in his reports on banking, currency, and manufacturers"** John Chamberlain, *The Roots of Capitalism (Indanapolis, IN: Liberty Fund, 1976), 85.*

PAGE 26: "can scarce be folly in that of a great kingdom" Adam Smith, *An Inquiry into the Nature and Causes of the Wealth of Nations*, bk. 4, ch. 2, http://www.ibiblio.org/ml/libri/s/SmithA_WealthNations_p.pdf. ȍ **"'are obliged to be oppressive and tyrannical'"** John Chamberlain, *The Roots of Capitalism (Indianapolis, IN: Liberty Fund, 1976), 42.* ȍ **"fell into a tannery pit while trying to explain division of labor to a friend" John Chamberlain,** *The Roots of Capitalism (Indianapolis, IN: Liberty Fund, 1976), 21.* **"'a burden to which Greek and Roman Shoulders proved unequal'"** Anti-Federalist No. 3, http://www.teachingamericanhistory.org/library/index.asp?document=1808. ȍ **"commanders often complained that their troops were 'almost naked'"** Robert E. Wright, Ph.D., *One Nation Under Debt: Hamilton, Jefferson, and the History of What We Owe* (New York: McGraw-Hill, 2008), 58.

PAGE 27: "The last resource then is finance" Robert E. Wright, Ph.D., *One Nation Under Debt: Hamilton, Jefferson, and the History of What We Owe* (New York: McGraw-Hill, 2008), 42. ȍ **"scraped together another $2 million from the Dutch"** Richard Beeman, *Plain, Honest Men: The Making of the American Constitution* (New York: Random House, 2010), 11, 15. ȍ **"bonds ranged from $1.04 to $804,000"** Robert E. Wright, Ph.D., *One Nation Under Debt: Hamilton, Jefferson, and the History of What We Owe* (New York: McGraw-Hill, 2008), 12, 248. ȍ **"in exchange for livestock, cloth, and other goods necessary to equip the army"** *See generally* "Signers of the Declaration, Biographical Sketches, Robert Morris, Pennsylvania," http://www.nps.gov/history/history/online_books/declaration/bio33.htm (accessed July 15, 2010). ȍ **"only good use for the bonds, the Brits said, was for wallpaper"** Robert E. Wright, Ph.D., *One Nation Under Debt: Hamilton, Jefferson, and the History of What We Owe* (New York: McGraw-Hill, 2008), 51.

PAGE 28: "'in war,' the Federalists wrote, 'the longest purse prevails'" Paula Backschneider, *Daniel Defoe: His Life (Baltimore: Johns Hopkins University Press, 1992),* 294. ȍ **"'vast unnecessary expenses continually incurred by its enormous vices'"** Samuel Langdon, *Government Corrupted by Vice, and Recovered by Righteousness* (Watertown, Mass., 1775). *See also:* Marvin Olasky, *Fighting for Liberty and Virtue: Political and Cultural Wars in Eighteenth-Century America* (Washington, D.C.: Regnery, 1995), 148. ȍ **"'is but swindling futurity on a large scale'"** Thomas Jefferson, "Letter to John Taylor, Monticello, May 28, 1816," in *The Writings of Thomas Jefferson*, ed. Paul Leicester, vol. 11 (New York: G.P. Putnam's Sons, 1892–1899), 533. ȍ **"take 'from the federal government the power of borrowing'"** Robert E. Wright, Ph.D., *One Nation Under Debt: Hamilton, Jefferson, and the History of What We Owe* (New York: McGraw-Hill, 2008), 13, 14. ȍ **"'if it is not excessive, will be to us a national blessing'" John Steele Gordon,** *Hamilton's Blessing: The Extraordinary Life and Times of Our National Debt* (New York: Walker & Company, 2010), 39.

PAGE 29: "'the reverse is the fate of those, who pursue an opposite conduct'" Alexander Hamilton, "The First Report on Public Credit, 1789," in *The Papers of Alexander Hamilton*, ed. Harold C. Syrett et al., vol. 6 (New York and London: Columbia University Press, 1962), http://www.wwnorton.com/college/history/archive/resources/documents/ch08_02.htm. ȍ **"'while Madison was so shy he seemed doomed to bachelorhood'"** Robert Allen Rutland, *James Madison: The Founding Father* (Columbia, MS: University of Missouri, 1997), 75. ȍ **"while Hamilton thought some level of debt could be a positive for the country; Madison hated the idea"** Robert Allen Rutland, *James Madison: The Founding Father* (Columbia, MS: University of Missouri, 1997), 75–76. ȍ **"since Hamilton was killed in a duel with Aaron Burr"** "Alexander Hamilton and Aaron Burr's Duel," accessed July 16, 2010, http://www.pbs.org/wgbh/amex/duel/peopleevents/pande17.html. ȍ **"'should always be accompanied with the means of extinguishment'"** Alexander Hamilton, "The First Report on Public Credit, 1789," in *The Papers of Alexander Hamilton*, ed. Harold C. Syrett et al., vol. 6 (New York and London: Columbia University Press, 1962), http://www.wwnorton.com/college/history/archive/resources/documents/ch08_02.htm. ȍ **"that cement would weigh America down with a reputation as a deadbeat borrower"** Robert E. Wright, Ph.D., *One Nation Under Debt: Hamilton, Jefferson, and the History of What We Owe* (New York: McGraw-Hill, 2008), 134. ȍ **"'and so moderate in their amount as never to be inconvenient'"** Alexander Hamilton, *The Works of Alexander Hamilton*, ed. Henry Cabot Lodge, vol. 1, Federal Edition (New York: G.P. Putnam's Sons, 1904), http://oll.libertyfund.org/?option=com_staticxt&staticfile=show.php%3Ftitle=1378&chapter=64156&layout=html&Itemid=27.

PAGE 30: "'to lead to great and convulsive revolutions of Empire'" Ron Chernow, *Alexander Hamilton* (New

York: Penguin Press, 2004), 300. ♁ **"used to retire 5 percent of the debt every year until it was paid off"** Ron Chernow, *Alexander Hamilton* (New York: Penguin Press, 2004), 300. ♁ **"'position too obviously true to require any illustration'"** Robert E. Wright, Ph.D., *One Nation Under Debt: Hamilton, Jefferson, and the History of What We Owe* (New York: McGraw-Hill, 2008), 87, 171. ♁ **"America enjoyed the 'highest credit rating in Europe'"** Robert E. Kelly, *The National Debt of the United States 1941 to 2008*, 2d ed. (Jefferson, N.C.: McFarland & Company, Inc., 2008), 15. ♁ **"'growing so rapidly that there can be no doubt of their solvency'"** John Steele Gordon, *Empire of Wealth: The Epic History of American Economic Power* (New York: Harper Perennial, 2005), 75. ♁ **"'sell his soul for money, and he would be right, for he would be exchanging dung for gold'"** Ron Chernow, *Alexander Hamilton* (New York: Penguin Press, 2004), 465.

PAGE 31: "Growth averaged just 1.9 percent a year" "GDP United States," accessed July 26, 2010, http://www.data360.org/graph_group.aspx?Graph_Group_Id=149. ♁ **"3.1 percent growth in 2010 and 3 percent growth in 2011"** Nancy Waitz, "Economists trim 2011 U.S. growth forecast," *Reuters*, March 10, 2010, http://www.reuters.com/article/idUSTRE6290Q020100310. ♁ **"has growth pegged at 2.2 percent a year going forward"** "The Obama Tax Trap—How some Republicans are preparing to walk right into it," *WSJ.com*, July 2, 2010, http://online.wsj.com/article/SB10001424052748703426004575338991852947182.html. ♁ **"a panic, ignited by speculators, erupted in the financial markets"** Robert E. Wright, Ph.D., *One Nation Under Debt: Hamilton, Jefferson, and the History of What We Owe* (New York: McGraw-Hill, 2008), 157. ♁ **"and the nationalization of a huge chunk of General Buggyworks"** Robert E. Wright, Ph.D., *One Nation Under Debt: Hamilton, Jefferson, and the History of What We Owe* (New York: McGraw-Hill, 2008), 158, 164. ♁ **"Wonder of all wonders, it worked"** Robert E. Wright, Ph.D., *One Nation Under Debt: Hamilton, Jefferson, and the History of What We Owe* (New York: McGraw-Hill, 2008), 158. ♁ **"'a free exercise of his industry and the fruits acquired by it'"** U.S. Treasury, "Fact Sheet on the History of the U.S. Tax System," accessed July 17, 2010, http://www.ustreas.gov/education/fact-sheets/taxes/ustax.shtml.

PAGE 32: "'are left unimproved for accelerating this valuable end'" George Washington, "Final State of the Union Address," December 7, 1796, http://www.thisnation.com/library/sotu/1796gw.html. ♁ **"Treasury Albert Gallatin floated bonds, which sold very well,"** Robert E. Wright, *Financial Founding Fathers: The Men Who Made America Rich* (Chicago: University of Chicago Press, 2006), 98–99. ♁ **"On May 2, 1803, the treaty was signed"** "Louisiana Purchase," accessed July 17, 2010 http://teacher.scholastic.com/activities/lewis_clark/purchase.htm. ♁ **"indicating that we've probably never paid the Dutch back for their investment"** "Louisiana Purchase Bonds Found," accessed July 17, 2010, http://www.offthekuff.com/mt/archives/001818.html.

PAGE 33: "the war debt (including about $25 million in state debts) had reached $75–80 million" Robert E. Kelly, *The National Debt of the United States 1941 to 2008*, 2d ed. (Jefferson, N.C.: McFarland & Company, Inc., 2008),15. ♁ **"the federal government owed about $225 per citizen"** Robert E. Kelly, *The National Debt of the United States 1941 to 2008*, 2d ed. (Jefferson, N.C.: McFarland & Company, Inc., 2008), 15. ♁ **"Forty-three thousand dollars per person"** Sarah Morgan, "The National Debt: What $13 Trillion Could Buy—For the Dollar Amount America Is in Debt, You Could Educate 68 Million Students at Yale or Buy a Dollar-Menu at McDonald's Every Day for the Next 115 Years," accessed July 26, 2010, http://articles.moneycentral.msn.com/SavingandDebt/ManageDebt/the-national-debt-what-13-trillion-dollars-could-buy.

Chapter 4: The Nineteenth Century

PAGE 34: "'increase the wants of the Government by unnecessary and profuse expenditures'" Andrew Jackson, "State of the Union Address, December 3, 1833," in *State of the Union Addresses of Andrew Jackson*, http://www.gutenberg.org/dirs/etext04/sujac11.txt.

PAGE 35: "Jackson had his servants haul the liquor out onto the White House lawn" John Steele Gordon, *Hamilton's Blessing—The Extraordinary Life and Times of Our National Debt* (New York: Penguin, 1998), 178. ♁ **"in 1824, he called it a 'national curse'"** Robert E. Wright, Ph.D., *One Nation Under Debt: Hamilton, Jefferson, and the History of What We Owe* (New York: McGraw-Hill, 2008), 269. ♁ **"'and ultimately destroy the liberty of our country'"** John Steele Gordon, *Hamilton's Blessing—The Extraordinary Life and Times of Our National Debt* (New York: Penguin, 1998), 59. *See also:* "Jackson's Ghost Looms Over Debt—Is Mr. Clinton's Budget Plan Worthy of Old Hickory?" http://www.cbsnews.com/stories/2000/02/07/national/main157689.shtml. ♁ **"'meet the intermediate interest of this additional debt without recurring to new taxes'"** Thomas Jefferson, "State of the Union Address, October 17, 1903," in *Thomas Jefferson, State of the Union Addresses* (Whitefish, MT: Kessinger Publications, 2004), 17.

PAGE 36: "but he continued to live by it after his eventual election" John Steele Gordon, *Hamilton's Blessing—The Extraordinary Life and Times of Our National Debt* (New York: Penguin, 1998), 59. ♁ **"both started a trend of paying off the debt"** Robert E. Wright, Ph.D., *One Nation Under Debt: Hamilton, Jefferson, and the History of What We Owe* (New York: McGraw-Hill, 2008), 270. ♁ **"continued the anti-frivolous spending views of our Founders"** Robert E. Wright, Ph.D., *One Nation Under Debt: Hamilton, Jefferson, and the History of What We Owe* (New York: McGraw-Hill, 2008), 269–84. ♁ **"'a few essential public goods, like defense'"** Robert E. Wright, Ph.D., *One Nation Under Debt: Hamilton, Jefferson, and the History of What We Owe* (New York: McGraw-Hill, 2008), 271. ♁ **"'Discernment, Employment, Freedom and God'"** Marvin Olasky, *Renewing American Compassion: A Citizen's Guide* (Washington, D.C.: Free Press, 1996). ♁ **"cost unfathomable sums of money each year"** Marvin Olasky, *Renewing American Compassion: A Citizen's Guide* (Washington, D.C.: Free Press, 1996).

PAGE 37: "for Alaska, the Gadsden Purchase and the land acquired in the Treaty of Guadalupe-Hidalgo" National Archives and Records Administration, "Teaching With Documents: The Treaty of Guadalupe Hidalgo," accessed July 13, 2010, http://www.archives.gov/education/lessons/guadalupe-hidalgo/. ♁ **"private Great Northern Railway was the most profitable"** "A Chicago Train Connecting Railroad—1930's–1940's: Great Northern Railway," accessed July 13, 2010, http://www.r2parks.net/gn.html. *See also:* "What was the Great Northern Railway?" accessed July 13, 2010, http://www.gnrhs.org/gn_history.htm. ♁ **"throw billions at Amtrak with no profitability in sight"** Jean Love, Wendell Cox and Stephen Moore, "Amtrak at Twenty End of the Line for Taxpayer Subsidies," *Cato Policy Analysis* 266 (Washington, D.C.: Cato Institute, 1996), http://www.cato.org/pubs/pas/pa-266.html. *See also*: Congressional Budget Office, "The Past and Future of U.S. Passenger Rail Service" (September 2003), http://www.cbo.gov/doc.cfm?index=4571&type=0&sequence=1 and Cato Institute, "Amtrak's Financial Shenanigans," accessed July 13, 2010, http://www.downsizinggovernment.org/amtraks-financial-shenanigans. ♁ **"his left arm was cut to the bone and his head was gashed open"** *Civil and Military History of Andrew Jackson* (New York: P. M. Dayis, 1825), 38, http://www.archive.org/stream/civilmilitaryhis00waldo/civilmilitaryhis00waldo_djvu.txt. *See also:* Sean Wilentz, *Andrew Jackson*, The American Presidents, ed. Arthur M. Schlesinger, Jr., and Sean Wilentz (New York: Times Books, 2006). ♁ **"once called the idea of mounting public debt 'harpy fangs'"** Robert E. Wright, Ph.D., *One Nation Under Debt: Hamilton, Jefferson, and the History of What We Owe* (New York: McGraw-Hill, 2008), 270. ♁ **"'and secure the blessings of freedom to our citizens'"** John Steele Gordon, *Hamilton's Blessing—The Extraordinary Life and Times of Our National Debt* (New York: Penguin, 1998), 61.

PAGE 38: "but Jackson himself stayed home" Robert E. Wright, Ph.D., *One Nation Under Debt: Hamilton, Jefferson, and the History of What We Owe* (New York: McGraw-Hill, 2008), 269. ♁ **"never spent more in a single year than $74.2 million (in 1858 dollars)"** John Steele Gordon, *Empire of Wealth: The Epic History of American Economic Power* (New York: Harper Perennial, 2005), 194. ♁ **"America has never spent *less* than $236.9 million"** John Steele Gordon, *Empire of Wealth: The Epic History of American Economic Power* (New York: Harper Perennial, 2005), 194. ♁ **"first time in history that any nation ever had a billion-dollar budget"** John Steele Gordon, *Empire of Wealth: The Epic History of American Economic Power* (New York: Harper Perennial, 2005), 194. ♁ **"that number had climbed to $1.5 million a day"** John Steele Gordon, *Empire of Wealth: The Epic History of American Economic Power* (New York: Harper Perennial, 2005), 192.

PAGE 39: The debt in 1843 was just $33 million. Robert E. Wright, Ph.D., *One Nation Under Debt: Hamilton, Jefferson, and the History of What We Owe* (New York: McGraw-Hill, 2008), 274. ♁ **"being funded 'largely (through) domestic financing'"** Jay Sexton, *Debtor Diplomacy: Finance and American Foreign Relations in the Civil War Era, 1837–1873* (Oxford: Clarendon Press, 2005), 19. ♁ **"'new mountains of debt would, likewise, be whittled away'"** Jay Sexton, *Debtor Diplomacy: Finance and American Foreign Relations in the Civil War Era, 1837–1873* (Oxford: Clarendon Press 2005), 113. ♁ **"Chase's public financing tactic successfully raised two-thirds of the Union's revenues"** James M. McPherson, *Battle Cry of Freedom: The Civil War Era* (New York: Oxford University Press, 2003), 443. ♁ **"'A NEW WAY TO PAY THE NATIONAL DEBT'"** W. S. Newlon, "A New Way to Pay the National Debt," *Chicago Tribune*, July 21, 1865, 2, http://pqasb.pqarchiver.com/chicagotribune/access/717500102.html?dids=717500102:717500102&FMT=CITE&FMTS=CITE:AI ♁ **"'oppressed by a debt which they owe to themselves'"** Abraham Lincoln, "State of the Union Address, December 6, 1864," http://www.usa-presidents.info/union/lincoln-4.html. ♁ **"(90 percent of our War of 1812 debt was held by citizens)"** Jay Sexton, *Debtor Diplomacy: Finance and American*

Foreign Relations in the Civil War Era, 1837–1873 (Oxford: Clarendon Press, 2005), 194. ŏ **"The numbers are 'imperfect'"** CBO Testimony, *Statement of Peter R. Orszag, Director, Foreign Holdings of U.S Government Securities and the U.S. Current Account, Before the Committee on the Budget U.S. House of Representatives* (June 26, 2007), 2, http://www.cbo.gov/ftpdocs/82xx/doc8264/06-26-ForeignHoldings.pdf. ŏ **"matched the entire amount the government was raising"** John Steele Gordon, *Empire of Wealth: The Epic History of American Economic Power* (New York: Harper Perennial, 2005), 194.

PAGE 40: "'the greatest obstacle I have ever met in my life'" Nathaniel Wright Stephenson, *An Autobiography of Abraham Lincoln Consisting of the Personal Portions of His Letters, Speeches, and Conversations* (New York: Bobs-Merrill Co., 1926), 12. ŏ **"'the rapid accumulation of National Debt . . . and the rapid deterioration of the National credit'"** Frederick J. Blue, *Salmon P. Chase: A Life in Politics* (Kent, OH: Kent State University Press, 1987), 163–64. ŏ **"a debt that he was not legally required to repay"** Nathan Wright Stephenson, *An Autobiography of Abraham Lincoln Consisting of the Personal Portions of Letters, Speeches, and Conversations* (New York: Bobbs-Merrill, 1926), 12. *See also:* Benjamin Thomas, *Abraham Lincoln: A Biography* (New York: Alfred Knopf, 1952), 37. ŏ **"astronomical rate of—ready for this?—10 percent!"** John Steele Gordon, *Empire of Wealth: The Epic History of American Economic Power* (New York: Harper Perennial, 2005), 195. ŏ **"'neither the President, his counsellors nor his commanding general seem to care'"** Frederick J. Blue, *Salmon P. Chase: A Life in Politics* (Kent, OH: Kent State University Press, 1987), 172. ŏ **"'the abyss of bankruptcy and ruin which yawns before us"** Frederick J. Blue, *Salmon P. Chase: A Life in Politics* (Kent, OH: Kent State University Press, 1987), 172.

PAGE 41: "the North passed the 'Legal Tender Act of 1862'" Tax History Museum, "The Civil War, 1861–1865," accessed July 13, 2010, http://www.taxanalysts.com/museum/1861-1865.htm. *See also:* "A Century of Lawmaking for a New Nation: U.S. Congressional Documents and Debates, 1774–1875," accessed July 13, 2010, http://memory.loc.gov/cgi-bin/ampage?collId=llsl&fileName=012/llsl012.db&recNum=376. ŏ **"so named because of the color of the ink that was used"** "Home Front," accessed July 13, 2010, http://civilwar.bluegrass.net/HomeFront/greenbacks.html. *See also:* "The Greenback Question," accessed July 13, 2010, http://www.taxanalysts.com/museum/1861–1865.htm. ŏ **"'legal tender notes' backed by the full faith and credit of the federal government"** "The Greenback Question," accessed July 13, 2010, http://www.taxanalysts.com/museum/1861–1865.htm. *See also:* Montgomery Rollins, *Money and Investments* (London: George Routledge & Sons, Ltd., 1917), http://chestofbooks.com/finance/investments/Money-Investments/Farthing-Financial-Bill.html. ŏ **"a 'great evil, and should be reformed as soon as possible.'"** Frederick J. Blue, *Salmon P. Chase: A Life in Politics* (Kent, OH: Kent State University Press, 1987), 303. ŏ **"Concerns over inflating took a back seat to concerns over existing"** "History of the Treasury, Secretaries of the Treasury, Salmon P. Chase (1861–1864)," accessed July 13, 2010, http://www.ustreas.gov/education/history/secretaries/spchase.shtml. ŏ **"boosting his name recognition enough to become president one day"** John Steele Gordon, *Empire of Wealth: The Epic History of American Economic Power* (New York: Harper Perennial, 2005), 196. *See also:* http://www.taxanalysts.com/museum/greenback.htm. ŏ **"stripped the removal-of-greenback provision from the act"** Frederick J. Blue, *Salmon P. Chase: A Life in Politics* (Kent, OH: Kent State University Press, 1987), 303.

PAGE 42: "THE PUBLIC DEBT AND WHO CREATED IT" "The Public Debt and Who Created It," *Chicago Tribune*, August 25, 1868. ŏ **"something called 'Dillistin's Bank Note Reporter'"** *Conspiracy Theories in American History: An Encyclopedia*, ed. Peter Knight, vol. 1 (Santa Barbara, CA: ABC-CLIO, 2003), 286. ŏ **"driving the private ones out of business"** *Conspiracy Theories in American History: An Encyclopedia*, ed. Peter Knight, vol. 1 (Santa Barbara, CA: ABC-CLIO, 2003), 287.

PAGE 43: "'produced a national debt and taxation unprecedented. . . . '" Abraham Lincoln, "Speech at Great Central Sanitary Fair, Philadelphia, Pennsylvania, June 16, 1864," in *Collected Works of Abraham Lincoln*, The Abraham Lincoln Association, ed. Roy P. Basler, vol. 7 (New Brunswick, N.J: Rutgers University Press, 1953), 395. ŏ **"Tough Love"** National Park Service, "Abraham Lincoln—From His Own Words and Contemporary Accounts," accessed July 14, 2010, http://www.nps.gov/history/history/online_books/source/sb2/sb2f.htm.

PAGE 44: "'as each had then, to establish them'" Abraham Lincoln, "Message to Congress in Special Session, July 4, 1861," in *Collected Works of Abraham Lincoln*, The Abraham Lincoln Association, ed. Roy P. Basler, vol. 4 (New Brunswick, N.J: Rutgers University Press, 1953), 432. ŏ **"understood the power and**

importance of economic growth as a method of paying down debt" Abraham Lincoln, "Annual Message to Congress, December 1, 1862," in *Collected Works of Abraham Lincoln*, The Abraham Lincoln Association, ed. Roy P. Basler, vol. 5 (New Brunswick, N.J: Rutgers University Press, 1953), 533–34. ♁ **"'delaying payment [on the nation's bills]'"** Abraham Lincoln, "Annual Message to Congress, December 1, 1862," in *Collected Works of Abraham Lincoln*, The Abraham Lincoln Association, ed. Roy P. Basler, vol. 5 (New Brunswick, N.J: Rutgers University Press, 1953), 533–34. ♁ **"'stood at $127 million, thanks to the War of 1812'"** Jay Sexton, *Debtor Diplomacy: Finance and American Foreign Relations in the Civil War Era, 1837–1873* (Oxford: Clarendon Press, 2005), 194. ♁ **"equal to about half of the country's entire GNP!"** John Steele Gordon, *Hamilton's Blessing—The Extraordinary Life and Times of Our National Debt* (New York: Penguin, 1998), 80–81. ♁ **"'and rigid responsibility in the public expenditures'"** Henry J. Ramond, *The Life and Public Services of Abraham Lincoln* (New York: Derby and Miller, 1865), 557.

PAGE 45: Clement Vallandigham Poster, "THE PEACE PARTY.; Mr. Vallandigham Reaffirms his Position," *The New York Times*, August 18, 1864, http://www.nytimes.com/1864/08/18/news/peace-party-mr-vallandigham-reaffirms-his-position-oracular-words-about-chicago.html.

PAGE 46: "'now more than ever in excess of public necessities'" Grover Cleveland, "State of the Union Address, December 6, 1886," http://www.teachingamericanhistory.com/library/index.asp?document=1286. ♁ **"'the government should not support the people'"** "Grover Cleveland Quotes and Quotations," accessed July 14, 2010, http://www.famousquotesandauthors.com/authors/grover_cleveland_quotes.html. ♁ **"a fairly significant number given that the population back then was only about 50 million"** Robert E. Wright, Ph.D., *One Nation Under Debt: Hamilton, Jefferson, and the History of What We Owe* (New York: McGraw-Hill, 2008), 162. ♁ **"even though he spent $7.2 million buying Alaska in 1867"** James R. Gibson, "Why the Russians Sold Alaska," *The Wilson Quarterly: Essays and Data on American Ethnic Groups*, ed. Thomas Sowell, vol. 3, no. 3 (Washington, D.C.: Woodrow Wilson International Center, 1979). ♁ **"'fanatically devoted to reducing the national debt and establishing a hard currency'"**Jay Sexton, *Debtor Diplomacy: Finance and American Foreign Relations in the Civil War Era, 1837–1873* (Clarendon Press: Oxford, 2005), 201. ♁ **"down to $2.2 billion—a cut of $500 million"** Robert E. Kelly, *The National Debt of the United States 1941 to 2008*, 2d ed. (Jefferson, N.C.: McFarland & Company, Inc., 2008), 20. ♁ **"a full 43 percent below the level it was at in 1865"** Robert E. Kelly, *The National Debt of the United States 1941 to 2008*, 2d ed. (Jefferson, N.C.: McFarland & Company, Inc., 2008), 20–23. ♁ **"'the only safe foundation for a monetary system'"** William Ralston Balch, *The Life of James Abram Garfield, Late President of the United States* (Philadelphia: Hubbard Bros., 1881), 564. ♁ **"surpluses for 28 straight years following the Civil War"** Burt Folsom, Jr., "Our Presidents and the National Debt," *The Freeman*, vol. 56, issue 6 (August 2006), http://www.thefreemanonline.org/columns/our-economic-past-our-presidents-and-the-national-debt/. ♁ **"the war debt had almost been paid off entirely"** John Steele Gordon, *Hamilton's Blessing—The Extraordinary Life and Times of Our National Debt* (New York: Penguin, 1998), 80–81. *See also:* Burton Folsom, Jr., "Our Presidents and the National Debt," *The Freeman*, vol. 56, issue 6 (August 2006), http://www.thefreemanonline.org/columns/our-economic-past-our-presidents-and-the-national-debt/.

Chapter 5: America's Debt Progresses the Wrong Way

PAGE 48: "nor any other mortal or mortals could have prevented this" William Bonner & Addison Wiggin, *The New Empire of Debt: The Rise of an Epic Financial Bubble* (Hoboken, N.J.: John Wiley & Sons, Inc., 2009), 95.

PAGE 49: "only U.S. president to hold a Ph.D. and to serve as president of Princeton University" "About Woodrow Wilson," accessed July 23, 2010, http://www.wilsoncenter.org/index.cfm?fuseaction=about.woodrow. ♁ **"held a White House screening of the infamous KKK movie, *The Birth of a Nation*"** "Jim Crow Stories," accessed July 23, 2010, http://www.pbs.org/wnet/jimcrow/stories_events_birth.html. ♁ **"Woodrow Wilson, son of a Confederate chaplain"** "28th President—Woodrow Wilson (1856–1924)," accessed July 23, 2010, http://www.presidentialavenue.com/ww.cfm. ♁ **"'my only regret is that it is all so terribly true'"** Richard Corliss, "Black Cinema: Micheaux Must Go On," *Time*, May 13, 2002, http://www.time.com/time/columnist/corliss/article/0,9565,237512,00.html. *See also:* Elvira Nieto, "Woodrow Wilson and White Supremacy: An Examination of Wilson's Racist and Antidemocratic Policies," accessed July 23, 2010, http://americanhistory.suite101.com/article.cfm/woodrow_wilson_and_white_supremacy#ixzz0uTfA132A and Tim Dirks, "The Birth of a Nation (1915)," accessed July 23, 2010, http://www.filmsite.org/birt.html. ♁

"Millions signed up to wear pointy white hoods" Richard Wormser, *The Rise and Fall of Jim Crow* (New York: St. Martin's Press, 2003), 121.

PAGE 50: "'no matter what he later said, was important'" Angela McGlowan, *Bamboozled: How Americans Are Being Exploited by the Lies of the Liberal Agenda* (Nashville, TN: Thomas Nelson, 2009), 160–61. ♁ **"and replaced them with whites"** Angela McGlowan, *Bamboozled: How Americans Are Being Exploited by the Lies of the Liberal Agenda* (Nashville, TN: Thomas Nelson, 2009), 159–60. ♁ **"executive orders to the Treasury Department and postmaster general to segregate the departments"** Angela McGlowan, *Bamboozled: How Americans Are Being Exploited by the Lies of the Liberal Agenda* (Nashville, TN: Thomas Nelson, 2009), 159–60. ♁ **"Teddy Roosevelt's record will stand forever"** "Jim Crow Stories," accessed July 23, 2010, http://www.pbs.org/wnet/jimcrow/stories_events_browns.html. *See also:* "Race Relations under Theodore Roosevelt," accessed July 23, 2010, http://www.u-s-history.com/pages/h943.html and Texas State Library and Archives Commission, "John Bartlett to Lanham, August 17, 1906," accessed July 23, 2010, http://www.tsl.state.tx.us/governors/rising/lanham-brownsville-1.html.

PAGE 51: "'to judge by his manor, a direct line to heaven'" H. W. Brands, *Woodrow Wilson* (New York, Henry Holt and Compnay, LLC, 2003), 25. ♁ **"'nor any other mortal or mortals could have prevented that'"** H. W. Brands, Woodrow Wilson (New York, Henry Holt and Company, LLC, 2003), 24–25. ♁ **"'imagine power as a thing negative, and not positive'"** Woodrow Wilson, *Constitutional Government in the United States*, Columbia University Lectures (New York: Columbia University Press, 1917), 106. ♁ **"does now whatever experience permits or the times demand'"** Woodrow Wilson, *The State: Elements of Historical and Practical Politics—A Sketch of Institutional History and Administration* (Boston: D. C. Heath & Co., 1894), 651. ♁ **"what he called the 'Fourth of July sentiments'"** Jonah Goldberg, *Liberal Fascism: The Secret History of the American Left, from Mussolini to the Politics of Meaning* (New York: Doubleday, 2007), 88. ♁ **"'put forward as fundamental principle'"** Jonah Goldberg, *Liberal Fascism: The Secret History of the American Left, from Mussolini to the Politics of Meaning* (New York: Doubleday, 2007), 86. ♁ **"'consistent with imperative governmental necessity'"** *Presidential Addresses and State Papers of William Howard Taft from March 4, 1909 to March 4, 1910*, vol. 1 (New York: Doubleday, Page and Company, 1910), 466.

PAGE 52: "'but under the [Darwinian] theory of organic life'" Woodrow Wilson, *The New Freedom: A Call for the Emancipation of the Generous Energies of a People* (New York: Doubleday, Page & Company, 1918), 47. ♁ **"'those sections pay most which enjoy most?'"** William Bonner & Addison Wiggin, *The New Empire of Debt: The Rise of an Epic Financial Bubble* (Hoboken, N.J.: John Wiley & Sons, Inc., 2006), 126. ♁ **"'make them as unlike their fathers as we can'"** Jonah Goldberg, *Liberal Fascism: The Secret History of the American Left, from Mussolini to the Politics of Meaning* (New York: Doubleday, 2007), 88. ♁ **"a 'second struggle for emancipation' and the need for a 'New Freedom'"** Melvin I. Urofsky, "Woodrow Wilson" in *Basic Readings in U.S. Democracy*, accessed July 23, 2010, http://usinfo.org/docs/democracy/32.htm. ♁ **"'interpret the Constitution according to the Darwinian principle'"** Jonah Goldberg, *Liberal Fascism: The Secret History of the American Left, from Mussolini to the Politics of Meaning* (New York: Doubleday, 2007), 88. ♁ **"EMPIRE STATE DEBT SHOWS RAPID RISE"** "Empire State Debt Shows Rapid Rise—Only $123,000 in 1893, It Was $6,577,000 in 1897 and $111,580,000 in 1912," *New York Times*, April 13, 1914,

PAGE 53: "'blind devotion to the Constitution'" Jonah Goldberg, *Liberal Fascism: The Secret History of the American Left, from Mussolini to the Politics of Meaning* (New York: Doubleday, 2007), 90. ♁ **"'a place for unrestricted individual enterprise'"** Jonah Goldberg, *Liberal Fascism: The Secret History of the American Left, from Mussolini to the Politics of Meaning* (New York: Doubleday, 2007), 92-93. ♁ **"'extravagance that we should fear being criticized for'"** *President Wilson's Addresses*, ed. George McLean Harper (New York: Henry Holt and Company, 1918), 126. ♁ **"'which research could discover and ingenuity could devise'"** Jonah Goldberg, *Liberal Fascism: The Secret History of the American Left, from Mussolini to the Politics of Meaning* (New York: Doubleday, 2007), 100. ♁ **"'plan and effect a redeeming transformation' of society"** Jonah Goldberg, *Liberal Fascism: The Secret History of the American Left, from Mussolini to the Politics of Meaning* (New York: Doubleday, 2007), 100.

PAGE 54: "'under the cover of a poor man's name?'" John Steele Gordon, *Hamilton's Blessing: The Extraordinary Life and Times of Our National Debt* (New York: Walker & Company, 2010), 81. ♁ **"he called the 'new symbol of wealth's arrogance'"** William C. Richards, *The Last Billionaire—Henry Ford* (New York: Charles Scriber's Sons, 1948), 18. ♁ **"'not just spiritually, but in material terms.'"** Henry Vedder, *Socialism* *and the Ethics of Jesus* (New York: MacMillan Company, 1912), 348. ȍ **"'constitutes the moral power in the propaganda of Socialism'"** Walter Rauschenbusch, *A Theology of the Social Gospel* (New York: MacMillan Company, 1922), 1–3. ȍ **"became a component of their social engineering mission"** Donald J. Pisani, "Reclamation and Social Engineering in the Progressive Era" in *Agricultural History*, vol. 57, no. 1 (January 1983): 46–63. ȍ **"promote the 'protection and stimulation of its mental, moral and physical manhood'"** Nancy K. Bristow, *Making Men Moral: Social Engineering During the Great War* (New York and London: New York University Press, 1996), 18–19. ȍ **"care for the poor and incapable, invoke sumptuary laws, educate the masses, enforce prohibition"** Larry Schweikart & Michael Allen, *A Patriot's History of the United States: From Columbus's Great Discovery to the War on Terror* (New York: Sentinel Trade, 2007), 503. **"President Wilson sees no prospect of a deficit in the United States Treasury"** "President Wilson Sees No Prospect of a Deficit in the United States Treasury," *Wall Street Journal*, February 1915.

PAGE 55: "'has much about it that is hateful, too hateful to last'" Woodrow Wilson, *The State: Elements of Historical and Practical Politics—A Sketch of Institutional History and Administration* (Boston: D.C. Heath & Co., 1894), 659. ȍ **"Balanced budgets were the norm"** Claire Suddath, "A Brief History of The U.S. Deficit," *Time.com*, August 25, 2009, http://www.time.com/time/nation/article/0,8599,1918390,00.html. ȍ **"From 1916 to 1919 total federal expenditures rose 2,494 percent"** U.S. Office of Management and Budget, "Table 1.1" in *President's Budget: Historical Tables* (Washington, D.C.: White House, 2010), http://www.whitehouse.gov/omb/budget/Historicals/. ȍ **"'in order that we may have a reduction of taxes for the next fiscal year'"** Calvin Coolidge, *State of the Union Addresses* (Whitefish, MT: Kessinger Publishing, 2004), 19, 20. ȍ **"was charged on incomes above $3,000 ($4,000 for married couples)"** Robert A. Wilson, "Personal Exemptions and Individual Income Tax Rates, 1913–2002," accessed July 24, 2010, http://www.irs.gov/pub/irs-soi/02inpetr.pdf. ȍ **"until they reached 7 percent on incomes over $500,000"** Robert A. Wilson, "Personal Exemptions and Individual Income Tax Rates, 1913–2002," accessed July 24, 2010, http://www.irs.gov/pub/irs-soi/02inpetr.pdf. ȍ **"only 350,000 1040 forms were filed in 1914"** John Steele Gordon, *Hamilton's Blessing: The Extraordinary Life and Times of Our National Debt* (New York: Walker & Company, 2010), 96. ȍ **"'will be impossible under this system'"** "Reserve Plan Bars Panics, Says Owen," *New York Times*, August 3, 1913, http://query.nytimes.com/mem/archive-free/pdf?_r=2&res=9B05EFDD113BE633A25750C0A96E9C946296D6CF.

PAGE 56: "A Greek Tragedy" Suzanne Daley, "Greek Wealth Is Everywhere but Tax Forms," *The New York Times*, May 2, 2010, http://www.nytimes.com/2010/05/02/world/europe/02evasion.html. ȍ **"jumped to 67 percent (and then to 77 percent the following year)"** Robert A. Wilson, "Personal Exemptions and Individual Income Tax Rates, 1913–2002," accessed July 24, 2010, http://www.irs.gov/pub/irs-soi/02inpetr.pdf. ȍ **"an increase of 227 percent"** U.S. Office of Management and Budget, "Table 1.1" in *President's Budget: Historical Tables* (Washington, D.C.: White House, 2010), http://www.whitehouse.gov/omb/budget/Historicals/. ȍ **"little public objection arose over the sharply raised taxes"** John Steele Gordon, *Hamilton's Blessing: The Extraordinary Life and Times of Our National Debt* (New York: Walker & Company, 2010), 96. ȍ **"now at 73 percent for the top bracket"** Robert A. Wilson, "Personal Exemptions and Individual Income Tax Rates, 1913–2002," accessed July 24, 2010, http://www.irs.gov/pub/irs-soi/02inpetr.pdf. ȍ **"only 21 people filed tax returns as millionaires"** Robert A. Wilson, "Personal Exemptions and Individual Income Tax Rates, 1913–2002," accessed July 24, 2010, http://www.irs.gov/pub/irs-soi/02inpetr.pdf. ȍ **"'such rates cannot be successfully collected'"** John F. Witte, *The Politics and Development of the Federal Income Tax* (Madison, WI: University of Wisconsin Press, 1985), 88.

PAGE 57: "Chart: State of the Union Match Game" All quotes from transcripts listed at *ThisNation.com*, http://www.thisnation.com/library/sotu/index.html.

PAGE 58: "the number had plunged to 225" Charles Adams, *For Good and Evil: The Impact of Taxes on the Course of Civilization* (Lanham, MD: Madison Books, 1992), 380. ȍ **"'more liars out of the American people than golf has'"** Charles Adams, *For Good and Evil: The Impact of Taxes on the Course of Civilization* (Lanham, MD: Madison Books, 1992), 401. ȍ **"the door is open to extortion"** Charles Adams, *For Good and Evil: The Impact of Taxes on the Course of Civilization* (Lanham, MD: Madison Books, 1992), 365. ȍ **"phony $26,000 deduction for payments to his wife"** Charles Adams, *For Good and Evil: The Impact of Taxes on the Course of Civilization* (Lanham, MD: Madison Books, 1992), 401. ȍ **"was reduced to $16 billion by 1930"** John Steele Gordon, *Hamilton's Blessing: The Extraordinary Life and*

Times of Our National Debt (New York: Walker & Company, 2010), 105. ♁ **"a one-year moratorium on repayments"** Finlo Rohrer, "What's a little debt between friends?," *BBC News Magazine*, May 10, 2006, http://news.bbc.co.uk/2/hi/uk_news/magazine/4757181.stm. ♁ **"not a trivial amount: $74 billion in today's dollars"** Finlo Rohrer, "What's a little debt between friends?," *BBC News Magazine*, May 10, 2006, http://news.bbc.co.uk/2/hi/uk_news/magazine/4757181.stm. ♁ **"Bond Issue Favored by President Wilson"** "Bond Issue Favored by President Wilson—To Meet Part of the Deficit Faced by United States Treasury," *The Atlanta Constitution*, December 30, 1916, 2. ♁ **"from 1921 to 1932, the longest run in history"** United States Department of the Treasury, "History of the Treasury—Secretaries of the Treasury—Andrew W. Mellon (1921–1932)," http://www.treas.gov/education/history/secretaries/awmellon.shtml. ♁ **"one of the most successful businessmen in American history"** "Andrew W. Mellon," *Encyclopedia Britannica Online*, accessed July 24, 2010, http://www.britannica.com/EBchecked/topic/374012/Andrew-W-Mellon. ♁ **"reducing the hefty national debt incurred during World War I"** "Andrew W. Mellon," *Encyclopedia Britannica Online*, accessed July 24, 2010, http://www.britannica.com/EBchecked/topic/374012/Andrew-W-Mellon. ♁ **"declared it 'the policy of the thriftless, the ne'er do-well'"** David Cannadine, *Mellon: An American Life*, (New York: Vintage Books, 2006), 318. ♁ **"calculated that the entire national debt could be extinguished by 1943"** David Cannadine, *Mellon: An American Life* (New York: Vintage Books, 2006), 315–18.

PAGE 59: "'the fundamental policy of the government since its beginning'" Andrew William Mellon, *Taxation: The People's Business* (New York: MacMillan Co., 1924), 25. *See also:* John Steele Gordon, *Hamilton's Blessing: The Extraordinary Life and Times of Our National Debt* (New York: Walker & Company, 2010), 103. ♁ **"'shifted from the market place to [government] administration'"** Marshall Dimock, "The Study of Administration" in *Political Science Quarterly*, vol. 31, no. 1 (New York: Academy of Political Science, February 1937): 30. ♁ **"he wrote, 'than to frame one'"** Woodrow Wilson, "The Study of Administration" in *Political Science Quarterly*, vol. 2, no. 2 (New York: Academy of Political Science, June 1887): 200.

Chapter 6: Hoover, Keynes, and FDR

PAGE 60: "six weeks in advance, what we are going to do" Burton W. Folsom, *New Deal or Raw Deal?: How FDR's Economic Legacy Has Damaged America* (New York: Threshold Editions, 2008), 103.

PAGE 61: "In October 1929 the stock market crashed" "The Stock Market Crash of 1929," accessed July 27, 2010, http://www.themoneyalert.com/stockmarketcrashof1929.html. *See also:* Claire Suddath, "Brief History of the Crash of 1929," *Time.com*, October 29, 2008, http://www.time.com/time/nation/article/0,8599,1854569,00.html. ♁ **"a very reasonable 6.3 percent"** Thomas Sowell, *The Housing Boom and Bust* (New York: Basic Books, 2009), 135. ♁ **"In 1931, one of the songs on America's lips was 'I've Got Five Dollars'"** Ella Fitzgerald, "I've Got Five Dollars," *Ella Fitzgerald: Rodgers & Hart Songbook*, vol. 1 (1931), http://www.rnh.com/song_detail.asp?id=41465&s=1. ♁ **"next year it was 'Brother, Can You Spare a Dime?'"** "Brother, Can You Spare A Dime," words and music by E.Y. Harburg and Jay Gorney, recorded by Bing Crosby, 1932. *See:* "A Depression-Era Anthem For Our Times," http://www.npr.org/templates/story/story.php?storyId=96654742 and Dude Walker's Music on Wheels, "Greatest Music Hits of 1932," accessed July 27, 2010, http://dudewalker.org/music/1932. ♁ **"a decrease of 53 percent in a matter of just a few years"** U.S. Office of Management and Budget, "Table 1.1" in *President's Budget: Historical Tables* (Washington, D.C.: White House, 2010), http://www.whitehouse.gov/omb/budget/Historicals/. ♁ **"'The finances of the Government are in sound condition'"** Herbert Hoover, *State of the Union Addresses* (Whitefish, MT: Kessinger Publishing, 2004), 5. ♁ **"engineer-turned-president who believed in the power of planning"** Herbert Hoover Library and Museum, "Herbert Clark Hoover: A Biographical Sketch," accessed July 27, 2010, http://hoover.archives.gov/education/hooverbio.html. ♁ **"also believed in the power of the 'cognitive elite' to solve society's ills"** Thomas Sowell, *The Housing Boom and Bust (New York: BasicBooks, 2009), 130–33.*

PAGE 62: "feed the people of Belgium during and in the buildup to World War I" Herbert Hoover Library and Museum, "Herbert Clark Hoover: A Biographical Sketch," accessed July 27, 2010, http://hoover.archives.gov/education/hooverbio.html. ♁ **"went from 24 to 63 percent during his administration"** Robert A. Wilson, "Personal Exemptions and Individual Income Tax Rates, 1913–2002," accessed July 27, 2010, http://www.irs.gov/pub/irs-soi/02inpetr.pdf. ♁ **"and will assure taxpayers of its temporary character"** Herbert Hoover, *State of the Union Addresses* (Whitefish, MT: Kessinger Publishing, 2004), 50. ♁ **"banks had to be closed**

down to keep depositors from draining all their cash" Steve Forbes and Elizabeth Ames, *How Capitalism Will Save Us: Why Free People and Free Markets Are the Best Answer in Today's Economy* (New York: Crown Business, 2009), 74. ◊ **"jumped to $2.7 billion just a year later"** U.S. Office of Management and Budget, "Table 1.1" in *President's Budget: Historical Tables* (Washington, D.C.: White House, 2010), http://www.whitehouse.gov/omb/budget/Historicals/. ◊ **"'are a continuous evolution of the Hoover measures'"** Thomas Sowell, *The Housing Boom and Bust* (New York: Basic Books, 2009), 132. ◊ **"deficit remained over $2.5 billion,"** U.S. Office of Management and Budget, "Table 1.1" in *President's Budget: Historical Tables* (Washington, D.C.: White House, 2010), http://www.whitehouse.gov/omb/budget/Historicals/. ◊ **"promised to give American families a 'new deal'"** "President Franklin Delano Roosevelt and the New Deal, 1933–1945," accessed July 27, 2010, http://lcweb2.loc.gov/ammem/ndlpedu/features/timeline/depwwii/newdeal/newdeal.html. ◊ **"FDR won in a landslide (472 electoral votes to 59)"** The American Presidency Project, "Election of 1932," accessed July 27, 2010, http://www.presidency.ucsb.edu/showelection.php?year=1932.

PAGE 63: "'policy makers to stop helping the jobless and start inflicting pain'" Paul Krugman, "The Pain Caucus," *New York Times*, May 31, 2010, A19, http://www.nytimes.com/2010/05/31/opinion/31krugman.html. ◊ **"'wrecked on the rocks of loose fiscal policy'"** John Chamberlain, *The Roots of Capitalism* (Indianapolis, IN: Liberty Fund, 1976), 259. ◊ **"'a continuation of that habit means the poorhouse'"** John Steele Gordon, *Hamilton's Blessing: The Extraordinary Life and Times of Our National Debt* (New York: Walker & Company, 2010), 114–15. ◊ **"swept 322 Democrats into the House compared with just 103 Republicans"** William Leuchtenburg, *Franklin D. Roosevelt and the New Deal, 1932–1940* (New York: Harper and Row, 1963), 116. ◊ **"inherited a debt of $22.5 billion in 1933 ($374 billion in today's dollars) and nearly doubled it"** "Historical Debt Outstanding—Annual 1900–1949," accessed July 27, 2010, http://www.treasurydirect.gov/govt/reports/pd/histdebt/histdebt_histo3.htm. ◊ **"he tried to ram through his court-packing scheme"** William Leuchtenburg, *Franklin D. Roosevelt and the New Deal, 1932–1940*, 233–38 (New York: Harper and Row, 1963). *See also:* William E. Leuchtenburg, *The Supreme Court Reborn: The Constitutional Revolution in the Age of Roosevelt* (New York: Oxford University Press, 1995), 134–42 and James T. Patterson, "A Conservative Coalition Forms in Congress, 1933–1939" in *The Journal of American History*, vol. 52, no. 4 (March 1966): 757–72, http://www.jstor.org/stable/1894345.

PAGE 64: "'this covenant with the taxpayers of this country'" John Boettiger, "Gov. Roosevelt Makes Pledge to Slash Taxes—Addresses Farmers From Four States," *Chicago Daily Tribune*, September 30, 1932. ◊ **"but he'd also increased the threshold for the top bracket from $100,000 to $5 million"** Robert A. Wilson, "Personal Exemptions and Individual Income Tax Rates, 1913–2002," accessed July 27, 2010, 219, http://www.irs.gov/pub/irs-soi/02inpetr.pdf. ◊ **"threshold plummeted from $5 million to $200,000"** Robert A. Wilson, "Personal Exemptions and Individual Income Tax Rates, 1913–2002," 219, accessed July 27, 2010, http://www.irs.gov/pub/irs-soi/02inpetr.pdf. ◊ **"rate went from 1.125 percent to 4 percent and then eventually to 19 percent"** Robert A. Wilson, "Personal Exemptions and Individual Income Tax Rates, 1913–2002," accessed August 17, 2010, http://www.irs.gov/pub/irs-soi/02inpetr.pdf. ◊ **"they still kept reelecting him"** "Franklin Delano Roosevelt (1882–1945)—Campaigns and Elections," accessed July 27, 2010, http://millercenter.org/academic/americanpresident/fdroosevelt/essays/biography/3. ◊ **"correlation between government spending and the amount of good the government could do"** "Constitution of the United States, Amendments 11–27," http://www.archives.gov/exhibits/charters/constitution_amendments_11-27.html#22. ◊ **"'creating a Kingdom of God on earth'"** William Leuchtenburg, *Franklin D. Roosevelt and the New Deal, 1932–1940* (New York: Harper and Row, 1963), 33. ◊ **"'been retained at the expense of the taxpayers'"** John Boettiger, "Gov. Roosevelt Makes Pledge to Slash Taxes—Addresses Farmers From Four States," *Chicago Daily Tribune*, September 30, 1932. ◊ **"not only became the 'greatest spending administration in peace times in all our history,'"** "FDR's Alphabet Soup," accessed July 29, 2010, http://www.ushistory.org/us/49e.asp. ◊ **"with the poor over the rich, the laborer over the capitalist"** Marvin Olasky, *The American Leadership Tradition: Moral Vision from Washington to Clinton Free Press* (New York: Free Press, 1999), 211. ◊ **"the 'lure of profit' caused by 'unscrupulous money changers'"** Larry Schweikart & Michael Allen, *A Patriot's History of the United States: From Columbus's Great Discovery to the War on Terror* (New York: Sentinel Trade, 2007), 556. *See also: Inaugural Addresses of the Presidents of the United States*, vol. 2: Grover Cleveland (1885) to Barack H. Obama (2009), rev. ed. (Bedford, MA: Applewood Books, 2009), 94.

PAGE 65: "felt '[l]ike a spy behind enemy lines'" Barack Obama, *Dreams of My Father: A Story of Race and*

Inheritance (New York: Crown Publishers, 2004), 135. ♁ **"'enter into the Kingdom of Heaven—if only he saved'"** Hunter Lewis, *Where Keynes Went Wrong: And Why World Governments Keep Creating Inflation, Bubbles, and Busts* (Mount Jackson, VA: Axios Press, 2009), 121. ♁ **"'sole . . . objective of all economic activity' was consumption"** John Maynard Keynes, *The General Theory of Employment, Interest and Money*, 104. ♁ **"'The more you eat your cake, the more cake [to eat]'"** Hunter Lewis, *Where Keynes Went Wrong: And Why World Governments Keep Creating Inflation, Bubbles, and Busts* (Mount Jackson, VA: Axios Press, 2009), 134.

PAGE 66: "or an 'orthodox' economist" Robert Lekachman, "The Radical Keynes" in *The Policy Consequences of John Maynard Keynes*, ed. Harold L. Wattel (Armonk, N.Y.: M. E. Sharpe, Inc., 1985), 36. ♁ **"could make 'a nation wealthy'"** Hunter Lewis, *Where Keynes Went Wrong: And Why World Governments Keep Creating Inflation, Bubbles, and Busts* (Mount Jackson, VA: Axios Press, 2009), 67. ♁ **"'we are beginning to despise it'"** Edward J. Nell, *Growth, Profits, and Property: Essays in the Revival of Political Economy* (Cambridge, United Kingdom: Cambridge University Press, 1980), 191. ♁ **"sometimes necessary but almost always undesired—doesn't really matter"** John Steele Gordon, *Hamilton's Blessing: The Extraordinary Life and Times of Our National Debt* (New York: Walker & Company, 2010), 132. ♁ **"'American people are on both sides of the balance sheet'"** Hunter Lewis, *Where Keynes Went Wrong: And Why World Governments Keep Creating Inflation, Bubbles, and Busts* (Mount Jackson, VA: Axios Press, 2009), 314.

PAGE 67: "'paid for with deficits rather than taxes'" Bruce Bartlett, *Reaganomics: Supply Side Economics in Action* (Westport, CT: Arlington House, 1981), 160. ♁ **"GOV. ROOSEVELT MAKES PLEDGE TO SLASH TAXES"** John Boettiger, "Gov. Roosevelt Makes Pledge to Slash Taxes—Addresses Farmers From Four States," *Chicago Daily Tribune*, September 30, 1932. ♁ **"'doubt the efficacy of an economy made up of small entrepreneurs and businesses'"** Roger M. Barrus, John H. Eastby, Joseph H. Lane Jr., David E. Marion and James F. Pontuso, *The Deconstitutionalization of America: The Forgotten Frailties of Democratic Rule* (Lanham, MA: Lexington Books, 2004), 70. ♁ **"'was supposed to perform, but never did.'"** Kathleen G. Donohue, *Freedom From Want: American Liberalism and the Idea of the Consumer* (Baltimore: The John Hopkins University Press, 2003), 210. **" 'I do not think that you can spend yourself rich'" he said."** John Steele Gordon, *Hamilton's Blessing: The Extraordinary Life and Times of Our National Debt* (New York: Walker & Company, 2010), 130.

PAGE 68: "Likewise, eminent economists such as Ludwig von Mises saw Keynes as 'the Santa Claus fable raised . . . to the dignity of an economic doctrine.'" John Chamberlain, *The Roots of Capitalism* (Indianapolis, IN: Liberty Fund, 1976), 263. ♁ **"draining our banks' reserves and creating anxiety among investors"** *See generally* William L. Anderson, "The New Deal and Roosevelt's Seizure of Gold: A Legacy of Theft and Inflation," pt. 2, *Freedom Daily* (September 2006), accessed July 30, 2010, http://www.fff.org/freedom/fd0609d.pdf. ♁ **"surrender their physical gold to the U.S. government in exchange for dollars"** "Executive Order 6102," accessed July 30, 2010, http://www.wellsfargonevadagold.com/confiscation-order.pdf. *See also:* The American Presidency Project, "Executive Order 6102—Requiring Gold Coin, Gold Bullion and Gold Certificates to Be Delivered to the Government, April 5, 1933," http://www.presidency.ucsb.edu/ws/index.php?pid=14611&st=&st1=. ♁ **"interest thereon is far less than it was in 1929'"** Franklin D. Roosevelt and Cortelle Hutchins, *State of the Union Addresses of Franklin Delano Roosevelt* (Whitefish, MT: Kessinger Publishing LLC, 2004), 98.

PAGE 69: "if a natural person, may be imprisoned for not more than ten years, or both" "Executive Order 6102," accessed July 30, 2010, http://www.wellsfargonevadagold.com/confiscation-order.pdf. *See also:* The American Presidency Project, "Executive Order 6102—Requiring Gold Coin, Gold Bullion and Gold Certificates to Be Delivered to the Government, April 5, 1933," http://www.presidency.ucsb.edu/ws/index.php?pid=14611&st=&st1=. ♁ **"'It is a lucky number,' he said, 'because it's three times seven'"** Arthur M. Schlesinger Jr., *The Coming of the New Deal, 1933–1935* (New York: Houghton Mifflin Company, 2003), 241. ♁ **"'I think they would really be frightened'"** Arthur M. Schlesinger Jr., *The Coming of the New Deal, 1933–1935* (New York: Houghton Mifflin Company, 2003), 241. ♁ **"'But above all, try something'"** Burton W. Folsom, *New Deal or Raw Deal?: How FDR's Economic Legacy Has Damaged America* (New York: Threshold Editions, 2008), 103. ♁ **"'from a temporary expedient to a permanent instrument of government'"** Larry Schweikart & Michael Allen, *A Patriot's History of the United States: From Columbus's Great Discovery to the War on Terror* (New York: Sentinel Trade, 2007), 561.

PAGE 70: "'enduring *institutions* to change the way the American economy operated'" Thomas Sowell, *The Housing Boom and Bust (*New York: Basic Books, 2009), 136. ȍ **"'means of . . . diminishing private control over the necessities of life'"** Arthur M. Schlesinger Jr., *The Age of Roosevelt: The Politics of Upheaval*, vol. 3 (Cambridge, MA: Houghton Mifflin Company, 1960), 379. ȍ **"The proposed provisions included:"** The American Presidency Project, "State of the Union Message to Congress, January 11, 1944," accessed July 30, 2010, http://www.presidency.ucsb.edu/ws/index.php?pid=16518. *See also:* Franklin D. Roosevelt Presidential Library and Museum, "1944 State of the Union Address: FDR's Second Bill of Rights or Economic Bill of Rights Speech," accessed July 30, 2010, http://www.fdrlibrary.marist.edu/archives/images/exerpt_c.jpg and http://www.fdrlibrary.marist.edu/archives/images/exerpt_d.jpg.

PAGE 71: "a book titled *The Second Bill of Rights: FDR's Unfinished Revolution and Why We Need It More Than Ever*" Cass R. Sunstein, *The Second Bill of Rights: FDR's Unfinished Revolution and Why We Need It More Than Ever* (New York: Basic Books, 2004). ȍ **"'PRESIDENT PROMISES TO CUT SPENDING'"** Warren B. Francis, "President Promises to Cut Spending—Cost Reductions and No New Tax or Borrowing Drive Assured by Aide," *Los Angeles Times*, November 22, 1939. ȍ **"'people came to expect the state to take care of things at home'"** William Bonner, Addison Wiggin, *The New Empire of Debt: The Rise and Fall of an Epic Financial Bubble* (Hoboken, N.J.: John Wiley & Sons, Inc., 2009), 134. ȍ **"many individuals unwittingly embraced the 'government-as-nanny-state' model"** Robert E. Wright, Ph.D., *One Nation Under Debt: Hamilton, Jefferson, and the History of What We Owe* (New York: McGraw-Hill, 2008), 278.

PAGE 72: "'restrictive, competitive, and deterrent government action on the other'" Gene W. Heck, *The Eclipse of the American Century: An Agenda for Renewal* (Lanham, MD: Rowman & Littlefield Publishers, Inc., 2008), 183. ȍ **"more than doubled federal spending, from $4.6 billion to $9.5 billion"** U.S. Office of Management and Budget, "Table 1.1" in *President's Budget: Historical Tables* (Washington, D.C.: White House, 2010), http://www.whitehouse.gov/omb/budget/Historicals/. ȍ **"by 1940 they were 9.1 percent"** John Steele Gordon, *Hamilton's Blessing: The Extraordinary Life and Times of Our National Debt* (New York: Walker & Company, 2010), 120. ȍ **"'TAFT TELLS HOW TO BALANCE NATIONAL BUDGET'"** Arthur Evans, "Taft Tells How to Balance National Budget—It Can Be Done, He Replies to Roosevelt Dare—Lists 5 Steps That Must Be Taken. Accepts President's Dare to Find a Way," *Chicago Daily Tribune*, January 6, 1940. ȍ **"had paid only $298 million into the U.S. Treasury."** Burton W. Folsom, *New Deal or Raw Deal?: How FDR's Economic Legacy Has Damaged America* (New York: Threshold Editions, 2008), 175. ȍ **"and the Federal Emergency Relief Act (FERA) funds was Harry Hopkins"** Eleanor Roosevelt National Historic Site, "Harry Lloyd Hopkins (1890–1946)," accessed July 30, 2010, http://www.nps.gov/archive/elro/glossary/hopkins-harry.htm. ȍ **"'realized that there was nothing for it but to be all-political'"** Robert E. Sherwood, *Roosevelt and Hopkins: An Intimate History*, rev. ed. (New York: Harper & Brothers, 1950), 68. ȍ **"as all of the dead presidents who came before him combined"** William Bonner, Addison Wiggin, *The New Empire of Debt: The Rise and Fall of an Epic Financial Bubble* (Hoboken, N.J.: John Wiley & Sons, Inc., 2009), 140.

PAGE 73: "'And an enormous debt to boot!'" Burton W. Folsom, *New Deal or Raw Deal?: How FDR's Economic Legacy Has Damaged America* (New York: Threshold Editions, 2008), 144. ȍ **"'meet the emergency spending for national defense'"** Franklin D. Roosevelt and Cortelle Hutchins, *State of the Union Addresses of Franklin Delano Roosevelt* (Whitefish, MT: Kessinger Publishing LLC, 2004), 108. ȍ **"tax *revenues* collected soared 82 percent"** Robert E. Kelly, *The National Debt of the United States 1941 to 2008*, 2d ed. (Jefferson, N.C.: McFarland & Company, Inc., 2008), 38–39. ȍ **"from $659 billion in 1940 to a jaw-dropping $3 trillion in 1946"** William Bonner and Addison Wiggin, *The New Empire of Debt: The Rise and Fall of an Epic Financial Bubble* (Hoboken, N.J.: John Wiley & Sons, Inc., 2009), 215. ȍ **"America's debt will represent 62 percent of the nation's economy"** "National debt soars to highest level since WWII," *USA Today*, June 30, 2010, http://content.usatoday.com/communities/onpolitics/post/2010/06/national-debt-soars-to-highest-level-since-wwii/1. ȍ **"'a narcotic, a subtle destroyer of the human spirit'"** Franklin D. Roosevelt and Cortelle Hutchins, *State of the Union Addresses of Franklin Delano Roosevelt* (Whitefish, MT: Kessinger Publishing LLC, 2004), 58.

Chapter 7: The 1960s and '70s

PAGE 74: "'I'll have them ngers voting Democratic for two hundred years'"** Ronald Kessler, *Inside the White House* (New York: Simon & Schuster Inc., 1996), 33.

PAGE 75: "Johnson told him, 'That's all right, son. It's my prerogative'" Cormac O'Brien, *Secret Lives of the U.S. Presidents: What Your Teachers Never Told You About the Men of the White House* (Philadelphia: Quirk Productions, Inc., 2004), 219. *See also:* Lisa Jardine, "Lyndon B Johnson: The Uncivil Rights Reformer," *The Independent*, January 21, 2009, http://www.independent.co.uk/news/presidents/lyndon-b-johnson-the-uncivil-rights-reformer-1451816.html. ♂ **"'made me wonder how that man had made it so far in the world'"** Doris Kearns, *Lyndon Johnson and the American Dream* (New York: Harper & Row, 1976), 241–42. *See also:* "Historical Notes: L.B.J.: Naked to His Enemies," *Time*, April 19, 1976, http://www.time.com/time/printout/0,8816,914063,00.html and Philip H. Melanson, Ph.D., *The Secret Service: The Hidden History of an Enigmatic Agency* (New York: Carroll & Graf Publishers, 2002), 290.

PAGE 76: "her husband 'loved people' and 'half the people in the world are women'" Ronald Kessler, *In the President's Secret Service: Behind the Scenes with Agents in the Line of Fire and the Presidents They Protect* (New York: Crown Publishers, 2009), 17. ♂ **"'every ignorant child educated, every jobless man employed'"** Doris Kearns, *Lyndon Johnson and the American Dream*, (New York: St. Martin's Press, 1991), 194. ♂ **"'even against bills that would have protected blacks from lynching'"** Robert A. Caro, *Master of the Senate: The Years of Lyndon Johnson*, vol. 3 (New York: Vintage, 2003), xv. ♂ **"'the pain and humiliation he could inflict at a moment's notice'"** Robert Parker and Richard L. Rashke, *Capitol Hill in Black and White* (New York: Dodd, Mead & Company, 1986), v, vi, 16, 23. ♂ **"'The current Federal budget for fiscal 1961 is almost certain to show a net deficit'"** John F. Kennedy, *State of the Union Addresses* (Whitefish, MT: Kessinger Publishing, 2004), 3, 5.

PAGE 77 : "by 1960 it had declined to less than 56 percent" Economic Report of the President: 2010 Report, "Table B-79—Federal Receipts, Outlays, Surplus or Deficit, and Debt, as Percent of Gross Domestic Product, Fiscal Years 1937–2011," accessed August 2, 2010, http://www.gpoaccess.gov/eop/2010/B79.xls. ♂ **"was just $740 million (compared to FDR's deficit of $15.9 billion in 1946 alone)"** U.S. Office of Management and Budget, "Table 1.1" in *President's Budget: Historical Tables* (Washington, D.C.: White House, 2010), http://www.whitehouse.gov/omb/budget/Historicals/. ♂ **"'but equality as a fact and equality as a result'"** LBJ and Equality of Outcome, "Commencement Address at Howard University: 'To Fulfill These Rights,'" June 4, 1965, http://www.hpol.org/lbj/civil-rights/. ♂ **"never spent any time in his adult life working in the private sector"** Lyndon Baines Johnson Library & Museum, "President Lyndon B. Johnson's Biography," accessed August 2, 2010, http://www.lbjlib.utexas.edu/johnson/archives.hom/biographys.hom/lbj_bio.asp#1930. ♂ **"'ALARMING RISE IN DEBT STRESSED BY SEN. BYRD'"** David Lawrence, "Alarming Rise in Debt Stressed by Sen. Byrd," *Los Angeles Times*, February 4, 1964, http://pqasb.pqarchiver.com/latimes/access/466008012.html?dids=466008012:466008012&FMT=ABS&FMTS=ABS:AI. ♂ **"saw it as a moneymaking opportunity"** George Melloan, *The Great Money Binge: Spending Our Way to Socialism* (New York: Threshold Editions, 2009), 49. ♂ **"targeting large voting blocs for political expediency"** *See generally* "Lyndon Baines Johnson (1908–1973)—Domestic Affairs," accessed August 2, 2010, http://millercenter.org/academic/americanpresident/lbjohnson/essays/biography/4.

PAGE 78: "'I want everyone to know he's a nger'"** Nicholas Lehmann, "On the Way with L.B.J.," *New York Times*, July 21, 1991, http://www.nytimes.com/1991/07/21/books/on-the-way-with-lbj.html. ♂ **"'after I have given them so much?'"** "Historical Notes: L.B.J.: Naked to His Enemies," *Time*, April 19, 1976, http://www.time.com/time/printout/0,8816,914063,00.html. See aso: William Henry Chafe, *The Unfinished Journey: America Since World War II*, 5th ed. (New York: Oxford University Press, 2003), 239. ♂ **"'desire for beauty and the hunger for community'"** Richard D. Heffner, *A Documentary History of the United States*, 7th ed. (New York: Penguin Group Inc., 2002), 415. ♂ **"'from all over the world to find those answers for America'"** Jonah Goldberg, *Liberal Fascism: The Secret History of the American Left, from Mussolini to the Politics of Change* (New York: Broadway Books, 2009), 231.

PAGE 79: "'GREAT SOCIETY' NOT A SOLVENT ONE" David Lawrence, "'Great Society' Not a Solvent One," *Evening Independent*, January 26, 1965, http://news.google.com/newspapers?id=Zb0NAAAAIBAJ&sjid=5VYDAAAAIBAJ. ♂ **"most Americans were strongly suspicious of federal power"** "History of the Park Service," accessed August 3, 2010, http://www.ti.org/npshist.html#RTFToC15. ♂ **"ration books specifying how much meat, gasoline, sugar, and other items they could purchase"** *The Home Front Encyclopedia: United States, Britain, and Canada in World Wars I and II*, eds. James Ciment and Thaddeus Russell, vol. 2 (Santa Barbara, CA: ABC-CLIO, 2007), 1000. *See also:* Steven Mintz and Susan Kellogg, *Domestic*

Revolutions: A Social History of American Family Life (New York: The Free Press, 1988), 159–60. ♁ **"collaborated to run the economy for the sake of winning the war"** Robert J. Samuelson, *The Good Life and Its Discontents: The American Dream in the Age of Entitlement, 1945–1995* (New York: Times Books, 1995), 25. ♁ **"Luxuries that were rare or nonexistent before the Depression . . . became commonplace"** Robert J. Samuelson, *The Good Life and Its Discontents: The American Dream in the Age of Entitlement, 1945–1995* (New York: Times Books, 1995), 38–39. ♁ **"suburban 'Levittowns' that had sprung up practically overnight"** Peter Bacon Hales, "Levittown: Documents of an Ideal American Suburb," accessed August 3, 2010, http://tigger.uic.edu/~pbhales/Levittown/. ♁ **"opened the college doors for millions of war veterans"** "The GI Bill's History—Born of Controversy: The GI Bill of Rights," accessed August 3, 2010, http://www.gibill.va.gov/post-911/history-timeline/. *See also:* "The GI Bill," accessed August 3, 2010, http://www.military.com/benefits/gi-bill. ♁ **"Polio was cured and antibiotics made people healthier"** Bernard Seytre and Mary Shaffer, *The Death of a Disease: A History of the Eradication of Poliomyelitis* (Piscataway, N.J.: Rutgers University Press, 2005). *See also:* Jeffrey Kluger, *Splendid Solution: Jonas Salk and the Conquest of Polio* (New York: Berkley Books, 2006). ♁ **"Robert Samuelson calls the 'Cult of Affluence'"** Robert J. Samuelson, *The Good Life and Its Discontents: The American Dream in the Age of Entitlement, 1945–1995* (New York: Times Books, 1995), 34. ♁ **"'helping the economically and the physically handicapped'"** Lyndon B. Johnson, *State of the Union Addresses*, ed. Andrew Johnson (Whitefish, MT: Kessinger Publishing, 2004), 3.

PAGE 82: "'man holds in his mortal hands the power to abolish all forms of human poverty'" *Inaugural Addresses of the Presidents of the United States, vol. 2: Grover Cleveland (1885) to George W. Bush (2005)*, rev. ed. (Bedford, MA: Applewood Books), 125. ♁ **"poverty was already falling and prosperity was already spreading"** U.S. Bureau of the Census, Current Population Reports, "Poverty in the United States," series P-60, no. 175 (Washington, D.C.: Government Printing Office, 1991), 2. ♁ **"reduce dependency enough to save tax dollars in the long run"** Thomas Sowell, *The Vision of the Anointed: Self-Congratulation as a Basis for Social Policy* (New York: BasicBooks, 1995), 9. ♁ **"'there's something fundamentally wrong about that'"** Jonathan Allen, "The Second Presidential Debate: CQ Politics' Bests and Mosts," *CQ Today Online News*, October 8, 2008. *See also:* Daniel P. L. Chong, *Freedom from Poverty: NGOs and Human Rights Praxis* (Philadelphia: University of Pennsylvania Press, 2010), 100. ♁ **"'declares unconditional war on poverty'"** Lyndon B. Johnson, *State of the Union Addresses*, ed. Andrew Johnson (Whitefish, MT: Kessinger Publishing, 2004), 4. ♁ **"'Total victory,' he said, was the only option"** Michael L. Gillette, *Launching the War on Poverty: An Oral History*, 2nd ed. (New York: Oxford University Press, 2010), xvii. ♁ **"and lead America 'upward to a Great Society'"** Richard D. Heffner, *A Documentary History of the United States*, 7th ed. (New York: Penguin Group Inc., 2002), 415. ♁ **"to redistribute their wealth to others"** Hunter Lewis, *Where Keynes Went Wrong: And Why World Governments Keep Creating Inflation, Bubbles, and Busts* (Mount Jackson, VA: Axios Press, 2009), 133.

PAGE 83: "Johnson and his team based their views on *The Other America*," Michael Harrington, *The Other America: Poverty in the United States* (New York: Touchstone, 1997). ♁ **"written by Michael Harrington, a self-professed socialist"** Herbert Mitgang, "Michael Harrington, Socialist and Author, Is Dead," *The New York Times*, August 2, 1989, http://www.nytimes.com/1989/08/02/obituaries/michael-harrington-socialist-and-author-is-dead.html. *See also:* Democratic Socialists of America, "Three Key US Socialists," accessed August 3, 2010, http://www.dsausa.org/about/DTH.html. ♁ **"claimed that millions of Americans were mired in poverty"** Michael Harrington, *The Other America: Poverty in the United States* (New York: Touchstone, 1997). ♁ **"'A fact can be rationalized and explained away; an indignity cannot'"** Michael Harrington, *The Other America: Poverty in the United States* (New York: Touchstone, 1997), 17–18. ♁ **"'from the socialist tradition of men like Michael Harrington'"** Maurice Isserman, *The Other American: The Life of Michael Harrington* (New York: PublicAffairs, 2000), 175. ♁ **"'an economy without poverty. Indeed, we are almost there!'"** Robert L. Heilbroner, *The Worldly Philosophers: The Lives, Times, and Ideas of the Great Economic Thinkers* (New York: Simon and Schuster, 1967), 256. ♁ **"In 1965, 43 percent of all black families fell under the $3,000 poverty line"** William Henry Chafe, *The Unfinished Journey: America Since World War II*, 5th ed. (New York: Oxford University Press, 2003), 230. *See also:* Gordon M. Fisher, "The Development and History of the Poverty Thresholds," *Social Security Bulletin* 55, no. 4, (1992) http://www.ssa.gov./history/fisheronpoverty.html. ♁ **"'got to get it during my honeymoon period'"** *The Unfinished*

Journey: America Since World War II, 5th ed. (New York: Oxford University Press, 2003), 229. ♁ **"'We must restore equilibrium to our balance of payments'"** Lyndon B. Johnson, *State of the Union Addresses*, ed. Andrew Johnson (Whitefish, MT: Kessinger Publishing, 2004), 77. ♁ **"Johnson rammed through a host of programs"** William Henry Chafe, *The Unfinished Journey: America Since World War II*, 5th ed. (New York: Oxford University Press, 2003), 229. ♁ **"Ted Kennedy called 1965 a 'breakout year' for the progressive agenda"** Edward Kennedy, *True Compass: A Memoir* (New York: Twelve, 2009), 137.

PAGE 84: "so many other voting blocs that could use a little extra cash" Larry Schweikart and Michael Patrick Allen, *A Patriot's History of the United States: From Columbus's Great Discovery to the War on Terror* (New York: Sentinel, 2004), 687–88. ♁ **"Charles Murray describes in his classic book, *Losing Ground*"** Charles A. Murray, *Losing Ground: American Social Policy, 1950–1980* (New York: Basic Books, 1984). ♁ **"they became less vigilant about preventing harmful behaviors"** Russ Roberts, "What Peltzman Found," November 15, 2006, http://cafehayek.com/2006/11/what_peltzman_f.html. ♁ **"In 1960, only 5.3 percent of all children in America were born out of wedlock"** "Testimony of Michael Tanner, Director of Health and Welfare Studies before the Committee on Finance United States Senate, Welfare Reform, March 9, 1995," accessed August 5, 2010, http://www.cato.org/testimony/ct-ta3-9.html. *See also:* Angela McGlowan, *Bamboozled: How Americans Are Being Exploited by the Lies of the Liberal Agenda* (Nashville, TN: Thomas Nelson, Inc., 2007), 9. ♁ **"Today that figure is around 40 percent"** Jessica Ravitz, "Out-of-wedlock births hit record high," *CNN.com*, April 8, 2009, http://edition.cnn.com/2009/LIVING/wayoflife/04/08/out.of.wedlock.births/index.html. ♁ **"S-CHIP was initially supposed to be for poor children"** Congressional Budget Office, "The State Children Health Insurance Program," (May 2007), vii, http://www.cbo.gov/ftpdocs/80xx/doc8092/05-10-SCHIP.pdf. ♁ **"a family of four making $77,175 per year was eligible for S-CHIP"** Noam M. Leavey, "Obama Signs into Law Expansion of S-CHIP Legislation for Children," *Chicago Tribune*, Feburary 5, 2009, http://www.chicagotribune.com/news/nationworld/chi-kids-health-care_thufeb05,0,30310.story.

PAGE 85: "In the 1960s, 25 percent of African-American babies grew up without a father" Kay S. Hymowitz, "The Black Family: 40 Years of Lies," *City Journal*, Summer 2005, http://www.city-journal.org/html/about_cj.html ♁ **"Today, 72 percent of black mothers are unwed"** Jessica Ravitz, "Out-of-wedlock births hit record high," *CNN.com*, April 8, 2009, http://edition.cnn.com/2009/LIVING/wayoflife/04/08/out.of.wedlock.births/index.html. *See also:* Angela McGlowan, *Bamboozled: How Americans Are Being Exploited by the Lies of the Liberal Agenda* (Nashville, TN: Thomas Nelson, Inc., 2007), 10. ♁ **"LBJ got 94 percent of the black vote, a record for presidential elections"** "When Did Blacks Start Voting Democratic?" http://www.factcheck.org/askfactcheck/when_did_blacks_start _voting_democratic.html. ♁ **"that stood until 2008, when Obama got 96 percent"** David Paul Kuhn, "Exit polls: How Obama won," *Politico*, November 5, 2008, http://www.politico.com/news/stories/1108/15297.html. ♁ **"In 1965, LBJ signed the Voting Rights Act"** Lyndon Baines Johnson Library & Museum, "President Lyndon B. Johnson's Biography," accessed August 5, 2010, http://www.lbjlib.utexas.edu/johnson/archives.hom/biographys.hom/lbj_bio.asp#1960. ♁ **"no Republican presidential candidate has ever gotten more than 15 percent of the black vote"** "When Did Blacks Start Voting Democratic?" accessed August 5, 2010, http://www.factcheck.org/askfactcheck/when_did_blacks_start_voting_democratic.html. ♁ **"rang up to an estimated $305.7 billion (in 2005 inflation-adjusted dollars)"** William Bonner, Addison Wiggin, *The New Empire of Debt: The Rise and Fall of an Epic Financial Bubble* (Hoboken, N.J.: John Wiley & Sons, Inc., 2009), 175. ♁ **"LBJ served in the U.S. Senate from 1948 to 1961"** Lyndon Baines Johnson Library & Museum, "President Lyndon B. Johnson's Biography," accessed August 6, 2010 http://www.lbjlib.utexas.edu/johnson/archives.hom/biographys.hom/lbj_bio.asp. ♁ **"'ARE ASHAMED TO KNOW YOU HAVE STOOD ON THE FLOOR AGAINST THEM TODAY'"** William Edward Leuchtenburg, *The White House Looks South: Franklin D. Roosevelt, Harry S. Truman, Lyndon B. Johnson* (Baton Rouge, LA: Louisiana State University Press, 2005), 247. ♁ **"Johnson watered it down in the Senate so it became largely unenforceable"** Randall Bennett Woods, *LBJ: Architect of American Ambition* (New York: The Free Press, 2006), 228.

PAGE 86: "worsened into a multigenerational *cycle* of poverty" Charles A. Murray, *Losing Ground: American Social Policy, 1950–1980* (New York: Basic Books, 1984). ♁ **"'We declared war on poverty and poverty won'"** *Why People Don't Trust Government*, eds. Joseph S. Nye Jr., Philip D. Zelikow, David C. King (Cambridge, MA: Harvard University Press, 1997), 21. *Also see generally* Robert Stacy McCain,

"Democrats Declare War on the Poor," *The American Spectator*, June 8 2009, http://spectator.org/blog/2009/06/08/democrats-declare-war-on-the-p. ŏ **"taking the total from 45 to 435 in just eight years"** "Nixon Forced to Inherit 'Great Society Spiral,'" *Herald-Tribune*, January 19, 1969, 7, http://news.google.com/newspapers?id=Ckg0AAAAIBAJ. ŏ **"committed advisors to Vietnam to fight off the communist insurgency"** "Vietnam: U.S. Advisors 1955–1965," accessed August 6, 2010, http://www.olive-drab.com/od_history_ vietnam_advisors.php. ŏ **"LBJ eventually expanded that to half a million"** Bryan Bender, "Papers Reveal JFK Efforts on Vietnam," *Boston Globe*, June 6, 2005, http://www.boston.com/news/nation/articles/2005/06/06/papers_reveal_jfk_efforts_on_vietnam/?page=full. ŏ **"'I'm sure we could work things out'"** William Doyle, *Inside the Oval Office: The White House Tapes From FDR to Clinton* (New York: Kodansha International, 1999), 157. ŏ **"Johnson and two civilian aides literally sat and handpicked the targets"** Mark Cloidfelter, *The Limits of Air Power: The American Bombing of North Vietnam* (New York: The Free Press, 1989), 122. ŏ **"'changing the North Vietnamese decision on intervention in the South'"** Randall Bennett Woods, *LBJ: Architect of American Ambition* (New York: The Free Press, 2006), 513.

PAGE 87: "view the bombing as 'seduction, not rape'" Doris Kearns, *Lyndon Johnson and the American Dream*, (New York: St. Martin's Press, 1991), 264. ŏ **"puzzled Johnson asks his aides, 'What does he [Ho] want?'"** Steven F. Hayward, *The Age of Reagan: The Fall of the Old Liberal Order, 1964–1980* (New York: Three Rivers Press, 2001), 113. ŏ **"'Old Ho can't turn me down,' he said to one aide"** Klaus P. Fischer, *America in White, Black, and Gray: the Stormy 1960s* (New York: The Continuum International Publishing Group, 2006), 182. ŏ **"But Ho Chi Minh, of course, did just that"** Robert Dallek, *Lyndon B. Johnson: Portrait of a President* (New York: Oxford University Press, 2004), 213. ŏ **"with a price tag of $61 billion per year"** William Bonner, Addison Wiggin, *The New Empire of Debt: The Rise and Fall of an Epic Financial Bubble* (Hoboken, N.J.: John Wiley & Sons, Inc., 2009), 160. ŏ **"'Hanoi could not have won the war'"** Richard H. Shultz, *The Secret War Against Hanoi: The Untold Story of Spies, Saboteurs, and Covert Warriors in North Vietnam* (New York: HarperCollins Publishers Inc., 1999), 205. ŏ **"'better chance to balance their family budgets"** Richard Nixon, *State of the Union Addresses* (Whitefish, MT: Kessinger LLC, 2004), 7.

PAGE 88: "has aptly called Nixon 'the Great Regulator'" Jonathan Rauch, "What Nixon Wrought: The Worst Presidency of the Century," *The New Republic*, May 16, 1994, http://www.jonathanrauch.com/jrauch_articles/nixon_20th_centurys_worst_president/. ŏ **"'and the Occupational Safety and Health Administration'"** Jonathan Rauch, "What Nixon Wrought: The Worst Presidency of the Century," *The New Republic*, May 16, 1994, http://www.jonathanrauch.com/jrauch_articles/nixon_20th_centurys_worst_president/. ŏ **"taking it from $37 billion to $100 billion (in 2009 dollars)"** U.S. Office of Management and Budget, "Table 3.2" in *President's Budget: Historical Tables* (Washington, D.C.: White House, 2010), http://www.whitehouse.gov/omb/budget/Historicals/. ŏ **"pushed community development spending by 206 percent"** Robert E. Kelly, *The National Debt of the United States 1941 to 2008*, 2d ed. (Jefferson, N.C.: McFarland & Company, Inc., 2008), 111–26. ŏ **"rose 246 percent and Medicaid spending climbed 120 percent"** Robert E. Kelly, *The National Debt of the United States 1941 to 2008*, 2d ed. (Jefferson, N.C.: McFarland & Company, Inc., 2008) 111–126. ŏ **"contributed to the inflationary chaos of the next decade"** Jonathan Rauch, "What Nixon Wrought: The Worst Presidency of the Century," *The New Republic*, May 16, 1994, http://www.jonathanrauch.com/jrauch_articles/nixon_20th_centurys_worst_president/. ŏ **"he tried to use wage and price controls to manage inflation"** Daniel Yergin and Joseph Stanislaw, *The Commanding Heights* (New York: Simon & Schuster, 2002), 60–64. *See also:* Steve Chapman, "Obama Embraces Nixonomics—The Folly of Imposing Wage and Price Controls," *Reason.com*, February 25, 2010, http://reason.com/archives/2010/02/25/obama-embraces-nixonomics. ŏ **"major Western powers had signed the Bretton Woods Agreement"** Addison Wiggin, "Bretton Woods Agreement," November 29, 2006, http://www.dailyreckoning.com.au/bretton-woods-agreement/2006/11/29/. ŏ **"President Charles de Gaulle of France started trading dollars for gold"** Adrian Ash, "A Crisis to Shatter the World," *Gold News*, November 10, 2007, http://goldnews.bullionvault.com/gold_dollar_France_Sarkozy_de_Gaulle_crisis_111020072. ŏ **under Nixon, it was a ridiculous 5,395"** Larry Schweikart & Michael Allen, *A Patriot's History of the United States: From Columbus's Great Discovery to the War on Terror* (New York: Sentinel Trade, 2004), 710.

PAGE 89: "1979 through 1981, when prices rose at a double-digit rate" David J. Lynch, "Book says inflation rates of 1970s could return," *USA Today*, January 18, 2009, http://www.usatoday.com/money/books/2009-01-18-book-review-great-inflation-aftermath_N.htm. ŏ **"'but they all had equal rights'"** Conrad Black,

Richard M. Nixon: A Life in Full (New York: PublicAffairs, 2007), 644. ǒ **"'[and] most Jews are disloyal'"** James P. Pfiffner, *The Character Factor: How We Judge America's Presidents* (College Station, TX: Texas A&M University Press, 2004), 141. *See also:* William Henry Chafe, *Private Lives/Public Consequences: Personality and Politics in Modern America* (Cambridge, MA: Harvard University Press, 2005), 271. ǒ **"'They turn on you. Am I wrong or right?'"** George Lardner Jr. and Michael Dobbs, "New Tapes Reveal Depth of Nixon's Anti-Semitism," *Washington Post*, October 6, 1999, http://www.washingtonpost.com/wp-srv/politics/daily/oct99/nixon6.htm. ǒ **"Triffin's Dilemma"** Walker Todd, "Triffin's Dilemma, Reserve Currencies, and Gold," December 31, 2008, http://www.aier.org/research/briefs/975-triffins-dilemma-reserve-currencies-and-gold. ǒ **"can't maintain a strong dollar if it also has to print mass amounts of currency"** Benjamin J. Cohen, "Bretton Woods System," accessed August 9, 2010, http://www.polsci.ucsb.edu/faculty/cohen/inpress/bretton.html. *See also:* Robert Triffin, *Gold and the Dollar Crisis: The Future of Convertibility*, rev. ed. (New Haven, CT: Yale University Press, 1961). ǒ **"leader of the British delegation? John Maynard Keynes"** Addison Wiggin, "Bretton Woods Agreement," November 29, 2006, http://www.dailyreckoning.com.au/bretton-woods-agreement/2006/11/29/ (accessed August 9, 2010).

PAGE 90: "operated under a theory called Mutual Assured Destruction" "Mutual Assured Destruction," accessed August 9, 2010, http://www.nuclearfiles.org/menu/key-issues/nuclear-weapons/history/cold-war/strategy/strategy-mutual-assured-destruction.htm. ǒ **"'REPORT SUGGESTS U.S. 'GO OFF GOLD' TO FIGHT DEFICITS'"** "Report Suggests U.S. 'Go Off Gold' to Fight Deficits—Gold Standard," *Los Angeles Times*, August 8, 1971, A1, http://pqasb.pqarchiver.com/latimes/access/640839292.html?dids=640839292:640839292&FMT=ABS&FMTS=ABS:AI (accessed August 9, 2010). ǒ **"'GOLD LOSES GLITTER AS NEW MONETARY STANDARD IS SOUGHT'"** "Gold Loses Glitter as New Monetary Standard Is Sought," *Sarasota Journal*, September 28, 1971, 15C, http://news.google.com/newspapers?id=5vceAAAAIBAJ&sjid=DY0EAAAAIBAJ (accessed August 9, 2010). ǒ **"predicted a world in which we would see the 'converging of interests'"** Carroll Quigley, *Tragedy and Hope: A History of the World in Our Time* (New York: Macmillan, 1966). ǒ **"'political system of each country and the economy of the world as a whole'"** Carroll Quigley, *Tragedy and Hope: A History of the World in Our Time* (New York: Macmillan, 1966), 1,210–11. ǒ **"a move that was later called 'the Great Grain Robbery'"** "Business: Another Soviet Grain Sting," *Time.com*, November 28, 1977, http://www.time.com/time/magazine/article/0,9171,919164,00.html.

PAGE 91: "'each balancing the other, not playing one against the other, an even balance'" Hedley Donovan, Henry Grunwald, Hugh Sidey and Jerrold Schecter, "The Nation: An Interview with the President: The Jury Is Out," *Time*, January 03, 1972, http://www.time.com/time/magazine/article/0,9171,879011-5,00.html. ǒ **"rose from 9.1 percent of GDP to 16.8 percent of GDP"** Office of Management and Budget, "Table 6.1—Composition of Outlays: 1940–2015" in *Historical Tables—Budget of the U.S. Government*, accessed August 9, 2010, 125, http://www.whitehouse.gov/sites/default/files/omb/budget/fy2011/assets/hist.pdf. ǒ **"the national debt also rose, from $293 billion to $909 billion"** Economic Report of the President: 2010 Report, "Table B-78—Federal Receipts, Outlays, Surplus or Deficit, and Debt, Fiscal Years 1943–2011," accessed August 9, 2010, http://www.gpoaccess.gov/eop/2010/B78.xls.

Chapter 8: Reagan, Bush, and Clinton

PAGE 92: "'trillion-dollar debt because we spend too much'" Ronald Reagan, *The Uncommon Wisdom of Ronald Reagan: A Portrait in His Own Words, ed. Bill Alder* (New York: Little, Brown, 1996).

PAGE 93: "wasn't eclipsed for another twenty-eight years" Burton Frierson, "Inflation Outlook Makes Consumers' Mood Grim," *reuters.com*, May 30, 2008, http://www.reuters.com/article/idUSN3031617020080530. ǒ **"likely they'd postpone a major purchase"** Louis Harris, "Economic Issue Still a Trouble Spot for Carter," *Chicago Tribune*, May 31, 1980, http://www.harrisinteractive.com/vault/Harris-Interactive-Poll-Research-ECONOMIC-ISSUE-STILL-ATROUBLE-SPOT-FOR-CARTER-1980-05.pdf. ǒ **"factories would be shutting down within months"** Louis Harris, "Americans More Concerned With the Recession Than With Inflation," *Chicago Tribune*, July 21, 1980, http://www.harrisinteractive.com/vault/Harris-Interactive-Poll-Research-AMERICANS-MORE-CONCERNED-WITH-THE-RECESSION-THAN-WITH-INFLATION-1980-07.pdf. ǒ **"making ends meet over the next six months"** Louis Harris, "Economic Mood Lightening Slightly Despite Belief that Country Is Still In a Recession," *Chicago Tribune*, September 22, 1980, http://www.harris interactive.com/vault/Harris-Interactive-Poll-Research-ECONOMIC-MOOD-LIGHTENING-SLIGHTLY-DESPITE-BELIEF-T-1980-09.pdf. ǒ **"favored overall cuts to federal spending"** Louis Harris,

"Majority of Americans Support Cuts in Federal Spending," *Chicago Tribune*, June 12, 1980, http://www.harris interactive.com/vault/Harris-Interactive-Poll-Research-MAJORITY-OF-AMERICANS-SUPPORT-CUTS-IN-FEDERAL-SPENDING-1980-06.pdf. ὃ **"cutting federal welfare spending"** Louis Harris, "Majority of Americans Support Cuts in Federal Spending," *Chicago Tribune*, June 12, 1980, http://www.harrisinteractive.com/vault/Harris-Interactive-Poll-Research-MAJORITY-OF-AMERICANS-SUPPORT-CUTS-IN-FEDERAL-SPENDING-1980-06.pdf.

PAGE 94: "'has the capacity to govern someone else?'" Ronald Reagan, "First Inaugural Address," (Speech, Capitol Building, Washington, D.C., January 20, 1981), http://bartelby.org/124/pres61.html. ὃ **"was just 13,266 pages"** Law Librarians' Society of Washington, D.C., "Annual Pages of Federal Register Published," in *LLSDC's Legislative Sourcebook* at *llsdc.com*, accessed August 1, 2010, http://www.llsdc.org/sourcebook/docs/fed-reg-pages.pdf. ὃ **"only 30 percent of the public believed that the government had grown too powerful"** David Frum, *How We Got Here: The 70's: The Decade That Brought You Modern Life—For Better or Worse* (New York: Basic, 2000), 283. ὃ **"now totaling 2.0 percent of GDP"** U.S. Office of Management and Budget, "Table 1.2," in *President's Budget: Historical Tables* (Washington, D.C.: White House, 2010), http://www.whitehouse.gov/omb/budget/Historicals/.

PAGE 95: "urban programs, and education programs, among others" Chris Edwards, "Federal Aid to the States: Historical Cause of Government Growth and Bureaucracy," *Policy Analysis* 593 (May 22, 2007), http://www.cato.org/pub_display.php?pub_id=8246. ὃ **"jumped from 30 percent to 40 percent"** David Frum, *How We Got Here: The 70's: The Decade That Brought You Modern Life—For Better or Worse* (New York: Basic, 2000), 283. ὃ **"jumped to 21.7 percent in 1980"** U.S. Office of Management and Budget, "Table 1.2," in *President's Budget: Historical Tables* (Washington, D.C.: White House, 2010), http://www.whitehouse.gov/omb/budget/Historicals/. ὃ **"Polls that year showed that a majority of the public was now ready to acknowledge"** David Frum, *How We Got Here: The 70's: The Decade That Brought You Modern Life—For Better or Worse* (New York: Basic, 2000), 283. ὃ **"spent most of his life to that point as a Democrat"** Ronald Reagan, *Speaking My Mind: Selected Speeches* (New York: Simon & Schuster, 1989), 25. ὃ **"beat Walter Mondale by the largest electoral margin in history"** Lou Cannon, *Reagan: The Role of a Lifetime* (New York: PublicAffairs, 2000), 434.

PAGE 96: "high of 20 percent in 1981" Federal Reserve Bank of New York, "Historical Changes of the Target Federal Funds and Discount Rates," *ny.frb.org*, accessed August 1, 2010, http://www.ny.frb.org/markets/statistics/dlyrates/fedrate.html. ὃ **"from $1.40 trillion to $1.68 trillion"** U.S. Office of Management and Budget, "Table 1.1," in *President's Budget: Historical Tables* (Washington, D.C.: White House, 2010), http://www.whitehouse.gov/omb/budget/Historicals/. Note: The figures cover 1981-1989 and I have adjusted them for inflation into 2009 dollars. The tax rate figure applies to two tax cut laws. The 1981 tax cuts gradually decreased the top rate from 70 percent to 50 percent, and the 1986 tax reforms further reduced it to 28 percent. ὃ **"individual income tax revenues expanded 13 percent"** U.S. Office of Management and Budget, "Table 2.1," in *President's Budget: Historical Tables* (Washington, D.C.: White House, 2010), http://www.whitehouse.gov/omb/budget/Historicals/. Note: The figures cover 1981-1989 and I have adjusted them for inflation into 2009 dollars. ὃ **"economy grew at an average rate of 3.4 percent a year"** Executive Office of the President and the Council of Economic Advisors, "Table B-4," in *2010 Economic Report of the President*, 111th Cong., 2nd sess. (Washington, D.C., 2010), http://www.gpoaccess.gov/eop/tables10.html. ὃ **"plummeted from 12.5 percent to 4.4 percent"** Executive Office of the President and the Council of Economic Advisors, "Table B-63," in *2010 Economic Report of the President*, 111th Cong., 2nd sess. (Washington, D.C., 2010), http://www.gpoaccess.gov/eop/tables10.html. ὃ **"unemployment rate fell from 7.1 percent to 5.5 percent"** Executive Office of the President and the Council of Economic Advisors, "Table B-35," in *2010 Economic Report of the President*, 111th Cong., 2nd sess. (Washington, D.C., 2010), http://www.gpoaccess.gov/eop/tables10.html. ὃ **"prime interest rate fell by one third"** Executive Office of the President and the Council of Economic Advisors, "Table B-73," in *2010 Economic Report of the President*, 111th Cong., 2nd sess. (Washington, D.C., 2010), http://www.gpoaccess.gov/eop/tables10.html. ὃ **"Productivity jumped 15 percent"** Executive Office of the President and the Council of Economic Advisors, "Table B-49," in *2010 Economic Report of the President*, 111th Cong., 2nd sess. (Washington, D.C., 2010), http://www.gpoaccess.gov/eop/tables10.html. ὃ **"S&P 500 leaped 124 percent"** Executive Office of the President and the Council of Economic Advisors, "Table B-95," in *2010 Economic Report of the*

President, 111th Cong., 2nd sess. (Washington, D.C., 2010), http://www.gpoaccess.gov/eop/tables10.html. ð **"contributions expanded 57 percent faster than inflation"** Dinesh D'Souza, *Ronald Reagan: How an Ordinary Man Became an Extraordinary Leader* (New York: Free Press, 1997), 116.

PAGE 97: "debt stood at $2.3 trillion (using 2009 dollars)" Treasury Direct, "Historical Debt Outstanding: Annual 1950–1999," *treasurydirect.gov*, accessed August 2, 2010, http://www.treasurydirect.gov/govt/reports/pd/histdebt/histdebt_histo4.htm. ð **"deficits in every single one of his eight years in office"** Treasury Direct, "Historical Debt Outstanding: Annual 1950–1999," *treasurydirect.gov*, accessed August 2, 2010, http://www.treasurydirect.gov/govt/reports/pd/histdebt/histdebt_histo4.htm. ð **"'serious about negotiating a down payment on the deficit'"** Storer Rowley, "Reagan Insists He'll Work To Cut Deficit," *Chicago Tribune*, January 28, 1984. ð **"'I'm trying to undo the "Great Society"'"** David Frum, *Dead Right* (New York: Basic, 1995), 47.

PAGE 98: "decided that reforming Medicare . . . was too politically risky" David Frum, *Dead Right* (New York: Basic, 1995), 49. ð **"eliminating the failed Comprehensive Employment and Training Act"** Dinesh D'Souza, *Ronald Reagan: How an Ordinary Man Became an Extraordinary Leader* (New York: Free Press, 1997), 102. ð **"we'll cut three dollars in spending"** Dinesh D'Souza, *Ronald Reagan: How an Ordinary Man Became an Extraordinary Leader* (New York: Free Press, 1997), 102–3. ð **"'least able to organize and protect themselves: the very poor'"** Michael Kinsley, "In the Land of the Magic Asterisk," *New York Times*, May 11, 1986, http://www.nytimes.com/1986/05/11/books/in-the-land-of-the-magic-asterisk.html. ð **"'Congress never cut spending by even a penny'"** Bruce Bartlett, "'Starve the Beast': Origins and Development of a Budgetary Metaphor," *Independent Review* 12, no. 1 (Summer 2007): 12.

PAGE 99: "fought to protect 'their turf' against budget cuts" David Frum, *Dead Right* (New York: Basic, 1995), 42. ð **"'This is the last stand on earth'"** Ronald Reagan, *Speaking My Mind: Selected Speeches* (New York: Simon & Schuster, 1989), 26. ð **"'We're going to go ahead with these [defense] programs'"** Peter Schweizer, *Reagan's War: The Epic Story of His Forty-Year Struggle and Final Triumph Over Communism* (New York: Doubleday, 2002), 139–40. ð **"'expense of my tax cutting program and my defense program'"** Dinesh D'Souza, *Ronald Reagan: How an Ordinary Man Became an Extraordinary Leader* (New York: Free Press, 1997), 104.

PAGE 100: "required slashing in excess of 40 percent from spending" John Samples, *The Struggle to Limit Government: A Modern Political History* (Washington, D.C.: Cato Institute, 2010), 139. ð **"'fell by 9.7 percent during his first term'"** Veronique de Rugy, "President Reagan: Champion Budget-Cutter," (paper, American Enterprise Institute for Public Policy Researcy, Washington, D.C., 2004), http://www.aei.org/paper/20675. ð **"increased 22 percent faster than inflation"** U.S. Office of Management and Budget, "Table 1.3," in *President's Budget: Historical Tables* (Washington, D.C.: White House, 2010), http://www.whitehouse.gov/omb/budget/Historicals/.

PAGE 101: "'we are going to begin to act, beginning today'" Ronald Reagan, "First Inaugural Address," (Speech, Capitol Building, Washington, D.C., January 20, 1981), http://bartelby.org/124/pres61.html.

PAGE 102: "'federal government to spend more than the federal government takes in'" Ronald Reagan, "First Inaugural Address," (Speech, Capitol Building, Washington, D.C., January 20, 1981), http://bartelby.org/124/pres61.html. ð **"got within one vote of the two-thirds majority needed"** U.S. Senate Republican Policy Committee, "S.J. Res. 1: Balanced Budget Constitutional Amendment," *rpc.senate.gov*, February 4, 1997, http://rpc.senate.gov/releases/1997/v5.htm. ð **"'And if it stops moving, subsidize it'"** Robert Andrews, ed., *The Columbia Dictionary of Quotations* (New York: Columbia, 1993), 263. ð **"'plus as much more as it can get away with'"** Milton Friedman, interview by Peter Robinson, "Friedman on the Surplus," *Hoover Digest* (Hoover Institution at Stanford University), no. 2 (2001), http://www.hoover.org/publications/hoover-digest/article/7863.

PAGE 103: "'Read my lips: no new taxes'" George Bush, Republican presidential candidacy acceptance speech (Republican National Convention, New Orleans, August 18,1988). ð **"'effort to reduce the Federal budget deficit'"** Peter T. Kilborn, "Bush Vows Talks on His First Day to Cut the Deficit," *New York Times*, November 23, 1988, http://www.nytimes.com/1988/11/23/us/bush-vows-talks-on-his-first-day-to-cut-the-deficit.html.

PAGE 104: "'you might not have to decide at all'" Michael Duffy and Dan Goodgame, *Marching in Place: The Status Quo Presidency of George Bush* (New York: Simon & Schuster, 1992), 92. ð **"it was the way he viewed his job"** Peter Schweizer and Rochelle Schweizer, *The Bushes: Portrait of a Dynasty* (New York:

Doubleday, 2004), 373–74. • **"then a 0.2 percent contraction in 1991"** U.S. Department of Commerce, Bureau of Economic Analysis, "Gross Domestic Product" in *National Economic Accounts, bea.gov,* accessed August 2, 2010, http://www.bea.gov/national/index.htm#gdp. • **"a 32 percent increase in just four years"** U.S. Office of Management and Budget, "Table 7.1," in *President's Budget: Historical Tables* (Washington, D.C.: White House, 2010), http://www.whitehouse.gov/omb/budget/Historicals/. • **"Social Security costs increased $72 billion (31 percent)"** U.S. Office of Management and Budget, "Table 3.1," in *President's Budget: Historical Tables* (Washington, D.C.: White House, 2010), http://www.whitehouse.gov/omb/budget/Historicals/. • **"Medicare outlays soared $46 billion (50 percent)"** U.S. Office of Management and Budget, "Table 3.1," in *President's Budget: Historical Tables* (Washington, D.C.: White House, 2010), http://www.whitehouse.gov/omb/budget/Historicals/. • **"interest payments . . . jumped up $30 billion (18 percent)"** U.S. Office of Management and Budget, "Table 3.1," in *President's Budget: Historical Tables* (Washington, D.C.: White House, 2010), http://www.whitehouse.gov/omb/budget/Historicals/.

PAGE 105: "'begins with the destruction of truth'" Bill Clinton, "Remarks by the President at the Dedication of the Thomas J. Dodd Research Center" (speech, Thomas J. Dodd Research Center at the University of Connecticut, Storrs, CT, October 15, 1995), http://www.ibiblio.org/pub/archives/whitehouse-papers/1995/Oct/1995-10-15-President-Remarks-at-Dodd-Research-Center-Dedication.

PAGE 106: "'largest one-year debt reduction in the history of the United States'" Kelly Wallace, "President Clinton Announces Another Record Budget Surplus," *Allpolitics* at *cnn.com,* September 27, 2000, http://archives.cnn.com/2000/ALLPOLITICS/stories/09/27/clinton.surplus/. • **"$223 billion this year alone"** Kelly Wallace, "President Clinton Announces Another Record Budget Surplus," *Allpolitics* at *cnn.com,* September 27, 2000, http://archives.cnn.com/2000/ALLPOLITICS/stories/09/27/clinton.surplus/. • **"'pay down $138 billion in national debt'"** Kelly Wallace, "President Clinton Announces Another Record Budget Surplus," *Allpolitics* at *cnn.com,* September 27, 2000, http://archives.cnn.com/2000/ALLPOLITICS/stories/09/27/clinton.surplus/. • **"'progress' on the debt over his two terms (in trillions):"** U.S. Office of Management and Budget, "Table 7.1," in *President's Budget: Historical Tables* (Washington, D.C.: White House, 2010), http://www.whitehouse.gov/omb/budget/Historicals/.

PAGE 107: "'deficit is much bigger now than it was when I said this'" Associated Press, "Clinton Backs Off Vow to Halve Debt," *St. Petersburg Times,* January 12, 1993. • **"intragovernmental debt goes up every single year"** U.S. Office of Management and Budget, "Table 7.1," in *President's Budget: Historical Tables* (Washington, D.C.: White House, 2010), http://www.whitehouse.gov/omb/budget/Historicals/. • **"Chart: A Surplus of Lies"** U.S. Office of Management and Budget, "Table 7.1," in *President's Budget: Historical Tables* (Washington, D.C.: White House, 2010), http://www.whitehouse.gov/omb/budget/Historicals. *See also,* U.S. Office of Management and Budget, "Table 1.4," in *President's Budget: Historical Tables* (Washington, D.C.: White House, 2010), http://www.whitehouse.gov/omb/budget/Historicals. *For public debt balances, see* U.S. Department of the Treasury, Bureau of Public Debt, http://www.treasurydirect.gov/govt/reports/pd/histdebt/histdebt.htm.

PAGE 108: "$320.4 billion over the eight-year period of 1993–2000" U.S. Office of Management and Budget, "Table 1.1," in *President's Budget: Historical Tables* (Washington, D.C.: White House, 2010), http://www.whitehouse.gov/omb/budget/Historicals/. • **"increasing by $1.6 trillion over that same period"** U.S. Office of Management and Budget, "Table 7.1," in *President's Budget: Historical Tables* (Washington, D.C.: White House, 2010), http://www.whitehouse.gov/omb/budget/Historicals/. • **"trust funds experienced a major influx of revenue"** Social Security Online, "Social Security and Medicare Tax Rates," *ssa.gov,* accessed August 3, 2010, http://www.ssa.gov/OACT/ProgData/taxRates.html. • **"surplus of $7.5 billion in 1985"** Social Security Online, "Fiscal Year Trust Fund Operations," *ssa.gov,* accessed August 3, 2010, http://www.ssa.gov/OACT/ProgData/fyOps.html. • **"more than doubled to $152 billion"** Social Security Online, "Fiscal Year Trust Fund Operations," *ssa.gov,* accessed August 3, 2010, http://www.ssa.gov/OACT/ProgData/fyOps.html.

PAGE 109: "'excites the spending predilection of politicians in both parties'" Hans F. Sennholz, "The Surplus Hoax," *Mises Daily at mises.org,* November 3, 2000, http://mises.org/daily/542. • **"'rest of the budget will have to subsidize Social Security'"** Lori Montgomery, "Recession Hurts Social Security Trust Fund," *cbsnews.com* from the *Washington Post,* March 31, 2009, http://www.cbsnews.com/stories/2009/03/31/politics/washingtonpost/main4906936.shtml. • **"costs on the national debt dipped by 1.0 percent of GDP"**

Calculations by Brian Riedl based on: U.S. Office of Management and Budget, "Table 3.2," in *President's Budget: Historical Tables* (Washington, D.C.: White House, 2010), http://www.whitehouse.gov/omb/budget/Historicals.

PAGE 110: "to $376 billion (adjusted for inflation in 2009 dollars)" Calculations by Brian Riedl based on: U.S. Office of Management and Budget, "Table 3.2," in *President's Budget: Historical Tables* (Washington, D.C.: White House, 2010), http://www.whitehouse.gov/omb/budget/Historicals. ♁ **"defense budget back up to only 4.9 percent of GDP"** U.S. Office of Management and Budget, "Table 8.4," in *President's Budget: Historical Tables* (Washington, D.C.: White House, 2010), http://www.whitehouse.gov/omb/budget/Historicals. ♁ **"deficit . . . would have been undeniable"** U.S. Office of Management and Budget, "Outlays by Superfunction and Function: 1940–2009," in *Historical Tables: Budget of the United States Government, Fiscal Year 2005* (Washington, D.C.: White House, 2004), 45–52. ♁ **"drove the NASDAQ index up by more than 450 percent"** Jorn Madslien, "Dotcom Bubble Burst: 10 Years On," *news.bbc.co.uk*, March 9, 2010, http://news.bbc.co.uk/2/hi/business/8558257.stm. ♁ **"than had occurred in the previous decade *combined*"** U.S. Office of Management and Budget, "Table 1.3," in *President's Budget: Historical Tables* (Washington, D.C.: White House, 2010), http://www.whitehouse.gov/omb/budget/Historicals. ♁ **"peacetime record of 20.6 percent of GDP"** U.S. Office of Management and Budget, "Table 1.3," in *President's Budget: Historical Tables* (Washington, D.C.: White House, 2010), http://www.whitehouse.gov/omb/budget/Historicals.

PAGE 112: "from 3.2 percent of GDP to 2.2 percent" U.S. Office of Management and Budget, "Table 8.4," in *President's Budget: Historical Tables* (Washington, D.C.: White House, 2010), http://www.whitehouse.gov/omb/budget/Historicals. ♁ **"'Not a dissent'"** Bob Woodward, *The Agenda: Inside the Clinton White House* (New York: Simon & Schuster, 1994), 84.

PAGE 113: "a different party from the one controlling congress" William A. Niskanen, "A Case for Divided Government," *cato.org*, May 7, 2003, http://www.cato.org/pub_display.php ?pub_id=3088. ♁ **"increased an average of 11.6 percent a year"** U.S. Office of Management and Budget, "Table 1.1," in *resident's Budget: Historical Tables* (Washington, D.C.: White House, 2010), http://www.whitehouse.gov/omb/budget/Historicals. ♁ **"spending declined by an average of 4.2 percent a year"** U.S. Office of Management and Budget, "Table 1.1," in *President's Budget: Historical Tables* (Washington, D.C.: White House, 2010), http://www.whitehouse.gov/omb/budget/Historicals. ♁ **"died before it could even be unveiled"** Steve M. Gillon, *The Pact: Bill Clinton, Newt Gingrich, and the Rivalry that Defined a Generation* (New York: Oxford, 2008).

Chapter 9: W. and O.

PAGE 114: "'matching good intentions with good results'" Fox News "Bush Pushes Economic Plan in Detroit," *foxnews.com*, February 9, 2005, http://www.foxnews.com/story/0,2933,146718,00.html.

PAGE 115: "'that the administration advocated on taking office a year ago'" Richard W. Stevenson, "In a Sign of Changing Times, Bush Calls for More Spending," *New York Times*, January 28, 2002, http://www.nytimes.com/2002/01/28/us/in-a-sign-of-changing-times-bush-calls-for-more-spending.html. ♁ **"Total Bush deficits: $3.3 trillion"** U.S. Office of Management and Budget, "Table 1.1," in *President's Budget: Historical Tables* (Washington, D.C.: White House, 2010), http://www.whitehouse.gov/omb/budget/Historicals/. Note: President Bush signed the FY 2002 through FY 2009 budgets into law, although these calculations omit the additional emergency legislation signed by President Obama shortly after taking office in 2009. ♁ **"(Bush's Real Deficits): $5.0 trillion"** U.S. Office of Management and Budget, "Table 7.1," in *President's Budget: Historical Tables* (Washington, D.C.: White House, 2010), http://www.whitehouse.gov/omb/budget/Historicals/. Note: This reflects the growth in the debt from the end of 2001 through the end of 2009, which covers the budgets signed by President Bush (net of the portion of 2009 debt resulting from President Obama's emergency legislation). ♁ **"Total Bush Spending: $20.5 trillion"** U.S. Office of Management and Budget, "Table 1.1," in *President's Budget: Historical Tables* (Washington, D.C.: White House, 2010), http://www.whitehouse.gov/omb/budget/Historicals/. Note: President Bush signed the FY 2002 through FY 2009 budgets into law, although these calculations omit the additional emergency legislation signed by President Obama shortly after taking office in 2009. ♁ **"Total Inflation-Adjusted Increase of the Federal Budget"** U.S. Office of Management and Budget, "Table 1.3," in *President's Budget: Historical Tables* (Washington, D.C.: White House, 2010), http://www.whitehouse.gov/omb/budget/Historicals/. Note: President Clinton figures are based on the growth from his inherited FY 1993 level (President George H.W. Bush's final budget) through his own final budget in FY 2001. President George W. Bush's figures are based on the growth from his inherited FY 2001 level through his final budget in FY 2009 (although these calculations omit the additional emergency legislation signed by President Obama shortly after taking office in 2009).

PAGE 116: "biggest spender since LBJ" Veronique de Rugy, "Spending Under George W. Bush" (working paper, Mercatus Center, George Mason University, Fairfax, VA, 2009), http://mercatus.org/sites/default/files/publication/WP0904 _GAP_Spending Under President George W Bush.pdf. ✪ **"that number had jumped to nearly $26,000"** Brian Riedl, "Federal Spending by the Numbers 2010," (report, The Heritage Foundation, Washington, D.C., 2010), http://www.heritage.org/research/reports/2010/06/federal-spending-by-the-numbers-2010. ✪ **"Chart: GWB in Context"** Original chart by Chris Edwards at the Cato Institute, data from U.S. Office of Management and Budget, "Table 1.1," in *President's Budget: Historical Tables* (Washington, D.C.: White House, 2010), http://www.whitehouse.gov/omb/budget/Historicals, *Note: Date excludes interest.*

PAGE 117: "and were the largest since 1981" Chris Edwards, "Tax Policy Under President Bush," *cato.org*, August 14, 2006, http://www.cato.org/pub_display.php?pub_ id=6621. ✪ **"economic growth rate doubled to 4.1 percent"** Brian Riedl, "Ten Myths About the Bush Tax Cuts," (report, The Heritage Foundation, Washington, D.C., 2007), http://www.heritage.org/Research/Reports/2007/01/Ten-Myths-About-the-Bush-Tax-Cuts. For job numbers see: U.S. Department of Labor, "Employment, Hours, and Earnings from the Current Employment Statistics Survey (National)," in *Databases and Tables, data.bls.gov*, accessed August 6, 2010. ✪ **"About $5.6 trillion of wealth evaporated"** World Federation of Exchanges, *1995–2002 Historical Monthly Statistics, world-exchanges.org*, accessed August 6, 2010, http://www.world-exchanges.org/statistics/historical-monthly. ✪ **"from more than 5,000 in 1999 to less than 2,000 by 2002"** Yahoo Finance, "Historical Prices," in *NASDAQ Composite (^IXIC), finance.yahoo.com*, accessed August 6, 2010, http://finance.yahoo.com/q/hp?s=%5EIXIC&a=01&b=5&c=1996&d=06&e=23 &f=2002&g=w&z=66&y=66. ✪ **"average of -4.1 percent a year from 2000 through 2003"** U.S. Office of Management and Budget, "Table 1.1," in *President's Budget: Historical Tables* (Washington, D.C.: White House, 2010), http://www.whitehouse.gov/omb/budget/Historicals/. ✪ **"fell by $250 billion between 2000 and 2003"** U.S. Office of Management and Budget, "Table 1.1," in *President's Budget: Historical Tables* (Washington, D.C.: White House, 2010), http://www.whitehouse.gov/omb/budget/Historicals/. ✪ **"'eight years of peace and prosperity'"** The Clinton Administration Cabinet, *Eight Years of Peace, Progress, and Prosperity* (Washington, D.C.: White House, 2001), http://clinton5.nara.gov/media/pdf/cabinet_accomps.pdf.

PAGE 118: "cost of the War on Terror to date . . . is over $1 trillion" CNN Wire Staff, "Report: Tab for 'War on Terrorism' Tops $1 Trillion," *cnn.com*, July 20, 2010, http://edition.cnn.com/2010/POLITICS/07/20/war.costs/index.html#fbid=WRepRYJuA7N&wom=true. **"he pushed it to over 4 percent of GDP."** Kiki Bradley and Robert Rector, Welfare Spendathon: House Stimulus Bill Will Cost Taxpayers $787 Billion in New Welfare Spending," heritage.org, February 6, 2009, http://www.heritage.org/ Research/Reports/2009/02/Welfare-Spendathon-House-Stimulus-Bill-Will-Cost-Taxpayers-787-Billion-in-New-Welfare-Spending. ✪ **"President Bush *still* would have spent $5 trillion more"** U.S. Office of Management and Budget, "Table 1.1," in *President's Budget: Historical Tables* (Washington, D.C.: White House, 2010), http://www.whitehouse.gov/omb/budget/Historicals/. ✪ **"one-third of all new spending under President Bush"** Brian Riedl, "Federal Spending by the Numbers 2008" (report, The Heritage Foundation, Washington, D.C., 2008), 4, http://www.heritage.org/Research/Reports/2008/02/Federal-Spending-By-the-Numbers-2008. ✪ **"first president to devote at least 3 percent of GDP"** Brian Riedl, "Federal Spending by the Numbers 2008" (report, The Heritage Foundation, Washington, D.C., 2008), http://www.heritage.org/Research/Reports/2008/02/Federal-Spending-By-the-Numbers-2008. ✪ **"Chart: Bush: The Spending Reality Gap"** Original chart by Chris Edwards at the Cato Institute, data from U.S. Government Printing Office, federal budgets for FY 2002 and FY 2011, http://www.gpoaccess.gov/usbudget/browse.html.

PAGE 119: "increased federal spending at an average of 3.7 percent a year" Calculated by Chris Edwards of the Cato Institute, based on: U.S. Office of Management and Budget *United States Budget, Fiscal Year 2002* (Washington, D.C.: White House, 2001), http://www.gpoaccess.gov/usbudget/fy02/pdf/budget.pdf. ✪ **"Clinton's actual average of 3.5 percent a year"** U.S. Office of Management and Budget, "Table 1.1," in *President's Budget: Historical Tables* (Washington, D.C.: White House, 2010), http://www.whitehouse.gov/omb/budget/Historicals/. ✪ **"voted for less overall spending from 2000 to 2005"** Stephen Moore and Stephen Slivinski, "The Return of the Living Dead: Federal Programs That Survived the Republican Revolution," *Policy Analysis*, no. 375 (July 24, 2000), http://www.cato.org/pubs/pas/pa375.pdf.

PAGE 120: "record $29 billion, nearly quadruple the 1994 level" Citizens Against Government Waste, "Pork-Barrel Report," *cagw.org*, accessed August 7, 2010, http://www.cagw.org/reports/pig-book/. ♁ **"due to their reputation as corrupt big spenders"** CNN's America Votes 2006, "U.S. House of Representatives/National/Exit Poll," *cnn.com*, accessed August 7, 2010, http://cnn.co.hu/ELECTION/2006/pages/results/states/US/H/00/epolls.0.html. ♁ **"nearly reached the depths of President Nixon's"** Wall Street Journal, "How the Presidents Stack Up," *wsj.com*, accessed August 7, 2010, http://online.wsj.com/public/resources/documents/info-presapp0605-31.html.

PAGE 121: "declared that there was no more wasteful spending left to cut" *Washington Times*, "Delay Declares 'Victory' in War on Budget Fat," *washingtontimes.com*, September 14, 2005, http://www.washingtontimes.com/news/2005/sep/14/20050914-120153-3878r/. ♁ **"even a nonbinding government waste commission"** *Commission on the Accountability and Review of Federal Agencies (CARFA) Act*, HR 2470, 109th Cong., 2nd sess. ♁ **"provided these interest groups with tens of thousands of earmarks"** Nicholas Confessore, "Welcome to the Machine: How the GOP Disciplined K Street and Made Bush Supreme," *Washington Monthly*, July/August 2003, http://www.washingtonmonthly.com/features/2003/0307.confessore.html.

PAGE 122: "sample constituent letter defending sugar subsidies" Michael Zehr, "Application Requirements for Legislative Correspondent Position," Office of Senator Mel Martinez, 2007. ♁ **"'The Republican Congressional Index: A Dozen Years of Success'"** Office of Senator Bill Frist, "The Republican Congressional Index: A Dozen Years of Success," press release, December 8, 2006. ♁ **"'Largest Federal Funding Increase . . . Linked to Reform'"** House Committee on Education and the Workforce Committee, "Largest Federal Funding Increase in History for K–12 Education Takes Effect, Linked to Reform," press release, July 1, 2002. ♁ **"bragged that GOP reforms had increased government dependency"** "RX Plans Good Prognosis," *Washington Times*, May 13, 2006, http://www.washingtontimes.com/news/2006/may/13/20060513-094640-3369r/. ♁ **"and even kicked off their congressional committees"** Tom A. Coburn, M.D. with John Hart, *Breach of Trust: How Washington Turns Outsiders Into Insiders* (Nashville, TN: Thomas Nelson, 2003). *See also* Linda Killian, *The Freshmen: What Happened to the Republican Revolution* (New York: Basic, 1999). ♁ **"John Gardner announced a full-scale study"** Associated Press, "Medicare May Cover Drug Costs," *Spartanburg Herald*, June 1, 1967. ♁ **"killed the idea, saying it was far too expensive"** Associated Press, "Senate Kills Prescription Drug Coverage," *Reading Eagle*, November 17, 1967.

PAGE 123: "Walker responded, 'Zip'" *60 Minutes*, "U.S. Heading for Trouble?: Comptroller Says Medicare Program Endangers Financial Stability," *cbsnews.com*, July 8, 2007, http://www.cbsnews.com/stories/2007/03/01/60minutes/main2528226 _page2.shtml. ♁ **"'expensive new program to pay for their prescription drugs'"** Bruce Bartlett, "Republican Deficit Hypocrisy," *forbes.com*, November 20, 2009, http://www.forbes.com/2009/11/19/republican-budget-hypocrisy-health-care-opinions-columnists-bruce-bartlett.html. ♁ **"currently underfunded by $7.2 trillion"** U.S. Department of the Treasury, Financial Management Service, *2009 Financial Report of the U.S. Government*, (Washington, D.C.: Department of the Treasury, 2009), 51, http://www.fms.treas.gov/fr/09frusg/09stmt.pdf.

PAGE 124: "'no one outside the House chamber could see what was going on'" Bruce Bartlett, "Republican Deficit Hypocrisy," *forbes.com*, November 20, 2009, http://www.forbes.com/2009/11/19/republican-budget-hypocrisy-health-care-opinions-columnists-bruce-bartlett.html. ♁ **"passed the bill with fifty-four votes"** U.S. Senate, "U.S. Senate Roll Call Votes: 108th Congress—1st Session," *senate.gov*, November 25, 2003, http://www.senate.gov/legislative/LIS/roll_call_lists/roll_call_vote_cfm. cfm?congress=108&session=1&vote=00459#position. ♁ **"Lindsey Graham . . . was one of them"** U.S. Senate, "U.S. Senate Roll Call Votes: 108th Congress—1st Session," *senate.gov*, November 25, 2003, http://www.senate.gov/legislative/LIS/roll_call_lists/roll_call_vote_cfm.cfm?congress=108&session=1&vote=00459#position. ♁ **"'And this generation is fulfilling our duty'"** Fox News, "Raw Data: Transcript of Bush Medicare Remarks," *foxnews.com*, December 8, 2003, http://www.foxnews.com/story/0,2933,105159,00.html.

PAGE 125: "Chart: Against Regulations" Veronique de Rugy, "Bush's Regulatory Kiss-Off," *Reason Magazine*, January 2009, http://reason.com/archives/2008/12/10/bushs-regulatory-kiss-off. ♁ **"all-time high of over 79,400 pages up from 64,438 pages"** Clyde Wayne Crews, "Ten Thousand Commandments 2009," *cei.org*, May 28, 2009, http://cei.org/studies-issue-analysis/ten-thousand-commandments-2009.

ǒ **"compliance with regulations cost $1.127 trillion in 2008"** Clyde Wayne Crews, "Ten Thousand Commandments 2009," *cei.org*, May 28, 2009, http://cei.org/studies-issue-analysis/ten-thousand-commandments-2009. ǒ **"tax revenue for that year was $304 billion"** U.S. Office of Management and Budget, "Table 2.1," in *President's Budget: Historical Tables* (Washington, D.C.: White House, 2010), http://www.whitehouse.gov/omb/budget/Historicals/. ǒ **"Bush *added* 91,196 people to the staff"** Veronique de Rugy, "Bush's Regulatory Kiss-Off," *Reason*, January 2009, http://reason.com/archives/2008/12/10/bushs-regulatory-kiss-off. ǒ **"'than any previous administration in U.S. history'"** Veronique de Rugy, "Bush's Regulatory Kiss-Off," *Reason*, January 2009, http://reason.com/archives/2008/12/10/bushs-regulatory-kiss-off. ǒ **"'BUSH PLEDGES EFFORT TO BALANCE BUDGET BY 2004'"** Mike Allen, "Bush Pledges Effort to Balance Budget by 2004," *Washington Post*, April 17, 2002.

PAGE 126: "our politicians gambled $3.7 trillion" David Lawder, "US Financial System Support Up $700 Bln in Past Year-Watchdog," *reuters.com*, July 21, 2010, http://www.reuters.com/article/idUSN2010140720100721. ǒ **"Chart: Guest Check!"** Barry Ritholtz, *Bailout Nation* (Hoboken, N.J.: John Wiley & Sons, 2009), 3.

PAGE 127: "'to save the free-market system'" "Bush Says Sacrificed Free-Market Principles to Save Economy," *breitbart.com*, December 16, 2008, http://www.breitbart.com/article.php?id=081216215816.8g97981o. ǒ **"mortgage guarantees was about 'one in a million'"** Joseph E. Stiglitz, Jonathan M. Orszag, and Peter R. Orszag, "Implications of the New Fannie Mae and Freddy Mac Risk-Based Capital Standard," *Fannie Mae Papers* 1, no.2 (March 2002), http://citeseerx.ist.psu.edu/viewdoc/download?doi=10.1.1.8.3820&rep=rep1&type=pdf. ǒ **"real unemployment rate is close to 18 percent"** U.S. Department of Labor, Bureau of Labor Statistics, "Alternative Measures of Labor Underutilization," news release, August 6, 2010, http://www.bls.gov/news.release/empsit.t15.htm. ǒ **"Incomes have continued to fall"** Joseph Curl, "Income Falls 3.2% During Obama's Term," *Washington Times*, April 13, 2010, http://www.washingtontimes.com/news/2010/apr/13/personal-income-falls-32-during-obamas-15-months/.

PAGE 128: "'Because I'm calling their bluff'" David Jackson, "Obama On Deficit and Debt Critics: 'I'm Calling Their Bluff,'" *USA Today*, June 28, 2010, http://content.usatoday.com/communities/theoval/post/2010/06/obama-signals-coming-battle-over-debt/1. ǒ **"'for us to do things that you could not do before'"** Gerald F. Seib, "In Crisis, Opportunity for Obama," *Wall Street Journal*, November 21, 2008, http://online.wsj.com/article/SB122721278056345271.html.

PAGE 129: "budgets stretched by 80, 90, and 100 percent" U.S. Office of Management and Budget, "Table 4.1," in *President's Budget: Historical Tables* (Washington, D.C.: White House, 2010), http://www.whitehouse.gov/omb/budget/Historicals/. ǒ **"'No, I'm not going to engage in that'"** Barak Obama, interview by the *New York Times*, "Obama's Interview Aboard Air Force One," *New York Times*, March 7, 2009, http://www.nytimes.com/2009/03/08/us/politics/08obama-text.html. ǒ **"'maximum tolerable proportion of taxation'"** Daniel J. Mitchell for the Cato Institute, "Spending Is Not Stimulus: Bigger Government Did Not Work for Bush and It Will Not Work for Obama," *Tax and Budget Bulletin*, no. 53 (February 2009), http://www.cato.org/pubs/tbb/tbb_0209-53.pdf.

PAGE 130: "larger stimulus package than the $130 billion he'd pitched" Peter Grier, "Obama Weighs a Supersized Stimulus Plan," *Christian Science Monitor*, December 22, 2008, http://www.csmonitor.com/USA/Politics/2008/1222/obama-weighs-a-supersized-stimulus-plan. ǒ **"payroll employment stood at 134.3 million"** U.S. Bureau of Labor Statistics, "Comparison of All Employees, Seasonally Adjusted, Before and After the March 2008 Benchmark," *bls.gov*, accessed August 8, 2010, ftp://ftp.bls.gov/pub/suppl/empsit.compaes.txt. ǒ **"by the first quarter of 2010 under each scenario"** Christina Romer and Jared Bernstein, "The Job Impact of the American Recovery and Reinvestment Plan," *politico.com*, January 9, 2010, http://www.politico.com/pdf/PPM116_ obamadoc.pdf. ǒ **"Jobs: 130.5 million (down 3.8 million)"** Paul Wiseman, "Long-Term Unemployed Fear Loss of Jobless Benefits," *USA Today*, July 15, 2010, http://www.usatoday.com/money/economy/employment/2010-07-15-unemployment15_CV_N.htm. ǒ **"Unemployment Rate: 9.5-10.1 percent"** U.S. Department of Labor, Bureau of Labor Statistics, "Labor Force Statistics from the Current Population Survey," in *Databases, Tables, and Calculators, bls.gov*, accessed August 8, 2010, http://data.bls.gov/PDQ/servlet/SurveyOutputServlet?data_ tool=latest_numbers&series_id=LNS14000000. Note: 10.1 percent was the peak rate. The unemployment rate was 9.5 percent as of the second quarter of 2010. ǒ **"that his plan would create 3.7 million jobs"** Lisa Lerer, Victoria McGrane, and Eamon Javers, "How Many New Jobs From Stimulus Plan? Your Guess Is as Good as Theirs," *Pittsburgh Post-Gazette*, January

14, 2009, http://www.post-gazette.com/pg/09014/941591-473.stm. ♁ **"rate they predicted without the stimulus 'disastrous'"** Paul Krugman, "Ideas for Obama," *New York Times*, January 2, 2009, http://www.nytimes.com/2009/01/12/opinion/12iht-edkrugman.1.19281918.html.

PAGE 131: "'it will help create 3 million to 4 million jobs'" Peter Orszag, interview by Jim Lehrer, *The NewsHour With Jim Lehrer*, PBS, February 5, 2009. ♁ **"'awfully tough to understand. This isn't it'"** Jared Bernstein, *Newsroom*, CNN, February 6, 2009. ♁ **"'This bill creates 3.5 million jobs'"** Senator Harry Reid, Press Conference (The Capitol, Washington, D.C., February 11, 2009). ♁ **"'3.5 million to 4 million jobs is a lot of jobs'"** Chuck Schumer, *Meet the Press*, NBC, March 8, 2009. ♁ **"'that's before you get to the financial recovery approach'"** Larry Summers, *Meet the Press*, NBC, January 25, 2009. ♁ **"'And I think that we're on track to do that'"** David Axelrod, *The Rachel Maddow Show*, MSNBC, February 9, 2002. ♁ **"'would be more than paid for by spending reductions'"** Matthew Benjamin, "Obama's Small Spending Limits, Big Tax Cuts May Worsen Deficit," *bloomberg.com*, July 29, 2008, http://www.bloomberg.com/apps/news ?sid=anGhCq5adqhU&pid=newsarchive. ♁ **"projected at a record $1.47 trillion"** Andrew Taylor, "White House Predicts Record $1.47 Trillion Deficit," *news.yahoo.com*, July 23, 2009, http://news.yahoo.com/s/ap/20100723/ap_on_bi_ge/us_budget_deficit_2. ♁ **"weren't even bothering to look for jobs"** U.S. Department of Labor, Bureau of Labor Statistics, "Employment Situation Summary," news release, August 6, 2010, http://www.bls.gov/news.release/empsit.nr0.htm.

PAGE 132: "'[the stimulus package] would work this well'" Ralph R. Reiland, "Obamanomics Thumped," *Pittsburgh Tribune-Review*, November 9, 2009, http://www.pittsburghlive.com/x/pittsburghtrib/opinion/s_651934.html. ♁ **"lost 221,000 jobs in June"** U.S. Department of Labor, Bureau of Labor Statistics, "Employment, Hours, and Earnings From the Current Employment Statistics Survey (National)," in *Databases, Tables, and Calculators, bls.gov*, accessed August 9, 2010. ♁ **"kept the unemployment rate from rising to 15 percent"** President Barack Obama, "Remarks by the President at a Town Hall Meeting on the Economy in Racine, Wisconsin," *whitehouse.gov*, June 30, 2010, http://www.whitehouse.gov/the-press-office/remarks-president-a-town-hall-meeting-economy-racine-wisconsin. ♁ **"a 1 percentage point impact on the unemployment rate"** Michael J. Boskin, "Obama's Economic Fish Stories," *Wall Street Journal*, July 21, 2010, http://online.wsj.com/article/SB1000142405 2748703724104575378751776758256.html. ♁ **"'OBAMA VOWS TO SLASH WASTEFUL U.S. SPENDING'"** Ross Colvin and Jeff Mason, "WRAPUP 5—Obama Vows to Slash Wasteful U.S. Spending," *forbes.com*, November 25, 2008, http://www.forbes.com/feeds/afx/2008/11/25/afx5743464.html. ♁ **"'folks laid off in this recession who really do need help'"** Alister Bull, "Obama Casts Republicans As Party of the Rich," *news.yahoo.com*, July 17, 2010, http://news.yahoo.com/s/nm/20100717/ts_nm/us_obama_republicans_3.

PAGE 133: "'for a total of 99 weeks'" Marc Lifsher, "California's Job Climate Stagnant in June," *Los Angeles Times*, July 17, 2010, http://www.latimes.com/business/la-fi-caljobs-20100717,0,3147798.story. ♁ **"national wealth increased by at least $9 trillion"** Board of Governors of the Federal Reserve System, *Flow of Funds Accounts of the United States: Annual Flows and Outstandings 1975–1984* (Washington, D.C.: Federal Reserve, 2010), http://www.federalreserve.gov/releases/z1/Current/annuals/a1975-1984.pdf. *See also:* Board of Governors of the Federal Reserve System, *Flow of Funds Accounts of the United States: Annual Flows and Outstandings 1985–1994* (Washington, D.C.: Federal Reserve, 2010), 95, http://www.federalreserve.gov/releases/z1/Current/annuals/a1985–1994.pdf.

PAGE 134: "'creation of the federal highway system in the 1950s'" Tom Barnes, "Rendell Cheers Obama's Huge Public Works Plan," *Pittsburgh Post-Gazette*, December 7, 2008, http://www.post-gazette.com/pg/08342/933401-178.stm#ixzz0uJuVQVJ2. ♁ **"'lay a solid foundation for future growth'"** Matthew Borghese, "Obama Pushes 'American Recovery and Reinvestment Plan' in Weekly Address," *allheadlinenews.com*, January 11, 2009, http://www.allheadlinenews.com/articles/7013672889#ixzz0uKHj6d6M. ♁ **"'my commitment to cover every single American'"** Aliza Marcus, "Obama Signs Children's Health-Care Expansion As 'Down Payment,'" *bloomberg.com*, February 4, 2009, http://www.bloomberg.com/apps/news?pid=newsarchive &sid=aKDDNupaESoo&refer=home. ♁ **"'a number no one thought about a year ago'"** Jackie Calmes and Brian Knowlton, "Biden Defends Expanded Recovery Plan," *New York Times*, December 21, 2008, http://www.nytimes.com/2008/12/22/us/politics/22stimulus.html. ♁ **"or 6 times the rate of inflation (21 percent)"** U.S. Department of Labor, Bureau of Labor Statistics, "Consumer Price Index," *bls.gov*, July 16, 2010. ♁ **"Federal Spending Increases from 2001 to 2009"** Brian Riedl, "Federal Spending by the Numbers 2009," (report, The Heritage Foundation, Washington, D.C., 2009), 5, http://www.heritage.org/research/reports/2009/07/federal-spending-by-the-numbers-2009. ✪ **"consuming 25 percent of national output, up from 20 percent"** U.S. Office of Management and Budget, *Mid-Season Review: Budget for the U.S. Government: Fiscal Year 2010* (Washington, D.C. White House, 2010), 20, http://www.gpoaccess.gov/usbudget/fy10/pdf/10msr.pdf. ✪ **"not be enough to cover the $1.5 trillion budget deficit"** David Jackson, "Obama On Deficit and Debt Critics: 'I'm Calling Their Bluff,'" *USA Today*, June 28, 2010, http://content.usatoday.com/communities/theoval/post/2010/06/obama-signals-coming-battle-over-debt/1.

PAGE 135: "'to get the deficit down to 3 percent of GDP'" Roberton Williams and Rosanne Altshuler, "5 Myths About Your Taxes," *Washington Post*, April 4, 2010, http://www.washingtonpost.com/wp-dyn/content/article/2010/04/01/AR2010040102287.html. *See also:* Rosanne Altshuler, Katherine Lim, and Roberton Williams, *Desperately Seeking Revenue* (Washington, D.C.: Tax Policy Center, 2010), http://www.taxpolicycenter.org/UploadedPDF/412018 _seeking_revenue.pdf. ✪ **"run the federal government for less than six months"** "The 2% Solution," *Wall Street Journal*, February 26, 2009, http://online.wsj.com/article/SB123561551065378405.html. *See also:* U.S. Office of Management and Budget, "Table 1.1," in *President's Budget: Historical Tables* (Washington, D.C.: White House, 2010), http://www.whitehouse.gov/omb/budget/Historicals/. ✪ **"a new top tax rate of 77 percent"** Roberton Williams and Rosanne Altshuler, "5 Myths About Your Taxes," *Washington Post*, April 4, 2010, http://www.washingtonpost.com/wp-dyn/content/article/2010/04/01/. ✪ **"would have to reach at least 18 percent"** "Europe's VAT Lessons," *Wall Street Journal*, April 15, 2010, http://online.wsj.com/article/SB10001424052702304198004575172190620528592.html. ✪ **"rising from 17.5 percent to 20 percent next year"** Reuters, "UK's Osborne Raises VAT to 20 Pct From 2011," *reuters.com*, June 22, 2010, http://www.reuters.com/article/idUSLDE65K0SX20100622. ✪ **"'extra spending cuts or income tax rises'"** Reuters, "UK's Osborne Raises VAT to 20 Pct From 2011," *reuters.com*, June 22, 2010, http://www.reuters.com/article/idUSLDE65K0SX20100622. ✪ **"'will have a negative effect on growth'"** Timothy Geithner, interview by Jake Tapper, *This Week*, ABC, July 25, 2010, http://abcnews.go.com/ThisWeek/week-transcript-geithner/story?id=11245464. ✪ **"grew $500 billion faster than inflation"** U.S. Office of Management and Budget, "Table 1.3," in *President's Budget: Historical Tables* (Washington, D.C.: White House, 2010), http://www.whitehouse.gov/omb/budget/Historicals/. ✪ **"studied the effects of the VAT in other countries"** Randall G. Holcombe, "The Value Added Tax: Too Costly for the United States," (working paper, Mercatus Center, George Mason University, Fairfax, VA, 2010), http://mercatus.org/sites/default/files/publication/VAT.Holcombe.pdf.

PAGE 136: "'very large and persistent positive output effects'" Christina D. Romer and David H. Romer, "The Macroeconomic Effects of Tax Changes: Estimates Based on a New Measure of Fiscal Shocks," (paper, University of California, Berkeley, 2007), http://www.econ.berkeley.edu/~cromer/RomerDraft307.pdf. ✪ **"'dealt another contradictory blow to the economy'"** Christina Romer, "Great Depression," (forthcoming entry in *Encyclopedia Britannica*, University of California, Berkeley, 2003), http://elsa.berkeley.edu/~cromer/great_depression.pdf. ✪ **"called for $42 *trillion* of government spending"** U.S. Office of Management and Budget, "Summary Tables," in *United States Budget, Fiscal Year 2010* (Washington, D.C.: White House, 2009), http://www.gpoaccess.gov/usbudget/fy10/pdf/budget/summary.pdf. ✪ **"national debt would rise by $9 trillion"** U.S. Congress, Congressional Budget Office, "Table 1.3," in *An Analysis of the President's Budgetary Proposals for Fiscal Year 2010* (Washington, D.C.: Congressional Budget Office, 2009), http://www.cbo.gov/ftpdocs/102xx/doc10296/06-16-AnalysisPresBudget_forWeb.pdf. ✪ **"PLEASE DON'T TELL OBAMA WHAT COMES AFTER A TRILLION"** *zazzle.com*, "Please Don't Tell Obama Bumper Sticker," http://www.zazzle.com/please_dont_tell_obama_bumper_sticker-128608622398518176.

PAGE 137: "'problems that have been put off for a very long time'" Barack Obama, interview by the *New York Times*, "Obama's Interview Aboard Air Force One," *New York Times*, March 7, 2009, http://www.nytimes.com/2009/03/08/us/politics/08obama-text.html. ✪ **"Over the following decade, it proposes to:"** Brian Riedl, "Obama Raises Taxes and Doubles the National Debt," *heritage.org*, March 9, 2010, http://www.heritage.org/Research/Reports/2010/03/Obama-Budget-Raises-Taxes-and-Doubles-the-National-Debt. *See also:* Congressional Budget Office, "Table 1.2," in *CBO's Estimate of the President's Budget* (Washington, D.C.: Congressional Budget Office, 2010), http://www.cbo.gov/ftpdocs/112xx/doc11280/Chapter1.shtml#1045449. ✪ **"Chart: Real vs. Claimed Deficits"** *For real deficits see:* Historical Debt Outstanding—Annual, "U.S. Department of the Treasury, Bureau of Public Debt," http://www.treasurydirect.gov/govt/

reports/pd/histdebt/histdebt.htm, *For claimed deficits, see:* Historical Tables of the U.S. Government, "U.S. Government Printing Office," http://www.gpoaccess.gov/usbudget/fy10/pdf/hist.pdf, 22.

PAGE 138: "some point in the future, never the present" Brian Reidl, "All the President's Tax Gimmicks," *heritage.org*, March 16, 2010, http://www.heritage.org/Research/Commentary/2010/03/All-the-Presidents-Budget-Gimmicks. ὂ **"than every president before him . . . combined"** Brian Reidl, "Obama Budget Raises Taxes and Doubles the National Debt," *heritage.org*, March 9, 2010, http://www.heritage.org/Research/Reports/2010/03/Obama-Budget-Raises-Taxes-and-Doubles-the-National-Debt. ὂ **"I'M SERIOUSLY SERIOUS"** Jackie Calmes, "Obama to Seek Spending Freeze to Trim Deficits," *New York Times*, January 25, 2010, http://www.nytimes.com/2010/01/26/us/politics/26budget.html.

PAGE 139: "OBAMA TO SEEK SPENDING FREEZE TO TRIM DEFICITS" Jackie Calmes, "Obama to Seek Spending Freeze to Trim Deficits," *New York Times*, January 25, 2010, http://www.nytimes.com/2010/01/26/us/politics/26budget.html.

Chapter 10: The Truth

PAGE 143: "spent more money than it has taken in" U.S. Office of Management and Budget, "Table 1.1," in *President's Budget: Historical Tables* (Washington, D.C.: White House, 2010), http://www.whitehouse.gov/omb/budget/Historicals/. ὂ **"Over the last 50 years . . . deficits in nine of them"** U.S. Office of Management and Budget, "Table 1.1," in *President's Budget: Historical Tables* (Washington, D.C.: White House, 2010), http://www.whitehouse.gov/omb/budget/Historicals/.

PAGE 144: "Chart: The $3.8 Trillion Budget" Shan Carter and Amanda Cox, "Obama's 2011 Budget Proposal: How It's Spent," *The New York Times*, February 2, 2010, http://www.nytimes.com/interactive/2010/02/01/us/budget.html.

PAGE 145: "Chart: Growing Faster than the Population" Historical Debt Outstanding—Annual, "U.S. Department of the Treasury, Bureau of Public Debt," http://www.treasurydirect.gov/govt/reports/pd/histdebt/histdebt.htm, *all debt adjusted for inflation to 2000 dollars.* ὂ **"'just 2 years ago'"** U.S. Government Accountability Office, *The Federal Government's Long-Term Fiscal Outlook: January 2010 Update* (Washington, D.C.: Government Accountability Office, 2010), http://www.gao.gov/products/GAO-10-468SP.

PAGE 146: "'largest single expenditure in the federal budget'" U.S. Government Accountability Office, *Understanding the Primary Components of the Annual Financial Report of the Government of the United States* (Washington, D.C.: Government Accountability Office, 2009), http://www.gao.gov/new.items/d09946sp.pdf. ὂ **"'political support for the tough decisions ahead'"** Editorial, "Waste, Fraud and the Truth," *New York Times*, May 24, 2010, http://www.nytimes.com/2010/05/25/opinion/25tue1.html.

PAGE 147: "interest we pay on the money we have to borrow to meet those commitments" U.S. Office of Management and Budget, "Summary Tables," in *United States Budget, Fiscal Year 2011* (Washington, D.C.: White House, 2010), http://www.whitehouse.gov/omb/budget/fy2011/assets/tables.pdf. ὂ **"2010 Selected Entitlement Spending"** Brian Riedl, *Federal Spending by the Numbers: 2010* (Washington, D.C.: Heritage Foundation, 2010), 5. ὂ **"'or do some combination of that'"** Dan Balz, "Obama's Debt Commission Warns of Fiscal 'Cancer,'" *Washington Post*, July 12, 2010, http://www.washingtonpost.com/wp-dyn/content/article/2010/07/11/AR2010071101956 _pf.html. ὂ **"Chart: Freebies vs. Freedom"** Brian Riedl, "Defense Spending Has Declined While Entitlement Spending Has Increased," *The Heritage Foundation's 2010 Budget Chart Book*, http://www.heritage.org/budgetchartbook/defense-entitlement-spending.

PAGE 148: "Chart: America's Shifting Priorities" D. Andrew Austin and Mindy R. Levit, "Trends in Discretionary Spending," *The Congressional Research Service*, February 22, 2010, http://assets.opencrs.com/rpts/RL34424_20100222.pdf. ὂ **"one-third went toward mandatory programs"** U.S. Office of Management and Budget, "Table 8.3," in *President's Budget: Historical Tables* (Washington, D.C.: White House, 2010), http://www.whitehouse.gov/omb/budget/Historicals/. ὂ **"(with defense comprising just one-fifth of all spending)"** U.S. Office of Management and Budget, "Table 8.3," in *President's Budget: Historical Tables* (Washington, D.C.: White House, 2010), http://www.whitehouse.gov/omb/budget/Historicals/. ὂ **"projected to double to 20 percent of GDP"** U.S. Congress. Congressional Budget Office, "Table 1.2," in *The Long-Term Budget Outlook*, 111th Cong., 1st Sess., 2009, Pub. No. 3216, http://www.cbo.gov/ftpdocs/102xx/doc10297/06-25-LTBO.pdf.

PAGE 149: "Chart: Change Is Not Always Good" Brian Riedl, "Federal Spending by the Numbers 2010," *The*

Heritage Foundation, June 1, 2010, http://www.heritage.org/research/reports/2010/06/Federal-Spending-by-the-Numbers-2010.

PAGE 150: "about 8.6 percent of our total revenue" U.S. Government Accountability Office, *The Federal Government's Financial Health: A Citizen's Guide to the Financial Report of the United States Government* (Washington, D.C.: Government Accountability Office, 2009), http://www.gao.gov/financial/fy2009/09frusg.pdf. *See also:* U.S. Office of Management and Budget, "Table 1.1" and "Table 3.1," in *President's Budget: Historical Tables* (Washington, D.C.: White House, 2010), http://www.whitehouse.gov/omb/budget/Historicals/. ♁ **"reaching 20 percent of revenue in 2020"** Jed Graham, "U.S. Debt Shock May Hit in 2018, Maybe As Soon As 2013: Moody's," *Investor's Business Daily*, May 5, 2010, http://www.investors.com/NewsAndAnalysis/Article.aspx?id=532490. ♁ **"add $845 billion in deficits"** U.S. Office of Management and Budget, "Table 3.1," in *Economic and Budget Analyses* (Washington, D.C.: White House, 2010), http://www.whitehouse.gov/omb/budget/fy2011/assets/econ_analyses.pdf. ♁ **"over 21 percent in 1980"** Board of Governors of the Federal Reserve System, "Bank Prime Loan Rate Changes: Historical Dates of Changes and Rates," *Federal Reserve Bank of St. Louis*, accessed July 12, 2010, http://research.stlouisfed.org/fred2/data/PRIME.txt.

PAGE 151: "set to exceed $20 trillion by 2020" U.S. Congress. Congressional Budget Office, "Table 1.2," in *An Analysis of the President's Budgetary Proposals for Fiscal Year 2011*, 111th Cong., 2nd Sess., 2010, Pub. No. 4111, http://www.cbo.gov/ftpdocs/112xx/doc11280/03-24-apb.pdf. ♁ **"record $45 billion in 2009"** Neil Irwin, "Federal Reserve Earned $45 Billion in 2009," *Washington Post*, January 12, 2010, http://www.washingtonpost.com/wp-dyn/content/article/2010/01/11/AR2010011103892.html. ♁ **"Chart: Putting Interest into Perspective"** Brian Riedl, "The Monthly Interest on the National Debt Is More Than Most Program Spending," *The Heritage Foundation's 2010 Budget Chart Book*, http://www.heritage.org/budgetchartbook/interest-spending.

PAGE 152: "Chart: Throwing Our Money Away" Brian Riedl, "Net Interest Spending Will Quadruple Over the Next Decade," *The Heritage Foundation's 2010 Budget Chart Book*, http://www.heritage.org/budgetchartbook/budget-net-interest-spending. ♁ **"CCC is the lowest rating offered by S&P"** Simon Rogers, "How Fitch, Moody's, and S&P Rate Each Country's Credit Rating," *The Guardian*, June 14, 2010, http://www.guardian.co.uk/news/datablog/2010/apr/30/credit-ratings-country-fitch-moodys-standard#.

PAGE 153: "ratings downgraded, all in April 2010" Bettina Wassener and Matthew Saltmarsh, "Fitch Downgrades Spain's Credit Rating," *DealBook blog at nytimes.com*, June 1, 2010, http://dealbook.blogs.nytimes.com/2010/06/01/fitch-downgrades-spains-credit-rating/. ♁ **"bailout package to calm nervous investors"** Matthew Craft, "Who Would Dare Downgrade U.S. Debt?" *forbes.com*, May 10, 2010, http://www.forbes.com/2010/05/10/rating-debt-us-greece-markets-bonds.html. ♁ **"S&P Credit Ratings and Outlooks"** Simon Rogers, "How Fitch, Moody's, and S&P Rate Each Country's Credit Rating," *The Guardian*, June 14, 2010, http://www.guardian.co.uk/news/datablog/2010/apr/30/credit-ratings-country-fitch-moodys-standard#zoomed-picture. ♁ **"Public Debt to GDP"** U.S. Central Intelligence Agency, "Country Comparison: Public Debt," in *The World Factbook* (Washington, D.C.: CIA, 2010), https://www.cia.gov/library/publications/the-world-factbook/rankorder/2186rank.html. ♁ **"Cost of Debt"** Buttonwood, "The Debt Trap: Ranking the Suspects," *Buttonwood's Notebook blog at economist.com*, February 1, 2010, http://www.economist.com/blogs/buttonwood/2010/02/debt_crisis_-_how_countries_rank.

PAGE 154: "slower than the Obama administration projects" James Quinn, "U.S. Credit Rating at Risk, Moody's Warns," *Telegraph*, February 4, 2010, http://www.telegraph.co.uk/finance/economics/7153180/US-credit-rating-at-risk-Moodys-warns.html. ♁ **"'first step toward solving them'"** Weiss Ratings, "Weiss Ratings Challenges S&P, Moody's, and Fitch to Downgrade Long-Term U.S. Debt," news release, May 10, 2010, http://www.weissratings.com/news-releases/general-2010-05-10.html. ♁ **"'beyond that we can not be so certain'"** Jed Graham, "U.S. Debt Shock May Hit in 2018, Maybe As Soon As 2013: Moody's," *Investor's Business Daily*, May 5, 2010, http://www.investors.com/NewsAndAnalysis/Article.aspx?id=532490.

PAGE 155: "stock price was already under four dollars" Edward Wyatt, "Enron's Many Strands: Warning Signs; Credit Agencies Waited Months to Voice Doubts About Enron," *New York Times*, February 8, 2002, http://www.nytimes.com/2002/02/08/business/enron-s-many-strands-warning-signs-credit-agencies-waited-months-voice-doubt.html. ♁ **"needs to raise 64 percent of its GDP"** Fiscal Affairs Department of the International Monetary Fund, *Fiscal Monitor, May 14th, 2010: Navigating the Fiscal Challenges Ahead* (Washington, D.C.: IMF, 2010), http://www.imf.org/external/pubs/ft/fm/2010/fm1001.pdf.

PAGE 156: "adjustments of less than 10 percent of their GDP" Fiscal Affairs Department of the International Monetary Fund, *Fiscal Monitor*, May 14, 2010: Navigating the Fiscal Challenges Ahead (Washington, D.C.: IMF, 2010), http://www.imf.org/external/pubs/ft/fm/2010/fm1001.pdf.

PAGE 157: "likely to reach $300 billion" Elizabeth McNichol and Nicholas Johnson for the Center on Budget and Policy Priorities, "Recession Continues to Batter State Budgets; State Responses Could Slow Recovery," *cbpp.org*, May 27, 2010, http://www.cbpp.org/cms/index.cfm?fa=view&id=711. ŏ **"'It would be enormously destructive'"** Kevin Sack, "Medicaid Cut Places States in Budget Bind," *New York Times*, June 7, 2010, http://www.nytimes.com/2010/06/08/us/08medicaid.html. ŏ **"'both cruel and counterproductive'"** Kevin Sack, "Medicaid Cut Places States in Budget Bind," *New York Times*, June 7, 2010, http://www.nytimes.com/2010/06/08/us/08medicaid.html. ŏ **"gap that will now likely be over $10 billion"** Kevin Sack, "Medicaid Cut Places States in Budget Bind," *New York Times*, June 7, 2010, http://www.nytimes.com/2010/06/08/us/08medicaid.html. ŏ **"compared with $172,000 for Kazakh debt"** Jim Christie and Peter Henderson, "California Debt Rating Cut as Cash Crunch Looms," *Reuters*, January 13, 2010, http://www.reuters.com/article/idUSTRE60C5Z620100114.

PAGE 158: "Charts: The State of Our States" State Debt Chart by Chris Edwards, The Cato Institute, with data from *Federal Reserve Board*, "Flow of Funds Accounts of the United States," March 1, 2010, Table D.3, http://www.federalreserve.gov/releases/z1/Current/, Note: 2010 data is estimated. State and Local Spending Chart by by Chris Edwards, The Cato Institute, with data from the *Bureau of Economic Analysis*, "National Income and Product Accounts," Table 3.3, http://www.bea.gov/national/nipaweb/index.asp.

PAGE 159: "the two richest men, Bill Gates and Warren Buffett" "Gates, Buffett to Megarich: Give It Up," *msnbc.msn.com*, June 16, 2010, http://www.msnbc.msn.com/id/37731478/ns/us_news-giving/. ŏ **"three months of interest on our national debt"** The Heritage Foundation, "The Monthly Interest Payment on the National Debt Is More Than Most Program Spending," *heritage.org*, accessed July 13, 2010, http://www.heritage.org/budgetchartbook/interest-spending. ŏ **"pensions are 'defined benefit' plans"** Andrew G. Biggs, *The Market Value of Public-Sector Pension Deficits* (Washington, D.C.: American Enterprise Institute, 2010), http://www.aei.org/docLib/2010RPOno1g.pdf.

PAGE 160: "return factored in by state pensions is 8 percent a year" Andrew G. Biggs, *The Market Value of Public-Sector Pension Deficits* (Washington, D.C.: American Enterprise Institute, 2010), http://www.aei.org/docLib/2010RPOno1g.pdf. ŏ **"the pension would be fully funded!"** Andrew G. Biggs, *The Market Value of Public-Sector Pension Deficits* (Washington, D.C.: American Enterprise Institute, 2010), http://www.aei.org/docLib/2010RPOno1g.pdf. ŏ **"'zero probability that benefits will not be paid in full'"** Andrew G. Biggs, *The Market Value of Public-Sector Pension Deficits* (Washington, D.C.: American Enterprise Institute, 2010), http://www.aei.org/docLib/2010RPOno1g.pdf. ŏ **"massive cuts in everything from education to health care"** Mary Williams Walsh, "In Budget Crisis, States Take Aim at Pension Costs," *New York Times*, June 19, 2010, http://www.nytimes.com/2010/06/20/business/20pension.html. ŏ **"reforms to existing pensions as well as future ones"** Mary Williams Walsh, "In Budget Crisis, States Take Aim at Pension Costs," *New York Times*, June 19, 2010, http://www.nytimes.com/2010/06/20/business/20pension.html.

PAGE 161: "receive an annual city pension of $76,440" Barbara Henry, "Carlsbad: Council to Reduce Police Retirement Benefits," *North County Times*, May 25, 2010, http://www.nctimes.com/news/local/carlsbad/article_6d50d589-bfab-56ef-820d-59123c42bc83.html. ŏ **"'payments to the pension fund—from the same pension fund'"** Danny Hakim, "State Plan Makes Fund Both Borrower and Lender," *New York Times*, June 11, 2010, http://www.nytimes.com/2010/06/12/nyregion/12pension.html. ŏ **"pay it back between 4.5 and 5.5 percent"** Danny Hakim, "State Plan Makes Fund Both Borrower and Lender," *New York Times*, June 11, 2010, http://www.nytimes.com/2010/06/12/nyregion/12pension.html.

PAGES 162–163: "Chart: A Global Pandemic" "Global Debt Comparison," *The Economist*, http://buttonwood.economist.com/content/gdc.

PAGE 164: "something that he calls a 'debt super cycle'" Garfield Reynolds and Wes Goodman, "U.S.'s $13 Trillion Debt Poised to Overtake GDP: Chart of the Day," *bloomberg.com*, June 4, 2010, http://www. bloomberg.com/news/2010-06-04/u-s-s-13-trillion-debt-poised-to-overtake-weigh-down-gdp-chart-of-day.html. ŏ **"Chart: Entering the Debt Super Cycle"** Garfield Reynolds and Wes Goodman, "U.S.'s $13 Trillion Debt

Poised to Overtake GDP," *Bloomberg.com*, June 4, 2010, http://www.bloomberg.com/news/2010-06-04/u-s-s-13-trillion-debt-poised-to-overtake-weigh-down-gdp-chart-of-day.html. ♁ **"Chart: The Wrong Kind of Growth"** Brian Riedl, "Net Interest Spending Will Quadruple Over the Next Decade," *The Heritage Foundation's 2010 Budget Chart Book*, http://www.heritage.org/budgetchartbook/growth-federal-spending.

PAGE 165: "Chart: Good Government, Bad Government" Chris Edwards, The Cato Institute, based on data from *The Bureau of Economic Analysis*, Table 1.1.10 "Percentage Share of Gross Domestic Product," http://www.bea.gov/national/nipaweb/TableView.asp?SelectedTable=14&Freq=Qtr&FirstYear=2008&LastYear=2010. ♁ **"'postponing them will only make them more difficult'"** Benjamin S. Bernanke, "Economic Challenges: Past, Present, and Future" (speech, Dallas Regional Chamber, Dallas, TX, April 7, 2010), http://www.federalreserve.gov/newsevents/speech/20100407a.htm.

PAGE 167: "Chart: The Cost of Delay" Douglas Elmendorf, "Statement before the United States Senate Committee on the Budget," The Long Term Budget Outlook, *Congressional Budget Office*, July 16, 2009, 20, http://www.cbo.gov/ftpdocs/104xx/doc10455/07-16-Long-TermOutlook_Testimony.pdf. ♁ **"'effect of changes in reserve requirement ratios'"** Federal Reserve Bank of St. Louis, "Series: BASE, St. Louis Adjusted Monetary Base," *Federal Reserve Bank of St. Louis*, accessed July 14, 2010, http://research.stlouisfed.org/fred2/series/BASE. ♁ **"Chart: The Next Bubble to Burst"** Federal Reserve Bank of St. Louis, "Series: BASE, St. Louis Adjusted Monetary Base," *Federal Reserve Bank of St. Louis*, accessed July 14, 2010, http://research.stlouisfed.org/fred2/series/BASE.

PAGE 168: "State and local debt: $2.5 trillion" Kevin Williamson, "The Other National Debt," *National Review*, June 21, 2010, http://article.nationalreview.com/436123/the-other-national-debt/kevin-williamson?page=1. ♁ **"State and local pensions (unfunded): $3 trillion"** Kevin Williamson, "The Other National Debt," *National Review*, June 21, 2010, http://article.nationalreview.com/436123/the-other-national-debt/kevin-williamson?page=1. ♁ **"Social security: $7.7 trillion"** Bruce Bartlett, "The 81% Tax Increase," *forbes.com*, May 15, 2009, http://www.forbes.com/2009/05/14/taxes-social-security-opinions-columnists-medicare.html. ♁ **"Medicare: $38 trillion"** Bruce Bartlett, "The 81% Tax Increase," *forbes.com*, May 15, 2009, http://www.forbes.com/2009/05/14/taxes-social-security-opinions-columnists-medicare.html.

PAGE 169: "'Not to speak is to speak. Not to act is to act.'" Epigraph. James H. Cone, "Theology's Great Sin: Silence in the Face of White Supremacy, in *Theology in Global Context: Essays in Honor of Robert Cummings Neville*, ed. Amos Yong and Peter G. Heltzel (New York: T&T Clark, 2004), 339.

Chapter 11: The Cover-Up

PAGE 170: "they lose, and you take their money'" Andru Luvisi, *practicenotincluded.com*, http://www.practicenotincluded.com/pni/three.card.monte.html.

PAGE 171: "'also are excluded from the cost of government operations'" U.S. Government Accountability Office, *Understanding the Primary Components of the Annual Financial Report of the United States Government* (Washington, D.C.: Government Accountability Office, 2010), http://www.gao.gov/new.items/d05958sp.pdf.

PAGE 172: "earmarked to pay future benefits" U.S. Government Accountability Office, *Understanding the Primary Components of the Annual Financial Report of the United States Government* (Washington, D.C.: Government Accountability Office, 2010), http://www.gao.gov/new.items/d05958sp.pdf.

PAGE 173: "Principles that are applied to public corporations were used" John Williams, "Commentary Number 282: Federal Government 2009 GAAP-Accounting," *shadowstats.com*, March 1, 2010, http://www.shadowstats.com/article/282-federal-2009-gaap-accounting.

PAGE 174: "'activities are considered off-budget'" U.S. Government Accountability Office, *Understanding the Primary Components of the Annual Financial Report of the United States Government* (Washington, D.C.: Government Accountability Office, 2010), http://www.gao.gov/new.items/d05958sp.pdf.

PAGE 175: "'and we're going to hold you to account'" Daniel Eisenberg, "Jail to the Chiefs?" *Time*, August 5, 2002, http://www.time.com/time/magazine/article/0,9171,333873, 00.html. ♁ **"'other than the Statements of Social Insurance'"** Gene L. Dodaro, *Statement of the Comptroller General of the United States*, (Washington, D.C.: Government Accountability Office, 2010), http://fms.treas.gov/fr/09frusg/09gao1.pdf.

PAGE 176: "currently totals about $8.6 trillion" U.S. Department of the Treasury, "Debt to the Penny and Who Holds It," *treasurydirect.gov*, accessed July 15, 2010, http://www.treasurydirect.gov/NP/BPDLogin?application=np. ♁ **"'*fiscal exposures* until payments are made'"** U.S. Government

Accountability Office, *Budget Issues: Accrual Budgeting Useful in Certain Areas but Does Not Provide Sufficient Information for Reporting on Our Nation's Longer-Term Fiscal Challenge*, (Washington, D.C.: Government Accountability Office, 2007), http://www.gao.gov/htext/d08206.html. ♁ **"currently totals about $8.6 trillion"** U.S. Department of the Treasury, "Debt to the Penny and Who Holds It," *treasurydirect.gov*, accessed July 15, 2010, http://www.treasurydirect.gov/NP/BPDLogin?application=np. ♁ **"currently equal about $4.5 trillion"** U.S. Department of the Treasury, "Debt to the Penny and Who Holds It," *treasurydirect .gov*, accessed July 15, 2010, http://www.treasurydirect.gov/NP/BPDLogin?application=np.

PAGE 177: "'government's finances than the budget does'" Bruce Bartlett, "It Doesn't Add Up," *National Review, April 10, 2002*, http://old.nationalreview.com/nrof_bartlett/Bartlett 041002.asp.

PAGES 178–179: "Chart: Government Accounting" "Understanding the Primary Components of the Annual Financial Report of the United States Government," *U.S. Government Accountability Office*, 32, http://www.gao.gov/new.items/d05958sp.pdf.

PAGE 181: "'The federal government will pay as it goes'" Speaker of the House Nancy Pelosi, speaking on the House floor on the passage of PAYGO legislation, on February 4, 2010, H.J. Res. 45, 111th Cong., 2nd sess., http://www.speaker.gov/newsroom/speeches?id=0241. ♁ **"'like families all across this great nation have to do'"** Congressman Baron Hill, "Hill's PAYGO Bill Soon to Become Law: Passed the House Today and Senate Last Week," press release, February 4, 2010, http://www.house.gov/apps/list/press/in09_hill/020410a.shtml. ♁ **"were limited to just 4 percent"** Veronique de Rugy, "Budget Gimmicks or the Destructive Art of Creative Accounting" (working paper, Mercatus Center, George Mason University, Washington, D.C., 2010), http://mercatus.org/sites/default/files/publication/Budget_Gimmick_WP1030.pdf. ♁ **"spent $700 billion *more* on entitlements than it cut or raised"** Brian Riedl, "PAYGO Is an Unworkable Gimmick," *heritage.org*, July 2, 2009, http://www.heritage.org/Research/Commentary/2009/07/PAYGO-is-an-unworkable-gimmick. ♁ **"'chasing higher spending with higher taxes'"** House. Republican Caucus Committee on the Budget, *Borrow-As-You-Go: Another Debt Ceiling Increase, Behind the Pay-Go Façade*, 111th Cong., 2nd Sess., 2010, http://www.house.gov/budget_republicans/press/2007/pr20100203paygo.pdf.

PAGE 182: "'we're going to have fiscal discipline'" President Barack Obama, "Renewing the American Economy," (speech, Cooper Union College, New York, NY, March 27, 2008), http://www.nytimes.com/2008/03/27/us/politics/27text-obama.html. ♁ **"more than 6 percent a year, Pay-Go can't touch it"** Brian Riedl, "PAYGO Is an Unworkable Gimmick," *heritage.org*, July 2, 2009, http://www.heritage.org/Research/Commentary/2009/07/PAYGO-is-an-unworkable-gimmick. ♁ **"counted only five years of spending"** Brian Riedl, "PAYGO Is an Unworkable Gimmick," *heritage.org*, July 2, 2009, http://www.heritage.org/Research/Commentary/2009/07/PAYGO-is-an-unworkable-gimmick. ♁ **"Deficit of Trust"** Pay-Go deficit Table *House Republican Caucus Committee on the Budget, Pay-As-You-Go: The Rule, or the Exception?*, 2, 111th Cong., 1st sess., 2009, http://www.house.gov/budget_republicans/press/2007/pr20090106 paygo.pdf.

PAGE 184: "and pass a budget by May 15" *Congressional Budget and Impoundment Control Act of 1974*, Public Law 93-344, 100th Cong., 1st sess. (July 12, 1974), http://www.rules.house.gov/archives/jcoc2y.htm. ♁ **"'finally passing a resolution on Oct. 9, 1990'"** The Committee for a Responsible Federal Budget, "Deadlines Are Made to Be Broken," *crfb.org*, March 9, 2010, http://crfb.org/blogs/deadlines-are-made-be-broken. ♁ **"'deficit and debt are spiraling out of control'"** The Committee for a Responsible Federal Budget, "Deadlines Are Made to Be Broken," *crfb.org*, March 9, 2010, http://crfb.org/blogs/deadlines-are-made-be-broken. ♁ **"'No longer will we hide its price'"** President Barack Obama, address to joint sessions of Congress, February 24, 2009, 111th Cong., 1st sess., http://www.whitehouse.gov/the_press_office/remarks-of-president-barack-obama-address-to-joint-session-of-congress/. ♁ **"Obama requested a $33 billon supplemental"** Mike Mount, "Gates Prods Congress on War Funding," *cnn.com*, June 16, 2010, http://www.cnn.com/2010/POLITICS/06/16/gates.war.funding/.

PAGE 185: "Chart: Emergency!" Veronique de Rugy, "The Never Ending Emergency: Trends in Supplemental Spending" (Policy Comment No. 18, Mercatus Center, George Mason University, Washington D.C., 2008), 5, http://mercatus.org/sites/default/files/publication/The_Never-Ending_Emergency.pdf. ♁ **"'from $1.3 billion in FY 1988 to $120 billion in FY 2007'"** Veronique de Rugy, "Budget Gimmicks or the Destructive Art of Creative Accounting" (working paper, Mercatus Center, George Mason University, Washington, D.C., 2010), http://mercatus.org/sites/default/files/publication/Budget_Gimmick_WP1030.pdf .

PAGE 186: "'payments to the public by $35 billion per year'" Congressional Research Service, *Supplemental*

Appropriations: Trends and Budgetary Impacts Since 1981, report prepared by Thomas L. Hungerford, 109th Cong., 1st sess., 2005, RL33134, http://assets.opencrs.com/rpts/RL33134_20051102.pdf. ō **"fund NASA and the EPA for an entire year"** U.S. Office of Management and Budget, "Summary Tables: Table S-11," in *United States Budget, Fiscal Year 2011* (Washington, D.C.: White House, 2010), http://www.whitehouse .gov/omb/budget/fy2011/assets/tables.pdf. ō **"payments were halted for six days"** Veronique de Rugy, "Budget Gimmicks or the Destructive Art of Creative Accounting" (working paper, Mercatus Center, George Mason University, Washington, D.C., 2010), http://mercatus.org/sites/default/files/publication/ Budget _Gimmick_WP1030.pdf.

PAGE 187: "'has not yet been performed'" U.S. Government Accountability Office, *The Federal Government's Financial Health: A Citizen's Guide to the Financial Report of the United States Government* (Washington, D.C.: Government Accountability Office, 2009), http://www.gao.gov/financial/ fy2009/09frusg.pdf. ō **"'individual budged cuts we'd actually approved'"** David A. Stockman, *The Triumph of Politics: Why the Reagan Revolution Failed* (New York: Avon, 1987), 135. ō **"cost $952 billion over the *next* ten years"** U.S. Congressional Budget Office, letter to the Chairman of the House Committee on Ways and Means, November 20, 2003, http://www.cbo.gov/ftpdocs/48xx/doc4808/11-20-MedicareLetter .pdf. ō **"a *permanent* new entitlement, not just a ten-year one"** Amy Fagan, "Estimates on Medicare Hit $2 Trillion: Prescription-Drug Benefit Promises 'Huge Costs,'" *Washington Times*, December 9, 2003. ō **"fund the program's commitments in perpetuity"** The Board of Trustees of the Federal Hospital Insurance and Federal Supplementary Medical Insurance Trust Funds, *2009 Annual Report of the Board of Trustees of the Federal Hospital Insurance and Federal Supplementary Medical Insurance Trust Funds* (Washington, D.C.: Federal Hospital Insurance and Federal Supplementary Medical Insurance Trust Funds, 2009), http://www.cms.gov/ReportsTrustFunds/downloads/tr2009.pdf.

PAGE 188: "they would have to close the Washington Monument" Gordon Tullock, Arthur Seldon, and Gordon L. Brady, *Government Failure: A Primer in Public Choice* (Washington, D.C.: Cato Institute, 2002), 60.

PAGE 189: "spend $38 million on iPods for schoolchildren" William Ahern, "In a New Low for Government Service, Michigan Threatens to Let the People Rot," *taxfoundation.org*, April 20, 2007, http://www .taxfoundation.org/news/show/22350.html. ō **"'a stunt designed to gain public support for raising taxes'"** Joseph Henchman, "California Governor Tries Washington Monument Ploy," *Tax Policy blog at taxfoundation.org*, January 15, 2008, http://www.taxfoundation.org/blog/show/22868.html. ō **"'or EMTs who die in the line of duty"** Tabor Now, "Abuse of Power in State Government Continues," news release, August 13, 2009, http://www.tabornow.com/news/27/27/RELEASE-Abuse-of-Power-in-State-Government-Continues. ō **"and lay off police officers and firefighters"** City of South Bend, Indiana, "Major Cuts to Hit Public Safety, Parks, All City Services," *ci.south-bend.in.us*, July 20, 2008, http://www.ci.south-bend.in.us/ news_detail_T13_R373.asp. ō **"'anarchy, literally, in the streets when the government shuts down'"** "Gov. Paterson in Stern Warning: Shutdown Over Budget Would Cause 'Unimaginable Chaos,' Crime in New York," *vosizneias.com*, June 10, 2010, http://www.vosizneias.com/57537/2010/06/10/albnay-ny-gov-paterson-in-stern-warning-shutdown-over-budget-would-cause-unimaginable-chaos-crime-in-new-york. ō **"'course in remedial economics at Allenwood Penitentiary'"** Michael Kinsley, "In the Land of the Magic Asterisk," *New York Times*, May 11, 1986, http://www.nytimes.com/1986/05/11/books/in-the-land-of-the-magic-asterisk.html.

PAGE 190: "debt limit was set at $43 billion" Brian Riedl, "Raise Debt Limit, but Attach Spending Caps," *heritage.org*, December 9, 2009, http://www.heritage.org/Research/Commentary/2009/12/Raise-Debt-Limit-but-Attach-Spending-Caps. ō **"291 times higher than the original 'limit'"** U.S. Office of Management and Budget, "Table 7.3," in *President's Budget: Historical Tables* (Washington, D.C.: White House, 2010), http://www.whitehouse.gov/omb/budget/Historicals/. ō **"Chart: Enabling Our Addiction"** Veronique de Rugy, "The Government's Endless Appetite for Spending," *Reason.com*, January 21, 2010, http://reason .com/archives/2010/01/21/the-governments-endless-appeti.

Chapter 12: The Murder Weapon

PAGE 193: "everything from government gridlock" "Special Interest Groups Not Entirely to Blame for Policy Malaise," *St. Petersburg Times*, October 7, 1992, http://news.google.com/newspapers?id=4PkNAAAAIBAJ. ō **"to overspending"** "Groups Spent 14,750 Hours Lobbying On Spending Limits: Backers Blame Special-Interest Opposition for Amendment's Defeat," *St. Paul Pioneer Press*, August 10, 2006. ō **"to stalled health-care reform"** Chuck Black, "Kennedy Denies Blame for Stalled Health Bill, Questions the Motives of His Critics," *Boston Globe*, June 22, 1996. ♁ **"to the demise of an energy tax"** Robert Siegel, "Special Interest Lobbyists 'Come Out of the Closet,'" *All Things Considered*, NPR, June 17, 1993. ♁ **"to the lack of immigration reform"** Editorial, "Congress to Blame for Immigration Fiasco," *San Jose Mercury News*, June 11, 1993. ♁ **"'THEY THRONG THE CORRIDORS OF THE CAPITOL'"** Associated Press, "'Lobbyist Swarm' Called Greatest in Years; They Throng the Corridors of the Capitol," *New York Times*, May 8, 1932.

PAGE 194: "lobbyists in Washington peaked at nearly 15,000" Open Secrets, "Lobbying Database," *opensecrets.org*, accessed August 11, 2010, http://www.opensecrets.org/lobby/index.php. ♁ **"yields on average $220 in return"** Bill Eggen, "Investments Can Yield More on K Street, Study Indicates," *Washington Post*, April 12, 2009, http://www.washingtonpost.com/wpdyn/content/article/2009/04/11/AR2009041102035.html. ♁ **"'from being lobbied by relatives'"** Matt Kelley and Peter Eisler, "Relatives Have 'Inside Track' in Lobbying for Tax Dollars," *USA Today*, October 17, 2006, http://www.usatoday.com/news/washington/2006-10-16-lobbyist-family-cover_x.htm.

PAGE 194: "mill around for a chance to bend his ear on an issue" Public Affairs Links, "A Brief History of Lobbying," *publicaffairslinks.co.uk*, accessed August 16, 2010, www.publicaffairslinks.co.uk/Help Guides/The History of Lobbying (guide1).doc. ♁ **"referred to one of the lobbies of the House of Commons"** Jesse Sheidlower, interviewed by Liane Hansen, "A Lobbyist by Any Other Name?" *Weekend Edition Sunday*, NPR, January 22, 2006, http://www.npr.org/templates/story/story.php?storyId=5167187.

PAGE 196: "urged them to send their own representatives" Peter Grier, "The Lobbyist Through History: Villainy and Virtue," *Christian Science Monitor*, September 28, 2009, http://www.csmonitor.com/layout/set/print/content/view/print/257882. ♁ **"congressman's son was just twelve years old"** Public Affairs Links, "A Brief History of Lobbying," *publicaffairslinks.co.uk*, accessed August 16, 2010, www.publicaffairslinks.co.uk/Help Guides/The History of Lobbying (guide1).doc. ♁ **"the Federal Regulation of Lobbying Act passed"** Peter Grier, "The Lobbyist Through History: Villainy and Virtue," *Christian Science Monitor*, September 28, 2009, http://www.csmonitor.com/layout/set/print/content/view/print/257882. ♁ **"'we're here for the people's interests'"** Frazier Moore, "Christiane Amanpour Takes On ABC News' 'This Week,'" *wtop.com*, August 1, 2010, http://www.wtop.com/?nid=114&sid=2016726.

PAGE 197: "blitz President Bush's plan to allow personal accounts for Social Security" American Federation of State, County, and Municipal Employees, "Lawmakers Vow to Oppose Privatizing Social Security," *afscme.org*, accessed August 11, 2010, http://www.afscme.org/11422.cfm. ♁ **"organized 224 events in sixty-five target districts in three weeks"** Americans United to Protect Social Security, press kit, *studentsforsocialsecurity.org*, June 16, 2005, http://www.studentsforsocialsecurity.org/learnmore/docs/socialsecurityjune16.pdf. ♁ **"supported by the American Federation of State, County, and Municipal Employees"** Brooks Jackson, "New Group, Old Habits," *factcheck.org*, January 27, 2006, http://www.factcheck.org/article372.html. ♁ **"'his new post is a return home'"** Chris Cilliza, "Woodhouse to DNC," *The Fix blog at washingtonpost.com*, June 20, 2008, http://voices.washingtonpost.com/thefix/eye-on-2008/woodhouse-to-dnc.html. ♁ **"'legislation coming out of the Obama White House'"** Americans United for Change, "About Us," *americansunitedforchange.org*, accessed August 11, 2010, http://www.americansunitedforchange.org/content/aboutus/.

PAGE 198: "'in no way constitutes a crisis'" National Committee to Preserve Social Security and Medicare, "Social Security Primer," *ncpssm.org*, accessed August 11, 2010, http://www.ncpssm.org/ss_primer/. ♁ **"white males are the ones who have easier jobs and can work longer"** Barbara Kennelly, interview by Scott Harris, *Counterpoint*, WPKN, Connecticut, July 12, 2010, http://www.ncpssm.org/video/bbk_wpkn.mp3. ♁ **"top recipient of money is Nancy Pelosi"** Open Secrets, "National Committee to Preserve Social Security: Recipients," *opensecrets.org*, accessed August 11, 2010, http://www.opensecrets.org/orgs/toprecips.php?id=D000000142&cycle=2010. ♁ **"launched to oppose the Vietnam War"** Gray Panthers, "Gray Panthers' Founding," *graypanthers.org*, accessed August 11, 2010, http://graypanthers.org/index.php?option=com_content&task=blogcategory&id=27&Itemid=17. ♁ **"'and democracy over institutions'"** Gray Panthers, "Mission/Vision/Values," *graypanthers.org*, Accessed August 11, 2010, http://graypanthers.org/index.php? option=com_content&task=view&id=32&Itemid=45. ♁ **"'from a progressive, even radical, point of view'"** Gray Panthers, "Gray Panthers Organize," *graypanthers.org*, accessed August 11, 2010, http://graypanthers.org/index.php?option=com_content&task =blogcategory&id=27&Itemid=17.

PAGE 199: "'and other measures that enhance the program'" Gray Panthers, "Issues: Family Security," *graypanthers.org*, accessed August 11, 2010, http://graypanthers.org/pdfs/Issues-Family_Seecurity.pdf. ♁ **"'discuss Medicare in our national or local groupings'"** Gray Panthers, "Issues: Health Care," *graypanthers.org*, accessed August 11, 2010, http://graypanthers.org/pdfs/Issues-Health.pdf. ♁ **"'through information, advocacy, and service'"** American Association of Retired Persons, "What We Do," *aarp.org*, accessed August 11, 2010, http://www.aarp.org/about-aarp/.

PAGE 200: "'its work to facilitate expanded coverage'" American Medical Association, "Access to Care," *ama-assn.org*, accessed August 11, 2010, http://www.ama-assn.org/ama/pub/advocacy/current-topics-advocacy/access-to-care.shtml/. ♁ **"using then-actor Ronald Reagan's voice"** Paul Krugman, "Raising the White Flag of Surrender—To Medicare," *The Conscience of a Liberal blog at nytimes.com*, October 3, 2008, http://krugman.blogs.nytimes.com/2008/10/03/raising-the-white-flag-of-surrender-to-medicare/?em. ♁ **"fought hard against any attempts to cut benefits"** Sam Stein, "American Medical Association Trying to Torpedo Health Care Reform Again," *huffingtonpost.com*, June 11, 2009, http://www.huffingtonpost.com/2009/06/11/american-medical-associat_n_214132.html. ♁ **"'and expand Medicare payments'"** Open Secrets, "American Medical Association: Summary," *opensecrets.org*, accessed August 11, 2010, http://www.opensecrets.org/orgs/summary.php?id=D000000068.

PAGE 201: "front organization for the pharmaceutical industry" AARP "Pulling Strings from Afar," *AARP Bulletin*, February 2003. ♁ **"'common sense solutions to the challenges of the future'"** The Seniors Coalition, "About," *seniors.org*, accessed August 11, 2010, http://www.senior.org/about.html. ♁ **"'the only way is through a Balanced Budget Amendment'"** *Balanced Budget Amendment to the Constitution*, H.J. Res.1, 104th Cong., 1st sess., Congressional Record 141, no. 27 (February 10, 1995), http://www.gpo.gov/fdsys/pkg/CREC-1995-02-10/html/CREC-1995-02-10-pt1-PgS2457.htm.

PAGE 202: "spent an average of $9,560 per lawmaker" "Lobbyists Report Spending $5,114,709, '69, 21% Over '68," *New York Times*, August 9, 1970. ♁ **"spent $6.4 million per lawmaker"** Open Secrets, "Lobbying Database," *opensecrets.org*, accessed August 16, 2010, http://www.opensecrets.org/lobby/index.php. Note: 2009 figure calculated by dividing total lobbying expenditures listed in database ($3.49 billion) and dividing by 535 (the number of members of the U.S. Congress).

PAGE 203: "'structure which is being built, but is by no means complete" Franklin Roosevelt, "Statement on Signing the Social Security Act," (speech, White House Cabinet Room, Washington, D.C., August 14, 1935), http://docs.fdrlibrary.marist.edu/odssast.html. ♁ **"'whether or not they have ever paid any Social Security taxes'"** Eileen Shanahan, "Senate Approves Benefits for All Aged 70 or More," *New York Times, March 9, 1966.*

PAGE 204: "'receive his benefit in dignity and self-respect'" David Kelley, *A Life of One's Own: Individual Rights and the Welfare State* (Washington, D.C.: Cato Institute, 1998), 140. ♁ **"'is in even worse shape than ours'"** Steven Erlanger, "Europeans Fear Crisis Threatens Liberal Benefits," *New York Times*, May 22, 2010, http://www.nytimes.com/2010/05/23/world/europe/23europe.html. ♁ **"'they're straight politics'"** Social Security Online, "Research Note #23: Luther Gulick Memorandum Re: Famous FDR Quote," *ssa.gov, July 21, 2005, http://www.ssa.gov/history/Gulick.html.* ♁ **"first person in history to receive regular monthly benefits"** Social Security Online, "Frequently Asked Questions," *ssa.gov*, accessed August 11, 2010, http://www.ssa.gov/history/hfaq.html.

PAGE 205: "'in a private way, and went to jail for it'" Paul Mallon, "News Behind the News," *Reading Eagle*, August 18, 1938. ♁ **"'total of $22,888.92 in Social Security benefits'"** Social Security Online, "Historical Background and Development of Social Security," *ssa.gov*, accessed August 12, 2010, http://www.ssa.gov/history/briefhistory3.html#idamay. ♁ **"'a structure . . . [that] is by no means complete'"** Franklin Roosevelt, "Statement on Signing the Social Security Act," (speech, White House Cabinet Room, Washington, D.C., August 14, 1935), http://docs.fdrlibrary.marist.edu/odssast.html. ♁ **"was age 65 or older"** Negative Population Growth, "Historical U.S. Population Growth by Year: 1900-1998," *npg.org*, accessed August 12, 2010, http://www.npg.org/facts/us_historical_pops.htm. ♁ **"had more than doubled to 12.8"** U.S. Bureau of the Census, "State and County QuickFacts," *census.gov*, accessed August 12, 2009, http://quickfacts.census.gov/qfd/states/00000.html. ♁ **"'nearly quadruple between 2000 and 2040'"** Urban Institute, "The U.S. Population Is Aging," *urban.org*, accessed August 12, 2010, http://www.urban.org/retirement_policy/agingpopulation.cfm.

PAGE 206: "gradually rise to 67 by 2025" Social Security Online, "Retirement Planner: Full Retirement Age," *ssa.gov*, accessed August 12, 2010, http://www.ssa.gov/retire2/retirechart.htm. ♁ **"earlier than most**

'experts' had been projecting" Mary Williams Walsh, "Social Security to See Payout Exceed Pay-In This Year," *New York Times*, March 24, 2010, http://www.nytimes.com/2010/03/25/business/economy/25social.html. ♁ **"because Congress already spent the money"** Mary Williams Walsh, "Social Security to See Payout Exceed Pay-In This Year," *New York Times*, March 24, 2010, http://www.nytimes.com/2010/03/25/business/economy/25social.html. ♁ **"the 'fund' will be completely exhausted"** Mary Williams Walsh, "Social Security to See Payout Exceed Pay-In This Year," *New York Times*, March 24, 2010, http://www.nytimes.com/2010/03/25/business/economy/25social.html. ♁ **"'rise in health care costs that plagues Medicare'"** Brian Reidl, "Facing America's Long-Term Entitlement Challenges Laid Out in the Financial Report of the United States Government," *heritage.org*, July 13, 2009, http://www.heritage.org/Research/Testimony/Facing-Americas-Long-Term-Entitlement-Challenges-Laid-Out-in-the-Financial-Report-of-the-United-States-Government.

PAGE 207: "in 1965, 70 Republicans voted in favor" Catharine Richert, "Dean Claims Social Security and Medicare Were Passed Without Republican Support," *politifact.com*, August 28, 2009, http://www.politifact.com/truth-o-meter/statements/2009/aug/28/howard-dean/dean-claims-social-security-and-medicare-were-pass/. ♁ **"'9 Republicans and 35 Democrats voted against it'"** Christine Hauser, "President Signs Medicare Bill Adding Prescription Drug Benefit," *New York Times*, December 8, 2003, http://www.nytimes.com/2003/12/08/politics/08CND-BUSH.html. ♁ **"'free the aged from the fear of financial hardship'"** United Press International, "Johnson Urges Medicare to Cost Many Billions," *Palm Beach Daily News*, January 8, 1965, http://news.google.com/newspapers?id=tPchAAAAIBAJ&sjid=hqEFAAAAIBAJ. ♁ **"'several billion dollars spread over this decade'"** United Press International, "Johnson Urges Medicare to Cost Many Billions," *Palm Beach Daily News*, January 8, 1965, http://news.google.com/newspapers?id=tPchAAAAIBAJ&sjid=hqEFAAAAIBAJ. ♁ **"calling it a '$6.5 billion bill'"** Associated Press, "LBJ Signs Medicare Bill: Truman Views Signing at Independence Home," *Spokesman-Review*, July 31, 1965, http://news.google.com/newspapers?id=WlQ0AAAAIBAJ&sjid=6gDAAAAIBAJ. ♁ **"a figure that even took projected inflation into account"** Steven Hayward and Erik Peterson, "The Medicare Monster: A Cautionary Tale," *Reason*, January 1993, http://reason.com/archives/1993/01/01/the-medicare-monster.

PAGE 208: "'estimates may prove to be quite a bit short of the mark'" William Clark, "U.S. Estimates Medicare Cost Far Too Low, Insurers Figure," *Chicago Tribune*, May 8, 1965. ♁ **"not $1.1 billion; it was $2.8 billion"** U.S. Office of Management and Budget, "Table 1.3," in *President's Budget: Historical Tables* (Washington, D.C.: White House, 2010), http://www.whitehouse.gov/omb/budget/Historicals/. ♁ **"wasn't 'several billion'; it was $13.2 billion"** U.S. Office of Management and Budget, "Table 1.3," in *President's Budget: Historical Tables* (Washington, D.C.: White House, 2010), http://www.whitehouse.gov/omb/budget/Historicals/. ♁ **"wasn't $12 billion; it was $98 billion"** U.S. Office of Management and Budget, "Table 3.2," in *President's Budget: Historical Tables* (Washington, D.C.: White House, 2010), http://www.whitehouse.gov/omb/budget/Historicals/. ♁ **"ten times more, even after factoring for inflation"** U.S. Office of Management and Budget, "Table 1.1," in *President's Budget: Historical Tables* (Washington, D.C.: White House, 2010), http://www.whitehouse.gov/omb/budget/Historicals/. ♁ **"'cost $131 billion more than originally forecast was reported today'"** "Big Increase in Medicare Costs Seen," *Chicago Tribune*, February 5, 1970. ♁ **"'reach 11.4 percent of GDP in 2083'"** Social Security and Medicare Board of Trustees, "A Summary of the 2010 Annual Reports," *ssa.gov*, August 5, 2010, http://www.ssa.gov/OACT/TRSUM/index.html. ♁ **"would have cost $1.63 trillion"** U.S. Department of Commerce, Bureau of Economic Analysis, "National Economic Accounts," *bea.gov*, accessed August 12, 2010, http://www.bea.gov/national/index.htm. ♁ **"an additional $10,000 a year in taxes"** Based on 115 million current U.S. households. U.S. Bureau of the Census, "Projections of Households by Type: 1995 to 2010, Series 1, 2, and 3," *census.gov*, accessed August 16, 2010, http://www.census.gov/population/projections/nation/hh-fam/table1n.txt.

PAGE 209: "finance most of the other 75 percent through tax revenues" U.S. Department of Health and Human Services, Centers for Medicare and Medicaid Services, "Medicare Part B Premium Costs in 2010," *medicare.gov*, November 2009, http://www.medicare.gov/Publications/Pubs/pdf/11444.pdf. ♁ **"will be spent on Medicare and Social Security alone"** Brian Riedl, "How Washington Is Spending Your Tax Dollars in 2010," *heritage.org*, April 9, 2010, http://www.heritage.org/Research/Commentary/2010/04/How-Washington-Is-Spending-Your-Taxes-in-2010. ♁ **"estimated to cost $400 billion over ten years"** Douglas Holtz-Eakin, letter to House Committee on Ways and Means Chairman William Thomas, November 20, 2003, http://www

.cbo.gov/ftpdocs/48xx/doc4808/11-20-MedicareLetter.pdf. ❍ **"'costs of Medicare and Medicaid are running way over original estimates'"** "Medicare Costs Over Estimates," *Hartford Courant*, July 2, 1969.

PAGE 210: "by Bush reducing it to $400 billion he fought really hard" Robert Pear, "Medicare Drug Benefit Plan is Proposed By 2 Democrats," *New York Times*, April 2, 2003, http://www.nytimes.com/2003/04/02/us/medicare-drug-benefit-plan-is-proposed-by-2-democrats.html. ❍ **"and to 26 percent by 2082"** U.S. Congress, Congressional Budget Office, *The Long-Term Budget Outlook*, 110th Cong., 1st sess., 2007, 5, http://www.cbo.gov/ftpdocs/88xx/doc8877/12-13-LTBO.pdf. Note: This represents the alternative fiscal scenario. ❍ **"for upper-income individuals, families, and corporations"** Peter R. Orszag, letter to Representative Paul Ryan, May 19, 2008, http://www.cbo.gov/ftpdocs/92xx/doc9216/05-19-LongtermBudget_Letter-to-Ryan.pdf. ❍ **"state Medicaid costs will double as well"** U.S. Congress, Congressional Budget Office, *The Long-Term Budget Outlook*, 110th Cong., 1st sess., 2007, 5, http://www.cbo.gov/ftpdocs/88xx/doc8877/12-13-LTBO.pdf. Note: This represents the alternative fiscal scenario. ❍ **"'work less, raise pensions, and erase deficits'"** Gregory Viscusi and Helene Fouquet, "Sarkozy Lifts Retirement Age to 62; Raises Highest Income-Tax Rate to 41%," *bloomberg.com*, June 16, 2010, http://www.bloomberg.com/news/2010-06-16/sarkozy-lifts-retirement-age-to-62-raises-top-income-tax-rate-one-point.html.

PAGE 211: "Chart: Consuming Every Dollar" Brian Riedl, "Entitlements Will Consume All Tax Revenues by 2052," *The Heritage Foundation's 2010 Budget Chart Book*, http://www.heritage.org/budgetchartbook/entitlements-historical-tax-levels. ❍ **"'pay pension payroll taxes for 40 years before retiring'"** Ben Wattenberg, "Baby Boom: The Demographic Deficit," *Cherokee County Herald*, December 27, 1995, http://news.google.com/newspapers?id=B3wwAAAAIBAJ&sjid=1j8DAAAAIBAJ.

PAGE 213: "from liberal activist group MoveOn.org, sent in July 2010" MoveOn.org, "Top Five Social Security Myths," *moveon.org*, July 2010, http://pol.moveon.org/ssmyths/index.html.

Chapter 13: Step One: The Rights of Man or Men?

PAGE 215: "'If not us, who? And if not now, when?'" Steven F. Hayward, *The Age of Reagan: The Conservative Counterrevolution, 1980–1989* (New York: Crown Forum, 2009), 182.

PAGE 216: "'The state is God'" Ludwig von Mises, *Omnipotent Government* (New Haven, CT: Yale University Press, 1944), 32.

PAGE 217: "'At peace with ourselves, our neighbors, and the world.'" *Ronald Reagan: The Great Communicator*, ed. Frederick J. Ryan Jr. (New York: HarperCollin, 1995), 2.

PAGE 218: "how the 'policies of the past' brought us to this point" Organizing for America, "Remarks of Senator Barack Obama: Response to the State of the Union, January 28, 2008," http://www.barackobama.com/2008/01/28/remarks_of_senator_barack_obam_43.php.

PAGE 220: "'ratified by all the States in the Union and has never been disannulled'" *Acts and Laws of the Commonwealth of Massachusetts* (Boston, MA: Wright & Potter, 1895), 70. ❍ **"'in the spirit of the Declaration of Independence'"** *Cotting v. Godard*, 183 U.S. 79 (1901), http://caselaw.lp.findlaw.com/scripts/getcase.pl?court=US&vol=183&invol=79.

PAGE 221: "declared that the rights of men were derived from government" Friedrich von Gentz, *The Origin and Principles of the American Revolution, Compared with the Origin and Principles of the French Revolution*, trans. John Quincy Adams (Philadelphia: Asbury Dickins, 1800).

PAGE 222: "'caused men to make laws [to protect themselves] in the first place'" Frédéric Bastiat, *The Law* (Minneapolis, MN: Filiquarian Publishing, LLC, 2005), 4. ❍ **"'individual rights supersede any public or social power'"** Ayn Rand, "Man's Rights," in *The Virtue of Selfishness* (New York: New American Library, 1964), 95. ❍ **"'cope with current problems and current needs'"** William Quirk and R. Bridwell, *Judicial Dictatorship* (New Brunswick, N.J.: Transaction Publishers, 2005), 7. ❍ **"'I have sneered at the natural rights of man'"** Thomas A. Bowden, "Elena Kagan: Could She Defend the Constitution's Purpose?" *Christian Science Monitor*, July 20, 2010, http://www.csmonitor.com/Commentary/Opinion/2010/0720/Elena-Kagan-Could-she-defend-the-Constitution-s-purpose. ❍ **"'NEW DEAL FORCING REASSESSMENT OF U.S. CONSTITUTION AS LIVING FORCE'"** A. Nettleton Jully, "New Deal Forcing Reassessment of U.S. Constitution as Living Force—Federal Judges' Rulings so Far Apart That Nation Look's to Supreme Court For Interpretation Rooseveltian Program Hinges on Flexibility of This Basic Code in American Social Structure," *Christian Science Monitor*, September 17, 1934, http://pqasb.pqarchiver.com/csmonitor_historic/access/305086112.html?dids=305086112:305086112&FMT=CITE&FMTS=CITE:AI.

PAGE 223: "'taking care of them, they must become happy'" Thomas Jefferson, "Letter to Thomas Cooper, November 29, 1802" in *The Writings of Thomas Jefferson, vol. 9, ed. Albert Ellery Bergh* (Washington, D.C.: The Thomas Jefferson Memorial Association, 1905), 342. ♁ **"implies that the alternative would be a 'dead' Constitution"** *See generally* Chris Blank, "Scalia Says 'Living Constitution' Reduces Democracy," March 6, 2008, http://www.law.com/jsp/article.jsp?id=1204716632734. ♁ **"to rewrite, not understand, key provisions of the Constitution'"** Richard A. Epstein, *How Progressives Rewrote the Constitution* (Washington, D.C.: Cato Institute, 2006), 135–36.

PAGE 224: "'should not be easier just because the individual in question is a judge'" William H. Rehnquist "The Notion of a Living Constitution," *Harvard Journal of Law & Public Policy* 29, no. 2 (2006): 414, http://www.law.harvard.edu/students/orgs/jlpp/Vol29_No2_Rehnquist.pdf. ♁ **"spelled out exactly how the Constitution could be updated"** U.S. Constitution, art. 5. ♁ **"'corrosive of the fundamental values of our democratic society'"** William H. Rehnquist "The Notion of a Living Constitution," *Harvard Journal of Law & Public Policy* 29, no. 2 (2006): 415, http://www.law.harvard.edu/students/orgs/jlpp/Vol29_No2_Rehnquist.pdf (accessed August 12, 2010). ♁ **"'and to forget about the citizens' interests'"** John O'Sullivan, *The President, The Pope and the Prime Minister: Three Who Changed the World* (Washington, D.C.: Regnery Publishing, Inc., 2006), 265.

PAGE 225: "'whose authority can be superseded by no power on earth'" "Founding Father on Religion in Government," accessed August 12, 2010, http://undergod.procon.org/view.resource.php?resourceID= 000070. ♁ **"more people dependent on the government than are paying taxes'"** Stephen Ohlemacher, "Nearly Half of U.S. Households Escape Fed Income Tax," April 7, 2010, http://finance.yahoo.com/news/Nearly-half-of-US-households-apf-1105567323.html. ♁ **"Franklin Roosevelt gave a speech called 'The Four Freedoms'"** "Franklin D. Roosevelt's Address to Congress, January 6, 1941," http://www.wwnorton.com/college/history/ralph/workbook/ralprs36b.htm. ♁ **"ask the question 'at whose expense?' after the right is proposed"** Ayn Rand, "Man's Rights," in *Capitalism: The Unknown Ideal* (New York: Dutton Signet, 1966), http://www.aynrand.org/site/PageServer?pagename=ari_ayn_rand_man_rights.

PAGE 226: "'who are imprisoned as a result of their own misdeeds'" Jess Bravin, "Kagan Backed Broad Interpretation of 14th Amendment," *WSJ.com*, May 16, 2010, http://online.wsj.com/article/NA_WSJ_PUB:SB10001424052748703745904575248620872377444.html. ♁ **"'which the government itself may not deprive the individual'"** Jess Bravin, "Kagan Backed Broad Interpretation of 14th Amendment," *WSJ.com*, May 16, 2010, http://online.wsj.com/article/NA_WSJ_PUB:SB10001424052748703745904575248620872377444.html. ♁ **"'precept that each individual is accountable for his actions'"** Vanessa Barker, *The Politics of Imprisonment: How the Democratic Process Shapes the Way America Punishes Offenders* (New York: Oxford University Press, 2009), 66.

PAGE 227: "'cannot conceive of truly ethical behavior and the acceptance of duties'" Wilhelm Röpke, *A Humane Economy: The Social Framework of the Free Market* (Chicago: H. Regnery Co., 1960), 172. ♁ **"'granted away to others, without their consent'"** Samuel Adams, *The Writings of Samuel Adams, ed. Harry Alonzo Cushing, vol. 1: 1764–1769* (New York: G. P. Putnam's Sons, Inc., 1904), 137. ♁ **"Susette Kelo involuntarily lost her land"** "Homes May Be 'Taken' for Private Projects," *MSNBC.com*, June 23, 2005, http://www.msnbc.msn.com/id/8331097/. ♁ **"(the others being National Security and Drug Reform)"** "Key Issues," http://www.aclu.org/key-issues, accessed August 12, 2010.

PAGE 228: "the entire parcel sits vacant and useless" Patrick McGeehan, "Pfizer to Leave City That Won Land-Use Case," *New York Times*, November 13, 2009, http://www.nytimes.com/2009/11/13/nyregion/13pfizer.html.

PAGE 229: "'imprinted by the finger of God on the heart of man.'" Samuel Adams, *The Writings of Samuel Adams, ed. Harry Alonzo Cushing, vol. 4: 1778–1802* (New York: G. P. Putnam's Sons, Inc., 1908), 356. ♁ **"free market to organize the bulk of economic activity"** Milton Friedman, *Capitalism and Freedom* (Chicago: University of Chicago Press, 2002), 9.

PAGE 230: "gap in giving was large: $2,210 for traditionalists, $642 for progressives" Arthur C. Brooks, *Who Really Cares: The Surprising Truth About Compassionate Conservatism* (New York: BasicBooks, 2006), 34. **"donated just 2.5 percent of his income to charity"** Franklin Delano Roosevelt's Tax Returns, http://www.taxanalysts.com/thp/presreturns.nsf/Returns/3F0BA87E176A72FA85256E430078A69A/$file/F_Roosevelt_1935.pdf.

Chapter 14: Step Two: Opportunity vs. Outcome

PAGE 232: "to try to make unequal things equal" *Unlike: Webster's Quotations, Facts and Phrases* (San Diego, CA: ICON Group International, 2008), 3.

PAGE 233: "'the happiest and the securest on whom the sun has ever shone'" Thomas Jefferson, "Letter to John Adams, October 28, 1813," in *The Writings of Thomas Jefferson*, vol. 13, ed. Albert Ellery Bergh (Washington, D.C.: The Thomas Jefferson Memorial Association of the United States, 1907), 403.

PAGE 234: "'believed in or tacitly accepted the morality of slavery'" Douglas L. Wilson, "Thomas Jefferson and the Character Issue," *The Atlantic Monthly*, November 1992, 57–74, http://www.theatlantic.com/past/docs/issues/96oct/obrien/charactr.htm. ŏ **"'long before freedom had entered into their conceptions'"** Alexis de Tocqueville, *Democracy in America*, trans. Henry Reeve, vol. 2 (New York: D. Appleton and Co., 1904), 789. ŏ **"'rather be equal in slavery than unequal in freedom'"** *Unlike: Webster's Quotations, Facts and Phrases* (San Diego, CA: ICON Group International, 2008), 3. ŏ **"'dedicated to the proposition that all men are created equal'"** *Encyclopedia of the American Civil War: A Political, Social, and Military History*, eds. David S. Heidler and Jeanne T. Heidler (New York: W. W. Norton & Company, Inc., 2000), 826.

PAGE 235: "'should have an equal opportunity to develop those talents'" Ashton Applewhite, William R. Evans III, Andrew Frothingham, *And I Quote: The Definitive Collection of Quotes, Sayings, And Jokes for the Contemporary Speechmaker*, rev. ed. (New York: St. Martin's Press, 2003), 78. ŏ **"one or the other, but not both at the same time."** F. A. Hayek, *The Constitution of Liberty* (Chicago: University of Chicago Press, 1960), 87. ŏ **"a metaphor for our whole way of life"** Israel Zangwill, *The Melting Pot: Drama in Four Acts*, act 1.

PAGE 236: "between 1990 and 2015, who live on less than $1 per day" Senate Committee on Foreign Relations, *The Global Poverty Act of 2007*, 110th Cong., 2d sess., 2008, S. 331, http://thomas.loc.gov/cgi-bin/cpquery/R?cp110:FLD010:@1(sr331). ŏ **"totaled 0.7 percent of our GNP, in addition to our existing foreign-aid budget"** Cliff Kincaid, "Obama's Global Tax Proposal up for Senate Vote," *aim.org*, February 12, 2008, http://www.aim.org/aim-column/obamas-global-tax-proposal-up-for-senate-vote/. ŏ **"You probably already guessed it: Barack Obama"** "S. 2433: Global Poverty Act of 2007," http://www.govtrack.us/congress/bill.xpd?bill=s110-2433. ŏ **"'and the Greeks believe in Greek exceptionalism'"** Ken Blackwell and Ken Klukowski, *The Blueprint: Obama's Plan to Subvert the Constitution and Build an Imperial Presidency* (Guilford, CT: Globe Pequot Press, 2010), 99. ŏ **"meant that the government was 'respecting people as equals'"** Jeremy Waldron, *God, Locke, and Equality: Christian Foundations of John Locke's Political Thought* (Cambridge, UK: Cambridge University Press, 2002), 9.

PAGE 237: "'passion for equality made vain the hope for freedom'" F. A. Hayek, *Individualism and Economic Order* (Chicago: University of Chicago Press, 1948), 31. ŏ **"Americans needed to engage in 'a reappraisal of values'"** David Ciepley, *Liberalism in the Shadow of Totalitarianism* (Cambridge, MA: Harvard University Press, 2006), 99. ŏ **"'The day of enlightened administration has come'"** Franklin D. Roosevelt and J. B. S. Hardman, *Rendezvous With Destiny: Addresses and Opinions of Franklin Delano Roosevelt* (New York: Dryden Press, Inc., 1944), 34. ŏ **"in terms of a changing and growing social order"** *Classics of American Political and Constitutional Thought*, eds. Scott J. Hammond, Kevin R. Hardwick and Howard L. Lubert, vol. 2: Reconstruction to the Present (Indianapolis, IN: Hackett Publishing Company, Inc., 2007), 408. ŏ **"'give even greater cause for social resentment'"** Wilhelm Röpke, *A Humane Economy: The Social Framework of the Free Market* (Wilmington, DE: Intercollegiate Studies Institute, 1998), 156.

PAGE 238: "'equality as a fact and *equality as a result*' (emphasis mine)." *Expanding Opportunity in Higher Education: Leveraging Promise*, eds. Patricia C. Gándara, Gary Orfield and Catherine L. Horn (Albany, N.Y.: State University of New York Press, 2006), 143. ŏ **"'to fulfill the fair expectations of man'"** Charles C. Lemert, *Dark Thoughts: Race and the Eclipse of Society* (New York: Routledge, 2002), 256. ŏ **"reach their conclusions behind a 'veil of ignorance'"** John Rawls, *A Theory of Justice*, rev. ed. (Cambridge, MA: Harvard University Press, 1999), 118. ŏ **"wealth should be distributed so that the worst off benefit the most"** John Rawls, *A Theory of Justice* (Cambridge, MA: Harvard University Press, 1971), 60–65.

PAGE 239: "'putting that much power in anyone's hands is enormously dangerous'" Ray Sawhill, "Black and Right—Thomas Sowell Talks About the Arrogance of Liberal Elites and the Loneliness of the Black Conservative," *Salon.com*, November 10, 1999, http://www.salon.com/books/int/1999/11/10/sowell/index.html. ŏ **"taxes to pay for public schools to give out iPods is probably unwise"** "Stimulus iPods Cause Debate—U.S.

senators list the plan among top 100 examples of wasteful spending," *ABCNEWS.com*, August 5, 2010, http://abcnews.go.com/Technology/video/stimulus-ipods-students-debate-11332414.

PAGE 240: "'what some ought to be willing to give, but not for what anyone can demand'" F. A. Hayek, *The Constitution of Liberty* (Chicago: University of Chicago Press, 1960), 101, http://www.woldww.net/classes/General_Philosophy/Hayek-equality.htm. ὃ **"'The grounds of this are virtue and talents'"** "Letter to John Adams, October 28, 1813" in *Political Thought in the United States: A Documentary History*, ed. Lyman Tower Sargent (New York: New York University Press, 1997), 161. ὃ **"not in sufficient degree to endanger the society"** Thomas Jefferson, *The Writings of Thomas Jefferson*, vol. 10, ed. Albert Ellery Bergh (Washington, D.C.: The Thomas Jefferson Memorial Association of the United States, 1905), iv–v.

PAGE 241: "H.R. 4287: Enhancing Livability for All Americans Act of 2009" *Enhancing Livability for All Americans Act of 2009*, 111th Cong., 1st sess., 2009, H. R. 4287, http://www.govtrack.us/congress/billtext.xpd?bill=h111-4287. ὃ **"H.R. 1321: Healthy Americans Act"** *Healthy Americans Act*, 111th Cong., 1st sess., 2009, H. R. 1321, http://www.govtrack.us/congress/bill.xpd?bill=h111-1321. ὃ **"H.R. 2233: Health Empowerment Zone Act of 2009"** *Health Empowerment Zone Act of 2009*, 111th Cong., 1st sess., 2009, H. R. 2233, http://www.govtrack.us/congress/bill.xpd?bill=h111-2233. ὃ **"H.R. 1040: A Living Wage, Jobs for All Act"** *A Living Wage, Jobs for All Act*, 108th Cong., 1st sess., 2003, H. R. 1040, http://www.govtrack.us/congress/bill.xpd?bill=h108-1040. ὃ **"H.R. 1500: Helping Families Afford to Work Act"** *Helping Families Afford to Work Act*, 111th Cong., 1st sess., 2009, H. R. 1500, http://www.govtrack.us/congress/billtext.xpd?bill=h111-1500. ὃ **"H.R. 4122: Graduation for All Act"** *Graduation for All Act*, 111th Cong., 1st sess., 2009, H. R. 4122, http://www.govtrack.us/congress/bill.xpd?bill=h111-4122.

PAGE 242: "you eventually become mediocre yourself" Matthew J. Franck, "Lawless Welfare State," *National Review*, May 17, 2010, 36. ὃ **"If envy exists, then so does inequality"** John Kekes, "Dangerous Egalitarian Dreams," *City Journal*, Autumn 2001, http://www.city-journal.org/html/11_4_urbanities-dangerous.html. ὃ **"One way to do that was through the progressive income tax"** John McDonald Hood, *Selling the Dream: Why Advertising Is Good Business* (Westport, CT: Praeger Publishers, 2005), 94. ὃ **"'the stronger is this envy of others, the heavier must be the tax'"** E. J. Mishan, "A Survey of Welfare Economics, 1939–1959," *The Economic Journal* 70, no. 278 (London: Macmillan and Co. Limited, 1960), 247. *See also:* James S. Duesenberry, *Income, Saving and the Theory of Consumer Behavior* (Cambridge, MA: Harvard University Press, 1967). ὃ **"And, just like that, everyone is equal"** Stephen Guest, *Ronald Dworkin* (Stanford, CA: Stanford University Press, 1991), 267C.

PAGE 244: "'not by what they lack but by what others have'" Harry Kalven and Walter J. Blum, *The Uneasy Case for Progressive Taxation* (Chicago: University of Chicago Press, 1953). ὃ **"'timid and industrious animals, of which the government is the shepherd'"** Alexis de Tocqueville, *Democracy in America, ed.* Bruce Frohnen (Washington, D.C.: Regnery Publishing, Inc., 2002), 627.

Chapter 15: Step Three: Faith in America

PAGE 246: *"'that God is just, that his justice cannot sleep forever'"* The Jefferson Monticello, Research & Collections, Quotations on the Jefferson Memorial, Panel Three, http://www.monticello.org/reports/quotes/memorial.html.

PAGE 248: "'for God is always right'" Marcus G. Raskin and Robert Spero, *The Four Freedoms Under Siege: The Clear and Present Danger from Our National Security State* (Westport, CT: Praeger Publishers, 2007), 134.

PAGE 249: "'in the next place oblige it to control itself'" Alexander Hamilton, James Madison, and John Jay, *The Federalist Papers (New Haven CT: Yale University Press, 2009)*, 264. ὃ **"'they have more need of masters'"** Benjamin Franklin, *The Autobiography of Benjamin Franklin*, volume 1: 1706–1757, ed. Mark Skousen, Ph.D. (Washington, D.C.: Regnery Publishing, Inc., 2007), xiv. ὃ **"Just 29 percent of people said 'religion'"** "An in-depth look at USA 's religious beliefs, practices," Survey question 5: "When it comes to questions of right and wrong, which of the following do you look to most for guidance?" (Total population bar), accessed August 19, 2010 http://www.usatoday.com/news/graphics/2008_pew_religion/flash.htm. ὃ **"Christian thinkers like Montesquieu and Blackstone"** Donald S. Lutz, "The Relative Influence of European Writers on Late Eighteenth-Century American Political Thought," *American Political Science Review* 78 (March 1984), 191. *See also:* William J. Federer's American Minute, "American Minute for September 17," http://www.amerisearch.net/index.php?date=2004-09-17&view=View. ὃ **"'wholly inadequate for the government of any other'"** Charles W. Colson, *God & Government: An Insider's View* *on the Boundaries Between Faith & Politics* (Grand Rapids, MI: Zondervan, 2007), 52. ♁ **"the French had (clear your throat) 'low moral character'"** John Eidsmoe, *Christianity and the Constitution: The Faith of Our Founding Fathers* (Grand Rapids, MI: Baker Book House Company, 1987), 383.

PAGE 250: "'impossible to make them conceive of one without the other'" Alexis de Tocqueville, *Democracy in America,* vol. 1, rev. ed., trans. Henry Reeve (New York: The Colonial Press, 1900), 310–11. ♁ **"'where a witness had been permitted to testify without such belief'"** Alexis de Tocqueville, *Democracy in America,* vol. 1, rev. ed., trans. Henry Reeve (New York: The Colonial Press, 1900), 311.

PAGE 251: "ten of the thirteen states had some provision recognizing Christianity" Data based on original reviews of state constitutions by researcher David Dougherty. ♁ **"'the public instructions in piety, religion, and morality'"** *The Founders' Constitution,* eds. Philip B. Kurland and Ralph Lerner, Massachusetts Constitution of 1780, pt. 1, arts. 3, http://press-pubs.uchicago.edu/founders/documents/amendI_religions38.html. ♁ **"'place of trust or profit in the civil department, within this State'"** *The Founders' Constitution,* eds. Philip B. Kurland and Ralph Lerner, North Carolina Constitution of 1776, arts. 32, http://press-pubs.uchicago.edu/founders/documents/amendI_religions29.html. ♁ **"'wall of separation between Church and State'"** "Jefferson's Letter to the Danbury Baptists," http://www.loc.gov/loc/lcib/9806/danpre.html.

PAGE 252: "amendment banning the government from sponsoring prayer?" David Limbaugh, *Persecution: How Liberals Are Waging War Against Christianity* (New York: HarperCollins Publishers Inc., 2004), 24. ♁ **"'then we will be a nation gone under'"** Gary Scott Smith, *Faith and the Presidency: From George Washington to George W. Bush* (New York: Oxford University Press, 2006), 337. ♁ **"'it is our duty to defend both'"** *The Quotable Founding Fathers: A Treasury of 2,500 Wise And Witty Quotations from the Men and Women Who Created America,* ed. Buckner F. Melton Jr. (Dulles, VA: Brassey's, 2004), 248. ♁ **"Twenty million more adults identified themselves that way in 2009 than in 2000"** Jane Lampman, "Survey Sees a Drift Away From Religion in America—The Percentage of Christians in the US Declined, While That of People with 'No Religion' Almost Doubled," *The Christian Science Monitor,* March 10, 2009, http://www.csmonitor.com/USA/Society/2009/0310/p01s02-ussc.html. ♁ **"'something to take command, to impose an occupation, a duty'"** José Ortega y Gassett, *Revolt of the Masses* (New York: W. W. Norton & Company, Inc., 1957), 136.

PAGE 253: "who said of religion, 'Let us put away childish things'" Christopher Lasch, *The Revolt of the Elites: And the Betrayal of Democracy* (New York: W. W. Norton & Company, Inc., 1995), 235. ♁ **"group of evangelical Christians, were 'peddlers of coercion'"** A. Bartlett Giamatti, "A Plea for Freedom and Tolerance," *The Day,* September 5, 1981, 16, http://news.google.com/newspapers?id=UwAhAAAAIBAJ&sjid=WHUFAAAAIBAJ. ♁ **"the cartoon was 'insensitive and exclusionary'"** Robert H. Bork, *Slouching Towards Gomorrah* (New York: Regan Books, 1997), 291. ♁ **"'message that the state prefers or otherwise endorses a certain religion'"** "Judges Rule Against Utah Highway Crosses for Fallen Troopers—Utah 's Attorney General Strongly Disagrees with Appeals Court," *Deseret News,* August 19, 2010, http://www.deseretnews.com/article/print/700058122/Judges-rule-against-Utah-highway-crosses-for-fallen-troopers.html.

PAGE 254: "attitude to religion ranges from indifference to active hostility" Christopher Lasch, *The Revolt of the Elites: And the Betrayal of Democracy* (New York: W. W. Norton & Company, Inc., 1995), 215. ♁ **"'It just covers everything. The Word."** Nicholas Ballasy, "Pelosi Says She Has a Duty to Pursue Policies in Keeping With The Values of Jesus, 'The Word Made Flesh,'" *CNSNews.com,* June 1, 2010, http://www.cnsnews.com/news/article/66208. ♁ **"'call to bring about the perfect kingdom of God'"** *American Progressivism: A Reader,* eds. Ronald J. Pestritto and William J. Atto (Lanham, MD: Lexington Books, 2008), 11. ♁ **"replace it with this idea that the state can somehow usher in God's will"** *See generally* James Patrick Scanlan, *Dostoevsky the Thinker* (Ithaca, N.Y.: Cornell University Press, 2002), 194–96. ♁ **"'the moral landscape necessarily changes'"** Jon Meacham, "The End of Christian America," *Newsweek,* April 4, 2009, http://www.newsweek.com/2009/04/03/the-end-of-christian-america.html. ♁ **"the one who is given five talents but does nothing with them"** Matt 25:15–30. ♁ **"George Orwell . . . commented that the hymn needed to be updated"** George Orwell, *The Orwell Reader: Fiction, Essays, and Reportage* (Orlando, FL: Harcourt, 1984), 368C.

PAGE 256: "succeed in this political building no better than the builders of Babel" Peter Grasso Jr., *In God We Betrayed* (Longwood, FL: Xulon Press, 2006), 33.

Chapter 16: Step Four: Decentralize and Disconnect

PAGE 258: "'turn over to the federal government responsibilities which are rightfully theirs'" Daniel Dyer, *Actions to Achieve Peace: What Every Citizen Can Do* (Raleigh, N.C.: Lulu Enterprises, Inc., 2008), 48.

PAGE 259: "number of federal regulators has more than tripled over the last fifty years" Kevin Hassett, "The Deregulation That Wasn't," *National Review*, August 16, 2010, 6.

PAGE 260: "'organized on the principles of decentralization management'" Company Overview, accessed August 15, 2010, http://www.investor.jnj.com/company-overview.cfm. ŏ **"'satisfy the unmet needs of patients or customers'"** "Johnson & Johnson CEO William Weldon: Leadership in a Decentralized Company," accessed August 15, 2010, http://knowledge.wharton.upenn.edu/mobile/article.cfm?articleid=2003&page=4. ŏ **"'Let's decentralize decision making wherever possible'"** Louis V. Gerstner, *Who Says Elephants Can't Dance?* (New York: HarperCollins Publishers Inc., 2002), 22. ŏ **"IBM's stock price increased by a factor of almost ten under his leadership" Thomas W. Malone,** *The Future of Work: How the New Order of Business Will Shape Your Organization, Your Management Style, and Your Life* (Boston: Harvard Business School Publishing, 2004), 111. ŏ **"they might understand the term *creative destruction*"** Joseph A. Schumpeter, *Capitalism, Socialism and Democracy* (New York: Harper, 1975), 82–85, http://transcriptions.english.ucsb.edu/archive/courses/liu/english25/materials/schumpeter.html. ŏ **"precisely because they were able to see that what Blockbuster was doing would soon no longer work"** Damon Darlin, "Always Pushing Beyond the Envelope," Everybody's Business, *New York Times*, August 8, 2010, http://www.nytimes.com/2010/08/08/business/08every.html?ref=technology.

PAGE 261: "'when the plan falls apart, when the enemy does something unexpected'" Army Leadership, "Be, Know, Do," *Leader to Leader*, no. 26, Fall 2002, 26, http://media.wiley.com/assets/70/47/jrnls_LTL_JB_rmy26.pdf. ŏ **"'delegate the necessary autonomy and then let them do the work'"** Army Leadership, "Be, Know, Do," *Leader to Leader*, no. 26, Fall 2002, 26, http://media.wiley.com/assets/70/47/jrnls_LTL_JB_army26.pdf. ŏ **"encouraging leaders to innovate and adapt based on the situation"** Dan Murphy, "New Commander, New Plan in Iraq," *Christian Science Monitor*, February 9, 2007, http://www.csmonitor.com/2007/0209/p01s03-woiq.html. *See also:* Linda Robinson, *Tell Me How This Ends: General David Petraeus and the Search for a Way Out of Iraq* (New York: PublicAffairs, 2008), 121. ŏ **"The Tenth Amendment, ratified in 1791, was created to act as a safety net"** Texas Governor Rick Perry, "States Rights Are Rapidly Eroding," accessed August 16, 2010, http://www.tenthamendmentcenter.com/2009/04/16/states-rights-are-rapidly-eroding/. ŏ **"'are reserved to the States respectively, or to the people'"** U.S. Constitution, amend.10, http://www.usconstitution.net/xconst_Am10.html.

PAGE 262: "'if established, be a *federal*, and not a *national* constitution'" James Madison, "The Federalist No. 39: Conformity of the Plan to Republican Principles," *Independent Journal*, January 16, 1788, http://www.constitution.org/fed/federa39.htm. ŏ **"elections are handled via electoral votes based on state population"** Thomas H. Neale, Government and Finance Division, "The Electoral College: How It Works in Contemporary Presidential Elections," September 8, 2003, http://fpc.state.gov/documents/organization/28109.pdf. ŏ **"'and the surest bulwarks against anti-republican tendencies'"** Thomas Jefferson, *The Jeffersonian Cyclopedia: A Comprehensive Collection of the Views of Thomas Jefferson*, ed. John P. Foley (New York and London: Funk & Wagnalls Company, 1900), 834. ŏ **"Article Six of the Constitution declares that the constitution itself is the supreme law of the land"** U.S. Constitution, art. 6, http://www.usconstitution.net/xconst_A6.html.

PAGE 263: "'acting individually or together, can effectively deal with them'" Edward H. Crane, *Cato Handbook for Policymakers*, 7th ed. (Washington, D.C.: Cato Institute, 2008), 70. ŏ **"James Madison vetoed a road and canal construction bill for being unconstitutional"** Burton W. Folsom Jr., "Madison's Veto Sets a Precedent," *The Freeman*, January 2008, http://www.thefreemanonline.org/columns/our-economic-past-madisons-veto-sets-a-precedent/. ŏ **"Alleviating poverty is the cause of my life"** Anne E. Kornblut, "Clinton Advisers Say Edwards Is a Threat," *Washington Post*, December 20, 2007, http://www.washingtonpost.com/wp-dyn/content/article/2007/12/19/AR2007121902494.html.

PAGE 264: "'Our objective: total victory'" Diana Nelson Jones, "Appalachia's War: The Poorest of the Poor Struggle Back," *Post-Gazette*, November 26, 2000, http://www.post-gazette.com/headlines/20001126appalachiamainnat2.asp. ŏ **"routinely scolded those looking for federal funds to enhance their local communities"** "The Founding of the United States, Wealth Creation, and the Constitutionality of Charity," accessed August 16, 2010, http://www.neoperspectives.com/foundingoftheunitedstates.htm. ♁ **"'fewer people will obtain their preference and more will be disappointed'"** Grover Rees III, "Federalism in the Supreme Court—The Fall of the House of Usery," *Regulation*, May/June 1983, 32n, http://www.cato.org/pubs/regulation/regv7n3/v7n3-7.pdf. ♁ **"'to argue for federalism now is to argue for greater local power'"** Lino A. Graglia, "In Defense of 'Federalism,'" *Harvard Journal on Law and Public Policy* 6 (1982): 23.

PAGE 265: "'Come and get it! Come and get it!'" Michael Levenson, "Bold Tax Vow Comes Back to Sting Patrick," *Boston Globe*, April 25, 2010, http://www.boston.com/news/local/massachusetts/articles/2010/04/25/bold_tax_vow_comes_back_to_sting_patrick/?page=2.

PAGE 266: "and most of them receive some kind of federal aid" Chris Edwards, "Federal Aid to the States—Historical Cause of Governmental and Bureaucracy," *Policy Analysis*, no. 593, May 22, 2007, 22, http://www.cato.org/pubs/pas/pa593.pdf. ♁ **"'$33.6 Million [in federal funds] for Community Development Block Grants'"** The Official Website of the Governor of Massachusetts, "33.6 Million for Community Development Block Grants," July 8, 2010, http://www.mass.gov/?pageID=gov3pressrelease&L=1&L0=Home&sid=Agov3&b=pressrelease&f=100708_community_development_grants&csid=Agov3. ♁ **"'$51 Million in Federal Education Funding'"** Office of the Governor, "Governor Doyle, Superintendent Evers Announce $51 Million in Federal Education Funding," June 18, 2010, http://www.wisgov.state.wi.us/journal_media_detail.asp?locid=19&prid=5215. ♁ **"'$540 Million in Public Safety Grant Requests to Improve Broadband Communications'"** New York State, Governor David A. Paterson, "Governor Paterson Announces $540 Million in Public Safety Grant Requests to Improve Broadband Communications," July 2, 2010, http://www.state.ny.us/governor/press/070210PublicSafety.html. ♁ **"'states cannot print money, as the federal government can"** Charles Fried, "Federalism—Why Should We Care?" *Harvard Journal of Law and Public Policy* 6, (1982–1983): 3.

PAGE 267: "Chart: The State Aid Boomerang" Chris Edwards, "Federal Aid to the States," The Cato Institute, *Policy Analysis*, No. 593, May 22, 2007, 3, http://www.cato.org/pubs/pas/pa593.pdf.

PAGE 268: "explains what a sham the idea of bureaucrats working for the greater good is" Thayer Watkins, "Public Choice Theory," accessed August 16, 2010, http://www.sjsu.edu/faculty/watkins/publicchoice.htm/. ♁ **"states were required to create, fund, and run highway departments"** Chris Edwards, "Federal Aid to the States: Historical Cause of Government Growth and Bureaucracy," *Policy Analysis*, no. 593 (May 22, 2007): 4–5, http://www.cato.org/pubs/pas/pa593.pdf. ♁ **"provide highway funds in exchange for states agreeing to their nanny-state regulations"** United States Government Accountability Office, "Surface Transportation—Restructured Federal Approach Needed for More Focused, Performance-Based, and Sustainable Programs," March 2008, 16, 67–68, http://www.gao.gov/new.items/d08400.pdf. ♁ **"'the men and women who educate our children or keep our communities safe'"** Matt Viser, "Obama signs $26b State Aid Bill After House OK—Mass. To Get $655m for Programs," *Boston Globe*, August 11, 2010, http://www.boston.com/news/nation/washington/articles/2010/08/11/obama_signs_26b_state_aid_bill_after_house_ok/.

PAGE 269: "'what the impact is and the potential unintended consequences'" Lisa Fleisher, "Christie Administration May Not Apply for $268M U.S. Education Aid," *NJ.com*, August 09, 2010, http://www.nj.com/news/index.ssf/2010/08/christie_administration_may_no.html. ♁ **"'bypass the state government' and flow straight to recipients chosen by the U.S. Department of Education"** Lisa Fleisher, "Christie Administration May Not Apply for $268M U.S. Education Aid," *NJ.com*, August 9, 2010, http://www.nj.com/news/index.ssf/2010/08/christie_administration_may_no.html.

PAGE 270: "Between 2000 and 2009, 1 out of every 7 New Yorkers left the state" Andy Soltis, "Tax Refugees Staging Escape from New York," *New York Post*, October 27, 2009, http://www.nypost.com/p/news/local/item _qb4pItQ71UXIc0i6cd3UpK.

PAGE 271: "'resistance to black advances clearly understood by white Southern voters'" Jack White, "Lott, Reagan and Republican Racism," *Time.com*, December 14, 2002, http://www.time.com/time/nation/article/0,8599,399921,00.html#ixzz0wKcoPNfp. ♁ **"'when it comes down to you and the blacks, we're with you'"** Bob Herbert, "Righting Reagan's Wrongs?," *New York Times*, November 13, 2007, http://www.nytimes.com/2007/11/13/opinion/13herbert.html. ♁ **"the top 10 percent finances over 70 percent of our country's revenue"** National Taxpayers Union, "Who Pays Income Taxes and How Much? Tax Year 2007," accessed August 15, 2010, http://www.ntu.org/tax-basics/who-pays-income-taxes.html.

PAGE 272: "'levels of access that fall below minimum national standards of adequacy" Howard Chernick,

"Federal Grants and Social Welfare Spending: Do State Responses Matter?," *National Tax Journal* 53, no. 1 (March 2000): 143, http://ntj.tax.org/wwtax/ntjrec.nsf/175d710dffc186a385256a31007cb40f/121932c37db6c66985256afc007f21d5/$FILE/v53n1143.pdf. ♁ **"wasn't even close: 71 percent supported it"** State of Missouri Primary Election, Proposition C, August 3, 2010, http://www.sos.mo.gov/enrweb/ballotissueresults.asp?eid=283. ♁ **"at least fourteen attorneys general are suing the federal government"** Warren Richey, "Attorneys General in 14 States Sue To Block Healthcare Reform Law," *Christian Science Moniter,* March 23, 2010, http://www.csmonitor.com/USA/Justice/2010/0323/Attorneys-general-in-14-states-sue-to-block-healthcare-reform-law. ♁ **"legislation declaring that federal regulations of firearms don't apply"** Kirk Johnson, "States' Rights Is Rallying Cry for Lawmakers," *New York Times,* March 17, 2010, New York ed., A1, http://www.nytimes.com/2010/03/17/us/17states.html?_r=2. ♁ **"reasserts the sovereignty of the state and seeks to curtail the power of the federal government"** Kirk Johnson, "States' Rights Is Rallying Cry for Lawmakers," *New York Times,* March 17, 2010, http://www.nytimes.com/2010/03/17/us/17states.html?_r=2.

Chapter 17: Step Five: A Taste of Their Own Medicine

PAGE 276: "'taking from our federal government the power of borrowing'" Arthur Bryant, *The American Ideal* (Freeport, N.Y.: Books for Libraries, 1969), 28. ♁ **"'and to provide new guards for their future security'"** U.S. Declaration of Independence, 2nd paragraph, http://www.ushistory.org/declaration/document/. ♁ **"'change the basic rules for the fiscal game'"** James M. Buchanan, "Clarifying Confusion About the Balanced Budget Amendment," *National Tax Journal* 48, no. 3 (September 1995), 347–55, http://ntj.tax.org/wwtax/ntjrec.nsf/009a9a91c225 e83d852567ed006212d8/68f7f882cd48d258852567ef0057a8a5/$FILE/v48n3347.pdf. ♁ **"'an explicit fiscal rule in the written constitution'"** James M. Buchanan, "Clarifying Confusion About the Balanced Budget Amendment," *National Tax Journal* 48, no. 3 (September 1995), 347–55, http://ntj.tax.org/wwtax/ntjrec.nsf/009a9a91c225e83d852567ed006212d8/68f7f882cd48d258852567ef0057a8a5/$FILE/v48n3347.

PAGE 277: "he proposed . . . a balanced-budget amendment in 2007" Senator Lindsey Graham, "Graham, DeMint Introduce Balanced Budget Constitutional Amendment," press release, November 13, 2007, http://lgraham.senate.gov/public/index.cfm?FuseAction=PressRoom.PressReleases&ContentRecord_id=3ab1d8d6-802a-23ad-4be5-c5a9217300e8.

PAGE 278: "'in short, amassing their own power'" S.A. Miller, "DeMint Tries to Ban 'Permanent Politicians,' *Washington Times,* November 11, 2009, http://www.washingtontimes.com/news/2009/nov/11/demint-revives-bill-to-ban-permanent-politicians/. ♁ **"and thirteen of the fifty-nine representatives showed up"** Ernest Sutherland Bates, *The Story of Congress: 1789–1935* (New York: Harper and Brothers, 1936). ♁ **"In 1815, members of Congress began receiving a salary"** Ernest Sutherland Bates, *The Story of Congress: 1789–1935* (New York: Harper and Brothers, 1936), 2–3.

PAGE 279: "'to find out what it means after you read the bill'" Nicholas Ballasy, "Conyers Sees No Point in Members Reading 1,000-Page Health Care Bill—Unless They Have 2 Lawyers to Interpret It for Them," *cnsnews.com,* July 27, 2009, http://www.cnsnews.com/public/content/article.aspx?RsrcID=51610.

PAGE 280: "'the buttons that you push and the levers that you pull'" Deb Price, "Crusader: Rep. Dingell to Become America's Longest-Serving Congressman," *Detroit News,* February 10, 2009, http://dingell.house.gov/pdf/090210.pdf. ♁ **"'I'd like to continue in the Senate'"** Caitlin Taylor and Huma Khan, "Robert C. Byrd, Senate's Longest-Serving Member, Dead at 92," *abcnews.com,* June 28, 2010, http://abcnews.go.com/Politics/robert-byrd-dead-92-senates-longest-serving-senator/story?id=6692830. ♁ **"Supreme Court ruled the practice unconstitutional"** Bruce Bartlett, "Don't Reinvent the Wheel," *Wall Street Journal,* March 13, 2006, http://online.wsj.com/article/SB114221992605496333.html.

PAGE 281: "'is sacredly obligatory upon all'" John R. Vile, *The Constitutional Amending Process in American Political Thought* (Westport, CT: Praeger, 1992). ♁ **"be amended by a simple majority of the popular vote"** John R. Vile, *The Constitutional Amending Process in American Political Thought* (Westport, CT: Praeger, 1992), 143.

PAGE 282: "sixty-five co-sponsors (all of them Republicans)" Govtrack.us, "H.R. 5323: Save America's Future Economy Act of 2010," *govtrack.us,* accessed August 17, 2010, http://www.govtrack.us/congress/bill.xpd?bill=h111-5323. ♁ **"unable to tweak the rules every time they want to make an exception"** Veronique de Rugy, "Budget Gimmicks or The Destructive Art of Creative Accounting," (working paper, Mercatus

Center, George Mason University, Fairfax, VA, 2010), http://mercatus.org/sites/default/files/publication/Budget_Gimmick_WP1030.pdf.

PAGE 283: "'shouldn't grow faster than the average family's budget'" Chris Edwards, "Federal Spending Limit," *cato-at-liberty.org*, June 1, 2010, http://www.cato-at-liberty.org/2010/06/01/federal-spending-limit/. ♁ **"'buried within larger spending packages'"** Editorial, "A Good Line-Item Veto," *Washington Post*, March 10, 2006, http://www.washingtonpost.com/wp-dyn/content/article/2006/03/09/AR2006030902109.html.

PAGE 284: "if they thought it was frivolous or unnecessary" Bruce Bartlett, "Don't Reinvent the Wheel," *Wall Street Journal*, March 13, 2006, http://online.wsj.com/article/SB114221992605496333.html. ♁ **"there had been a 'peaceful turn of events'"** John Steele Gordon, "Impoundment," *americanheritage.com*, September 28, 2006, http://www.americanheritage.com/blog/20069_28_488.shtml. ♁ **"in funds for things like housing and education"** John Steele Gordon, "Impoundment," *americanheritage.com*, September 28, 2006, http://www.americanheritage.com/blog/20069_28_488.shtml. ♁ **"'authorization would have been constitutional'"** *Clinton v. City of New York*, 95 F. Supp. 168 (D.C. Cir. 1998), http://www.law.cornell.edu/supct/html/97-1374.ZX.html.

PAGE 285: "he used to make $193,400 a year" Fredreka Schouten, "Doors Still Revolving Between Capitol, Lobbyists," *USA Today*, March 22, 2009, http://www.usatoday.com/news/washington/2009-04-21-lobbying_N.htm. ♁ **"'43% of former lawmakers became lobbyists'"** Fredreka Schouten, "Doors Still Revolving Between Capitol, Lobbyists," *USA Today*, March 22, 2009, http://www.usatoday.com/news/washington/2009-04-21-lobbying_N.htm. ♁ **"Republicans lost seats 6-to-1 that cycle"** *Fredreka Schouten, "Doors Still Revolving Between Capitol, Lobbyists," USA Today*, March 22, 2009, http://www.usatoday.com/news/washington/2009-04-21-lobbying_N.htm.

PAGE 286: "'brothers, sisters, sons, daughters, in-laws and more'" Sharyl Attkisson, "Family Ties Bind Federal Lawmakers to Lobbyists," *cbsnews.com*, June 25, 2010, http://www.cbsnews.com/stories/2010/06/25/eveningnews/main6618973.shtml. ♁ ***"All in the Family"*** Sharyl Attkisson, "Family Ties Bind Federal Lawmakers to Lobbyists," *cbsnews.com*, June 25, 2010, http://www.cbsnews.com/stories/2010/06/25/eveningnews/main6618973.shtml.

PAGE 287: "one dissenting vote in the House" "Congress' Role in War," *USA Today*, May 18, 2005, http://www.usatoday.com/news/nation/2002-10-08-congress-war.htm. ♁ **"'on the path toward fiscal reform and responsibility'"** The White House, Office of the Press Secretary, "President Obama Establishes Bipartisan National Commission on Fiscal Responsibility and Reform," press release, February 18, 2010, http://www.whitehouse.gov/the-press-office/president-obama-establishes-bipartisan-national-commission-fiscal-responsibility-an.

PAGE 288: "'we'll get back to you later'" Louis Jacobson, "Obama Flip-Flops on Use of Presidential Commissions," *politifact.com*, July 1, 2010, http://www.politifact.com/truth-o-meter/statements/2010/jul/01/barack-obama/obama-flip-flops-use-presidential-commissions/. ♁ **"(Ann Fudge, former CEO of Young & Rubicam)"** Jonathan Weisman, "Obama: Four Diverse Picks for Debt Panel," *Washington Wire* blog at *wsj.com*, February 26, 2010, http://blogs.wsj.com/washwire/2010/02/26/obama-four-diverse-picks-for-debt-panel/. ♁ **"'in 17 of them at the same time if you try hard enough'"** Robert Harold Schuller and Paul David Dunn, *The Power of Being Debt Free: How Eliminating the National Debt Could Radically Improve Your Standard of Living*, (Nashville, TN: Thomas Nelson, 1985).

PAGE 289: "reelection rates run upwards of 90 percent" Open Secrets, "Reelection Rates Over the Years," *opensecrets.org*, accessed August 18, 2010, http://www.opensecrets.org/bigpicture/reelect.php. ♁ **"called the design a 'Gerry-mander'"** Kenneth Dautrich, David A. Yalof, Charldean Newell, David Prindle, and Mark Shomaker, *American Government: Historical, Popular, and Global Perspectives* (Boston: Wadsworth, 2000), 165. ♁ **"'common sense which the founders set for us'"** Henry J. Abraham, *The Judiciary: The Supreme Court in the Governmental Process* (New York: New York University, 1996), 207. ♁ **"can't come from the 'political class'"** Christian Whiton and Larry Greenfield, "The End of Gerrymandering," *Weekly Standard*, November 25, 2008, http://www.weeklystandard.com/Content/Public/Articles/000/000/015/854xppnl.asp.

PAGE 290: "Chart: Gerrymander-Sham-Mockery!" Created based on data from *The National Atlas of the United States*, http://www.nationalatlas.gov/natlas/Natlasstart.asp.

PAGE 291: "'one or more jurors to serve in some court'" Thomas Jefferson, *The Jeffersonian Cyclopedia: A Comprehensive Collection of the Views of Thomas Jefferson, ed. John P. Foley* (New York: Funk and

Wagnalls, 1900), 213. ŏ **"only 7 percent of those in the private sector"** Jonathan Cohn, "Why Public Employees Are the New Welfare Queen," *New Republic*, August 8, 2010, http://www.tnr.com/blog/jonathan-cohn/76884/why-your-fireman-has-better-pension-you.

PAGE 292: "'unionized public work force in many states and cities'" Daniel Henninger, "The Fall of the House of Kennedy," *Wall Street Journal*, January 21, 2010, http://online.wsj.com/article/SB1000142405274870432010457501501051 5688120.html. ŏ **"from fundraising when they're in session"** National Conference of State Legislators, "Limits on Contributions During the Legislative Session," *ncsl.org*, January 25, 2010, http://www.ncsl.org/default.aspx?tabid=16544.

Chapter 18: Step Six: Scalpels, Hatchets, and Chainsaws

PAGE 296: "'The only question is how to spend it'" Chris Moody, "Van Jones: Stop Worrying About the Deficit. The Government Can Just Take More Money From Rich Companies," *The Daily Caller*, July 24, 2010, http://dailycaller.com/2010/07/24/van-jones-stop-worrying-about-the-deficit-the-government-can-just-take-more-money-from-rich-companies/.

PAGE 298: "To update Barack Obama's line" Amanda Carpenter, "Obama Reacts to Biden's Crisis/Plumber Gaffes," *townhall.com*, October 22, 2008, http://townhall.com/blog/g/6f278df3-8de1-4ef0-913f-0741530f7b60. ŏ **"Over the first year, it would save $15 billion (out of a $1.5 trillion estimated deficit)"** "Obama Seeks Partial Three-Year Spending Freeze," *Foxnews.com*, January 26, 2010, http://www.foxnews.com/politics/2010/01/25/obama-seek-freeze-budget/. ŏ **"I'll take the $15 billion"** Roger Runningen and Brian Faler, "Obama Raises 2010 Deficit Estimate to $1.5 Trillion," *Bloomberg*, August 25, 2009, http://www.bloomberg.com/apps/news?pid=newsarchive&sid=aNaqecavD9ek.

PAGE 299: "federal employees receive a staggering $42,000 or more" Dennis Cauchon, "Federal Workers Earning Double Their Private Counterparts," *USA Today*, August 10, 2010, http://www.usatoday.com/money/economy/income/2010-08-10-1Afedpay10_ST_N.htm. ŏ **"grown from 66 percent in 2000 to 101 percent in 2009"** Tad DeHaven, "Federal Employees Continue to Prosper," accessed August 21, 2010, http://www.cato-at-liberty.org/federal-employees-continue-to-prosper/ŏ **"compensation (salaries and benefits) for federal employees is 50 percent higher"** Dennis Cauchon, "Federal Workers Earning Double Their Private Counterparts," *USA Today*, August 10, 2010, http://www.usatoday.com/money/economy/income/2010-08-10-1Afedpay10_ST_N.htm. ŏ **"would save almost $47 billion in 2011"** James Sherk, "Inflated Federal Pay: How Americans Are Overtaxed to Overpay the Civil Service," *Center for Data Analysis Report* no. 10-05, http://www.heritage.org/Research/Reports/2010/07/Inflated-Federal-Pay-How-Americans-Are-Overtaxed-to-Overpay-the-Civil-Service.

PAGE 300: "Total Expected Revenue: $2,567" Office of Management and Budget, "Table 1.1—Summary of Receipts, Outlays, and Surpluses or Deficits (-): 1789–2015" in *Historical Tables—Budget of the U.S. Government*, 23, http://www.whitehouse.gov/sites/default/files/omb/budget/fy2011/assets/hist.pdf. ŏ **"Mandatory spending: ($2,165)"** Office of Management and Budget, "Table 8.5—Outlays for Mandatory and Related Programs: 1962–2015" in *Historical Tables—Budget of the U.S. Government*, 154, http://www.whitehouse.gov/sites/default/files/omb/budget/fy2011/assets/hist.pdf. ŏ **"Expected interest payments: ($251)"** Office of Management and Budget, "Table 8.5—Outlays for Mandatory and Related Programs: 1962–2015" in *Historical Tables—Budget of the U.S. Government*, 154, http://www.whitehouse.gov/sites/default/files/omb/budget/fy2011/assets/hist.pdf. ŏ **"Constitutional priorities"** Office of Management and Budget, "Table 3.1—Outlays by Superfunction and Function: 1940–2015" in *Historical Tables—Budget of the U.S. Government*, 23, http://www.whitehouse.gov/sites/default/files/omb/budget/fy2011/assets/hist.pdf.

PAGE 301: "pay for federal employees has grown 36.9 percent since 2000. Private-worker pay? 8.8 percent" Dennis Cauchon, "Federal Workers Earning Double Their Private Counterparts," *USA Today*, August 10, 2010, http://www.usatoday.com/money/economy/income/2010-08-10-1Afedpay10_ST_N.htm. ŏ **"which would save $2.2 billion"** Dennis Cauchon, "Federal Workers Earning Double Their Private Counterparts," *USA Today*, August 10, 2010, http://www.usatoday.com/money/economy/income/2010-08-10-1Afedpay10_ST_N.htm. ŏ **"in plain view, it says: *Working to Save the Planet*"** U.S. Department of Energy, *Agency Financial Report*, Fiscal Year 2009, http://www.cfo.doe.gov/cf12/2009PARafr.pdf.

PAGE 302: "President Clinton pushed that exact idea more than fifteen years ago" Steve Chapman, "Unplug the DOE!—Why Clinton Should Abolish the Department of Energy," *Slate*, November 28, 1996, http://www.slate.com/id/2392. ŏ **"'will not be easy, but we know it can be done'"** U.S. Department of Energy,

"Secretary Chu Auto Loan Announcement (Full Remarks)," June 23, 2009, energy.gov/news/7496.htm. • **"aimed at 'weatherizing' homes for 'low-income families and creating green jobs'"** U.S. Department of Energy, *Agency Financial Report*, Fiscal Year 2009, 10, http://www.cfo.doe.gov/cf12/2009PARafr.pdf. • **"'economic uncertainty, U.S. dependence on oil, and the threat of a changing climate'"** U.S. Department of Energy, "Message From the Secretary" in *Agency Financial Report*, Fiscal Year 2009, http://www.cfo.doe.gov/cf12/2009PARafr.pdf.

PAGE 303: "a DOE Task Force recommended privatizing those labs" Steve Chapman, "Unplug the DOE!—Why Clinton Should Abolish the Department of Energy," *Slate*, November 28, 1996, http://www.slate.com/id/2392. • **"a federal program to help low-income families with education subsidies"** Don Wolfensberger, "The Evolving Federal Role in Education: An Introductory Essay" ("Congress and Education Policy: ESEA at 40," Congress Project Seminar, Woodrow Wilson International Center for Scholars, March 15, 2005), 12–15, http://www.wilsoncenter.org/events/docs/education-intro.pdf. • **"'had thought we would not see happening to education is happening here'"** Casey J. Lartigue Jr., "Dems of Cheney's School," Cato, August 25, 2000, https://www.cato.org/dailys/08-25-00.html. *See also:* John E. Berthoud, "Who Got It Right? What Proponents and Opponents of the Creation of the Department of Education Promised & Predicted," Thomas B. Fordham, March 1, 1996, http://www.edexcellence.net/detail/news.cfm?news_id=149&id=.

PAGE 304: "'meddle in everything. I do not want that'" David Boaz, *The Politics Of Freedom: Taking on the Left, the Right, and Threats to Our Liberties* (Washington, D.C.: Cato Institute, 2008), 145. • **"'as it attempts to establish uniformity throughout the Nation'"** John E. Berthoud, "Who Got It Right? What Proponents and Opponents of the Creation of the Department of Education Promised & Predicted," Thomas B. Fordham, March 1, 1996, http://www.edexcellence.net/detail/news.cfm?news_id=149&id=. • **"'the nature of American education, which is characterized by diversity'"** David Boaz, "The Reagan Budget: The Deficit that Didn't Have to Be," *Policy Analysis*, no. 13, August 10, 1982, http://www.cato.org/pubs/pas/pa013.html. • **"'not wanting to embarrass the president'"** *Cato Handbook for Congress: Policy Recommendations for the 108th Congress* (Washington, D.C.: Cato Institute, 2003), 296, http://www.cato.org/pubs/handbook/hb108/hb108-28.pdf. • **"initial budget was $13.1 billion (in 2007 dollars) and it employed 450 people"** Mona Charen, "Wanting to Abolish the Department of Education Is Not Radical," *National Review Online*, June 11, 2010, http://www.nationalreview.com/articles/229936/wanting-abolish-department-education-not-radical/mona-charen. • **"estimated budget is $107 billion"** Office of Management and Budget, "Table 4.1—Outlays by Agency: 1962–2015" in *Historical Tables—Budget of the U.S. Government*, 83, http://www.whitehouse.gov/sites/default/files/omb/budget/fy2011/assets/hist.pdf. • **"'department has a jaw-dropping 4,800 employees"** Mona Charen, "Wanting to Abolish the Department of Education Is Not Radical," *National Review Online*, June 11, 2010, http://www.nationalreview.com/articles/229936/wanting-abolish-department-education-not-radical/mona-charen. • **"89.4 percent of the department's employees were deemed "nonessential" and were sent home"** John E. Berthoud, "Who Got It Right? What Proponents and Opponents of the Creation of the Department of Education Promised & Predicted," Thomas B. Fordham, March 1, 1996, http://www.edexcellence.net/detail/news.cfm?news_id=149&id=. • **"more than 130 bills were introduced to Congress to create the Department of Education"** D. T. Stallings, *A Brief History of the United States Department of Education: 1979–2002* (Durham, N.C.: Center for Child and Family Policy, Duke University, 2002), 3, http://www.childandfamilypolicy.duke.edu/pdfs/pubpres/BriefHistoryofUS_DOE.pdf. • **"'a presidential candidate—Jimmy Carter—for the first time in the history of the organization'"** *D. T. Stallings, A Brief History of the United States Department of Education: 1979–2002* (Durham, N.C.: Center for Child and Family Policy, Duke University, 2002), 3, http://www.childandfamilypolicy.duke.edu/pdfs/pubpres/BriefHistoryofUS_DOE.pdf. • **"'simply don't need the aggravation of taking them on'"** *Cato Handbook for Congress: Policy Recommendations for the 108th Congress* (Washington, D.C.: Cato Institute, 2003), 296, http://www.cato.org/pubs/handbook/hb108/hb108-28.pdf.

PAGE 305: "math scores are up just one percent" Mona Charen, "Wanting to Abolish the Department of Education Is Not Radical," *National Review Online*, June 11, 2010, http://www.nationalreview.com/articles/229936/wanting-abolish-department-education-not-radical/mona-charen. • **"'doesn't really help the kids, who needs us?'"** Greig M. O'Brien and Charles Peters, "Why The Right May Be Right: After Two Decades, Why Is the Department of Education Still Ignoring the Basic Problems Plaguing Our Public Schools?," *Washington Monthly*, April 1, 1997, http://www.thefreelibrary.com/Why+the+Right+may+be

+right%3a+after+two+ decades%2c+why+is+the+Department...-a019279947. ő **"'the kind of educational system that such arrangements produce'"** *Cato Handbook for Congress: Policy Recommendations for the 108th Congress* (Washington, D.C.: Cato Institute, 2003), 295, http://www.cato.org/pubs/handbook/hb108/hb108-28.pdf. ő **"'determine the education of our children."** Dan Lips, "Reagan's ABCs," *cato.org*, accessed August 21, 2010, http://www.cato.org/research/education/articles/reagan.html.

PAGE 306: "'formally completed in 1996 with the 160,000-mile national highway system'" Gabriel Roth, "The Rise in Federal Intervention," in *Federal Highway Funding*, accessed August 21, 2010, www.downsizing government.org/transportation/highway-funding. ő **"2005 highway bill that contained 6,376 earmarks that cost $24 billion"** Jeff Jacoby, "The Republican Pork Barrel," *Boston Globe*, August 4, 2005, http://www.boston.com/news/globe/editorial_opinion/oped/articles/2005/08/04/the_republican_pork_barrel/.

PAGE 307: "Republicans controlled Congress that year" Jeff Jacoby, "The Republican Pork Barrel," *Boston Globe*, August 4, 2005, http://www.boston.com/news/globe/editorial_opinion/oped/articles/2005/08/04/the_republican_pork_barrel/. ő **"would save $93 billion over the next decade"** CBO, *Budget Options*, vol. 2, August 2009, http://www.cbo.gov/ftpdocs/102xx/doc10294/08-06-BudgetOptions.pdf. ő **"*Federal agriculture subsidies*: $10–30 billion a year"** Chris Edwards, "Overview," in *Agricultural Subsidies*, June 2009, www.downsizinggovernment.org/print/agriculture/subsidies. ő **"more than $15 billion in wasteful spending and payments of $1.3 billion"** Sarah Cohen, "Deceased Farmers Got USDA Payments—Study Faults Lack Of Case Reviews," *Washington Post*, July 23, 2007, Washingtonpost.com/wp-dyn/content/article/2007/07/22/AR2007072201128.html.

PAGE 308: "Former NBA star Scottie Pippen and David Letterman have also been on the gravy train" Bill Sanderson, Rich Harvest—Wealthy NYers Get Fed Farm $ubsidies," *New York Post*, December 12, 2007, http://www.nypost.com/p/news/regional/item_CJFLY7vhXTChpbaTPwQr5J. ő **"estimates that this would save us $1 billion right away, and perhaps $3 billion over the long term"** Rand National Defense Research Institute and Rand Arroyo Center "Privatizing Military Production," Research Brief, accessed August 21, 2010, http://rand.org/pubs/research_briefs/RB9048/RB9048.pdf.

PAGE 309: "Great Britain privatized London's Heathrow Airport" BAA plc, accessed August 21, 2010, http://www.fundinguniverse.com/company-histories/BAA-plc-Company-History.html. ő **"Taxpayers coughed up $685 million"** Robert W. Poole, Jr. and Chris Edwards, "A Brief History of Federal Funding," in *Airports and Air Traffic Control*, June 2010, http://www.downsizinggovernment.org/transportation/airports-atc. ő **"cost $155 million to build and includes service from several discount airlines"** Branson Airport Fact Sheet, 1, http://www.flybranson.com/docs/BransonAirportFactSheet.pdf (accessed August 21, 2010). *See also:* Christine Negroni, "Branson Opening Nation's only Privately Funded Commercial Airport," *Dallas Morning News*, May 11, 2009, http://www.dallasnews.com/sharedcontent/dws/bus/stories/DNbranson_11bus.State.Edition1.c23c71.html. ő **"would save us about $10.7 billion over the next decade"** CBO, *Budget Options*, vol. 2, August 2009, 96, http://www.cbo.gov/ftpdocs/102xx/doc10294/08-06-BudgetOptions.pdf. ő **"top marks for efficiency and safety"** Chris Edwards, "Infrastructure," in *Privatization*, February 2009, http://www.downsizinggovernment.org/privatization. ő **"want to fund corporate welfare programs or pay billionaires to grow food"** Yasha Levine, "The Making of Manhattan's Elite Welfare Farmers," *New York Press*, June 15, 2010, http://www.nypress.com/article-21342-the-making-of-manhattans-elite-welfare-farmers.html.

PAGE 310: "Medicaid, where $24 billion, or nearly eight cents of every dollar, was 'improperly spent'" Tom Cohen, "White House Reports Billions of Improper Payments in 2009," *CNN*, November 18, 2009, http://www.cnn.com/2009/POLITICS/11/18/government.improper.payments/index.html. ő **"22 percent of them, representing $123 billion in annual spending"** Brian Riedl, "50 Examples of Government Waste," WebMemo on Federal Budget no. 2642, October 6, 2009, http://www.heritage.org/Research/Reports/2009/10/50-Examples-of-Government-Waste#_edn4. ő **"Total ten-year savings: $931 million"** CBO, *Budget Options*, vol. 2, August 2009, 38, http://www.cbo.gov/ftpdocs/102xx/doc10294/08-06-BudgetOptions.pdf. ő **"Total ten-year savings: $7.9 billion"** CBO, *Budget Options*, vol. 2, August 2009, 42, http://www.cbo.gov/ftpdocs/102xx/doc10294/08-06-BudgetOptions.pdf. ő **"Total ten-year savings: $10.9 billion"** CBO, *Budget Options*, vol. 2, August 2009, 72, http://www.cbo.gov/ftpdocs/102xx/doc10294/08-06-BudgetOptions.pdf. ő **"Total ten-year savings: $18.8 billion"** CBO, *Budget Options*, vol. 2, August 2009, 121, http://www.cbo.gov/ftpdocs/102xx/doc10294/08-06-BudgetOptions.pdf.

PAGE 311: "everybody endeavors to live at the expense of everybody else" *Social Science Quotations: Who Said What, When, and Where, eds. David L. Sills and Robert King Merton* (New Brunswick, N.J.: Transaction Publishers, 2000), 12. ♁ **"It's called the 'Roadmap for America's Future'"** Representative Paul D. Ryan, Ranking Member, Committee on the Budget, *A Roadmap for America's Future, A Plan To Solve America's Long-Term Economic and Fiscal Crisis, version 2.0, January 2010,* http://www.roadmap.republicans.budget.house.gov/UploadedFiles/Roadmap2Final2.pdf. ♁ **"'while denying that you're doing any such thing"** Paul Krugman, "Ryan On Medicare," The Conscience of a Liberal, *New York Times,* August 14, 2010, http://krugman.blogs.nytimes.com/2010/08/14/ryan-on-medicare/.

PAGE 312: "'owed air-conditioning, cars, telephones, televisions'" Adam Liptak, "Reticent Justice Opens Up to a Group of Students," Sidebar, *New York Times,* April 14, 2009, http://www.nytimes.com/2009/04/14/us/14bar.html?_r=1&ref=clarence_thomas.

PAGE 314: "'by placing under every one what his own eye may superintend, that all will be done for the best" *Thomas Jefferson, The Jeffersonian Cyclopedia,* ed. John P. Foley (New York: Funk & Wagnalls Company, 1900), 836. ♁ **"'Violence and disorder, not surprisingly, rose alarmingly'"** Charles J. Sykes, *A Nation of Victims: The Decay of the American Character* (New York: St. Martin's Press, 1992), 243.

PAGE 315: "to create 'internalized inhibitions, reinforced by social sanctions'" James Q. Wilson and Richard Herrnstein, *Crime and Human Nature: The Definitive Study of the Causes of Crime* (New York: The Free Press, 1985), 431. ♁ **"[alcohol consumption] fell from 10 gallons to 2.1 gallons [per person] a year'"** Charles J. Sykes, *A Nation of Victims: The Decay of the American Character* (New York: St. Martin's Press, 1992), 243. ♁ **"'It is in violation of the traditions of America'"** Representative Paul D. Ryan, Ranking Member, Committee on the Budget, *A Roadmap for America's Future, A Plan To Solve America's Long-Term Economic and Fiscal Crisis,* version 2.0, January 2010, 14, http://www.roadmap.republicans.budget.house.gov/UploadedFiles/Roadmap2Final2.pdf.

PAGE 316: "'when payroll receipts fall short of benefits" Paul Krugman, "Social Security Finances," The Conscience of a Liberal, *New York Times,* August 13, 2010, http://krugman.blogs.nytimes.com/2010/08/13/social-security-finances/. ♁ **"five million state and local workers who are exempt from the Social Security system"** Carrie Lips, "State and Local Government Retirement Programs: Lessons in Alternatives to Social security," SSP no. 16, March 17, 1999, http://www.cato.org/pubs/ssps/ssp-16es.html. ♁ **"have their money put into conservative fixed-rate guaranteed annuities instead"** Ray Holbrook and Alcestis Oberg, "Galveston County: A Model for Social Security Reform," National Security for Policy Analysis, Brief Analysis no. 514, April 26, 2005, http://www.ncpa.org/pdfs/ba514.pdf. ♁ **"that same worker would get around $1,645 a month"** "Counties Opt Out of Social Security?," *Foxnews.com,* October 29, 2009, http://www.foxnews.com/story/0,2933,570311,00.html. ♁ **"'really more of a political issue rather than an economic issue'"** "Counties Opt Out of Social Security?," *Foxnews.com,* October 29, 2009, http://www.foxnews.com/story/0,2933,570311,00.html.

Chapter 19: Step 7: Declare War on Defense Dollars

PAGE 318: "'nothing is too great for Allah'" "Bin Laden: Goal Is To Bankrupt U.S.—Al-Jazeera Releases Full Transcript of Al Qaeda Leader's Tape," *CNN,* November 1, 2004, http://www.cnn.com/2004/WORLD/meast/11/01/binladen.tape/.

PAGE 319: "'undergo the fatigues of supporting it'" Mark A. Sauter and James Jay Carafano, *Homeland Security: A Complete Guide To Understanding, Preventing, and Surviving Terrorism* (New York: McGraw Hill Companies, Inc., 2005), 3. ♁ **"'Government always finds a need for whatever money it gets'"** Richard A. Viguerie, *Conservatives Betrayed: How George W. Bush and Other Big Government Republicans Hijacked the Conservative Cause* (Los Angeles: Bonus Books, 2006), 231. ♁ **"'national debt is our biggest national security threat'"** Rick Berman, "Here's a Scary Idea: The Debt Is Our Top National Security Threat," *Atlanta Journal-Constitution,* August 11, 2010, http://www.ajc.com/opinion/heres-a-scary-idea-590097.html. ♁ **"'Restore fiscal responsibility'"** David Ignatius, "How Debt Imperils National Security," *Washington Post,* May 23, 2010, http://www.washingtonpost.com/wp-dyn/content/article/2010/05/21/AR2010052103260.html.

PAGE 320: "'we can't have a strong military if we have a weak economy'"U.S. Department of Defense, Office of the Assistant Secretary of Defense (Public Affairs), News Transcript, "Media Availability with Secretary Gates en Route to Kansas City, Missouri," May 7, 2010, http://www.defense.gov/Transcripts/

Transcript.aspx?TranscriptID=4621. • **"'is a dollar we can't spend on what we do need'"** U.S. Department of Defense, Office of the Assistant Secretary of Defense (Public Affairs), News Transcript, "Media Availability with Secretary Gates en Route to Kansas City, Missouri," May 7, 2010, http://www.defense.gov/Transcripts/Transcript.aspx?TranscriptID=4621. • **"'a national security threat, one of the greatest we know of'"** Jake Sherman, "Steny Hoyer Aims To Turn Terror Tables on GOP," *politico.com*, June 28, 2010, http://www.politico.com/news/stories/0610/39085.html. • **"'*a national debt of 44 billions of dollars*'"** Willard Edwards, "Debt Is Greatest Defense Threat, America Warned—44 Billion Dollar Total Cited by Republicans," *Chicago Daily Tribune*, March 12, 1940, 4, http://pqasb.pqarchiver.com/chicagotribune/access/466373502.html?dids=466373502:466373502&FMT=ABS&FMTS=ABS:AI. • **"'[We must do this] in the next ten or fifteen years."** Joseph Stalin, *Leninism (London: Lawrence & Wishart, 1940), 634.* • **"participated in that bankrupting of the Soviets while they occupied Afghanistan,"** "Bin Laden: Goal Is To Bankrupt U.S.—Al-Jazeera Releases Full Transcript of Al Qaeda Leader's Tape," *CNN*, November 1, 2004, http://www.cnn.com/2004/WORLD/meast/11/01/binladen.tape/. • **"'numbers estimated to total more than a trillion dollars'"** "Bin Laden: Goal Is To Bankrupt U.S.—Al-Jazeera Releases Full Transcript of Al Qaeda Leader's Tape," *CNN*, November 1, 2004, http://www.cnn.com/2004/WORLD/meast/11/01/binladen.tape/. • **"a good portion of our national debt is owed to China"** Department of the Treasury/Federal Reserve Board, "Major Foreign Holders of Treasury Securities," August 16, 2010, http://www.ustreas.gov/tic/mfh.txt. • **"dump Fannie Mae and Freddie Mac securities as a form of economic warfare against us"** Michael McKee and Alex Nicholson, "Paulson Says Russia Urged China To Dump Fannie, Freddie Bonds," *bloomberg.com*, January 29, 2010, http://www.bloomberg.com/apps/news?pid=newsarchive&sid=afbSjYv3v814.

PAGE 321: "made clear that as a form of retaliation they might stop buying our debt" Judy Shelton, "The United States: Debtor and Leader?: Why Lech Walesa Is Right To Worry About Declining American Influence," Opinion, *Wall Street Journal*, February 16, 2010. • **"'the resulting product does likewise'"** Thomas G. Paterson, J. Garry Clifford, Shane J. Maddock, Deborah Kisatsky, and Kenneth J. Hagan, *American Foreign Relations: A History*, vol. 2: Since 1895, 7th ed. (Boston, MA: Wadworth, 2010), 276. • **"'costs between [$]10 (billion dollars) and $15 billion and has 6,000 lives on it.'"** U.S. Department of Defense, Office of the Assistant Secretary of Defense (Public Affairs), News Transcript, "Media Availability with Secretary Gates en Route to Kansas City, Missouri," May 7, 2010, http://www.defense.gov/Transcripts/Transcript.aspx?TranscriptID=4621. • **"'put himself or herself in harm's way for the rest of us'"** Ronald Reagan, *Speaking My Mind: Selected Speeches* (New York: Simon & Schuster Inc., 1989), 281. • **"'If giving us a pay cut will help our country, cut our pay'"** Ronald Reagan, "Remarks and a Question-and-Answer Session With Editors of Gannett Newspapers on Domestic and Foreign Policy Issues," December 14, 1983, http://www.reagan.utexas.edu/archives/speeches/1983/121483e.htm.

PAGE 322: "'I wouldn't cut their pay if I bled to death'" Ronald Reagan, "Remarks and a Question-and-Answer Session With Editors of Gannett Newspapers on Domestic and Foreign Policy Issues," December 14, 1983, http://www.reagan.utexas.edu/archives/speeches/1983/121483e.htm. • **"sergeant-level employee with five years of experience receives $37,104"** "Basic Pay—Effective January 1, 2010," 1, accessed August 17, 2010 http://www.dfas.mil/militarypay/militarypaytables/2010WebPayTable34.pdf. • **"poverty level for a family of three was $17,163 per year"** Institute for Research on Poverty, "The Census Bureau's Poverty Thresholds for 2008," accessed August 17, 2010, http://www.irp.wisc.edu/faqs/faq1.htm. • **"pays a minimum of $51,000 for the first year"** James Sherk, "Inflated Federal Pay: How Americans Are Overtaxed To Overpay the Civil Service," The Heritage Foundation, Center for Data Analysis Report #10-05, accessed August 17, 2010, http://www.heritage.org/Research/Reports/2010/07/Inflated-Federal-Pay-How-Americans-Are-Overtaxed-to-Overpay-the-Civil-Service#_ftnref7. • **"'and usurp the standard of freedom'"** William H. Seward, *Life of John Quincy Adams* (Whitefish, MT: Kessinger Publishing LLC, 2004), 132–33. • **"says we are to 'provide for the common defense'"** U.S. Constitution, preamble, http://caselaw.lp.findlaw.com/data/constitution/preamble/.

PAGE 323: "'reducing the deficit and getting the debt under control'" Andrew Quinn, "Clinton Spotlights U.S. Debt as Diplomatic Threat," Reuters, May 27, 2010, http://www.reuters.com/article/idUSN2714967820100527.

PAGE 324: "'preserve its freedom in the midst of continual warfare'" James Madison, *Selected Writings of James Madison, The American Heritage, ed. Ralph Ketcham* (Indianapolis, IN: Hackett Publishing Company, Inc., 2006), 236. • **"'SOVIET BORROWS HEAVILY AS OIL AND DOLLAR FALL'"** Clyde H.

Farnsworth, "Soviet Borrows Heavily as Oil and Dollar Fall," *New York Times*, December 3, 1987, http://www.nytimes.com/1987/12/03/world/soviet-borrows-heavily-as-oil-and-dollar-fall.html?pagewanted=all. ♁ **"The actual combat represents just 20 percent"** CBO Testimony, Statement of Peter Orszag, Director, "Estimated Costs of U.S. Operations in Iraq and Afghanistan and of Other Activities Related to the War on Terrorism," Before the Committee on the Budget, U.S. House of Representatives, October 24, 2007, http://www.cbo.gov/ftpdocs/86xx/doc8690/10-24-CostOfWar_Testimony.pdf. *See also*: Linda J. Bilmes and Joseph E. Stiglitz, "The Iraq War Will Cost Us $3 Trillion, and Much More," *Washington Post*, March 9, 2008, http://www.washingtonpost.com/wp-dyn/content/article/2008/03/07/AR2008030702846.html. ♁ **"'to subdue the enemy without fighting is the acme of skill"** Jay M. Shafritz, *Words on War: Military Quotations From Ancient Times to the Present* (New York: Prentice Hall, 1990), 101.

PAGE 325: "succeeded in kicking the Soviets out of those countries without any American soldiers being put at risk" Charles Krauthammer, "The Reagan Doctrine," *Time*, April 1, 1985, http://www.time.com/time/magazine/article/0,9171,964873,00.html. ♁ **"'more important than missiles and satellites in meeting crises yet to come . . .'"** William J. Casey, *The Secret War Against Hitler* (New York: Berkley Books, 1989), xiv. ♁ **"'can and should expect closer, harsher scrutiny'"** Adam J. Hebert, "The Pentagon's War on Overhead," *AirForce-Magazine.com*, August 2010, http://www.airforce-magazine.com/MagazineArchive/Pages/2010/August 2010/0810issbf.aspx. ♁ **"the Pentagon budget is now double—in real terms—what it was in 1998"** Lawrence J. Korb and Christopher A. Preble, "Cut Defense Spending," *The National Interest*, June 16, 2010, http://nationalinterest.org/commentary/cut-defense-spending-3572. ♁ **"declared the Pentagon's accounting system to be 'high-risk'"** *See generally* Scot J. Paltrow. "The Pentagon's $1 Trillion Problem," *Portfolio.com*, April 14 2008, http://www.portfolio.com/news-markets/national-news/portfolio/2008/04/14/Pentagons-Accounting-Mess/. ♁ **"We know it's gone," he said, "but we don't know what they spent it on."** "The War On Waste—Defense Department Cannot Account For 25% Of Funds—$2.3 Trillion," *CBS Evening News*, January 29, 2002, http://www.cbsnews.com/stories/2002/01/29/eveningnews/main325985.shtml. ♁ **"a total of $102 billion that Gates is trying to cut, almost all from overhead"** Tim Kauffman, "DoD Comptroller: Cutting Staff, Managers Possible," *FederalTimes.com*, June 13, 2010, http://www.federaltimes.com/article/20100613/DEPARTMENTS01/6130305. ♁ **"'My supervisor asking me why I care about doing a good job'"** "The War On Waste—Defense Department Cannot Account For 25% Of Funds—$2.3 Trillion," *CBS Evening News*, January 29, 2002, http://www.cbsnews.com/stories/2002/01/29/eveningnews/main325985.shtml.

PAGE 326: "he says, the Pentagon simply wrote off the missing money" "The War On Waste—Defense Department Cannot Account for 25% of Funds—$2.3 Trillion," *CBS Evening News*, January 29, 2002, http://www.cbsnews.com/stories/2002/01/29/eveningnews/main325985.shtml. ♁ **"'who they've sold stuff to, who owes them, who they owe'"** "The Pentagon's Broken Book-keeping," *DefenseIndustryDaily.com*, February 28, 2006, http://www.defenseindustrydaily.com/the-pentagons-broken-bookkeeping-01945/. ♁ **"announcing that the Pentagon was unable to track $2.3 trillion worth of transactions"** "The War On Waste—Defense Department Cannot Account for 25% of Funds—$2.3 Trillion," *CBS Evening News*, January 29, 2002, http://www.cbsnews.com/stories/2002/01/29/eveningnews/main325985.shtml. ♁ **"they cannot account for a full 25 percent of their annual expenditures"** "The War On Waste—Defense Department Cannot Account for 25% of Funds—$2.3 Trillion," *CBS Evening News*, January 29, 2002, http://www.cbsnews.com/stories/2002/01/29/eveningnews/main325985.shtml. ♁ **"it cannot account for $8.7 billion in Iraqi funds"** Liz Sly, "Pentagon Can't Account for $8.7 Billion in Iraqi Funds," *Los Angeles Times*, July 26, 2010, http://articles.latimes.com/2010/jul/26/world/la-fg-iraq-funds-20100727. ♁ **"'loose change in [the Pentagon], without having to hit the taxpayers.'"** "The War On Waste—Defense Department Cannot Account for 25% of Funds—$2.3 Trillion," *CBS Evening News*, January 29, 2002, http://www.cbsnews.com/stories/2002/01/29/eveningnews/main325985.shtml. ♁ **"'unnecessary, and duplicative defense spending that does nothing to make our nation safe'"** Lawrence J. Korb and Christopher A. Preble, "Cut Defense Spending," *The National Interest*, June 16, 2010, http://nationalinterest.org/commentary/cut-defense-spending-3572.

PAGE 327: "I'm No SecDef, But . . ." Erik Prince, founder of Xe, in an e-mail interview with author, August 9, 2010.

PAGE 328: "'problems that we need to confront for the future.'" "CIA Director: Deficit a Threat to National Security," November 10, 2009, http://www.youtube.com/watch?v=rYznF6mVTcA, 0'17" to 1'18".

PAGE 329: "'thus become the chief menace to our national security'" James R. Schlesinger, *The Political Economy of National Security: A Study of the Economic Aspects of the Contemporary Power Struggle* (New York: Praeger, 1960), 258. ♁ **"consumes about 40 percent of its annual budget in overhead costs" Adam J. Hebert, "The Pentagon's War on Overhead,"** *AirForce-Magazine.com,* August 2010, http://www.airforce-magazine.com/MagazineArchive/Pages/2010/August 2010/0810issbf.aspx.

PAGE 330: "Congress has a 16 percent approval rating" Rasmussen Reports, "Congressional Performance—16% Say Congress Doing A Good or Excellent Job; 56% Say Poor," August 9, 2010, http://www.rasmussenreports.com/public_content/politics/mood_of_america/congressional_performance. ♁ **"funding for private contractors would be reduced by 10 percent in each of the next three years"** Dana Hedgpeth, "Defense Secretary's Planned Cuts Upset Investors and Defense Contractors," *Washington Post,* August 11, 2010, http://www.washingtonpost.com/wp-dyn/content/article/2010/08/10/AR2010081006290.html. ♁ **"'They're going to come full force'"** Bill Myers, "Local Defense Contractors Prepare for Lean Times," *Washington Examiner,* August 11, 2010, http://www.washingtonexaminer.com/economy/Local-defense-contractors-prepare-for-lean-times-1008943-100385829.html#ixzz0wh9r0gNk. ♁ **"by one outside estimate, it's approximately 790,000"** Dana Hedgpeth, "Defense Secretary's Planned Cuts Upset Investors and Defense Contractors," *Washington Post,* August 11, 2010, http://www.washingtonpost.com/wp-dyn/content/article/2010/08/10/AR2010081006290.html. ♁ **"not only save the Pentagon $135 billion over five years"** Roxana Tiron, "House Armed Services Leaders Aim To Cut Pentagon Waste, Fraud," The Hill, April 13, 2010, http://thehill.com/news-by-subject/defense-homeland-security/91965-house-defense-leaders-up-the-ante-on-pentagon-reform. ♁ **"'*why voters are right to worry about America's debt crisis*'"** Niall Ferguson, "An Empire at Risk," December 15, 2009, http://www.niallferguson.com/site/FERG/Templates/ArticleItem.aspx?pageid=226.

Chapter 20: Step Eight: Spit Ourselves Out of the System

PAGE 332: "'prime consideration in too many economic decisions'" William J. Federer, *The Interesting History of Income Tax* (St. Louis: Amerisearch, 2004), 119.

PAGE 333: "'bear lighter tax burdens than those on the outside'" Charles Adams, *For Good and Evil: The Impact of Taxes on the Course of Civilization* (New York: Madison, 1993), 448.

PAGE 334: "could agree on how much the family owed in taxes" Steve Forbes, *Flat Tax Revolution: Using a Postcard to Abolish the IRS* (Washington, D.C.: Regnery, 2005), 7. ♁ **"'in any other way, could be borne with ease'"** Arthur B. Laffer, *Return to Prosperity: How America Can Regain Its Economic Superpower Status* (New York: Threshold, 2010), 173. ♁ **"received wrong answers or no answer at all"** Jeff Schnepper, "Why the Tax System Drives Me—and You—Crazy," *moneycentral.msn.com,* accessed August 20, 2010, http://moneycentral.msn.com/content/taxes/p82372.asp.

PAGE 335: "'TAX-ON-RICH' BILL PASSED IN SENATE" Warren B. Francis, "'Tax-on-Rich' Bill Passed in Senate; Expansion Beaten," *Los Angeles Times,* August 16, 1935. ♁ **"'existing wealth in relatively stable forms'"** Milton Friedman, *Capitalism and Freedom* (Chicago: University of Chicago Press, 1982), 173. ♁ **"more than 9 million words long"** Steve Forbes and Elizabeth Ames, *How Capitalism Will Save Us: Why Free People and Free Markets Are the Best Answer in Today's Economy* (New York: Crown, 2009), 153. ♁ **"nearly 4 million full-time workers"** U.S. Department of the Treasury, Internal Revenue Service, *National Taxpayer Advocate: 2009 Annual Report to Congress, Volume One* (Washington, D.C.: IRS, 2009), http://www.irs.gov/pub/irs-utl/1_09_tas_arc_vol_1_preface_toc_msp.pdf. Note: TAS analysis of IRS data shows that U.S. taxpayers and business spend about 7.6 billion hours a year complying with the filing requirements of the Internal Revenue Code. It would require 3.8 million workers to consume 7.6 billion hours, effectively making the "tax industry" one of the largest industries in the United States.

PAGE 336: "about $1.2 trillion in personal income taxes" Steve Forbes and Elizabeth Ames, *How Capitalism Will Save Us: Why Free People and Free Markets Are the Best Answer in Today's Economy* (New York: Crown, 2009), 154. ♁ **"will cost us $338 billion this year"** Tax Foundation, "Total Federal Income Tax Compliance Costs, 1990–2015," *taxfoundation.org,* October 26, 2006, http://www.taxfoundation.org/research/show/1962.html. ♁ **"to more than 7 million in 2005"** J. Scott Moody, Wendy P. Warcholik, and Scott A. Hodge, "The Rising Cost of Complying with the Federal Income Tax" (report, The Tax Foundation, Washington, D.C., December 2005), http://www.taxfoundation.org/files/sr138.pdf. ♁ **"'progress bringing down our long-term deficits'"** Jake Tapper, "Treasury Secretary Says Letting Bush Tax Cuts for Rich

Expire Will Not Slow Economic Growth," *Political Punch* blog at *abcnews.com*, July 24, 2010, http://blogs.abcnews.com/politicalpunch/2010/07/treasury-secretary-says-letting-bush-tax-cuts-for-rich-expire-will-not-slow-economic-growth.html.

PAGE 337: "less from that group than they were expecting" Laura Smitherman, "Top Payers Fade Away," *Baltimore Sun*, May 14, 2009, http://articles.baltimoresun.com/2009-05-14/news/0905130138_1_higher-tax-bracket-individual-income-franchot. ♁ **"most of that money will just sit idle" Paul Krugman, "America Goes Dark,"** *New York Times*, August 8, 2010, http://www.nytimes.com/2010/08/09/opinion/09krugman.html?_r=1. ♁ **"'is the cause of the poverty of the poor'"** Ludwig von Mises *Planning for Freedom: Let the Market System Work* (Indianapolis, IN: Liberty Fund, 2009), 36.

PAGE 338: "not Massachusetts, California, or even Florida, but *Fiji*" "Kennedy Divides Merchandise Mart," *Chicago Tribune*, March 22,1947. ♁ **"That's about .0004 percent"** Michael Jensen, "Managing the Kennedy Millions," *New York Times, June 12, 1977.*

PAGE 339: "'encouraging flight of jobs and outsourcing'" "Alan Keyes and Barack Obama Debate, Hosted By Illinois Radio Network," *keyesarchive.com*, October 12, 2004, http://www.keyesarchives.com/transcript.php?id=367. ♁ **"'a rising tide lifts all the boats'"** William Safire, *Safire's Political Dictionary* (New York: Oxford, 2008), 627.

PAGE 340: "'changes in the marginal tax rates in both directions'" David Ranson "The Revenue Limits of Tax and Spend," *Wall Street Journal*, May 17, 2010, http://online.wsj.com/article/SB10001424052748704608104575217870728420184.html. ♁ **"between 1950 and 2009 averaged 17.9 percent"** U.S. Office of Management and Budget, "Table 2.3," in *President's Budget: Historical Tables* (Washington, D.C.: White House, 2010), http://www.whitehouse.gov/omb/budget/Historicals/. ♁ **"maxed out at 20.6 percent (in 2000)"** U.S. Office of Management and Budget, "Table 2.3," in *President's Budget: Historical Tables* (Washington, D.C.: White House, 2010), http://www.whitehouse.gov/omb/budget/Historicals/. ♁ **"to a high of 92 percent over that time period"** Robert A. Wilson, "Personal Exemptions and Individual Income Tax Rates, 1913–2002," http://www.irs.gov/pub/irs-soi/02inpetr.pdf (accessed July 24, 2010). ♁ **"Chart: The Top Tax Rate Ruse"** Robert A. Wilson, "Personal Exemptions and Individual Income Tax Rates, 1913–2002," http://www.irs.gov/ pub/irs-soi/02inpetr.pdf (accessed July 24, 2010); *See also:* U.S. Office of Management and Budget, "Table 1.2," in *President's Budget: Historical Tables* (Washington, D.C.: White House, 2010), http://www.whitehouse.gov/omb/budget/Historicals/.

PAGE 341: "whopping 71 percent of the federal income taxes" Steve Forbes and Elizabeth Ames, *How Capitalism Will Save Us: Why Free People and Free Markets Are the Best Answer in Today's Economy* (New York: Crown, 2009), 148. ♁ **"'International Business Machines, and Citigroup combined'"** David Keating, "A Taxing Trend: The Rise in Complexity, Forms, and Paperwork Burdens" (policy paper, National Taxpayers Union, Alexandria, VA, April 15, 2010), http://www.ntu.org/ntu-pp-127-tax-complexity-2010.pdf. ♁ **"*negative* 6.6 percent in federal income tax"** Congressional Budget Office, "Historical Effective Federal Tax Rates: 1979 to 2006," *cbo.gov*, April 2009, http://www.cbo.gov/ftpdocs/100xx/doc10068/effective_tax_rates_2006.pdf. ♁ **"paid 103.6 percent of the taxes collected"** Congressional Budget Office, "Historical Effective Federal Tax Rates: 1979 to 2006," *cbo.gov*, April 2009, http://www.cbo.gov/ftpdocs/100xx/doc10068/effective_tax_rates_2006.pdf.

PAGE 342: "lower the corporate tax rate by 10 to 15 percentage points" Dan Mitchell, "America Will Now Be the Unquestioned World Leader . . . But in the Wrong Way," *danieljmitchell.wordpress.com*, June 15, 2010, http://danieljmitchell.wordpress.com/2010/06/15/america-will-now-be-the-unquestioned-world-leader-but-in-the-wrong-way/. ♁ **"in the European Union is now less than 25 percent"** Eurostat European Commission, Taxation and Customs Union, *Taxation Trends in the European Union: Data From EU Member States and Norway* (Brussels: European Commission, 2009), http://epp.eurostat.ec.europa.eu/cache/ITY_OFFPUB/KS-DU-09-001/EN/KS-DU-09-001-EN.PDF. ♁ **"'achieve a balanced budget in the fiscal year 1953'"** Felix Belair, Jr., "Sales Tax Backed to Balance Budget; But C.E.D. Favors Use Only if Necessary—Eisenhower's Views Seen in Report," *New York Times*, April 22, 1952, http://select.nytimes.com/gst/abstract.html?res=F50716FC385F177 B93C0AB178FD85F468585F9.

PAGE 343: "allowed them to report higher false profits" Steve Forbes and Elizabeth Ames, *How Capitalism Will Save Us: Why Free People and Free Markets Are the Best Answer in Today's Economy* (New York: Crown, 2009), 151. ♁ **"only about 12 percent of federal revenues"** U.S. Office of Management and Budget,

"Table 2.1," in *President's Budget: Historical Tables* (Washington, D.C.: White House, 2010), http://www.whitehouse.gov/omb/budget/Historicals/. ♁ **"'Incremental change will not be adequate'"** Alan Greenspan, "U.S. Debt and the Greece Analogy," *Wall Street Journal*, June 18, 2010, http://online.wsj.com/article/SB10001424052748704198004575310962247772540.html.

PAGE 344: "'let me know the amount of the balance due'" President Franklin Delano Roosevelt, tax return, March 15, 1938, http://taxbase4.tax.org/thp/presreturns.nsf/Returns/A5959101FDF7DEEE85256E430078B2BA/$file/F_Roosevelt_1937.pdf.

PAGE 345: "two postcards: one for households and one for businesses" Steve Forbes and Elizabeth Ames, *How Capitalism Will Save Us: Why Free People and Free Markets Are the Best Answer in Today's Economy* (New York: Crown, 2009), 153. ♁ **"'less profitable at 19 percent than at 40 percent'"** Robert Ernest Hall and Alvin Rabushka, *The Flat Tax*, (Stanford, CA: Hoover Institution, 1995), 155. ♁ **"'absolutely essential if the budget is to be balanced'"** Walter Lippmann, "Increased Income Tax Rate Only Solution to U.S. Budget Problem," *Los Angeles Times, March 6, 1959.* ♁ **"'the ones that minimize taxable income'"** Robert Ernest Hall and Alvin Rabushka, *The Flat Tax*, (Stanford, CA: Hoover Institution, 1995), 155–56.

PAGE 346: "and that the tax code was too complex" Robert Ernest Hall and Alvin Rabushka, *The Flat Tax*, (Stanford, CA: Hoover Institution, 1995), 72–74. ♁ **"'Prevent Individuals From Escaping All Federal Payments'"** Rodney Crowther, "Income Tax on Rich Expected in Surtax Bill: Measure Would Prevent Individuals From Escaping All Federal Payments," *Baltimore Sun*, July 2, 1969. ♁ **"'far more important than any tax break'"** Robert Ernest Hall and Alvin Rabushka, *The Flat Tax*, (Stanford, CA: Hoover Institution, 1995), 158. ♁ **"stands at about 67 percent of the population"** Bob Tedeschi, "A Falling Homeownership Rate," July 16, 2010, http://www.nytimes.com/2010/07/18/realestate/18mort.html.

PAGE 347: "'effect a flat tax in such a positive way'" Associated Press, "Bush Touts Estonia's Flat Tax," *msnbc.com*, November 28, 2006, http://www.msnbc.msn.com/id/15935317/38479203.

Conclusion

PAGE 350: "enough to conquer the whole of America" Manoj Sharma, *History of World Civilization* (New Delhi: Anmol Publications, 2005), 516. ♁ **"'any of the qualifications necessary to make a good soldier'"** William Bradford Reed, *Life and Correspondence of Joseph Reed* (Philadelphia: Lindsay and Blakiston, 1847), 223. ♁ **"'as fast as their feet could carry them'"** Marvin Olasky, *Fighting for Liberty and Virtue: Political and Cultural Wars in Eighteenth-Century America* (Washington, D.C.: Regnery, 1996), 141.

PAGE 351: "'wrong which will be imposed upon them'" William Voegeli, "The Meaning of the Tea Party," *Claremont Review of Books*, Spring 2010, http://www.claremont.org/publications/crb/id.1704/article_detail.asp.